THE BEST OF GERMANY

Second Edition

Directed by
André Gayot

Translation and Adaptation
Marianne Benz, Heidi Ellison,
Linda Healey, Reine-Marie Melvin

Coordination
Alain Gayot

German-Language Guide:

Directed by
Johannes Heyne

Editor-in-Chief
Manfred Kohnke

Paris ▪ Los Angeles ▪ New York ▪ London ▪ Munich ▪ San Francisco

Bring You

The Best of Chicago
The Best of Florida
The Best of France
The Best of Germany
The Best of Hawaii
The Best of Hong Kong
The Best of Italy
The Best of London
The Best of Los Angeles
The Best of New England
The Best of New Orleans
The Best of New York
The Best of Paris
The Best of San Francisco
The Best of Thailand
The Best of Toronto
The Best of Washington, D.C.
The Best Wineries of North America

The Food Paper
Tastes Newsletter

Published by Gault Millau, Inc.
5900 Wilshire Blvd.
Los Angeles, CA 90036

Please address all comments regarding
The Best of Germany to:
Gault Millau, Inc.
P.O. Box 361144
Los Angeles, CA 90036

Editorial Assistance: Sam Martin, Dennis Schaefer, Jan Zastrow

Page Layout and Design: Mad Macs Communications

Maps Courtesy of: German Wine Information Bureau, Huber Kartography/Baedecker

Library of Congress Cataloging-in-Publication Data

Deutschland. English
The best of Germany/directed by André Gayot; translation and adaptation, Marianne Benz ... [et al .]; coordination, Alain Gayot; German-language guide, directed by Johannes Heyne; editor-in-chief, Manfred Kohnke. — 2nd ed.
p. cm.
Translation of: Deutschland.
Includes index.
Cover Title: Gayot's The best of Germany.
ISBN 1-881066-15-0: $20.00
1. Germany—Guidebooks. 2. Restaurants—Germany—Guidebooks.
I. Gayot, André. II. Kohnke, Manfred. III. Title. IV. Title:
Gayot's The best of Germany
DD16.D3813 1995
914.304'879—dc20

95-4219
CIP

Printed in the United States of America

CONTENTS

THANK YOU

We would like to extend a very dear thanks to those who helped to make this book possible: Marita Kallfez at Lufthansa Airlines; Carol Sullivan at the German Wine Information Bureau.

RIGHTS

DISCLAIMER

THE NEW TASTE OF GERMANY

It's time to forget the clichés about food in Germany. Of course Germans are still patriotically fond of their beer and wurst, but no more so than are partisans of neighboring nations on the Continent proud of their own respective indigenous cuisines.

The culinary revolution that swept France almost 25 years ago was felt in Germany too. From the North Sea to Lake Constance, the new wave of gastronomic innovation left its tangible—and very tasty—traces, which have by now influenced fine cooks everywhere in the country.

Since the last edition of our guide to the restaurants of Germany, the quality of German cuisine has continued to improve and today there are more spectacularly good restaurants to be found than ever before. Only a handful of years ago, we were astonished to discover how German chefs had studied the new tastes that had already conquered the palates of neighboring countries, and how they adapted them in a creative style of cooking that retained a "gemütlich" German character. Today, first-rate modern German cooking is no longer a new phenomenon. In fact, it can be found everywhere.

Top German restaurants can now be favorably compared with those of neighboring nations. Of course, the recession that hit Western Europe so hard in recent years has not spared Germany. Diners in German restaurants, as elsewhere on the Continent and in the U.S. too, have become cautious and reluctant to spend the way they did in the past. Chefs had to respond to consumers' heightened sensitivity to price if they were to survive in the difficult economy.

Many restaurants have responded to this challenge by offering attractive menus at lower prices. You will find this book filled with reviews of such establishments. In some cases, where quality has been sacrificed to cost controls, we were forced to note the decline of the dining rooms in question.

Economic concerns aside, there have been countless changes on the fine dining front in Germany since our last edition. We have worked with determination to remain abreast of the ever-changing landscape and are pleased to bring to you our current judgments of both the best values and the very best dining experiences available in Germany today. In addition, we have prepared a guide to many of Germany's best wineries. And, of course, we provide hotel recommendations to help you choose the most appropriate lodging for your stay.

Needless to say, the reunification of this long-divided nation has had a profound impact on all of German culture, cooking and dining customs included. Vigorous efforts are being made in restaurants in the eastern regions of Germany to make up for lost time. We are pleased to encourage these efforts by reporting to you on many of the most successful ones to date.

Guten Appetit!

André Gayot

Our Rating System

What decides the rating of a restaurant? What is on the plate is by far the most important factor. The quality of basic ingredients is among the most telling signs of a restaurant's culinary status. It requires a great deal of commitment and money to stock the finest grades and cuts of meat and the finest quality of fish. Quality restaurants also attune themselves to seasonal produce, whether it is local berries or truffles from Italy. Freshness is all-important, too, and a telling indication of quality. This means not only using fresh rather than frozen fish, for example, but also preparing everything from scratch at the last possible moment, from appetizers through desserts.

What else do we look for? Details are telling: If sauces are basically all the same, you know that the kitchen is taking shortcuts. The quality of the bread on the table is always a tip-off; similarly house wine can speak volumes about the culinary attitude and level of an establishment. Finally, among the very finest restaurants, creativity and influence can be determining factors. These features, however, are relatively unimportant for simply good restaurants, where the quality and consistency of what appears on the plates are the central factors.

Our rating system works as follows: Restaurants are ranked in the same manner that French students are graded, on a scale of 1 to 20. The rankings reflect only our opinion of the food; the decor, service, wine list and atmosphere are commented on within each review. Restaurants that are ranked 13/20 and above are distinguished with toques (chefs' hats) according to the table below. For a complete index of every restaurant in the book by rating, please see the "Toque Tally" on pages 8 and 9.

Exceptional
(ratings of 19/20 and 19.5/20)

Excellent
(ratings of 17/20 and 18/20)

Very good
(ratings of 15/20 and 16/20)

Good
(ratings of 13/20 and 14/20)

Keep in mind that we are comparing Germany's restaurants to the very best in the world. Also, these ranks are relative. A 13/20 (one toque) may not be a superlative ranking for a highly reputed (and very expensive) restaurant, but it is quite complimentary for a small place without much culinary pretension.

Toques in red denote restaurants serving modern cuisine; toques in black denote restaurants serving traditional food.

At the end of each restaurant review, prices are given—either à la carte or menus (fixed-price meals) or both. A la carte prices are those of an average meal (a starter, a main course, and a dessert) for one person, including service and a half bottle of relatively inexpensive wine. Lovers of great Bordeaux, Burgundies and Champagnes will, of course, face stiffer tabs. The menu prices quoted are for a complete multicourse meal for one person, including service but excluding wine (unless otherwise noted). These fixed-price menus often give diners on a budget a chance to sample the cuisine of an otherwise expensive restaurant.

Prices in red denote restaurants that offer particularly good value.

A SAMPLING OF THINGS TO COME...

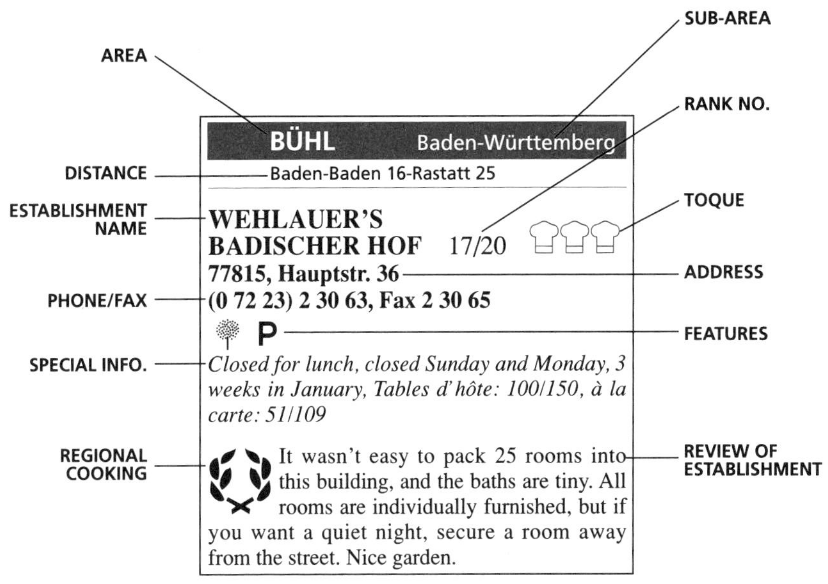

Hotels

Our opinion of the comfort level and appeal of each hotel is expressed in a ranking system, as follows:

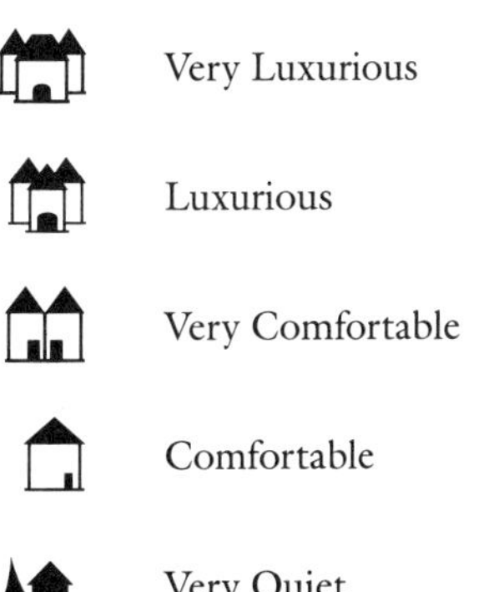

Symbols in red denote charm.

Hotel prices listed are for complete range of rooms, from the smallest singles to the largest doubles; suite prices are also given when possible. These prices are per room, not per person. Half-board and full-board prices, however, are per person. All of the main rooms have baths and/or showers unless otherwise indicated.

Sadly, prices continue to creep up, so some places may have become more expensive than our estimates by the time you visit. If you expect to pay a little more-you may end up being pleasantly surprised!

TOQUE TALLY

TOP RESTAURANTS: FOOD RATING

19.5/20

Schwarzwaldstube
Schweizer Stuben
Tantris
Zur Traube

19/20

Le Canard
Kurhausstüberl
Restaurant Dieter Müller
In Schloßhotel Lerbach
Restaurant Jörg Müller
Restaurant Winkler
Waldhorn

18/20 

Auberge Le Concarneau
Bamberger Reiter
Bareiss
In Hotel Bareiss
Benedikt
In Hotel Résidence
Brückenkeller
Cheval Blanc
In Hotel Gregor
Colombi
Da Gianni
Die Ente Vom Lehel
In Nassauer Hof
Essigbrätlein
Gasthaus Glockenbach
Goldener Pflug
Le Gourmet
Hessler
Hirschen
Hostellerie Bacher
Imperial
L'orchidee
In Hotel Zur Post
Landhaus Baur
Landhaus Scherrer
In Burg-Hotel Stromburg
Rockendorf's Restaurant
Schloss Höfingen
Stern's Restaurant
In Hotel Georgenhof
Taverna La Vigna
Valkenhof
Victorian
Wald & Schlosshotel
Friedrichsruhe
Le Val D'or
Waldhotel Sonnora

17/20 

Alte Stadtmühle
Altes Forsthaus Beck
Anna E Sebastiano
Aubergine
Berghotel Baader
Bründlhof
Capricorne
In Hotel Schwarzer Bock
Cölln's Austernstuben
Delice
Der Schafhof
Die Ulrichshöhe
La Forge
In Schmiedegasthaus
Gala
Grand Slam
Grashoff's Bistro
Graues Haus
Hotel 3 Stuben
Kleines Restaurant
Königshof
Kurhotel Zum Löwen
Gehrke
Landgasthof Adler
Landhaus Götker
Landhaus Köpp
La Mairie
Maxwell
Ölmühle
Orangerie
In Parkhotel Völklingen
Petersilie
Ponte Vecchio
La Provence
Raub's Restaurant
Rest. Marcobrunn
In Schloß
Reinhartshausen
Schützenhof
Schwarzer Hahn
In Deidesheimer Hof
Speismeisterei
Steinheuers Rest. Zur
Alten Post
3 Stuben
Toddy's
Villa Fayence
Waldhorn
Wehlauer's
Badischer Hof
Wielandshöhe
Winzerstübchen
Zur Krone
In The Hotel Zur Krone

16/20 

Acquarello
Al Pino
Alt-Luxemburg
Alte Schenke
Alte Villa
Ana E Bruno
Apicius
In Jagdhaus
Eiden Am See
Averbeck's Giebelhof
Bauernstube
Bistro Ente Vom Lehel
In Nassauer Hof
Bistro Terrine
Bistrot 77
Bomke
Büdel's Restaurant
Calla
Dichterstub'n
In Parkhotel Egerner Hof
Die Insel
In The Hotel Corso
Die Trüffel
In Hotel Maritim
Dorfstuben
Endtenfang
In Hotel Fürstenhof
Fischereihafen-
Restaurant
Flohr's Restaurant
Galleria
Grüns Restaurant
Häckermühle
Halbedel's Gasthaus
Hefter
Himmeltoss
Historisches Eck
Historisches Gasthaus
Zur Stube
Hotellerie Hubertus
Hoyerberg Schlössle
Hummer-Stübchen
Im Schiffchen
Jägerstüberl
Kaminstube
Köhlerstube
Kölner Hof
Krautkrämer
Krone
Krone Assmannshausen
Kronnenschlössen
L'ecole
Landgast Am Königsweg
Landhaus Mühlenberg
Landhaus St. Urban
Langer's
Schlemmerstuben
Luther

Le Maître
Martin's Gute Stube In Winzerhof
Massimiliano
Le Moissonier
Oberländer Weinstube
Orangerie In Martim Seehotel
Osteria Enoteca
Pan Zu Erbach
Poppenborg
Restaurant Français
Restaurant Oblinger By The Old Seagate
Ristorante Rossini
Rôtisserie Dubs
Schaller In Hotel Coburger Hof
Scheid
Schwanen
Seehotel Sieber
Sepp Halbritter's Landgastahus
St. Magnuszimmer In Gasthaus Krone
Tafelhaus
Tappes Restaurant
Ulrich's Klostergalerie
La Vigna
Villino
Waldhotel Post
Waldschlössl
Wullenwever
Zirbelstuben In Hotel Victoria
Zum Adler
Zum Blauen Fuchs
Zum Hugenotten In The Hotel Inter-Continental

15/20

Aalschokker
Achterdiek
Adler Wirtschaft
Alpenhof Murnau
Alpenschlössle
Alte Apotheke
Alte Schmiede
Altes Pfarrhaus
Altes Zollhaus
Ambiance Am Dom In The Hotel
Excelsior Ernst
Andresen's Gasthof
Arnspitze
Auberge In Hotel Henneberger Haus
Auberge Délices
Bakkarat In The Machsee Casino
Bammes
Biermann's Restaurant
Bistro In Kaiser Karl Hotel
Bistro Bamberger Reiter
Botheler Landhaus
Brasserie Bruno
Brenner's Park-Hotel
Burgrestaurant Staufeneck
La Chandelle In Hotel Mondial
Le Carat
Le Chalet
C+W Gourmet
Damperhof
Das Caroussel
Das Fäßle
Das Weisse Haus
Davert-Jagdhaus
De Balzac In Hotel Becher
Der Leeberghof
Die Mühle
Dobler's Restaurant L'epi D'or
Domherrenhof
Feiler
La Fontaine In Hotel Ludwig Im Park
Forsthaus Ilkahöhe
Frühsammer's Gasthaus
Funk
Fürstenhof
Gala In Parkhotel
Gallo Nero
Garden-Restaurant
Gasthof Brink
Goldene Kugel
Gourmet-Restaurant Wagner
Graugans In The Hyatt Regency
Halali
Haus Rödgen
Haus Waldsee
Heimathof Nolle
Hermannsdorfer Schweinsbräu
Hirsch
Hirsch-Weinstuben
Histor. Wirthaus An Der Lahn
Höerhof
Hohenhaus
Hotel Abtei
Hotel Adler
Hotel Neumühle
Hunsingers Bouillabaisse
Ifen-Hotel
Il Ristorante
Inzlinger Wasserschloss
Käfer-Schänke
Kleines Landhaus
Klosterschenke
Krausler-Feine Speisen In The Bergcafé
Kräutergarten
Krone
Kupferkanne In Hotel Erbguth's Landhaus
Kurfürstliches Amthaus
Landgasthof Alte Post
Landhaus Ammann
Landhotel Schlosswirtschaft
Lehenstube In Hotel Schloß Lehen
Markgräfler Hof
Metzler's Gasthof
Orangerie In Nassauer Hof
Pades Restaurant
Papillion In The Sheraton
Pension Corveyblick
Pesel
Le Petit Poisson
Pfälzer Stuben In The Hotel Zur Krone
Puth's Ambiente
Résidence
Ressmann's Restaurant
Rest. Vogelherd In Schloßhotel Oberstotzingen
Restaurant Bado La Poêle D'or
Restaurant Im Logenhaus
Ristorante Bei Grazi
Ritter St. Georg
Rolink's Alte Mühle
Rosi's Restaurant
Rôtisserie Landhaus Leick
Rützelerie Geiss
Schaarscmidt-Alte Krone
Schiffchen
Schillinghof
Schloss Bevern
Schloss Loersfeld
Schloss Schwansbell
Schloss Wilkinhege
Schloss-Restaurant In Schlosshotel Bühlerhöhe
Schlossgass' 16
Schober
Schwarzer Adler
Schwarzer Adler
Schwarzwälder
Schweizer Stuben In Kirschberg-Schlössl
September
Siebelnhof
Silberburg
Sonne
Sonne
Spago
Storchen-Nest
La Table
Tao
Tönsings Kohlenkrug
Top Air
Trio
V.M. 1
La Vigna
Villa Duttenhofer (L'etoile)
Villa Hammerschmeide
Villa Leonhardi
Walhaus Ohlenbach
Walk'sches Haus
Wein Wolf
Weinhaus Stern
Wilder Mann
Zum Alde Gott
Zum Alten Rentamt
Zum Hirschen
Zum Ochsen
Zum Watkorn
Zur Krone

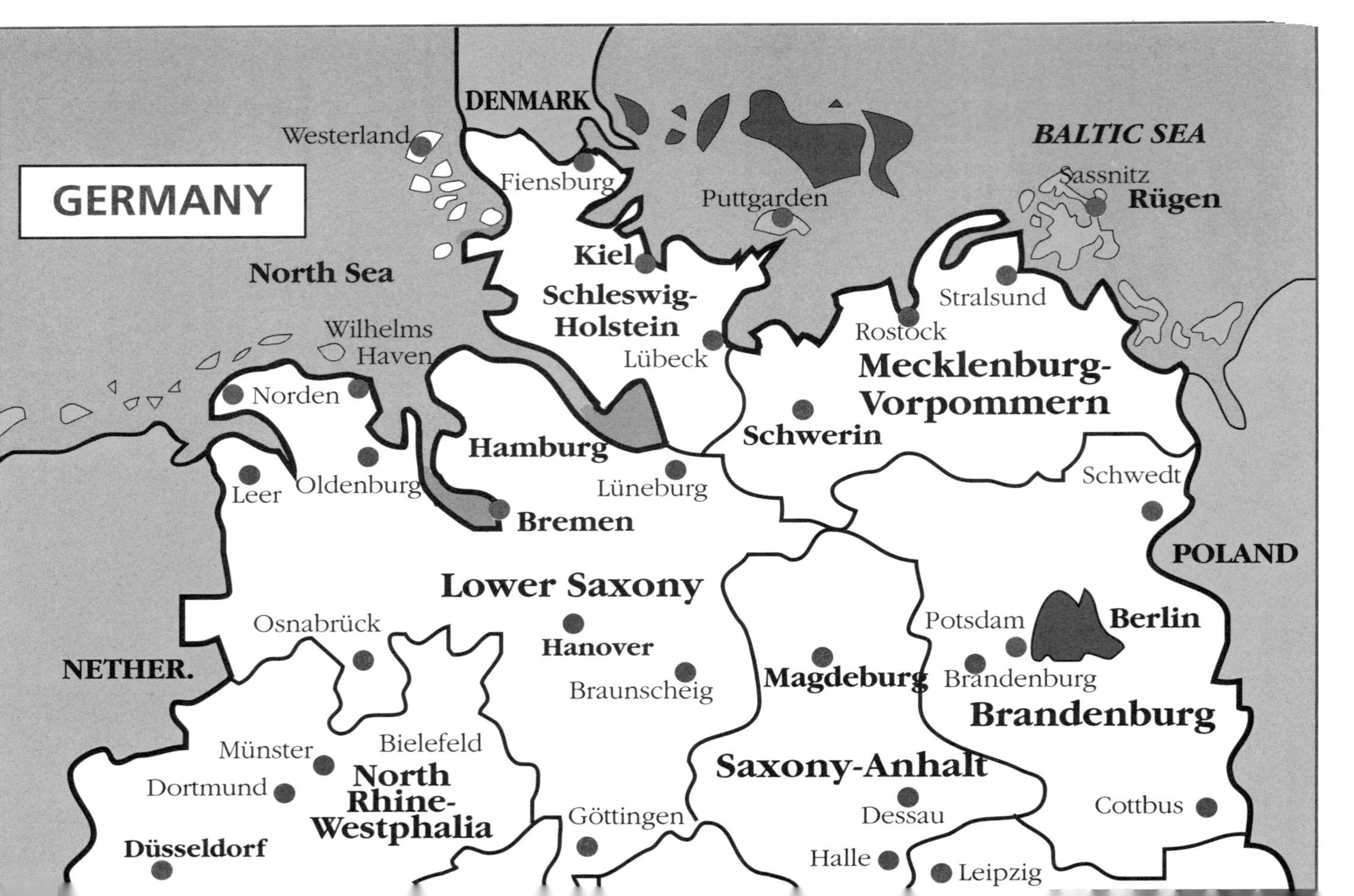
GERMANY
DENMARK
BALTIC SEA
North Sea
Westerland
Fiensburg
Puttgarden
Sassnitz
Rügen
Kiel
Schleswig-
Holstein
Lübeck
Stralsund
Rostock
Mecklenburg-
Vorpommern
Schwerin
Wilhelms
Haven
Norden
Hamburg
Leer
Oldenburg
Lüneburg
Bremen
Schwedt
POLAND
Lower Saxony
Osnabrück
Hanover
Braunscheig
Potsdam
Berlin
Brandenburg
Brandenburg
Magdeburg
NETHER.
Münster
Bielefeld
Dortmund
North
Rhine-
Westphalia
Düsseldorf
Göttingen
Saxony-Anhalt
Dessau
Halle
Leipzig
Cottbus

Kassel
Aachen
Cologne
Bonn
Koblenz
BELG.
Hesse
Limburg
Frankfurt
Wiesbaden
Rhineland
Palatinate
Mainz
LUX.
Saarland
Saarbrücken
Weimar
Erfurt
Eisenach
Jena
Gera
Thuringia
Suhl
Meissen
Dresden
Saxony
Chemnitz
Plauen
Coburg
Aschaffenburg
Bamberg
CZECH
REPUBLIC
Würzburg
Bayreuth
Heidelberg
Nuremberg
Rothenburg
on Tauber
Heilbronn
Karlsruhe
Regensburg
Bavaria
FRANCE
Stuttgart
Baden-Baden
Ingolstadt
Passau
Landshut
Donauwörth
Baden-
Württemberg
Augsburg
Munich
Freiburg
Friedrichshafen
Kempten
Oberammergau
Garmisch-Partenkirchen
AUSTRIA
SWITZERLAND
Mittenwald
© AGP

Symbols Chart

Symbol	Meaning
	BAR
	BATH/WC/TOILET
	CAFÉ
	FAX CONNECTION IN ROOM
	FITNESS CENTER
P	FULL-BOARD
	GARAGE
	GOLF COURSE
1/2P	HALF-BOARD
/	INDOOR/OUTDOOR POOL
	KITCHEN OPEN LATE
App.	LUXURY APART./ SUITES
	NUMBER OF ROOMS
P	PARKING LOT/GARAGE
	PARTICULARLY PEACEFUL
	REGIONAL COOKING
res.	RESERVATIONS ACCEPTED
	RIDING AVAILABLE
	SAUNA
	SEA-SWIMMING PERMITTED
	SHOWER/WC/TOILET
	SPA (CURATIVE) TREATMENTS
	SUPERVISED CHILD PLAY AREA
	TAP ROOM
	TELEVISION IN ROOM
	TENNIS
	TERRACE/GARDEN
	WINE/BAR

GERMANY

AACHEN NRW

Köln 70-Brüssel 140

LE CANARD 12/20

52062, Bendelstr. 8-32
(02 41) 3 86 63, 2 30 18, res.

Closed Sunday and Monday, one week during Carnival and before Whitsunday. Tables d'hôte: 57 L, 98 D, à la carte: 61-99

This is a stylish restaurant with an uneven culinary offering. The hors d'oeuvres were individually tasty, but the combination of herring, salmon, duck, carpaccio, shrimp and potato salad on one plate was just plain weird. The near-disaster of an almost burnt salmon gratin with spinach was compensated for by the wonderful Scottish saddle of lamb that harmonized well with the accompanying ratatouille. The green apple with baked gorgonzola crust was a sensation! The choice of wines is small but sensible.

GALA 17/20

52062, Monheimsallee 44
(02 41) 15 3 13, Fax (02 41) 15 85 78 res.

Closed for lunch, closed Sunday, Monday. Tables d'hôte: 95-125, à la carte: 64-104, Tables d'hôte with wine: 140-195

"Eccentric" is a good way to describe this restaurant in Aachen's casino. The glamorous lighting is spectacular, and Salvador Dali's "Gala" is a treat for the eye, but the endlessly tinkling electronic piano is hard on the ears. Happily, chef Maurice de Boer's cooking is a delight for a gourmet's palate. Although the first course of sweetbreads with a lovely salad was insipid, it was followed by delicious marinated foie gras with onion marmalade, an excellent fillet of anglerfish in sorrel butter and terrific truffled pigeon breasts and legs. Dining here does not require hitting the jackpot: A four-course dinner with wine costs 140 DM on weekdays. Be sure to reserve a table for weekends. Maître d'hôtel Jörg Wössner, an expert on German wine, is the perfect host and turns every meal into a gala.

ST. BENEDIKT 14/20

8 km southeast
in 52076 Kornelimünster
Benediktusplatz 12
(0 24 08) 28 88, Fax 28 88

Closed for lunch, closed Sunday, Monday, 3 weeks during the North Rhine-Westphalia summer school holiday, Tables d'hôte: 75-98, à la carte: 53-79

Gisela Kreus is the motivated cook and her husband the charming host in this beautiful old house with a trellis of yellow roses at the front door. Fresh and light dishes are characteristic of the cuisine. We enjoyed chicken-liver parfait on pears as an appetizer, fish and vegetables rolled up in a rice leaf, Scottish salmon with vegetable vinaigrette and an absolutely tender and light fillet of lamb with Burgundy sauce. The vegetables, meat and fish offered here are grown and raised in the region. The sauces are harmonious and the cheeses wonderfully ripe and mellow. Try the desserts—they're something else! Be sure to reserve beforehand in this popular little restaurant.

STEIGENBERGER QUELLENHOF

52062, Monheimsallee 52
(02 41) 15 20 81 , Fax 15 45 04

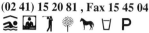

160, **S** 185/260, **D** 280/420,
APP 440/850, **½P** +45, **P** +80

Grand and elegant, this traditional hotel with its quiet and tastefully furnished rooms is close to the casino, conference center and spa gardens. The hotel gives directly onto the spa, which offers massage, solarium and beauty treatments. There is a breakfast buffet and an ambitious restaurant.

ACHERN Baden-Württ.

Offenburg 20 - Baden-Baden 29

GÖTZ SONNE-EINTRACHT 12/20

77855, Hauptstr. 112
(0 78 41) 64 50, Fax 64 56 45

Tables d'hôte: 39/44L, 69/120D, à la carte: 38/86

August Götz still serves expensive wines in tiny glasses. But this is just one of the reasons guests have a hard time trying to feel at home here. Traditional cuisine is the kitchen's forte, unexperimental but featuring time-tested regional dishes like marinated veal, white tripe, venison ragout and a Black Forest trout for 34 DM. If you order the prix-fixe menu, you're in for a roller-coaster ride. We needed a magnifying glass to find the smoked duck's breast in our appetizer, but didn't need any help in deciding that the dressing on our lamb's lettuce with soggy chicken liver was much too sour. Some highlights were tasty shrimp soup, excellent veal fillet with morel cream sauce and lovely spaetzle. The service was good.

GÖTZ SONNE-EINTRACHT

77855, Hauptstr. 112
(0 78 41) 64 50, Fax 64 56 45

P

55, **S** 89/189, **D** 130/190,
APP 260/320, **½P** +42, **P** +69

In this cheerful and sunny hotel, Gustl Götz continues a 350-year-old family tradition of hospitality. The rooms are elegantly appointed. A romantic story linking the Götz family to the royal house of Thailand inspired Lehár's opera "Land des Lächelns." Restaurant.

KININGER'S HIRSCH

77855, Orsteil Oberachern
Oberacherner Str. 26
(0 78 41) 2 15 79, Fax 2 92 68

Closed Monday, closed for lunch Tuesday. Tables d'hôte: 41/78, à la carte: 28/62

Germany needs more restaurants like this one. This place isn't one of the top gourmet spots, but is still very popular for a number of good reasons: it serves a variety of good and honestly prepared dishes at relatively low prices. At simply but precisely set tables, you can order daily specials chalked up on the slate. A few of them, like the antipasto platter or marinated salmon with rösti, show that Bernhard Kiniger is ambitious and can satisfy more than the demands usually made of a plain country eating place. You can get a taste of this when you order his very special wine-vinegar aperitif made with orange-blossom honey! The wine list features regional wines and a few international bottles. Wines by the glass come in the classic *viertele*, holding about a quarter-liter. The service isn't bad.

AHAUS Nordrhein-Westfalen

Gronau 16 - Coesfeld 19

REST. WILDER WEIN IN THE HOTEL RUDOLPH 14/20

48683, Coesfelder Str. 21-23
(0 25 61) 91 10, Fax 91 13 00 res.

P

Closed Sunday. Tables d'hôte: 38/65L, 98D, à la carte: 37/70

While the "Ratsstübchen" on the premises caters to those who want a quick lunch or a plain dinner, the restaurant's new exclusive conception has left room for only five tables seating 24 guests. The exquisite floral decoration, though, is as opulent as ever, the service is as pleasant and professional and the prices on the wine list as reasonable as before. This cuisine offers no flamboyant surprises, but sticks to modern classic recipes with seasonal accents.

RATSHOTEL RUDOLPH
48683, Coesfelder Str. 21-23
(0 25 61) 91 10, Fax 91 13 00
 P
40 beds, **S** 148/158, **D** 196/206,
APP 266, **½P** +43, **P** +76

This postmodern-style hotel, centrally located yet quiet, offers comfortable rooms and beautifully equipped suites. There is also a solarium, fitness facilities, bowling alleys and bike rental. Opulent breakfast buffet and first-class service.

AHRENSHOOP Meckl.-Vorp.

Rostock 45

CAFÉ BUHNE 12 12/20
18347, Grenzweg 12
(03 82 20) 2 32, res.
Closed Thursday. Tables d'hôte: 40, à la carte: 25/34

Don't expect grande cuisine here or fine details, but you can be sure of carefully prepared and absolutely fresh produce. The restaurant, on a cliff overlooking the sea, is as plain and unadorned as the dishes you can choose from the handwritten menu. We had pike-perch fillet from an Ahrenshoop fisherman, little plaice fillets poached in vegetable broth and a steamed salmon with dill sauce. We loved this unartificial food just as much as the fantastic view of the ocean. A choice of eight Franconian wines from the famous Bürgerspital are stored in special refrigerators that keep the bottles at just the right temperature.

CAFÉ NAMENLOS 12/20
18347, Dorfstr. 44
(03 82 20) 8 01 56, Fax 8 03 83
 P
Closed: 11 - 24 December. Tables d'hôte: 60, à la carte: 24/55

This café offers good and hearty regional fare. We liked fillet of bass with vegetable julienne, delicately steamed pike-perch fillet with hollandaise sauce and tender fillet of venison. When the house is full and people eat on the terrace as well, the service staff can't keep up. The wine list could be improved.

HAUS AM MEER
18347, Dorfstr. 36
(03 82 20) 8 08 16, Fax 8 06 10
 P
24 beds, **S** 128/210, **D** 148/228,
APP 220/260, **½P** +25

The spa was rebuilt in 1970 and offers newly decorated modern rooms. Two adjoining houses on the beach form the hotel.

AIDLINGEN Bad.-Württ.

Sindelfingen 6-Calw 14

ALTE VILLA 16/20
71134, Deufringen
Aidlingerstr. 36
(0 70 56) 28 72, Fax 44 72 res.
P
Closed for lunch, Tuesday through Saturday. Closed Monday, 1-15 January. Tables d'hôte: 45/98, à la carte: 41/79

Ever since Erika Molkeke took over the kitchen of this beautiful Art Nouveau establishment, she has been cooking her way up the culinary ladder. Deceptively simple dishes are prepared with loving care and few frills. Several dishes went beyond the realm of mere food to become sensual poetry: marinated salmon with potato pancakes and creamy horseradish; perfectly dressed salads with quail's breast and Serrano ham; *Gaisburger Marsch* (a Swabian-style stew) of shrimps with spaetzle, accompanied by a potato and vegetable julienne; and bass served on a bed of spinach with homemade mushroom noodles. Perhaps the most stunning dish was the hare, marinated sauerbraten-style, with a delicate sauce and cèpe risotto. The saddle of venison with truffles and Brussels sprouts was absolute perfection. Choice cheeses, delicious desserts, and dainty petits fours rounded off a first-class dinner. The service was agreeable, and the wine cellar is well-stocked with international vintages at reasonable prices. Wine can be ordered by the glass or half bottle.

ALBSTADT Baden-Württ.

Tübingen 45-Konstanz 104

LINDE 12/20
72458, Orsteil Ebingen
Untere Vorstadt 1
(0 74 31)5 30 61, Fax 5 33 22

P

Closed: 23 December through 7 January; last three weeks of the Bad.-Württ. summer school holiday. No Credit Cards. Tables d'hôte: 49/63L, 78/105D, à la carte: 32/83, Tables d'hôte with wine: 49

The Linde has a cozy, homey atmosphere and attentive service, but the efforts of the kitchen are not always up to par. A salmon steak with ratatouille and chopped tomatoes was excellent, and a fillet of venison with mushrooms and pancakes with plums nicely done, but what was described on the menu as coffee with fancy pastry turned out to be weak espresso with biscuits. A respectable selection of relatively reasonable European wines is available by the bottle or by the glass.

LINDE
72458, Orsteil Ebingen
Untere Vorstadt 1
(0 74 31) 5 30 61, Fax 5 33 22

 P

23, **S** 105/150, **D** 178/205

Closed Saturday, Sunday; 23 December through 7 January; last three weeks of the Bad.-Württ. summer school holiday, No Credit Cards

This is a hospitable establishment, whose individually furnished rooms with their modern amenities express the personality of the owner, Kurt Hettler. The furniture is either antique or timelessly functional. The rooms in this beautiful old framework house aren't very spacious, but cleverly laid out.

ALKEN Rheinl.-Pfalz

Koblenz 21-St. Goar 33

BURG THURANT 13/20 
56332, Moselstr. 16
(0 26 05) 35 81, res.

Closed for lunch, closed Monday. à la carte: 28/57

Don't look for this restaurant up in the Thurant castle. It's located at the foot of the vineyards in an old stone house with tower on the Moselle promenade. In the rustic dining room, with its old baking oven and open fireplace, Gabi and Peter Kopowski serve imaginative refined regional cuisine: delicious chanterelles with noodles, trout fried in almond butter, succulent eel with parsley potatoes and *tafelspitz* Moselle-style with an excellent sauce. The wine list features mostly Moselle wines, but some fine wines of other regions as well. Don't hesitate to take advantage of the surprisingly modest prices. There are five idyllic guest rooms.

ALSDORF NRW

Jülich 12-Aachen 13

DIE INSEL
IN THE HOTEL CORSO 16/20 
52477, Burgstr. 30
(0 24 04) 90 40, Fax 90 41 80 res.

Closed for lunch. Tables d'hôte: 79/145, à la carte: 53/90. Tables d'hôte with wine: 109/195

The talented young cook Alexander Melicker has learned his craft well from chef Heinz Winckler in Aschau. He's an excellent cook who keeps both feet on the ground. His menu is much too laconic for snobs; veal fillet with asparagus, iced tomatoes with angler medallions, oxtail in red-wine sauce and cheese soufflé with strawberry sauce don't sound particularly exciting. Don't be fooled! Our prix-fixe menu (under 100 DM) began with an amusing appetizer: consommé in an eggcup, a spoonful of foamy angler mousse and a tiny ham doughnut. Then Melicker got serious: a fabulous roulade of smoked salmon with chive sauce, savory blood pudding with sour cream and salad, wonderfully done char filled with squash on pesto and pike-perch and red beets with horseradish cream, followed by a farmyard duck fried whole with a super sauce we wouldn't have been ashamed to sip out of the sauceboat. The Austrian-Bohemian dessert platter left us flabbergasted. The chic and stylish interior doesn't leave diners much room to move around in. You sit either in cozy nooks or at the bar, where places are also set. The wine list includes wines from Germany, France, Italy and Spain (about two dozen can be ordered in half-bottles as well) at reasonable prices.

ALT-DUVENSTEDT SH

Flensburg 8

TÖPFERHAUS

2491 Alt-Duvenstedt
(0 43 38) 4 02, Fax 5 51

P

47, **S** 120/190, **D** 180/260,
APP 230/260, **½P** +55

TÖPFERHAUS 11/20

2491 Alt-Duvenstedt
(0 43 38) 4 02, Fax 5 51

 P

Tables d'hôte: 45L, 60D, à la carte: 38/72

This imposing hotel and restaurant complex situated on the shores of the Bistensee is surrounded by pristine nature. Although the restaurant seats 70, it does not feel crowded because there are several pleasant dining rooms. The menu changes daily and offers two (expensive) gourmet dinners. Unfortunately, culinary standards have definitely sunk since the departure of chef Ralf Chalas. The wine cellar offers a good choice of renowned German, French and Italian vintages but is dominated by higher-priced Bordeaux. The waiters, while attentive and friendly when present, are not easy to find in such a large restaurant.

ALTENSTADT Bayern

Illertissen 1-Memmingen 24

LANDHOTEL SCHLOSSWIRTSCHAFT 15/20

89281, Illereichen
Kirchplatz 2
(0 83 37) 80 45, Fax 4 60

 P

Closed: Sunday evening, Monday. Tables d'hôte: 86 L, 155/175 D, à la carte: 66/110

Eberhard Aspacher advertises "lively and honest German cooking." We would have forgiven him his high prices if his performance had been as good as it used to be. He hasn't lost any of his professionalism, but his cooking has become complacent. The chickpea crème with baby lobster was sadly unimaginative and the calf's tongue with perfectly done saddle of lamb just seemed lost. His superb foie gras parfait, though, revealed what Aspacher is capable of (if he doesn't try to do too many things at once). But we shook our heads in honest bewilderment when we tasted the wonderful but lukewarm consommé of guinea fowl and the insipid carrots and celery served with an otherwise impeccable turbot.

LANDHOTEL SCHLOSSWIRTSCHAFT

89281, Illereichen
Kirchplatz 2
(0 83 37) 80 45, Fax 4 60

11, **S** 106, **D** 150/220,
APP 280, **½P** +50, **P** +110

The same loving care that went into the creation of the restaurant is evident in this small hotel, which offers all one could ask for, including absolute quiet. A popular place for business meetings.

ALTUSREID BW

Kempten 14-Leutkirch 18

LANDGASTHOF ALTE POST 15/20

87452, Ortsteil Kimratshofen
Am Kirchberg 2
(0 83 73) 81 11, Fax 81 13

P

Closed Tuesday. Tables d'hôte: 48L, 89D, à la carte: 41/75

The accomplishments of this country inn are homogeneous: it is elegantly and simply furnished, with an impeccable, uninflated cuisine and amiable and competent service. This restaurant is an oasis in the culinary area around Kempten. The small but attractive menu excited our imagination. We tasted crème of mushrooms, fresh crab chowder with seaweed, lovely green salads, delicious veal schnitzel with lime sauce and parmesan risotto and an impressive Pichelstein stew. If you want wine, don't call for the wine list (they don't have one) but the competent owner, who can help you.

AMÖNEBURG Hessen

Stadtallendorf 11-Marburg 15

DOMBÄCKER 14/20 

35827, Am Markt 18
(0 64 22) 37 55, Fax 5 14 95 res.

 P

Closed for lunch Monday, closed 1 week in January, 2 weeks during the Hessen summer school holiday. Tables d'hôte: 42/46L, 68/78 D, à la carte: 36/68

The Dombäcker always offers the perfect setting for a pleasant dinner, whether you sit outside on the terrace in summer (in the middle of the marketplace) or inside in winter in front of a roaring fire. Ulrich Schulist offers light and sometimes inventive dishes that can also occasionally be hearty and savory. The farmyard duck we had, though, was a total failure. On the other hand, we enjoyed a lovely mousse of scallops, calf's kidneys in mustard cream sauce with crisp rösti, correctly done fish (halibut, lemon sole, striped mullet and salmon) with Riesling butter and a delicate mousse, parfait and sorbet made of strawberries. The service and wine list are adequate.

AMORBACH Bayern

Anschaffenburg 47-Heilbronn 67

DER SCHAFHOF 17/20 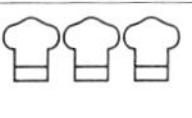

63916, Im Otterbachtal
(0 93 73) 80 88, Fax 41 20

Tables d'hôte: 65/150, à la carte: 48/94

There is a splendid view over a valley from this beautiful country inn, but the motivated young staff seems to have its eyes set on heaven. The subtly elegant harmony of the food here pleases all the senses. Try the turbot and spiny lobster served in a delicate tarragon sauce, the truffled roulade of foie gras, or the perfectly prepared John Dory in yogurt flavored with herbs and cucumber. The house symbol, a sheep, is painted on the plates and served on them as well. Highlights included a juicy, exquisitely seasoned saddle of lamb and a tender loin of lamb in a cheese crust, served with thyme-flavored potatoes. Meals can be splendidly topped off with a marvelous millefeuille of wild strawberries or ravioli stuffed with Muenster cheese. Specialties of the house include grilled piglet roulade filled with sausage and roast lamb served with cabbage, and fresh trout from a nearby pond. In summer, snacks can be ordered on the terrace. The wine cellar offers good German and French vintages, and the head waiter is willing to help customers choose affordable wines.

DER SCHAFHOF 

63916, Im Otterbachtal
(0 93 73) 80 88, Fax 41 20

P

23, **S** 160/225, **D** 180/250,
APP 325/350, **1/2P** +75, **P** +135

The hotel's modern management provides guests with more worldly pleasures than did the Benedictines who used to run this estate in the 18th century. Cupid could have furnished many of the unabashedly romantic rooms of this Relais & Châteaux hotel. No wonder more and more weddings and banquets are held here. And no wonder an annex has become necessary to accommodate these guests. The main building has remained unchanged.The idyllic Odenwald is balm for the stressed soul of the city businessman, and offers recreation for those who want to stay active: carriage drives in summer and sleighing in winter. Cozy breakfast room and buffet with homemade marmalades and honey.

VICTORIA 14/20 

63916, Johannesturmstr. 10
(0 93 73) 73 15,

Closed Monday and Tuesday. No Credit Cards. Tables d'hôte: 49/54, à la carte: 32/62

The light and airy surroundings of this restaurant provide the perfect ambience for enjoyable eating. All ingredients are chosen with the utmost care and prepared with an eye for detail. Favorite dishes on the menu included tagliatelle with chanterelles and cream of chives, aspic of *Tafelspitz* with a fresh herb dip, rabbit livers with lentils in balsamic vinegar and iced cucumber with shrimp and coriander. The small but choice wine list offers quite a few wines by the glass. Anne-Kathrin Zöllner's refreshing personality makes dining here a delightful experience.

AMRUM Schleswig-Holstein

Autofähre: (0 46 81) 80 40

PESEL 13/20 

in 25946 Norddorf
Nei Stich 16
(0 46 82) 24 74, Fax 41 58

P

Closed for lunch, closed Monday, mid-January through mid-February. A la carte: 28/59

Here you get an idea of what Germans mean when they talk about their Sunday parlor. The lovingly decorated dining rooms flaunt Frisian flair without kitsch. A communicative little aperitif bar as well as uncomplicated friendly service quickly make guests feel at home. Göran Quedens offers refined and high-quality regional cuisine at fair prices. His redfish in a crust of sesame seeds with lovely homemade mayonnaise, perfectly fried lamb fillets with potato gratin and herring with tomato coulis were very tasty. Nicely stocked wine list with prices typical of the island. Five tastefully furnished rooms and sumptuous breakfast with seafood and sparkling wine.

SEEKISTE 12/20

in 25946 Nebel
Smääljaat 2
(0 46 82) 6 40, Fax 14 21

Closed for lunch, closed Monday, 18 November through 19 December and 10 January through 18 February. Tables d'hôte: 38/76, à la carte: 28/65. No Credit Cards

This pub offers the most creative and original cuisine on the island. Everything is fresh and tasty, for instance the Frisian zarzuela (different fish fillets steamed in a broth of tomato and garlic) or the sheep-cheese gratin with herbs. Best of all are the fried potatoes. The service is attentive and quick, and remains pleasant even when it's busy. The wine list offers a small but respectable choice of wines.

ANDERNACH Rheinl.-Pf.

Koblenz 15-Remagen 20

HOTEL-RESTAURANT ALTE KANZLEI 12/20

56626, Steinweg 30
(0 26 32) 4 44 47, Fax 49 48 65 res.

Closed for lunch, closed Sunday, 23 December through 6 January. A la carte: 28/55. No Credit Cards

Pubs in vaulted cellars are usually poorly ventilated, dense with smoke and full of forced German joviality. But not this one—the owners, from Baden, have decorated their restaurant with wit and loving care. The cook doesn't want to tickle gourmets' palates; he wants to feed his hungry guests. We liked cheese soup, roast beef with onions, leg of lamb with mint sauce and *tafelspitz* with red beets. The choice of wines is small but good.

PUTH'S AMBIENTE 15/20 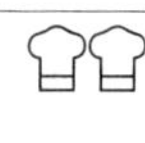

56626 Am Helmwartsturm 4-6
(0 26 32) 49 20 47, Fax 4 55 47 res.

P

Closed Sunday. Tables d'hôte: 65/115, à la carte: 33/76

Puth's restaurant comes in two versions. The Gothic vaulted cellar, the "Ratsstuben," serves only evening dinner; the light "Ambiente" above offers the same menu at noon as well. The dishes range from hearty and savory blood pudding ravioli with creamed sauerkraut to elegant veal fillet with duck-liver parfait and truffled sauce. The lobster with beans and puréed potatoes and leeks lies somewhere in between.The prix-fixe menu we had featured regional dishes with a distinct Mediterranean flair. A somewhat oily appetizer of headcheese with fried potatoes was followed by fabulously fried angler, colorfully arranged on a plate with ratatouille, basil gnocchi and pesto. This was followed by excellently marinated sauerbraten of lamb with potato dumplings and red cabbage. The finale was a French-Italian duet of champagne crème and grappa zabaglione, accompanied by fresh berries and our enthusiastic applause for a harmonious and imaginative meal. The service is amiable, the hotel of the restaurant elegant and the choice of wines tempting. Some 14 wines can be ordered by the glass.

ANGELBACHTAL BW

Heilbronn 40-Mannheim 44

SCHLOSS MICHELFELD 12/20

74918, Ortsteil Michelfeld
Friedrichstr. 2
(0 72 65) 70 41/2, Fax 2 79 res.

Closed for lunch Tuesday through Friday, closed Monday. Tables d'hôte: 54/88, à la carte: 46/87

The idyllic villages of the Kraichgau are home to many romantic manor houses like this one that seem meant to be transformed into fine restaurants. Customers pass through an imposing portal, and after being seated on the terrace or in the dining room with its stucco ceiling, they expect a fine meal. After this promising beginning, however, the food was a disappointment. The goose livers were drowned in balsamic vinegar, and the venison schnitzel and fillet of beef had an odd smell. In spite of the seasonal abundance of berries, cherries, peaches and apricots, only tropical fruits were offered on the menu.

ANZING Bayern

Markt Scwaben 4-München 20

ZUM KIRCHENWIRT 11/20

85646, Högerstr. 2
(0 81 21) 30 33, Fax 4 31 59

Closed Monday, 1—20 August, à la carte: 15/45

This *Gaststube* obviously caters to hearty Bavarian appetites. But the gargantuan portions are not the only thing that keeps regulars coming back for more. The hospitable innkeeper butchers his own top-quality meat, making for a memorably succulent roast pork—best at midday, when it is fresh from the oven—garnished with tasty potato dumplings. The soup with liver dumplings and noodles was a savory treat. Everything here is served with a smile, including the affordable wines.

Some establishments change their closing times without warning. It is always wise to check in advance.

ARNSTADT Thüringen

Erfurt 20-Suhl 40

STADTHOTEL MON PLAISIR

99310, Lessingstr. 21
(0 36 28) 73 91 11, Fax 73 92 22

37 rooms, **S** 130/150, **D** 170/190,
APP 205/245, **1/2P** +40, **P** +80

The rooms are simply but adequately furnished, the service friendly and breakfast ample. Restaurant.

VESTE WACHSENBURG 14/20

5 km northwest
in 99310 Holzhausen
Auf dem Burgberg
(0 36 28) 7 42 40 , Fax 74 24 88

Tables d'hôte: 45-73, à la carte: 33-69

The Wagner family's newly renovated restaurant provides an elegant setting for its excellent French cuisine. Try the appetizer of fresh goat cheese with olive oil, basil and tomato; scallops au gratin served with a tasty salad; the fragrant asparagus consommé with plump mushroom dumplings; the delicately seasoned stewed duck; or the lamb fillet in lemon sauce. The moderately priced wine list features vintages from around the world. All this is accompanied by quiet background music provided by a classical pianist. The only thing that struck the wrong note here was an excessive amount of butter on the rice. The well-chosen wine list is international and moderately priced.

ASCHAFFENBURG Bayern

Frankfurt 42-Würzburg 73

SCHLOSSGASS' 16 15/20

63739, Schloßgasse 16
(0 60 21) 1 23 13, res.

Closed for lunch Monday through Saturday, closed Wednesday night, closed from mid-February through 10 March, Tables d'hôte: 76, à la carte: 30-77

In this pretty 400-year-old house, the court tailor used to make clothes for the residents of the castle above. Andreas Cetin and his charming wife have made it into a quaint and romantic little gourmet restaurant. The menu offers a choice of witty prix-fixe meals and promising standards à la carte. Whatever you choose has vitality and class, combining the power of Wagner with the delicacy of Chopin. We were entranced by our appetizer: shrimp in a fantastic coconut and coriander sauce. Andreas Cetin's ambitions lead him to display his great cooking in little details, for instance his aromatic snail soup and finely balanced green salad with wafer-thin slices of beef carpaccio. His cod with lime and thyme sauce and his mousseline of smoked trout with honey and quince sauce were superb, the venison and lamb perfect. Cetin's sauces are inspirations.The wine list is small and compact, but shows the same attention to fine detail as the food. More than a dozen wines available by the glass offer good taste for relatively little money.

SONNE 15/20

8 km north in 63867
JohannesbergHauptstr. 2
(0 60 21) 47 00 77, Fax 41 39 64 res.

Closed Monday, closed from late August through mid-September. Tables d'hôte: 88-128, à la carte: 48-89

You recognize Friedel Meier's roguish sense of humor on the menu. He trips you up with his word games and makes you curious, but doesn't forget the point of his little culinary jokes when he serves his amusing but always tasty and original dishes. His Asiatic fish dishes are prepared with finesse, and the small delicacies he serves are always pleasant surprises, for instance foie gras in puff pastry with currant sauce. We enjoyed lovely, lightly smoked sweetbreads with velvety rucola sauce, loved the delicate foie gras on corn tortilla and were entranced by his savory "lamb-dumpling idea" and his "desserts for deserters." We like the Sonne best in summer, when we can enjoy our food in the garden with a view of the village chapel. There's also a special menu for light dishes outside as well as a collection of light wines, and a low-priced prix-fixe lunch during the week. The service is attentive and unpretentious. The red wines served by the glass are a few degrees too warm, but the large choice of good bottles at reasonable prices makes up for it.

SONNE

8 km north in 63867
JohannesbergHauptstr. 2
(0 60 21) 47 00 77, Fax 41 39 64

8 rooms, **S** 68/78, **D** 118

Closed from late August through mid-September

This 150-year-old country mansion offers simply but adequately furnished rooms that guarantee a quiet night's rest after a sumptuous meal in the restaurant.

ASCHAU

Prien 12-Rosenheim 22

RESTAURANT WINKLER 19/20

83229, Kirchplatz 1
(0 80 52) 1 79 90, Fax 17 99 66 res.

Tables d'hôte: 145L, 165/195D, à la carte: 66/129

If first impressions are telling, then Heinz Winkler's restaurant must be among the best. Evi Winkler's charm, the spaciously arranged and tastefully set tables and the lovely terrace with a marvelous view of the idyllic mountain landscape deserve compliments. So does the reasonably priced wine list: a 1982 Château Pichon-Lalande was 100 DM cheaper than at Scherrer's in Hamburg, but the list should include more of the best German wines. Because of his year-round job as hotelier and businessman, we didn't want to make our test too hard for Heinz Winkler; we put our menu away and let him suggest a prix-fixe meal. Our resume: everything is better, and much is almost perfect. But we failed to experience the kind of extraordinary taste sensations we could rave about.After last year's appetizer (marinated thin slices of foie gras, green salad and brioche), we had red mullet with a slightly sour ratatouille (not exactly a revelation), followed by perfect ravioli with little morels, a slightly baroque but superb turbot in potato crust with fresh mushrooms and marvelous pigeon with herbs. On our next visit, we ordered à la carte, and got wonderful pigeon breast on artichokes with herbs and duckling with mustard-seed sauce. The sole with leeks and chanterelles was a classic dish, as was the lovely saddle of suckling lamb, which we liked better than the saddle of venison offered us at a time when game was totally out of season (but still in the deep freeze?). Even if Winkler won't start a new culinary revolution with his cooking, his accomplishments are nonetheless first-class. Our last meal began with a memorable appetizer: three quails' eggs wrapped in salmon slices, each stuffed with caviar, lobster or chanterelles. The cauliflower parfait with prawns was excellent, and the John Dory in coriander sauce as difficult to surpass as the lobster with cèpes or the truffled turbot. The desserts are absolutely perfect, from cheese dumplings with stewed rhubarb, apricot or plum to cheese soufflé with apricot, pear or cherry sauce.

RESIDENZ HEINZ WINKLER

83229, Kirchplatz 1
(0 80 52) 1 79 90, Fax 17 99 66

32, **S** 180/550, **D** 220/450,
APP 450/580

White marble floors and precious Oriental rugs lead the way to spacious hotel rooms with style. Before and after enjoying chef Winkler's cuisine, you can use nearby footpaths for walks and sports or visit the beauty spa in the hotel. Breakfast: 30 DM.

ASPACH Bad.-Württ.

Backnang 3 -Ludwigsburg 20

LAMM 14/20

71546, Ortsteil Großaspach
Hauptstr. 23
(0 71 91) 2 02 71, Fax 2 31 31

P

Closed for dinner Sunday, closed Monday, 3 weeks in the Bad.-Württ. summer school holiday. Tables d'hôte: 35/45L, 65/86D, à la carte: 36/68. No Credit Cards

A fixed-price three-course meal is no longer offered here, and diners must beware of huge portions when ordering à la carte. A terrine of salmon and pike-perch with a fines herbes sauce was followed by a warm carpaccio of *tafelspitz* with lamb's lettuce, an aromatic consommé with delicious Swabian ravioli, pike-perch fillet with a delicate crawfish sauce, a perfectly cooked breast of duck with cassis sauce and potatoes au gratin, and refreshing sherbets with fresh fruit. Some great vintages had disappeared from the wine list, but no bottle costs more than 100 DM.

ASPERG Baden-Württ.

Ludwigsburg 5 - Stuttgart 19

RESTAURANT SYMPHONIE IN THE HOTEL ADLER 13/20

71679, Stuttgarter Str. 2
(0 71 41) 6 30 01, Fax 6 30 06 res.

Closed for lunch, closed Sunday, Monday, 1 week in January, 4 weeks during the Bad.-Württ. summer school holiday. Tables d'hôte: 96, à la carte: 42/84

What a pleasant surprise to discover a marked improvement in a previously mediocre kitchen! An attractive tomato terrine with pesto, fried scallops with sesame-seed dressing, a finely seasoned pheasant consommé with dumplings and the fish pot-au-feu proved that standards are rising here. The overcooked tournedos, the only reminder of the past, were easily overlooked when followed by a delightful terrine of oranges with Grand Marnier and frozen yogurt served by the friendly, efficient staff. Württemberg vintages dominate the reasonably priced wine list.

HOTEL ADLER

71679, Stuttgarter Str. 2
(0 71 41) 6 30 01, Fax 6 30 06

65, **S** 135/185, **D** 196/220,
APP 250/280, **1/2P** +35, **P** +60

In planning a modern addition to this historic 135-year-old hotel, the builder achieved harmony between the old and the new. The rooms, with their tasteful mahogany furniture, are small but elegant. The service is pleasantly attentive. Family-run, this hotel has a very personal touch. Breakfast room for nonsmokers and swimming pool.

SCHAARSCMIDT-ALTE KRONE 15/20 

71679, Königstr. 15
(0 71 41) 6 58 00 , Fax 6 51 43 res.

P

Closed for lunch Saturday, closed Sunday, 3 weeks during the Bad.-Württ. summer school holiday. Tables d'hôte: 41/78, à la carte: 38/72, No Credit Cards

Eating at this restaurant located in a beautiful house in the middle of a sleepy town is an all-round pleasure. Hostess Eveline Schaarschmidt receives customers with great warmth and charm and graciously recommends moderately priced wines from the best estates. The pleasures continue with chef Klaus Schaarschmidt's butterfish (arranged like an igloo over mashed potatoes), raw sea urchins marinated in olive oil and lemon pepper, aromatic cream of walnut soup, green asparagus with saddle of veal and a savory mustard sauce, and an excellent terrine of olives and cheese with a tasty red onion dressing. The fragrant rum mousse melts in the mouth. Espresso was served with dainty pastries at the end of the meal.

ATTENDORN NRW

Lüdenscheid 37-Siegen 45

LE PÂTÉ 13/20

3 km southwest
in New-Listernohl
57439, Alte Handelsstr. 15
(0 27 22) 75 42, 7 01 94, Fax 7 01 36 res.

Closed for lunch, closed Monday, 3 weeks during the NRW summer school holiday. Tables d'hôte: 75/107, à la carte: 41/75

This establishment has retained its reputation as the best restaurant in this region, and its cuisine still offers impeccable boredom. None of the dishes was disappointing, but there wasn't one among them that swept us off our feet. The only new "idea" we noticed was potato gratin as a new side dish for fish—something we didn't like at all. But when the red mullet is prepared as insipidly as ours was last time, we don't speculate about harmonizing side dishes. The service is correct and offers guests a comprehensive wine list. Compared to the wide range of top Bordeaux wines, the choice of German wines is meager.

AUGSBURG Bayern

München 67 - Ulm 80

CHEVAL BLANC IN HOTEL GREGOR 18/20 

7 km southeast
86179, Stadtteil Haunstetten
Landsberger Str. 62
(08 21) 8 00 50, Fax 80 05 69 res.

P

Closed for lunch, closed Sunday, Monday, first week in January, month of August. Tables d'hôte: 115/140, à la carte: 50/93

Talented young chef Franz Fuchs can hold his own among the top three dozen restaurants in Germany. Diners are welcomed with two appetizers: nicely seasoned veal tartare with quail's egg, and a sardine fillet with potato slices on fennel, served with gazpacho. Those are just teasers for the delights to come: a consommé with feather-light pigeon-liver dumplings, quail's legs and crawfish with green asparagus, delicately seasoned John Dory with crispy rice cakes, and cabbage roulade with fresh cod. Fuchs also has a way with rabbits, and his desserts are ingenious—an exquisite crunchy crêpe with almond parfait or bittersweet mango in a rice leaf with blancmange, for example.The wine list offers a wide choice of French vintages and has retained its moderate prices. The service is nothing short of perfect.

HOTEL GREGOR 

7 km southeast
86179, Stadtteil Haunstetten
Landsberger Str. 62
(08 21) 8 00 50, Fax 80 05 69

 **P**

40 (35), **S** 100/120, **D** 140/170, **APP** 180

This elegantly appointed hotel on the southern outskirts of the city can easily be reached from the Stuttgart-Munich highway. The rooms all have balconies and are equipped with modern comforts. We liked the quieter rooms toward the back.

DIE ECKE 13/20 

86150, Elias-Holl-Platz 2
(08 21) 51 06 00, Fax 31 19 92 res.

Tables d'hôte: 33L, 69D, à la carte: 33/80

Works by Augsburg painters decorate the walls of this restaurant, which happens to be located in the former home of the "Ecke" artists' association. Owner Georg Zink's light cooking has a decided Mediterranean influence. A well-seasoned gazpacho complements perfectly a venison consommé, a fish terrine and salmon carpaccio with seaweed salad. Saltimbocca was served in traditional style, with Parma ham and sage. Game shows up frequently and in all its variations on the menu. For dessert, the classic apple tart with vanilla ice cream is highly recommended. The service can sometimes be a little too hurried, especially around closing time.The wine list offers a respectable selection of French and Italian vintages.

RESTAURANT OBLINGER BY THE OLD SEAGATE 16/20

86152, Pfärrle 14
(08 21) 51 86 62 , Fax 3 07 02 res.

Closed for dinner Sunday, closed Monday, Tables d'hôte: 29/48, à la carte: 26/71

Oblinger's has been revamped, and its blend of regional cooking and haute cuisine, along with careful preparation, a new name and moderate prices, has turned out to be a winning combination in Augsburg. Highlights of the its light cuisine are veal paillard with prawns and watercress salad, and shrimp with celery and olive oil. The tender sweetbreads with morels, a delicate roulade of brook trout, and grilled calf's heart with fried watercress cakes are also a success. Pork is flavored with marjoram and served with spinach and vegetable cakes, and the traditional Swabian roast comes with cheese spaetzle. Crispy ducks are fried whole, and cabbage is seasoned with aromatic pimpernel. Desserts well worth trying are the cream cheese with strawberry purée or the unusual poppy-seed noodles with rhubarb and pistachio rice.The service was agreeable, and low-priced wines from all over the world are available by the glass, half-bottles or bottle.

STEIGENBERGER DREI MOHREN 

86150, Maximilianstr. 40
(08 21) 5 03 60, Fax 15 78 64

107, **S** 225/259, **D** 270/340, **APP** 375/490, **1/2P** +36, **P** +71

In the heart of old Augsburg, this hotel exhibits old-fashioned elegance. The rooms are effectively soundproofed, unobtrusively furnished and comfortable. Restaurants.

AURICH Niedersachsen

Emden 25 - Wilhelmshaven 51

WALDHOF WIESENS 14/20

5 km east in Ortsteil Wiesens
26605, Zum alten Moor 10
(0 49 41) 6 10 90/0, Fax 6 65 79

Tables d'hôte: 38/68, à la carte: 32/67

A visit to this comfortable restaurant merits a detour through a dense forest. Meals are served in the surrounding park when the weather permits. The kitchen deserves praise for its use of fresh produce, competent food preparation and presentation of regional dishes. Regional specialties can be had at very fair prices and include a summer salad with Greetsiel shrimps, fillet of pork in mustard sauce with green beans, and fruit soup with whipped vanilla cream. The beef carpaccio was excellent, but a grilled fillet of fish was overwhelmed by onions in a red wine sauce. The wine cellar offers a good choice of vintages. Hotel:One wing of this lovely and typical country house is reserved for guests who want to stay overnight. The tastefully furnished rooms and enchanting suites have terraces overlooking the park and forest. Prices range from 75 to 250 DM.

AYING Bayern

Bad Aibling 21 - München 25

BRAUEREIGASTOF

85653, Zornedinger Str. 2
(0 80 95) 7 05, Fax 20 53 res.

Closed mid-January through 3 February. Tables d'hôte: 40L, 80D, à la carte: 27/79

 An ideal brewery for the wide variety of beers served in the rustic *Gaststube* or in the pretty garden behind the house. The high-priced Bavarian specialties should be avoided in favor of the cheaper and somewhat better pancake soup and well-seasoned ox-tongue salad. About all that can be said for the desserts is that they are copious. Simply furnished rooms can be rented at number 18, and there is a beer garden across from it.

BADEN-BADEN Baden-Württ.

Karlsruhe 36-Stuttgart 120

ALLEE-HOTEL BÄREN

76534, Hauptstr. 36
(0 72 21) 70 21 11, Fax 70 21 13

   P

80, **S** 125/210, **D** 195/345, **APP** 380, **1/2P** +44, **P** +65

This attractive family-run hotel is situated in a splendid park. Free admission to both the Caracalla and the Turkish Baths. Transfer from the hotel.

BAD-HOTEL ZUM HIRSCH

76530, Hirschstr. 1
(0 72 21) 93 90, Fax 3 81 48

58, **S** 130/160, **D** 230/280, **1/2P** +44, **P** +76

This 300-year-old hotel, situated near the old part of town, has kept its nostalgic spa-hotel grandness even under the new Steigenberger management and has added modern comfort and attentive service. All bathrooms are provided with running thermal water. The public areas are just as attractive as the hotel rooms. A noble establishment.

BELLAVISTA "DA UMBERTO" 13/20

76530, Langestr. 40-42
(0 72 21) 2 98 00, Fax 3 13 38 res.

P

Tables d'hôte: 45L, 85D, à la carte: 57/108

Umberto Campanelli's Italian restaurant is recommended with reservations. The location in a pedestrian area that is rather sinister at night is unfortunate, and the prices are unduly high – 110 DM for a three-course meal, dessert not included. Why come here then? For the warm Italian hospitality and the inventive cuisine. Most dishes are perfectly prepared. The potato stew with chard was truly impressive, and the chef has his way with lamb fillets and all kinds of pasta. The only jarring note here is the occasional appearance of such un-Italian elements as caviar or radishes.The choice wines here are served just as they should be.

BOCKSBEUTEL 13/20

76534, Ortsteil Varnhalt
Umweger Str. 103
(0 72 23) 5 80 31/2, Fax 6 08 08 res.

 P

Closed Monday. Tables d'hôte: 39/95, à la carte: 44/88

With its elegant decor and view of the Rhine plateau, this restaurant attracts everyone from small-time business-people to millionaires like publisher Hubert Burda. Owner and hostess Christa Springmann is knowledgeable about wine, and her husband cooks the classic cuisine. During hunting season, fresh pheasant from the Rhine meadows, savory hare ragout and the famous Baden-Baden-style saddle of venison are available. The young staff is informed about the best regional vintages, but apart from that, can barely distinguish red wine from white. In the summer, meals are served on the terrace.

BRENNER'S PARK-HOTEL 15/20

76530, Schillerstr. 6
(0 72 21) 90 00, Fax 3 87 72

P

Tables d'hôte: 72/94L, 105D, à la carte: 72/108

In spite of major renovations, the new decor of the restaurant here leaves much to be desired, even if we admit that the partitioning of large rooms with oversized plants is a matter of taste.The cuisine could also use some inspiration. Time stands still in the kitchen of Brenner's Park Hotel, even though a new menu is printed daily and the à la carte dishes always use seasonal products. Chef Albert Kellner is known for his fine sauces, and the tasteless sauce served with the terrine of quail and foie gras was a great disappointment. The anglerfish was fresh, but its consistency was unpleasant. The morels served with the venison fillet were better than the meat itself. These lapses were forgiven, however, at a taste of the top-notch prawns with basil and homemade noodles, the fried Mediterranean fish with mixed salad, the delicately seasoned lamb fillet, and the inimitable ice cream soufflé. The service here is assiduously attentive, and the wine list brings a sparkle to the eye of the connoisseur. There is also an impressive selection of after-dinner drinks.

BRENNER'S PARK-HOTEL

76530, Schillerstr. 6
(0 72 21) 90 00, Fax 3 87 72

100, **S** 330/650, **D** 450/980,
APP 1220/2600, **1/2P** +80/115, **P** +135/170

The service here is assiduously attentive, and the wine list brings a sparkle to the eye of the connoisseur. There is also an impressive selection of after-dinner drinks. On the bank of a stream in a park shaded by old trees stands one of the world's most majestic hotel palaces. Behind the classicistic façade, a century-old hotel tradition is kept alive, aristocratic down to the last minute detail. With true aplomb, the house calls itself the "spa of spas." Backing up that claim are comprehensive programs for guests who want to combine health and holiday, or for those accompanying a convalescent family member. The hotel maintains its own beauty farm, spa clinic and Roman salon. Even breakfast is noble at 35 DM.

DER KLEINE PRINZ

76530 Lichentaler Str. 36
(0 72 21) 34 64, Fax 3 82 64
P
39, **S** 195/275, **D** 295/295,
APP 425/750

The loveliest hotel in Baden-Baden is also the most original. The pretty little rooms and suites have been completely refurnished with handcarved artifacts and decorated with verve and charm. A hotel for people who want to make romantic dreams come true. Restaurant.

PAPALANGI 12/20

76530 Lichentaler Str. 13
(0 72 21) 3 16 16,
Closed for dinner Sunday, closed Monday. A la carte: 36/75

Shortly before this allegedly most elegantly decorated restaurant in Baden-Baden opened, the landlord absconded with millions. But scandal hasn't hurt the restaurant's owner, Peter Wehlauer, whose talented interior decorator combined postmodern elements with the typical flair of Baden-Baden. The beautiful courtyard seating 60 guests is particularly romantic. If you're afraid to cross the threshold of such an elegant establishment, a look at the low prices on the menu is reassuring. There's Viennese schnitzel , plaice, grilled and roasted meat and a few excursions into modern cuisine (prawns and shrimps). The service is pleasant and the wine list reasonably priced.

PAVEL POSPISIL'S RESTAURANT MERKURIUS 14/20

76534, Ortsteil Varnhalt
Klosterbergstr. 2
(0 72 23) 54 74, Fax 6 09 96 res.
 P
Closed Monday, closed for lunch Tuesday, Tables d'hôte: 45/100, à la carte: 45/87. Tables d'hôte with wine: 45/130, No Credit Cards

Pavel Pospisil has always been a regional champion of good cooking, and he deserved every point of his 17/20 rating. Something seems to have gone seriously wrong, however. Perhaps Pospisil feels called to higher things than just serving good food in Varnhalt. His Baden-Baden customers are sulking and no longer frequent the restaurant. Pospisil tries to keep his remaining customers by entertaining them instead of feeding them well. Over a series of visits, the food and service were too inconsistent to criticize in detail. Based on an overall judgement, Pospisil will keep his toque for another year.

RESTAURANT SCHLOSS NEUWEIER 13/20

76534, Ortsteil Neuweier
Mauerbergstr. 21
(0 72 23) 5 79 44, Fax 5 89 33 res.

Closed Tuesday, 22-25 December, Tables d'hôte: 39L, 78/130D, à la carte: 39/83

Cross the drawbridge into the romantic courtyard of this little castle and you might feel you have entered the Middle Ages. But the clatter of the cash register and loud telephone conversations will snap you back to modern-day reality quickly enough. There is a tendency to exaggerate here—too much butter and seasoning is used, and fried foods are overcooked. Still, this is a good address for those who like regional food. All that is missing is a little finesse and originality. The extensive wine list will not disappoint those who enjoy local vintages.

STAHLBAD 13/20

76530, Augustaplatz 2
(0 72 21) 2 45 69, Fax 39 02 22 res.

Closed Sunday, Monday, Tables d'hôte: 130D, à la carte: 55/98

The Stahlbad, centrally located on the Augusta Platz, qualifies as an institution in Baden-Baden because of its good food and wine, its atmosphere and its charming, obliging owner, who is a well-known personality in Baden-Baden. She has gone overboard with her prices, however: 45 DM for goulash is out of this world! High prices like this demand exceptional quality, not just the most beautiful garden in this part of the country. The restaurant risks losing its toque if this trend continues.That said, the sole with fresh lamb's lettuce and potato salad was of choice quality, and even the expensive goulash tasted good, although the meat in it was not of the highest quality. The pancake in the consommé was better than the broth itself. The salmon tartare was seasoned with subtlety, the foie gras terrine was outstanding, and the breast of duck was cooked to pink perfection.

STEIGENBERGER EUROPÄISCHER HOF

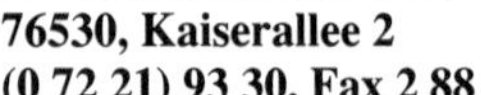

76530, Kaiserallee 2
(0 72 21) 93 30, Fax 2 88 31

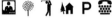

131 rooms, **S** 175/285, **D** 270/470, **APP** 550/2500, **½P** +55, **P** +85

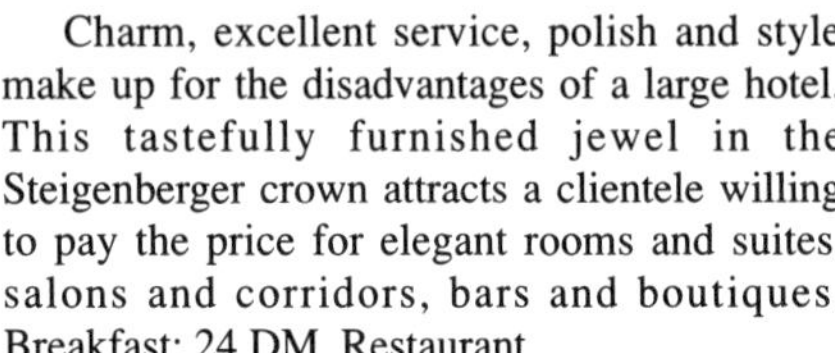

Charm, excellent service, polish and style make up for the disadvantages of a large hotel. This tastefully furnished jewel in the Steigenberger crown attracts a clientele willing to pay the price for elegant rooms and suites, salons and corridors, bars and boutiques. Breakfast: 24 DM. Restaurant.

TRAUBE 12/20

76534, Ortsteil Neuweier
Mauerbergstr. 107
(0 72 23) 5 72 16 , Fax 67 64 res.

Closed Wednesday. Tables d'hôte: 78, à la carte: 34/83

Competition is keen in Baden-Baden and has forced more than one restaurant to try to stimulate business with new ideas. Importing oysters from the faraway ocean just doesn't fill the bill, however. Even the eternal tinkling of Richard Claydermann over the restaurant's loudspeakers couldn't make them any fresher. Everything else here was delicious and of consistently high quality, including the delicately home-smoked salmon with cream cheese, lamb's lettuce with a delicate vinaigrette, and specially prepared foie gras. Venison pops up often on the menu, and is served with appetizing side dishes. The service is friendly and accommodating, and the wine list makes a good impression.

ZUM ALDE GOTT 15/20

76534, Ortsteil Neuweier
Weinstr. 10
(0 72 23) 55 13, Fax 6 06 24 res.

Closed Thursday, closed for lunch Friday, closed 9-31 January. Tables d'hôte: 70/100L, 90/145D, à la carte: 66/102

Some restaurants owe their reputation to their wonderful setting. Here you can sit on the terrace and watch the evening sun go down behind picturesque vineyards. An idyll like this might makes some customers happy, but it is not enough for those who demand first-rate food. The first let-down was stale bread, the next salty cucumber carpaccio accompanied by sole and scampi. Various attempts to turn regional specialties into haute cuisine were miserable failures. Consolations included the pleasant tartness of delicate foie gras and artichokes, and exquisite little cakes served with the coffee.The service is prompt and efficient, and hostess Ilse Serr pleasant and helpful. The wine list leaves nothing to be desired.

ZUM ENGEL

76534, Ortsteil Neuweier
Mauerbergstr. 62
(0 72 23) 5 72 43, Fax 6 04 09 res.

P

Closed Monday, Tuesday, 3 weeks in March. A la carte: 25/38

True gourmets (or those who think they are) may smile disdainfully at this rustic *Weinstube*, and some might even laugh out loud. But they would be wrong, because this modest establishment offers good quality at very moderate prices. Eduard Fröhlich reigns over the vineyards and wine cellar, and his wife Gerti cooks such classics as sauerbraten, schnitzel and steak. Her salads are legendary. This is the best of its kind in Baden-Baden.

BADENWEILER BW

Basel 40-Freiburg 40

RÖMERBAD

79410, Schloßplatz 1
(0 76 32) 7 00, Fax 7 02 00

84, **S** 240/330, **D** 380/480,
APP 520/600, **½P** +65, **P** +95

Solid turn-of-the-century quality is the keynote here. The park is splendid, the service obliging and the rooms bright and spacious. If you want a bit of quiet, you can send the kids to the supervised playground while you take a stroll through the gardens or a dip in the pool. In these surroundings, you're almost morally obligated to dress for dinner. Five golf courses within 15 to 60 minutes. Children's discount.

SCHWARZMATT 14/20 

79410, Schwarzmattstr. 6a
(0 76 32) 60 42, Fax 60 47

P

Tables d'hôte: 55/65L, 85/125D, à la carte: 49/79

There's only one address for spa guests in search of gourmet dining, and that's the Schwarzmatt complex. Spacious and festively decorated dining rooms, outstanding service and Roland Schulz's cuisine create the luxurious ambience so congenial to relaxed wining and dining. Regional dishes are featured as well as classic recipes, but all use fresh seasonal produce. We liked smoked duck's breast, grilled prawns with green salad, cream of cauliflower soup, a superbly done saddle of lamb with ratatouille and desserts that looked as delicious as they tasted. The large wine list emphasizes regional wines.

SCHWARZMATT 

79410, Schwarzmattstr. 6a
(0 76 32) 60 42, Fax 60 47

41, **S** 215, **D** 340/376,
APP 390/440, **½P** +20

A gem of a hotel with individually styled rooms and a comprehensive sports and recreation program. Beauty farm, boutique and wonderful footpaths for walks in the country. Excursions to Basel, Freiburg and Alsace. Breakfast: 25 DM.

BAIERSBRONN BW

Freundenstadt 7 - Stuttgart 100

BAREISS IN HOTEL BAREISS 18/20 

72270, Ortsteil Mittletal
Gärtenbühlweg 14
(0 74 42) 4 70, Fax 4 73 29 res.

Closed Monday, Tuesday, 6 June through 7 July, 27 November through 24 December. Tables d'hôte: 140/180, à la carte:70/118

We couldn't conceal our surprise: the restaurant has been extravagantly redecorated with incredibly good taste (and a lot of money). In the midst of such cherry wood and marble, silk and precious antiques, we hardly dared ask the question that hovered uppermost in our minds: How well do you have to cook in the most elegant restaurant in Germany? Claus-Peter Lumpp has managed not to let the superb ambience overwhelm his cooking. His imaginative cuisine sometimes runs a little wild, but we'd rather try new creations that the usual standards given de luxe treatment. If he thinks a little more before he cooks, he'll avoid such aberrations in taste (and looks) as his sole with prawns on mozzarella and tomatoes. New dishes that need subtle seasoning also need a lot of practice. We're looking forward to seeing Lumpp develop his great talent. The wine list offers a choice of 700 fabulous wines.

DORFSTUBEN 16/20

72270, Ortsteil Mittletal
Gärtenbühlweg 14
(0 74 42) 4 70, Fax 4 73 29

Closed Monday, Tuesday, 6 June through 7 July, 27 November through 24 December. A la carte: 26/63

These rebuilt 18th-century cottage rooms are a beautiful, picturesque setting for the cuisine served here. Guests enjoy hearty and savory regional dishes like stew and cream cheese, Black Forest trout and ham, soup with pancake strips and a game platter. The highlight is the *Murgtäler brotzeit* with a little bit of everything. Both atmosphere and cuisine are inviting, but the small rustic chairs are definite drawbacks for taller and heavier folks, who'd better choose a bench instead. Beer and regional wines by the glass are offered with the rustic meals, but you can also choose from the comprehensive wine list of the Bareiss.

KAMINSTUBE 16/20

72270, Ortsteil Mittletal
Gärtenbühlweg 14
(0 74 42) 4 70, Fax 4 73 29

Closed Monday, Tuesday, 6 June through 7 July, 27 November through 24 December. Tables d'hôte: 49/105, à la carte: 39/82

This restaurant in an elegant country style offers refined regional cuisine. The three daily prix-fixe meals are usually interesting, as are the vegetarian prix-fixe, a prix-fixe for for two and a children's plat du jour. Some highlights of the menu were marinated sea trout with mustard and dill sauce, fillet of beef with asparagus in vegetable vinaigrette, trout in all variations, duck's breast with potato and apple gratin and venison medallions with juniper-berry sauce. More than a dozen regional wines can be ordered by the glass as well as six château wines, but you can take a peek at the Bareiss wine list as well.

HOTEL BAREISS IM SCHWARZWALD

72270, Ortsteil Mittletal
Gärtenbühlweg 14
(0 74 42) 4 70, Fax 4 73 29

P

100, **S** 195/335, **D** 360/590,
APP 530/780, **1/2P** +10, *Suites from 800*
No Credit Cards

The spa hotel with its superlative comfort and excellent sports and recreation program is almost always full. Impressive cuisine as well as yoga, massage, dancing lessons and diet menus add to the sense of well-being. The rooms are elegant and well equipped, the service perfect, the boutique glamorous and the jewelry shop exquisite. Library. Wine-tasting in a cellar with 18,000 bottles. Excursions in a rebuilt 1928 Ford bus.

RESTAURANT SCHLOSSBERG IN HOTEL SACKMANN 14/20

12 km north in Schwarzenberg
72270, Murgtalstr. 602
(0 74 47) 28 90, Fax 28 94 00 res.

 P

Closed for lunch, closed Monday, Tuesday, 1—21 February, 2—15 August. Tables d'hôte: 95/125, à la carte: 53/95

Jörg Sackmann is always good for a rating of 17/20, but it can't have escaped him that his kitchen staff doesn't work up to par when he's not there. And one of his duties is to see that they do. Scallops with a penetrating deep-fried odor, impossible venison and rubbery salmon mousse were only some "highlights" of our meal. The 12/20 the kitchen staff earned at our last visit and the 17/20 Sackmann usually deserves average out to 14/20. Guests who want to eat well here had better call first to see if the chef is on hand.

SCHWARZWALDSTUBE IN HOTEL TRAUBE TONBACH 19.5/20

72270, Tonbachstr. 237

(0 74 42) 49 26 65, Fax 49 26 92 res.

P

Closed Monday, Tuesday, 9-31 January, 31 July through 22 August. Tables d'hôte: 155/195, à la carte: 70/128

Some cooks are inspired by their own success; others are motivated by their guests to become better and better. Harald Wohlfarth, like a perpetual motion machine, doesn't need anyone or anything to drive him on.Still, even while Germany's best cook is working full-steam, he hates being conspicuous and prefers standing in his kitchen from morning till night to advertising himself on public-relations tours. The only time his conspicuous talent shows is on his plates. His aspics and terrines are unsurpassed in Germany; his lobster fried in its shell is first-class and his iced orange foam a taste sensation. Guests who prefer more luxurious-sounding dishes can order potato stuffed with caviar, onion jelly with white Alba truffles or pigeon cutlet with Périgord truffles and foie gras with truffled sauce.With his unparalleled expertise in classic French cuisine. Wohlfarth could play with international recipes if only he wanted to, but maybe he's too serious to try. So we admire the lovely things he creates with a product, for instance sweetbreads when morels are in season: He serves sweetbreads with morels and asparagus in an open ravioli, arranges glazed sweetbreads with sesame leaves and morels as a millefeuille or composes a ragout of sweetbreads, morels and foie gras with asparagus chartreuse. Nothing is too complicated or too extravagant for Wohlfarth; he stuffs breast of guinea fowl with truffles and foie gras, wraps it in a leaf of savoy cabbage and serves it perfectly done in a light puff-pastry crust.Kitchen, cellar and service are so provokingly perfect in the Schwarzwaldstuben that they pass even the ultimate tests. How about trying each of the three dozen cheeses for ripeness? How about putting aside the list of 600 wines and asking for one to go with grilled scampi and Oriental spices? Or simply asking for buttered toast with truffles? Nothing in the world would embarrass the masterful staff in this paradise of a restaurant.

KÖHLERSTUBE 16/20

72270, Tonbachstr. 237

(0 74 42) 49 26 65, Fax 49 26 92 res.

Closed Thursday. Tables d'hôte: 49L, 85/119D, à la carte: 44/83

We had Heiner Finkbeiner's promise that the high standard of cooking here wouldn't change, even if the chefs did. The new cook, Bernd Schlecht, does his best to keep that promise. He prepares that combination of traditional and modern classic dishes, seasonal and regional specialities that makes this restaurant so popular. Everything he creates is light and flavorful. We were just as happy with our Swabian salads and ragout of ox cheeks in Lemberg sauce as with deceptively simple dishes like lentils with duck, beef with horseradish and red beets and ox-tongue salad with radishes. Friendly service and a great wine list make us sure we've spent an evening in one of the best family restaurants in Germany.

BAUERNSTUBE 16/20

72270, Tonbachstr. 237

(0 74 42) 49 26 65, Fax 49 26 92 res.

Closed Monday, Tuesday, 9—31 January, 31 July through 22 August. A la carte: 35/63

This is probably the only bistro where ladies are surprised with an orchid (or something equally exquisite) when they leave—at least on Saturdays. Not only women but also men leave this à la carte restaurant with smiles on their faces. One can order from the Köhlerstuben menu here, and also eat traditional Swabian dishes the way Grandma used to make. We liked roast blood pudding, beef consommé, deluxe *Gaisburger Marsch* and more. Wine list and service as in the Köhlerstube.

TRAUBE TONBACH

72270, Tonbachstr. 237
(0 74 42) 49 20, Fax 49 26 92

175 rooms, **S** 168/227, **D** 325/510,
APP 441/546, **1/2P** +23, **P** +45
No Credit Cards

In the course of two centuries, this once-unassuming building has become the non-plus-ultra of spa and holiday hotels. With more than ample space, the rooms offer the comfort of a luxurious country mansion. The service is incomparable: breakfast in bed includes the daily weather report. If it's pouring outside, don't worry. With a library, cinema, table tennis, billiards and more at your disposal, you can't fail to enjoy the domain of host Willi Finkbeiner, a perfectionist in the best sense of the word.

BALDUINSTEIN Rheinl. - Pf.

Limburg/Lahn 10 - Koblenz 62

KLEINES RESTAURANT 17/20

65558, Bahnhofstr. 24
(0 64 32) 8 10 91, Fax 8 36 43 res.

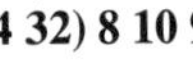

Closed for lunch, closed Monday, Tuesday, three weeks followiing Ash Wednesday. Tables d'hôte: 95/139, à la carte: 42/86

The more rustic dining room of the former Kaminstube has been surreptitiously added to the refined little gourmet restaurant that looks like a library. The service in both rooms is thoughtful and discreet. In front of the tiled stove of the Kaminstube, lunch as well as dinner is served, whereas in the Kleines Restaurant you can order (reservations only!) a festive and fabulous prix-fixe meal. The menu for both offers one four- or five-course meal and two dozen à la carte dishes, all prepared expertly with first-class produce. The generous salads are always astutely seasoned (ours was served with pieces of crispy quail); only the artichoke salad with glazed sweetbreads was dressed a little too sourly to go with our wine. Mediterranean vegetables with fillet of lamb was an eye-catcher and a taste sensation at the same time. Striped mullet on an mound of asparagus accompanied by two delicate sauces and fried artichoke slices with loin of lamb on ratatouille ravioli were excellent, and the saddle of venison with savoy cabbage and spaetzle outstanding.The wine list (41 pages) includes hundreds of wines from famous wine regions. A choice of 50 half-bottles makes it possible for lone diners and couples to drink several kinds of wine with their meal. The choice of digestifs is sensational.

HOTEL ZUM BÄREN

65558, Bahnhofstr. 24
(0 74 42) 8 10 91, Fax 8 36 43

P

10 rooms, **S** 75/80, **D** 150/160,
Closed three weeks following Ash Wednesday

Hotels are rare in the beautiful landscape on the shore of the Lahn river. The Buggles have equipped 10 rooms without extravagant frills but with every comfort for traveling guests—some with a wonderful view of the romantic Lahn valley.

BAMBERG Bayern

Nürnberg 60 - Würzburg 80

BAROCK-HOTEL AM DOM

96049, Vorderer Bach 4
(09 51) 5 40 31, Fax 5 40 21

P

19 rooms, **S** 98/100, **D** 140/155,
Closed 6 January through 6 February

This town palace in the Baroque style has a unique location: in the heart of old Bamberg and yet absolutely quiet. Breakfast is served beneath the historic vaulted ceilings.

IL BASSANESE 14/20

96049, Obere Sandstr. 32
(09 51) 5 75 51, res.
Closed 1 June through 6 September, No Credit Cards, Tables d'hôte: 60/120, à la carte: 50/77

Gabriele Tonin has borrowed not only the name of his hometown, Bassano del Grappa, for his restaurant, but also its traditional fish-based cuisine. The charming owner insists on absolutely fresh fish, so the choice of dishes on the menu is small. You will not go wrong if you follow his recommendations. The antipasti might be marinated squid, grilled sardines and mussels in wine, followed by grilled fish with just a little lemon as the main course. This is not haute cuisine, but honest *cucina italiana*. Avoid the meat dishes and desserts, which can be disappointing.The wine list is limited to the typical repertoire of Italian restaurants, with a few bottles of higher quality.

NATIONAL

96052, Luitpoldstr. 37
(09 51) 2 41 12, Fax 2 24 36

41, **S** 97/110, **D** 157/179,
APP 220, **1/2P** +24, **P** +45

This hotel on a busy thoroughfare is a 10-minute walk from the old part of town. There are quiet rooms if you ask for them. The rooms are tastefully furnished, the baths almost luxurious. Excellent service and generous breakfast buffet. Restaurant.

BARGUM Schleswig-Holstein

Niebüll 19 - Husum 27

ANDRESEN'S GASTHOF 15/20

25842 Bargum/ near the B5 motorway
(0 46 72) 10 98, Fax 10 99 res.

Closed Monday, Tuesday, closed for lunch Wednesday and Thursday, mid-January through mid-February, late October through mid-November. Tables d'hôte: 50L, 95/150D, à la carte: 60/104

We don't envy the new chef Thomas Teigelkamp, who has stepped into the shoes of his talented and imaginative predecessor. Besides two prix-fixe meals, Teigelkamp offers a comprehensive choice of dishes à la carte, many with a distinctly Mediterranean accent and some that even play with Asian influences. We had an excellent, tender lobster gratin with chanterelles and spinach, tasty kid from Goldelund with green beans and olive dumplings (which took a bit of getting used to) and an uninteresting choice of insipid cheeses. Teigelkamp prepares regional produce very carefully, without destroying natural flavor, like a discreet (nondescript?) tasting sweetbread parfait with asparagus or marinated mini-eggplants with smoked angler (which could have used some seasoning). The crispy fried dorado with its dominating red-pepper sauce didn't tickle our palate, and whether or not the sheatfish deserved its intensive orange and olive marinade was highly debatable. The performance of the kitchen doesn't merit these high prices (yet). But as long as Elke Andresen retains her dry humor, she's as dear to us as ever.

ANDRESEN'S GASTHOF

25842 Bargum/ near the B5 motorway
(0 46 72) 10 98, Fax 10 99

5, **S** 95, **D** 175,
Closed mid-January through the beginning of February. 1 week during autumn

After enjoying the excellent cuisine and fine wines, you can stay the night in pleasant and comfortably furnished rooms. Breakfasts here are refreshingly hearty.

BAYREUTH

Nürnberg 90 - Würzburg 166

BAYERISCHER HOF

95444, Bahnhofstr. 14
(09 21) 7 86 00, Fax 2 10 85

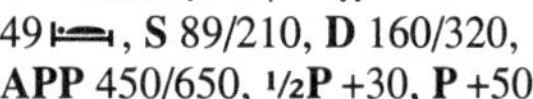

49, **S** 89/210, **D** 160/320,
APP 450/650, **1/2P** +30, **P** +50

Everybody who's anybody in German high society and show business has stayed at this hotel at some time or other. Prices correspond to the individual quality of the rooms and are quite reasonable off-season.

RESTAURANT CUVÉE IN HOTEL EREMITAGE 13/20

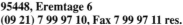

95448, Eremtage 6
(09 21) 7 99 97 10, Fax 7 99 97 11 res.

Closed for lunch, closed Sunday, Monday, the month of February. Tables d'hôte: 62/92, à la carte: 37/76

The Cuvée has found a new home in an idyllic setting on the grounds of the Bayreuth Hermitage (the residence of a former military governor and his clever wife Wilhelmine). In a carefully renovated sandstone building, Wolfgang and Brigitte Hauenstein manage a *Biergarten,* a simple *Gasthof,* a hotel and a gourmet restaurant. Perhaps thatis one thing too many. The quality and originality of the restaurant seem to have suffered as a result. The menu descriptions are mouthwatering, but although Wolfgang Hauenstein faithfully followed his recipes, his personal touch was missing.The meager wine list offers unremarkable German and Italian vintages. Service is attentive but impersonal.

HOTEL EREMITAGE
95448, Eremtage 6
(09 21) 7 99 97 10, Fax 7 99 97 11

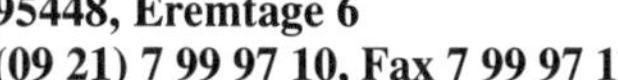

6 rooms, **S** 95/150, **D** 180/220

You can't bed yourself down like the Countess Wilhelmine, who used to stay here, because postmodern furniture has replaced the noble four-posters of the hotel's six bedrooms. But the view from the windows into the quiet and lovely park still evokes bygone idylls.

SCHLOSSHOTEL THIERGARTEN
95406, 6 km south in Thiergarten
(0 92 09) 98 40 , Fax 9 84 29

Tables d'hôte: 56/65, à la carte: 43/68

The Schloss Thiergarten is made to soothe the souls of stressed city dwellers. Approaching the castle through meadows and fields, you leave the hectic hubbub of city life far behind. From the old orchard and the gorgeous hall with its beautifully laid tables, we expected to spend a wonderful, romantic evening. We were sadly disappointed on our last visit. But things are supposed to have changed for the better, since Anton Dötzer took over the kitchen—too late to test for this edition. The wine list is irreproachable but conventional, and offers a choice of standards.

SCHLOSSHOTEL THIERGARTEN

95406, 6 km south in Thiergarten
(0 92 09) 98 40 , Fax 9 84 29

8 rooms, **S** 130/150, **D** +56,
1/2P +56, **P** +112

This historic hunting lodge with its domed roof and stucco work by Domenico Caddenazi has spacious, expensively furnished rooms and every modern comfort. The service—even during the Wagner festival—is of the same quality and is topped off by the charming atmosphere created by the owners.

BEDERKESA Nieders.

Bremerhaven 20 - Cuxhaven 43

WALDSCHLÖSSCHEN BÖSEHOF 13/20

27624, Hauptmann-Böse-Str. 19
(0 47 45) 94 80, Fax 94 82 00

Tables d'hôte: 30/39L, 50/90D, à la carte: 39/68

This little château in the forest provides a fairy-tale setting for the Manke family restaurant. The cuisine aspires to elegance, but a hungry wanderer can still treat himself to simple pleasures like marinated herring and fried potatoes.The soups, especially the eel soup, were delectable, as were the delicate salmon mousse, the sauces and the fish. The chicken was hearty and plump and tasted just like a farm-raised chicken should. Nice desserts rounded off a good dinner. Special requests were met with speed and good nature. The choice of wines is acceptable and not overly expensive.

WALDSCHLÖSSCHEN BÖSEHOF

27624, Hauptmann-Böse-Str. 19
(0 47 45) 94 80, Fax 94 82 00

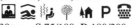

30 rooms, **S** 75/100, **D** 180/200,
1/2P +30, **P** +38

There's always a reason to spend the night in these beautiful and perfectly quiet surroundings, or even to stay a few days. Most of the nicely appointed, comfortable rooms face south. Solarium.

BELLHEIM Rheinl. - Pfalz

Germersheim 6 - Landau 14

BRAUSTÜBL 12/20
76756, Hauptstr. 78
(0 72 72) 7 55 00, Fax 7 40 13 res.

P

Closed Monday and Tuesday. Tables d'hôte: 40L, 90D, à la carte: 30/74

The interior of this brewery's restaurant is as rustic as the colorful dirndls the staff wears, and as countrified as the savory cuisine. You can order maties (marinated) herring here and all standard beef, veal and game dishes, and find a few refined creations on the menu as well. Guests can count on good, dependable-quality plain fare without frills and flourishes. The wine list includes a wide variety of regional wines and a good choice of wines by the glass.

BAD BELLINGEN BW

Müllheim 10 - Lörach 18

LANDGASTOF SCHWANEN 11/20
79415, Rheinstr. 50
(0 76 35) 13 14 , Fax 23 31

P

Closed Tuesday, closed for lunch Wednesday. A la carte: 20/71

This country inn isn't trying to be a gourmet restaurant. The clever owner also caters to the wishes of his dieting spa clientele, always on the lookout for an enjoyable and low-priced meal. The restaurant also provides them with its own wines and brandies. The wide variety of dishes is more significant than any one outstanding culinary performance. Besides many *plats du jour*, the Schwanen is proud of its fish, game and asparagus when in season.

BERCHTESGADEN Bayern

Salzburg 20 - München 163

BERGGASTOF VORDERBRAND
83471, Schönau am Königssee
Vorderbrandweg 91
(0 86 52) 20 59,

P

A la carte: 13/38

The Berggasthof is situated in a meadow high on a hill above Berchtesgaden. After a steep climb to reach it, the visitor is rewarded with an enchanting view of the valley below. This rustic *gasthof* is just the thing for tired, hungry voyagers in search of a tasty, hearty, homemade meal and a good night's sleep in a simply furnished room.

HOTEL GEIGER
83471, Ortsteil Stanggaß
Berchtesgadener STr. 103-115
(0 86 52) 96 55 55, Fax 96 54 00

P

55, **S** 100/180, **D** 160/300,
APP 300/600, **1/2P** +30

Over the last hundred years, the renowned Geiger has undergone frequent renovations, but the lounges still retain their rustic and cozy charm. The rooms are simply furnished and bathrooms are adequate. The beds often creak, and the springs reminded us of sleepless nights in France. The new rooms of the are furnished in a rustically elegant style and offer a breathtaking view of the mountains of the Berchtesgaden National Park.In the restaurant, smokers are relegated to the back dining room, consoled only by a lone zither player, while non-smokers are rewarded with lovely tables in the new winter garden. The restaurant offers hotel standards of more or less acceptable quality.

BERGISCH GLADBACH NRW

Köln 16 - Bonn 37

DAS FACHWERKHAUS 13/20
51429, Ortsteil Bensberg
Burggraben 37
(0 22 04) 5 49 11, Fax 5 76 41 res.

P

Closed for lunch, closed Monday, 10 days at the beginning of January, 3 weeks during the NRW summer school holiday, No Credit Cards. Tables d'hôte: 85, à la carte: 51/78

This pretty little gingerbread house out of Hansel and Gretel is larger than it seems from the outside. It's amazing how many tables fit in here! With a full house, however, Toni Richerzhagen has problems in his tiny half-timbered kitchen; when there's no time to pay attention to fine details or exact cooking times, guests pay for mishaps. Appetizers cost more than 20 DM and main dishes at least 40 DM. But we don't want only to criticize. We had flawlessly prepared vitello tonnato, salad with shrimps, prawns and squid and – as the highlight of the season – veal fillet with fresh morels and puréed truffles. Aspic of *tafelspitz,* pigeon in balsamic vinegar and entrecôte in pink pepper cream are favorites here, and if the guests didn't get their opulent pasta and their creamy soup they'd start a riot. The service sometimes can't keep up with the pace. The wine cellar contains some treasures.

GRAPPOLO D'ORO 14/20

51467, Ortsteil Schilgen
Nittumer Weg 7
(0 22 02) 87 30, Fax 86 20 46 res.

P

Tables d'hôte: 48/76, à la carte: 34/63

The golden grapes featured in his restaurant's name aren't too presumptious for Emilio Lattarulo. You'd have to look far and wide to find a better restaurant in this region. In contrast to the un-Italian understatement outside, inside guests find typical Mediterranean flair. The encyclopedic listing of Italian standard dishes is (and right they are!) ignored by the regular guests, who order one of the 15 *plats du jour*, for example vegetable strudel or cèpes risotto, angler with tomatoes and fresh garden herbs or salmon with Pommery and mustard sauce, Angus beef with ratatouille or goose leg with chestnut gnocchi.The Italian owner buys high-quality produce and Bernd Liedtke, a cosmopolitan chef from Burscheid, prepares light and flavorful dishes. His pasta converted us; his lovely desserts enchanted us. And his brilliantly done John Dory with a sauce of exquisite subtlety took our breath away. We only managed to applaud.The wine list with (naturally) an emphasis on Italian wines is interesting. The service is very quick.

RESTAURANT DIETER MÜLLER IN SCHLOßHOTEL LERBACH 19/20

51469, Ortsteil Heidkamp
Lerbacher Weg
(0 22 02) 20 40, Fax 20 49 40 res.

Closed Sunday and Monday, 1—17 January, 16 July through 7 August. Tables d'hôte: 99L, 148/198D, à la carte: 90/129

A few disturbing moments in a first-class German restaurant that carries the name of one of the world's best cooks: The parking attendant treats our car with far more respect than he treats us, the charming wife of the owner serves us warm champagne, and the friendly young lady who helps us choose our wines is obviously relieved to discover that we know more about them than she does. Chef Dieter Müller demands exorbitant prices for his choice wines and charges 65 to 88 DM for a main course, but he skimps not only on the salary of a capable sommelier but also on the service staff, which is friendly but inattentive and hopelessly disorganized.The first sign of life from the kitchen was underwhelming: herring salad with too thickly sliced cucumbers. A much simpler restaurant would be ashamed to serve this to its customers.The produce here is of top quality, but the chef practices rigid economies. The turbot and saddle of lamb, for instance, were on both the à la carte menu and the fixed-price menu. While fish, lobster, foie gras and fowl were offered, there was no game, veal or beef. This made it difficult to select courses without repetition.The quail and foie gras dishes, however, showed what the kitchen is capable of. The terrine of foie gras and pigeon breasts with mushroom cake and jellied praline was superb. Every element of this famous composition deserves more points than the restaurant's overall rating. Before Dieter Müller gets a complex about the state of his cooking, we would like to thank him for his delectable Mediterranean salad with seafood aspic and mille-feuille of tomatoes and scallops, the vegetable fondue with tripe in champagne and fried scampi, the turbot fillet with lobster and morels in champagne, and the breast of duck with fried black pudding on creamed Savoy cabbage. They represent the height of Dieter Müller's artistry. We hope to celebrate his accomplishments without any reservations next time.

RESTAURANT SCHLOSSCHÄNKE IN SCHLOßHOTEL LERBACH

51469, Ortsteil Heidkamp
Lerbacher Weg
(0 22 02) 20 40, Fax 20 49 40

Tables d'hôte: 33/54L, 86D, à la carte: 47/68, Tables d'hôte with wine: 33/132

The Schlosschänke is located in the basement of this castle-hotel, and the cuisine does not rise to any great heights either. While super-chef Dieter Müller has nothing to do with the food that comes out of this kitchen, it should be of some concern to him as the Schlosschänke is billed as the "counterpoint" to his gourmet restaurant, also located in the hotel.The young and ambitious new chef Bernd Stollenwerk was crowned with three toques as chef of Cologne's Ambiance, and his Schlosschänke menu is appealing: fresh fowl in aspic with potatoes, cucumbers and chili mayonnaise; fried red mullet with ratatouille and gazpacho; anglerfish with leeks, tomatoes and baked mushrooms; glazed duck on a ragout of rhubarb and shallots. Stollenwerk's personal touch was missing from all this, however. We will reserve judgment and omit the rating this time. The service is enthusiastic, and the wine cellar well-stocked.

SCHLOSSHOTEL LERBACH

51469, Ortsteil Heidkamp
Lerbacher Weg
(0 22 02) 20 40, Fax 20 49 40

P

54, **S** 290/480, **D** 380/580, **APP** 780/1280

This is pure luxury: in the midst of a gigantic park, the hotel offers very spacious and individually furnished rooms. Technical equipment for businessmen is available, as is a beauty farm, jogging paths, bike rental and fishing. Children up to 12 years of age are free if accompanied by a paying adult.

WALDSTUBEN IN WALDHOTEL MANGOLD 14/20

51429, Ortsteil Bensberg
in Milchborntal
(0 22 04) 5 40 11, Fax 5 45 00 res.

Closed Sunday and Monday. Tables d'hôte: 48/120, à la carte: 37/82

In an idyllic location in the middle of Bensberg, a young and talented cook surprised us with culinary creations that would have guaranteed a sensation in one of the big cities. Maybe they would cause a sensation here as well, if public and critic attention weren't riveted on Dieter Müller and his Schloss Lerbach. But we don't want to compare the Schloss with the familiar Hotel Mangold, which is neither a luxury hotel nor an architectural gem. And Gerhard Krämer has only begun his career. He restrains his creativity from flying too high, but serves highlights of classic cuisine. One of them was a fabulous oxtail consommé with thyme quenelles—a masterpiece of flavorful precision. We also liked the crèpinette of quail filled with spinach and duck's liver. The side dishes are imaginative and amusing, for instance black and white ravioli with fried prawns. Wonderful sauces and desserts and correctly priced wines (many available by the glass) confirm our good impression.

BERLIN

Hannover 282-Hamburg 290
Frankfurt 550-München 600

ABENDMAHL 13/20

10997, Kreuzberg
Muskauer Str. 9
(0 30) 6 12 51 70, res.

Closed for lunch, No Credit Cards. A la carte: 34/59

The allusion to the Lord's Supper in the restaurant's name isn't supposed to spoil the appetite of devout Christians, but instead provide just a pinch of decorative blasphemy. Saints' pictures, devotional candles and a holy-water font make up part of the eccentric decor appreciated by mostly young diners. Besides creating original names for his food, Udo

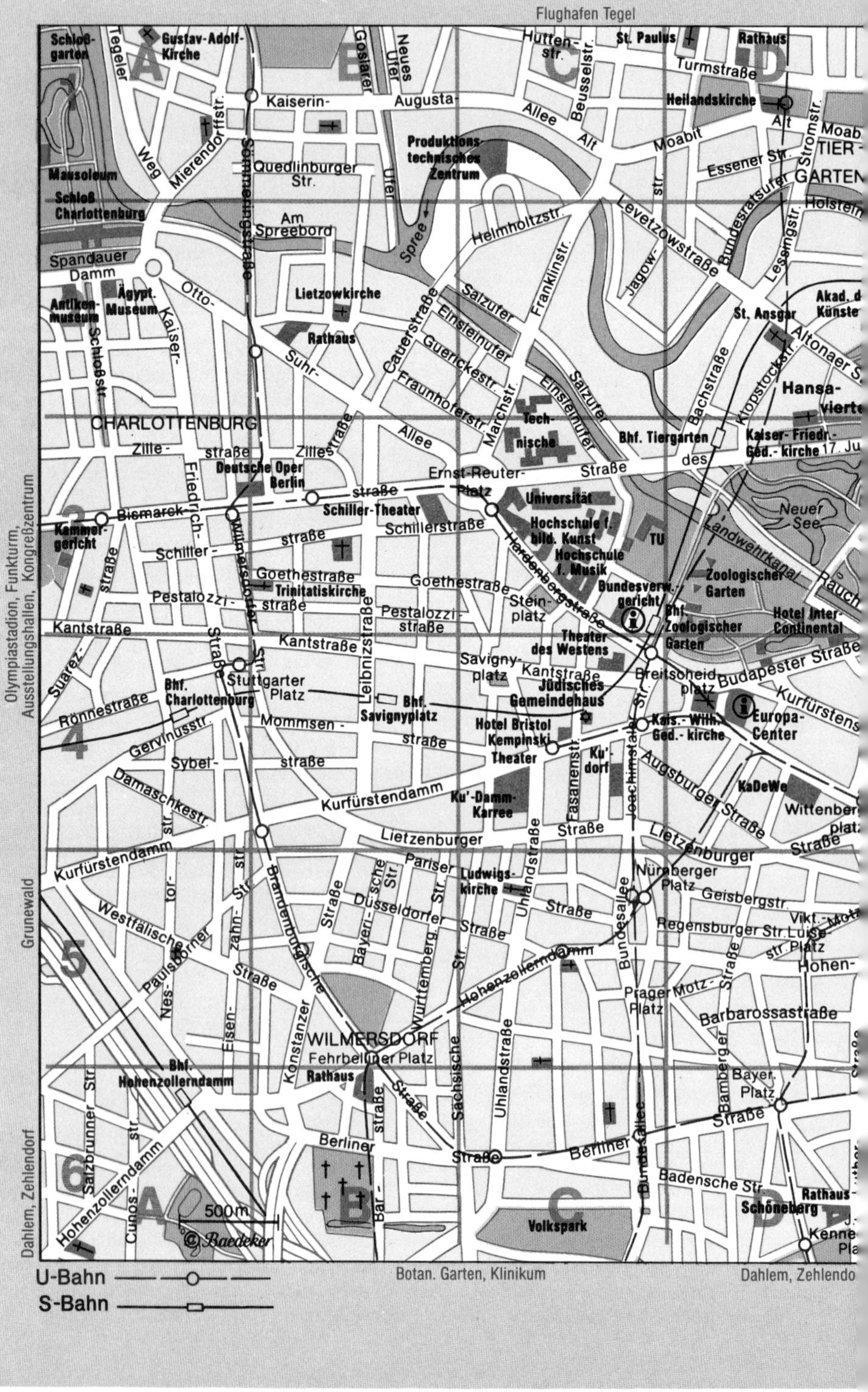

Flughafen Tegel

Schloß-garten
Gustav-Adolf-Kirche
Tegeler Weg
Mierendorffstr.
Kaiserin-Augusta-Allee
Goslarer Ufer
Neues Ufer
Hutten-str.
Beusselstr.
St. Paulus
Rathaus
Turmstraße
Heilandskirche
Alt Moabit
Stromstr.
Moabit
TIER-GARTEN
Essener Str.
Bundesratsufer
Quedlinburger Str.
Produktions-technisches Zentrum
Mausoleum
Schloß Charlottenburg
Am Spreebord
Spree
Helmholtzstr.
Levetzowstraße
Holstein
Lessingstr.
Spandauer Damm
Otto-Suhr-Allee
Sömmeringstraße
Lietzowkirche
Jagow-str.
Franklinstr.
Salzufer
Einsteinufer
Antiken-museum
Ägypt. Museum
Kaiser-Friedrich-Straße
Schloßstr.
Rathaus
Cauerstraße
Guerickestr.
Fraunhoferstr.
Marchstr.
Akad. d. Künste
St. Ansgar
Altonaer Str.
Bachstraße
Klopstockstr.
Hansa-viertel
CHARLOTTENBURG
Technische Universität
Bhf. Tiergarten
Kaiser-Friedr.-Ged.-kirche
Straße des 17. Juni
Zillestraße
Deutsche Oper Berlin
Ernst-Reuter-Platz
Bismarckstraße
Schiller-Theater
Schillerstraße
Neuer See
Kammer-gericht
Wilmersdorfer Str.
Hochschule f. bild. Kunst
TU
Landwehrkanal
Hochschule f. Musik
Hardenbergstraße
Goethestraße
Trinitatiskirche
Bundesverw.-gericht
Zoologischer Garten
Rauchstr.
Pestalozzistraße
Steinplatz
Bhf. Zoologischer Garten
Hotel Inter-Continental
Kantstraße
Theater des Westens
Leibnizstraße
Savignyplatz
Budapester Straße
Suarezstr.
Stuttgarter Platz
Bhf. Charlottenburg
Bhf. Savignyplatz
Jüdisches Gemeindehaus
Breitscheidplatz
Kurfürstenstr.
Rönnestraße
Gervinusstr.
Mommsenstraße
Hotel Bristol Kempinski
Kais.-Wilh.-Ged.-kirche
Europa-Center
Sybelstraße
Theater
Fasanenstr.
Ku'dorf
Joachimstaler Str.
Augsburger Straße
Damaschkestr.
Kurfürstendamm
Ku'-Damm-Karree
KaDeWe
Wittenbergplatz
Lietzenburger Straße
Kurfürstendamm
Pariser Str.
Ludwigs-kirche
Uhlandstraße
Nürnberger Platz
Geisbergstr.
Olympiastadion, Funkturm, Ausstellungshallen, Kongreßzentrum
Westfälische Str.
Brandenburgische Straße
Bayerische Str.
Düsseldorfer Straße
Württemberg. Str.
Bundesallee
Regensburger Str.
Viktoria-Luise-Platz
Motzstr.
Grunewald
Paulsborner Str.
Nestorstr.
Eisenzahnstr.
Konstanzer Straße
Hohenzollerndamm
Prager Platz
Hohen-
Barbarossastraße
WILMERSDORF
Fehrbelliner Platz
Rathaus
Sächsische Str.
Bhf. Hohenzollerndamm
Bamberger Str.
Bayer. Platz
Salzbrunner Str.
Cunostr.
Berliner Straße
Badensche Str.
Rathaus Schöneberg
Kennedy-Platz
Dahlem, Zehlendorf
Hohenzollerndamm
500 m
© Baedeker
Barstraße
Volkspark
Botan. Garten, Klinikum
Dahlem, Zehlendorf

U-Bahn
S-Bahn

Hamburger Bahnhof

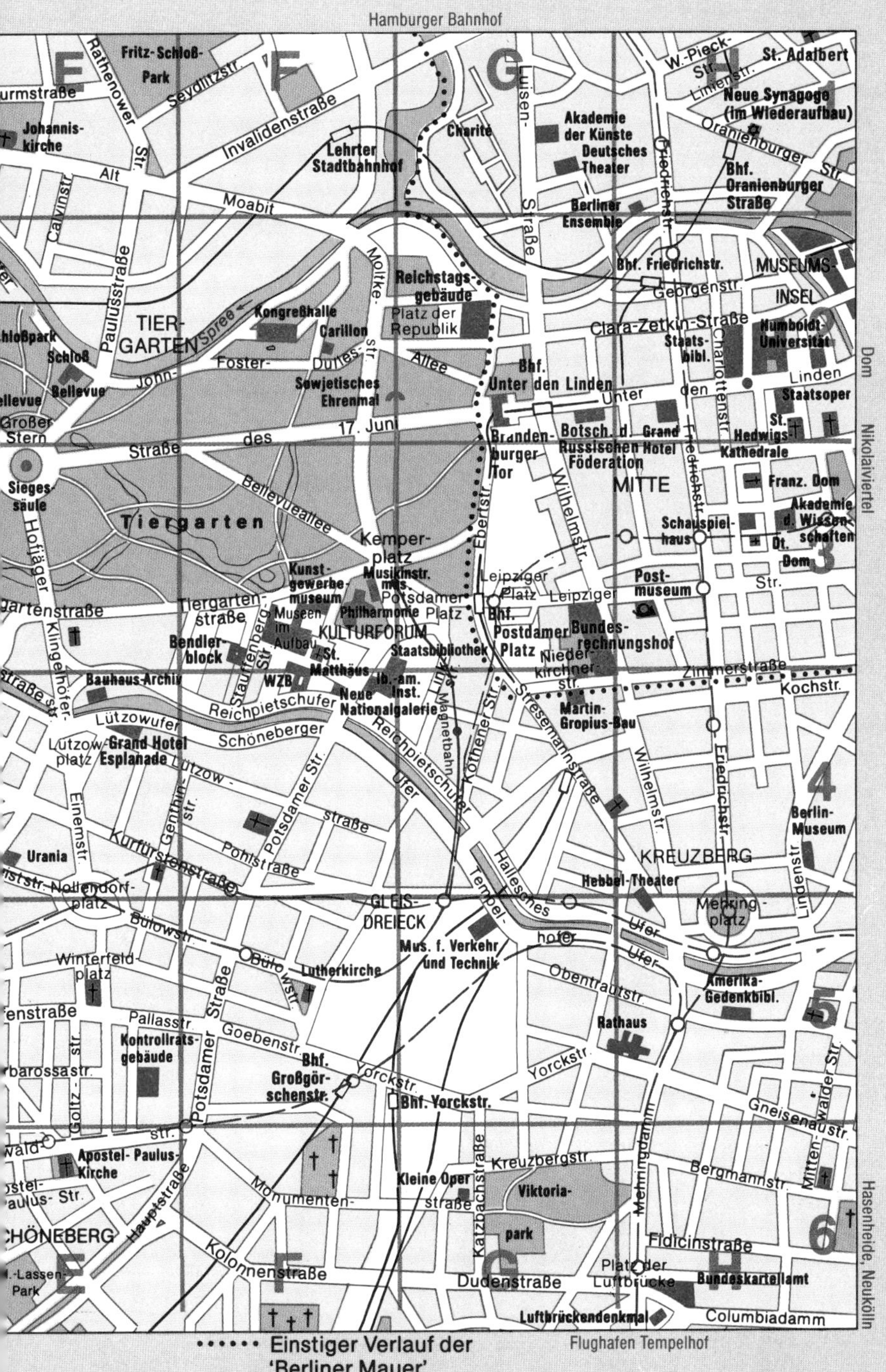

•••••• Einstiger Verlauf der 'Berliner Mauer'

Flughafen Tempelhof

Dom

Nikolaiviertel

Hasenheide, Neukölln

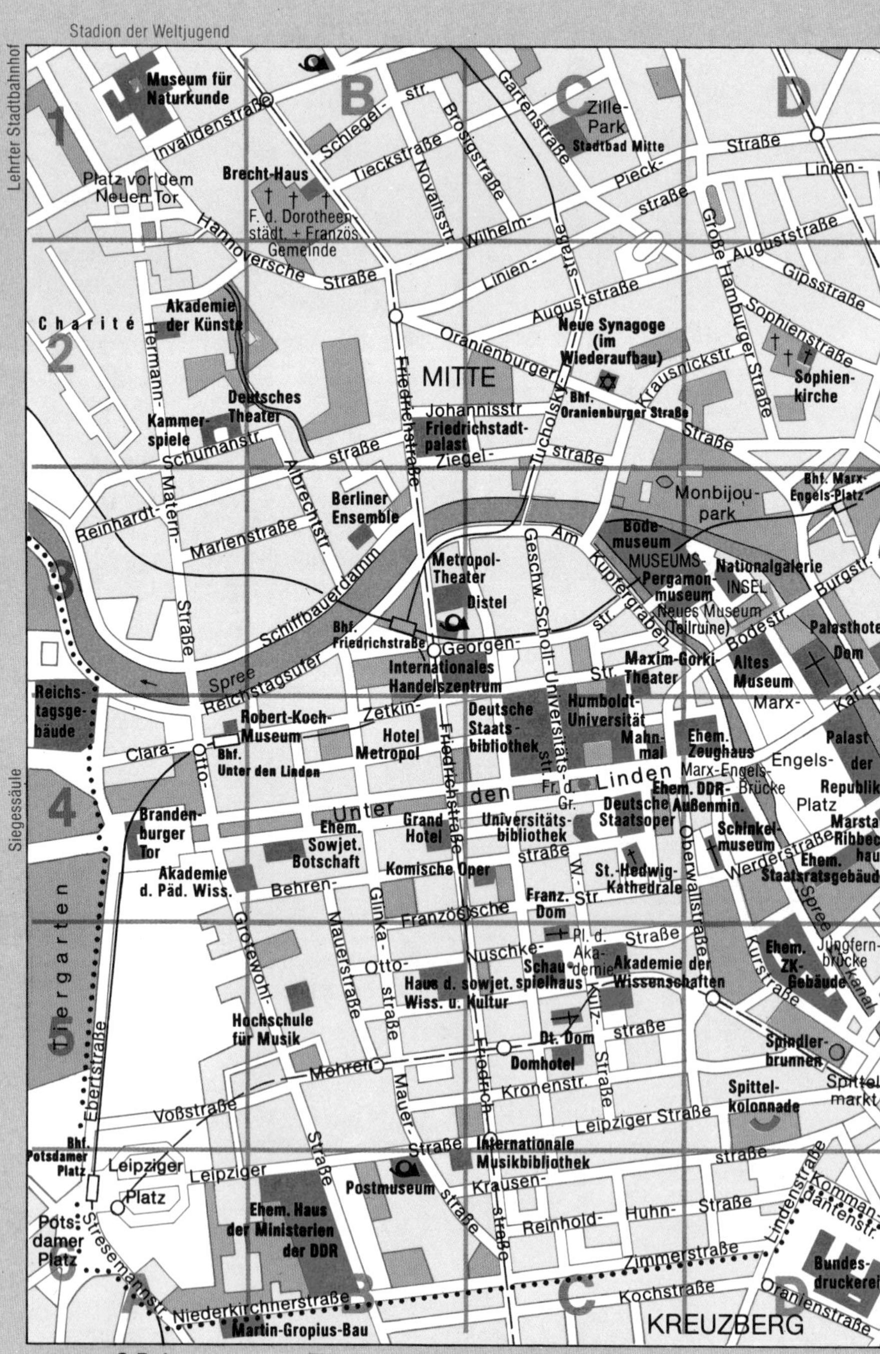

S-Bahn

Einstiger Verlauf der 'Berliner Mauer'

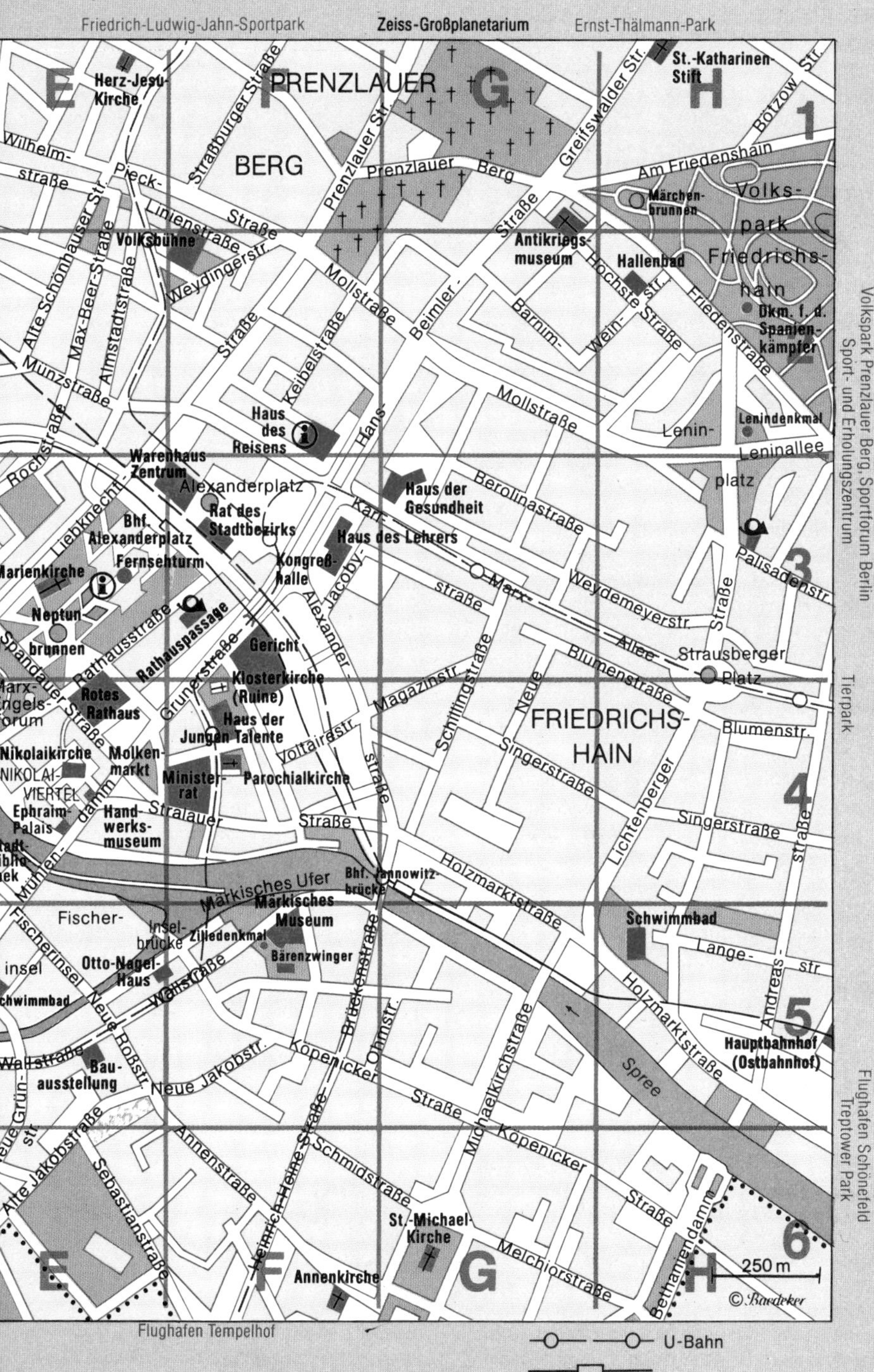

Friedrich-Ludwig-Jahn-Sportpark
Zeiss-Großplanetarium
Ernst-Thälmann-Park
E
F
G
H
1
3
4
5
6
PRENZLAUER
BERG
FRIEDRICHS-
HAIN
Herz-Jesu-
Kirche
St.-Katharinen-
Stift
Volksbühne
Antikriegs-
museum
Märchen-
brunnen
Hallenbad
Volks-
park
Friedrichs-
hain
Dkm. f. d.
Spanien-
kämpfer
Lenindenkmal
Leninallee
Lenin-
platz
Haus
des
Reisens
Warenhaus
Zentrum
Alexanderplatz
Rat des
Stadtbezirks
Bhf.
Alexanderplatz
Haus der
Gesundheit
Haus des Lehrers
Fernsehturm
Kongreß-
halle
Marienkirche
Neptun-
brunnen
Rathauspassage
Gericht
Klosterkirche
(Ruine)
Rotes
Rathaus
Haus der
Jungen Talente
Nikolaikirche
NIKOLAI-
VIERTEL
Molken-
markt
Minister-
rat
Parochialkirche
Ephraim-
Palais
Hand-
werks-
museum
Bhf. Jannowitz-
brücke
Märkisches Ufer
Märkisches
Museum
Fischer-
insel
Insel-
brücke
Zilledenkmal
Otto-Nagel-
Haus
Bärenzwinger
Schwimmbad
Bau-
ausstellung
Hauptbahnhof
(Ostbahnhof)
Spree
St.-Michael-
Kirche
Annenkirche
Strausberger
Platz
Wilhelm-Pieck-Straße
Linienstraße
Weydingerstr.
Straßburger Straße
Prenzlauer Str.
Prenzlauer Berg
Greifswalder Straße
Am Friedenshain
Bötzow Str.
Mollstraße
Keibelstraße
Hans-Beimler-Straße
Barnim-
Höchste Str.
Wein-Straße
Friedenstraße
Alte Schönhauser Str.
Max-Beer-Straße
Almstadtstraße
Münzstraße
Rochstraße
Liebknecht-
Karl-Marx-Allee
Berolinastraße
Weydemeyerstr.
Palisadenstr.
Blumenstraße
Blumenstr.
Jacoby-
Alexander
Rathausstraße
Grunerstraße
Spandauer Straße
Marx-Engels-Forum
Magazinstr.
Voltairestr.
Schillingstraße
Neue
Singerstraße
Lichtenberger
Andreas-
straße
Stralauer Straße
Mühlendamm
Holzmarktstraße
Lange-
str.
Fischerinsel
Wallstraße
Neue Roßstr.
Neue Jakobstr.
Köpenicker Straße
Brückenstraße
Ohmstr.
Michaelkirchstraße
Neue Grün-
str.
Alte Jakobstraße
Sebastianstraße
Annenstraße
Heinrich-Heine-Straße
Schmidstraße
Melchiorstraße
Bethaniendamm
250 m
© Baedeker
Volkspark Prenzlauer Berg, Sportforum Berlin
Sport- und Erholungszentrum
Tierpark
Flughafen Schönefeld
Treptower Park
Flughafen Tempelhof

U-Bahn

Einenkel has a captivating way with fish. His fish soup with fennel and shrimp quenelles, fresh shrimp in sesame seeds and ray wing with balsamic vinegar and olives were outstanding. His vegetarian dishes (no meat on the menu!) are nothing to write home about. The waiters don't pretend to be the stars of this "in" restaurant, but take good care of their customers instead. The wine list is barely adequate.

ALTES ZOLLHAUS 15/20

10961, Kreuzberg
Carl-Herz-Ufer 30
(0 30) 6 92 33 00, Fax 6 92 35 66 res.

P

Closed for lunch Sunday and Monday, closed 2 weeks in January and July. Tables d'hôte: 70/100, à la carte: 44/79

This beautiful, half-timbered house on the Landwehrkanal is a historic monument, and the kitchen inside has made progress. Hearty regional classic dishes have been refined and made lighter, and new combinations provide surprising taste sensations. While the marinated veal shank was luscious and tender and the salmon on asparagus salad with a mild vinaigrette superb, the cream of kohlrabi soup drowned any taste of the champagne it contained. The whiff of cinnamon in the red cabbage gave a lovely, crisp Brandenburg farmyard duckling style and polish. The strawberry charlotte would have been better with riper fruit. Unlike the cuisine, the wine list has an international profile and emphasizes German and French vintages, although we also found wines from Italy, Spain, California and Lebanon. Helpful and uncomplicated service.

ALT-LUXEMBURG 16/20

10627, Charlottenburg
Windschiedstr. 31 [A3]
(0 30) 3 23 87 30, res.

Closed for lunch, Sunday, Saturday from May to August, Monday from September to April. Tables d'hôte: 115/145, à la carte: 57/94

Karl Wannemacher stays true to classic haute cuisine, come what may. But don't mistake loyalty to tradition for a lack of ideas, because eating here is never boring (apart from some desserts). His strictly classic compositions attempting to create new harmony with few ingredients have become more exuberant under new Asian influences. Point and counterpoint of Wannemacher's dishes are his exquisite sauces. The dark and slightly sweet secret potion he serves on his fried foie gras is something to get ecstatic about. Combining a lovely lemongrass sauce with sweetbread-stuffed ravioli was sheer genius. Aromatic basil sauce joined a fried gurnard to sweet-and-sour squash. As highly as we esteem Wannemacher's expertise in preparing sauces, fish and meat, we must sadly admit that his side dishes are disappointing.True to its name, the wine list carries a few Luxembourg wines, though German and French names predominate. Many good wines can be had by the glass as well. The service can sometimes be a little strict in denying polite requests.

AM FASANENPLATZ 13/20

10719, Wilmersdorf
Fasanenstr. 42 [C5]
(0 30) 8 83 97 23,

Closed Sunday and Monday. Tables d'hôte: 46L, 58/90D, à la carte: 37/72

We like this restaurant, its attentive and obliging service and its unpretentious and honestly good cuisine. We found German and Austrian dishes on the modest menu, some with a Mediterranean touch. Our savory Swabian ravioli soup was as delicious as the tender *tafelspitz* that followed it, or the swordfish fried in lemon butter. A little more attention to seasonal products would have left a more favorable impression than strawberries and blueberries offered in the middle of a snowy winter.We missed this refreshing down-to-earth attitude on the exotic wine list, which includes such rarities as a white wine from China and a Chilean red wine, but we liked the choice of 15 wines by the glass.

ANA E BRUNO 16/20

14059, Cahrlottenburg
Sophie-Charlotten-Str. 101 [A3]
(0 30) 3 25 71 10, Fax 3 22 68 95

Closed for lunch, Sunday, Monday, 10 days in January, 3 weeks during the summer. Tables d'hôte: 94/125, à la carte: 44/82

This is the most interesting Italian restaurant in town. While the charming Ana Arcones looks after her guests, Bruno Pellegrini turns his kitchen into a laboratory. With scientific accuracy and inspiration, our experimental genius meticulously works out new recipes.Pellegrini's "nuova cucina" has left purely Italian dimensions far behind. You can order classic roast beef with a marinade of fine herbs as well as typically Italian veal fillet with foamy tuna sauce or pasta with radicchio and shrimps. Ana e Bruno has maintained its characteristic lines with perfectly done, highly flavorful and harmonious creations, even though Pellegrini's strong point, his undogmatic tolerance, can also be his weakness. A strained vegetable soup with croûtons as an appetizer is ludicrous, and the zucchini soufflé (a tiny green pudding decorated with three white truffle slices) is a caricature of nouvelle cuisine.The wine list is a book you can spend all evening reading. If you'd rather drink wine, trust the sound advice of Bruno Pellegrini.

BACCO 13/20

10789, Wilmersdorf
Marburger Str. 5 [D4]
(0 30) 2 11 86 87, Fax 2 11 52 30 res.

Closed Sunday, Tables d'hôte: 60L 80/120D, à la carte: 39/80

In contrast to most of the tourist traps in the vicinity of the Gedächtniskirche, this little Italian restaurant offers pasta, fish and meat of good quality. The sauces harmonize and the dishes are perfectly done. Traditional Italian cuisine is prepared without risky experiments – and without much love for either desserts or side dishes, which are both rather unimaginative. The wine list offers an acceptable choice of well-known Italian wines.

BAMBERGER REITER 18/20

10777, Wilmersdorf
Regenburger Str. 7 [D5]
(0 30) 2 18 42 82, Fax 2 14 23 48 res.

Closed for lunch, closed Sunday and Monday, 1—14 January. Tables d'hôte: 145/185, à la carte: 70/108

If you really want to enjoy a good meal—and the emphasis is on enjoyment—you've found the right place. This is no place for false snobbery and strained formality. The dining rooms are comfortable and cosy (even the creaking floorboards sound friendly) and the young staff gladly does everything to make you feel at home. More than 350 choice and fairly priced wines are in the cellar. Franz Raneburger doesn't need a festive setting to celebrate his cuisine. His cooking indulges in no artistic flights of fancy. Raneburger's pigeon terrine with shiitake mushrooms is his most daring creation. Instead, he brings the essentials of European cuisine to your table in ultimate perfection. Nothing sounds particularly spectacular—fried angler with pesto, quail consommé, lobster with asparagus, saddle of venison with spaetzle—but everything is pure enjoyment. Only rarely does something not quite come up to snuff, like raw scallops that succumbed to an overwhelming lime vinaigrette. Raneburger's desserts are fabulous.

BISTRO BAMBERGER REITER 15/20

10777, Wilmersdorf
Regenburger Str. 7 [D5]
(0 30) 2 13 67 33, Fax 2 14 23 48 res.

Closed for lunch, Sunday, Monday, 1—14 January. Tables d'hôte: 68/83, à la carte: 45/73, No Credit Cards

This doesn't look like a bistro. With its elegant furniture and distinguished ambience, it seems more like a luxury restaurant. But the cuisine meets bistro expectations, even though perfectionist Franz Raneburger supervises the kitchen. Lamb pâté with baked fruit and squash kernels, stuffed eel with crispy fried potatoes or calf's liver with puréed potatoes and celery root are all wonderfully uncomplicated dishes. You can order haute cuisine—fine fish with lobster sauce or shrimp ravioli with champagne sauerkraut—as well. So what's the difference between the elegant bistro and the main restaurant? Simply this: here the dishes are a little less perfect and extravagant, and a lot less expensive.

C+W GOURMET 15/20

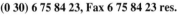

15732, Eichwalde
Banhofstr. 9
(0 30) 6 75 84 23, Fax 6 75 84 23 res.

Closed for lunch except for Sunday, Monday, Tuesday, 24 December through 10 January, 14 days during the Berlin Summer school holiday, No Credit Cards. Tables d'hôte: 60/80, à la carte: 40/68

You can get sushi, pizza and Greek gyros on every corner in Berlin, but you'll have a hard time finding well-done regional cooking. In the true pioneer spirit, Carmen Krüger and Wolfgang Haase have established such a restaurant on the southeastern outskirts of the city. The name of the restaurant is as irritating as the cool and functional decor (white tiles and black furniture), but the food is comfortably rustic in style. Leave scruples about calories and cholesterol behind when you eat here, because you'll get plenty of both. We loved the homemade blood pudding with a delicious rösti crust, pike-perch with savory potatoes fried in lots of bacon and breaded sweetbreads. Don't miss the classic thick cream of potato soup with crayfish and the crispy pigeon on savoy cabbage with carrots and potatoes. If you don't like beer, let Wolfgang Haase suggest one of the choice wines on his list.

CRISTALLO 14/20

14167, Zehlendorf
Teltower Damm 52
(0 30) 8 15 66 09, Fax 8 15 20 23

Closed for lunch every day except Sunday Tables d'hôte: 79, à la carte: 38/79, Tables d'hôte with wine: 89

A creative and dynamic treatment of *cucina italiana* isn't always popular with the guests of a traditional Italian restaurant. Daniele Pasolini satisfies both regular customers and gourmets keen on experimenting. His menu reads like a best-seller list of Italian dishes, but his "specialties of the month" show what his ambitious kitchen is capable of. The "specialties" could use a bit more concentration, though. The tagliolini with shrimps, cubed potatoes and asparagus slices would have been fantastic if the shrimps hadn't been so dry. Too much chili marred the taste of the aromatic tomato sauce with tender squid and diced zucchini that came with tiny strozzapreti. Such carelessness is the exception rather than the rule, however. The anger medallions and the imaginative desserts show that the cuisine is on its way up.The large choice of wines competes with the wide variety on the menu and offers everything from a simple vino di tavola to a first-class Barolo. The service is charming and adroit.

DON CAMILLO 13/20

14059, Charlottenburg
Schloßstr. 7-8 [A2]
(0 30) 3 22 35 72 res.

Closed Wednesday, 15 July to 15 August, No Credit Cards, Tables d'hôte: 80/120L, à la carte: 38/75

Instead of asking for the menu, ask what the kitchen recommends. Nimble waiters will carry all the fresh produce the cook has to offer to your table for you to pick and choose from. The cèpes in white wine and garlic were a light and delicious appetizer, as were the marinated celery and mushrooms carpaccio. The pasta is more imaginatively prepared than the fish and meat courses; the impressively large choice here attempts to compensate for the lack of creativity. Only dessert brought a surprise: besides the classic sweets on the dessert cart, we also found a bowl with potatoes, with which the waiter created a "special dessert" at our table. The Soave offered by the glass is drinkable, but the choice of wines remains inadequate.

FIORETTO BEI CARMERS 14/20

10623, Charlottenburg
Charmerstr. 2 [C3/4]
(0 30) 3 12 31 15

Closed for lunch Saturday, Sunday, month of July. A la carte: 42/96

Doris Burneleit doesn't impress her guests with faddish originality, but tries to make the most of the original tastes of her ingredients. Freshness and top quality are prerequisites for good cooking here, so that even an all-time classic like insalata caprese with sun-ripened tomatoes and buffalo cheese tastes like a new creation. Doris Burneleit can be proud of her delicious asparagus soup, too, but she should have left her shrimps in the ocean. The pasta here is always highly commendable, like the superb strozzapreti with fresh scampi and flavorful pesto. Doris Burneleit's talents aren't obvious enough in her main courses; the turbot in potato crust was dry and the lamb fillets would have been more at home at a barbecue. A light vanilla and mint pudding with fresh berries for dessert swept us off our feet again. Part of the Fioretto's success is due to its attentive and pleasant service. But even they couldn't turn off the Italian tenor on the tape. A Ceretto Barolo from the small but expertly stocked wine list consoled us.

FIRST FLOOR 13/20

10789, Wilmersdorf [D4]
Budapester Str. 42/Eur.-Center
(0 30) 25 02 10 20, Fax 2 62 65 77 res.
P

Closed for lunch Saturday, closed Sunday. Tables d'hôte: 60L, 75/125D, à la carte: 52/103

The "First Floor" doesn't just sound chic, it also tells you where to go if you want to eat in the Palace Hotel. With an ostentatious and posh new decor (no expense spared), the management has followed the example of the Intercontinental and tried to upgrade its restaurant with lots of polished silver, extravagant woodwork, discreet and exclusive lighting and lush fabrics. A banal cuisine, however, without any creative taste sensations, doesn't fit into the new surroundings. All too often vegetables are purely decorative and sauces dull. Tender oxtail was delicious, even though we could see but not taste the truffles on the puréed potatoes. With an impressive choice of cheese and lovely desserts, our meal ended better than it began.Not only the kitchen has to improve here. The wine list could use more moderately priced wines in addition to the proud names we found, although we were pleasantly surprised at the number of half-bottles offered. The service has been effectively drilled.

FRÜHSAMMERS GASTHAUS 15/20

14129, Zehlendorf
Matterhornstr. 101
(0 30) 8 03 27 20, Fax 8 03 37 36

Closed for lunch, 2 weeks in January and during the Berlin summer school holiday. Tables d'hôte: 46/78, à la carte: 180

Peter Frühsammer has found a new hobby: when he's not in his kitchen: he raises Galloway beef on the southern outskirts of Berlin and dreams of a country farm where he can open a new restaurant. We hope he realizes his dream soon, because with only a part-time cook the cuisine in his restaurant suffers. He still buys the best regional and seasonal products, but his dishes are prepared with a definite lack of interest and inspiration. His superb haunch of venison with spaetzle, delicious roasted shoulder of suckling lamb and lovely Viennese schnitzel prove that the maestro hasn't lost his touch. But gritty salad without vinaigrette, tasteless spinach soup with oysters and insipid pancakes filled with lobster and asparagus sadly disappointed us.The wine list offers choice wines from Germany, Italy and France. The wines that accompany the courses of the prix-fixe menu are offered by the glass.

LE GRAND RESTAURANT SILHOUETTE 14/20

10117, Stadtmitte
Friedrichstr. 158-164 [B4]
(0 30) 23 27 45 00, Fax 23 27 33 62 res.
P

Closed for lunch, closed Sunday, Monday, 9 July to 17 August. Tables d'hôte: 145/175, à la carte: 66/108

From the window you can see countless cranes building a new future for this city. Inside the restaurant of the Maritim Hotel, the ambience reminded us of the 1970s: a tired couple danced to the old pop songs of a run-down combo and the stiffly servile waiters presented "madame" with orchids in a paper box. Chef Rolf Schmidt obviously feels at home in this restaurant, more anyway than in his kitchen. His staff, though, manages well without him. The breast of guinea fowl had a nice, crispy crust and the angler was perfectly done. If some of the promising creations taste a little flat, it's probably because the ingredients themselves lack flavor. The lemon-grass sauce didn't taste like lemon grass and basil wasn't anything more than green. If Schmidt promises truffles, he shouldn't irritate us with cheap and tasteless products.The wine list offers an international choice of wines.

GRAND SLAM 17/20

14193, Grunewald
Gottfried-von-Cramm-Weg 47
(0 30) 8 25 38 19, Fax 8 26 63 00 res.

 **P**

Closed for lunch, Sunday, Monday, 1 to 17 January, 24 July to 10 August. Tables d'hôte: 125/175, à la carte: 64/105

The obstinate extravagance of this intimate restaurant, well-frequented by members of an exclusive tennis club, scorns any thought of a recession. A perfectly trained host of waiters fulfills every wish, and a lot of extras, from wonderful bread and a variety of appetizers to lovely petits fours and pâtisserie with coffee, make a visit here worthwhile. Johannes King has finally found his individual style. Oysters, truffles, caviar, lobster and foie gras still belong to the repertoire, but the luxury products aren't (mis)used to hide a lack of creativity. On the contrary, King's marinated calf's tongue with watercress-blossoms and an intensive aroma of truffles or his convincing combination of foie gras and morel ravioli were superb. His impressive bouillabaisse salad didn't remind one much of the famous French stew; in different, delectable sauces we had lovely salmon, John Dory, sole, redfish and shrimps.The exquisite choice of cheeses as well as the well-stocked wine list deserve praise.

HARLEKIN IN THE GRAND HOTEL ESPLANADE 13/20

10785, Tiergarten
Lüzowufer 15 [E4]
(0 30) 25 47 80, Fax 2 65 11 71 res.

P

Closed for lunch, closed Sunday. Tables d'hôte: 90/145, à la carte: 57/98

With a touch of "too much," the originally good cooking in this hotel's restaurant suffers serious setbacks. Why couldn't the kitchen leave the perfectly done angler cheeks with flavorful pesto alone? They could have easily done without pale tomatoes and a ludicrous little mound of caviar! Three extremely chewy and surely superfluous slices of duck's breast destroyed the wonderful impression of the exquisite tomato soup. And whatever possessed our cook to serve delicious squab and mushrooms risotto with the tiny corncobs you usually find in a glass of mixed pickles? Highlights were fried John Dory in ginger and curry sauce, pigeon in pastry with an abundance of white truffles and chocolate terrine with orange slices.The wine list of the Esplanade offers only a few medium-priced wines and many well-known names from Germany and France. The service is well-trained.

HEISING 14/20

10789, Schöneberg
Rankstr. 32 [D4]
(0 30) 2 13 39 52, 3 02 55 15,
Fax 3 02 41 86 res.

P

Closed for lunch, closed Sunday. A la carte: 89, No Credit Cards

The first time you step into this unassuming little restaurant, you'll probably think you're in the Heisings' living room. Dark furniture, beautifully set tables, hand-painted porcelain and moiré on the walls create an intimate atmosphere, and the Heisings make their guests feel at home. The cuisine here has exactly the old-fashioned touch we like. There's only one four-course prix-fixe menu, but you can choose the courses individually. We liked watercress soup, rabbit fillets and green salad with goat's cheese or duck confit. Heising doesn't always attain the finesse of his exquisite fried quail on grapes with a delicate filling of gingerbread and shallots, but all dishes are well-prepared. His faithful use of decorative cocktail tomatoes and parsley bouquets is touching.

HEMINGWAY'S 14/20

14193, Grunewald
(0 30) 8 25 45 71, Fax 89 00 62 70 res.

P

Closed for lunch. Tables d'hôte: 95/130, à la carte: 54/90

Grunewald's gastronomy builds up the ego of a swell(ed) clientele: the owner shakes hands with his guests, the service exhibits dignified phlegm, the menu is—where size and price are concerned—exorbitant, and the glamorous decorating scheme makes those who already live in similar surroundings feel at home.If you want to make an impression on your dinner guests, order the lobster salad. It's prepared at the table like a true Las Vegas spectacle. But the cuisine doesn't actually need to put on a show for snobs. The shrimp and garlic soup is an high-wire act between light charm and strong seasoning. Although creativity reaches its peak with a saddle of veal and shiitake mushrooms, all standards are finely balanced and professionally prepared, like liver of suckling kid with zucchini, Brandenburg lamb in a pine-nut crust, delicate fillet of bass with lobster butter and sole in lime sauce.The guests here fail to be impressed by the exorbitant prices of champagne and wine. Some bottles under 100 DM are offered.

KÖNIGIN LUISE IN OPERNPALAIS 13/20

10117, Stadtmitte
Unter den Linden 5 [C4]
(0 30) 2 38 40 16, Fax 2 00 44 38 res.

Closed for lunch, closed Monday, 3 weeks during the Berlin summer school holiday. Tables d'hôte: 58/75, à la carte: 44/76

The Baroque splendor of the dining room takes you back to the pomp of past centuries without letting the cuisine catapult you back into cruel reality. The decor smacks strongly of Disney World, but with the grand Zeughaus for a background even a little kitsch looks good. The menu reveals a lot of creativity and ambition, and the wine list is stocked with a passable choice of German and French wines. Beautiful arrangements and daring experiments, however, don't disguise the fact that the cook's feet sometimes leave the ground – for instance, when he serves deep-fried melon balls in a savory lobster soup. The vegetable aspic with duck's breast and mustard sauce was excellent. The desserts are in keeping with the season.

MARIO 13/20

10629, Charlottenburg
Liebnizstr. 43 [B4]
(0 30) 3 24 35 16 res.

Closed Saturday, à la carte: 38/84

Sometimes the quality goes up, sometimes down. The only thing you can depend on here is the high prices. The best food is served here on weekdays, when there are only a few customers. With a little luck, you may get perfectly fried quail with a delicious sauce and rucola salad, chanterelles and cèpes or tender saddle of lamb with garlic and green beans. None of the pastas leaves a lasting impression. The wine list offers an interesting choice of Italian wines at reasonable prices.

MAXWELL 17/20

10717, Wilmersdorf
Helmstedter Str. 9 [D5]
(0 30) 8 54 47 37, Fax 8 54 47 37 res.

Closed for lunch. Tables d'hôte: 98, à la carte: 51/79

In Berlin, wherever gourmet cuisine deserves its name, it's celebrated with pomp and circumstance. But there are exceptions to this rule, and one of these is Maxwell's, where a relaxed atmosphere, unpretentious service and fine gourmet cooking have undergone a rare symbiosis. The decor doesn't have to be glamorous when the cuisine is. Some highlights were quail with sautéed mushrooms in balsamic vinegar with coriander, watercress soup, and poularde with honey and ginger sauce. Uwe Popall plays with strong flavors and borrows some ideas from Asiatic as well as Mediterranean cuisine without flying off into abstruse experimental spheres. His talent and inspiriation conform to the taste and the wishes of his guests. The wine list offers nothing comprehensive, but a few carefully chosen wines, one of which is always adequate for the high-quality food ordered.

MERZ 13/20

10785, Schöneberg
Schöneberger Ufer 65 [F4]
(0 30) 2 61 38 82 res.

Closed for lunch Saturday and Sunday, closed Monday. No Credit Cards, à la carte: 34/60

Things are looking up for this restaurant on the banks of the Schöneberger River. The menu has grown and become more interesting, and the prices have gone down to a reasonable level. But nothing tastes as exciting as the way it's described on the menu. Good and solid bistro fare is this restaurant's forte. Mediterranean dishes are served here as well as game, lovely salads and little snacks for in between. The cook should pay more attention to cooking times and temperatures. But his desserts were delicious.

PARKRESTAURANT IN THE HOTEL STEINBERGER BERLIN 13/20

10789, Wilmerdorf
Los-Angeles-Platz 1 [D4]
(0 30) 2 12 77 55/47, Fax 2 12 77 97

P

Closed for lunch except Sunday, closed for dinner Sunday, closed Monday. A la carte: 44/76

Steigenberger's Parkrestaurant still adheres to the philosophy that made its cooking something special. Sauces are created on oil bases and are often enriched with exotic seasonings. The kitchen, once ambitious and precise, had grown a bit lax on our last visit. The fried prawns were half raw and cold, and the angler with ginger oil and sprouts so dry and salty that we sent it back. The second try was proof enough that Peter Griebel can do better: the angler looked and tasted delicious, almost as good as the duck's breast on sugar peas with peach sauce and gnocchi that followed it. Main fish courses are available in a smaller version as appetizers. The professional service also offers many wines by the glass, whereas the wine list features well-known names.

PONTE VECCHIO 17/20

10585, Charlottenburg
Spielhagenstr. 3 [B3]
(0 30) 3 42 19 99 res.

Closed for lunch except Sunday, closed Thursday, 4 weeks during the Berlin summer school holiday, 1—10 January. Tables d'hôte: 80, à la carte: 37/89

We have yet to take our first look at the menu here. We'd rather wait patiently for Valter Mazza's personal recommendations. Somehow he seems to know exactly what you'd like and suggests a meal that provokes a highly satisfied sigh after every course. Zucchini flower stuffed with ricotta, lobster with rucola, tagliatelle with chanterelles, roast rabbit—the dishes here are unpretentious, almost simple, and afford an evening of gourmet enjoyment. Careful shopping for high-quality produce, the outstanding craftmanship of a motivated kitchen staff and a little something that is sometimes called intuition, talent or genius are the ingredients of this successful recipe. The wine list offers many well-known Italian wines, but its standard is not on a par with the cuisine.

REINHARDS

10178, Stadtmitte
Poststr. 28 [E4]
(0 30) 2 42 52 95, Fax 2 42 41 02 res.

Closed Christmas Eve, à la carte: 34/60

This restaurant profits from a lack of competition in the eastern part of town. Customers seem to feel at home in the bistro ambience of this popular restaurant, which is highly frequented from morning till late at night seven days a week. They apparently put up with the sometimes rough treatment the staff subjects them to. We were asked to fill up a table where it would have been difficult to find a place for a wine cooler! If you arrive 10 minutes after the time you reserved a table, your reservation is cancelled. The food ranges from unremarkable to irritating.

RESTAURANT IM LOGENHAUS 15/20

10714, Wilmersdorf
Emserstr. 12-13 [C5]
(0 30) 87 25 60, Fax 8 61 29 85 res.

P

Closed for lunch, closed Sunday. Tables d'hôte: 82/104, à la carte: 44/73

An extravagant interior doesn't hide the fact that the Steinhorst and Fehrenbach duo has run out of ideas. The kitchen offers last year's best-sellers: we experienced a true déjà-vu evening with veal fillet and morels, lamb saddle and ratatouille and striped mullet under a crust of herbs. We wouldn't mind eating the same thing a hundred times over if it were done to perfection. All ingredients are finely balanced to harmonize with each other, but the cooking times and temperatures are unprecise and result in unpleasant surprises, for instance overdone potatoes, dry guinea fowl and underdone shrimps.Proof of fine taste is the interesting choice of German wines. The service is correct.

ROCKENDORF'S RESTAURANT 18/20

13469, Waidmannslust
Düstrehaupstr. 1/Ecke Waidmannsluster Damm
(0 30) 4 02 30 99, Fax 4 02 27 42 res.

Closed: Sunday, Monday, month of July, 22 December to 6 January. Tables d'hôte: 110/175, à la carte: 175/220

No doubt this was and is the very best restaurant in Berlin. And we don't want to insult it, let alone depose its gourmet majesty. Rockendorf is a brilliant cook with a perfectly organized restaurant; his technical perfection, sureness of taste, culinary imagination, discerning choice of products and—last but not least—his untiring efforts to promote fine cuisine with regional roots have been praised time and time again. Rockendorf's inventively composed six- to nine-course prix-fixe meals are astoundingly light. The well-stocked wine cellar can even offer a connoisseur some surprises, especially if he orders champagne. The staff is competent and works quickly and flawlessly without losing any of its charm and good humor.But, we're sorry to say, Rockendorf doesn't always realize his full potential. Sometimes he loses his nerve and his creative concentration in arranging superfluous frills. An exquisitely savory tomato essence with cheese dumplings really didn't need that insipid little lobster cookie with a hood of lobster aspic and a teaspoonfull of fennel and lobster salad. After raving about his savory and aromatic veal shanks with artichokes and beans, we can't help but be disappointed with a dry veal roulade filled with a strip of paprika and accompanied by chanterelles and kohlrabi. The desserts used to be better: our peach gratin with strawberries and white chocolate was too sweet and soggy. The cherry terrine with the walnut parfait could have been tangier.

TRATTORIA À MUNTAGNOLA 13/20

10777, Schöneberg [D5]
Fuggerstr. 27
(0 30) 2 11 66 42

A la carte: 30/58

Here is what we've all been looking for: a trattoria in the best Italian style with checkered tablecloths, friendly service and honest vino da tavola. "La mamma" cooks and the whole family helps. Mamma shrugs her shoulders at light nuova cucina and is loyal to the regional cuisine of her native home, the Basilicata, an almost forgotten region in the deepest south of Italy. Some rustic specialties are puréed broad beans with dandelion greens, wonderful fusilli with bread crumbs fried in olive oil, and lots and lots of garlic. Mamma isn't afraid of inconsequence and prepares (with bravado!) her famous castrato alla pastorale (mutton in savory sauce) with ecologically raised sheep from a German heath. The modest prices are within the range of an original trattoria.

TRIO 15/20

14059, Charlottenburg
Klausenerplatz 14 [A4]
(0 30) 3 21 77 82 res.

Closed for lunch, closed Wednesday, Thursday. Tables d'hôte: 52/88, à la carte: 38/67, No Credit Cards

Siegfried Stier doesn't have to fight for existence even during a recession. His consistently high performance in the kitchen, a pleasant rapport with his customers and fair prices have secured many regular diners. Good, fresh ingredients are used to produce uncomplicated dishes we would love to eat every day: goat-liver mousse with sugar peas, coalfish with saffron sauce, saddle of lamb with vegetable tart, sheatfish with red beets and potato cakes. The vegetarian dish was as unimaginative as last year's.The wine list emphasizes wines from Baden and Bordeaux and offers many half-bottles.

UDAGAWA 14/20

12163, Steiglitz Feuerbacherstr. 24
(0 30) 7 92 23 73 res.
Closed for lunch, closed Tuesday, No Credit Cards. Tables d'hôte: 95, à la carte: 40/110

The soul of a nation becomes apparent in its cooking. But not all restaurants are successful ambassadors for their countries. The Udagawa is a convincing representation of Japanese philosophy, puristic and strict: a fish is a fish is a fish, and it is best consumed raw and unadulterated. As the cook doesn't have to consider cooking times and temperatures, he can concentrate on the artistic presentation of his sushi. Tempura Moriavase—king prawns, fish and vegetables fried in crispy dough with a sauce of soy, ginger and spicy wasabi—perhaps suits a European palate better.

ZUM HUGENOTTEN IN THE HOTEL INTER-CONTINENTAL 16/20

10714, Wilmersdorf
Budapester Str. 2 [D4]
(0 30) 26 02 12 63, Fax 2 60 28 07 60 res.

P

Closed for lunch, closed Sunday, Monday, 3 weeks in January, 3 weeks in July/August. Tables d'hôte: 105/145, à la carte: 62/102

After a complete renovation, not much more than the name has remained of the old Hugenotten. The newly decorated dining rooms are more pleasant and comfortable than before. Walls are wood-paneled, floors covered with thick rugs and oil paintings, and extravagant floral decorations create the ambience of culture and distinction that American tourists appreciate in Europe. The "Hugo" is ambitious and aims high. The rules of luxury restaurants are strictly adhered to: ubiquitous and discreet service by a large staff, two *amuse bouches*, a pre-dessert after the main course (a superfluous fad, we thought), excellent petits fours with coffee and a gift of pralinés at the end of the meal.We looked for a hair in the soup, but didn't find one. Chef Jürgen Reiske exhibits true virtuosity and meets our high expectations. He tries out new compositions with expertise and imagination. Sometimes they work; sometimes they don't. His scallops on tomatoes and artichokes combined with wafer-thin slices of tender calf's tongue were sensational, whereas a lobster aspic with wild asparagus seemed rather insipid. His angler fillet in cider sauce with kohlrabi spaghetti was fantastic, but his sweetbreads coated with rösti and accompanied by rucola mousse was a failure. Behind the enormous wine list, restaurant critics can take copious notes unobserved, but normal guests will find it an encumbrance. The choice of wines is oriented toward the ambitions of the restaurant: top quality at top prices.

HOTELS

BERLIN HILTON

10117, Mohrenstr. 30 [B5]
(0 30) 2 38 20, Fax 23 82 42 69

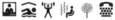

502 beds, **S** 170/395, **D** 210/445,
APP 600/1500

This hotel is a postmodern gem on historic grounds near the old Gendarmenmarkt. It's an ideal spot for those who want to steep themselves in Berlin history and architecture, but frequented more by businessmen, who find here a perfectly equipped conference center. Squash, bowling, beauty farm and hairdresser. Restaurants and discotheque. Breakfast: 30 DM.

BRISTOL-KEMPINSKI

14059, Charlottenburg
Kurfürstendamm 27 [C4]
(0 30) 88 43 40, Fax 8 83 69 75

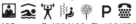

315 beds, **S** 340/480, **D** 390/530,
APP 600/1200

The spacious hotel lobby, a nostalgic reminder of old-fashioned grand hotels, has achieved a fresh new image by installing chic boutiques. The rooms are comfortable and have soundproofed windows. Hotel bar, restaurant, 24-hour room service. Breakfast: 17-30 DM.

GRAND HOTEL ESPLANADE

10785, Tiegarten
Lützowufer 15 [E4]
(0 30) 25 47 80, Fax 2 54 11 71

P

402 beds, **S** 409/499, **D** 488/578,
APP 679/2229, **½P** +50, **P** +100

The soundproofed and air-conditioned rooms are slightly smaller than the terrace of the Grand Suite. Children up to 12 years old stay for free. Hairdresser. House doctor. Library with 4,000 art books. Boutique. Harry's New York Bar. The hotel has its own restaurant and convention ship for 120 passengers. Breakfast: 29 DM.

HOTEL BERLIN

10714, Wilmersdorf
Lützowplatz 17 [E4]
(0 30) 2 60 50, Fax 26 05 27 16

490, **S** 220/320, **D** 245/345,
APP 450/1500, **1/2P** 40, **P** +80

The hotel sports an attractive lobby with gorgeous Oriental rugs. The service is courteous and deferential and almost all rooms have soundproofed windows. The new Kurfürsten wing houses conference rooms and fitness facilities, a hairdresser and beauty farm. Breakfast: 27 DM. Restaurant.

HUMBOLDT-MÜHLE

13507, Tegel
An der Mühle 5-9
(0 30) 43 90 40, Fax 43 90 44 44

123, **S** 210/260, **D** 250/320,
APP 380/500, **1/2P** +25/35, **P** +60/70

The old tower of the Humboldt mill is a historic monument—and the second hotel the Sorat chain has opened in Berlin. Lake Tegel is at your door, and a short walk brings you into the middle of a wood. You won't need 10 minutes to get to the city by autobahn. Most of the rooms are in an addition built onto the tower. They're modern and comfortable. The hotel's motor yacht anchored on the lake seats 12 guests. Bike and motorcycle rental. Shuttle service to Tegel airport. Restaurant. Breakfast: 23 DM.

INTER-CONTINENTAL

10787, Wilmersdorf
Budapester Str. 2 [D4]
(0 30) 2 60 20, Fax 2 60 28 07 60

511, **S** 335/485, **D** 385/535,
APP 650/2500

The largest of Berlin's luxury hotels, with a view over the Tiergarten and only three minutes from the Kurfürstendamm, offers every comfort. The glass entrance to the huge lobby is remarkable. Around-the-clock room service is offered, as well as a swimming pool, thermal baths and fitness facilities. The rooms are functionally and comfortably furnished. Breakfast: 29 DM.

MARITIM

10117, Stadtmitte
Friedrichstr. 158-164 [B4]
(0 30) 2 32 70, Fax 23 27 33 62

349, **S** 355/535, **D** 480/660,
APP 730/3400, **1/2P** +45, **P** +85

As a representative palace built in the former German Democratic Republic with Japanese money and know-how, this hotel has everything from modern facilities to the exclusive ambience you can expect in a luxury hotel. Flawless service, roof terrace, 11 restaurants and bars, 24-hour room service. Breakfast: 28 DM.

PALACE

10789, Wilmersdorf [D4]
Budapester Str. 42/Eur.-Center
(0 30) 2 50 20, Fax 2 62 65 77

321, **S** 280/450, **D** 330/500,
APP 650/2600, **1/2P** +35, **P** +70

The Palace is behind the Gedächtniskirche in the Europa Center, where you can shop and stroll in any weather. An elegant Gobelin tapestry invests the lobby with a palatial atmosphere. The rooms are luxuriously furnished. Bars, café, Tiffany's, rustic restaurant. Breakfast: 26 DM.

RADISSON PLAZA

10178, Karl-Liebnecht-Str. 5
(0 30) 2 38 28, Fax 23 82 75 90

567, **S** 290/350, **D** 340/400,
APP 400/1200,

Some 65 million DM have been invested to bring the former palace hotel facing the museums and the Domplatz up to international standards. The renovated rooms are coolly elegant and equipped with modern technology. Cuisine and wine cellar are on the way up. Breakfast: 27 DM.

RIEHMERS HOFGARTEN

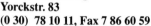

10965, Kreuzberg
Yorckstr. 83

(0 30) 78 10 11, Fax 7 86 60 59

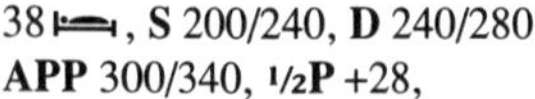

38, **S** 200/240, **D** 240/280,
APP 300/340, **½P** +28,

The former Hindenburg residence is now an in-spot for nightclubbers and those who want to experience the scene in Kreuzberg. The spacious rooms are functional. Breakfast is served here. Bar. Restaurant.

SCHLOSSHOTEL VIER JAHREZEITEN

14193, Grunewald
Brahmsstr. 6-10
(0 30) 89 58 40, Fax 89 58 48 00

39, **S** 545/595, **D** 635/685,
APP 950/3500

After extravagant restoration (30 million DM), the former Hotel Gerhus seems like a noble English country mansion with lovely old furniture, dark wood paneling, silver and decorative brocades and breakfast in the winter garden. Karl Lagerfeld's ideas have inspired the decorating scheme, and the designer himself has furnished his own suite (which can be rented when he's not there). This venerable hotel built in 1912 also offers such modern amenities as a PC-connection, two telephones and a fax machine (on demand) in every room. Ambitious restaurant.

SCHWEIZERHOF INTER-CONTINENTAL

10787, Wilmersdorf
Budapester Str. 21-31 [D4]
(0 30) 2 69 60, Fax 2 69 69 00

430, **S** 295/445, **D** 345/495,
APP 450/1800

A fitness and physiotherapy department, guaranteed to get the weariest guest going again, has been added to the largest hotel swimming pool in Berlin. Convenient central location near the Kurfürstendamm. 24-hour room service. Breakfast: 29 DM.

SORAT ART HOTEL

10719, Wilmersdorf
Joachimstaler Str. 28-29 [C4]
(0 30) 88 44 70, Fax 88 44 77 00

75, **S** 230/250, **D** 270/290,
½P +35, **P** +65

This hotel provides the right ambience for traveling design fiends. Unusual styling from door handles to coat hangers and traces of Wolf Vostell throughout characterize this hotel, frequented largely by the media and advertising set. This hotel is situated on one of the noisiest corners of the city. Breakfast: 25 DM.

SORAT HOTEL GUSTAVO

10409, Prenzlauer Berg
Prenzlauer Allee 169
(0 30) 44 66 10, Fax 44 66 16 61

123, **S** 190/270, **D** 240/310,

This is the first hotel with a comfortable upper-middle-class standard in this section of Berlin. Paintings of fabulous creatures created by the Spanish artist Gustavo are featured in the guest rooms, and his amusing wooden faces decorate the breakfast room. Soundproofed windows shut out most of the noise from the busy Prenzlauer Berg.

BESCHEID Rheinl. - Pfalz
Trittenheim 8 - Hermeskeil 12

MALERKLAUSE 14/20

54413, in Hofecken
(0 65 09) 5 58, Fax 10 82

Closed Monday, closed for lunch Tuesday through Friday, 2—18 January, 4—11 September. Tables d'hôte: 58/78, à la carte: 29/80, No Credit Cards

A couple of young winegrowers tipped us off to this restaurant a couple of years ago, and it turned out to be a real find. Hans-Georg Lorscheider serves good food at unbeatable prices. Unfortunately, we are not the only ones in on the secret, and crowds are heading here as well.Our last meal was superb: a tasty foie gras terrine with an *Auslese* (late-harvest wine) aspic, followed by perfectly done lobster in walnut and vinegar dressing, a juicy fillet of angler with spinach, and an opulent dessert. Hats off to Lorscheider, who sometimes cooks for 25 customers with just a single helper in the kitchen.The wine list offers the best Rieslings from the Moselle at relatively low prices, many other German wines and the better Bordeaux (priced accordingly).

BIEBELRIED Bayern

Würzburg 12

RESTAURANT LEICHT 13/20

97318, Würzburger Str, 3
(0 93 02) 8 14, Fax 31 63

P

Closed Sunday, à la carte: 29/63

This traditional inn has developed into a comfortable hotel, well-frequented because of its advantageous location near the autobahn. The menu offers regional specialities from Franconia as well as international cuisine. A staff in pretty dirndls brings to your table game from the nearby forests, pike-perch and salmon, plum parfait and apple pancakes as well as a choice of "digestifs"—the powerful fruit brandies of the house.

BIELEFELD NRW

Hannover 110 - Dortmund 112

AUBERGE LE CONCARNEAU 18/20

33659, Ortsteil Senne
Museumhof Senne
Buschkampstr. 75
(05 21) 49 37 17, Fax 49 33 88 res.

P

Closed for lunch, closed Sunday and holidays, Monday, 3 weeks during the NRW Easter holiday, 3 weeks during the NRW summer school holiday and 1 week during the autumn holiday., Tables d'hôte: 110/160, à la carte: 70/103

After long years of apprenticeship in the best French restaurants, Ernst Heiner Hüser now celebrates haute cuisine in the renovated barn of an old Westphalian farmhouse. A rather conservative cook with a disciplined imagination, Hüser offers French classics. His warm duck salad, Irish salmon with champagne butter and Challans duck with green pepper were flawlessly prepared and sublime in taste. Hüser's sweetbread salad with deep-fried artichokes was very savory, whereas his turbot was exquisitely delicate. Don't miss the excellent salad of fresh herbs with French ocean snails, only offered for a few weeks in summer, or the lovely scallops with shrimps and celery. Hüser's semolina pudding with purèed raspberries was sublime, but his potpourri of dessert miniatures is unsurpassed. Regular guests familiar with Hüser's repertoire should wait till the maestro himself comes to the table to ask, "What shall I cook for you?"The service is discreet but efficient and the wine list, with a comprehensive choice of French wines, remains one of the strong points of this restaurant. Low and moderately priced wines are listed together with great names from Burgundy and Bordeaux. A choice of wines by the glass can be individually arranged with each prix-fixe meal.

BUSCHKAMP 14/20

33659, Ortsteil SenneMuseumhof
SenneBuschkampstr. 75
(05 21) 49 28 00, Fax 49 33 88

 P

Tables d'hôte: 64/68, à la carte: 21/63

This old half-timbered farmhouse has been rebuilt in the middle of a historic landscape museum. A prix-fixe meal on the Buschkamp lawn is one of the loveliest summer enjoyments we know. The chef of the gourmet Auberge has recruited talented help, and with sous-chef Ange Kötter guarantees refined regional cuisine. The famous potato soup with cream and poppy seed was delectable, and we loved our smoked spare-ribs and fried potatoes. We were overjoyed to see that the tasty regional classics were still on the menu: first-class pig's ears and snout with lentils and fresh herbs. Newcomers should try the Westphalian prix-fixe menu. Beer goes well with the dishes here, but the wine list also offers sufficient wines by the glass from all German regions. The service is friendly and quick.

KLÖTZER'S KLEINES RESTAURANT 12/20

33602, Ritterstr. 33

(05 21) 6 89 54, Fax 6 93 21 res.

Closed for dinner Saturday, closed Sunday, Monday, à la carte: 33/71

If you like a lot of mahogany and don't mind paying 135 DM for a teaspoonful of Ossetra caviar with a piece of potato pancake, you might feel at home here. We don't, but we haven't yet given up all hope. Luxury products abound on the menu, which offers rich food rather than imaginative cooking. We like to remember a good pâté of foie gras and some well-done vegetables, but the rest we'd like to forget. The service is nimble and friendly and the wine list offers a good choice of wines by the glass.

MANUFAKTUR

33602, Feilenstr. 31

(05 21) 17 79 99, res.

No Credit Cards. Tables d'hôte: 35D, à la carte: 28/37

The ground floor of a former shirt-collar factory now houses a combination restaurant, bistro, café, pub and cocktail bar. Wooden benches and a few relics of the old factory as well as a copper bar create an attractive ambience. We were enthralled by the fantastic breakfast served here. Small lunch and dinner menus offer popular standards such as poularde breast with orange slices and green salad, potato and zucchini pancake with garlic sauce, veal ragout with noodles, saddle of lamb with beans and potatoes seasoned with thyme, crème caramel and white mousse with puréed raspberries. No highlights, but well-done and moderately priced. The wine list is meager, the bartenders behind the cocktail bar more (or less) talented.

SEEKRUG

33611, Lohheide 22a

(05 21) 8 10 81

A la carte: 23/52

On the shore of the Obersee, where Bielefelders like to make excursions, Alois Hülser has renovated a wonderful old 17th-century house with outbuildings and opened a marvelous beer garden. The Seekrug seats 1,200 outside and offers a variety of popular dishes and snacks for hungry visitors: a veritable schnitzel parade and insipid salads that have nothing at all do to with the cuisine the family offers in town (Auberge, Buschkamp). The service is sometimes disorganized and the wine list offers a white, a red and a rosé wine.

BIETIGHEIM-BISSINGEN BW

Stuttgart 24 - Heilronn 25

ZUM SCHILLER 13/20

74321, Stadtteil Biettigheim

Marktplatz 5

(0 71 42) 4 10 18 , Fax 4 60 58 res.

Closed Sunday, closed for lunch Monday, closed 1 week at Easter and 3 weeks during the Bad.-Württ. summer school holiday. Tables d'hôte: 48/69L, 98/125D, à la carte: 32/80

We recognized many favorite dishes on the menu here, including rutabaga and apple soup, foie gras with blood pudding, pike-perch and salmon terrine with beans, a hearty roe-deer consommé with ricotta ravioli and spaetzle, and roast duck with dumplings and red cabbage. A respectable Mecklenburg pike came with a risotto of red beets that was marred by an irritating horseradish sauce. The dessert mousse was not as light and fluffy as it should have been.The food prices on the handwritten menu (ask one of the friendly waitresses to help you read it) seemed unnecessarily high, while those on the extensive wine list were surprisingly moderate.

BINGEN Rheinland-Pfalz

Bad Kreuznach 15 - Mainz 30

BRUNNENKELLER 13/20

55411, Vorstadt 60

(0 67 21) 1 61 33, 1 06 63, Fax 1 61 33 res.

Closed for lunch Friday and Saturday, closed Sunday, 3 weeks during the NRW summer school holiday. Tables d'hôte: 35/45L, 65/100D, à la carte: 38/75

Since the plastic pond and the artificial flowers have been cleared away, this cellar restaurant has become more attractive. The department-store background music didn't irritate us half as much as the poor ventilation in the gallery that let us smell exactly what was cooking in the kitchen. After a rabbit galantine that could have used a little more seasoning, Heiko Bergner's excellent sprout salad with nut oil showed his passion for vegetarian dishes. His savory saffron ravioli stuffed with sweetbreads and served with champagne sauce and breast of poularde with nut sauce were highlights, whereas the rack of lamb creole lacked flavor. The service was friendly and competent. The wine list had shrunk to a choice of two dozen wines from all sorts of regions. The waiter's explanation that the regular wine list wasn't available during Jean-Pierre Mazur's vacation filled us with misgivings. Does Heiko Bergner's partner take the keys to the wine cellar with him when he's on holiday?

WEINSTUBE KRUGER-RUMPF

4 km southwest
55424, Münster-Sarnsheim
0Rheinstr. 47
(0 67 21) 4 38 59, Fax 4 18 82

Closed Monday, closed 25 December through 25 January, 2 weeks during the Rheinl.-Pf. summer school holiday. A la carte: 22/43. Tables d'hôte with wine: 60

This new *Weinstube* is exactly what it should be. The surroundings are agreeable—large rooms with tiled stoves and high, stuccoed ceilings—and the traditional regional fare is highly enjoyable. On the menu are homemade aspics, potatoes with basil and three different sauces, and a local cheese-based dish with onion dressing. In addition to wines from his own well-known cellars, Kruger-Rumpf offers other top-quality German vintages.

BINZEN Baden-Württ.

Lörrach 8 - Basel 11

MÜHLE 14/20

79589, Mühlenstr. 26
(0 76 21) 60 72, Fax 6 58 08 res.

Closed Sunday and holidays. No Credit Cards. Tables d'hôte: 45/50L, 78/99D, à la carte: 37/85

Hansjörg Hechler's historic mill is an exemplary gourmet oasis and the only thing worthy of notice in this town. Guests like to sit in the lovely garden outside or in one of the rustically or elegantly comfortable dining rooms. Hechler only works with fresh market produce and the best of the region, and buys the rest of his ingredients in France. Even the most fastidious guests from nearby Switzerland feel at home here and pounce on the outstanding foie gras terrine, which deserves a rating of 18/20 every time. Fine dishes like this serve as credentials for Hechler's talents as a cook. On the whole, though, more savory and strongly seasoned dishes characterize his cuisine, like dandelion greens with wild boar ham, trout mousse, angler Provençal or succulent saddle of lamb. The choice of cheeses could use more attention. The service is obliging and the wine list emphasizes regional wines.

BISCHOFSWIESEN Bayern

Berchtesgaden 5

GRAN SASSO 13/20

83483, Hauptstr. 30
(0 86 52) 82 50, Fax 82 50 res.

Closed for lunch every day except Sunday, closed Monday, 2 weeks at Whitsunday. Tables d'hôte: 90/95, à la carte: 37/68

Judging by the all-round excellence of their attractive new restaurant, Pasquale Fieni and Lucio Giancola must be feeling right at home now. Their light, imaginative Italian cuisine emphasizes ocean fish and crustaceans. Only a single fresh-water fish manages to make an appearance, well-hidden in the delicious ravioli. The wonderful pasta alone makes the journey to Bischofswiesen worthwhile. In addition to the usual veal and beef, Gran Sasso offers ostrich for those who are watching their cholesterol. The tiramisu and the sherbets are exquisite, and the wines are carefully selected Italians at moderate prices. The service is discreet and charming.

BLANSINGEN Bad.-Württ.

Lörrach 15 - Müllheim 20

TRAUBE 14/20

79588, Alemannenstr. 19
(0 76 28) 82 90/9, Fax 87 36 res.

Closed Tuesday, closed for lunch Wednesday . Tables d'hôte: 36/56L, 64/98D, à la carte: 47/83

The Traube is just the right place for purist gourmets who delight in fine detail and appreciate style and taste. The restaurant lies off the main road, high on the Isteiner Klotz in the little village of Blansingen. The Blansingen wines, sold by the cooperative here, are already famous, and the Traube is becoming more and more popular. Many gourmet guests come from Basel and enjoy Georg Albrecht's cooking. The old and massive building isn't decorated in the usual rustic style, but is furnished with cherry and walnut chairs and tables that contrast nicely with the whitewashed walls. Our asparagus salad with stuffed saddle of hare, cream of garlic soup with toast and herbs, pike-perch soufflé with spinach and carrot noodles and lamb piccata as well as date doughnuts with mango coulis and lemon curd were flawlessly prepared.

BLAUFELDEN Bad.- Württ.

Rothenburg 20 - Würzburg 90

ZUM HIRSCHEN 15/20

74572, Hauptstr. 15
(0 79 53) 3 55 res.

P

Closed Monday. Tables d'hôte: 98/128, à la carte: 30/90

The baguette was accompanied by dripping butter, radishes, cherry tomatoes and quail's eggs. It was followed by an impressive stuffed pig's foot with warm lentil salad, surrounded by lettuce and celery laced with an exquisite vinaigrette. The egg roll with prawns and lobster sauce was a success, but the stuffed pigeon looked crispier than it actually was. The beautifully garnished chocolate log with almond sauce and jellied grapefruit was superb. On the down side, the lukewarm coffee was served with dry cake. Chef Manfred Kurz has been cooking his way through regional recipes in Blaufelden for 15 years, and his low prices are a marvel. The service is amiable and highly competent. Noble wines can be had at relatively moderate prices, and excellent wines are available by the glass. The 18 quiet, modern rooms here can also be recommended.

BLIESKASTEL Saarland

Zweibrücken 12-Homburg 12

GUTSHOFJUNKERWALD 12/20

66440, Ortsteil Niederwürzbach
Am Weiher
(0 68 42) 70 77

 P

Closed Monday. Tables d'hôte: 69, à la carte: 37/70

This former manor house is located on the shore of the Würzbach pond and is surrounded by forest. Outside there are landscaped grounds and a lovely terrace, inside a comfortable, rustic ambience. Traditional dishes and regional specialties are offered here at moderate prices, like Bliesgau rabbit ragout with dumplings and endive salad, discreetly seasoned asparagus salad with smoked salmon, concentrated beef consommé with carpaccio, succulent saddle of veal with caramelized lemon slices and white and brown mousse with a coulis of red berries. The service is pleasant and the wine list includes a small but adequate choice of affordable wines.

BOCHUM NRW

Dortmund 16 - Wuppertal 30

BRINKHOFF'S STAMMHAUS 12/20

44805, Stadtteil Harpen
Harpener Hellweg 157
(02 34) 23 35 49,

 P

Closed for lunch, closed Tuesday. No Credit Cards. Tables d'hôte: 60, à la carte: 46/76

It is a well-kept secret that two of the many beer brewers here have also opened attractive restaurants. One of the better addresses is Brinkhoff's Stammhaus, located in a handsome Art Nouveau-style brick building with a wood-paneled interior. The creative (though not always reliable) cooking eschews simple fare. For example, the breast of duck is marinated in coriander and honey and served with shiitake mushrooms. Applause for the fresh, fruity mousse of tomatoes, the hearty potato and carrot soufflé, the wonderfully seasoned salads and the fluffy rhubarb strudel with vanilla parfait. We just hope our charming waitress did not recommend the gray, tasteless fillet of lamb because the kitchen wanted to get rid of it. Until Brinkhoff's Stammhaus deserves its toque, we will praise the choice wine list, with its French and Italian accents, and honor the fact that all bottles under 50 DM can be ordered by the glass.

STADTPARK RESTAURANT 14/20

44791, Klinikstr. 41-45
(02 34) 50 70 90, Fax 5 07 09 99 res.

 P

Closed Monday, 27 December through 16 January. Tables d'hôte: 45/50L, 70D, à la carte: 36/71

When Wolfgang Markloff comes out of his kitchen to advise his guests, the usual stiffness and formality fades out of this elegant restaurant (with terrace). Markloff's Hessian boisterousness creates a friendly and familiar atmosphere, and when he verbosely (and with a little justified conceit) explains his various culinary compositions, every gesture reveals him to be a passionate cook who's probably still stirring a pudding in his sleep. Savory and hearty regional recipes are his forte, and his guests like his ingenious variations and his fair prices—main courses cost less than 40 DM.Gourmet eating has to be fun, says Markloff. Indeed, we enjoyed his pike with cider and watercress sauce and pumpernickel gratin as well as his sheatfish soufflé with nut and rye noodles, sautéed rabbit and piglet in savoy cabbage with beer sauce and his pear and fig tart with almond soufflé. Lovely hors d'œuvres are artistically arranged, and we could have hugged the maestro after we tasted his lime soup with red and green pepper! The service is agreeably motivated and the expertly stocked wine list includes eight respectable wines by the glass.

STAMMHAUS FIEGE 12/20

44787, Bongardstr. 23
(02 34) 1 26 43

Closed for dinner Sunday, closed Thursday, 3 weeks during the NRW summer school holiday. Tables d'hôte: 78, à la carte: 38/70

In their brewery restaurant, the Schwinnings manage to satisfy both their regular customers, who insist on good, plain fare and a beer to go with it, and inquisitive gourmets, who are looking for better things. Fish soup and pike dumplings belong to the repertoire, as well as an excellent and unusual oxtail aspic with Trappist beer jelly and mediocre squid stuffed with salmon farce and served with watercress mousse. Such fabulous desserts as lime parfait with figs and caramel sauce or iced and truffled pralinés with white chocolate cream deserve two toques! Besides beer, you can get respectable wines by the glass.

BONN Nordrhein-Westfalen

Köln 28 - Düsseldorf 78 - Frankfurt 175

BELLEVUECHEN 13/20

14 km south in 53424 Rolandseck
Bonner Str. 68 near the B9 motorway
(02 22 28) 79 09 res.

 P

Closed Monday, Tuesday, 2 weeks in January, NRW autumn school holiday. Tables d'hôte: 55, à la carte: 44/62

The Bellevuechen, opposite the art gallery in Rolandseck's train station, is a gem. Manfred and Uschi Zozin take great pains to please their guests. Market produce is prepared fresh in discreetly nouvelle style. You may have the distinct impression you've eaten all this before, but a closer look at the careful compositions reveals a different kind of fowl with salad, other sauces and unusual side dishes with fish and meat. The Riesling soup with fish and herbs belongs to the time-tested repertoire, and so do the sautéed calf's kidneys in cognac cream. But the guests appreciate these well-prepared standards and like the low prices. The wines are cleverly chosen.

BIERHOFF IN HOTEL BRISTOL

53113, Prinz-Albert -Str. 2/ Poppelsdorfer Allee
(02 28) 2 69 80

 P

A la carte: 37/68

The Günnewigs try to bring more color into their restaurant with a lovely buffet and a variety of international dishes. In summer you can sit on the terrace and enjoy coffee and delicious cakes.

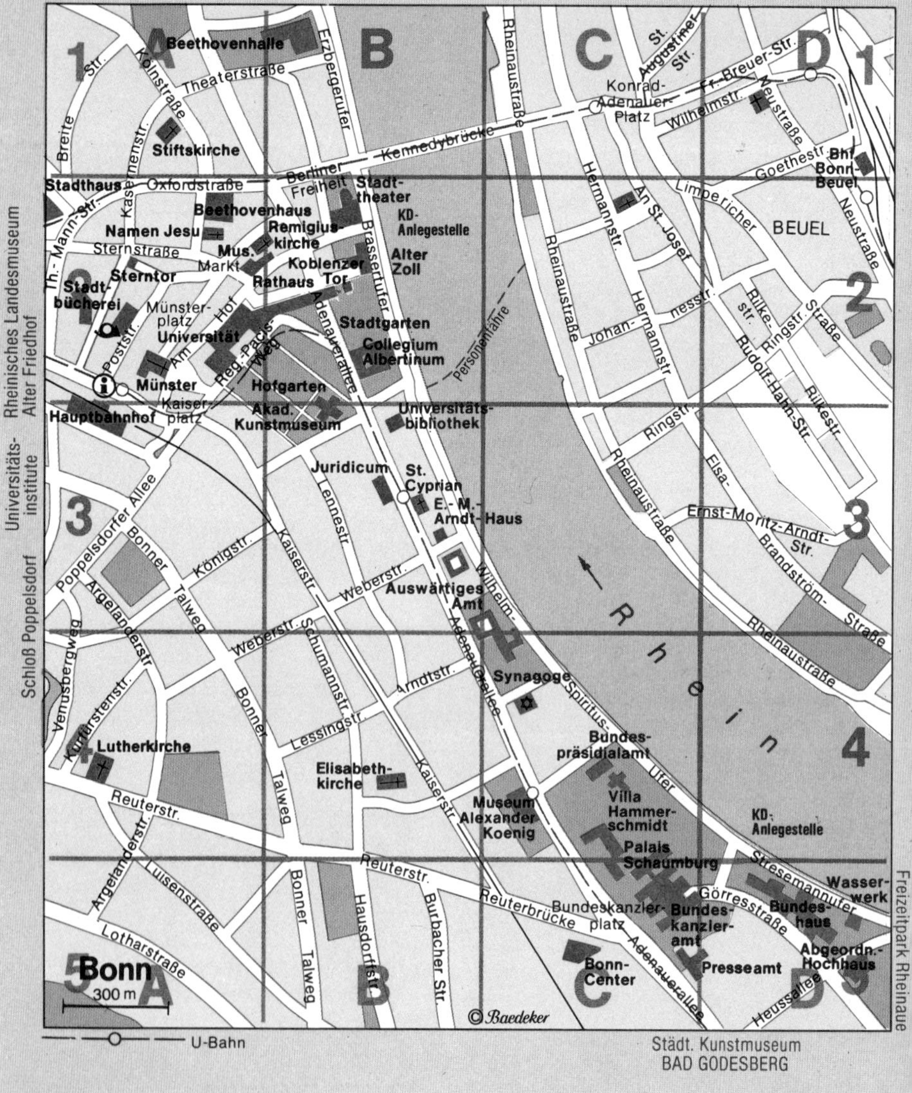

Bonn

300 m

U-Bahn

© Baedeker

Rheinisches Landesmuseum

Alter Friedhof

Universitäts-institute

Schloß Poppelsdorf

Freizeitpark Rheinaue

Städt. Kunstmuseum BAD GODESBERG

A B C D

1 2 3 4 5

Beethovenhalle
Theaterstraße
Kölnstraße
Breite Str.
Kasernenstr.
Stiftskirche
Erzbergerufer
Rheinaustraße
St. Augustiner Str.
Konrad-Adenauer-Platz
Fr.-Breuer-Str.
Wilhelmstr.
Neustraße
Kennedybrücke
Bhf Bonn-Beuel
Goethestr.
Stadthaus
Oxfordstraße
Berliner Freiheit
Stadttheater
KD-Anlegestelle
Alter Zoll
Th.-Mann-Str.
Beethovenhaus
Namen Jesu
Remigiuskirche
Mus.
Sternstraße
Markt
Koblenzer Tor
Rathaus
Sterntor
Stadtbücherei
Münsterplatz
Poststr.
Universität
Am Hof
Reg.-Pacis-Weg
Adenaueralle
Brassertufer
Stadtgarten
Collegium Albertinum
Personenfähre
Hermannstr.
An St. Josef
Limpericher
BEUEL
Johannesstr.
Rilkestr.
Ringstr.
Rudolf-Hahn-Str.
Münster
Kaiserplatz
Hauptbahnhof
Hofgarten
Akad. Kunstmuseum
Universitätsbibliothek
Juridicum
St. Cyprian
E.-M.-Arndt-Haus
Lennéstr.
Kaiserstr.
Elsa-Brandström-Straße
Ernst-Moritz-Arndt-Str.
Poppelsdorfer Allee
Bonner Talweg
Königstr.
Weberstr.
Auswärtiges Amt
Wilhelm-Spiritus-Ufer
Rhein
Argelanderstr.
Venusbergweg
Schumannstr.
Arndtstr.
Adenauerallee
Synagoge
Kurfürstenstr.
Lutherkirche
Lessingstr.
Bundespräsidialamt
Elisabethkirche
Museum Alexander Koenig
Villa Hammerschmidt
Palais Schaumburg
Reuterstr.
Hausdorffstr.
Burbacher Str.
Reuterbrücke
Stresemannufer
Görresstraße
Bundeskanzlerplatz
Bundeskanzleramt
Bundeshaus
Wasserwerk
Abgeordn.-Hochhaus
Presseamt
Bonn-Center
Luisenstraße
Lotharstraße
Heussallee

BISTRO IN KAISER KARL HOTEL 15/20

53119, Vorgebirgsstr. 59
(02 28) 69 69 67/8, Fax 63 78 99

Closed for lunch Saturday and Monday, closed Sunday, 3 weeks at Carnival. Tables d'hôte: 50L, 75D, à la carte: 41/71

Friendly service, attractive cuisine and low prices make young people feel at home in this bistro par excellence. Decorated in a lightly elegant Art Nouveau style, the restaurant is very popular and reservations are necessary. The cuisine is fresh and seasonal and offers nothing fancy or artistic, just good and honest gourmet dishes, from nouvelle cuisine to German regional fare. There's always a sauce that gives a touch of genius to delicate rabbit aspic and green salad, hearty fried blood pudding with puréed apples, angler and salmon wrapped in green leaves and venison cutlet. We loved a wonderful creation of warm chocolate pudding with strawberry mousse and papaya salad. Many wines by the glass are offered at moderate prices.

CÄCILIENHÖHE 13/20

53177, Stadtteil Bad Godesberg
Goldbergweg 17
(02 28) 32 10 01/2, Fax 32 83 14 res.

Closed for lunch Saturday, closed Sunday. Tables d'hôte: 38/90, à la carte: 48/70, Tables d'hôte with wine: 60/100

Eating at Bruno's is like going to the theater, some customers say. The view from his windows is one of the most beautiful in Bonn, and the scenery a perfect setting for the acts to follow. Star of the show is Bruno Pierini, who presents the wonderful things you won't find on the menu with a great deal of rhetoric and charm. A standing ovation for the highlights of our meal, which included delectably dressed salads Italian-style, and especially the tender calf's liver and excellent baby turbot and potatoes with rosemary. The service is circumspect, nimble and polite.

LA CASTAGNA 13/20

53117, Stadtteil Buschdorf
Buschdorfer Str. 38
(02 28) 67 33 04, Fax 68 72 39 res.

Closed for lunch Saturday. Tables d'hôte: 90, à la carte: 41/77

A noticeably cheerful team runs this restaurant, which has become very popular in Bonn. The menu is always seasonal, but most guests follow the suggestions of the staff. Lentil salad with lamb carpaccio, black noodles with saffron and scampi or beef carpaccio over a delicious salad—everything was prepared fresh. The turbot was accompanied by the same garlic, tomato and basil sauce as the angler medallions (even if the latter was announced with a wine sauce), but both fish dishes were fresh and tasty. The cheese (exclusively Italian) is good, the pannacotta better. The wine list is adequate. Reservations are necessary, especially in summer.

LE GALOPIN 13/20

53127, Stadtteil Lengsdorf
Provinzialstr. 35
(02 28) 25 46 38

Closed for lunch Friday and Saturday, closed Sunday. Tables d'hôte: 29/39

In the bistro of Le Marron, we enjoyed the ambience of this little brasserie looking out over a green garden. The cuisine is plainer but no less good than in the restaurant next door. The service is especially friendly and the diners cheerful. Only the prix-fixe meals and wines commended on the slate are served. You have a choice of three appetizers, a soup, two fish and three main courses, two desserts and cheese. For example, you can have oysters when in season, brook trout in delicate wine sauce with leaf spinach and rice, aromatic chervil soup, saddle of lamb with gnocchi and beans, ripe cheeses and a fruity orange terrine.

GUTEN APPETIT 12/20

Chinesisches Speisehaus
53111, Am Boeselagerhof 15 [B2]
(02 28) 63 77 34

Tables d'hôte: 60/175, à la carte: 31/59

This friendly Cantonese restaurant is open when the opera (directly opposite) lets out. The aesthetic cuisine includes prix-fixe meals from four to nine courses, besides à la carte dishes typical of different Chinese provinces. We liked our scallops and Chinese lobster, roast pork and, of course, delicious Peking duck.

HALBEDEL'S GASTHAUS 16/20

53173, Stadtteil Bad Godesberg
Rheinallee 47
(02 28) 35 42 53, Fax 35 42 53 res.

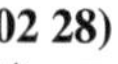

Closed for lunch, closed Monday, 3 weeks during the NRW summer school holiday. Tables d'hôte: 97/118, à la carte: 58/93

This beautiful villa in Art Nouveau style opens its doors and welcomes you almost as a private guest of the house. The service is nostalgically dressed, but works with modern efficiency.The Halbedels are masters of the gourmet scene in Bonn, and their finely balanced compositions are always pure enjoyment. Especially recommendable is the five-course prix-fixe menu with appropriate wines expertly chosen by Rainer-Maria Halbedel. After an interesting appetizer, the kitchen combines respectable bourgeois fare with restrained nouvelle cuisine: the first fresh chanterelles prepared just the way you like them, tender suckling kid liver with rucola, lasagna of salmon and kohlrabi with caviar, great bass with a light garlic sauce, flawlessly done saddle of young wild boar and a wonderful goat cheese soufflé with rhubarb compôte.The wine list is formidable and offers the best from Germany and France as well as choice rarities.

HERRENHAUS BUCHHOLZ 12/20

10 km northwest in 53347 Alfter
Buchholzweg 1
(02 28)6 00 05/6, Fax 6 13 69 res.

Tables d'hôte: 50/75L, 65/120D, à la carte: 43/84

This manor house is located in the middle of asparagus country—and that's what you'll get, if you arrive in season. Outside of asparagus, the menu offers, for instance, pigeon consommé, red snapper in shrimp sauce with original wild rice pancakes and calf's liver with onions and apples. All portions are more than generous, and the desserts are something for a sweet tooth. The wine list offers a good choice of wines by the glass.

ISOLA D'ISCHIA 13/20

53175, Stadtteil Bad Godesberg
Brandenburgerstr. 4A
(02 28) 37 52 52 res.

Closed Monday, à la carte: 40/77

Not only journalists like to eat in this little Italian restaurant. Without any kind of extravaganzas, the cuisine keeps to its traditional recipes. Don't be afraid to ask for daily specials or desserts. You can always order the delicious homemade pasta or fresh fish, displayed on a platter for you to select. The choice of wines by the glass is satisfactory and the service friendly and helpful.

KORKEICHE 12/20

53177, Stadtteil Lannesdorf
Lyngsbergstr. 104
(02 28) 34 78 97, 36 32 14 res.

Closed for lunch Saturday, closed Monday, mid-January through the beginning of February. Tables d'hôte: 42/79, à la carte: 28/69

The owner of this lovely half-timbered house has given the Korkeiche a new cook and new impetus. Regional dishes like sauerbraten and blood pudding are prepared here, but we also had a salmon cassata wrapped in a leaf of savoy cabbage and saddle of lamb with honey and vinegar. In summer you can eat in the pretty ivy-covered courtyard. Nice service and competent advice in choosing wines.

KRÄUTERGARTEN 15/20

10 km west in 53343 Wachtberg-Adendorf
Töpferstr. 30
(02 28) 75 78, Fax 75 78 res.

Closed for lunch Saturday, closed Sunday, Monday, 14 days at Carnival, during the Nordr.-Westf. summer school holiday. No Credit Cards. Tables d'hôte: 48L, 83/108D, à la carte: 50/78

We admire the light cuisine here, which uses a lot of herbs yet insists on classic bases (butter galore!). The menu is an appetizer in the true sense of the word. We started our meal with a smoked salmon terrine on yellow lentils with curry sauce and thyme, followed by a mousseline of wild herbs with snails that was just as perfect as the artichoke filled with seafood. Whether you've ordered turbot suprême, smoked rabbit leg with plums or fillet of ox with Asian seasoning, herbs and mushrooms, all dishes are served with delectable and remarkable sauces. The choice of cheeses is wonderful and the desserts simple but with great finesse: lavender and honey crèpes with peaches, sweet marzipan cherries with chocolate soufflé or iced champagne with various sherbets.The comprehensive wine list offers many good French and German wines, some of which are also served by the glass. Thursday's prix-fixe menu for 88 DM includes wine.

LE MARRON 13/20

53225, Stadtteil Lengsdorf
Provinzialstr. 35
(02 28) 25 32 61, Fax 25 30 28

 P

Closed for lunch Friday and Saturday, closed Sunday. Tables d'hôte: 126D, à la carte: 52/86

The menu sounded exciting and we were eager for culinary adventures, especially since we'd found out that Wilhelm Niedenhoff, a genial cook from Cologne, had taken over the kitchen. However promising the dishes sounded —turbot breaded with coconut, quail's "ham" with Italian paprika in white pepper sauce or potato and leek soup with fried potato salad and blood pudding—the products were not of the usual top quality, and more attention should have been paid to cooking times and temperatures. Nothing reminded us of the previous culinary fireworks.The ambience, though, is still comfortably elegant here, and the service pleasant and obliging. We hope Niedenhoff finds his way back to his old form. Maybe the toque we gave him (mostly out of pity) will motivate him.

MATERNUS

53175, Stadtteil Bad Godesberg
Löbestr. 3
(02 28) 36 28 51 res.

Closed Sunday. A la carte: 38/73

Ria Maternus is the perfect hostess and her guests represent an international Who's Who. In her traditional German restaurant you can enjoy such dishes as sauerbraten with raisins, marinated herring on pumpernickel with onions or sole Nantua, all simple and plain but good food. The light Moselle wines and Ria Maternus's charm always tempt us to come back.

LE PETIT POISSON 15/20 

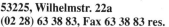

53225, Wilhelmstr. 22a
(02 28) 63 38 83, Fax 63 38 83 res.

Closed for lunch, closed Sunday and Monday. Tables d'hôte: 80/120, à la carte: 43/92

Nobody knows better how to cook fish in Bonn than Ludwig Reinarz, who belongs to the top ranks in the capital city. Everything takes a little longer when the restaurant is full. We didn't mind, but the service could have been more diligent in filling our wine glasses from time to time while we waited. The appetizer was an exquisite hint of what the kitchen is capable of. This time, we had Gravad salmon with a mustard sauce that harmonized perfectly with the slightly sweet, purple potato, followed by oysters baked in curry zabaglione. Everything filled us with delight: the salmon tartare in cream with chives, délice of sea bream with lobster ravioli and angler in potato crust. If you don't like fish, there's salad with Bresse rabbit on lentils with vinaigrette or oxtail ragout with cèpes.The comprehensive choice of wines doesn't offer many half-bottles or wines by the glass.

RISTORANTE CARLO RUGGIERO 12/20

53129, Stadtteil Dottendorf
Kessenicherstr. 100-102
(02 28) 23 77 00, Fax 23 77 00 res.

 P

Closed Tuesday, 3 weeks during the NRW summer school holiday. Tables d'hôte: 55L, 75D, à la carte: 37/86

Good Italian cooking alone doesn't draw guests anymore, unless a regional accent, a special ambience or a personal touch of the padrone makes it attractive. Ruggiero's meets all these qualifications. His restaurant is light and pleasant, decorated in a more cool than rustic style. Fish fans trust

Ruggiero, who always serves something new, imaginative and fresh, for example a slice of grilled swordfish sprinkled with olive oil or salmon medallions with saffron. The prix-fixe menu suggestions change daily. Desserts, cheese and wines are Italian. If you haven't found the right wine on the wine list, Ruggiero will get a special bottle from his cellar.

HOTELS

BRISTOL

53113, Prinz-Albert-Str. 2/
Poppelsdorfer Allee [A3]
(02 28) 2 69 80, Fax 2 69 82 22

  P

120, **S** 250/315, **D** 320/400,
APP 520/1600, **1/2P** +35, **P** +75

The Bristol offers pleasantly redecorated, air-conditioned rooms in a relatively quiet location in the center of town. Restaurants, bar, garden, meeting and banquet rooms. Solarium. Breakfast: 25 DM.

DOMICIL

53111, Thomas-Mann-Str. 24+26
(02 28) 72 90 90, Fax 69 12 07

 P

42, **S** 180/360, **D** 250/410,
APP 420/460, **1/2P** +40, **P** +80

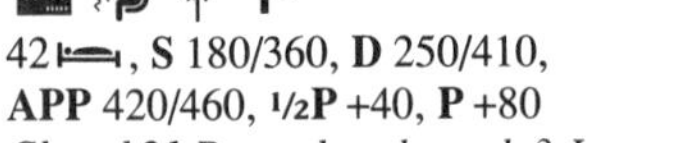

Closed 21 December through 3 January

A talented architect combined several older buildings to create a gem of a hotel with the charm of a private dwelling. Breakfast: 21 DM.

KÖNIGSHOF

53111, Adenauerallee 9 [B2]
(02 28) 2 60 10, Fax 2 60 15 29

 P

138, **S** 200/225, **D** 280/290,
APP 300/360,

Quietly and centrally located on the Rhine and near the Hofgarten, this hotel has always been attractive. Besides comfortably cozy rooms, it offers a pleasant bar and a terrace facing the river.

MARITIM

53175, Stadtteil Bad Godesberg
Godesberger Allee
(02 28) 8 10 80, Fax 8 10 88 11

 P

412, **S** 245/423, **D** 298/488,
APP 580/1800, **1/2P** +40, **P** +70

This modern hotel with its high technical standards is centrally located. The quiet rooms have even numbers. The hotel claims to be luxurious, but we found the service to be at best nonchalant. Massage, solarium, hairdresser, boutiques and restaurants.

RHEINHOTEL DREESEN

53179, Stadtteil Bad Godesberg
Rheinstr. 45-49 [C3]
(02 28) 8 20 20, Fax 8 20 21 53

 P

74, **S** 195/295, **D** 270/370,
APP 510, **1/2P** +38

This 100-year-old hotel is located amid the quiet of the embassy buildings on the Rhine, where the subdued puttering of ships sends you to sleep. Guests like the old-fashioned flair in the bar and the salons, but the rooms are modern, some even equipped for businessmen. Conference rooms, restaurant and garden with chestnut trees.

STEIGENBERGER HOTEL VENUSBERG

53127, An der Casselsruhel
(02 28) 28 80, Fax 28 82 88

 P

85, **S** 235/285, **D** 320/360,
APP from 360, **1/2P** +40, **P** +79

This two-story hotel, designed like a French manor house, was built in the middle of a wood without felling a single one of the old trees. It offers a marvelous view of Bonn, the Rhine valley and the Siebengebirge. Bar, solarium, massage, bike rental and restaurant.

BOPFINGEN Baden-Württ.

Nördlingen 12-Aalen 23

SONNE 15/20

73441, Am Markt
(0 73 62) 9 60 60, Fax 96 06 40 res.

P

Closed for dinner Sunday, closed for lunch Monday, 24 December through 2 January, 1—11 July. Tables d'hôte: 44/99, à la carte: 26/68

Chef Otto Sperber cannot survive on the strength of the few gourmets in Bopfingen, so he offers a double bill of fare: his steady customers get their roasts and tripe and *Maultaschen* (Swabian-style ravioli), while the gourmets can choose carpaccio of deer with red lentils and Parmesan, shrimp salad with watercress, tasty pink dolphin fish on spinach, anglerfish with chopped tomatoes and asparagus with fresh hollandaise sauce, and prettily garnished homemade ice-cream *Gugelhupf* (a cake made with raisins and almonds). The menu deserves praise.The impressive service staff is attentive, friendly and competent. Hostess Heide Sperber is an expert on the wines in her cellar, which offers the finest vintages at remarkably reasonable prices. The hotel has comfortably furnished rooms.

BOTHEL Niedersachsen

Rotenburg/Wümme 8-Bremen 51

BOTHELER LANDHAUS 15/20

27386, Hemsbünder Str. 10
(0 42 66) 15 17 res.

  P

Closed for lunch, closed Sunday and Monday. Tables d'hôte: 55/97, à la carte: 48/80

This lovely country house with flower-filled window boxes conceals a fine restaurant. A broccoli terrine with whipped chervil cream was served as an appetizer, followed by buckwheat rolls with salmon and caviar, and asparagus with buckwheat pancakes with chives and hollandaise on top. Everything is subtly creative, attractively presented, and carefully prepared. The first courses set very high standards that the unspectacular main dishes did not live up to. The unpretentious service is pleasant.

BOTTROP Nordrhein-Westfalen

Oberhausen 8 - Essen 11

PETIT MARCHÉ 12/20

46244, Ortsteil Kirchhellen
Hauptstr. 16
(0 20 45) 32 31

Closed Sunday, à la carte: 39/72

There are few reasons to go out of your way to visit Bottrop, but if you happen to be there, you can dine well at the Petit Marché. The flaky crust on the cream of lobster soup was filled with (pressed and canned) crab meat, but the seafood chowder was very tasty. The mushrooms with noodles also came out of a tin, but the fillet of ray wing with lime sauce was nice and fresh, and the saddle of lamb seasoned with rosemary was perfectly done.There is a respectable choice of wines, and if you treat yourself to a bottle of Fetzer's fumé blanc, you might even forget you are in Bottrop!

BRAUBACH Rheinland-Pfalz

Lahnstein 6 - St. Goarshausen 25

ZUM WEISSEN SCHWANEN 12/20

56338, Brunnenstr. 4
(0 26 27) 5 59, Fax 88 02 res.

 P

Closed for lunch, closed Wednesday, 22 December through 8 January, month of July. Tables d'hôte: 45/60, à la carte: 29/63

The historic building has style, and the inn exudes the kind of comfortable coziness Germans like to call *gemütlichkeit*. The traditional German cooking offered here has its attractions. We liked our savory potato and sauerkraut soup with blood pudding, boiled beef with fresh horseradish, the "best of wild boar" with red cabbage and rack of lamb with mustard and Pernod sauce. The generous side dishes—fried potatoes or delicious dumplings— were overwhelming.The wine list offers more than other inns in town. On a busy day the service is sometimes overtaxed.

BRAUNSCHWEIG Nieders.

Hannover 45-Hildesheim 45

BRABANTER HOF 14/20

38100, Güldenstr. 77
(05 31) 4 30 90

This beautiful and comfortable Art Deco restaurant still has a small menu and a hardly mentionable wine list, but the reception and service are extraordinarily pleasant and the way the kitchen prepares the dishes is worth a standing ovation. After a lovely sweetbread ravioli as appetizer, we tried a lobster salad with orange sauce that was nearly perfect. Sweet-pea soup with shrimps was outstanding, and the salmon tranche under its delicious potato crust was well done, even if (like the angler following) not absolutely fresh. Out of curiosity we tasted the combination of chicken and duck on mushrooms—and were pleasantly surprised.

DEUTSCHES HAUS

38100, Ruhfäutschenplatz 1
(05 31)1 20 00, Fax 1 20 04 44

   P

85, **S** 129/147, **D** 198/222,
APP 219/360, **½P** +30, **P** +60

All of the quiet rooms face south and afford a view of the cathedral, built in 1195. This former guest house of the dukes of Braunschweig is spacious and tastefully decorated.

MERCURE ATRIUM

38102, Berliner Platz 3
(05 31) 7 00 80, Fax 7 00 81 25

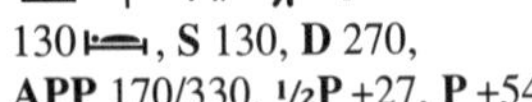

130, **S** 130, **D** 270,
APP 170/330, **½P** +27, **P** +54

Centrally located just 100 meters from the train station, the Mercure Atrium has a concrete façade that leads one to expect an office building rather than a fine hotel. A view of the quiet courtyard compensates for the drab exterior. Ample breakfast buffet. Restaurant.

RITTER ST. GEORG 15/20

38100, Alte Knochenhauerstr. 12-13
(05 31) 4 66 84, Fax 1 38 30 res.

Closed Sunday. Tables d'hôte: 45L, 50/155D, à la carte: 52/87

The main attraction for children in this historic framework house is the genuine medieval suit of armor. They can even bang on it, and nobody minds (much), as the younger set is welcome here. The best food in Braunschweig is served here under a colorfully painted medieval ceiling: a marvelous mousse of smoked trout, a fantastic green salad with marinated salmon and different kinds of caviar, fresh and tasty haddock served with a mountain of spinach, and juicy and tender loin of lamb with beans. The chocolate mousse could have been more delicate, but the cappuccino helped us forget about it.

BREMEN Bremen

Hamburg 119-Hannover 125

AM DEICH 68 12/20

28199, Am Deich 68
(04 21) 5 97 96 82 res.

Closed for lunch, closed 15 August to 2 September. No Credit Cards, à la carte: 30/62

Till now, the only thing worth mentioning in this artistic little inn was the loud music. On our last visit, the food was good and moderately priced. We liked the carrot and honey soup with walnuts and the marinated olives as appetizers. The homemade ravioli could have been a little less al dente, but the leg of rabbit with ratatouille and rosemary potatoes was perfect. There are draught beers available, but you can also do well if you drink wine: for example a 1992 Chardonnay from Pojer and Sandri for 38 DM.

BIERLACHS 13/20

28199, Langemarckstr. 38-42
(04 21) 5 90 20, Fax 50 74 57 res.

P

A la carte: 28/70

An amazing lack of fine fish restaurants remains a mystery in this seaport town. The clear, generously garnished fish soup is a popular appetizer, but it wasn't always served as hot as it should have been. A succulent timbale of shrimps and smoked eel was a welcome alternative. The fish was always absolutely fresh and carefully prepared, but in no way as attentively presented as it deserved. Fish was simply piled on plates and the salads tasted much better than they looked.The choice of wines isn't grand, but intelligent and low-priced. The variety of grappas beats the desserts anytime and the service is pleasant and competent.

BREMEN MARRIOTT

28195, Hillmannplatz 20
(04 21) 1 76 70, Fax 1 76 72 38

228, **S** 290/320, **D** 340/370,
APP 500/750, **1/2P** +40, **P** +80

Where once the venerable Hillmann Hotel stood, the luxurious Bremen Plaza, built in 1985 and taken over by Marriott, now welcomes its guests. The approach to this centrally located hotel is a bit difficult for travelers. Boutiques and shops, bistro, garden and restaurant. Breakfast: 26 DM.

CARVALHO

28195, Kolpingstr. 14
(04 21) 3 36 50 80

No Credit Cards. Tables d'hôte: 35, à la carte: 17/37

You can eat good food here long past midnight. The ambience is pleasant and the music not too loud. Nor do you have to pay nightlife prices for all of this. The tapas are commendable and the red and white wines moderately priced. The choice of liquors and brandies from southern countries is impressive and unequaled in Bremen.

L'ECHALOTE 14/20

28215, Hollerallee 90
(04 21) 3 78 96 27, Fax 3 78 96 00 res.

P

Closed for lunch, closed Sunday, Monday, closed July through mid-August. Tables d'hôte: 88/108, à la carte: 65/97

With its excellent service, elegant ambience and good food, this is one of the few restaurants in Bremen we can recommend for dinner. The food prices are not exactly cheap, but the wines are more reasonable than we expected.If you like soup, we advise you to order the cream of potato with fish. We had a good salad with red mullet, and delicious anglerfish stuffed with lobster. The meat dishes deserve no criticism. Our favorits was tender sweetbreads with wonderful fresh vegetables. Even the desserts have improved.The headwaiter is extremely solicitous of his customers, almost too solicitous for those who like a little privacy during their meal. This restaurant may not be able to compete with the ambience of the Parkrestaurant in Bremen, but its kitchen takes top marks every time.

GRASHOFF'S BISTRO 17/20

28195, Contrescarpe 80/ Hillmann-Passage
(04 21) 1 47 40, Fax 30 20 40 res.

Closed for dinner, closed Sunday. Tables d'hôte: 50, à la carte: 50/78

If only all trendy bistros had Grashoff's quality! The usually staid and stiff Bremen inhabitants suddenly sit close together here and obviously have fun. They have good reason to be happy, because the lunch they get is excellent. We had a superb crayfish soup as well as an exquisitely delicious lobster on homemade spaghetti. Guests can choose from a variety of salads—all superbly dressed with the finest oils and vinegars—or order tagliatelle with fresh morels, but they always eat the best. As dessert we recommend unforgettable caramel ice cream with fresh roasted almonds and the outstanding blueberry crèpes.Very good if limited wine list, and quick and unconventional service.

MARITIM

28215, Hollerallee 90
(04 21) 3 78 90, Fax 3 78 96 00

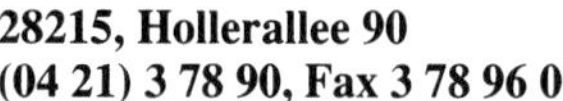

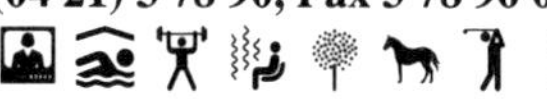

261, **S** 245/395, **D** 298/438,
APP 600/1200, **1/2P** +40, **P** +68

Located on a busy street facing the Bürgerpark, the Maritim, which opened its doors 1992, isn't as quiet as the Park-Hotel just a few minutes away. The service is much better, however, and its 12 conference and banquet rooms are more modern. The rooms are adequately furnished. Breakfast: 25 DM.

MEIEREI BÜRGERPARK 13/20

28209, Im Bürgerpark
(04 21) 3 40 86 19, Fax 21 99 81

 P

Tables d'hôte: 59/79L 98/106D, à la carte: 48/87

The "Meierei," located in Bremen's wonderful Bürgerpark, is one of the most beautiful restaurants in the city. On summer evenings, the view from the terrace is so wonderful that it almost compensates for the sometimes unreliable cooking.That said, however, our previous criticisms of the cooking and service seem to have resulted in some improvements. In the tastefully redecorated rooms, a new team now looks after the customers, andthe food has also improved. We started with parsnip soup and a delicate avocado salad. While the consommé of guinea fowl seemed a little flat, the braid of salmon and sole was as excellent, as was the sliced fillet of beef in balsamic vinegar. Homemade noodles made a delicious side dish, and the desserts and petits fours are outstanding.There is a good choice of wines by the glass; most bottles are overpriced, except the Swiss vintages, which we recommend.

L'ORCHIDEE IN HOTEL ZUR POST 18/20

28195, Banhofsplatz 11
(04 21) 3 05 98 88, Fax 3 05 95 91 res.

P

Closed for lunch, closed Sunday, Monday, 2 weeks at Easter, 4 weeks during the Bremen summer school holiday Tables d'hôte: 97/137, à la carte: 55/94

The desolate square in front of the main train station could not be a more inappropriate setting for this elegant restaurant. The aristocratic decor of the Orchidee harmonizes with its perfect service and creative, first-class cooking. The unusual appetizers—including terrine of baby chicken and foie gras with truffled mayonnaise, and roulade of sturgeon with caviar dressing—cannot be overpraised. The restaurant employs a separate chef just for the first courses. The fish soup was exceptionally fresh and intense - a true masterpiece. Meat dishes are prepared as carefully as the fish. The saddle of venison with potato cakes was a perfect composition. The desserts are of the finest quality, and the choice of wines is irreproachable. A real orchid never comes cheap, however, and neither does this one.

PARK-RESTAURANT 13/20

28209, Im Bürgerpark
(04 21) 3 40 80, Fax 3 40 86 02 res.

P

Tables d'hôte: 70/90, à la carte: 50/98. Tables d'hôte with wine: 114/150

This elegant restaurant is primarily patronized by customers of the hotel, but occasionally a few citizens of Bremen find their way here and indulge themselves. The numerous waiters are not as stiff-necked as they were a few years ago, and they do their best, but the service is often just not good enough. As for the cuisine, it is perhaps too conservative. The salad with lobster and fried liver was good but conventional, and the same could be said for the green asparagus with chervil. The saddle of lamb in a crust of herbs was perfect, as well it should be after so many years on the menu. The desserts are often great, sometimes disappointing. There is an extensive wine list, and the wines by the glass are of good quality.

PARK-HOTEL

28209, Im Bürgerpark
(04 21) 3 40 80, Fax 3 40 86 02

150, **S** 305/320, **D** 435/520,
APP 580/1600,

Surrounded by the lovely Bürgerpark, this hotel seems far away from the noise of the city. The public areas are elegantly appointed with beautiful carpets and tasteful furniture. The spacious rooms and suites are comfortable, although some rooms in the new wing are apt to be small and dark. The Bürgerpark affords numerous opportunities for strolling, jogging, cycling and riding.

RATSKELLER
Im Alten Rathaus
28195, Am Markt 1
(04 21) 32 16 76, Fax 3 37 81 21 res.

Tables d'hôte: 61/75, à la carte: 47/79

By all rights, this centrally located restaurant in the cellar of the honorable Rathaus should play a central role in Bremen's culinary scene, but for the moment, it is not to be. Waiters serve meatball soup (announced as consommé of *tafelspitz*) with such forbiddingly formal style that one would expect them to be serving a king. The red snapper was excessively chewy, and the accompanying spaghetti was overdone. What can be said about the desserts, except that they were boring? On the positive side, the choice of wines is one of the best in Germany. We recommend that this ostensibly chic restaurant and the funny little booths called "Priölken" be bypassed in favor of the scoured wooden tables of the main hall, where hearty specialties are served. If the waiter happens to be too stressed to serve you, as is usually the case here, call the manager. He's nice.

SCANDIC CROWN

28195, Böttcherstr. 2
(04 21) 3 69 60, Fax 3 69 69 60

235, **S** 215/265, **D** 265/340, **APP** 340/400, **½P** +30, **P** +60

In the heart of Bremen, this hotel offers modern and comfortable rooms. The remarkably immense entrance hall has a glass ceiling, and one of the salons has been decorated by an Bremen expressionist.

SEWASTOPOL AM SCHWARZEN MEER
28205, Am Schwarzen Meer 27
(04 21) 49 42 99, Fax 4 98 81 83 res.

Closed for lunch. No Credit Cards, à la carte: 23/41

The owners of this former pub are called Mick and Laci, and are refugees from the Balkan countries. The don't want to offer just food to eat, but food for thought as well. One of the soups, for instance, is called "nowji borschtsch—for the honor of the bandit Petljura;" an appetizer is named "muschik—beloved of all honest people and workers." What exactly "colchose-nostalgie" is, you'll have to find out for yourself. The choice of 30 different vodkas (at moderate prices) is considered sensational even by Russian experts.

TOPAZ 14/20
28203, Ostertorsteinweg 70/71
(04 21) 7 76 24, Fax 7 76 15

Closed Sunday. No Credit Cards, à la carte: 26/53

The owners of this former pub are called Mick and Laci, and are refugees from the Balkan countries. The don't want to offer just food to eat, but food for thought as well. One of the soups, for instance, is called "nowji borschtsch—for the honor of the bandit Petljura;" an appetizer is named "muschik—beloved of all honest people and workers." What exactly "colchose-nostalgie" is, you'll have to find out for yourself. The choice of 30 different vodkas (at moderate prices) is considered sensational even by Russian experts.

VILLA VERDE 14/20
28205, Weserstadion
(04 21) 3 05 91 00, Fax 4 98 73 07 res.

Closed Sunday, Monday, 1 to 22 January, 3 weeks during the Bremen summer school holiday. Tables d'hôte: 47L, 87/107D, à la carte: 50/101

After a not very auspicious beginning, Villa Verde has developed into a respectable gourmet restaurant. The prices have gone up along with the quality: the food is as expensive here as it is at the Orchidee – not surprising since they have the same owner. If we had to choose between them, we would pick the Orchidee just because it is more attractively decorated.After a mousse of asparagus with Persian caviar, we enjoyed a smooth cream of nettle soup with a delicious king prawn swimming in it. The marinated salmon with apples and pink grapefruit is popular, but we preferred the salmon with the classic Nordic sauce that contains mustard and honey. Don't miss the Bresse fowl with fried green asparagus - delicious and plentiful!The choice of wines is large and knowledgeably arranged; the service is a treat.

ZUR SCHLEUSE

un 28865 Lilienthal
Truperdeich 35
(0 42 98) 20 25 res.

 P

Closed Monday, Tuesday, month of October, No Credit Cards. Tables d'hôte: 19/38L, à la carte: 17/48

The Bavarians in Munich probably couldn't suppress a condescending grin, but Bremen really has its own beer garden, even if they call it by a different name. The inn Zur Schleuse is located on the shore of the Wümme, surrounded by old trees. Well-known lawyers, TV journalists, average Bremen citizens and astonished tourists sit here side by side. Guests don't arrive by car, since the approach on the winding street is a bit difficult. Nobody has high expectations of the cuisine. The consommé was salty, the salad drowned in dressing and the steak was prepared the way the cook liked it and not how the guest wanted it. Regional specialties are your best bet here. We recommend water, beer and rye whisky instead of wine. Like a beer garden, the Schleuse is most charming in summer.

BRILON Nordrhein-Westfalen

Meschede 18-Paderborn 20

HAUS WALDSEE 15/20

7 km south in 59929 Guldenhagen
Am Waldfreibad
(0 29 61) 33 18 res.

P

Closed Monday. Tables d'hôte: 69/80, à la carte: 34/69

This restaurant stands in a romantic setting beside the open-air swimming pool in Brilon-Guldenhagen. But it's not easy to find, especially at night. A lot of old, dark wood, a typical stone façade, tiles, comfortable tables and benches, soft lighting and a cheerful decor create a rustic and homey ambience. The service is quick and helpful and the wines are really low-priced with a international selection and many half-bottles and wines by the glass. Our prix-fixe meal included a savory and splendid mousse of smoked trout with green sauce followed by calf's tail consommé and à point fried pike-perch fillet with crayfish sauce and leeks al dente, and a superbly tender and succulent loin of venison with delicious fresh cèpes and (slightly sticky) homemade spaetzle.If you've imbibed too much of those incredibly low-priced wines, spend the night in one of the five comfortable and quiet rooms offered here.

BRUCKMÜHL Bayern

Bad Aibling 10-Rosenheim 21

GROSSER WIRT 12/20

83052, Ortsteil Kirchdorf
Am Griesberg 2
(0 80 62) 12 49, Fax 58 88 res.

 P

Closed Thursday. Tables d'hôte: 30/33L, 30/60D, à la carte: 18/59

This rustic, country *Gasthof* on the main road to München-Rosenheim specializes in warm Bavarian hospitality. The large dining rooms are wood-paneled, and the terrace is sheltered from the noisy street. This is a good address for travelers, who can always get a hot meal here. The menu includes hearty dishes like smoked fillet of trout, eel soup, fillet of pike, roasted duck or goose, and game.Respectable wines can be had by the glass, and some bottles are priced very moderately. The service is helpful and friendly.

BAD BRÜCKENAU

Fulda 33-Würzburg 76

ALTE VILLA 12/20

8 km southwest
in 97799 Zeitlofs-Rupboden
Kohlgraben 2
(0 97 46) 6 31 , Fax 12 47

 P

Closed for lunch Wednesday through Friday, closed Monday and Tuesday, 13 February through 3 March. Tables d'hôte: 69L, 93D, à la carte: 35/64

After an indifferent yogurt and vegetable terrine and a compact and clammy mushroom pâté, we at last found something to enjoy: a wonderfully tasty squash soup with ginger, garnished with cream and slivered almonds. The saddle of veal was tender and succulent, the vegetables nondescript and the plum terrine for dessert tasteless.The service is friendly but too busy to advise diners. The large wine list offers an abundant choice of half-bottles and wines by the glass.

BUCKOW Brandenburg

Berlin 60-Frankfurt/Oder 41

BERGSCHLÖSSCHEN 12/20

15377, Königstr. 38
(03 34 33) 5 73 12, Fax 5 74 12

Tables d'hôte:40, à la carte: 22/44

The idyllic natural landscape of the Märkische Schweiz attracted Emperor Friedrich Wilhelm IV and Bertolt Brecht. Since the Wall fell in Germany, some new restaurants are also attracting a number of weekend tourists. The Schlösschen high above this romantic hamlet is one of them. The ambience is comfortable and familiar in historic surroundings, and the kitchen serves good-quality food, appetizingly presented but without any creative highlights. We liked the chicken breast with excellent orange sauce and crispy fried quail in a nest of potatoes. The service is a bit shy, the wine list carefully compiled.

BERGSCHLÖSSCHEN

15377, Königstr. 38
(03 34 33) 5 73 12, Fax 5 74 12

14 rooms, **S** 100, **D** 140/160, **APP** 200,

With romantic turrets and bay windows, this family-run hotel promises peace and quiet. The rooms are elegant and provide all modern amenities as well as marvelous views from the terraces and balconies. The ample breakfast buffet (15 DM) can also be enjoyed on the terrace. The service is the best in the region.

BÜHL Baden-Württemberg

Baden-Baden 16-Rastatt 25

DIE GRÜNE BETTLAD 13/20

77815, Blumenstr. 4
(0 72 23) 2 42 38, Fax 2 42 47 res.

Closed Sunday and Monday, 23 December through mid-January, 2 weeks during the Bad.-Württ. summer school holiday. Tables d'hôte: 69/90, à la carte: 41/87

Little snail pans hanging from the ceiling, hot-water bottles as lamp stands and slit copper pitchers as lighting fixtures are part of the nostalgic decor (or folkloric masquerade?) of this restaurant. The centerpiece of this little half-timbered house is, of course, the historic four-poster bed (bettlad) that gives the restaurant its name.Modern regional cuisine is offered in this romantic setting. Peter Günther served delicious venison saddle, duck's breast, lamb and rabbit fillets, carpaccio of smoked Black Forest trout and char from Lake Constance. Our *tafelspitz* terrine came out the fridge, but we liked our salmon in Riesling sauce and cheese soufflé with strawberries and puréed fruit.Wine is expensive, but the friendly service can't help that.

DIE GRÜNE BETTLAD

77815, Blumenstr. 4
(0 72 23) 2 42 38, Fax 2 42 47

6 rooms, **S** 135/160, **D** 180/200, **APP** 210/250,
Closed 23 December through mid-January, 2 weeks in the Baden-Württemberg summer school holiday

Similar to the adjoining restaurant in style and congeniality, this is a thoroughly inviting hotel. The rooms in this 300-year-old framework house are extravagantly furnished, some with four-poster beds.

GUDE STUB

77815, Dreherstr. 9
(0 72 23) 84 80, Fax 90 01 80

A la carte: 33/80

 This is where star cook Ludwig Bechter has disappeared to, after giving up the Imperial kitchen of the Bühlerhöhe. Instead of serving grande cuisine in a half-empty restaurant, he wanted to cook good regional dishes for a (hopefully) full house in the valley. We couldn't test his menu yet, but regional cooking is a tradition in this 200-year-old half-timbered house with six small dining rooms in the middle of town.

IMPERIAL 18/20 IN SCHLOSSHOTEL BÜHLERHÖHE

77815, Schwarzwaldhochstr. 1
(0 72 26) 5 50, Fax 5 57 77 res.

Closed for lunch every day except Sunday, closed Wednesday, Thursday and 3 weeks in January. Tables d'hôte: 148L, 165D, à la carte: 70/125

This restaurant caters to an international gourmet clientele, and its quality shows in the exquisitely set tables and the fine ingredients used in the kitchen. After Chef Dieter Bechter's sudden departure, sous-chef Wolfgang Müller took over the kitchen. In Bechter's absences in the past, Müller was always good for a rating of 18/20. We'll see how it goes.The Imperial served us one of the best lamb shoulders (with fresh vegetables and cèpes) we have ever eaten —it deserves a 19.5 rating. The dumplings in a hearty veal-shank stew were not as light as they should have been, and the scallop and truffle mille-feuille and the Bresse-pigeon pie with foie gras terrine were lacking in originality. The price of a bottle of wine begins at 32 DM. Among the 40 different wines listed is a 1947 Château Petrus (price only upon inquiry)! The choice of wines seemed a bit haphazard and shows the need for a capable sommelier—an absolute must in a house with such a reputation!The staff is well-trained and keeps smiling even after two or three strenuous hours.

SCHLOSS-RESTAURANT IN SCHLOSSHOTEL BÜHLERHÖHE 15/20

77851, Schwarzwaldhochstr 1
(0 72 26) 5 50, Fax 5 57 77 res.

🌳 P

Tables d'hôte: 65/115, à la carte: 62/104

The first thing that strikes you here is the fantastic view, especially on a sunny day when the sky is a brilliant azure.The menu – with both regional specialities and international dishes – is intriguing, but the quality of the cooking is as changeable as the weather here. A nicely fried pigeon came with delicious squash sliced a little too thickly. The saddle of fresh piglet was perfectly done, and the *tafelspitz* soup and the stuffed duckling leg were very tasty, but the pike-perch with a whole-grain crust would please only the most hard-bitten health freak.The service is charming, and the wines carefully chosen.

SCHLOSSHOTEL BÜHLERHÖHE

77815, Schwarzwaldhochstr. 1
(0 72 23) 5 50, Fax 5 57 77

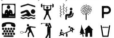

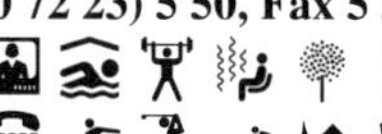

90 rooms, **S** 300/450, **D** 490/690,
APP 1150/2400, **½P** +80, **P** +140

Following its renovation, this legendary luxury hotel in an 18-hectare park offers the finest accommodations money can buy. The convention center is equipped with modern technology. A spa clinic, putting green and beauty farm are part of the complex.

PLÄTTIG-HOTEL

77815, Schwarzwaldhochstr. 1
(0 72 26) 5 53 00, Fax 5 54 44

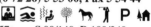

57 rooms, **S** 90/140, **D** 180/240,
APP 260/320, **½P** +28

Like the neighboring Bühlerhöhe, the 100-year-old Plättig Hotel has been renovated. The old-fashioned façade now contains comfortably modernized rooms and public areas. Fine terraces. The Plättig Hotel is several categories lower than the more luxurious hotels of the Grundig group. Restaurant.

WEHLAUER'S BADISCHER HOF 17/20

77815, Hauptstr. 36
(0 72 23) 2 30 63, Fax 2 30 65

Closed for lunch, closed Sunday and Monday, 3 weeks in January. Tables d'hôte: 100/150, à la carte: 51/109

In spite of its elegant ambience, customers still feel comfortably at home here, thanks to the scrupulous attention they receive from the staff. Occasionally it was a bit too attentive, and we sometimes had the feeling that the waiters were eavesdropping on our conversations.The menu here has something for everyone from the gourmet to the traveling salesman who wants his Wiener schnitzel. Such good, simple fare does not seem out of place here. The various varieties of bread served were delicious. The parfait of sturgeon was a little coarse, but the scallops with vermouth-and-butter sauce were nothing short of perfect. A new trend that we appreciate is the combination of roasted and fried versions of the same thing; here, the ribs of lamb served with leg of lamb were exquisite. The pastry is excellent, and there is an interesting choice of wines, including Baden's best vintages at reasonable prices.

WEHLAUER'S BADISCHER HOF

77815, Hauptstr. 36
(0 72 23) 2 30 63, Fax 2 30 65

P

25, **S** 110/160, **D** 240/295, **APP** 315

It wasn't easy to pack 25 rooms into this building, and the baths are tiny. All rooms are individually furnished, but if you want a quiet night, secure a room away from the street. Nice garden.

BÜRGSTADT Bayern

Miltenberg 2-Würzburg 65

WEINHAUS STERN 15/20

63927, Hauptstr. 23-25
(0 93 71) 26 76, Fax 6 51 54 res.

Closed for lunch everyday except Saturday and Sunday, closed Thursday, 2 weeks in February and August, Tables d'hôte: 75, à la carte: 27/69

This *Weinhaus* does not look like a temple of gourmet cuisine, but in a modest yet determined way, chef Klaus Markert is cooking his way up with an imaginative, cosmopolitan cuisine that defies classification. Most of his customers are regular customers who just want "something ordinary" to eat. A gourmet dinner here must be ordered several days in advance. Be prepared for a unique experience. Markert might be feeling exotic and serve a Thai dish seasoned with lemongrass and chili peppers. Or la pièce de résistance could be fresh fish steamed Japanese-style in rice leaves. His fantastically seasoned Arabian dishes are nothing short of amazing. In spite of all this world-hopping, Markert's cuisine never seems trendy or artificial. He is equally at home with classic cuisine like saddle of lamb or venison—everything is perfectly prepared and seasoned. The choice of wines reveals the good taste of Markert's sister Heidi and lists the best vintages the region has to offer. The service is pleasant and capable, and there is a summer terrace at the back of the house. A good address for anyone who appreciates good food more than ideological culinary principles.

WEINHAUS STERN

63927, Hauptstr. 23-25
(0 93 71) 26 76, Fax 6 51 54

13, **S** 55/75, **D** 98/125, **1/2P** +25

This renovated wine tavern now includes 13 lovely and individually furnished rooms. If you want to sleep late, make sure you get a room facing the garden. Breakfast is an experience in the historic public rooms.

BURBACH Nordrh.-Westf.

Dillenburg 18-Siegen 21

D'R FIESTER-HANNES

8 km east in Holzhausen
57299, Flammersbacher Str. 7
(0 27 36) 39 33 res.

 P

Closed for dinner Monday, closed Tuesday. Tables d'hôte: 49/80, à la carte: 40/76

The previous owners, pioneers of gourmet cooking in this region since 1975, have given up and moved to Miltenberg. A successor for their restaurant, awarded a

toque these past years, hadn't been appointed by the time this guide went to press. But it's no secret that a small hotel complex is being added and that the restaurant reopens in May 1995.

BURGHAUSEN Bayern

Altötting 15-Salzburg 56

BAYERISCHE ALM 12/20

84489, Robert-Koch-Str. 211
(0 86 77) 98 20, Fax 98 22 00

 P

Closed Friday, closed for dinner Sunday during the winter. Tables d'hôte: 48, à la carte: 24/65

Reisinger's Hotel Bayerische Alm sits high above the picturesque medieval town of Burghausen, with a view of the largest German citadel below. The restaurant is comfortable, and the terrace is pleasant and shady.The straightforward Bavarian cuisine is prepared with a refreshingly light touch. The fillet of roe-deer with kohlrabi and the tender roast kid with warm potato salad were fine first courses, and brook trout in white wine with risotto and duck breast with raspberry sauce are excellent choices for the main course.The wine list offers a choice of Austrian vintages, regional wines and moderately priced French wines. The service is prompt and friendly.

BURGWALD Hessen

Marburg 18-Korbach 44

BURGWALD-STUBEN 13/20

35099, Ortsteil Ernsthausen
Marburger Str. 25
(0 64 57) 80 66, Fax 10 76

P

Closed for lunch every day except Sunday, closed Wednesday. Tables d'hôte: 45/105, à la carte: 39/77, No Credit Cards

This nondescript restaurant on the busy main street of Ernsthausen has earned its toque. At our last visit, Ruth Oertel cooked with class and concentration—good produce, prepared lightly, seasoned correctly and cooked à point. The watercress soup with quail's egg was a bit thin but savory, and was followed by excellent fried turbot with Italian vegetables and delicious lime sauce, pike-perch with flawlessly prepared asparagus and tender poached beef fillet with a fabulous green sauce. We loved our delectable dessert potpourri of parfaits and mousses!The service is obliging, and the wine list and menu moderately priced.

CALW Baden-Württemberg

Pforzheim 28-Stuttgart 40

ULRICH'S KLOSTERGALERIE 16/20

75365, Wildbader Str. 2
(0 70 51) 56 21, Fax 5 17 95 res.

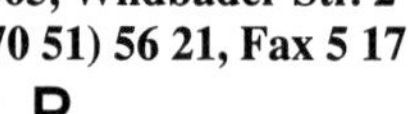 P

Closed for dinner Sunday, closed Monday, 3 weeks during the Bad.-Württ. summer school holiday. Tables d'hôte: 55/98, à la carte: 44/82

Customers cannot help but feel at home in this lovely gallery, and the exquisitely composed dishes are a delight for the eye and the palate.An appetizer of king prawns with artichoke tarts and tomato purée was magnificent, as was a delicate composition of salmon and pike-perch with two kinds of caviar and fresh chives. A venison dish topped with cream was wonderfully flavorful and mild at the same time. A fresh scallop tart with saffron, and a tender fillet of young boar with a liver mousse (an ideal combination!) were part of a superlative main course. Top-quality cheese and a basil parfait with biscuits and fruit rounded off this wonderful dinner. The service here is perfect.Choice wines of international renown, reasonably priced, can be had from the cellar of the ancient monastery that houses this fine restaurant.

KLOSTERSCHENKE 15/20

75365, Wildbader Str. 2
(0 70 51) 56 21, Fax 5 17 95 res.

 P

Tables d'hôte: 35/40, à la carte: 25/56

A restaurant that serves ingenious regional specialities in a cultivated, comfortable atmosphere and that has moderate prices and especially friendly service—what more can you ask for? A few recommendations, all guaranteed to make the fussiest gourmet happy: homemade pasta with cèpes, snail soup, fried fish with herb cream, and delectable variations on chocolate mousse. Also outstanding is the roulade of anglerfish, stuffed with lobster and served with a sumptuous sauce, a vegetable bouquet and watercress potatoes (17/20!). The veal marinated in Riesling is tender and savory - and the taste of the wine even comes through. Dainty homemade pastries were offered with excellent coffee.The German and international wines were reasonably priced.

KLOSTER HIRSAU
75365, Wildbader Str. 2
(0 70 51) 56 21, Fax 5 17 95

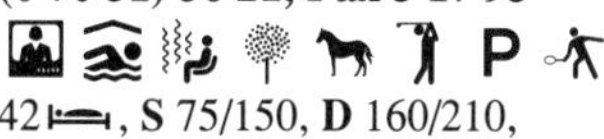

42, **S** 75/150, **D** 160/210,
1/2P +35, **P** +60

The former inn of the neighboring Benedictine monastery has been transformed into a hotel that prides itself on its "elegant hospitality." The rooms in the new wing are the most comfortable. Swimming pool and skittle alley are in the building. Indoor golf.

CASTROP-RAUXEL — NRW
Dortmund 10-Düsseldorf 85

GOLDSCHMIEDING 14/20
44575, Ringstr. 97
(0 23 05) 3 29 31, Fax 1 59 45

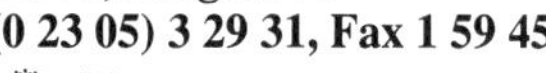

 P

Closed for lunch Saturday, closed Monday. Tables d'hôte: 49/69L, 69/132D, à la carte: 48/94

Castrop's best restaurant is in an old manor house. It is a treat to go there on cold winter evenings when the ancient fireplace, built in 1597, spreads warmth throughout the rooms. Goldschmieding had its golden days in the 1980s, and current chef Martin Heinrich is still trying valiantly to live up to the high standards of his predecessors. His succulent fillet of pikeperch with a tangy sauce was a great success, as were his lamb fillets with a piquant mustard sauce. The creamed roast of veal with fresh vegetables was nothing to rave about, however, and the char with arugula simply flat. The good choice of wines is as praiseworthy as ever.

SCHLOSSHOTEL GOLDSCHMIEDING

44575, Dortmunder Str. 55
(0 23 05) 1 80 61/63, Fax 3 13 20

43, **S** 176/196, **D** 246/286,
APP 390, **1/2P** +29, **P** +54

This, the only chic hotel in Castrop-Rauxel, is beautifully situated and has well-appointed guest rooms, a bistro and bar.

CELLE — Niedersachsen
Hannover 44-Hamburg 120

L'AUBERGE 12/20
29223, Winsener Str. 10
(0 51 41) 5 14 53

P

Tables d'hôte: 64/98

This beautiful large half-timbered house with a French name has stricken the traditional French onion soup from its menu and is on its way to a lighter and better cuisine. Quantity still beats quality by far, but things are looking up. Our potato pancake with salmon tartare would have fed half a school class, and the stewed rather than fried duck liver with soggy lentils, marbled pork chops with delicious rösti and lovely green beans were filling and not much else. Fatigued and stuffed, we discovered many wines by the glass in the arbitrarily stocked wine list.

ENDTENFANG IN HOTEL FÜRTSTENHOF 16/20

29221, Hannoversche Str. 55/56
(0 51 41) 20 10, Fax 20 11 20 res.

 P

Tables d'hôte: 55L, 98/145D, à la carte: 48/106

This ostentatiously decorated restaurant overflows with obviously well-to-do diners. There has always been much to criticize in the past, but this time we were pleasantly surprised. The prices are still astronomically high (a lobster costs 100 DM, and more modest main courses about 50), and the wine list could do with a little less quantity and a lot more quality, but the old-fashioned service was attentive and charming.The food is now prepared with more loving care and greater precision. Iced oxtail soup with caviar and a rabbit first course were excellent. The quail variations, pigeon pot-au-feu and fresh salmon with rice leaves rated 17/20. The sauces could be improved with less cream and more character.It is a happy surprise to find that the gap between price and performance is narrowing here.

FÜRTSTENHOF 

29221, Hannoversche Str. 55/56
(0 51 41) 20 10, Fax 20 11 20

76 rooms, **S** 170/280, **D** 200/400, **APP** 335/480, **½P** from 55

This country palace, built in 1670 on the orders of Duke Wilhelm, embodies the pomp and splendor of the Baroque period in northern Germany. The elegant entrance hall and the reception area are located in the former palace, whereas the comfortable rooms are in the modern hotel wing. The hungry guest can choose between the Endtenfang and the rustic Kutscherstube. A unique bar is located in the cellar. "A Relais et Châteaux hotel."

RISSMAN'S FEINSCHMECKERTREFF 12/20

29221, Am Heiligen Kreuse
(0 51 41) 2 54 54,

Closed Sunday. Tables d'hôte: 35L, 60/90D, à la carte: 35/70

The name of this restaurant near the old part of town announces that it is a meeting place for gourmets. Well, they may come for the nearly perfect service, the pleasant decor and the fairly reasonable prices, but it is unlikely that they would be attracted by the inadequate wine list or the uneven cooking. The thickly sliced marinated salmon just tasted salty, and the garden herbs in the soup had started to turn brown. Still, the parfaits are excellent.

CHEMNITZ Sachsen

Dresden 65-Leipzig 73

BIJOU IN HOTEL CHEMNITZER HOF 12/20

09111, Theaterplatz 4
(03 71) 68 40, Fax 6 25 87

Tables d'hôte: 35L, 50D, à la carte: 31/60

After extensive renovation, this restaurant reopened in the fall of 1994, so that we couldn't test it for this guide. The management intends to serve the needs of an international clientele.

CHEMNITZER HOF 

09111, Theaterplatz 4
(03 71) 68 40, Fax 6 25 87

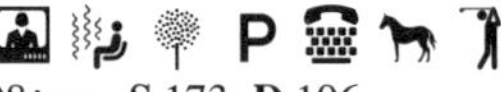

98 rooms, **S** 173, **D** 196, **APP** 320, **½P** +25, **P** +55

This hotel was erected 1930 in the Bauhaus style. The small rooms and suites, although they don't quite meet modern standards, are nevertheless clean and habitable. The prices are inappropriately high, though. Restaurants. Pleasant service. Breakfast: 22 DM.

BRASSERIE IN HOTEL MERCURE KONGRESS 10/20

09111, Brückenstr. 19
(03 71) 68 30, Fax 68 35 05

The cuisine here has hit rock bottom. The only thing we found fit to admire was our waiter, who agreed with all our complaints and still remained more than friendly up to the bitter end—hats off to him! We will give this restaurant a wide berth in the future. On top of everything else, the meager wine list offers no reason to come back.

MERCURE KONGRESS 

09111, Brückenstr. 19
(03 71) 68 30, Fax 68 35 05

386 rooms, **S** 149/185, **D** 179/225, **APP** 295/400, **½P** +30, **P** +60

The renovated rooms are still small but comfortably equipped, and the new bathrooms leave nothing to be desired. Restaurants, cafés, bars, fitness facilities, solarium and massage.

BURGHOTEL RABENSTEIN 14/20

09117, Grünaer Str. 2
(03 71) 85 65 02, Fax 85 05 79

Tables d'hôte: 35/49, à la carte: 19/63

On summer days, customers have to fight their way through the crowd in this pretty garden restaurant. Grilled trout, sausages, saddle of veal and lamb ribs attract a lot of hungry diners.Inside, the restaurant is quieter. An appetizer of marinated salmon was followed by a duck terrine, which could have done with a bit more seasoning, served with a well-dressed salad. The cèpe consommé was excellent, the fillet of sole good but not spectacular. The medallions of wild boar were perfectly done and came with a superb sauce and a gratin of potatoes and mushrooms. The nougat parfait with tropical fruit and a sauce of rose hips was likable.The service was obliging, friendly and prompt, and the chefs here are willing to make an effort to satisfy their customers. The wine list is arranged with loving care—vintages are described in detail and priced moderately.

BURGHOTEL RABENSTEIN

09117, Grünaer Str. 2
(03 71) 85 65 02, Fax 85 05 79

20, **S** 135/185, **D** 250/290, **APP** 300/395

This centrally located but quiet small hotel is the most beautiful and exclusive establishment in Chemnitz. Rooms, apartments and suites are comfortably and stylishly equipped. Bar, restaurant, café.

REFUGIUM IN HOTEL DOMICIL 13/20

6 km northwest in 09232
HartmannsdorfAm Berg 3
(03 37 22) 9 54 61, Fax 9 54 76 res.

Tables d'hôte: 30/40, à la carte: 25/52

Light and modern with large windows, a lovely terrace and unusual lighting—this is how the new restaurant presents itself. The new service staff is appropriately quick and young, pleasant and correct, and the wine cellar is stocked with first-class wines from renowned international estates at moderate prices (half-bottles and champagnes are expensive, though). At our last visit, a large number of guests kept the kitchen pretty busy. Maybe that's why the asparagus and roast beef salad seemed more like a ragout. The rest of our meal was not great cuisine, but respectably good cooking, for example a lovely light omelet with herbs, salmon and zucchini and delicious venison medallions with smoked beef and mushrooms.

DOMIZIL

6 km northwest in 09232
HartmannsdorfAm Berg 3
(03 37 22) 9 54 61, Fax 9 54 76

88, **S** 130/240, **D** 210/270

This attractive new building offers pleasant and plainly furnished rooms, very friendly and obliging service and conference rooms with modern technology. Bar.

VILLA POSTHOF 13/20

09116, Zwickauer Str. 154
(0 37 27) 38 29

Tables d'hôte: 39/49, à la carte: 18/44

This charming little restaurant is housed in a beautiful villa with a summer terrace and conservatory. The service is competent and pleasant; the wine list offers German, French and Italian wines at remarkably low prices.The kitchen of the Villa Posthof is fond of fresh herbs. We found them on our asparagus salad with ham and apple, in our wonderful consommé with vegetables and pancake strips and on poached African perch with cauliflower gratin. Our loin of lamb braised with thyme and garlic was delicious, but a little spongy. As dessert we recommend "Kirschplotzer" for those who like cherries.

COBURG Bayern

Bamberg 45-Hof 90

SCHALLER IN HOTEL COBURGER HOF 16/20

96450, Ketschendorfer Str. 22
(0 95 61) 2 50 74, Fax 2 88 74

 P

Closed for lunch, closed Sunday. Tables d'hôte: 95/115, à la carte: 51/84, No Credit Cards

Ever since the untiring Ulrich Schaller took his son-in-law on board, this flagship of fine regional gourmet cooking has gained momentum. With the extra help, Schaller can realize his often original ideas. His delicately marinated wild boar with salad was absolutely tender, and his sheatfish (a type of catfish) with a crust of squash seeds and olives was a rare experience of flavorful harmony. Schaller uses regional products so that his menu reflects the seasons. Asparagus, suckling lamb, young deer, fresh berries and mushrooms were some of the highlights tasted on a recent visit. The chefs have been experimenting with Asiatic cuisine, and we found tempura and pike-perch seasoned with ginger on the menu. There is a wide choice of dishes on the menu, and they are all beautifully prepared and cooked. Dessert lovers will suffer pangs of indecision when forced to choose among baked plum strudel, cream cheese dumplings and fig tempura. The owner is happy to guide his customers, suggesting dishes and appropriate wines from the choice wine list. He is also responsible for the marvellous bouquets of flowers that add charm to the otherwise plain decor.

COCHEM Rheinl.-Pfalz

Koblenz 50-Trier 88

PARKHOTEL VON LANDENBERG 12/20

56812, Ortsteil Sehl
Sehler Anlagen 1
(0 26 71) 71 10, Fax 83 79 res.

 P

Closed 5 January through 15 March. à la carte: 28/80

The dining room with its noble fireplace, crystal chandeliers, heavy furniture and a lovely view onto parklike grounds creates an elegant ambience. Friedhelm Prinz, who after years of cooking on an ocean liner has finally found a port, is a good cook, but his choice and combinations of ingredients are a bit arbitrary. Though he always prepares his dishes fresh, his cuisine reminds us of the time when mandarin oranges were used to decorate lamb's lettuce. Imaginative cooking doesn't just mean unusual combinations. Venison with large pieces of green peppers and mango in pastry crust, for instance, accompanied by morels, cherries, mushrooms, red cabbage and a pink currant sauce shows uncertainty, not creativity. House wines from the Landenberg estate are offered, as well as second-class international vintages. The service is professional and pleasant.

COESFELD NRW

Borken 27-Münster 39

VALKENHOF 18/20

48653. Mühlenstr. 25
(0 25 41) 8 77 34, Fax 8 77 79 res.

 P

Closed Monday. Tables d'hôte: 48L, 105D, à la carte: 56/92

We hate to gush, but not one of the superbly prepared dishes here earns a rating of less than 17/20, and most of them merit far more. The scallops, gently marinated in lime juice and olive oil and served on a bed of avocados, were wonderful, and the fried foie gras with poached rhubarb and a breathtaking dark sauce was brilliant. A Brittany lobster with Savoy cabbage was subtly perfumed with herbs and kumquats, and the variations of duck with two sauces were fantastic. Even the desserts have improved greatly.The service was impeccable, and the excellent wine list features French wines as well as an intelligent choice of the best German vintages.Because Coesfeld is a little out of the way, we recommend room reservations in the nearby Hotel zur Mühle.

COTTBUS Brandenburg

Dresden 95-Berlin 132

FÜRST PÜCKLER IN HOTEL BRANITZ 13/20

4 km southeast in 03042 Branitz
Heinrich-Zille-Str.
(03 55) 7 51 00, Fax 71 31 72

P

Tables d'hôte: 28/42, à la carte: 19/48

The ambience here approaches the regal. The rich Serbian soup, full of fresh vegetables, sliced egg custard and meat is served appropriately in a silver dish. The ingenious sauces show great attention to detail: a sour cream sauce served with pike-perch, a pepper sauce for a tender hare, and a Béarnaise sauce with a fillet of pork.The wine list has been improved by the addition of quality wines from France and a wider choice of wines by the glass.

HOTEL BRANITZ

4 km southeast in 03042 Branitz
Heinrich-Zille-Str.
(03 55) 7 51 00, Fax 71 31 72

201 rooms, **S** 170/216, **D** 226/256,
APP 480

Built in the functional and plain style the socialist republic favored, this drawn-out hotel complex behind the Branitz park has modern and pleasant rooms and a conference center that features the latest technology.

CUXHAVEN Niedersachsen

Bremerhaven 45-Stade 74

BADHOTEL STERNHAGEN 13/20

27476, Cuxhavener Str. 86
(0 47 21) 43 40, Fax 43 44 44 res.

Closed for lunch Wednesday through Friday, closed Monday, Tuesday, 15 January through 12 February, 15 November through 24 December. Tables d'hôte: 45/75L, 125D, à la carte: 48/95

An impressive view of the ocean, with incoming and outgoing ships and Neuwerk Island across the shallows, makes this restaurant unique. The unusually friendly service and cuisine deserving of a toque are further attractions. The mostly older couples who frequent the dining room appreciate the somewhat dietetic cooking, but we missed taste and seasoning in our shrimp mousse, lentil soup and angler wrapped in spinach beets. An exquisitely tender poularde stuffed with curds and herbs would have been a highlight if it had been more strongly seasoned. The desserts are nice but not sensational.The wine list is flawless and even offers wines from Israel at reasonable prices.

BADHOTEL STERNHAGEN

27476, Cuxhavener Str. 86
(0 47 21) 43 40, Fax 43 44 44

 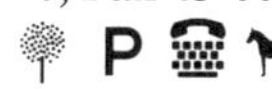

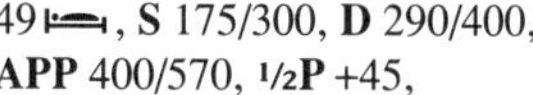

49 rooms, **S** 175/300, **D** 290/400,
APP 400/570, **1/2P** +45,
Closed 15 November through 24 December

This hotel affords a wonderful view of the North Sea, and has its own beach. It offers the finest in comforts for its well-heeled clientele. Comfortable rooms guarantee a pleasant, if expensive, stay here.

KUR-STRAND-HOTEL DUHNEN

27476, Duhner Strandstr. 5-7
(0 47 21) 40 30, Fax 40 33 33

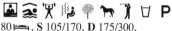

P

80 rooms, **S** 105/170, **D** 175/300,
APP 285/440, **1/2P** +30, **P** +50

Over the years this house on the sea promenade has become a comfortable spa-hotel offering a swimming pool, solarium, fitness room and restaurant. All rooms and suites facing the sea have balconies and are pleasantly furnished.

DARMSTADT Hessen

Frankfurt 28-Mannheim 55

MARITIM KONFERENZHOTEL

64295, Rheinstr. 105
(0 61 51) 87 80, Fax 89 31 94

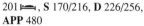

P

352 rooms, **S** 215/325, **D** 272/398,
APP 470, **1/2P** +40, **P** +70

Of all the chain hotels in the Rhine-Main region, the Maritim (opened in 1982) is the most elegant—and just a 15 minute drive from the airport. No expense has been spared in the decoration: marble stairs all the way from the top floor to the basement car park and opulently furnished rooms with all the amenities of a modern hotel, including a skittle alley, a wonderful bar and restaurants.

WEINMICHEL 11/20

64230, Schleiermacherstr. 10-12
(0 61 51) 2 90 80, Fax 2 35 92

P

Tables d'hôte: 43/53L, 76/89D, à la carte: 44/84

Besides this restaurant, the bustling businessman Karl Eisele runs three wine stores in Darmstadt and Frankfurt. He's done much to improve the modest culinary level in Darmstadt. But his many activities haven't done his cuisine any good: the quality of the food has gone down. None of the dishes we tried at our last visit had any taste at all, and the sauces were thin and insipid. The overdone sheatfish in a pink excuse for a red beet sauce fell apart on our plate, whereas the lamb in an undefined broth defied our efforts to chew it tender.The decor lacks charm, and so does the service. The wine list sounds exciting, but after getting flat sparkling wine and warm red wine, we didn't dare order anything else.

WEINMICHEL 

64230, Schleiermacherstr. 10-12
(0 61 51) 2 90 80, Fax 2 35 92

P

74, **S** 146/186, **D** 238

This is a very pleasant, well-run house with newly renovated and lovingly furnished rooms. The rooms aren't luxuriously equipped, but the prices are moderate. Good wine cellar and a nice area for tastings. Good breakfast buffet.

DARSCHEID Rheinl.-Pfalz

Daun 6-Cochem 30

KUCHER'S LANDHOTEL 13/20

54552, Karl-Kaufmann-Str. 2
(0 65 92) 6 29, Fax 35 77 res.

 P

Closed Monday, closed for lunch Tuesday, closed 5-20 January. Tables d'hôte: 52L, 68/120D, à la carte: 46/78

The restaurant in back of the wine shop offers a wine list that alone is worth a detour. Connoisseur Kucher has collected great and choice wines from all over Europe and loves to hold private tastings with his guests. If his expertise also extended to the food he cooks, we would be satisfied. As it is, his creativity leads him to combine tastes that just don't harmonize. For instance, the Beluga caviar with a carpaccio of red beets and scallops went perfectly with the vegetable, but managed to kill the subtle taste of the raw scallops. Our delicious saddle of lamb was accompanied by an almost-cold, red and sour sauce, and the angler fillet was swamped with a sauce of olives, dried tomatoes and capers. Highlights were the desserts, guinea fowl terrine with asparagus and duck liver.The service is helpful and well-informed.

KUCHER'S LANDHOTEL 

54552, Karl-Kaufmann-Str. 2
(0 65 92) 6 29, Fax 35 77

14, **S** 60/65, **D** 120/130,
1/2P +28

Closed 5—20 January

Martin and Heidi Kucher's hotel, surrounded by pastures and forests with lovely hiking paths, offers simply furnished and scrupulously clean rooms as well as bike rental and tennis courts 150 meters from the hotel. Good and ample breakfast buffet.

DAUFENBACH Rheinl.-Pfalz

Trier 12

LANDHAUS MÜHLENBER 16/20 

54313, Mühlenberg 2
(0 65 05) 87 79 res.

 P

Closed for lunch every day except Sunday, closed Monday and Tuesday, 2 weeks in January and June, 1 week in September, Tables d'hôte: 83/110, à la carte: 58/91

Unobtrusively but obstinately, Ulrike and Harald Stoebe have cooked their way to the top of the region's rankings. Their pretty little house in the middle of a forest, the quiet and pleasant service and the sensitive harmony of the cuisine make this restaurant attractive. Ulrike Stoebe is one of the few self-taught cooks who have reached this degree of perfection. We started with seafood and lemon sauce, seasoned with Indian spices, followed by excellent warm calf's tongue with potato salad, asparagus and salsa verde, as well as ricotta ravioli, a classic of the house. Even the most daring combinations seldom failed to harmonize. The white beans with the delicious dorado and angler on tomato sauce could have been less al dente, but a finely balanced and exquisite pear sorbet and flawless saddle of venison and wild boar fillet in Barolo with savoy cabbage and peas were magnificent highlights of a superb meal. Stoebe's wine list is by no means comprehensive, but intelligently stocked. As there are only a few half-bottles and wines by the glass, we recommend asking for the specials.

KURFÜRSTLICHES AMTSHAUS

54550, Auf dem Burgberg
(0 65 92) 30 31, Fax 49 42

42 rooms, **S** 115/155, **D** 210/260, **1/2P** +50

Closed 8—22 January

Guests at this antiques-furnished hotel are in no hurry to leave. They would like to linger in the comfortable, tastefully decorated rooms with their beautiful views of the landscape and spend more time in the swimming pool set in volcanic rock, the whirlpool bath and the solarium.

DAUN Rheinl.-Pfalz

Bonn 90-Saarbrücken 140

KURFÜRSTLICHES AMTHAUS 15/20

54550, Auf dem Burgberg
(0 65 92) 30 31, Fax 49 42 res.

Closed Monday, Tuesday, 8—22 January.
Tables d'hôte: 51L, 85D, à la carte: 60/110

A veritable fireworks of wonderful ideas inspires the cuisine here and makes high prices acceptable. The beautiful exterior of the house isn't the only feature that surpasses everything for miles around. Our mild and delicate salmon tartare with asparagus mousse deserved a high rating, as did the fresh scallops with marinated seaweed and tomato sauce. A delicious lobster was served with endive salad, and lamb liver (with superfluous capers) was accompanied by pesto noodles as well as onions with lemon. Our panaché of fine fish was formidable—four different kinds of fish, each prepared extravagantly like a separate dish—and was equaled in quality only by exquisite pigeon variations. The comprehensive wine list is well stocked with Mosel-Saar-Ruwer wines, Bordeaux and Burgundies. The service is competent and keeps smiling even when the house is full.

DEGGENDORF Bayern

Passau 68-Regensburg 80

GRAUER HASE 14/20

94469, Untere Vorstadt 12
(09 91) 77 70 res.

P

Tables d'hôte: 35/85, à la carte: 25/59

This elegantly rustic restaurant under new management serves a new creative Bavarian cuisine at (new!) moderate prices. Almost all of the produce and ingredients used are bought locally and the cooking is wonderful, for instance the mushroom consommé with light liver dumplings or a *tafelspitz* soup with julienne and spicy stuffed *pfannkuchenradln*. The recipe for the duck liver cake with orange ragout is a souvenir from the Charivari, where Kerscher once headed the kitchen staff. The other thing he has brought with him is his preference for fish. His *guglhupf* of native fish and his Pichelsteiner fish stew were as delicate as his pike-perch in potato pancake or his red mullet fillet with spinach and tomato risotto. For those who don't like fish, the suckling pig is a must, as is the Viennese schnitzel and the breast of poularde with leeks in Riesling and homemade noodles.The wine list offers a wide variety at moderate prices: not a single bottle costs more than 100 DM. The service is pleasant and professional.

DEIDESHEIM Rheinl.-Pfalz

Bad Dürkheim 14-Saarbrücken 110

GASTHAUS ZUR KANNE

67146, Weinstr. 31
(0 63 26) 9 66 00, Fax 96 60 96

Tables d'hôte: 33/98, à la carte: 31/70

The oldest inn in this region has returned to its roots. In the 12th century it started as a hostelry with many functions; now refined cuisine, a bistro-type restaurant, a wine garden, a cozy parlor for celebrations and a terrace are housed under one roof. All the dining rooms have different ambiences, but the same menu is offered in each. You can order a light meal or a snack from the evening menu all day. Besides that, there's a menu with classic and regional dishes, ranging from beef carpaccio and salmon tranche to stuffed breast of veal with tarragon sauce.The wine list is well-stocked with the owner's wines from the Dr. Bürklin-Wolf vineyard, but also offers a goodly number of other regional and some international wines.

SCHWARZER HAHN IN DEIDESHEIMER HOF 17/20

67146, Am Marktplatz 1
(0 63 26) 18 11, Fax 76 85 res.

Closed for lunch, closed Sunday and Monday. Tables d'hôte: 100/150, à la carte: 60/119

The departure of Chef Nagy left a hole that hadn't been filled at our last visit. We had promised him and his maître d' Gamblin an 18/20 rating this time, but since they both left, cuisine and service show serious shortcomings. If a dish is oversalted, it's probably a coincidence, at most bad luck. But when more than half of the dishes are spoiled by such a "mishap," then it can only be pure carelessness and the artistic arrangement of the food doesn't console us a bit. After salty red mullet, the *guglhupf* of smoked salmon and asparagus mousse earned a rating of 17/20 (even if the asparagus mousse was a bit oversalted). Our bass with saffron risotto was perfect, even though the sauce with it had been reduced too much and become just a salty (again!) vegetable broth. The only dish that hadn't been blizzarded with the salt shaker was the most impossible one: the "best of kid" was a mountain of bones with hardly any meat on them. After a nicely done saddle of lamb, we had edges of duck's breast and salty carrots with courgettes. Thank goodness there were tolerable cheeses and marvelous desserts to feed the (still) hungry! We haven't given up hope, but if this keeps up, we'll have to lower the rating to the deserved 15/20.The wine list is the best in this area and well stocked with champagne, Bordeaux, Burgundies and regional wines.

WEINSTUBE ST. URBANIN DEIDESHEIMER HOF 14/20

67146, Am Marktplatz 1
(0 63 26) 18 11, Fax 76 85 res.

Closed 1—6 January, 10—24 July. Tables d'hôte: 49/79, à la carte: 40/77

The old original restaurant of the Hahn family has remained true to its traditional good standards of cooking, a combination of regional dishes, small à la carte choices and one refined prix-fixe menu. The plats du jour are usually recommendable, but the regional specialties offered are not necessarily better than in other restaurants along the wine route. The service is friendly, but sometimes has difficulty matching dishes with the hungry guests who ordered them.We tried delicious fried salmon with insipid salmon mousse, good scampi and lovely sole, nicely dressed salad with well-seasoned rabbit fillets, savory mushroom and chicken liver terrine, tough and salty *tafelspitz*, greasy lamb cutlets and a strange tasting mocha crème with chocolate zabaglione.The wine list is well-stocked with regional wines and quite a few good wines by the glass.

DEIDESHEIMER HOF

67146, Am Marktplatz 1
(0 63 26) 18 11, Fax 76 85

APP 330/400,
Closed 1—6 January, 10—24 July

An intrinsic part of the old town, this hotel, like the surrounding buildings, breathes unpretentious prosperity. To please the gourmets who dine at its restaurant, the Schwarzer Hahn, the hotel has redecorated one floor, using imaginative layouts to avoid the usual uniformity of hotel rooms.

DENZLINGEN Baden-Württ.

Freiburg 9-Offenburg 60

REBSTOCK-STUBE 14/20 

79211, Hauptstr. 74
(0 76 66) 20 71, Fax 79 42 res.

P

Closed Sunday and Monday except holidays, 1—15 August. Tables d'hôte: 45/65L, 65/100D, à la carte: 37/80

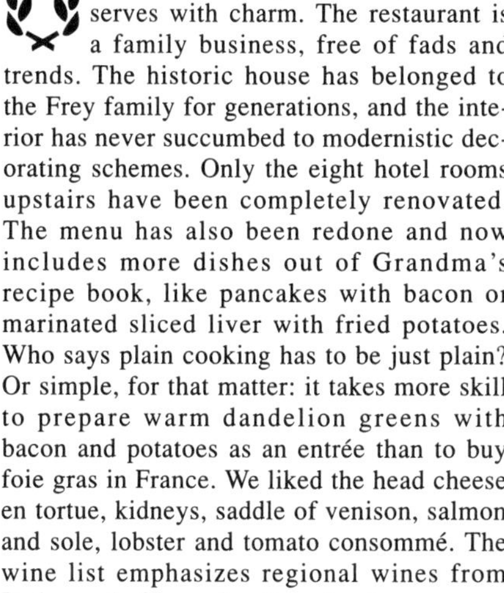

He cooks with perfection, and she serves with charm. The restaurant is a family business, free of fads and trends. The historic house has belonged to the Frey family for generations, and the interior has never succumbed to modernistic decorating schemes. Only the eight hotel rooms upstairs have been completely renovated. The menu has also been redone and now includes more dishes out of Grandma's recipe book, like pancakes with bacon or marinated sliced liver with fried potatoes. Who says plain cooking has to be just plain? Or simple, for that matter: it takes more skill to prepare warm dandelion greens with bacon and potatoes as an entrée than to buy foie gras in France. We liked the head cheese en tortue, kidneys, saddle of venison, salmon and sole, lobster and tomato consommé. The wine list emphasizes regional wines from Baden and offers a few French wines.

DESSAU Sachsen-Anhalt

Leipzig 60-Magdeburg 64

FÜRST LEOPOLD IN STEIGENBERGER AVANCE HOTEL 14/20 

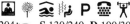

06814, Friedensplatz
(03 40) 2 51 50, Fax 2 51 51

P

Tables d'hôte: 35/70, à la carte: 29/62

The entrance to this restaurant is through the lobby of the Steigenberger Hotel. The dining rooms are spacious and modern and have small tables with comfortable chairs. There's a buffet for appetizers and self-service for salads and desserts. We tried steamed turbot fillet with a light cream sauce and excellently done duck's breast with artichoke hearts and two kinds of sauces, and a lovely banana mousse with delicious cassis sauce. All dishes were garnished and presented with loving care and pride. We could watch the cooks at work through the window between kitchen and restaurant—and were impressed with their professional nonchalance and expertise.The small international wine list is high-priced.

STEIGENBERGER AVANCE HOTEL 

06814, Friedensplatz
(03 40) 2 51 50, Fax 2 51 51

 P

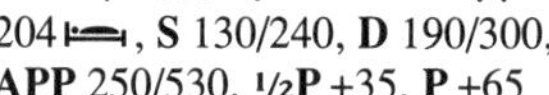

204, **S** 130/240, **D** 190/300,
APP 250/530, **½P** +35, **P** +65

This extravagant new building is located in the heart of Dessau and has exquisitely furnished spacious rooms and suites. The lobby has a piano bar, comfortable upholstery and modern paintings. All rooms have a hookup for fax machines, and the conference facilities have modern equipment. Breakfast: 20 DM.

DETTELBACH Bayern

Würzburg 20-Bamberg 62

HIMMELSTOSS 16/20 

97337, Bamberger Str. 3
(0 93 24) 47 76, Fax 49 69

Closed Tuesday, closed for lunch Wednesday. Tables d'hôte: 32/38L, 48/85D, à la carte: 24/65

Chef Herbert Kuffer makes no compromises when he cooks. He goes far beyond the conservative regional style of cooking, experimenting instead with more cosmopolitan cuisines. The resulting blend of native and foreign dishes, regional produce and exotic spices is a work of culinary art. There are two four-course fixed-price menus that are served with a good choice of regional wines. It is possible to order just a glass of wine and a snack, and there is a midnight menu for nightowls. A few examples of Kuffer's creative cuisine: terrine of fresh goat cheese with watercress and rice salad and a vinaigrette of honey and papaya, cream of potato soup with king prawns and a shot of lime juice, scallops sautéed in lemon and thyme and accompanied by discreetly flavorful orange butter. The cheerful atmosphere that prevails in the kitchen infects the customers in this subtly rustic *Gaststube*, which has been carefully renovated in keeping with the historic surroundings. The service is always circumspect and good-humored.The wine list is too heavy on the house's own wines and lacking in quality vintages from other regions. The food deserves better.

DIERHAGEN Meckl.-Vorp.

Ahrenshoop 7-Rostock 36

BLINKFÜER 13/20

18347, Schwedenschanze 20
(03 82 26) 8 03 84/6, Fax 8 03 92 res.

 P

Tables d'hôte: 35/52L, 42/68D, à la carte: 25/56, Tables d'hôte with wine: 38/82

This is the best restaurant on the peninsula. It offers regional game dishes like venison medallions with mushrooms and green pepper sauce and baked walnuts or rabbit leg with cognac plum sauce and fried herb dumplings. Seafood here means fish from the nearby ocean. We had delightful baby cod with a light herb sauce and succulent roulade of pike-perch and salmon in savoy cabbage.We thought the desserts were better last year. The service is pleasant and the wine list is improving.

SVEN LOHSSE

18347, Schwedenschanze 20
(03 82 26) 8 03 84/6, Fax 8 03 92

28 rooms, **S** 95/110, **D** 145/175,
APP 190/225, **½P** +20, **P** +40

This new hotel stands sentinel over the Fischland Darss-Zingst peninsula, and offers above-average comfort for discriminating holidaymakers and business travelers. The hotel is equipped with a solarium and fitness center, and there are ideal surfing and sailing conditions on the nearby ocean and in Bodden. Bicycles and picnic baskets can be rented. The breakfast buffet is opulent.

DILLENBURG Hessen

Siegen 30-Wetzler 31

BARTMANNS HAUS 12/20

35683, Untertor 3-4
(0 27 71) 78 51 res.

P

Tables d'hôte: 55/105, à la carte: 32/72

Theo Friedrich promises light Mediterranean cuisine in his menu, but the dishes we ordered here were still as rich, heavy and filling as ever. Two courses were more than enough for us. We don't mind Friedrich's splurges with butter and cream, but does he have to thicken his sauces with flour, too? After a nondescript appetizer platter, thick cream of asparagus soup, nice cèpes ravioli, overdone turbot and a leg of lamb, we waived dessert, which rarely happens. Friedrich's forte is more classic dishes, like salad with quail's breast and fillet of beef with nice fried potatoes. A special menu offers a few regional specialities and some snacks.We liked the large wine list more and the somewhat lame service less than before.

LANDHAUS AM ERLENHECK

35684, Ortsteil Frohnhausen
Erlenheck 1
(0 27 71) 3 29 93, Fax 3 56 06

 P

Closed for lunch Saturday, closed Wednesday. Tables d'hôte: 32/68, à la carte: 25/66

Viola Pfaff and Ralf Dörr belong to that army of young and ambitious cooks and restaurant employees who, after years of apprenticeship in renowned houses, want to strike out on their own. But they're not making any of the usual mistakes: their cuisine and the prices they charge are far from exalted. The Landhaus am Erlenheck already has the best reputation far and wide. We're reserving judgment till next time, but from what we tried, the Landhaus could deserve a toque in any case. Dörr's light sauces, expert desserts, salmon and duck's breast gave us an impression of his capabilities. The small wine list includes some excellent German Riesling at relatively low prices. The service is attentive and pleasant.

DILLINGEN Bayern

Donauwörth 27-Ulm 49

STORCHEN-NEST 15/20 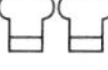

6 km southeast in Frstingen
89407, Demleitnerstr. 6
(0 90 71) 45 69, Fax 61 80 res.

 P

Closed Monday and Tuesday. Tables d'hôte: 35/40L, 68/98D, à la carte: 37/82

This restaurant has a comfortable, woodsy interior and a beautiful garden outside. It is impossible not to admire the courage it takes to offer haute cuisine in the middle of this culinary no-man's-land. Unfortunately, what is on the menu is not always available. We tried to swallow our chagrin and enjoyed the familiarly seasoned gazpacho, homemade venison terrines, and young chicken with shallots, beans, mashed carrots and potato pancakes. Homemade coconut, strawberry and walnut ice creams with fresh fruit were delicious, as was the aromatic sherbet of elderberry blossoms. The small wine list offers wines by the glass and bottles of international wines at reasonable prices. The service is attentive and pleasant, although at times touchingly helpless.

DINKELSBÜHL Bayern

Nürnberg 81-Würzburg 105

ZUM KLEINEN OBRISTEN IN HOTEL EISENKRUG 14/20

91550, Dr.-Martin-Luther-Str. 1
(0 98 51) 5 77 00, Fax 57 70 70 res.

 P

Closed Monday and Tuesday, 3 weeks in January. Tables d'hôte: 39/119D, à la carte: 52/92

Neither his cuisine nor his stuffy restaurant is as cosmopolitan as self-confident globetrotter Martin Scharff believes them to be. In addition to his gourmet restaurant, he runs a hotel, a restaurant for crowds of tourists in a historic vaulted cellar and another guest house. Perhaps he is spreading himself too thin. Fresh dill on marinated salmon is not original, overcooked vegetables not in the least creative, heavy sauces and overcooked asparagus not innovative. We did appreciate the fact that the courses of the three gourmet fixed-price menus can be ordered à la carte, but what we read on the menu was often more exciting than what we finally found on our plates: rack of lamb with herbs in a pastry crust, suckling calf with albufera sauce (a creamed sauce made with broth and red paprika butter) and morel-stuffed ravioli, sheatfish (a type of catfish) with red beets, and pike-perch with a sauce of olives and tomatoes. Each dish was traditionally prepared. Asiatic spices might promise new taste sensations, but in fact they were used only for decorative purposes.Martin Scharff can cook, but he will have to set some priorities for himself.Less on the comprehensive wine list would have been more. Many of the standard wines found in simpler restaurants could be omitted.

DISSEN Nordrhein-Westfalen

Herford 12-Minden 20

HEIMATHOF NOLLE 15/20

49201, Norte 83
(0 54 21) 44 50 , Fax 22 52 res.

Closed for lunch every day except Sunday, closed Monday and Thursday, 2 weeks during the summer and winter. Tables d'hôte: 48/85, à la carte: 47/78

When Christa Stubenreich welcomes her guests with natural charm, they soon feel at home in this cheerful and comfortable restaurant. Norbert Stubenreich likes to prepare dishes that don't need subtle seasoning, sauces or dressings to taste good. He cooks honest regional fare with seasonal products according to old recipes. Stubenreich's cuisine is as refined as his lovely old house, and both toques fit better than ever—except when he tries more international or complicated dishes. Not even some precious bottles from his well-stocked cellar can help him then.

BAD DOBERAN Meckl.-Vorp.

Rostock 16-Wismar 41

KURHOTEL BAD DOBERAN

18209, Ortsteil HeiligendammAm Kamp
(03 82 03) 30 36, Fax 21 26

62, **S** 135/165, **D** 160/280,

Located in the first German sea resort, this hotel was built in 1793 as a guest house for Herzog Friedrich Franz von Mecklenburg. In 1992, the historic rooms were renovated in the traditional style, and the hotel rooms were modernized. The hotel offers shoeshine, laundry and babysitting services, and a solarium. Riding lessons, carriage drives, yachting and sailing courses can be arranged. Café, restaurants. Opulent breakfast buffet: 20 DM.

DONZDORF Baden-Württ.

Göppingen 13-Geislingen 14

DE BALZAC IN HOTEL BECHER 15/20

73072, Schloßstr. 7
(0 71 62) 2 00 50, Fax 20 05 55

 P

Closed Sunday and holidays, closed Monday, 2 weeks in January, 3 weeks during the Bad.-Württ. summer school holiday. Tables d'hôte: 73/108D à la carte: 51/85

Diners are in for a pleasant shock here: the comprehensive wine list offers the finest German and French vintages (even aged grand crus) at moderate prices. Chef Winfried Müller prepares culinary creations to match and serves them competently on elegantly set tables. We ordered the daily fixed-price menu: wonderful headcheese salad, variations of scallops (carpaccio, tartare and fried) with gnocchi and green asparagus, and delicate Swabian bread soup; a lovely sea bream fried in butter with capers and served with cucumbers and leeks; loin of lamb with thyme, green peas and potato gratin; cheese, and poached pear with exquisite vanilla ice cream. Müller's kitchen staff also cooks meals for two neighboring restaurants—Becher and Bauernstuben—which emphasize regional cuisine.

DORNSTETTEN Bad.-Württ.

Freundenstadt 8-Stuttgart 87

DIE MÜHLE 15/20

2.5 km northeast in Hallwangen
72280, Eichenweg 23
(0 74 43) 63 29, res.

 P

Closed Wednesday, closed for lunch Thursday. Tables d'hôte: 77/115, à la carte: 42/80

Chef Horst Gaiser, who cooks in a tiny kitchen, has never disappointed us. We enjoyed rolled fillet of sole with tiny croutons, excellent fish in vinaigrette, and delicate foie gras with apple slices and Sauterne sauce. The cream of potato soup with fresh marjoram could have used more seasoning. The brill with lobster served with baked endives and a mild velouté of wine was a masterpiece. So was the delicious soup of passion fruit with pineapple, strawberries, kiwis, mangos, orange slices and fresh vanilla ice cream. Exquisite petits fours were served with good coffee.It would take some time to fully appreciate the extensive choice of wines, offered at surprisingly moderate prices.

DORNUM Niedersachsen

Aurich 11-Esens 14

LEBER'S RESTAURANT IN THE BENINGA-BURG AT DORNUM 13/20

26550, Beningalohne 2
(0 49 33) 29 11 , Fax 23 01 res.

P

Closed Monday from October through May. Tables d'hôte: 40/110D , à la carte: 39/95, No Credit Cards

Since Wolfgang Leber moved to this medieval citadel, he seems to have resigned himself to compromising his standards to please his touristic clientele. A few examples: shrimp cocktail, beef tips in curry sauce with spaetzle, turbot in pastry crust, and a captain's plate with fried fish. It is especially difficult to understand why he uses frozen shrimp instead of buying them fresh practically on his own doorstep. Leber still aspires to a high standard, but has left his creativity far behind. The wine cellar offers a number of very good wines by the glass. The service staff does its best, whereas the chef sometimes shows an entire lack of interest in his customers.

DORSTEN Nordrhein-Westfalen

Gladbeck 17-Recklinghausen 20

HENSCHEL 14/20

46284, Ortsteil Hervest
Borkener Str. 47 (B224)
(0 23 62) 6 26 70, res.

P

Closed for lunch Staurday, closed first week in January, 2 weeks during the NRW summer school holiday. Tables d'hôte: 55/68L, 80/146D, à la carte: 60/92

Lobster, caviar and foie gras are intrinsic to the Henschel family's culinary repertoire. While the competition lowers prices in the hope of attracting new customers, this restaurant demands almost 50 DM for a main course. Still, diners are getting their money's worth: the portions are immense and every meal begins and ends with wonderfully staged "special effects." One of these is the trilogy of appetizers: scampi parfait, lobster in aspic and terrine of salmon with lobster. The meal ends with coffee and a wagon load of delicious tarts to choose from. In between, Mrs. Henschel treats us to sweetbread-filled ravioli in a consommé of chanterelles, roast fillet of ox with a sauce of snails and leeks, and grapes prepared as parfait or served with honey zabaglione. All this brings the restaurant pretty close to a second toque. Alfred Henschel's list of the finest international wines is remarkable and includes about 40 half-bottles and even a grand cru by the glass. The service in this elegant restaurant is friendly and capable.

DORTMUND NRW

Düsseldorf 83-Köln 95

ALTER BAHNHOF 11/20

44369, Stadtteil Huckarde
Altfriedstr. 16
(02 31) 39 19 30,

 P

Closed for lunch Saturday and Sunday, closed Monday. Tables d'hôte: 52/59L, 84/114D, à la carte: 50/91, Tables d'hôte with wine: 150

Refined cuisine has chugged to a standstill in this renovated railway station. Gourmet fare is on the menu but can be found in only a few dishes. A promising appetizer (rabbit livers with kidneys and kohlrabi mousse), followed by a salad of lobster with apples and celery and seasoned with cider vinaigrette, led us to expect more of the same quality. We were badly disappointed. The lukewarm combination of turbot, sole, lobster and crayfish was not even fresh, and the rack of lamb consisted of little more than a few bones. The international choice of wines leaves much to be desired. The owners also manage a bar with a beer garden on the side.

BURKHARDT'S RESTAURANT 12/20

44287, Stadtteil Aplerbeck
Köln-Berliner-Str. 63
(02 31) 44 87 79, Fax 44 88 53

Closed Monday, 1—10 January. Tables d'hôte: 50/70, à la carte: 43/68, No Credit Cards

Burkhard Middeke's light and unpretentious new bistro with an ambitious cuisine and not-so-ambitious prices is part of a dynamic new trend. He doesn't charge more than 35 DM for a main course, but his astounding repertoire evokes great and costly gourmet temples. Middeke takes pains in shopping for and preparing his (not always first-class) products. He offers three and five-course surprise prix-fixe meals. We were off to a brilliant start with our ray wing on asparagus and roquette salad dressed with vermouth sauce, followed by an excellent cream soup of Jerusalem artichokes with chervil and tasteless lamb slices. Angler and prawns could have been more al dente—and fresher, too! Most of the 32 wines can be ordered by the glass. The esthetics of the interior rely on the contrast between a renovated turn-of-the-century façade and a modern and functional decor inside.

CASTELLINO IN HOTEL RÖMISCHER KAISER 14/20

44135, Betenstr. 20
(02 31) 5 43 24 35, Fax 5 43 24 42 res.

Closed for lunch Saturday, closed Sunday, 2 weeks during the NRW summer school holiday. Tables d'hôte: 59L, 93D, à la carte: 55/84

Dortmund's gourmets are regular customers here, and they think everything is just wonderful. We do not agree. The pastries leave much to be desired, and not every culinary composition is a complete success. Still, chef Clemens Hemmer-Hiltenkamp has no problem earning his 15/20 rating, even if he is judged only on the strength of his savory terrine of guinea fowl with endives and piquant dried tomatoes, or his risotto of spring vegetables with fresh chanterelles, plenty of butter and Parmesan cheese. His duck's liver with muscat aspic, fish with traditional Tuscany stew, and saddle of lamb with a crust of olives and red-chicory ravioli demonstrate that it is not authenticity that he is searching for, but a creative new cuisine with Italian inspiration.Perhaps that explains why the wine list is heavy on Italian vintages.

LENNHOF

44227, Stadtteil Barop
Menlinghauser Str. 20
(02 31) 7 57 26, Fax 75 93 61

P

38, **S** 140/180, **D** 190/225,
APP 250/300

This is a highly frequented convention center that is also popular with families who have something to celebrate. The rustic decor is not entirely authentic. There is a bar and restaurant, and weekend specials are available for tennis players and gourmets.

LA TABLE 15/20

44265, Stadtteil Hohensyburg
Hohensyburgstr. 200
in the Spielbank
(02 31) 9 77 70 34, Fax 9 77 70 77 res.

P

Closed for lunch, closed Monday. Tables d'hôte: 96/118, à la carte: 64/96

As disenchantment sets in, the pomp and splendor of postmodern architecture can seem simply arrogant. The gastronomic flagship of the casino in Dortmund, however, hasn't been touched by this disillusionment. La Table defends its reputation as an oasis of quiet enjoyment, far away from one-armed bandits and capricious roulette wheels. The elegant decor is not ostentatious and the service is excellent without being stiff and formal.Since Thomas Bühner has found his own style, he's not afraid to indulge in culinary caprices. He smokes scallops, injects parsley into a pike-perch in Chablis and serves an Albufera sauce with rabbit instead of fowl. He plays with Asiatic flavors—and wins! His champagne soup with turbot quenelles tastes of lemon grass; five different Chinese spices flatter a lovely bass; and tandoori and teriyaki transform angler with curry and beef fillet in Burgundy into exotic dishes that are worth three toques. The delicious desserts bring you back to Europe.The sensational wine list may have left out a few wines, but nobody's missed them yet.

WITTEKINDSHOF

2 km east in Ortsteil Gardenstadt
44141, Westfalendamm 270
(02 31) 59 60 81, Fax 51 60 81

P

65, **S** 210/250, **D** 260/30,
APP 390/550, **1/2P** +39, **P** +77

Located on the busy Westfalendamm, this historic hotel with its massive slate roof is tucked away behind lovely rhododendron hedges. The rusticity of the hotel's otherwise elegant interior is too pompous for our taste, but is mercifully absent in the well-appointed guest rooms. Restaurant. Breakfast: 20 DM.

DREIEICH Hessen

Langen 4-Frankfurt 13

LE MAÎTRE 16/20

63303, Siemensstr. 14
(0 61 03) 8 20 85, Fax 8 49 66 res.

 P

Closed for lunch, closed Sunday and Monday, 10 days in January, 3 weeks in the Hess. summer school holiday. Tables d'hôte: 68/115, à la carte: 58/85

Chef Dieter Schmidt could have seen himself in our plates after each course; in our enthusiasm over his fantastic cooking we wiped them clean every time. Our enchantment started with the appetizer, a delicate white tomato soufflé, and continued with raw marinated fennel salad, every leaf of which had a bouquet of fresh herbs, and climaxed in perfectly fried red mullet fillet and superb angler medallions with mussel ravioli and two lovely sauces. The heath-raised duckling alone would have guaranteed our return. The sauces were all so perfectly composed we'd have to sing a hymn to describe them adequately. Cheese and pâtisserie are unsurpassed in this region. Guests can choose from 100 choice wines and many wines by the glass. Besides that, there are wonderfully fresh draught beer and remarkable digestifs. The beautifully set tables with tasteful silver cutlery let us forget the drabness of the restaurant surroundings in the middle of an industrial area. The service is unobtrusive and dependable.

DRESDEN Sachsen

Görlitz 62-Leipzig 125-Berlin 200

CANALETTO 11/20

01097, Große Meißner Str. 15
(03 51) 5 66 26 48, Fax 5 59 97 res.

P

Closed for lunch, closed Sunday and Monday. Tables d'hôte: 75/150, à la carte: 51/89

The only thing of high caliber we found here were the prices. The prestigious restaurant in the Hotel Maritim has a long way to go before the quality of the cuisine can match these prices. We were served good but ice-cold carpaccio of salmon and turbot with just a trace of truffled vinaigrette and salad, fresh and light lobster bisque with caviar, somewhat overdone breast of guinea fowl stuffed with chanterelles, and dark brown fritters with syrupy cream.The international wine list is inconsistently priced. Many items are too expensive, especially champagne, mineral water (a small bottle for 17 DM!) and wines by the glass.

DAS CAROUSSEL 15/20

01097, Neustadt
Rähnitzgasse 19
(03 51) 4 40 33, Fax 4 40 34 10 res.
Tables d'hôte: 58, à la carte: 37/68

This renovated Baroque building erected in 1730 houses a restaurant with a beautiful ambience. The light and airy rooms featuring the finest materials, lovely fabrics and elegant furniture as well as the friendly and competent service of a young staff create the perfect setting for gourmet enjoyment. This is exactly the cuisine a city like Dresden needed, from the fried headcheese and sweetbreads with lamb's lettuce and croûtons to the fabulous dessert creations. We enjoyed flavorful tomato soup with cheese quenelles and basil, truffled tagliatelle, succulent angler medallions with lentils and straw potatoes, heavenly veal fillet with asparagus and a dessert platter featuring two chocolate terrines with black raspberry sauce, cheese dumplings with caramel and little pastry boats filled with lovely wild strawberries, followed by the best coffee and delicious pralinés. The few but choice wines from Germany, France and Italy are surprisingly low-priced, as are the fine wines by the glass.

ERLWEIN RESTAURANT 11/20

01067. Theaterplatz 3
(03 51) 49 81 60, Fax 4 98 16 88
Closed 3 weeks in July/August. Tables d'hôte: 95, à la carte: 65/144

The gruesome decor of this new restaurant documents somebody's appalling taste. But don't let the light green walls hung with bad imitations of Manet and petrol-colored chairs irritate you. Save that for your meal. The service is pleasant and the waiters are dressed in tails, probably to justify the exorbitant prices: courses range from 51 to 84 DM. If you're obstinate enough, you may find out there's a prix-fixe menu. We had liver terrine with morels, an insipid pheasant consommé, Leipziger Allerlei with soggy morels and battered-looking crayfish, nicely done veal medallions with lovely tomatoes and an unmentionable dessert. The wine list is a loose-leaf collection with high prices.

MARCOLONIS VORWERK 14/20

01099, Bautzner Str. 96
(03 51) 5 67 11 68, Fax 57 91 80

 P

Closed for dinner Sunday. Tables d'hôte: 70/90, à la carte: 29/61

You'll have to be on the lookout for this historic building that Count Camillo Marcolini, director of the art academy here and the famous porcelain factory, bought in 1785. In two especially beautiful vaulted dining halls, Klaus Dieter Brüning's dishes are served at exquisitely set tables. We enjoyed excellent fried veal kidneys with different-colored paprika, onions, bacon and fresh marjoram; cucumber soup with shrimps seasoned with dill; and savory piccata of spiny lobster served with light tomato sauce and lemon balm. The beautiful arrangement of the food, often decorated with blooms of various flowers, contributed to our enjoyment. The homemade "Dresdner grütze," a sort of cold sweet soup with a delicate vanilla sauce, deserved extra praise. Pleasant and competent service. The small international wine list is moderately calculated, except where the champagne is concerned.

RISTORANTE ROSSINI 16/20

01067, An der Frauenkirche 5
(03 51) 4 84 17 41 , Fax 4 84 17 00
Tables d'hôte: 42/80, à la carte: 32/67

The unparalleled view of the Elbe river and the landscape around Dresden from this restaurant soothes the nerves, but the skittish staff puts them on edge again. The steep price increases on the menu and the wine list were another irritation.The appetizer consisted of a dry pastry shell (as big as a thimble) filled with ham and decorated with three little watercress leaves (cute!). Overdone slices of guinea fowl (or was it chicken breast?) and tomato soup with soggy croutons followed. The pike-perch fillet with dill cream and the chicken with spiny lobster were good but not exceptional in any way. We should perhaps take away Schloss Eckberg's toque, but we are going to give it the benefit of the doubt for now and hope that our experience was an exception to the rule.

SCHLOSS ECKBERG 13/20

01099, Bautzner Str. 134
(03 51) 5 25 71, Fax 5 53 79 res.

Tables d'hôte: 48L, 68/120D, à la carte: 42/76

The unparalleled view of the Elbe river and the landscape around Dresden from this restaurant soothes the nerves, but the skittish staff puts them on edge again. The steep price increases on the menu and the wine list were another irritation.The appetizer consisted of a dry pastry shell (as big as a thimble) filled with ham and decorated with three little watercress leaves (cute!). Overdone slices of guinea fowl (or was it chicken breast?) and tomato soup with soggy croutons followed. The pike-perch fillet with dill cream and the chicken with spiny lobster were good but not exceptional in any way. We should perhaps take away Schloss Eckberg's toque, but we are going to give it the benefit of the doubt for now and hope that our experience was an exception to the rule.

LA VIGNA 13/20

in 01445 Radebeul
Nizzastr. 55

(03 51) 8 32 10, Fax 8 32 14 45

Tables d'hôte: 45/70, à la carte: 50/90

This elegant restaurant is extravagantly built, equipped and furnished. Modern paintings and lighting create an exclusive ambience. The young ladies of the service staff were so friendly and helpful that we gladly overlooked some snags. The comprehensive international wine list seemed a matter of course in this luxury ambience. The kitchen recommended tender and wonderfully marinated lamb fillet with an aromatic sauce, poached turbot with a sauce of (dried!) morels, and poularde breast with maple syrup and green asparagus. The adjacent wonderful terrace restaurant belongs to the La Vigna as well.

HOTELS

BÜLOW RESIDENZ

01097, Neustadt
Rähnitzgasse 19
(03 51) 4 40 33, Fax 4 40 34 10

31, **S** 290, **D** 340, **APP** 420

This is the most exquisite hotel in town. In the rooms of this Baroque town house, everything is of the finest. Bedrooms and bathrooms are extravagant and luxurious. The conference rooms have modern equipment. First-class (late) breakfast: 25 DM. The service is perfect and the cellar bar has an inviting atmosphere.

DRESDEN HILTON

01067, An der Frauenkirche 5
(03 51) 4 84 10, Fax 4 84 17 00

333, **S** 350/405, **D** 400/455, **APP** 650/780, **½P** +45, **P** +93

The noble entrance hall is an immediate indication of the style and savoir faire of this modern hotel. The gigantic complex in the heart of the Saxon metropolis was designed by the Swiss architect Fenngel and opened in 1990. The interior decor is an effective combination of dark-stained wood, shiny chrome and radiant white paired with elegant gray, and the Saxon hospitality of the old Dresdner Hof is still apparent even though Hilton now owns the place. Rooms, apartments and maisonettes are individually decorated in an elegant modern style. Dresden's artistic and cultural treasures are just steps away, and the complex's 15 restaurants, cafés and bistros offer everything from gourmet dining to a quick cup of coffee. There is also a large convention center with sophisticated technology. Breakfast costs 29.50 DM, and non-smoking rooms are available.

FLAMBERG HOTEL HOFLÖSSNITZ

in 01445 Radebeul
Nizzastr. 55
(03 51) 8 32 10, Fax 8 32 14 45

202, **S** 290/330, **D** 350/410,
APP 540/800, **½P** +30, **P** +60

This grand building on the outskirts of Dresden flaunts a posh lobby with bar, bistro-café-restaurant and a lovely view into a courtyard with Mediterranean flair. Fitness center. Some baths are dark, and many of the televisions are cheap products. Breakfast: 25 DM.

MARITIM HOTEL BELLEVUE DRESDEN

01097, Große Meißner Str. 15
(03 51) 5 66 20, Fax 5 59 97

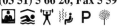

340, **S** 277/387, **D** 318/448,
APP 530/1200, **½P** +45, **P** +80

This hotel is part of a chain but is still one of the most beautiful in Germany. It is a model of culture and hospitality—stylish, elegant and dignified. It has a charming and romantic Baroque courtyard, and rooms and suites have views of the Elbe river and the historic silhouette of the city. We were delighted with the decor and ambience of the rooms, many of which are furnished with antiques. All rooms and apartments have air-conditioning and exquisite baths. There is a convention and banquet center with all necessary technical equipment, and the attractive lobby can be used for presentations. There are also salons, fitness center, solarium, saunas, bowling alley, jogging path and non-smoking rooms.

MARTHA HOSPIZ

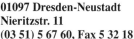

01097 Dresden-Neustadt
Nieritzstr. 11
(03 51) 5 67 60, Fax 5 32 18

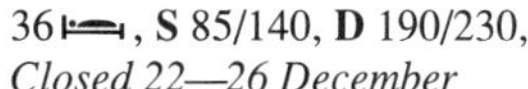

36, **S** 85/140, **D** 190/230,
Closed 22—26 December

The Martha Hospiz is located in the new part of town, only a few minutes' walk from the Neumarkt, the Semperoper and the Brühl terraces. Parking is easy in this quiet side street. The rooms, redecorated in 1991, are not very large but are comfortable and clean. The service is personal and friendly. In short, this is a commendable, relatively low-priced alternative to a palatial hotel. In the rustic restaurant, Zum Kartoffelkeller, you will discover what the Saxons can do with potatoes.

SCHLOSS ECKBERG

01099, Bautzner Str. 134
(03 51) 5 25 71, Fax 5 53 79

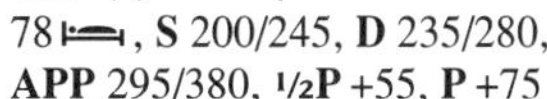

78, **S** 200/245, **D** 235/280,
APP 295/380, **½P** +55, **P** +75

This is a romantic, neo-Gothic château in the middle of a large, sheltered park complete with sculptures and a picturesque pond full of water lilies. Situated high above the Elbe river, it has a marvelous view of the Saxon countryside. Reservations are necessary for the château, where the rooms are larger and better equipped than in the new wing, the Haus Eckberg. Amenities: fitness center, friendly service, great breakfasts.

DÜREN Nordrhein-Westf.

Aachen 30-Köln 35

HEFTER 16/20

52351, Kreuzstr. 82
(0 24 21) 1 45 85, Fax 1 45 85 res.

Closed for lunch Sunday, closed Monday, Tuesday, 2 weeks in January/February and during the NRW summer school holiday. Tables d'hôte: 80L, 90/130D, à la carte: 43/88, No Credit Cards

The fact that you have to ring the doorbell to be admitted to this restaurant makes it not so much exclusive as very private. And, in fact, we do have the impression that the Hefters are giving a dinner not for paying guests but for good friends in their originally styled villa. First-class ingredients are prepared with concentration and expertise. One of Hefter's typical compositions is his Bresse pigeon stuffed with foie gras and sweetbreads and accompanied by sensational vegetable purée, potato gratin and kohlrabi. His wafer-thin scampi carpaccio harmonizes with the caviar cream, and the delicately fried pikeperch comes with a savory potato and chive sauce with capers and lovely leaf spinach. Manfred Hefter doesn't want to cook differently than his colleagues, just better than most of them—and he does. Roswitha Hefter supervises her service staff unobtrusively and efficiently. The well-stocked wine list emphasizes German and French wines, including rare Burgundy from Romanée-Conti. For lunch we recommend the low-priced businessmen's prix-fixe menu.

DÜSSELDORF Nordrhein-Westf.

Köln 47-Hannover 295

AALSCHOKKER 15/20

40489, Stadtteil Kaiserswerth
Kaiserswerther Markt 9
(02 11) 40 39 48, Fax 40 36 67 res.
Closed for lunch, closed Sunday, Monday, Easter. Tables d'hôte: 158, à la carte: 55/148

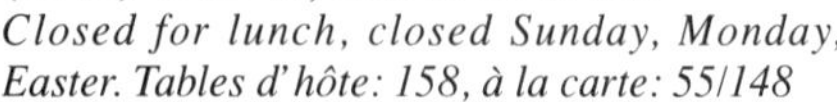

We feel more at home downstairs, where Madame Bourgeuil does the honors with a ready professional smile. Things are more relaxed than in the pseudoaristocratic den above, but the cuisine is just as good, or even better, because you don't have to be a VIP to eat well here. We enjoyed our refined regional cuisine in more spacious and uncramped surroundings than upstairs. The Zeltinger fish potpourri was delicious and, at the same time, highly amusing: the potpourri consisted of only two kinds of fish, salmon and cod. The repertoire includes *labskaus* (a stew made of salted meat, salted herring, red beets and pickles—very popular with sailors) from Hamburg, sweet and sour lobster, foie gras variations, strong-tasting salmon tartare and somewhat dry duck roulade. The prix-fixe menu includes wine.

BENKAY IN HOTEL NIKKO

40210, Immermannstr. 41 [D4]
(02 11) 83 40 , Fax 16 12 16
Tables d'hôte: 65/95, à la carte: 25/77

This Japanese restaurant serves the usual sushi, sashimi and tempura – and for the especially brave, *kinpira gobou* (seasoned black salsify) and subtle fish soups. After extensive rebuilding, the Benkay reopened in late summer 1994, too late for us to test it.

BREIDENBACHER ECK 12/20

40213, Heinrich-Heine-Allee 36
(02 11) 1 30 30, Fax 1 30 38 30 res.

Tables d'hôte: 68, à la carte: 41/83

This dependable restaurant has always catered to the tastes of its conservative Düsseldorf clientele, who prefer good traditional quality fare to fancy gourmet dining. But on our last visit we discovered a progressive (subversive?) influence on the menu. The calf's liver isn't prepared "Berlin style" anymore, but served audaciously in a sesame seed crust. Has the saddle of lamb with pesto, tomato salsa and Roman dumplings infiltrated staid German cuisine?We can sound the "all clear": salads, fillets and soups with *tafelspitz* are still prepared with the usual accuracy, and the time-tested desserts popular with the regular customers haven't changed. The service could use a little freshening up. The very good wines by the glass are moderately priced.

LA CAPANNINA 12/20

40476, Frankenstr. 27
(02 11) 44 16 52
Closed Saturday, closed for lunch Sunday. A la carte: 48/76

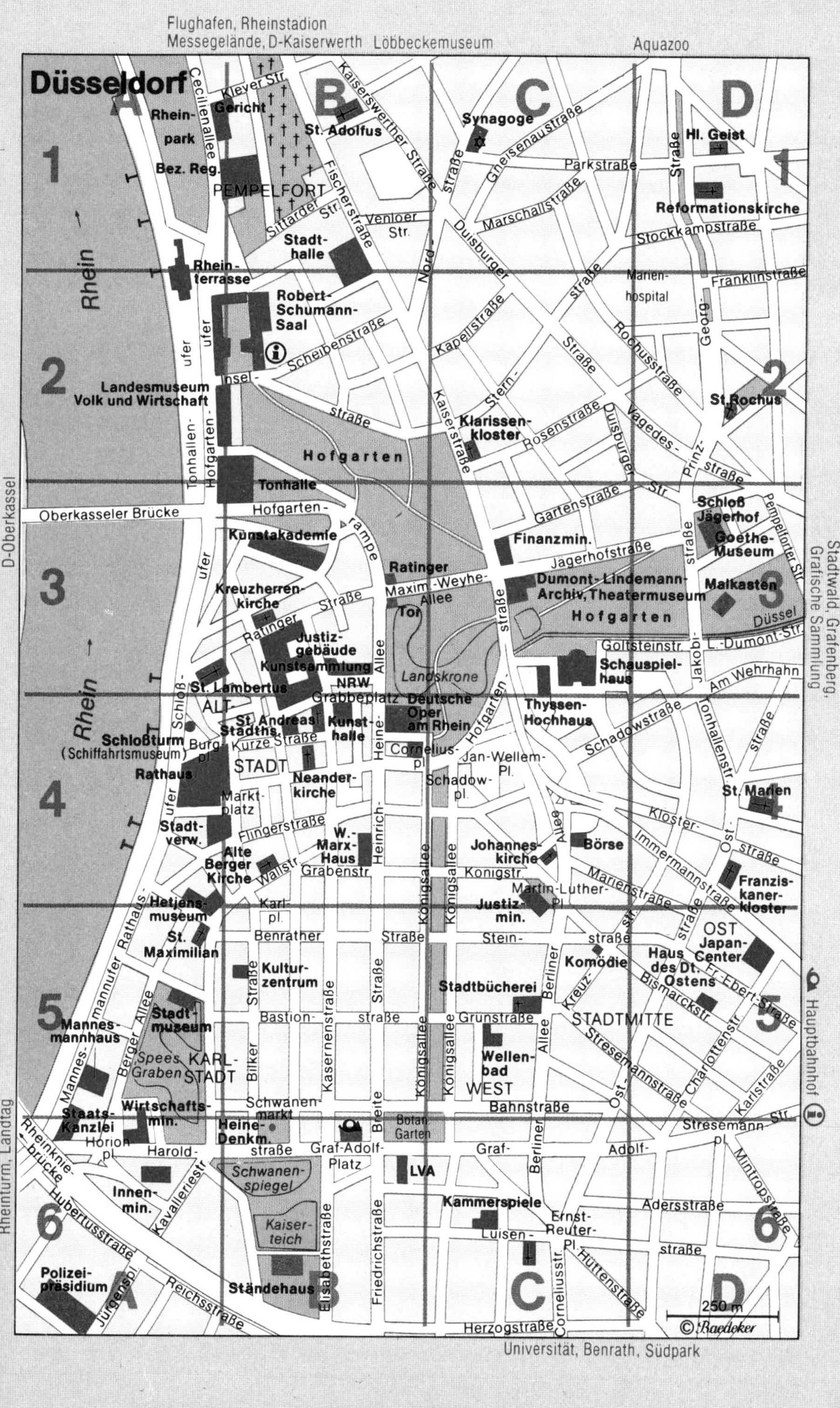

Düsseldorf

Flughafen, Rheinstadion
Messegelände, D-Kaiserwerth
Löbbeckemuseum
Aquazoo

A B C D
1 2 3 4 5 6

Klever Str.
Cecilienallee
Gericht
Rhein-
park
Bez. Reg.
PEMPELFORT
Sittarder Str.
St. Adolfus
Kaiserswerther Straße
Fischerstraße
Venloer Str.
Synagoge
Gneisenaustraße
Nordstraße
Parkstraße
Marschallstraße
Duisburger Straße
Hl. Geist
Reformationskirche
Stockkampstraße
Frankinstraße
Marien-
hospital
Georg-Straße
Stadt-
halle
Rhein-
terrasse
Rhein
Robert-
Schumann-
Saal
Scheibenstraße
Kapellstraße
Rochusstraße
Inselstraße
ufer
Landesmuseum
Volk und Wirtschaft
Tonhallen-
Hofgarten-
Sternstraße
Klarissen-
kloster
Rosenstraße
Kaiserstraße
Vagedes-
Straße
St. Rochus
Prinz-
Georg-Straße
Hofgarten
Tonhalle
Oberkasseler Brücke
Hofgarten-
rampe
Gartenstraße
Duisburger Str.
Schloß
Jägerhof
Pempelforter Str.
Goethe-
Museum
D-Oberkassel
Kunstakademie
Finanzmin.
Jägerhofstraße
Ratinger
Tor
Maxim.-Weyhe-
Allee
Dumont-Lindemann-
Archiv, Theatermuseum
Malkasten
Stadtwald, Grafenberg,
Grafische Sammlung
Kreuzherren-
kirche
Ratinger Straße
Hofgarten
Düssel
Golfsteinstr.
L.-Dumont-Str.
Justiz-
gebäude
Kunstsammlung
NRW
Landskrone
Jakobistraße
Schauspiel-
haus
Am Wehrhahn
St. Lambertus
ALT-
Grabbeplatz
Deutsche
Oper
am Rhein
Thyssen-
Hochhaus
Schadowstraße
St. Andreas
Stadths.
Kunst-
halle
Schloßufer
Schloßturm
(Schiffahrtsmuseum)
Burgpl.
Kurze Straße
Cornelius-
pl.
Jan-Wellem-
Pl.
Hofgartenstraße
Tonhallenstr.
STADT
Heinrich-Heine-Allee
Rathaus
Markt-
platz
Neander-
kirche
Schadow-
pl.
St. Marien
Stadt-
verw.
Flingerstraße
W.-
Marx-
Haus
Johannes-
kirche
Allee
Börse
Kloster-
straße
Immermannstraße
Oststraße
Alte
Berger
Kirche
Wallstr.
Grabenstr.
Königsallee
Königstr.
Martin-Luther-
Pl.
Marienstraße
Franzis-
kaner-
kloster
Hetjens-
museum
Rathausufer
Karl-
pl.
Justiz-
min.
OST
St.
Maximilian
Benrather Straße
Steinstraße
Japan-
Center
Kultur-
zentrum
Komödie
Haus
des Dt.
Ostens
Fr.-Ebert-Straße
Hauptbahnhof
Mannesmannufer
Stadtbücherei
Bismarckstr.
Kasernenstraße
Berliner Allee
Kreuzstraße
Stadt-
museum
Bastion-
straße
Grünstraße
STADTMITTE
Mannes-
mannhaus
Berger Allee
Spees
Graben
KARL-
STADT
Bilker Straße
Wellen-
bad
WEST
Stresemannstraße
Charlottenstr.
Karlstraße
Mannesmannufer
Wirtschafts-
min.
Schwanen-
markt
Breite Straße
Botan.
Garten
Bahnstraße
Ost-
straße
Staats-
kanzlei
Heine-
Denkm.
Stresemann-
pl.
Horion-
pl.
Harold-
straße
Graf-Adolf-
Platz
Graf-Adolf-
Straße
Rheintum, Landtag
Rheinknie-
brücke
Schwanen-
spiegel
LVA
Innen-
min.
Kavalleriestr.
Kammerspiele
Adersstraße
Mintropstraße
Hubertusstraße
Kaiser-
teich
Elisabethstraße
Friedrichstraße
Luisen-
straße
Ernst-
Reuter-
Pl.
Hüttenstraße
Polizei-
präsidium
Jürgensplatz
Reichsstraße
Ständehaus
Corneliusstr.
250 m
Herzogstraße
© Baedeker

Universität, Benrath, Südpark

This is a pleasantly decorated restaurant without the usual Italian kitsch. Although the antipasti are not any better here than in other Italian restaurants, the pasta dishes are wonderful. Best of all is the irresistible charm of owner Paolo Biagianti, who makes you feel like an old friend. It is pure enjoyment to hear him recommend wines or to watch him dress a fruit salad. The staff, on the other hand, seems annoyed when customers want to order.

CAVEAU (MÖVENPICK)
40212, Königsallee 60 [C5]
(02 11) 32 03 14,

Closed for lunch Sunday

The successful recipe of this former vaulted wine cellar, situated in the Mövenpick-complex on the famous Königsallee, is simple. Self-service, a choice of about 15 wines by the glass, moderately priced snacks and light bistro-type meals make this a nice place to eat a little something or to conduct private wine tastings.

EDO 13/20
40547, Stadtteil Oberkassel
Am Seestern 3
(02 11) 59 10 82/3, Fax 59 13 94 res.

Closed Sunday. Tables d'hôte: 20/80L, 85/160D, à la carte: 44/97

A wooden teahouse and a Japanese garden complete with waterfall make up a little Tokyo in the middle of Düsseldorf. There is a tempura room with tables and chairs; a teppanyaki room, where the customers sit at a bar facing the cook; and (by special reservation) a tatami room with traditional Japanese service. The service is friendly, but there are some language problems. Avoid the desserts and the expensive but mediocre wines and have tea, beer or sake instead. Kampai!

FÜCHSCHEN
40213, Ratinger Str. 28/30 [B3]
(02 11) 8 40 62, Fax 32 45 47

A la carte: 12/21

Everybody should know by now: If you value your health, your purse and your mind, don't eat in Düsseldorf's Altstadt, and drink only at a few chosen locations. One of the places where you can do both without coming to harm is the original brewery pub Füchschen. The fresh draught beer is praised by connoisseurs and consumed by enthusiasts. The Füchschen butchers its own pork and beef and serves hearty and savory plain fare. Don't let the rough wooden tables, your boisterous neighbors or the familiar service irritate you. It's all part of the ambience.

GUISEPPE VERDI 14/20
40595, Stadtteil Benrath
Paulistr. 5
(02 11) 7 18 49 44, Fax 7 18 20 53 res.

P

Tables d'hôte: 78/100, à la carte: 48/86. Tables d'hôte with wine: 130/150

Not surprisingly, the music of Maestro Verdi (on CD) welcomes customers to this tastefully decorated restaurant with dark wood paneling, a red ceiling, white curtains and rough plastered walls. Pasquale Messere offers stimulating, imaginative Italian cuisine, including a carpaccio of duck's breast with a sauce of anchovies and olives, and superb pasta with seafood. The pasta with a foie gras sauce and the lamb roast with garlic and rosemary were well-balanced culinary compositions. For a finale, we recommend sheep's cheese with honey and pears. Da capo!The choice of Italian wines is excellent, the service rapid and discreet.

HUMMER-STÜBCHEN 16/20
40547, Stadtteil Lörick
Bonifatiusstr. 35
(02 11) 59 44 02, Fax 5 97 97 59 res.

P

Tables d'hôte: 159, à la carte: 84/125

It is just a short walk from the Landhaushotel through a pretty forest down to the yacht harbor and the banks of the Rhine, but most customers do not want to take more than the few steps from the parking lot to the restaurant. The lovely pastel decor and opulent floral arrangements cannot hide the fact that the tables are set much too close together; you can't help hearing your neighbors' conversations. The waiters run a quick slalom around the chairs, destroying any illusion that you are enjoying an idyll on the banks of the Rhine. The cuisine is superb, made with only the choicest and most luxurious ingredients. Chef Peter Nöthel probably couldn't cook a cream of potato soup without putting lobster, foie gras and truffles in it! No wonder that the least-expensive main course costs 59 DM.The foie gras praline was a delicious appetizer, but the truffles, quince jelly and brioche served with it were overkill. The salad of lobster with chanterelles was exquisite, but did not need to be followed by lasagne with (another) lobster and (more) truffles? For customers who are shocked by the prices on the magnificent wine list, we'll let you in on a secret: moderately priced wines by the glass are available but not listed on the menu.

IM SCHIFFCHEN 16/20

40489, Stadtteil Kaiserswerth
Kaiserswerther Markt 9
(02 11) 40 10 51, Fax 40 36 67 res.

Closed for lunch, closed Sunday and Monday. Tables d'hôte: 164/196, à la carte: 83/194

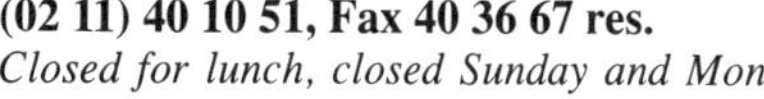

In a historic building erected in 1733, Claude Bourgueil runs two restaurants at the same time. We visited the beletage [query] paneled with cherry wood, which offers a showy version of classic French cuisine. The diners Bourgueil treats as VIPs think he's the best cook in Germany. He doesn't know us. Most of those who climb the steep stairs to sit in the cramped and inhospitable Schiffchen, where the diners at the next table have to (over) hear everything you're saying, are convinced that expensive food must be good food and usually order the super prix-fixe menu with a great many courses. We obnoxiously ordered à la carte and had an exquisite appetizer, a salmon mousse with lobster wrapped in seaweed with chive sauce, followed by variations of foie gras. Some, like the fried foie gras, were delicate; others, like the musty and fatty terrine, almost inedible. The combination of sweetbreads and snails with truffled butter was a fabulous marvel of exquisite taste, whereas the little Brittany lobster steamed in camomile was almost raw, the nicely done Bresse pigeon breast tasteless under an almost burnt crust and the saddle of lamb stringy and without aroma. The modest champagne of the house is poured with a ceremony befitting (at least) a Roederer Cristal. The high-carat wine list is appreciated by businessmen with liberal expense accounts.

KÖ-STÜBLI

40212, Königsallee 60 [C5]
(02 11) 13 22 40, Fax 32 80 58 res.

 P

Closed Sunday, à la carte: 36/65

If you want to escape from the bustle of the Königsallee, just dive into this quietly idyllic little restaurant with its pretty terrace. The small menu offers mainly seafood (flawlessly prepared), bouillabaisse, lamb ribs and Angus steak. Caviar variations are a popular specialty. Champagne and wines by the glass can be ordered from the reliable Mövenpick list.

LIBANON RESTAURANT 12/20

40213, Bergerstr. 19-21 [B4]
(02 11) 32 95 93

Tables d'hôte: 52/94, à la carte: 27/38

The Libanon Restaurant on the Berger Strasse is one of the exceptions to our rule never to eat in Düsseldorf's chaotic Altstadt. This culinary oasis, however, with its marble, Oriental mirrors and lamps, fountains and opulent shrubbery seems like an exotic seraï. Grilled lamb cutlets, beef tartare, fabulously succulent chicken, warm sheep cheese in pastry crust, puréed eggplants and chick-peas are highlights of the original Arabic cuisine offered here. Belly dancing is an unavoidable "treat" Wednesday to Saturday.

LIGNANO 13/20

40597, Stadtteil Benrath
Hildenere Str. 43
(02 11) 7 11 89 36, Fax 7 11 89 59 res.

P

Closed for lunch Saturday, closed Sunday. Tables d'hôte: 74/95, à la carte: 44/73

You do not have to know exactly where Lignano is on the map of Italy to enjoy this place. Decorated in soft pastel colors, this restaurant has nothing to do with folkloristic trattorias with fishing nets and seashells on the walls. There is a small choice of à la carte dishes and two fixed-price menus. The pasta dishes have just the right consistency, and we can also recommend the fresh sturgeon with its light butter sauce, the perfectly prepared saddle of lamb and the tangy grapefruit sorbet.The service is charmingly attentive, and the excellent wine list features fine vintages from Friaul and Piemont but offers only a meager selection of half-bottles and wines by the glass.

MENUETT 10/20
40213, Corneliusplatz 1 [C4]
(02 11) 1 38 10, Fax 1 38 15 70 res.

P

Tables d'hôte: 63L, 85/115D, à la carte: 44/99

The new name of the former Rôtisserie in Steigenberger's Parkhotel is misleading. The cuisine reminds one more of a heavy-footed polonaise than the light steps of a rococo dance. On nice summer evenings you can sit on the lovely terrace; otherwise, guests often feel a little lost in the grand dining hall, at the mercy of a staff that doesn't even manage to serve a few guests without mishaps.Monstrous compositions are characteristic of the menu, for example: sheatfish fillet fried in herbs with marinated lentils and barley, and a potato and cabbage omelet. The specialties of the day aren't always pleasant surprises. The eggplant lasagna with grilled John Dory on *tafelspitz* had all flavor cooked out of it and the kohlrabi soufflé with lamb cutlets tasted watered down and warmed up.

MEUSER
40547, Stadtteil Niederkassel
(02 11) 55 12 72 res.

Closed for lunch, closed Monday, 2—24 July. No Credit Cards, à la carte: 18/38

Meuser's is an institution in Düsseldorf. The sixth generation serves the famous dark draft beer (called Altbier) in the historic house built in 1641. Little seems to have changed since then. Stockbrokers, art students and salesgirls sit side by side at scoured wooden tables and enjoy pancakes with bacon and pickles (at 18 DM for two people) with their beer. On very busy days (almost every day), when there is only standing room left in the courtyard, the waiters tend to get a little confused.

NAPALAI 13/20
40212, Königsallee 60 [C5]
(02 11) 32 50 81, Fax 8 64 21 17 res.

Closed for lunch Monday. Tables d'hôte: 61/138, à la carte: 37/76

This Thai restaurant deserves its popularity. The large and dusky dining room on the first floor, with a lot of teak and green plants, is almost always full. The waitresses in Asiatic dress are exceptionally polite, nimble and efficient and the seasoning of the Thai dishes (milder for European palates) is explained in the menu. Try one of the prix-fixe suggestions if you want to get a taste of the great variety of Thai cooking. We liked our duck with green curry, chicken with ginger and shrimps with fried rice noodles. The vegetables in coconut milk are fabulous and the mushroom soup with chicken delicious. Don't expect too much of wines or desserts.

DAS RESTAURANT 13/20
40474, Karl-Arnold-Platz 5
(02 11) 45 53 11 36, Fax 4 55 31 10 res.

Tables d'hôte: 48L, 79D, à la carte: 34/70

The interior of international-hotel elegance and the lovely view into the garden is unchanged, but since Michael Hau left his kitchen in the hands of his sous-chef, the cuisine steers a zigzag course through international dishes. Sometimes it drifts a little starboard toward Asia, but curried chicken with basmati rice sweeps nobody off his feet anymore. At other times the accent is more local, and guests can enjoy a Düsseldorf mustard roast, an indigent terrine of lobster and squab with dull salad greens and a watery cream of red lentil soup. This zigzag course, however, may also bring you to happier gourmet grounds, for instance to fried king prawns with ginger mousse or an excellently done (if tiny) saddle of lamb under a crust of yogurt and basil.

ROBERTS BISTRO 14/20

40219, Wupperstr. 2
(02 11) 30 48 21

Closed Sunday, Monday, 1 week at Easter, first part of the NRW summer school holiday, 1 week following 22 December. No Credit Cards, à la carte: 29/59

The popularity of Robert Hülsmann's bistro has not abated. Although the decorating scheme of this street-corner pub has all the charm of an office building, the cream of Düsseldorf society still stands in line to get a seat at one of the wobbly tables covered with paper napkins. When they finally get in, they have a choice of more than 50 dishes on a menu that includes a salt cod mousse with Savoy cabbage, crab and grilled sausages, but no desserts. Some of the bistro dishes have become classics: warm duck giblets, a seafood dish with oysters, crabs and shrimps, the skate with butter or a dish called "the best," with sweetbread, tongue, foie gras and salad. Everything is prepared with exacting care, generous portions and reasonable prices. On Saturday mornings, a great breakfast is served. The wine list is nailed to the wall, but that does not mean the prices are low. The staff does its best, as quickly as possible.

ROSATI

40474, Felix-Klein-Str. 1
corner of Kaiserswerther Str.
(02 11) 4 36 05 03, Fax 45 29 63 res.

 **P**

Closed for lunch Saturday, closed Sunday. Tables d'hôte: 49L, 98D, à la carte: 45/77

Remo and Renzo Rosati can count on their fans and their regular guests. This ristorante is pleasant, almost elegant, the wines are affordable and the service is so confiding and friendly that we overlook some lapses. Antipasto and desserts aren't better than those of other Italian restaurants, but the pasta is always fresh and truly al dente. You can order food to go in the adjacent Rosatidue.

SAVINI 13/20

40221, Stromstr. 47
(02 11) 39 39 31, Fax 39 17 19

P

A la carte: 44/72

Now that the facade has been "lifted," the old Interconti looks much more attractive. It even has a new sunken swimming pool with an adjoining garden. The air-conditioned rooms have all been completely renovated and are comfortable, even though the bathrooms are still tiny. If you can afford to spend more money, take suites 736/738 or 836/838. Amenities include a solarium, masseur and fitness center. Lufthansa has its own check-in counter here. For a bite or a drink, try the Café de la Paix or the Bar Kürassier Lounge. Breakfast: 28.50 DM.

VICTORIAN 18/20

40212, Königstr. 3a [C4]
(02 11) 32 02 22, Fax 13 10 13 res.

Closed Sunday and holidays. Tables d'hôte: 55/85L, 130/160D, à la carte: 57/110

This gourmet restaurant on a little side street off the famous Königsallee is the cream of the crop in Düsseldorf. The functionally styled restaurant is on the first floor, with a beautiful banquet hall in pastel shades above. Is this the best kitchen in Düsseldorf? We've heard some complaints but couldn't find a fault, try as we might. The kitchen staff cooks flawlessly: the red mullet was perfect, the anglerfish with green peppers just lovely. The saddle of venison was as outstanding as the ragout with chanterelles and leek aspic. The fillet of lamb with a crust of olives seemed a little tame in comparison. More exciting were the appetizer of turbot with a potato crust served with spinach and truffles and the daring but delectable breast of pheasant with foie gras stuffing served with sauerkraut and champagne.The service is perfect, and the sommelier is both competent and charming.

BISTRO IM VICTORIAN 13/20

40212, Königstr. 3a [C4]
(02 11) 32 02 22, Fax 13 10 13

Closed Sundays from May through September. A la carte: 28/69

What used to be the Victorian Lounge has been transformed into a bistro with something of a waiting-room atmosphere.The intelligently composed menu includes dishes that are changed daily. The foie gras terrine with apple was superb. We were also pleased with Sevruga caviar with potato salad, liver dumplings with sauerkraut, fine fish and baked tripe. Typical bistro fare is also available: lamb's lettuce with scampi, pasta with vegetables and crabs. Beside the noble wines on the comprehensive list, there is also draft beer from a Duisburg brewery.The service is prompt and pleasant.

HOTELS

BREIDENBACHER HOF

40213, Heinrich-Heine-Allee 36
(02 11) 1 30 30, Fax 1 30 38 30

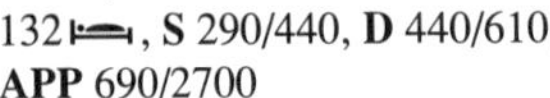

132, **S** 290/440, **D** 440/610,
APP 690/2700

This is no doubt the most extravagant hotel in the capital of North Rhine-Westphalia. Just a few minutes away from the Königsallee, the Altstadt (Old Town) and the banking and business quarter, the hotel still seems more like a private residence. Toned-down colors dominate throughout, and the baths are done in white marble. Everything is decorated true to the hotel's motto: smooth elegance enhanced with exquisite antiques. Every room exhibits its own special flair. The suites impress with the finest materials, private saunas and such lavish extravagances as gilt faucets. The service is ever-present but discreet. Valet parking, room service round the clock and secretarial service are available. A grand breakfast is served in the Grill Royal. The bar and the lobby/lounge are as elegant as the rest.

HILTON

40474, George-Glock-Str. 20
(02 11) 4 37 70, Fax 37 77 91

372, **S** 325/525, **D** 385/565,
APP 675/2350

Situated in the relative peace of a park, the Hilton is easy to reach from the city or the airport thanks to its own highway exit. The public rooms are remarkable: the Grand-Pix-Bar, the Oriental nightclub "1001" and the immense ballroom, the scene of many a Mardi Gras celebration in Düsseldorf. The executive floors have a separate check-in counter. The air-conditioned rooms all have personal computers and fax machines and have nothing in common with the usual ready-made standard of the chain. The service is run smoothly and effectively around the clock, and some staff members even speak Arabic and Japanese! There is a supermodern business center, and guests can even borrow jogging suits and shoes. Breakfast: 29 DM.

SAS ROYAL SCANDINAVIA HOTEL

40474, Karl-Arnold-Platz 5
(02 11) 4 55 30, Fax 4 55 31 10

309, **S** 215/575, **D** 255/653,
APP 595/2950, **1/2P** +39, **P** +78

Now that the facade has been "lifted," the old Interconti looks much more attractive. It even has a new sunken swimming pool with an adjoining garden. The air-conditioned rooms have all been completely renovated and are comfortable, even though the bathrooms are still tiny. If you can afford to spend more money, take suites 736/738 or 836/838. Amenities include a solarium, masseur and fitness center. Lufthansa has its own check-in counter here. For a bite or a drink, try the Café de la Paix or the Bar Kürassier Lounge. Breakfast: 28.50 DM.

STEIGENBERGER PARK-HOTEL

40213, Corneliusplatz 1 [C4]
(02 11) 1 38 10, Fax 1 38 15 70

P

160, **S** 325/425, **D** 430/590,
APP 850/1650, **1/2P** +50

The monumental Park-Hotel, built at the turn of the century, has a first-class location right next to the opera house. The corridors are spacious, and the rooms and suites, most of which have French windows or balconies, are comfortable. The lobby, with its café-lounge, Étoile Bar and adjoining restaurant, is elegant without being showy. Twenty-four-hour service and two parking attendants are available.

DUISBURG

Essen 20-Düsseldorf 24

ANATOLL

47056, Neudorfer Markt 2-4
(02 03) 35 66 37 res.

No Credit Cards. Tables d'hôte: à la carte:

This restaurant offers plain but good Turkish fare with absolutely fresh salads, homemade bread and wonderful compositions of yogurt and goat cheese. Of course, you can order such typical German-Turkish dishes as köfte, kebab and döner. More authentic and much better, however, are the dishes that feature roast lamb with tomatoes and garlic and—why not?—the hearty soup with tripe.

ARLBEGER HOF 13/20

42249, Stadtteil Buchholz
Arlberger Str. 39
(02 03) 70 18 79, Fax 79 64 02 res.

Closed for lunch, closed Sunday, first part of the NRW summer school holiday. No Credit Cards. Tables d'hôte: 59/98, à la carte: 41/75

We were a bit taken aback by the colorful Tyrolean-style gable painted on the wall, but otherwise the interior of this restaurant is subtly decorated and comfortably elegant. The owner's cooking hovers between rustic Austrian fare and the finest gourmet cuisine. That means he offers rack of lamb and turbot with seaweed as well as calf's brains with lentils. The terrine of brook trout and lobster was prepared with a fine hand, but fried black pudding with fresh marjoram, sauerkraut and Riesling was more of a pleasure. If a full house keeps you waiting for a table, pass the time by trying the famous Austrian wines from the Wachau and the Burgenland, which are sold by the glass or by the bottle.

DETTMANN'S RESTAURANT 14/20

47055, Kalkweg 26
(02 03) 72 57 90, Fax 72 92 13 res.

Closed for lunch Saturday, closed Monday, 1—15 January. Tables d'hôte: 59L, 62/75D, à la carte: 41/74

The gourmets of this region now have another good address. Once a pub that only offered plain fare, this nicely furnished restaurant with an attentive young service staff now cooks hearty traditional regional dishes, vegetarian meals (leek soup with goat cheese) and gourmet cuisine (fish strudel with lobster). Some combinations seem a little forced, such as squid salad with green asparagus and zucchini blossoms, or fried terrine of guinea fowl and morels with roasted foie-gras cubes. The choice of wines is surprisingly good and moderately priced.

DUISBURGER HOF

47051, Neckarstr. 2
on König-Heinrich-Platz
(02 03) 33 10 21, Fax 33 98 47

111, **S** 185/265, **D** 280/380,
APP 435/635, **1/2P** +40, **P** +75

This quiet (for a city) hotel remains number one in Duisburg. In spite of zealous redecorating of the rooms and the spacious corridors, it still seems old-fashioned. The relatively large baths usually have windows looking out on the world. Wide gastronomic variety is available in the restaurant.

GASTHOF BRENDEL 13/20

47229, Stadtteil Friemersheim
Kaiserstr. 81
(02 03) 4 70 16, res.

No Credit Cards. A la carte: 25/60

Instead of serving lobster and foie gras, Chef Dirk Brendel puts the emphasis on the regional products he buys from his neighbors. He won't tell you where to buy it, but he'll give you cleaned tripe to carry home if you want it. For his countrified bistro dishes, he doesn't skimp on arugula or romaine lettuce. The blood pudding is first class, and the calf's brains with a crust of shallots and mustard is just as hearty, but slightly lacking in refinement. Some regional dishes are described in German dialect on the menu. The menu is too large for the small kitchen staff, who have problems with fish and mediocre desserts. There is a very respectable choice of wines, including 18 wines by the glass.

LA PROVENCE 17/20

47051, Hohe Str. 29
(02 03) 2 44 53, res.
Closed for lunch Saturday, closed Sunday, 10—23 April, 2 weeks during the NRW summer school holiday, 22 December through 7 January. No Credit Cards. Tables d'hôte: 93L, 105/140D, à la carte: 56/98

In a neighborhood populated with grocery stores, Turkish fast-food restaurants and belly-dancing studios, Klaus-Theo Friederichs offers gourmet food for those are unable to travel to Provence in France to enjoy its fine cooking. The small restaurant, with its elegantly set tables and beamed ceiling, creates an intimate atmosphere. The cuisine is grand, but not pompous. And when chef Theo Friederichs comes out of his kitchen to help you choose from the menu, you feel like a friend of the family. Some classic dishes are in great demand, including the superbly prepared pigeon with chanterelles, the heavenly turbot with lentils and truffled noodles, and the raw salmon slices with champagne sauce. The kohlrabi purée with lobster and the flavorful cream of curry soup with anglerfish were exquisite. Friederichs offers his customers an unparalleled selection of cheeses.

LA VILLA 12/20

47058, Mülheimer Str. 213
(02 03) 33 04 80
P
A la carte: 36/67

This Italian restaurant, located between the university and the zoo, is a nice place in summer, when you can sit outside and enjoy pasta al dente or a lovely salad. The antipasto and fresh and tasty fish are prepared without frills in a traditional Italian way. Very pleasant service and a respectable choice of Italian wines.

WEBSTER

47051, Dellplatz 14
(02 03) 2 30 78, Fax 28 40 79 res.

Closed 24—29 December. A la carte: 21/45

On weekends, young people overrun this brewery inn and the service staff is slightly out of breath. Take a large draught of the lovely mellow light or dark beer fresh from the tap, or try the seasonal specialties. The kitchen serves plain fare from noon till 11 p.m.

WEISSES GASTHAUS 12/20

47199, Grafschafter Str. 197
(0 28 41) 8 1 11, Fax 85 10 res.
Closed for lunch, closed Monday. A la carte: 33/66

Duisburg has its pastoral spots. This beautiful old house near the river is furnished with plain wooden tables and has a dining terrace in back and a beer garden under old chestnut trees. Regular customers drive up in their Mercedes or run in on their sneakers to feed on simple spaghetti or the traditional *pillekuchen,* a pancake with sliced potatoes. But you can also have nicely roasted lamb or fresh lobster. The service is so-so, and you are better off ordering a perfectly drawn beer than one of the middling wines.

DURBACH Baden-Württ.

Offenburg 7-Baden-Baden 54

REBSTOCK 12/20

77770, Halbgütle 256
(07 81) 48 20, Fax 48 21 60 res.
P
Closed for dinner Sunday during the winter, closed Monday, 15 January through 15 February, first week in August. Tables d'hôte: 35/68, à la carte: 30/65

At the end of the valley behind Durbach stands this restaurant, which has developed into an impressive gastronomic complex over the years. The extensive parking lot gives you an idea of how many visitors two restaurants, a conference center, a hotel and large terrace under immense trees can accommodate. That's one of the reasons why coordinating kitchen and service is sometimes difficult. Franz Baumann offers everything that's anything: duck, sweetbreads, steaks and fillets and fish and game in many different versions as well as Swabian specialties. The wine list features French vintages and regional wines.

ZUM RITTER 13/20

77770, Badische Weinstr. 1
(07 81) 3 10 31, Fax 4 19 75 res.

P

Closed for lunch Monday. Tables d'hôte: 48/130, à la carte: 41/88

Chef Wilhelm Brunner seems just as inflexible as an almost immovable knight ("Ritter") in his clumsy armor. He serves the same cuisine he served years ago, with the same highlights and even the same flaws. His shrimp cocktail with endive salad is still dressed with a penetrating sauce, and foie gras pralinés and fresh lobster remain time-tested standard dishes. We'd like to see more regional classics. The wine list includes pages of Durbach wines and a few French and Italian names. The service is competent. Just one thing has changed here: the three-course prix-fixe menu starts at 48 DM.

ZUM RITTER

77770, Badische Weinstr. 1
(07 81) 3 10 31, Fax 4 19 75 res.

  P

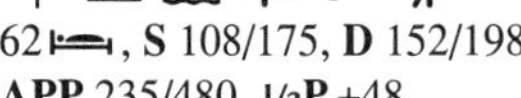

62, **S** 108/175, **D** 152/198,
APP 235/480, **1/2P** +48

This half-timbered house is about 400 years old and has been run as *Gasthof* by the Brunner family since 1901. Renovated on a grand scale just a short time ago, it offers true luxury in the country. A walk through the vineyards begins at the back doorstep. Prices go up in holiday season.

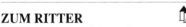

EBERBACH Baden-Württ.

Heidelberg 33-Heilbronn 55

TALBLICK 14/20

69430, Ortsteil Brombach
Geisbergweg 5
(0 62 72) 14 51, Fax 31 55 res.

P

Closed for lunch every day except Sunday, closed Monday, Tuesday, 7—31 January, 10—30 July. Tables d'hôte: 85, à la carte: 28/74, No Credit Cards

Take the road through Hirschhorn to get to this lovely restaurant in the middle of a beautiful forest populated by deer, hare, fox and and the occasional forest ranger. Siegfried Haberstroh's success lies in his combination of traditional recipes and regional specialities (game, of course) in his fine cuisine. We sampled the delicate salmon, served with fresh fried potato cakes and garnished with applesauce and horseradish, and superb consommé with excellent marrow quenelles. All seafood was absolutely fresh; the perfectly prepared fillet of sole with spiny lobster tails was a highlight. The entrecôte was marvelous, but the asparagus a little underdone. The kitchen deserves applause—and a higher rating.The rather small wine list includes affordable vintages, and the service is attentive, friendly and unpretentious.

EBERSBERG Bayern

Wasserburg 22-München 31

SIEGHARTSBURG 12/20

85560, Sieghartstr. 8
(0 80 92) 2 11 2

Closed for dinner Sunday, closed Monday, 1—15 January, à la carte: 29/64

Situated right in the middle of a pretty town, this restaurant has a wood-paneled interior and comfortably furnished dining room. The service is pleasant and dependable, and the kitchen staff cooks with a kind of serene competence. The prices are not low, but portions are large and most dishes dishes are well prepared: cream of morel soup, for instance, with a pastry crust, carpaccio with fried quail's egg, or salad with asparagus in a spicy marinade. The boned and truffled quail with duck livers was a pleasant surprise, as was the hare with spaetzle and cranberries. The desserts, however, are unimaginative.The wine cellar offers a choice of 20 vintages and some good, moderately priced wines by the glass.

ECKERNFÖRDE Schl.-Holst.

Schleswig 20-Kiel 30

KIEKUT 12/20

24340, Altenhof
(043 51) 4 13 10, Fax 49 24 res.

 P

Closed Tuesday, closed for dinner Wednesday, month of February, 2 weeks in November. Tables d'hôte: 59/79D, à la carte: 28/67

The classic fresh cuisine served here in this compact little thatched cottage on the beach is popular with both natives and tourists. We liked our generously garnished fish soup, plaice fried in butter and tasty saddle of lamb raised on the salt meadows here. If you get tired of fighting off flies in the rustically furnished dining room, you can sit on a lovely terrace in the summer. The choice of wines is adequate and the service is quick and helpful.

EGGENFELDEN Bayern

Passau 74-München 120

BACHMEIER 13/20

84307, Schöauer Str. 2
(0 87 21) 30 71, Fax 30 75

P

Tables d'hôte: 30/35L 75/95D, à la carte: 34/66

The trendy Bachmeier in Eggenfelden can be depended on for high quality. The semolina dumpling soup is simple and good, as are the fresh salad with delicious marinated *tafelspit,* the tasty fish dumplings with vegetables, the first-class fillet of beef with shallots and crisply roasted potatoes, the saddle of lamb with fine herbs, and the rabbit leg. Meals are topped off with light desserts.The small wine list is stocked with German wines, nice Austrian vintages from the Wachau, and Italian and French wines at reasonable prices. The service is attentive and correct.

BACHMEIER

84307, Schöauer Str. 2
(0 87 21) 30 71, Fax 30 75

P   

40 , **S** 75/85, **D** 110/130,
APP 130, **½P** +28, **P** +45

The hosts describe their accommodations as ranging from *"gemütlich"* (cozy, hospitable and homey) to luxurious—whatever that means. An old-fashioned charm pervades the bedrooms, whereas the convention rooms are modern and functional. The breakfast room could be a little more gemütlicher. There is a fitness center. The Bachmeiers also run the lounge of the nearby 18-hole golf course.

EGGSTÄTT Bayern

Seebruck 13-Rosenheim 26

LANDHAUS EGGSTÄTT 12/20

83125, Frühlingstraße
(0 80 56) 8 96

 P

Tables d'hôte: 25/35, à la carte: 21/62

Midway between Prien and the old Benedictine monastery of Seeon you'll find an quiet oasis for gourmet enjoyment in Eggstätt. The dining rooms are comfortable furnished, the terrace is lovely and the menu enticing. We liked our savory venison consommé with ham quenelles and an appetizing tartare of herring marinated in red wine with potato pancake. Besides angler fried in butter and John Dory or sheatfish poached in a beet consommé, gourmets find game galore. We enjoyed saddle of venison coated with pumpernickel, breast of pheasant wrapped in bacon with raisins and wild duck's breast in potato crust. The wines are moderately priced, and the service is pleasant and attentive.

EHRENBERG Hessen

Wasserkuppe 9-Mellrichstadt 24

ZUR KRONE

36115, Seiferts
Eisenacher Str. 24
(0 66 83) 2 38, Fax 14 82

Closed Wednesday, à la carte: 19/39

The mountains and valley of the Rhön region draw hikers in summer and skiers in winter. The restaurants here are much less inviting than the landscape, with one exception. The ambitious "Krone" in the little village of Ehrenberg offers its guests hearty regional fare made from homegrown products. The savory lamb sausages with leeks and potatoes with pear mustard are a must, as are the "Rhöner Hirtenpfanne" with minced lamb, savoy cabbage, crème fraîche and potatoes and the "Rhönlammtiegel," in which pieces of lamb are marinated in cider and honey. The trout are caught in the nearby ponds. The desserts are as good as Grandma used to make. The service is quick and attentive. Homemade cider and beer are served; there's no wine list.

EICHENZELL Hessen

Fulda 7

ZUR ALTEN BRAUEREI 14/20

2.5 km west in Löschenrod
36124, Frankfurter Str. 1
(0 66 59) 12 08

Closed for lunch Saturday, closed Monday. Tables d'hôte: 34L, 68/120D, à la carte: 32/71, Tables d'hôte with wine: 35/68, No Credit Cards

The Hübsch family seems to have followed our advice—the cooking is now simper but better. French cuisine has not been completely banished from the menu, however. Brittany lobster, Charolais beef and native game and fowl are all available. With dishes like slivered veal in cream, breast of ox, and three kinds of fillet, the restaurant tries to cater to the tastes of a new clientele that does not want to spend more than 30 DM for a main course. After an excellent salad, we were disappointed with the variety of first courses heaped in a confused mess on our plate. The turbot with kohlrabi cream and leeks was first class, but the fillet of suckling calf fried with duck liver in a hearty Sauterne sauce was as disappointing as the desserts. Many things are nearly perfect here, however: the service is pleasant, the decor is elegant and the wine list is comprehensive. One minor gripe: the menu is written on a first-grade level, which is sometimes amusing but more often irritating. The cuisine deserves better. Until chef Robert Hüsch stops entertaining his customers at the expense of his cooking, a second toque is out of the question.

EICHHORST Brandenburg

Eberswalde 18

JAGDSCHLOSS HUBERTUSSTOCK 13/20

16244, northwest of the village
(03 33 63) 5 00, Fax 5 02 55 res.

A la carte: 27/70.

A bellowing stag shows the way to this simple, modern restaurant in an old manor house where good cooking is flawlessly served. We liked our juicy breast of ox, fresh saddle of hare with homemade nut spaetzle, poached pike-perch with mustard sauce, and lightly fried whitefish from Uckermark. The four-course fixed-price meal was a delicious composition of brook trout remoulade, consommé of guinea fowl, fillet of beef with potato gratin and orange soufflé.The choice of wines by the glass is good. The wine cellar has been stocked with additional vintages from France and Italy.

JAGDSCHLOSS HUBERTUSSTOCK

16244, northwest of the village
(03 33 63) 5 00, Fax 5 02 55 res.

17, **S** 50/180, **D** 90/180,
APP 170/350, **1/2P** +35, **P** +70

Prussia's King Friedrich Wilhelm IV built this hunting château in 1849 in the middle of a heath in the true Bavarian style. Aristocrats of the highest nobility spent their honeymoons in these rooms, and prominent German politicians planned international conferences here. Hunting trips can be arranged—as well as sailing on the Werbelinsee, riding in Sarnow, bike rental, billiards, and visits to the monastery of Chorin and the biggest ship lift in Europe. The two suites are unusually roomy and have fireplaces dating from Kaiser Wilhelm's time. The modern apartments in the nearby woods are more comfortable than they look.

EICHSTÄTT Bayern

Ingolstadt 27-Nürnberg 93

ADLER

85072, Markplatz 22
(0 84 21) 67 67/9, Fax 82 83

P

38, **S** 110/140, **D** 150/210,
APP 180/210
Closed 15 December through 15 January

The polished golden eagle over the door, the trademark of this hotel, looks out over the historic town marketplace. The almost 300 year old Baroque building has been completely rebuilt true to historic detail, but with every modern comfort added. The studios offer a particularly attractive view of the marketplace. Architects like to book room 38 far in advance, because its exposed original framework is actually part of the decorating scheme! There is a solarium, and breakfast is served in light, airy salons.

DOMHERRENHOF 15/20

85072, Domplatz 5
(0 84 21) 61 26, Fax 8 08 49

P

Closed Monday, mid-January through mid-February. Tables d'hôte: 35/45L, 85/98D, à la carte: 41/81.

Restaurant critics lead a hard life! After tasting 30 or more saddles of lamb with potato gratin and ratatouille, we are tempted to attribute a fast-food attitude to some gourmet cooks. The same dishes seem to appear on nearly every menu. The Domherrenhof offers a welcome respite from those run-of-the-mill "gourmet" dishes (although even here we were not spared the ubiquitous saddle of lamb with potato gratin and ratatouille!). But we love this light and airy Roccoco-style restaurant, where a pleasant, competent staff serves savory, classic cuisine. Rupert Waldmüller does not like fads and creates his classic dishes with a strong regional accent. Tops on our list were the two kinds of pasta with black truffles, delicious mashed potatoes with sour cream and caviar, tasty bouillabaisse with fish from a nearby brook, and a rib roast of lamb (with the eternal potato gratin and ratatouille!). Rupert Waldmüller does not set off culinary fireworks, but you can spend a wonderful evening in his restaurant. And that is an important part of good eating. The wine list offers some very nice aged Bordeaux at moderate prices and an interesting choice of German wines.

EISENACH Thüringen

Erfurt 48 - Kassel 89

GLOCKENHOF 14/20

99817, Grimmelgasse 4
(0 36 91) 23 40 , Fax 23 41 31

Closed Sunday. Tables d'hôte: 25L, 35/38D, à la carte: 36/48. Tables d'hôte with wine: 37

We enjoy every visit to this charming old frame house with its Art Nouveau flair and a gallery that exhibits the works of local painters. The service is pleasant, and the charming hosts are always present. Rainer Danz's talents as a cook were evident in the duck breast with salad, an outstanding consommé with vegetables and noodles, carefully prepared salmon with asparagus and hollandaise sauce, tender fillet of lamb with leeks, and a gratin of mushrooms and cheese with a sauce that was just lightly seasoned with garlic. Thuringian specialities are also offered.Many German and a few French vintages can be found on the wine list, but the choice of wines by the glass is especially commendable: 36 different wines costing between 3.50 and 7 DM! Wines by the bottle are also moderately priced.

GLOCKENHOF

99817, Grimmelgasse 4
(0 36 91) 23 40 , Fax 23 41 31

22, **S** 135/150, **D** 130/180,
APP 230, **1/2P** +25, **P** +40

This is a clean, family-run hotel with attractive, modern and comfortably furnished rooms and pleasant service. First-class breakfast buffet: 17 DM.

HOTEL FÜRSTENHOF 12/20

99817, Luisenstr. 11-13
(0 36 91) 77 80, Fax 29 36 82

Tables d'hôte: 42L, 39/105D, à la carte: 31/65

The elegant dining room of this hotel has kept its Art Nouveau flair, but the kitchen has to try a little harder to meet the expectations that go with this lovely ambience. Our angler seasoned with aniseed was delicious, but the lobster with saffron a little soft and soggy. We enjoyed the saddle of venison with red cabbage and a touch of rosemary and the apple and chestnut confit. The choice of desserts includes homemade pistachio ice cream and a fruit terrine in aspic, prettily garnished with fresh fruit.The wine list features international scope and high prices.

HOTEL FÜRSTENHOF

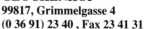

99817, Luisenstr. 11-13
(0 36 91) 77 80, Fax 29 36 82

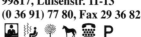

51, **S** 185/240, **D** 225/265,
APP 300/370, **1/2P** +25, **P** +55

Almost every room affords a lovely view of the Wartburg and Eisenach. The furnishings exude atmosphere and are all beautifully made by hand. The rooms are spacious, the bathrooms modern and comfortable. Friendly service.

WEINRESTAURANT TURMSCHÄNKE IN HOTEL KAISERHOF 14/20

99817, Wartburgallee 2
(0 36 91) 21 35 13, Fax 20 36 53

P

Closed for lunch, closed Sunday. Tables d'hôte: 55/78, à la carte: 36/67

Once you've climbed the steep staircase to the tower of the Nikolaitor, you'll be rewarded with an elegant ambience, a lovely view of the Karlsplatz and Luther monument, a good choice of wines (some a little young) and an agreeable cuisine.The lentil salad that accompanied our fried scampi could have used stronger seasoning, but the cold cucumber soup with shrimps and dill was tasty, and our striped mullet with an excellent tomato and zucchini side dish and a sauce of squid and red beets was almost perfect. The saddle of venison with exquisite sauce, chanterelles and oyster mushrooms looked as wonderful as it tasted. The pear marinated in red wine was a soggy (and sorry) companion for our cheese, and the peach with baked vanilla ice cream and puréed raspberries could have been peeled first.The service is pleasant.

HOTEL KAISERHOF

99817, Wartburgallee 2
(0 36 91) 21 35 13, Fax 20 36 53

P

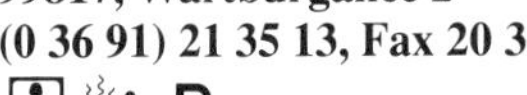

64, **S** 130/150, **D** 170/220, **APP** 280, **1/2P** +22, **P** +44

This formerly pompous but lately run-down Kaiserhof has been renovated on a large scale, preserving its neo-Renaissance style. Restaurants.

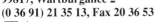

ELTVILLE Hessen

Wiesbaden 14 - Mainz 16

ADLER WIRTSCHAFT 15/20

4 km west in
65347, Hattenheim
Hauptstr. 31
(0 67 23) 79 82, Fax 8 78 67 res.

P

Closed for lunch, closed Sunday and Monday. Tables d'hôte: 72, à la carte: 40/63

This place is extremely popular in the Rheingau, not least because the proprietor likes people and can cook if he has a mind to. Franz Keller's cuisine is unconventional, but doesn't succumb to modern fads. The first courses are opulent and original, but warm and cold dishes are served at the same time. Nobody seems to mind, though, and groups of customers at large tables have fun tasting and exchanging various dishes. The dishes à la carte are a melange of Italian, Provençal and regional German cuisine. The lentil salad with quail's breast, the cassoulet and the rabbit roasted in olive juice were just great. The wine list features the best wine-growing regions and offers a low-priced choice of the house's own wines.

KRONENSCHLÖSSCHEN 16/20

4 km west in Hattenheim
65347, Rheinallee
(0 67 23) 6 40, Fax 76 63 res.

 P

Closed the month of February. Tables d'hôte: 58L, 105/135D, à la carte: 49/94

Patrik Gimpel's performance in the kitchen of this little château is worth two toques. But it takes more than culinary efforts to make diners actually feel like kings of the castle. This restaurant has no soul, no guiding spirit to answer questions, make suggestions or take care of complaints. Anonymous waitresses dressed in something like widows' weeds whisk through somber salons and discourage anything but whispered conversations. No wonder most guests prefer the more lively bistro with its pretty terrace, especially in summer. Only the food provides true enjoyment here, even if the menu offers little variety apart from the excellent prix-fixe meal. All dishes, though, are imaginative and close to perfection, like our highly aromatic ricotta and tomato ravioli with basil, outstanding quail confit with white beans and pesto, finely balanced champagne and mustard soup with sautéed sweetbreads and truly superb strudel of king prawns, scallops and squash compôte. The Stilton marinated in port was a little acrid, but the rhubarb tart with vanilla ice cream was delicious.The wine list emphasizes Rheingau wines and offers only a few nondescript wines by the glass.

KRONENSCHLÖSSCHEN 

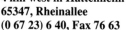

4 km west in Hattenheim
65347, Rheinallee
(0 67 23) 6 40, Fax 76 63

18, **S** 220/290, **D** 250/390,
APP 390/680, **1/2P** +70, **P** +120

The owners have renovated their little château in the heart of the Rheingau as stylishly and exclusively as the enchanting Krone in Assmansshausen. Each room is furnished individually in the best of taste and with every imaginable luxury: marble bathrooms, works of art and fine rugs. The suites have whirlpools and saunas. Breakfast: 22 DM.

PAN ZU ERBACH 16/20

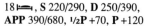

65346, Ortsteil Erbach
Erbacher Str. 44
(0 61 23) 6 35 38, Fax 42 09

Closed Wednesday, Shrove Tuesday, Tables d'hôte: 28/125, à la carte: 49/81, Tables d'hôte with wine: 86/135

The Greek god Pan would like this congenial restaurant bearing his name. The cuisine is fresh and aromatic, and reminds guests of extravagant picnics in green parks. The zucchini piccata with tomato noodles in tarragon sauce was light and lovely, and the smoked sheatfish on lentils delicate and harmonious. The stuffed shoulder of venison with potato ravioli, aspic of kid and elderberry blossom parfait evoked associations of lovely forests and green meadows. Chef Heckl transforms even time-tested sauces that elsewhere usually drown in their own mediocrity—for instance a Frankfurt green sauce or a horseradish sauce.The menu offers a number of exciting à la carte dishes, but the prix-fixe meals are real treats: a small country meal can be had for 28 DM, a four-course refined prix-fixe menu for 60 DM and a surprise prix-fixe menu for 85 DM. The grand gourmet menu with wine costs 125 DM and is a good example of reasonably priced fine food.An absolute must is the gourmet brunch that begins Sunday mornings at 11:00, a steal at 75 DM. The service is agreeably uncomplicated and cheerful, the restaurant elegant and comfortable. The wine list offers a large number of Rheingau wines at moderate prices and a good choice of wines by the glass.

REST. MARCOBRUNN IN SCHLOSS REINHARTSHAUSEN 17/20

65337, Ortsteil Erbach
Hautpstr. 43
(0 61 23) 67 64 32, Fax 67 64 00 res.

Closed for lunch except Sunday, closed for dinner Sunday, closed Monday and Tuesday, closed the month of January, Tables d'hôte: 85/150, à la carte: 64/109

A photographer of cuisine art would have fun with Jochen Wissler's carefully created and beautifully arranged dishes. The appetizer is something to see: we had a tiny shish kebab of kidney pieces and mushrooms, a doll-sized roulade of stuffed quail, a mini potato with crème and a spot of caviar. The original fried headcheese terrine with marinated potato slices was superb, and the clear consommé garnished with succulent pieces of pigeon, mushrooms, sweet onion ravioli and foie gras sheer poetry. The lobster tempura with an exotic ratatouille was flawlessly prepared and our warm smoked salmon on lentils was indescribably flavorful. Wissler cooks with great sensitivity and uncompromising perfection and is the best of a handful of good cooks in the Rheingau.The service is as perfect as the cuisine. Sommelier Kurt Bichler offers a prize-winning collection of 650 wines.The Schlosskeller offers plainer regional fare.

SCHLOSS REINHARTSHAUSEN 

65337, Ortsteil Erbach
Hautpstr. 43
(0 61 23) 67 64 32, Fax 67 64 00

53, **S** 290/340, **D** 340/390,
APP 420/950,
Closed the month of January

After massive rebuilding and renovations, this formerly nondescript château can no longer be overlooked. The late owner invested more than a million marks per bed. Tons of marble and lots of fine parquetry went into this elegant hotel with its banquet and conference rooms, a grand ballroom and creative arts center. The precious paintings rescued from the château's past could fill a museum. There is a sunny conservatory, chic bar, extensive terrace and a marvelous view of the Rhine. Breakfast: 20 DM.The renowned wine cellar has also been renovated and includes a wine shop, a historic cellar with old and rare vintages and a large banquet room for auctions and wine tastings.

EMDEN Niedersachsen

Leer 28 - Oldenburg 95

MUSEUMSSTUBE 12/20

26721, Hinter dem Rahmen 5a
(0 49 21) 2 86 97

Closed for dinner Sunday, closed Monday. Tables d'hôte: 45/75L, à la carte: 31/63

A visit to Henri Nannen's art gallery always makes a trip to Emden worthwhile, and now you can also eat in the same building. We had high hopes and thought the excellent quality of the modern art exhibited here would inspire the cuisine. Nothing doing. The appetizer was a dull beginning, followed by an unimaginative first course. The dry pike-perch and the tough duck's breast obviously came out of the microwave. The sauces, though, were surprisingly good. A mediocre wine list rounds off an uninteresting picture.

EMMENDINGEN BW

Kenzingen 11 - Freiburg 14

KRONE 13/20

3 km northeast in Maleck
79312, Brandelweg 1
(0 76 41) 84 96, Fax 5 25 76 res.

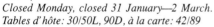

Closed Monday, closed 31 January—2 March. Tables d'hôte: 30/50L, 90D, à la carte: 42/89

Heinrich Will justifies his relatively high prices by the high quality of the product he prepares. For our part, we're always ready to spend a few more marks for opulent accommodations, silver cutlery and elegantly set tables. After all,the flamingos in the park outside have to live, too. The classic cuisine also deserves its merit (and prices). There's plenty of fish and lobster, a great variety of different meats, fowl and game, respectable side dishes, carefully balanced sauces and fresh salads. We found a warm salad with king prawns, salmon in green sauce with noodles, and lovely tangy rhubarb variations especially commendable. The large wine list features French and German wines and many digestifs. Pleasant service.

WINDENREUTER HOF

3 km east in 79312 Windenreute
Rathauseweg 19
(0 76 41) 40 85/87, Fax 5 32 75

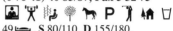

49, **S** 80/110, **D** 155/180,
½P 40, **P** +55

This hotel, with its beautiful and peaceful setting, is perfect for a relaxing holiday. The rooms are well-appointed and each has a balcony affording a lovely view of the Rhine Valley. There are also conference rooms, making this a favorite location for seminars and business meetings. The service is discreet and competent. Restaurant.

ENDINGEN Baden.-Württ.

Breisach 20 - Freiburg 26

SCHINDLER'S RATSSTUBE 12/20

79346, Marktplatz 10
(0 76 42) 34 58

Closed for dinner Sunday, closed Monday. Tables d'hôte: 28/89, à la carte: 30/78

Wine regions generally attract many star cooks, but not the Kaiserstuhl. Schindler's Ratsstube, located on the historic marketplace of Endingen, is one of the few restaurants that try to meet the gourmet demands of fine cuisine. Ignore the numerous showcases with nonsensical bric-à-brac and concentrate on the menu. Max Schindler's strong point is regional cuisine, and he serves hearty and savory dishes, for instance liver and oxtail, Swabian ravioli and variations of ham. Guests can also order more refined food, like duck's breast, excellent venison terrine, succulent fillet of pork with fabulous mushroom ragout, spaetzle and vegetables.Schindler's choice of Kaiserstuhl wines is unsurpassed.

ENZKLÖSTERLE BW

Wildbad 12 - Freundenstadt 28

ENZTALHOTEL 14/20 

75557, Freundenstädter Str. 67
(0 70 85) 1 80, Fax 16 42

Closed Wednesday and Thursday, closed 1—20 December. Tables d'hôte: 50/80, à la carte: 40/73

Extensive redecorating has made an already pleasant setting even prettier and has apparently inspired chef Kurt Braun and his kitchen staff. The gourmet menu started with subtly seasoned shrimp salad with tomato mousse, nicely fried fish (salmon, red mullet and sole) with parsley cream and caviar, and a frothy soup of parsnips with red beet juice. Perfectly poached fillet of pike-perch on spinach with a wonderful champagne sauce, and venison medallions with cream of port and thyme followed. Ice cream and orange slices concluded a wonderful meal. The Swabian clientele also find their beloved lamb's lettuce, brook trout and beef roast on the menu.The choice of German, French and Italian wines at moderate prices is interesting. The service is pleasant and efficient.

ENZTALHOTEL 

75557, Freundenstädter Str. 67
(0 70 85) 1 80, Fax 16 42

50, **S** 110/125, **D** 160/225, **APP** 220/290, **1/2P** +25, **P** +35 *Closed 1—20 December, No Credit Cards*

If you want to spend a relaxing holiday, this is the place for you. The hotel's recreation program offers a variety of sports and activities all year round. The peaceful setting in the picturesque Black Forest; the recently renovated, exquisite apartments; the spacious and elegant lobby with fireplaces and a bar; the breakfast room and restaurant and, last but not least, the modest prices make your stay here a genuine pleasure.

We are always interested to hear about your discoveries, and to receive your comments on ours. Please feel free to write to us, stating your opinions clearly.

EPPINGEN BW

Heilbronn 26 - Pforzheim 37

RESTAURANT FALKENSEE 14/20 

75031, Ortsteil Richen
Berwanger Str. 29
(0 72 62) 18 73, Fax 18 73

Closed for lunch Friday and Saturday, closed Thursday. A la carte: 36/68, No Credit Cards

A visit to this nice little restaurant is always enjoyable. The owner's wife has especially good taste in colors and furnishings, and is also an expert at choosing reasonably priced wines from the well-stocked cellar. In his one-man kitchen, Stefan Karadensky cooks without fault or flaw. Shrimp salad with tomato mousse, for instance, delicious watercress soup, extremely tender fried anglerfish fillets seasoned with saffron and served with chard, lovely saddle of veal and good white chocolate mousse with an excellent fruit sauce.

ERDING Bayern

Freising 16-München 35

ERDINGER WEISSBRÄU

85435, Lange Zeile1
(0 81 22) 1 22 08 , Fax 28 91

A la carte: 19/46, No Credit Cards

The Erdinger Weissbräu can be found in a charming, picturesque old part of town. Under the arches in the vaulted cellar of this restaurant, you can order the well-known *Weissbier* that is brewed here. From 9 in the morning till 1 a.m., customers can enjoy typical Bavarian hospitality as waitresses in traditional dirndl skirts serve pork roast, roast duck or pike-perch fillet.

ERFTSTADT NRW

Euskirchen 18 - Köln 20

RESTAURANT HANS JOSEF ZINGSHEIM 13/20

50374, Ortsteil Kierdorf
Goldenbergstr. 30
(0 22 35) 8 53 32 res.

Closed for lunch except Sunday and holidays, closed Wednesday, Tables d'hôte: 40/60L, 80/115D, à la carte: 36/89, No Credit Cards

Zingsheim doesn't take things easy. For some years now, he's been living the dream of grande cuisine in the country, advertising himself as the leading chef in the region between Köln, Bonn and Aachen. We admire his self-confidence, especially in view of the mediocre cooking we had to put up with on our last visit. The beef carpaccio was seasoned solely with mounds of parmesan, and the tafelspitz was tough and stringy. The kitchen saved on salt for the potatoes and compensated with mountains of tasteless greenhouse salad. If this renovated village inn doesn't want to lose its toque, all dishes must be at least as good as the tasty bass with bacon and butter sauce or the honey crème with eggnog. Zingsheim insists on reservations. Make sure there isn't a large, disturbing celebration planned. The wine list is remarkable, whereas the service could be improved.

ERFURT Thüringen

Leipzig 115 - Kassel 137

CASTELL 13/20

99092, Hermann-Müller-Str. 2
(03 61) 55 67 68, Fax 66 67 68 res.

Closed for lunch, closed for dinner Sunday. Tables d'hôte: 42/76

The performance of the kitchen staff of this beautiful restaurant leaves much to be desired. The fried sweetbreads with a delicate port sauce was not accompanied by the announced fresh salad sprouts but by cold beans and lentils, and the fish soup was flavorless. Still, the anglerfish medallions with (tasteless) mussels in a lightly seasoned curry sauce were outstanding, and the breast of pheasant with cassis cream and young vegetables was very good. Desserts like cream cheese ravioli with orange slices or homemade Grand Marnier ice cream and tropical fruit tasted as good as they looked. We especially enjoyed the fresh warm apple tart and grapes with our coffee. The wine cellar is stocked with international vintages. Customers can choose from a nice selection of half bottles and many good wines by the glass that do not cost a fortune. The service is charming and competent.

ERFORDIA IN HOTEL ERFURTER HOF 12/20

99084, Am Bahnhofplatz 1-2
(03 61) 53 10, Fax 6 46 10 21

P

A la carte: 34/64

Its new decor makes this restaurant elegant and comfortable. The service is pleasant and almost perfect, but the chef arrogantly ignores his customers. We had a very good asparagus salad, calf's tail soup with chervil quenelles, tasty fried sole with spinach, nicely done duck's breast with an almost bitter raspberry vinegar accompanied by underdone sugar peas and a potato crêpe, followed by an opulent fruit gratin with cassis ice cream. The wine list confines itself to a choice of 40 wines from Germany, France and Italy.

ERFURTER HOF

99084, Am Bahnhofplatz 1-2
(03 61) 53 10, Fax 6 46 10 21

173, **S** 200/250, **D** 250/380,
APP 450/500, **1/2P** +28, **P** +50

This house is part of a German hotel chain and is recommended not only for its prime location near the railroad station but for its friendly and pleasant atmosphere. The rooms, suites and apartments of this hotel, built around the turn of the century, have for the most part been renovated and offer all modern amenities. This Grand Hotel offers luxury and proverbial Thuringian hospitality. It has a number of restaurants and cafés as well as the famous Regina Bar, where you can drink and dance till four in the morning. Breakfast and service are first-class: 25 DM.

HOTEL CYRIAKSBURG 12/20

99094, Cyriakstr. 37
(03 61) 6 43 83 72, Fax 6 43 83 73

Closed for dinner Sunday. Tables d'hôte: 35L, 36/55D, à la carte: 25/54

The waitresses make themselves scarce here, but we finally found one who gave us a table. What was announced on the menu as yogurt dressing on marinated asparagus and shrimps turned out to be a simple vinaigrette, and the chicken consommé lacked flavor. The sole with sliced kohlrabi was accompanied by rice, the veal medallions in a sauce of red wine by potatoes. The fresh strawberries with whipped cream seemed a lame excuse for dessert.

HOTEL CYRIAKSBURG
99094, Cyriakstr. 37
(03 61) 6 43 83 72, Fax 6 43 83 73

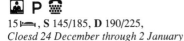

14, **S** 93/163, **D** 183/206,
APP 206/266

This house is part of a German hotel chain and is recommended not only for its prime location near the railroad station but for its friendly and pleasant atmosphere. The rooms, suites and apartments of this hotel, built around the turn of the century, have for the most part been renovated and offer all modern amenities. This Grand Hotel offers luxury and proverbial Thuringian hospitality. It has a number of restaurants and cafés as well as the famous Regina Bar, where you can drink and dance till four in the morning. Breakfast and service are first-class: 25 DM.

ZUM BÄREN
99084, Andreasstr. 26
(03 61) 2 11 13 74 , Fax 2 86 98

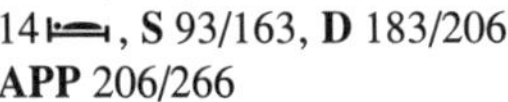

15, **S** 145/185, **D** 190/225,
Cloesd 24 December through 2 January

This house is part of a German hotel chain and is recommended not only for its prime location near the railroad station but for its friendly and pleasant atmosphere. The rooms, suites and apartments of this hotel, built around the turn of the century, have for the most part been renovated and offer all modern amenities. This Grand Hotel offers luxury and proverbial Thuringian hospitality. It has a number of restaurants and cafés as well as the famous Regina Bar, where you can drink and dance till four in the morning. Breakfast and service are first-class: 25 DM.

ERLANGEN Bayern
Nürnberg 18 - Bamberg 40

ALTSTADT
91054, Kuttlerstr. 10
(0 91 31) 2 70 70, Fax 2 82 46

APP 125/180,
Closed 24 December through 3 January

Situated in the center of town, this small hotel offers a pleasant alternative to large and representative houses. Pleasant service and agreeable atmosphere. The redecorated rooms in back are the quietest. Ample breakfast buffet.

BASILIKUM 14/20
91052, Äubere Brucker Str. 90
(0 91 31) 2 73 33, Fax 3 77 88

P

Closed for lunch Saturday, closed Monday. Tables d'hôte: 48/62L, 82/95D, à la carte: 48/84

The trendy interior decorating scheme of this restaurant hints at a lack of a clearly defined image. Its name suggests Italian cooking, but Stephan Unger's cuisine, even though it has a definite Italian touch, has become international. The aroma of Mediterranean herbs and olives accompanies a meal, sauces are lightly seasoned with olive oil, and fish and shellfish are expertly grilled and served with plenty of greens and lovely vinaigrettes. Although his cooking has become simpler and fresher, Unger is still far from the pure, uncompromising cuisine of Southern Europe. Instead, he conforms to the taste of his customers, who prefer international gourmandise with a touch of Italy. On the wine list you'll find famous names and renowned wines of sometimes excellent quality.

GASTHAUS POLSTER 14/20
91056, Ortsteil Kosbach
Am Deckersweiher 26
(0 91 31) 7 55 40, Fax 75 54 45 res.

P

Tables d'hôte: 40L, 73/120D, à la carte: 32/78

It is a well-known fact that Hans Polster cooks well, but he seems intent on proving to himself (and to the world), that he is also a successful businessman. After numerous extensions and alterations of his restaurant, he has now built a country hotel with 13 rooms. His cooking could have used a bit of renovating, too. In fact, the cuisine here ranges from good to excellent. What is irritating is the evident lack of new ideas. Everything looks and tastes the same as it did years ago. Polster's noncommittal international gourmet cuisine leaves no room for creativity. The wine list offers standard good vintages for gourmet meals. The service is more dutiful than pleasant. Those who don't like surprises will like it here.

WEINTRÖDLER 14/20

91054, Ältstädter Kirchenplatz 2
(0 91 31) 2 71 80, Fax 2 71 83

Closed Sunday, Monday, first week in January, 3 weeks in September, Tables d'hôte: 39/46D, à la carte: 32/52, No Credit Cards

A wine merchant does business behind the sandstone facade of this historic house, and an excellent restaurant is also located here. In the small bistro that seats only 25 diners, a young team confines itself to the essentials. Customers sit at scoured wooden tables, use steel cutlery, drink out of functional glasses and pay about half the usual price for such good food. The menu is simple, offering only three or four first courses, a soup and fish course, two main courses and two desserts, but the high quality of the dishes more than makes up for the lack of choice. All the soups contain the quintessence of the products they are made of. The first courses are unusual compositions: fennel with basil and salmon, for instance, or fried sardines with olive mayonnaise. The risotto and pasta dishes are delicious. The main courses are creative but always harmonious, and neither sauces nor side dishes serve mere decorative purposes. Some of our favorite dishes were the wonderful fried fresh cod served with fresh beans, oven-roasted lamb with a tasty ratatouille, and entrecôte with potatoes fried in olive oil and rosemary. The fruit mille-feuille were superb.The comprehensive wine list offers wines at moderate prices and includes some interesting rarities. The charming service makes you feel like a regular customer. The best seats are next to the windows, which have a wonderful view of the idyllic Erlanger Altstadt.

ZUM STORCHENNEST 14/20

9 km north in 91083 Baiersdorf
Hauptstr. 41
(0 91 31) 8 26, Fax 57 44 res.

Closed Sunday, Monday 2—10 January, 3 weeks in August. Tables d'hôte: 85/98, à la carte: 49/81

The days when this restaurant's chef tried to imitate the trendy dishes of prominent colleagues are over. Now Volker Biermann cooks without frills, paying strict attention to his ingredients. Customers can choose from a few à la carte dishes and two fixed-price menus, but the chef respects individual wishes. The Mediterranean menu is a classic, and the haute cuisine is prepared without pomp or pretension. Biermann's fish is first class and his vegetable dishes outstanding. The latter have nothing to do with the sometimes colorful and rarely tasty niceties that often serve only to garnish a main dish. His salads too are more than decoration, always flavorful and served with fresh herbs. You might not find fantastic creativity in Biermann's cuisine, but you'll remember his dishes long after you've left his restaurant.The small but comprehensive annotated wine list is appreciated by wine experts.

ESCHWEGE Hessen

Götingen 55 - Eisnach 36

HOTEL SCHLOSS WOLFSBRUNNEN 14/20

4 km east
in 37376 Meinhard-Schwebda
(0 56 51) 30 50, Fax 30 53 33 res.

 **P**

Tables d'hôte: 25/45L, 52/110D, à la carte: 38/76

A great entrance, noble knights' hall and a mirrored salon impress guests and prepare them for the sumptuous elegance of the dining rooms. In keeping with the splendid ambience of this restaurant, the service is first-class, the wine list magnificent and the kitchen promises "the best." We were served well-fried angler medallions with parsley sauce, ratatouille and vegetable millefeuille, savory calf's tail consommé with excellent sweetbread ravioli, breaded veal roulade stuffed with Parma ham and cheese and accompanied by well-seasoned rosemary sauce and an immense portion of strawberry gratiné with champagne sorbet.

HOTEL SCHLOSS WOLFSBRUNNEN

4 km east
in 37376 Meinhard-Schwebda
(0 56 51) 30 50, Fax 30 53 33

65, **S** 150/245, **D** 195/305,
APP 295/395, **½P** +38, **P** +65

This beautiful hotel is located on a hill above town in the middle of lovely and quiet grounds with a beautiful view over the Werra valley. It offers a grand lobby with fireplace, a number of elegant salons and individually furnished rooms with all modern amenities and spacious bathrooms. Library, bar, pleasant terrace.

ESSEN NRW

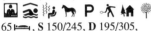

Düsseldorf 32 - Dortmund 38

BENEDIKT IN HOTEL RÉSIDENCE 18/20

45219, Stadtteil Kettwig
Auf der Forst 1
(0 20 54) 89 11, Fax 8 25 01 res.

Closed for lunch, closed Sunday, Monday, 1—7 January, 3 weeks weeks during the NRW summer school holiday. Tables d'hôte: 139/175

The Benedikt was the second restaurant to open in the Hotel Résidence, but only chronologically. Gourmets know that Benedikt's cuisine is more creative and subtler, and the courses of a meal more harmonious than the more classic kitchen of the Résidence. European and Oriental gourmet cooking have have formed an astounding symbiosis here. The traditional French sequence of courses is strictly adhered to, but elements of Thai (sculptured fruit and vegetables) and Japanese (preparation of produce and harmony of flavors) cuisine have been cleverly incorporated. This was the first time we tried foie gras wrapped in won-ton dough and steamed. The salmon sashimi and tagato with saffron formed a harmonious concert of characteristic flavors, and the finely drawn contrast between steamed foie gras and grapefruit was enchanting. In addition to Chinese and Vietnamese influences, the Benedikt also uses Indian spices. The saddle of lamb in tandoori with marinated plums was fantastic, and the pike-perch fried with bananas and served with curry sauce and red-beet noodles tasted as exquisite as it looked.The service and the choice of wines are beyond reproach.

RÉSIDENCE 15/20

45219, Stadtteil Kettwig
Auf der Forst 1
(0 20 54) 89 11, Fax 8 25 01 res.

 P

Closed for lunch, closed Sunday, Monday, 1—7 January, 3 weeks weeks during the NRW summer school holiday. Tables d'hôte: 125/168, à la carte: 70/115

The Bühlers' Art Nouveau villa looks deceptively plain from the outside, but the cuisine that is served inside is as high-class as can be found. The elegant interior is just made for luxurious dining. In summer, customers can eat on the terrace if they don't mind the terribly uncomfortable chairs. The table decorations were creative but discreet, the menus tastefully printed.We've praised Heinz Bach's creativity and consistently excellent performance in the kitchen many times before, so this time we were surprised at the fluctuating quality of the dishes he served us. The often-copied but never-equaled harmony of different flavors he used to achieve has turned into pure cacophony. Consider such exotic compositions as roast duck with glazed rhubarb, kohlrabi and poppyseed pancakes in mocha sauce! Instead of the usual light appetizer, we got a rubbery mass of green peppers and stuffed cucumbers. The sweetbread-filled ravioli with excellent tomato essence were floury and the stuffing hard to identify. The venison cutlet was tough, and its red wine sauce too thick. The galantine of quail's breast and foie gras was simply tasteless. As a peace offering, the kitchen offered us an outstanding plum soufflé, delicious brioches and tasty buns.The large staff provides attentive service, and you can trust the recommendations of the unobtrusive and immensely capable sommelier.

HOTEL RÉSIDENCE

45219, Stadtteil Kettwig
Auf der Forst 1
(0 20 54) 89 11, Fax 8 25 01

P

18, **S** 179, **D** 240, **APP** 350

Closed 1—7 January, 3 weeks weeks during the NRW summer school holiday. Tables d'hôte: 139/175

The rooms in this old villa in a lovely, wooded area of town are not what one would call spacious, but all have mini-bars and color televisions hidden away behind mirrored cupboards. Extras include a complimentary carafe of sherry on arrival and an apple when you leave.

BONNE AUBERGE 13/20

45130, Witteringstr. 92
(02 01) 78 39 99 res.

Closed for lunch Saturday, closed Sunday.Tables d'hôte: 70/119, à la carte: 47/87

This light and pleasant restaurant deserves its name. While the decor and the wine list have distinct Italian accents, the cuisine offers classic French dishes. We liked our delicious variations of lobster and our excellent carpaccio of salmon and angler with green salad. Some dishes need only a little more attention to cooking times and temperatures to be really superb. Especially commendable are light and dainty dishes such as caviar with corn crèpes and chive sauce or enticing mango sorbet with champagne. The service was satisfactory.

LA BUVETTE 14/20

45239, Stadtteil Werden
An der Altenburg 30
(02 01) 40 80 48 res.

Closed for lunch except Sunday. Tables d'hôte: 78/119, à la carte: 59/91, No Credit Cards

This gingerbread house on top of a mountain seems to come right out of "Hansel and Gretel." Inside, it is rustic but elegant and charming. In winter, guests gather around a grand old fireplace in the dining room, and in summer take the air on the idyllic terrace.The kitchen has ended its Asiatic revels and now uses Japanese elements sparingly—in the lobster tempura or the ox teriyaki, for instance. Most dishes are European, but seasoned with more courage and competence than before. Saddle of venison with chanterelles or guinea fowl with gnocchi are good examples. The appetizer was especially lovely: marinated fish tartare with red beets and cucumber. Charmingly attentive service made our stay pleasant. The wine list is well chosen, but high-priced. Some wines are offered by the glass.

EMILE 13/20

45128, Emilienstr. 2
(02 01) 79 13 18 res.

P

Closed Sunday, closed 22 December through 5 January. Tables d'hôte: 25/75, à la carte: 44/68

This restaurant has an uninhibited and cheerful ambience that keeps drawing us back. Every time we come, we find the same relaxed atmosphere and friendly service. Tino Battistella is always willing to find a nice bottle of wine for his customers.Hungry diners cannot go wrong if they follow the menu suggestions chalked on a slate. Our latest meal consisted of duck liver with cassis, and scampi in white wine. The tagliolini with duck ragout and the grilled fresh fish were also excellent. Those who do not want a full meal are welcome to order oysters with their Pinot bianco.

ESSEN-SHERATON

45128, Huyssenallee 55
(02 01) 1 00 70, Fax 1 00 77 77

P

205, **S** 295/495, **D** 360/560,
APP 650/1455, **½P** +50, **P** +99

The tasteful elegance of this Sheraton's interior is a welcome relief from the standard insipid design of other international hotels. The rooms facing the park have the nicest views, but all boast soundproofed windows, air-conditioning and a hair dryer in the bathroom. The hotel includes a piano bar, fitness club and the chic "Papageno" disco.

LA FONTAINE 13/20

45127, Hagen III
(02 01) 22 71 67, res.

Closed Sunday and holidays, closed for dinner Monday. Tables d'hôte: 23/39L, 70D, à la carte: 36/72

This restaurant (in a midtown bank building) helps you forget about the hectic bustle of the big city. The low-priced lunch menus and a respectable choice of wines were appealing, and the pasta, scallops and grilled bass were tasty. The soup with basil and the saddle of lamb were also quite good, although the latter was a bit overdone. Add dependably delicious desserts (wonderful sherbets!) and correct service, and what more could you ask for in a bank?

G'NAU 11/20
45134, Stadtteil Steele
Stiftplatz 1
(02 01) 47 27 36, res.

P

Closed for lunch, closed Monday, à la carte: 21/54

The oldest house in Essen has a new style. The modernized rooms are meant to attract more young people, who can also sit on the lovely summer terrace. But on the way to new horizons, the cuisine has lost its direction: onion tart or lamb cutlets, noodles with fish or salmon with sugar peas—that is the question! In the meantime, we tried such absurdities as "little herb and garlic hamburgers with cèpes sauce"—which in turn tried our patience.The wine list has been drastically cut back, and so has the choice of wines by the glass. The service could be more professional.

LA GRAPPA 14/20
45128, Rellinghauser Str. 4
(02 01) 23 17 66, Fax 22 91 46 res.

Closed for lunch Saturday, closed Sunday. Tables d'hôte: 55L, 82D, à la carte: 53/80

The owner has a selection of 561(!) different kinds of grappa. And you don't even have to drink and drive, because this restaurant is situated at the backdoor of Essen's train station. On our plates we found lobster and king prawns with two kinds of sauces, and turbot with a lovely butter sauce. Chef Srour Hafem's nonchalant cuisine exhibits Italian and French influences. He prepares perfect al dente tagliolini as well as a delicate carpaccio of turbot with hot pepper sauce. We also liked such simple dishes as smoked mozzarella with anchovies. The desserts are colorful, and the Italian staff is friendly and efficient. The choice of wine is good, but not cheap. Wines by the glass are served, and a little taste of grappa is always welcome (if not obligatory with such a choice at hand). We recommend the menus that include wine.

KÖLNER HOF 16/20 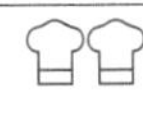
45145, Duisburger Str. 20
(02 01) 76 34 30, res.

Closed Monday, Closed for lunch Tuesday, closed 2 weeks in January. Tables d'hôte: 79/120, à la carte: 48/87

We've often given this restaurant on a street corner a hard time, but those days are now over. The interior is now much more elegant, the service is professional and charming, and the choice of wines is superb. On top of all that, Heinz Furtmann's cuisine is getting better every year. Applause for his savory soup with fresh peas and lobster and for his deceptively simple truffled noodles. The borscht with duck was superb, the bass with fresh cèpes and red wine butter daring but good, and the pigeon breast with black salsify astounding. The fresh berry strudel was nice and light, and the rhubarb gratin with woodruff-and-yogurt ice cream was fantastic.

OASE 12/20
45130, Stadtteil Rüttenscheid
Friederikenstr. 45-47
(02 01) 77 07 91, Fax 77 08 63 res.

P

Closed Monday, closed 19 December through 20 January. Tables d'hôte: 18/32L, 42/70D, à la carte: 31/66

What makes generations of regular guests throng to this former ice-cream parlor in Rüttenscheid? It can't be the provokingly cheerless and uncomfortable ambience or the insipid desserts that have kept drawing them for the last 25 years. Maybe it's the perfect service or the fresh and crispy pizza buns. In any case, the dishes here are fresh and accurately prepared and, on top of that, low-priced. Salads are generously apportioned, pastas are always dependably al dente, and lamb, duck or bass well-done. There are some good wines by the glass.

SCHLOSS HUGENPOET 14/20

45219, Stadtteil Kettwig
August-Thyssen-Str. 51
(0 20 54) 1 20 40 , Fax 12 04 50 res.

Closed 24 December though 7 January. Tables d'hôte:115L 155D, à la carte: 60/110

This magnificent castle with ancient stone fireplaces, marble stairs and antique-furnished dining rooms on the banks of the Ruhr river is just the right setting for grand dinners and festive banquets. At Hugenpoet, time seems to have stood still. Thomas Mann's Buddenbrooks would have liked the saddle of venison, veal or lamb and the grilled salmon with béarnaise sauce as much as we did. On the down side, the sole with green asparagus lacked character, the oxtail soup was a little too tangy, and the sauce that came with the oxtail with chanterelles was much too rich.The waiters, even if they happen to be in a great hurry, always manage to drag their feet aristocratically. The choice of wines is excellent, but expensive if ordered by the glass.

SCHLOSS HUGENPOET

45219, Stadtteil Kettwig
August-Thyssen-Str. 51
(0 20 54) 1 20 40 , Fax 12 04 50

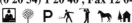

19, **S** 265/365, **D** 330/470,
APP 750, **1/2P** +75, **P** +120
Closed 2—7 January

This 300-year-old castle on the water, located in a park in the Ruhr Valley near Essen, is undoubtedly one of the most impressive German "Relais et Châteaux" hotels and a popular setting for weddings and other celebrations. The interior boasts a magnificent entrance hall with marble floors and a marble staircase, nobly furnished restaurant and salons full of art treasures. The rooms are spacious and mostly furnished with antiques.

WEINHAUS MICHL

45130, Stadtteil Rüttenscheid
Elfriedenstr. 17
(02 01) 77 27 56 res.

Closed for lunch Saturday, closed Sunday, 2 weeks during Christmas/New Year season, à la carte: 22/56

This *Weinhaus* in Rüttenscheid is not easy to find, but that is not necessarily a drawback. Only real connoisseurs would make the effort to come here. Both service and cuisine have improved, and the kitchen staff can even offer passable cheese ravioli, a variety of salads and warm goat cheese. But the best reason for coming here is the comprehensive and exquisite choice of wines. The wine list is a who's who of all the wine-growing regions in Germany, and the prices are fair. There is also a stock of international vintages.

ZEITUNGSENTE 12/20

45128, Sachsenstr. 30
(02 01) 23 66 08, Fax 23 66 63 res.

Closed for lunch Saturday, closed Sunday. Tables d'hôte: 39L, 90D, à la carte: 37/75

This lovely and comfortable renovated bistro-restaurant is located in the same building that houses Essen's daily press. You'll find few journalists here from the offices above, but more young people who have become regular guests. The Tunisian staff is well-trained and pleasant.The Italian-inspired cuisine is still searching for its own style. We had marvelous antipasto and nondescript fish, lovely homemade pasta, delicious squab with Barolo sauce and boring desserts. Our excellent lobster in savory broth and heavenly tasty and succulent fillet of beef made us suspect fine talent (as yet) buried in the kitchen.The prices of the prix-fixe meals are moderate, and so are those of the wines. Where else can you get a dozen good French, Italian, and Californian wines for under 30 DM? Or a choice of five top champagnes for less than 75 DM?

ETTLINGEN Bad.-Württ.

Karlsruhe 9-Baden-Baden 37

ERBPRINZ 14/20

76275, Rheinstr. 1
(072 43) 32 20, Fax 1 64 71

Closed for dinner Sunday, closed Monday. Tables d'hôte: 45L, 82/130D, à la carte: 45/88

This lovely and comfortable renovated bistro-restaurant is located in the same building that houses Essen's daily press. You'll find few journalists here from the offices above, but more young people who have become regular guests. The Tunisian staff is well-trained and pleasant.The Italian-inspired cuisine is still searching for its own style. We had marvelous antipasto and nondescript fish, lovely homemade pasta, delicious squab with Barolo sauce and boring desserts. Our excellent lobster in savory broth and heavenly tasty and succulent fillet of beef made us suspect fine talent (as yet) buried in the kitchen.The prices of the prix-fixe meals are moderate, and so are those of the wines. Where else can you get a dozen good French, Italian, and Californian wines for under 30 DM? Or a choice of five top champagnes for less than 75 DM?

ERBPRINZ

76275, Rheinstr. 1
(072 43) 32 20, Fax 1 64 71

42 rooms, **S** 125/220, **D** 180/260, **APP** 295/350

The staff of this venerable hotel does its best to ensure the comfort of each guest from arrival to departure. The rooms are tastefully appointed and comfortable.

WEINSTUBE ZUM ENGELE 14/20

76275, Kronenstr. 13
(0 72 43) 1 51 56, 1 28 52, Fax 46 73

Tables d'hôte: 45L, 75D, à la carte: 40/76

It is heartening to see that Edwin Hartmaier's restaurant is well frequented. His new chef and his moderately priced fresh cuisine without frills have attracted an enthusiastic clientele. We were pleasantly surprised with a regional version of the typically Alsatian terrine of chicken livers with a marmalade of figs and mustard (17/20!). In contrast, the pike-perch and the dull sauce that went with it were without interest. As a rule, meat courses are better than fish here; a good example is the great fillet of Angus beef with balsamic vinegar and dumplings. The desserts and pastries have gotten much better, and the caramelized lime parfait with strawberries was fantastic.

EURASBURG Bayern

Seeshaupt 13-Starnberg 24

SPRENGENÖDER ALM 12/20

82547 Eurasburg
(0 81 79) 7 21/2, Fax 15 23 res.

Closed Monday, Tuesday, 1 January through 15 February. No Credit Cards, à la carte: 25/60

Not far from the Starnberger See, high up over Eurasburg, a restaurant sits on a green alpine pasture. The view from the terrace bordered by large trees is stupendous. The accommodations are Bavarian rustic, as is the cooking. Don't bother to come here on a sunny Sunday or on a holiday, however. Bavarians are willing to wait two hours for their pork roast, but are you? The wine list offers moderately priced wines by the glass and a respectable choice of German, French, Italian, Austrian and Spanish wines by the bottle.

FIEFBERGEN Schl.-Holst.

Schönberg 4 - Kiel 23

SOMMERHOF 14/20

24217, Am Dorfteich 11
(0 43 44) 66 85, Fax 44 98 res.

Closed for lunch, closed Monday, 3 weeks in October/November, last 2 weeks in February. Tables d'hôte: 69/89, à la carte: 40/61, No Credit Cards

This lovingly restored old stone house draws more and more gourmets every year. The Sommerhof's popularity is mainly due to its young chef Volker Specht, who keeps refining his regional cuisine. Our appetizer, stuffed rabbit leg with pesto, indicated lofty ambitions. We had lovely quail with lentils, succulent North Sea turbot with oxtail sauce and beet noodles, and were entranced with lovely desserts such as chocolate cake with creamy banana ice and light coconut mousse or buttermilk sorbet with baked plums and delightful apricot sorbet.The service is relaxed and familiar. The wine list offers moderately priced wines from Germany, France and Italy.

FISCHBACHTAL Hessen

Dieberg 15 - Darmstadt 20

LANDHAUS BAUR 18/20

64405, Lippmannweg 15
(0 61 66) 83 13, Fax 88 41 res.

 P

Closed Monday, closed for lunch Tuesday, 3 weeks in January, 2 weeks in October. Tables d'hôte: 65/110L, 150/160D, à la carte: 68/100, No Credit Cards

The cheerful, charming atmosphere of this place seems to inspire both the chef in the kitchen and his customers in the dining room. Albert Baur takes hearty regional recipes and makes deliciously light dishes out of them. This was true even for saddle of piglet stuffed with blood pudding and liver sausage. With an eye to minute detail, he designs dishes with dense flavors, like Allgäu ox with chanterelles and young Savoy cabbage. Exciting flavors are harmoniously combined in the red mullet from Brittany with crawfish sauce and curry oil. Other ingenious dishes that deserve applause: fried calf's liver and foie gras with wheat sprouts and an entrancing turnip sauce, pig's feet aspic and lobster tartare with puréed peas and salad, saddle of rabbit and tripe, and elegant pike-perch with scalloped carrots and coriander. Our saddle of venison was accompanied by an exciting sauce of rosemary and lavender. The exquisite cheese selection was followed by a spectacular dessert of fresh cherries, sweet rice chips and peach ice cream with delicate almond cream. The menu lists only two fixed-price meals, but each dish can be ordered à la carte. The charming and competent service contributed to our enjoyment. The wine list includes many vintages from the little-known Hessische Bergstrasse wine region nearby. Try them by the glass with your meal. The liqueurs are also excellent.

FISCHEN Bayern

Oberstdorf 6 - Kempten 33

GASTHOF KRONE 13/20

87538, Auf der Insel 1
(0 83 26) 2 87, Fax 93 51 res.

 P

Closed Monday, Tuesday, 2—12 April, 6—20 November. Tables d'hôte: 50, à la carte: 27/56

Kurt Podobnik is proud of the many prizes and medals he has received for good cooking, and displays them in the entrance to his restaurant. He has a reputation for well-prepared, down-to-earth cuisine, and his ravioli, cheese spaetzle and cèpe noodles have made the Krone famous in the region. We liked cream of potato soup with mushroom ravioli, a Provençal fish dish and a precisely done steak with rösti.

KUR-UND SPORTHOTEL SONNENBICHL

3 km south in
87538, Ortsteil Langenwang
Sägestr. 19
(0 83 26) 99 40, Fax 99 41 80

P

54 rooms, **S** 86/104, **D** 158/222,
APP 254/284, **1/2P** +25, **P** +45

Closed 19 April through 5 May, No Credit Cards

This especially comfortable and reasonably priced hotel offers a peaceful setting and warm hospitality. The Alpine style of the building with its flower boxes, balconies and terraces is carried over into the rooms. A passageway connects the hotel to the adjoining sanatorium.

KUR-UND SPORTHOTEL TANNECK

87538, Maderhalm 20
(0 83 26) 99 90, Fax 99 91 33

P

62 rooms, **S** 129/169, **D** 199.338,
APP 258/399, **1/2P** +18, **P** +33

Closed 5 November through 20 December

The wonderful, exclusive setting of this hotel with its stupendous view of the surrounding mountains and valleys is complemented by the Alpine style of its interior decoration. Besides a splendid swimming pool, the hotel offers fitness facilities, a hairdresser, restaurant and guided mountain hikes.

LANGER'S SCHLEMMERSTUBEN 16/20

3 km west in Obermaiselstein
87538, Paßstr. 2
(0 83 26) 95 00, Fax 94 96

Closed Tuesday, closed for lunch Wednesday, 2 weeks at the end of January and at the beginning of December. Tables d'hôte: 89/135, à la carte: 33/102, No Credit Cards

Armin Langer cooks as superbly as ever—and doesn't let his guests wait too long for the next course. The menu offers only two prix-fixe meals. After an enticing appetizer of herb butter on crispy bread and flavorful salmon terrine with curry crème, we enjoyed a delicious tomato soup with pine nuts, light and tangy asparagus terrine with basil, flawless pike-perch fillet with lobster, fresh spinach beets, risotto and a savory Chardonnay crème. The cheese dumplings with melted butter, rhubarb confit and grape ice cream was nearly perfect. The impressive wine list offers quite a few wines by the glass. The service is charmingly Bavarian.

ZUM KITZEBICHL 12/20

in 87538 Bolsterlang
(0 83 26) 96 06

P

Apart from the folksy music droning from the restaurant's loudspeakers, the ambience is rustic and comfortable. The Ritzingers take pains to please all sorts of diners, for example those who are counting calories, fans of grandma's cooking and children. The high quality of the produce, though, doesn't always guarantee convincing cuisine. The turkey breast with curry sauce, fruit and rice is something tourists would probably appreciate more than we did, but our cream of chanterelle soup with leek strips was fabulous. We also liked fillet of Angus beef in a sauce of green pepper, whereas the salads were simply disappointing.The wine list is adequate.

FÖHR (INSEL) Schl.-Holst.

Fähre van Dagenbüll 45 min.
Platzreservierung (0 46 81) 80 40

ALTES PASTORAT 14/20

in 25938 Süderende
(0 46 83) 2 26, 2 50, res.

Closed for lunch, closed October through Easter. Tables d'hôte: 95

The guests fall in readily with Hussein El-Dessouki's ways: after an aperitif at 7:00, the (daily changing) five-course prix-fixe meal begins at 7:30 p.m. sharp. Our discreet host and cook served us saddle of lamb marinated in herbs, garlic and olive oil, excellently prepared lobster with celery mousse, succulent pigeon breast with exquisite cassis sauce and cabbage with a touch of cumin. We enjoyed the freshly prepared dishes and savored the original flavors of the ingredients used.The service in the two dining rooms, which are tastefully decorated with antiques, is amiably familiar. The remarkable wine list offers first-class German white wines and an ample selection of nicely aged Bordeaux at fair prices.

ALTES PASTORAT

in 25938 Süderende
(0 46 83) 2 26, 2 50

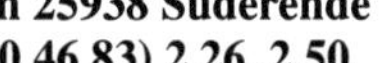

5 rooms, **S** 280/300, **D** 500/550,
APP 560/600

Closed October through Easter, Suite price includes 1/2P, No Credit Cards

This former vicarage, built in the 16th century, is surrounded by old elm trees and lindens. It has a cozy library furnished with antiques and offers comfortable rooms and apartments. Breakfast is more than ample and five o'clock tea is free.

LUISENHOF

in 25938 Utersum/Hedehusum
Poolstich 5
(0 46 83) 12 21, Fax 12 23

5 rooms, **S** 180/200, **D** 260/300,

Closed 15 October through 20 December, 5 January through Easter

This thatched farmhouse, built in 1635, was renovated a few years ago and turned into a lovely little country hotel. Tastefully furnished rooms with marble bathrooms.

FRANKFURT Hessen

Bonn 175-Saarbrücken 190 - Nürnberg 222

AVOCADO—LE BISTRO 14/20

60313, Hochstr. 27
(0 69) 29 28 67 res.

Closed Sunday. Tables d'hôte: 52/80, à la carte: 41/85

This smartly decorated bistro is one of the nicest restaurants in Frankfurt. Its lovely terrace seems like a mirage in the bustle of downtown Frankfurt. Flavorful Mediterranean cuisine and refined plain fare were harmoniously combined: on one hand, angler fried in olive oil with tomatoes, green olives, garlic and fresh herbs; on the other, cabbage roulade stuffed with minced meat in a truffled sauce. Saddle of lamb with a crust of mustard and herbs, plain sole, spinach and ricotta ravioli and baked goat cheese with salads were some of the slightly varied standards sadly in need of new creative impulse. Our untrained memory has yet to remember all 10 of the dishes and their ingredients that were rattled off at our table, but we're working on it—with the help of the nice staff. The wine list didn't contribute to our enjoyment: some wines were extravagantly priced; others were not of the best vintages. Red wines were served too warm and the wines by the glass were too expensive.

BISTROT 77 16/20

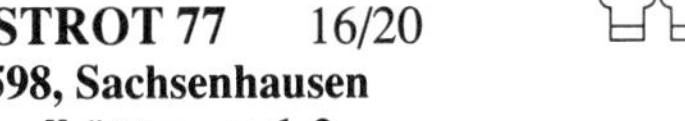

60598, Sachsenhausen
Ziegelhüttenweg 1-3
(0 69) 61 40 40 , Fax 7 24 08 85 res.

Closed for lunch Saturday, closed Sunday 23 December through 4 January, 3 weeks during the Hessen summer school holiday. Tables d'hôte: 48L, 100/130D, à la carte: 40/94. Tables d'hôte with wine: 100

Classic French cuisine with a regional touch characterizes the relaxed and enjoyable ambience of this restaurant. Simple dishes can be just great, for example œufs en Meurette, when the yolk of the poached eggs flows together with the light red wine sauce, or ragout of young wild boar. "Calf's liver Lyonnaise" doesn't sound exciting on the menu, but you can be sure Dominique Mosbach will make something spectacular out of this classic dish. In any case, all sauces are perfectly balanced: light, delicate, but extremely flavorful and expressive. Wednesdays, the fish soup is worth a little celebration, and Thursdays the Mosbachs serve a regional prix-fixe menu with dishes from Périgord, Provence or other parts of France. A special lunch menu and the changing regional prix-fixe meals have fair prices. The wine list doesn't only stock noble Bordeaux and rarities, but also offers modestly priced Alsatian house wines.

BRÜCKENKELLER 18/20

60331, Schützenstr. 6
(0 69) 28 42 38, 28 50 92, Fax 29 60 68 res.

Closed for lunch, closed Sunday and holidays, 23 December through 7 January. Tables d'hôte: 90/138, à la carte: 60/119

The cuisine in this elegantly decorated, vaulted cellar restaurant exudes vitality and a love of life, and every bite is pure enjoyment. The deceptively rustic dishes on the menu are prepared so delicately as to partake of the finest cuisine, for example strudel of blood pudding with sauerkraut sauce, stuffed oxtail or cheeks of beef in red wine sauce. The ingenious simplicity of poached egg with white truffles was irresistible, and the perfection of a scrumptious saddle of rabbit with squash exciting. Courageous new ideas were carried out with expertise, like pork cheeks with black truffles, for instance. Sauces and side dishes complement the natural flavors of the main products and create harmonious dishes like red mullet with rosemary crème or sautéed rabbit with sage. After Alfred Friedrich's spectacular appetizers and main courses, his pâtisserie seems "only" good, except, of course, for his unbelievably creamy curd dishes.The service is efficient even if the house is full, and has become more self-confident and relaxed.

CAFÉ SCHIRN

60311, Römerberg 6a [F4]
(0 69) 29 17 32, Fax 2 97 85 03

A la carte: 24/58

The enormous popularity of this glassed-in café with its 40-meter-long bar is only partly due to its unusual ambience and strategic location

Fernmeldeturm,
Deutsche Bundesbank

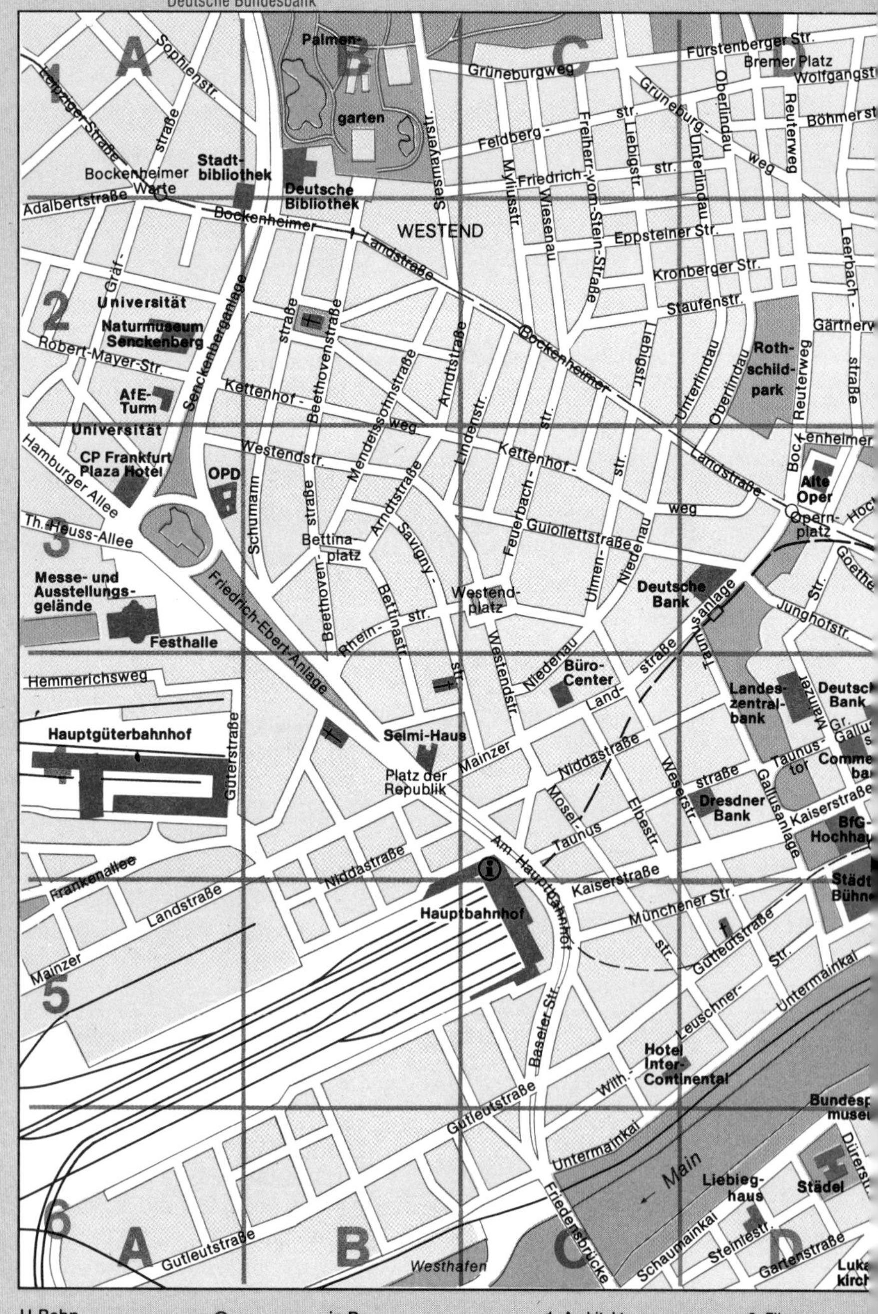

U-Bahn ——— ——— ——○— — — — in Bau

1 Architekturmuseum 2 Filmmuseum

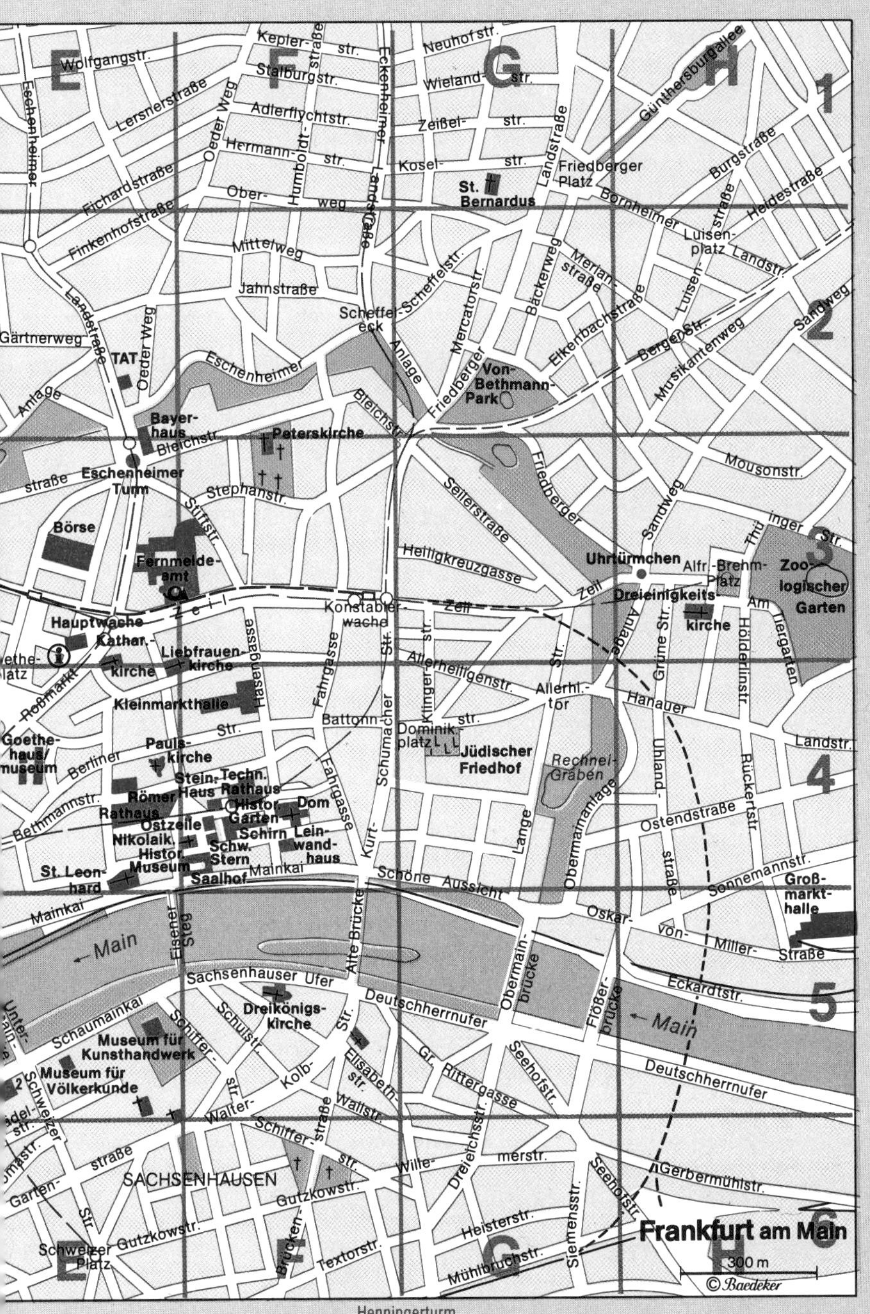
Frankfurt am Main
300 m
© Baedeker
E
F
G
H
1
2
3
4
5
6
Wolfgangstr.
Kepler-str.
Neuhofstr.
Stalburgstr.
Wieland-str.
Günthersburgallee
Eschenheimer Landstraße
Lersnerstraße
Oeder Weg
Humboldtstraße
Adlerflychtstr.
Zeißel-str.
Hermann-str.
Kosel-str.
Eckenheimer Landstraße
Friedberger Landstraße
Friedberger Platz
Burgstraße
Fichardstraße
Ober-weg
St. Bernardus
Bornheimer Landstr.
Heidestraße
Finkenhofstraße
Mittelweg
Luisenplatz
Luisenstraße
Merianstraße
Bäckerweg
Mercatorstr.
Scheffelstr.
Jahnstraße
Scheffeleck
Elkenbachstraße
Sandweg
Gärtnerweg
TAT
Anlage
Eschenheimer Anlage
Friedberger Anlage
Bergerstr.
Musikantenweg
Von-Bethmann-Park
Bleichstr.
Bayerhaus
Peterskirche
Mousonstr.
Eschenheimer Turm
Stephanstr.
Stiftstr.
Seilerstraße
Thüringer Str.
Börse
Fernmeldeamt
Heiligkreuzgasse
Uhrtürmchen
Alfr.-Brehm-Platz
Zoologischer Garten
Zeil
Konstablerwache
Dreieinigkeitskirche
Am Tiergarten
Hauptwache
Kathar.-kirche
Liebfrauenkirche
Goethe-platz
Roßmarkt
Hasengasse
Fahrgasse
Klingerstr.
Allerheiligenstr.
Allerh.-tor
Grüne Str.
Hölderlinstr.
Kleinmarkthalle
Battonnstr.
Hanauer Landstr.
Goethehaus/museum
Paulskirche
Berliner Str.
Dominik.-platz
Jüdischer Friedhof
Rechneigraben
Uhlandstraße
Rückertstr.
Steinhaus
Techn. Rathaus
Römer
Rathaus
Histor. Garten
Dom
Bethmannstr.
Kurt-Schumacher-Str.
Lange Str.
Obermainanlage
Ostendstraße
Ostzeile
Nikolaik.
Schirn
Leinwandhaus
Histor. Museum
Schw. Stern
St. Leonhard
Saalhof
Mainkai
Schöne Aussicht
Sonnemannstr.
Großmarkthalle
Oskar-von-Miller-Straße
Main
Eiserner Steg
Alte Brücke
Obermainbrücke
Flößerbrücke
Eckardtstr.
Sachsenhauser Ufer
Dreikönigskirche
Deutschherrnufer
Schaumainkai
Schifferstr.
Schulstr.
Museum für Kunsthandwerk
Elisabethenstr.
Gr. Rittergasse
Seehofstr.
Museum für Völkerkunde
Kolbstr.
Wallstr.
Walter-Kolb-Str.
Schifferstraße
Schweizer Str.
Dreieichsstr.
Wille-merstr.
Gerbermühlstr.
Sachsenhausen
Gutzkowstr.
Siemensstr.
Gartenstr.
Heisterstr.
Schweizer Platz
Brückenstr.
Textorstr.
Mühlbruchstr.
Henningerturm
S-Bahn
in Bau

between the cathedral and the central and picturesque "Römer." Frankfurters like the good quality of the food and the modest prices—and the fact that you can get the best snacks and small dishes in town. Guests can choose among 20 different tapas: "just a bite to eat" means duck's breast in honey and ginger; wonton with salmon, vegetables and sprouts; Chinatown chicken with teriyaki dip; sushi; scampi with garlic; angler with potatoes and much more. These snacks are the size of appetizers and you can order three for about 20 DM. The restaurant kitchen isn't as deftly sure in the preparation of its dishes as the bistro's. Young guests who frequent the café in the evenings like the loud music. Afternoons are quieter, when whole families come to eat the delicious cakes.The dozen wines by the glass were of less-than-mediocre quality, but some bottles are passable, for instance the Sauvignon blanc from New Zealand and the Australian Chardonnay. The service is relaxed, pleasant and untrained.

ERNO'S BISTRO 14/20

60323, Liebigstr. 15 [C2]
(0 69) 72 19 97, Fax 17 38 38 res.

Closed Saturday, Sunday, mid-June through mid-July, 23 December through the end of the first week of January. Tables d'hôte: 50L, 98D, à la carte: 62/108

This "in" bistro offers dishes that are much more extravagant than its name implies. The daily changing menu offers fine French cuisine. Guy Bastian's strong points are his finely balanced salads and his lovingly prepared and arranged appetizers, like zucchini and avocado slices with fried scampi, or Greek vegetables with stuffed breast of poularde. Interesting and exotic was the marinated turbot with red lentils and coriander. Bastian's rack of lamb with a crust of mustard and parsley is the best in Frankfurt.The wine list offers a comprehensive choice of French wines at moderate prices. The service is familiar.

GARGANTUA 13/20

60323, Liebigstr. 47
(0 69) 72 07 19, Fax 72 07 17 res.

Closed for lunch Saturday, closed Sunday, 3 weeks at Christmas. Tables d'hôte: 38L, 85/110D, à la carte: 58/89

The dishes that come out of the Trebes's kitchen have always been good and enticing plain fare. Trebes cooks according to his own rules, but exhibits a fine sense of taste in letting his main products keep their natural flavors, just enhancing them with fresh herbs or exotic spices, new oils and vinegar preparations. His "blackened tuna" with terrifically hot Japanese horseradish and ginger is a favorite with his guests. A Mediterranean touch was obvious in the pesto we had with our scampi and beans and in the saffron risotto with duck liver. The main courses come in generous portions; you might end up sharing a dish when ordering a whole meal. The lunch prix-fixe menu is super for 38 DM.The wine list is well-stocked but expensive for a bistro, even though there are some wines by the glass.

HOFGARTEN 13/20

60311, Am Kaiserplatz [E4]
(0 69) 21 58 06, Fax 21 59 00

P

Closed Sunday. Tables d'hôte: 52L, à la carte: 32/77

When the sun is shining, we can always recommend this place. One of the most centrally located and most beautiful terraces in Frankfurt combines comfort with Mediterranean flair. The kitchen offers unremarkable food, but the cocktails with fresh fruit are commendable. The service is nimble and pleasant.

KNOBLAUCH 13/20

60323, Staufenstr. 39 [C2]
(0 69) 72 28 28, Fax 72 97 15 res.

Closed Saturday and Sunday, No Credit Cards. Tables d'hôte: 29L, 42D, à la carte: 37/60

Some of the ducks' breasts can't help being smoked in clouds of Gitane fumes, but it's all part of the atmosphere of this lively *gaststube*. Bohemian charm is combined with good cooking, and makes this restaurant one of the most popular in Frankfurt. The Alsatian cuisine is succulent and savory from the first bite to the last, without being unrefined or rustic. Some people only need an Alsatian blood pudding or a sauerkraut salad with sausage to be happy. We had savory braised leg of goose and delicious squab and were in seventh heaven. The choice of wines needs to be improved, especially the wines offered by the glass. The service is nonchalant and quick.

LAUDA 14/20

60313, Gr. Bockenheimer Str. 52 [D3]
(0 69) 29 46 94 res.

P

Closed Sunday and holidays. Tables d'hôte: 80, à la carte: 40/78

This is one of the few dependable Italian restaurants in Frankfurt. The pasta is always deliciously al dente, the sauces flawlessly prepared, fish and meat perfectly done. Our riviolettini were served in a light gorgonzola sauce, and a distinct but delicate wine sauce accompanied our lovely sole fillets. Maria Lauda has a sure hand for precise seasoning and a good sense of flavors. The menu of the restaurant above is also available in the more turbulent bistro below. The beletage [query] is too elegant to offer pasta and other little delicacies. The bistro's service is relaxed and friendly, but in the restaurant the maître d' maintains a stiff upper lip. The wine list offers fewer faddish wines and more bottles for connoisseurs. Besides three first-class Spumantes, there are 25 kinds of grappa to choose from.

DIE LEITER 13/20

60313, Kaiserhofstr. 11 [D3]
(0 69) 29 21 21, Fax 29 16 45

P

Closed Sunday. Tables d'hôte: 44L, à la carte: 23/73

Most of the restaurants in downtown Frankfurt are full of surprises: you never know what you're getting. The Leiter has a reputation for being an "in" bistro frequented by rich sports-car drivers. People aren't usually aware that behind its façade this clever little bistro offers good and dependable cuisine. Its chefs have cooked in renowned restaurants and serve well-known dishes with finesse, for example tortelloni filled with fresh spinach and lentils with a mascarpone and gorgonzola sauce. The pasta is always good here and the fillet tips of beef and angler medallions superb. The prix-fixe lunch for 44 DM is a steal. There are a dozen moderately priced and good wines by the glass to choose from, but red wines (mostly Italian) were served much too warm. The service is charming and/or competent.

MAINGAU 14/20

60594, Sachsenhausen
Schifferstr. 38-40 [F6]
(0 69) 61 07 52, Fax 62 07 90

P

Closed Saturday, closed for dinner Sunday, 4 weeks weeks during the Hesse summer school holiday. Tables d'hôte: 36L, 84D, à la carte: 33/68, Tables d'hôte with wine: 84

If this place were were located out in the country rather than in a drab side street in Sachsenhausen, it would be a popular excursion for countless city dwellers. Döpfner shows a preference for regional dishes, knows how to prepare hearty and savory food with a light hand and is open to new ideas. His style of cooking combines creative plain bourgeois fare with regional finesse. Sachsenhäuser potato and sauerkraut strudel with liverwurst sauce and baked blood pudding is a favorite. We loved such full-bodied creations as lamb sausage with lentils and roasted potatoes with thyme, or venison from the Taunus in walnut crust.The finely balanced salmon tartare was delicious and the variations of fine fish excellent. The exquisite sauces are served in saucières, so that we could surreptitiously sip them with our spoons. Praliné parfait and rhubarb gratin rounded off our meal.The wine list offers good wines at reasonable prices. Besides finding wines from New Zealand, Australia and Chile, you may also land a catch like the great Château Talbot we had at a special price.

OSTERIA ENOTECA 16/20

60489. Rödelheim
Arnoldshainer Str. 2
(0 69) 7 89 22 16 res.

Closed for lunch Saturday, closed Sunday, 22 December through 8 January. Tables d'hôte: 95, à la carte: 56/85

We wonder at the diners who grumble at the high prices here. After all, Frankfurt's best, most creative, most beautiful and most Italian of Italian restaurants isn't giving away food for free.From fine linen on the tables to the lovely little sugar bowls, everything has been imported from Tuscany to create an authentic atmosphere. Only the glasses are of the finest Tyrolean manufacture. Grissini, four kinds of bread and olive dip were as enticing as our appetizer, a delicate cheese dumpling in a lovely tomato and basil coulis. The remarkable antipasti are artistic little compositions, for example fried gamberoni with puréed potatoes laced with grappa and accompanied by sweet pepperoni sauce. Besides lovely pasta ideas and superb risotto, everything chef Carmelo Greco and his staff cook seems to be a success. The John Dory with fennel sauce tasted light and delicate, red mullet with lime risotto was perfect and turbot with pesto, beans and polenta just great. Not only was the rabbit perfectly done, each side dish was a work of art. The highlight of our last visit was a braised shoulder of wild boar, marinated five days in red wine herbs and vegetables. The desserts are dependably delicious.The wine list offers more than 250 different well-chosen Italian wines, but the choice of bottles under 70 DM could be larger. No open wines are listed, but may usually be had for the asking.

PAPILLON IN THE SHERATON 15/20

60549, Flughafen Terminal Mitte
(0 69) 69 77 12 28, Fax 69 77 24 18 res.

P

Closed for lunch Saturday, closed Sunday and holidays, 2 weeks in August. Tables d'hôte: 58L, 130D, à la carte: 72/129

Thanks to inventive and enthusiastic Klaus Böhler, creative cuisine has taken over the kitchen of the comfortably elegant airport restaurant. With rapid efficiency, the kitchen staff realizes the many ideas of their chef, for instance baramundi fish with saffron sauce and lemon risotto, or glazed duck's breast with soy mousse. Sometimes guests are surprised with (delicious) gags, like high-class vinegar for an aperitif. (Not a gag: reserve a parking space when you book a table here!) Flavorfully steamed lamb fillet and beech-smoked pigeon breast served with lentil ravioli were our favorites last time. The fried John Dory with marinated onions, tomato and basil sauce and stuffed eggplant roulade was excellent. Some dishes were curiously devoid of temperament, though: noncommittal sole fillets, sticky rice, irritatingly tangy orange noodles and a boringly respectable veal paillard. Dishes without an Asiatic touch often lacked flavor; some seemed ready-made and not absolutely fresh. The service is very attentive and always there when you need it. The wine list includes an excellent wine by the glass, a first-class rosé from Château Simone.

PREMIERE 13/20

60313, Konrad-Adenauer-Str. 7
(0 69) 2 98 11 72, Fax 2 98 18 12 res.

P

Closed for lunch, closed 4 weeks during the summer. Tables d'hôte: 86/130, à la carte: 47/95

A fresh ocean breeze fills the sails of the house's flagship: from the general-store type restaurant offering anything that didn't bite back, an ambitious fish restaurant has developed. Only two of the 20 dishes on the menu include meat. Heinz Imhoff's light fish cuisine, though, is enriched with a lot of butter and cream. The prices have been lowered but still remain high. Special gourmet days with prix-fixe meals and a collection of wines guarantee enjoyment at fair prices. Our creamy lentil soup with black truffles was a good start, the sole in caviar sauce nice but not exciting and the potato spaghetti with it good just for a gimmick. The stuffed char with tomato and rosemary butter was a bit overdone, and the sauce could have used more flavor. In fact, a lot of dishes could have done with more verve and temperament. The menu promised taste sensations the kitchen couldn't deliver. The stiff and formal atmosphere of this first-class restaurant is livened up by the determinedly relaxed service, centered on the comic talent of the headwaiter.

RESTAURANT FRANÇAIS 16/20

60311, Am Kaiserplatz
(0 69) 21 58 06, Fax 21 59 00 res.

P 

Closed for lunch Saturday, closed Sunday and Monday except during the Fair, 6 weeks during the Hesse summer school holiday. Tables d'hôte:105, à la carte: 64/98

The grand old lady of Frankfurt's hotel scene shows some worried lines on her fine and striking face, but she still manages to keep her dignity. In the midst of shrill and modern Frankfurt, we always enjoy strolling along the old-fashioned and timelessly styled corridors and halls of the Frankfurter Hof till we get to the restaurant with its dramatically styled entry. Inside, the elegant decor has a comfortable Parisian flair. Even though the cuisine has undergone apparent Italian and Asiatic influences, the menu is still written in French. Heinz Schiebenes and his sous-chef Burkhard Lidlar served dishes that all deserved a rating of 16/20: meltingly tender millefeuille of foie gras, veal *tafelspitz* with sweet mustard mousse; superbly done turbot with crayfish and green asparagus and truffled mousse; succulent lamb baked in pesto and served with mashed potatoes and herbs as well as braised artichokes; and, finally, fabulous saddle of venison with apple vinegar and honey, mushroom dumplings and pears with beans. The wine list is sadly in need of improvement, but the sommelier always finds a bottle to surprise you with, like our sensational Mas de Daumas Cassac from Languedoc.

SCHLUND

60320, Eschersh. Landstr. 347
(0 69) 5 60 18 95 res.

Closed for lunch everyday except Sunday, closed Monday and Tuesday, No Credit Cards. Tables d'hôte: 36/50, à la carte: 25/59

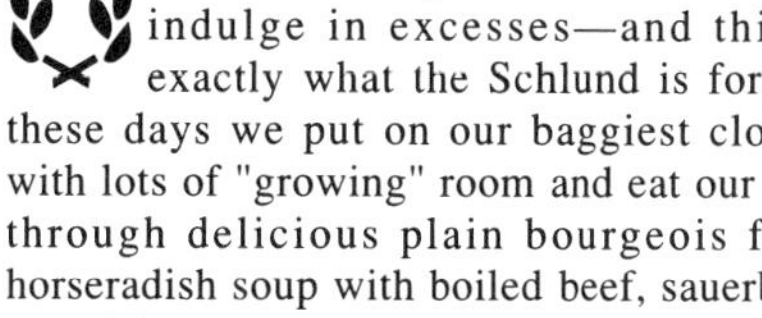

There are days when we have to indulge in excesses—and this is exactly what the Schlund is for. On these days we put on our baggiest clothes with lots of "growing" room and eat our way through delicious plain bourgeois fare: horseradish soup with boiled beef, sauerbraten with lentils and spaetzle, beef tongue, Swabian ravioli, potato pancakes with blood pudding and apples, tripe in red wine sauce and much, much more. Besides regional wines, you can also order French, Italian and Austrian wines, but we've always been satisfied with the choice of 13 wines by the glass. The Schlunds are looking for a successor, who we hope will carry on.

VILLA LEONHARDI 15/20

60325, Zeppelinallee 18 [B1]
(0 69) 74 25 35, Fax 74 04 76 res.

Closed Saturday, Sunday, 23 December through 9 January. Tables d'hôte: 45L, 98D, à la carte: 48/87

Surrounded by an idyllic park, this enchanting villa in the heart of the city doesn't attract the chic nouveau riche, but a sober gourmet clientele who want quality instead of whimsy. We appreciated the combination of Mediterranean finesse and German cleverness apparent in such dishes as stuffed saddle of rabbit with warm lentil salad, lemon sole with oyster ravioli, ray wing in jellied yogurt and turbot coated with herbs.The marinated beef and veal in olive tapenade was prepared with sensitivity and care, and tasted much better than many carpaccios. Chef Thomas Quecke carried out pert new ideas with bravado, like his pike shish kebab on rutabagas, but he's also an expert at classic dishes: his succulent goose with red cabbage and dumplings was first-class, and his roast of prime beef rib just right for very hungry gourmets. Quecke makes creative and delicious desserts. We enjoyed poppy-seed mousse with plums in Armagnac, semolina roulade with zabaglione and warm apricot strudel with almond cream and Burgundy ice cream. The service is discreet and competent. The wine list is intelligently stocked but needs to be revised.

VINI DI VINI

60323, Liebigstr. 27 [C2]
(0 69) 72 26 69, Fax 17 20 21

Closed Saturday and Sunday, à la carte: 20/62

In this smart little place located in Frankfurt's renowned Westend, guests can spend an enjoyable evening tasting good wines. The uncomplicated bar-like ambience and, in summer, the terrace with its long wooden benches create a convivial atmosphere. There are more than 100 Italian wines to choose from. Most of the dozen wines offered by the glass are respectable reds as well. A few simple dishes can be ordered to accompany the wines here, for example rabbit liver with fettucine, saddle of lamb with shallot sauce and fried potatoes and tortelloni with tomato and pesto.

WEIDEMANN 14/20

60528, Niederrad
Kelsterbacher Str. 66
(0 69) 67 59 96, Fax 67 39 28

Closed for lunch Saturday, closed Sunday. Tables d'hôte: 48L, 89/108D, à la carte: 41/89

In spite of rising popularity and high praise from critics, this restaurant still unpretentiously upholds its high standards in the kitchen, in the wine cellar and among its staff. Dependable consistency, however, doesn't prevent creative ideas from being realized. Apart from about 20 standard dishes on the menu, the kitchen offers a choice of just about as many daily specials. We liked dorado in a salt crust and lamb coated with herbs, osso buco and calf's liver, and recommend delicious "salt" variations, for instance angler fillet in salt crust with garlic and rosemary oil and rib-eye steak baked on ocean salt. We'll order a double portion of scrumptious squid in garlic sauce next time! Scallops wrapped in bacon with sweet roquette were as superb as salt cod in tomato and paprika sauce. An apple parfait and pear mousse with peppermint zabaglione rounded off our meal. The wine list offers an attractive choice of Italian and Spanish wines and a few recommendable wines by the glass. The service is quick and discreetly amiable.

HOTELS

ARABELLA GRAND HOTEL

60313, Konrad-Adenauer-Str. 7
(0 69) 2 98 10, Fax 2 98 18 10

378, **S** 295/550, **D** 365/620,
APP 1100/2400

This isn't the largest hotel in Frankfurt by far, but the "grand" isn't going to far if applied to the noble and elegant accommodations. The lobby with its Rhapsodie-Bar has the elegance of a luxury ocean liner, and the rooms each have a marble bathrooms and three telephones. Groups of 50 can reserve their own floor. 24-hour room service, ballroom, banquet and convention rooms with modern technology, sushi bar and Chinese restaurant, brasserie and *Bierstube*. Breakfast: 29.50 DM.

FORTE GRAND PARKHOTEL

60329, Wiesenhüttenplatz 28/38
(0 69) 2 69 70, Fax 2 69 78 84

P

296, **S** 298/548, **D** 378/548,
APP 578/789, **1/2P** +36, **P** +56

This hotel consists of two buildings, the Park hotel and the "Tower." The latter is the original old building with spacious and well-appointed rooms as well as luxurious suites. The room prices in the new section are substantially lower; the rooms are more uniform, but still very comfortable. Fitness center, restaurant, bar. Breakfast: 25 DM.

FRANKFURTER HOF

60311, Am Kaiserplatz
(0 69) 2 15 02 , Fax 21 59 00

P

350, **S** 324/524, **D** 389/589,
APP 879/1279

This fashionable hotel, called the "flagship of the Steigerberger Corporation," offers rooms in 30 different categories from dark and depressing to bright and pleasant. Besides 24-hour room service, shoe-shine and hairdresser, the hotel offers a beautiful lobby, two bars and room for 1,000 guests if you want to celebrate a party in one of the salons. The Presidential Suite has five rooms and butler service.

GRAVENBRUCH KEMPINSKI

11 km southeast in
63263 Neu-Isenburg
(0 61 02) 50 50, Fax 50 54 45

288, **S** 240/520, **D** 240/520,
APP 650/2200

"A luxury hotel with the atmosphere of a country house in a 15-hectare park" is how this hotel is described in its brochure, and that is exactly what it is. The demands of the most fastidious guests are satisfied here. Restaurant with terrace facing the park. Breakfast: 29 DM.

HESSISCHER HOF

60325, Friedr.-Ebert-Anlage 40
(0 69) 7 54 00, Fax 7 54 09 24

  P

117, **S** 240/545, **D** 300/605,
APP 695/1755

The luxurious Hessischer Hof is a popular hotel with visitors to the Frankfurt fairs. The house has been gradually expanded over the years, with the result that the rooms come in all shapes and sizes. All are stylishly appointed and supplied daily with fresh fruit and mineral water. Special requests should be directed to the staff, but be sure to ask the price. Shoe-shine service, restaurant. Tourist groups are not accommodated. Breakfast: 28 DM.

INTER-CONTINENTAL

60329, Wilh.-Leuschner-Str. 43
(0 69) 2 60 50, Fax 25 24 67

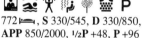

772, **S** 330/545, **D** 330/850,
APP 850/2000, **1/2P** +48, **P** +96

This is the largest hotel in Frankfurt, probably the most impersonal, but surely one of the most luxurious. The rooms are comfortable and have soundproofed windows. If you're willing to spend in one night what other people earn in a week, you can even enjoy the splendor of one of the four apartments found on each floor. This city-within-a-city includes chic boutiques, a bank, jewelry shop, round-the-clock service and check-in counters for Lufthansa. Breakfast: 21.50 or 32 DM (buffet).

MAINGAU

60594, Sachsenhausen
Schifferstr. 38-40 [F6]
(0 69) 61 70 01, Fax 62 07 90

100, **S** 70/120, **D** 140/180

This family hotel is situated in a quiet side street away from Sachsenshausen's night-life. Visitors to the Frankfurt Fair can combine business with pleasure here, enjoy cider in sociable surroundings or drop into the impressive museums nearby.

SHERATON

60549, Flughafen Terminal Mitte
(0 69) 6 97 70, Fax 69 77 22 09

 P

1050, **S** 395/585, **D** 425/615,
APP 800/3400

This is Europe's largest hotel, and often seems more like a cruise ship at anchor. The lines in front of the reception desk are sometimes longer than those at Lufthansa check-in counters. There are cinemas, bars, beer pubs, nightclubs, gourmet restaurants, shops and much more. The soundproof windows in the more than 1,000 rooms prevent guests from being disturbed by airport or autobahn noise, and the upper floors offer (provided you're on the right side) a marvelous view of jets taking off and landing. Many rooms have been elegantly redecorated; most are functionally furnished. Breakfast: 24-34 DM (Continental, buffet, Japanese).

STEIGENBERGER FRANKFURT AIRPORT

60549, Unterschweinsteige 16
(0 69) 6 97 50, Fax 69 75 25 05

 P

436, **S** 285/455, **D** 340/490,
APP 570/2500

Those of us spoiled by Steigenberger hotels will have difficulty getting used to the sterile atmosphere of this one. The rooms are all adequately equipped, but not exactly lovingly furnished. The location of the hotel at the edge of a forest is attractive, though. The hotel has its own casino as well as a nightclub, drugstore, solarium, computer service and a pleasant coffee shop. Check- in for Lufthansa and free bus service to and from the airport is available.

FRANKFURT/ODER Brand.

Berlin 92 - Dresden 200

KONGRESSHOTEL FRANKFURTER HOF

15230, Logenstr. 2
(03 35) 5 53 60, Fax 5 53 65 87

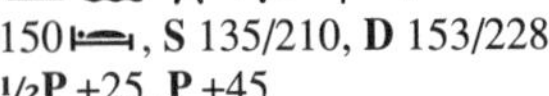

150, **S** 135/210, **D** 153/228,
1/2P +25, **P** +45

This sterile house could use some of the flair of its Steigenberger namesake in Frankfurt/Main. The hotel is ideal for conventions and offers a number of rooms for business meetings, comprehensive service and modern technology. Fitness club, solarium, hairdresser and beauty farm.

FRASDORF Bayern

Salzburg 64 - München 77

LANDGASTHOF KARNER 13/20

83112, Nußbaumstr. 6
(0 80 52) 40 71, Fax 47 11 res.

Closed 24 and 25 December. Tables d'hôte: 57L, 103D, à la carte: 55/97

Why are the prices of this beautiful country restaurant so exorbitantly high? They are not justified in any way by the quality of the food served.We'd rather do without an appetizer if it tastes as leathery as the tiny quiche we had. The soup with bitter watercress and dry salmon slices was disappointing. The side dishes were not always what the menu promised. Instead of fried rice cakes with our John Dory and lobster, we were nonchalantly served cooked potatoes, and we needed a magnifying glass to find the artichokes that were supposed to accompany the fish - they were buried under a mountain of green peas! The duck's breast with a salad of morels and potatoes, the veal roulade with morels, and the fillet of beef with celery gratin were much better, and the strawberry terrine with rhubarb was beyond reproach.The wine list is fine, but the service is so-so.

LANDGASTHOF KARNER

83112, Nußbaumstr. 6
(0 80 52) 40 71, Fax 47 11

25, **S** 110/165, **D** 185/200,
1/2P +58, **P** +115
Closed 24 and 25 December

One of the Flair hotel chain, this tasteful and homey country hotel offers comfortable rooms, a wonderful garden and many opportunities for sailing on the Chiemsee, riding, mountain hiking and skiing.

FREIAMT Bad. Württ.

Freiburg 25

FORELLENSTÜBLE

79348, Im Vorhof 7
(0 76 45) 3 45 res.

 P

Closed for dinner Sunday, closed Monday morning, closed Thursday, à la carte: 24/44, No Credit Cards

Guests come here to eat fresh trout—what else? Located outside of town on a meadow and close to a brook, this former mill (behind an imposing Bavarian-style house) is very rustically furnished. The whole family is on hand to serve the guests, who appreciate the low prices and the fresh trout, served either fried, boiled or smoked with potatoes and salad. We also recommend the generous ice cream portions for dessert, regional wines offered by the glass and home-brewed brandies. The service is very busy and often grumpy.

FREIBURG Bad. Württ.

Basel 67 - Karlsruhe 135

COLOMBI 18/20

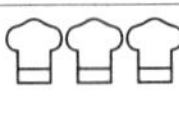

79098, Am Colombi-Park
(07 61) 2 10 60, Fax 3 14 10 res.

Tables d'hôte: 47/56L, 89/153D, à la carte: 60/110

Progress has not spared Freiburg. An American fast-food chain has even taken up residence at one of the medieval gates to the city. Luckily, Roland Burtsches keeps old traditions alive in his formidable

Colombi Hotel. Compared with the performance of other highly rated establishments in Germany, this hotel and its restaurants are simply grand. The ambience is elegant and comfortable, and the freshness of the produce used in the kitchen and its preparation are beyond comparison.Some highlights of Alfred Klink's cuisine are a mosaic of salmon and scallops marinated in lime with caviar, chartreuse and salad of white and green asparagus with lobster medallions and champagne vinaigrette, headcheese-filled ravioli in parsley juice, turbot with lentils and onions, tender fried pigeon breasts stuffed with Savoy cabbage, lamb noisettes with ravioli potatoes, almond soufflé with zabaglione, apple sherbet and vanilla ice cream. We could go on, but we will stop there. Klink's cooking is perfect every time. He even adjusts his dishes to harmonize with the wine you've ordered! The only thing we can find to complain about are the petits fours, which are a little below standard. If the capable sommelier is not there, follow the expert advice of the owner or the headwaiter. The wine list offers regional specialities as well as Italian and French vintages at reasonable prices. The service is irreproachable.

COLOMBI 

79098, Am Colombi-Park
(07 61) 2 10 60, Fax 3 14 10 res.

119 rooms, **S** 260/290, **D** 350/370,
APP 430/1360, **½P** +45,
Tables d'hôte: 47/56L, 89/153D, à la carte: 60/110

This is the top hotel in Freiburg. The rooms are elegant, and new conference and seminar rooms have been added as well as a grand swimming pool with fitness club, solarium and beauty farm. Breakfast: 22 DM.

EICHHALDE 14/20 

79104, Stadtteil Herdern
Stadtstr. 91
(07 61) 5 48 17, Fax 5 43 86 res.

Closed for lunch Saturday, closed Tuesday. Tables d'hôte: 56/86, à la carte: 52/78

Eichhalde's competent new owner, Karola Isele, and her friendly service staff and expert kitchen team deserve praise. Chef Matthias Dahlinger can now show off what he learned in Hamburg and Berlin. Occasionally, his cooking hits a sublime note, as in the fresh pike-perch and asparagus salad with a delicate vinaigrette. But he also has his weaknesses. The exquisitely prepared anglerfish was accompanied by too thickly sliced ratatouille. The roasted lamb with beans, however, was outstanding.The discerning wine list includes moderately priced regional wines.

KÜHLER KRUG 12/20

79100, Satdtteil Günterstal
Torplatz 1
(07 61) 2 91 03, Fax 2 97 82 res.

Closed Wednesday, Thursday, 3 weeks in July. Tables d'hôte: 38/65, à la carte: 35/80

If we were asked to name a good restaurant in Freiburg, we'd recommend the Kühler Krug, an unexciting and down-to-earth kind of place, where a staid and conservative clientele would probably take fright if the decor were more modern. Regional dishes and creations with a toned-down Mediterranean touch are served in spacious dining rooms. Halibut, salmon and pike-perch with homemade noodles and Riesling sauce are tasty standards, but the fish terrine is worth a rating of 15/20. The consommé with marrow quenelles deserves praise, as does the delicious breast of guinea fowl.

MARKGRÄFLER HOF 15/20

79098, Gerberau 22
(07 61) 3 25 40, Fax 3 79 47 res.
Closed Sunday and Monday. Tables d'hôte: 39/89, à la carte: 48/92

This establishment is restaurant, bar, *Weinstube* and wine library at the same time. But don't let a little bit of havoc bother you. So what if the flower bouquets are as dry as dust, and there are cobwebs on the empty bottles of fine Bordeaux that decorate the tables. The full bottles of fine Bordeaux offered on the excellent wine list are of top quality, as are the rare Gutedel wines of this region.The cuisine deserves both toques. The first courses were promising. We had Osiestra caviar with finely chopped egg and fresh fried potato pancakes. We recommend a little Tokay or Ruländerauslese with the terrine of foie gras with Sauterne jelly, followed by delicious fresh fried bass with peppers. The plat du jour for lunch—*tafelspitz* with horseradish, potatoes and vegetables—was also tasty.

OBERKIRCH'S WEINSTUBEN

79098, Münsterplatz
(07 61) 3 10 11, Fax 3 10 31

Closed Sunday and holidays, closed the month of January. Tables d'hôte:28/36L, à la carte: 31/73

The oldest traditional *gasthaus* on the Münsterplatz has been owned by the same family for generations. This is the wine tavern in Freiburg, frequented by inhabitants as well as former students of the university here. Forty tables are reserved every week for regular guests! The kitchen serves plain fare, but that's not why people visit this place, anyway. The 19 regional wines by the glass are offered in typical vierteles (a glass holding about one-fourth of a liter) and the prices are relatively low.

PANORAMAHOTEL MERCURE

am Jägerhäusle
79104, Wintererstr. 89
(07 61) 5 10 30, Fax 5 10 33 00

85, **S** 170/225, **D** 190/275,
1/2P +40, **P** +80

Recently renovated, this hotel has an almost perfect setting. The intriguing glass-and-concrete architecture is set in a quiet forest above the town. The rooms, although somewhat small, have spacious bathrooms as well as balconies facing south with a lovely view. Swimming pool, rooms for conventions and seminars, massage, restaurant.

SCHILLER 12/20

79104, Stadtstr. 91
(07 61) 70 33 30, Fax 7 03 37 77 res.

Tables d'hôte: 50D, à la carte: 31/59

Freiburg's youngest bar-bistro-restaurant exhibits an attractive Parisian flair in its ambience and cuisine. Guests sit close together and like it. The menu is small and offers rustic and tasty dishes à la bœuf bourguignon and company. The wine list is well stocked, the service quick and cheerful.

FREINSHEIM Rhl.-Pf.

Mannheim 20 - Kaiserslautern 40

LUTHER 16/20

67248, Hauptstr. 29
(0 63 53) 20 21, Fax 83 88 res.

Closed for lunch, closed Sunday, 3 weeks during the Rhl.-Pf. summer school holiday. Tables d'hôte: 130, à la carte: 58/88

Impossible acoustics are the only drawback in this old cellar with its beautiful vaulted ceiling: you can clearly hear every word spoken in the room. But aside from that, we have only positive things to report, from the quiet location in the historic part of town to the attentive service, which only needs a capable sommelier to advise guests about the surprisingly well-stocked wine list. NB: on our last visit the sleepy kitchen crew couldn't be bothered to serve the large prix-fixe menu after 8 p.m. Guests who reserve a table at 8:30 should bear this in mind.We had to put a few question marks after some courses we enjoyed. The zucchini roulade with pike-perch was served ice-cold, and the king prawns with lovely asparagus was accompanied by a sour salad. White beans al dente with a succulent and perfectly fried rack of lamb isn't everybody's favorite. Highlights of our meal were an excellent salmon carpaccio with herbs and olive oil and an artistic dessert of caramelized strudel with strawberry coulis and ice cream of passion fruit and curds.

LUTHER

67248, Hauptstr. 29
(0 63 53) 20 21, Fax 83 88

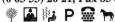

23 rooms, **S** 110/150, **D** 160/250
Closed 3 weeks during the Rhl.-Pf. summer school holiday

While one dozes under old walnut trees, life can be perfect in this idyllic atmosphere. The rooms are nicely furnished and you can stroll to the pretty Altstadt and view the old city wall.

FREUDENSTADT — BW

Stuttgart 90 - Freiburg 91

KURHOTEL SONNE AM KURPARK

72250, Turnhallestr. 63
(0 74 41) 60 44, Fax 63 00

37 rooms, **S** 120/170, **D** 200/260,
APP 290, **½P** +29, **P** +41

This hotel is located in the very heart of town and offers a standard of luxury unique in Freudenstadt. There are two restaurants, the more rustic Sonnenstüble and the fancier Exquisit, and a new pub. Diet programs under medical supervision.

WARTECK 14/20

72250, Stuttgarter Str. 14
(0 74 41) 74 18, Fax 29 57
Closed Tuesday. Tables d'hôte: 50/120, à la carte: 33/80

You'll find this comfortable little restaurant just a few steps away from the marketplace. Ursula Glässel and her friendly young staff serve at nicely laid tables. Appetizing dishes included headcheese salad with sweetbreads and tongue and a finely balanced vinaigrette, fresh cod wrapped in an omelet with a tomato purée, saddle of veal with asparagus and fresh hollandaise, sherbets of cassis, raspberries and mangoes with berries and tropical fruit. Swabian specialities and other dishes were available à la carte.The wine cellar is stocked with the best regional wines, grands crus and international vintages. The prices of half-bottles and outstanding wines by the glass are very pleasing.

FREYUNG — Bayern

Passau 34

BIERHÜTTE

8 km northwest in 94545 Hohenau
Bierhütte 10
(0 85 58) 3 15/9, Fax 23 87

43 rooms, **D** 99/139, **S** 150/210,
APP 230/300, **½P** +32, **P** +64

This is one of the oldest hotels in the Bavarian forest. In the course of its long history it's been, among other things, a brewery, a glassworks and a hunting lodge for visiting nobility from Passau. Today, the Bierhütte is part of a hotel complex featuring comfortable rooms with balconies, conference rooms, a solarium and fitness facilities. The surrounding park with its large pond is perfect for sunbathing and strolls.

LANDGASTHAUS SCHUSTER 13/20

94078, Ort 19
(0 85 51) 71 84

P

Closed Monday, closed for lunch Tuesday, closed 9—19 January, 1—15 August. Tables d'hôte: 35L, 35/87D, à la carte: 28/66, No Credit Cards

The façade of this country inn doesn't convince us that gourmet food is served here, but once inside, we believe it almost possible. Comfortable chairs, terra-cotta tiles, nice floral decoration and discreet classical music create a convivial ambience for fine dining. The menu offers rustic Bavarian food and internationally known dishes. The chef exhibits courage in seasoning his courses and prepares his food respectably. The service is remarkably hospitable, but the wine list could use more profile.

FRIEDEWALD — Hessen

Bad Hersfeld 13 - Bad Salzungen 49

ZUM LÖWEN 11/20

36289, Hauptstr. 17
(0 66 74) 7 36, 12 80, Fax 86 35

Closed Monday. Tables d'hôte: 25/55, à la carte: 32/59

This restaurant once had a toque but lost it. And it looks as if it will stay that way. The only thing we really appreciated was the fine buttermilk mousse with herbs (which deserved 13/20) at the beginning of the meal. The owners' country hotel does a good business, and perhaps that explains why they are not concentrating on the cuisine. Red currants turned up in three out of five courses, and baked potatoes in two. The fillet of beef was tough, and the dessert beyond description. If things don't get better, we'll content ourselves with ordering some choice wines from the remarkable wine list next time we go there.

FRIEDLAND Niedersachsen

Kassel 42 - Braunschweig 115

SCHILLINGHOF 15/20

37133, Ortsteil Gieß Schneen
Lappstr. 14
(0 55 04) 2 28, Fax 2 18 res.

 P

Closed Monday, Closed for lunch Tuesday, closed 1-14 January, 3 weeks during the Nieders. summer school holiday. Tables d'hôte: 55/95 à la carte: 36/89

The comfortable Schillingshof is a family business. Stephan Schilling cooks, his brother Thomas tends the well-stocked wine cellar, and his sister-in-law supervises the service with somewhat brittle charm. Stephan Schilling fully deserves his two toques. He prepares meals for large and small appetites, offering all of his main courses as half-portions or à la carte. The Schillings try to comply with the tastes and desires of all their customers. For those who do not like salmon and tuna sashimi, there is the duck, for instance, which can be ordered with side dishes other than lemongrass noodles, honey/soy sauce and Chinese cabbage. Veal with tuna sauce *(vitello tonnato)*, and turbot with three kinds of peppers are something special, and the tomato-and-pepper sauce with marinated sheep cheese tasted wonderful. But the grilled swordfish with ginger noodles developed its characteristic flavor very hesitatingly, simply because the enchanting sauce stole the show.

FRIEDRICHSHAFEN BW

Ravensburg 20 - Lindau 29

BUCHHORNER HOF 12/20

88045, Friedrichstr. 33
(0 75 41) 20 50, Fax 3 26 63

P

Tables d'hôte: 28/92, à la carte: 27/83. Tables d'hôte with wine: 40/160

In these conservative and plain old Swabian rooms, the genuine and pleasant hospitality we experienced really deserved better cooking Try as we might, we couldn't overlook everything, for example warm white wine and stinginess with bread and butter, overdone pike-perch and fall vegetables in spring. The wine list offers respectable wines by the glass and some fine bottles from France. The menu lists down-to-earth classics such as somewhat boring hors d'œuvres, angler, pork fillet and fruit flambé. Guests with normal appetites do best to order smaller portions. Some low-priced prix-fixe menus and modest plats du jour cater to guests with less money to spend.

SIEBEN SCHWABEN 12/20

6 km north in Ailingen
88048, Hauptstr. 37
(0 75 41) 5 50 98/9, Fax 5 69 53 res.

P

Closed for lunch. Tables d'hôte: 32/65, à la carte: 18/43

This is the right place to go if you want to enjoy an original, hearty Swabian meal in comfortable surroundings. Of course, the kitchen does more than just cook filling regional dishes. Although the menu offers an international repertoire from carpaccio to châteaubriand, we preferred fresh fish from the lake and the best Swabian ravioli far and wide. Consistently good was the roast beef with onions, and the spaetzle outstanding, whereas the desserts were nothing special.The service is pleasant and amiable, and the wine list emphasizes bottles and wines by the glass from Baden-Württemberg.

SIEBEN SCHWABEN

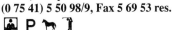

6 km north in Ailingen
88048, Hauptstr. 37
(0 75 41) 5 50 98/9, Fax 5 69 53 res.

P

28, **S** 90/120, **D** 135/160,
½P +19
Closed 2 weeks in January/February

If you don't want to spend the night in the middle of a noisy town, you'll enjoy a quiet rest in the Hellers' well-cared for hotel. It's located in an orchard high above Friedrichshafen. From the rustically furnished rooms you have a nice view of the town, the Bodensee and the Swiss Alps. We especially liked apartments 23 and 25.

TRAUBE 13/20

6 km north in Ailingen
88048, Ittenhauser Str. 4
(0 75 41) 5 30 63

P

Closed Thursday. Tables d'hôte: 22/65, à la carte: 24/63

Constant endeavor reaps its reward, and we hope the Traube keeps the toque we hesitatingly gave it. Sometimes we missed butter with our bread; other times there was more gelatin than chocolate in the white mousse. We shouldn't have shown our enthusiasm about the cheapest main course on the menu (the marinated tripe in Trollinger sauce with lovely fried potatoes) so openly, since we don't know if it's being offered next year at its old price of 16 DM. In any case, the low prices of this plain and down-to-earth restaurant are one its main attractions.The cuisine caters more to the fine palates of gourmets than to ravenous guests, although they won't starve, either. The side dishes are good, but not spectacular: homemade noodles or salads in hearty vinaigrette. We'd appreciate more creative desserts than parfaits, mousses and tiramisù.The didactic wine list is *comme il faut,* and the service is helpful and competent.

BAD FRIEDRICHSHALL BW

Heilbronn 10

LEHENSTUBE IN HOTEL SCHLOSS LEHEN 15/20

74177, Ortsteil Kochendorf
Hauptstr. 2
(0 71 36) 40 44, Fax 2 01 55

P

Closed Sunday, Monday. Tables d'hôte: 79/98, à la carte: 37/93

This castle and its kitchen are just magnificent. Tables with discreet gray cloths are laid with the finest porcelain, glassware and silver. Friedheinz Eggensperger's performance in the kitchen is consistently good. Variations of salmon were followed by variations of sweetbreads. Our slightly smoked pigeon with mushroom noodles was formidable, done to a turn, and looked as sensational as it tasted. Shish-kebab of turbot and lobster was excellent, although the saffron rice it came with was underdone. We loved the lamb cutlets with (also underdone) white beans, tasty carrots, turnips and zucchini. After a choice of five superbly ripened country cheeses, we almost capitulated in the face of the immense choice of desserts. The international wines are reasonably priced.

SCHLOSS LEHEN

74177, Ortsteil Kochendorf
Hauptstr. 2
(0 71 36) 40 44, Fax 2 01 55

27, **S** 90/125, **D** 165/210,
APP 210

Recent renovations and the addition of bathrooms in each room have made this hotel more comfortable, and the ample breakfast buffet provides a good start to the day. Renaissance buildings don't have balconies, but a marvelous view of the surrounding park from the windows compensates for this. Restaurant.

FRIESENHEIM BW

Lahr 5 - Offenburg 13

MÜHLENHOF 12/20

77948, Ortsteil Oberweier
Oberweier Hauptstr. 32
(0 78 21) 63 20, Fax 63 21 53

Closed Tuesday, closed 3 weeks in January and August. Tables d'hôte: 40/58, à la carte: 24/50

A new hotel tract has been added atop the Mühlenhof, so now the restaurant calls itself a country inn. The restaurant has been redecorated, too, and presents itself as elegant and rustic at the same time.The kitchen cooks for every taste, for spendthrifts and splurgers. The six-course prix-fixe menu is good value for 56 DM. Small appetites are satisfied with good à la carte dishes, and if you come after 2 p.m. you can still get lunch. We started with quail's egg on bacon with watercress and green sauce, followed by salmon ravioli in Riesling crème, and finished with saddle of veal with sweetbreads and kohlrabi drowned in a sea of white sauces. Nice desserts, assiduous service and a wine list that needs revision.

FÜRTH Bayern

Nürnberg 7 - München 175

FORTSHAUS

90768, Ortsteil Dambach
Zum Vogelsang 20
(09 11) 77 98 80, Fax 72 08 85

P

107, **S** 190, **D** 270,
APP 450/800, **1/2P** +40, **P** +75

This hotel is frequented primarily by those who attend seminars and conferences here. The rooms are elegant, and the location in the Fürth-Dambach Forest is lovely. The former private residence of Max Grundig nearby has been turned into the convention center "Grundig Park." Fitness facilities, hiking paths. Restaurant.

KUPFERPFANNE 14/20

90762, Königstr. 85
(09 11) 77 12 77, Fax 77 76 37 res.

P

Closed Sunday and Monday. Tables d'hôte: 85, à la carte: 55/87

The Kupferpfanne was once the shining defender of refined Franconian cooking. Today, the cuisine is correct but offers only the unexciting gourmet fare found the world over. Lamb's lettuce with croutons, the usual beef carpaccio, Maine lobster, Wiener schnitzel with buttered asparagus, lamb saddle with a crust of herbs, baked turbot—everything was prepared perfectly. But what ever happened to the creativity and esprit that were once Erwin Weidenhiller's trademarks? The prices are still high, even though today's cuisine tastes like a faded copy of one-time greatness. We remember the inspired cuisine and the marvelous evenings we spent here, and hope Erich Weidenmiller finds new impetus. One consolation: the wine cellar is brilliantly stocked.

FÜSSEN Bayern

Kempten 40 - München 120

ALPENSCHLÖSSLE 15/20

87629, Bad Faulenbach
Alatseestr. 28
(0 83 62) 40 17, Fax 3 98 47 res.

Closed Tuesday. Tables d'hôte: 24/28L, 78/98D, à la carte: 35/76, No Credit Cards

Good things usually aren't far away, so Hermine Hummel, charming owner of this lovely and idyllically located hotel, is a little sad when her house guests eat out. This is the best restaurant in Füssen and Hermine Hummel's cook, Thomas Kopp, is really good. Some highlights of our last visit: an exquisite composition of succulent lamb fillet slices and black olive sauce with ratatouille accompanied by an outstanding Château Loyasson, followed by an excellent cream of prawn soup and capped by angler cutlet with champagne sauce and fresh asparagus.The ambience is stylish and discreetly charming, the service attentive and the wine list comprehensive, even in the choice of half-bottles. French and Italian wines are offered at moderate prices.

Remember to reserve your table or your room in advance, and please let the restaurant or hotel know if you cannot honour your reservation.

ALPENSCHLÖSSLE

87629, Bad Faulenbach
Alatseestr. 28
(0 83 62) 40 17, Fax 3 98 47

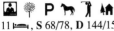

P

11, **S** 68/78, **D** 144/150,
1/2P +33, **P** +43
No Credit Cards

Pine, cherry wood and knotty oak give this hotel a rustic and comfortable charm. Some of the most beautiful lakes for swimming are located nearby, as are the castles Neuschwanstein and Hohenschwangau.

FISCHERHÜTTE 12/20

5 km northwest
in 87629 Hopfen am See
Uferstr. 16
(0 83 62) 71 03

The location of this restaurant on the shore of the Hopfensee is enchanting, but the cuisine, which caters to crowds of tourists, is much less exciting. The menu offers unremarkable standards. The kitchen could use new impetus.

GASTHOF ZUM SCHWANEN 12/20

87629, Brotmarkt 4
(0 83 62) 61 74

Closed for dinner Sunday, closed Monday, month of November, 2 weeks during the spring. Tables d'hôte: 20L, 25/40D, à la carte: 17/40, No Credit Cards

Everything's right with the world when you step into this friendly *gasthaus* in the old section of Füssen. Customers immediately feel at home here. The menu confirmed our good first impression. We tried well-seasoned garlic soup and consommé with *flädle* (shredded pancake), tasty Swabian ravioli, excellent homemade pork sausage, juicy pork roast and saddle of venison with spaetzle. The warm apple strudel fresh from the oven was especially tasty.The small but well-stocked wine cellar surprised us with moderately priced, high-quality wines from Germany, France and Italy. The service was attentive and friendly.

LANDHAUS ENZENSBERG 13/20

5 km north in
87629 Hopfen am See
Höhenstr. 53
(0 83 62) 40 61/2, Fax 3 91 79 res.

Closed Monday, expected to close either January or April. Tables d'hôte: 25/35L, 65/88D, à la carte: 25/81, No Credit Cards

High on a southern slope above the Hopfensee (the Riviera of the Allgäu), there is a pretty whitewashed country house with flowered balconies, green and blue window shutters and a wonderful terrace. The restaurant is decorated with light-colored wooden paneling. There is a nice little beer bar as well. For remarkably low prices, we ordered a flavorful consommé with al dente vegetables, venison schnitzel with Calvados cream and Savoy cabbage and morels, saddle of lamb with Gorgonzola crust, and fillet of beef in onion sauce with ravioli. The side dishes could use a little more attention: The artichokes were overdone, the cèpe spaghetti too heavy, and the creamed sauce with the veal fillet too thin. The desserts, however, were light and enjoyable.The wine list offers wines by the glass at reasonable prices and a good choice of wines by the bottle from Germany, France and Italy. The owner was much friendlier than the ladies who served our meal.

LANDHAUS ENZENSBERG

5 km north in
87629 Hopfen am See
Höhenstr. 53
(0 83 62) 40 61/2, Fax 3 91 79

P

10, **S** 75/90, **D** 160/220,
APP 220/320, **1/2P** +35, **P** +52
Expected to close month of January, No Credit Cards

The spacious rooms of this elegant country manor house are well-equipped. Marble bathrooms, tiled floors and comfortable furniture make guests feel at home.

FULDA Hessen

Frankfurt 103 - Würzurg 108

GOLDENER KARPEN 14/20

36037, Simpliciusplatz 1
(06 61) 7 00 44, Fax 7 30 42 res.

P

Tables d'hôte: 45/98, à la carte: 34/82

A carp is a fish that lives in fresh water and avoids strong currents, that is more at home in quiet ponds than flowing rivers. But this Goldener Karpfen (golden carp) makes its way through today's strong culinary currents with easy nonchalance. The experienced kitchen staff juggles trendy cuisine and classic dishes, but rarely loses its balance. First courses and desserts have become more interesting, and only small "accidents" prevent the awarding of a second toque. The cucumber soup was a little on the heavy side, the beef tips with mustard sauce were not as tender as they should have been, and the accompanying dumplings could have been lighter. We had nothing but praise for the terrine of chanterelles with cherries, the salmon terrine with sour cream, fresh tomato soup with basil and fillet of veal, marinated salmon with caviar cream and seaweed, delicate crêpe with sweetbreads and chanterelles, and carefully fried fresh halibut with potato gratin and an unobtrusive garlic sauce. The delicious desserts all deserved a rating of 15/20. The service is perfect, and the wine cellar is especially well stocked.

GAGGENAU Baden-Württ.

Baden-Baden 16-Karlsruhe 30

ADLER 14/20

76571, Ortsteil Ottenau
Hauptstr. 255
(0 72 25) 37 06 res.

P

Closed for dinner Sunday, closed Monday, 1 week before Shrove Tuesday, 3 weeks during the Bad.-Württ. summer school holiday. Tables d'hôte: 39/90, à la carte: 29/67, No Credit Cards

Black Forest cuisine is usually very down-to-earth. On our last visit to the Adler, we ran into a *schlachtfest,* a traditional celebration after the butchering of a pig. We stayed and had delicious stuffed pig's feet, blood pudding broth and *schlachtplatte* (an assortment of sausages and pork), and we were singing the cook's praises when we finished. When game is in season, try the hare or venison with spaetzle, roasted wild boar, pheasant with sauerkraut, or roasted wild duck. All the dishes here have a distinct regional touch and are savory and very good.After taking a peek at the skimpy wine list, we ordered a draft beer. The service is friendly and welcoming.

PARKHOTEL GAGGENAU

76555, Konrad-Adenauer-Str. 1
(0 72 25) 6 70, Fax 7 62 05

P

63 rooms, **S** 118/159, **D** 159/227,
APP 220/287, **½P** +35, **P** +60

This hotel is without a doubt the most beautiful and striking building in town. It is built in what the Swiss architect Julius Dahinden calls the "futuristic desert style," and has become one of the emblems of Gaggenau, just like the trademark of a famous German car manufacturer (Mercedes-Benz) here. Bar, dancing, restaurant. Breakfast: 19.50 DM.

TRAUBE MICHELBACH 13/20

76571, Ortsteil Michelbach
Lindenstr. 10
(0 72 25) 7 62 63, Fax 7 02 13 res.

 P

Tables d'hôte: 50/85, à la carte: 42/78

This restaurant is a refuge for easygoing sensualists. It has a romantic atmosphere, with its wooden beams and paneling, and the owner's friendly attentions make this one of our favorite places to sit, eat and drink. The cuisine is nothing to rave about, but Jean-Pierre Recht serves cleverly seasoned and skillfully prepared Alsatian specialities. The fried foie gras was of unusually good quality, and the bass and sole with saffron and butter sauce was almost poetry. The lamb ribs were excellent, too. The desserts are served on the traditional wagon, which does not mean that they are not good. The wine list is comprehensive reasonably priced.

GAIENHOFEN BW

Radolfzell 11

SEERESTAURANT SCHLÖSSLI 12/20

78343, Ortsteil Horn/Höri
Hornstaader Str. 43
(0 77 35) 20 41

 P

Tables d'hôte: 62, à la carte: 40/68

This castle on the lakeshore, called by the diminutive *Schlössli,* is really the distinguished Schloss Hornstaad. An inviting beer garden faces the shore, and the interior is far from formal or stuffy. There's a rustic *bauernstube* and a sort of bar-bistro-pub combination, but gourmets eat in an elegant glassed-in winter garden. We couldn't quite share the unmitigated enthusiasm of Schlössli fans who rave about the cuisine here, but we must admit that nowhere else between Lindau and Radolfzell have we found a restaurant with such a splendid view offering such good quality at low prices. The highlight of our four-course prix-fixe meal was rack of lamb with zucchini lasagna and garlic. The à la carte choice includes Belgian endive salad with grilled scampi and two sauces, fried duck liver with thyme and floating island with honey cream.The service is pleasant and the wine list small but choice, with 19 wines available by the glass.

GARMISCH-PARTENK. Bay.

Mittenwald 18 - Innsbruck 55

ASCHENBRENNER

82467, Loisachstr. 46
(0 88 21) 5 80 29, Fax 48 05

 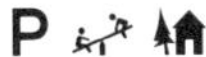

23, **S** 75/100, **D** 130/190

If you like typical turn-of-the-century charm, you'll enjoy this hotel, which is a mixture of modern comfort and *fin-de-siècle* appeal. The rooms are spacious and comfortable, and the wood-paneled breakfast room is lovely. The hotel is two minutes away from the spa and four minutes from the center of town.

CLAUSINGS POSTHOTEL

82467. Marienplatz 12
(0 88 21) 70 90, Fax 70 92 05

45, **S** 120/180, **D** 160/220,
APP 240/450, **1/2P** +35, **P** +50

This hotel is located in the middle of bustling Garmisch, just where a traditional Bavarian post office belongs. If you're susceptible to the charm of old buildings, you'll feel at home in the individually decorated rooms furnished with antiques. Glassed-in breakfast terrace, beer garden, fitness center, discotheque and restaurant.

GRAND-HOTEL SONNENBICHL (BLUE SALON) 14/20

82467, Burgstr. 97
(0 88 21) 70 20, Fax 70 21 31 res.

 P

Tables d'hôte: 40/80, à la carte: 38/73

The restaurant has been redecorated, and the good old days seem to have returned. The kitchen seems to have been reborn as well. We found some snags (scampi shells in the wonton pastry and hard cheese croutons in the sorrel soup) but, on the whole, we were satisfied. We had lobster cocktail and smoked breast of goose, pike-perch with fennel sauce, steamed seafood, veal schnitzel in lemon sauce and veal fillet with tomatoes and mozzarella. The wide range of wines and champagnes is (more or less) reasonably priced. The service staff could do with a little coaching.

GRAND-HOTEL SONNENBICHL

82467, Burgstr. 97
(0 88 21) 70 20, Fax 70 21 31

93, **S** 100/200, **D** 200/300,
APP 350/900, **1/2P** +40, **P** +65

The hotel in this complex has been known for generations as the Golf Hotel Sonnenbichl and is one of the leading hotels in the region. The rooms are spacious and comfortably furnished, and most have balconies with a wonderful view of the

Alps. A large terrace, which is used as a café in the afternoons, is located at the rear of the house. Solarium, fitness center, massage, bicycles.

OBERMÜHLE

82467, Mühlstr. 22
(0 88 21) 70 40, Fax 70 41 12

P

93, **S** 195/240, **D** 250/325, **½P** +35, **P** +55

Although located a few minutes from the center of town, this hotel is an oasis of peace and quiet. The rooms are well-furnished and comfortable and offer all modern amenities, including an indoor pool, a bar and cozy lounges.

PARTENKIRCHNER HOF

82467, Bahnhofstr. 15
(0 88 21) 5 80 25, Fax 7 34 01

P

65, **S** 130/180, **D** 170/210, **APP** 270/450, **½P** +45

Closed 15 November through 15 December

This very popular hotel, located near the train station, tries to combine elegance with comfort. Six million DM have been invested recently to assure more class and comfort. The rooms are somewhat small (we recommend those facing the garden), but the restaurant and lobby are furnished with choice antiques. The apartments in the Haus Wetterstein annex are furnished in 19th-century country style. Very ample breakfast buffet.

POSTHOTEL PARTENKIRCHEN 14/20

82467, Ludwigstr. 49
(0 88 21) 5 10 67/8, Fax 7 85 68 res.

P

Tables d'hôte: 32/78, à la carte: 26/76

Ironically enough, finding a typical Bavarian hotel in Garmisch-Partenkirchen can be very difficult. The Posthotel is one. Built in the 15th century, it was a post stop for many years and has been owned by the same family for four generations. We recommend the rooms in the new annex, since they have direct access to the sun deck.

POSTHOTEL PARTENKIRCHEN

82467, Ludwigstr. 49
(0 88 21) 5 10 67/8, Fax 7 85 68

P

60, **S** 115/170, **D** 190/290, **APP** 350

Once you get used to the oppressive wooden ceiling and the wood paneling, the Alte Posthalterei in the Posthotel Partenkirchen is a comfortable restaurant. There was a fresh wind in the kitchen that sent a few surprises to our table, such as asparagus tips with ham mousse and red wine jelly.The consommé with *flädle* (pancake strips) was as delicate as could be. The anglerfish with seasoned tomatoes was a complete success, as were the lamb noisettes with beans, and the boiled fillet of beef with horseradish and spinach. Red currant pancakes with cinnamon ice cream and orange gratin concluded an excellent meal.The wine list offers well-known vintages from Germany, France and Italy, plus a wide choice of champagnes. If only the prices were a bit lower! The service is the Achilles' heel of the Posthotel—sometimes sloppy and, when the restaurant is full, unnecessarily hasty.

QUEENS HOTEL RESIDENCE

82467, Mittenwalder Str. 2
(0 88 21) 75 60, Fax 7 42 68

P

117, **S** 160/226, **D** 230/302, **APP** 290/382, **½P** +37, **P** +74

The interior decoration and many works of art make these small, typically Bavarian rooms inviting. The hotel offers everything a guest could want. Tourist groups are welcome here. Breakfast buffet.

REINDL'S RESTAURANT IN HOTEL PARTENKIRCHNER HOF 14/20

82467, Bahnhofstr. 15
(0 88 21) 5 80 25, Fax 7 34 01 res.

Closed 15 November through 15 December. Tables d'hôte: 335/45L, 110D, à la carte: 36/73

We are always drawn back to Reindl's, where the reception in the tastefully decorated dining rooms is pleasant and considerate, and the service is quick and attentive.Reindl's daughter Marianne Holzinger has taken over the kitchen, and we were impressed with the piquant fish soup (with plenty of fish), the spicy lentil soup with scampi, the fresh eel from the nearby Walchensee, char, whitefish, salmon and anglerfish (fried whole only). Lobster is only available for two people. A classic coq au vin, tender truffled fillet of beef, and calf's kidneys in sweet and sour sauce were pure pleasure. For dessert, there is a variety of homemade ice creams and sherbets, crème caramel and fresh fruit salad.The prices of the wines are incredibly low.

RESTAURANT HUSAR 12/20

82467, Fürstenstr. 25
(0 88 21) 17 13 res.

P

Closed for lunch every day except Sunday, closed Monday, month of August. Tables d'hôte: 30/50L, 40/80D, à la carte: 42/85

Good honest cooking is served in this historic building with its folksy painted gables and comfortable rustic decor (wood everywhere!). We can't complain about quality or quantity, but the food is much too expensive. Tasty dished included nettle soup with crème fraîche and fish soup seasoned with Pernod. Delicious king prawns, a specialty of the house, can be ordered baked, fried or poached with dill. The choice of main courses include *tafelspitz* or grilled veal with morel sauce, saddle of rabbit or lamb, or schnitzel of venison with spaetzle and cranberries. The desserts are fruity, and the service is pleasant.The wine list offers good wines by the glass and reasonably priced wines by the bottle.

STAUDACHER HOF

82467, Höllentalstr. 48
(0 88 21) 5 51 55, Fax 5 51 86

37 rooms, **S** 80/155, **D** 85/130, **APP** 150/160

Closed 23 April through 7 March

"Your home in Garmisch," claims the house brochure, which hits the nail on the head. Located on a quiet little side street in Garmisch, this little hotel with its twin white turrets looks as cozy and comfortable on the outside as it is inside. Solarium. Particularly friendly service. Breakfast: 18 DM.

GAU-BISCHOFSHEIM RP

Mainz 10 - Alzey 39

WEINGUT NACK 12/20

55296, Pfarrstr. 13
(0 61 35) 30 43/4, Fax 83 82 res.

Closed for lunch every day except Sunday, closed Tuesday. Tables d'hôte: 85/125, à la carte: 46/85

The facade of this former wine estate radiates dignity and elegance, but once you're inside, this historic building looks as if it has seen better days. The dining room is decorated with arty bric-a-brac and kitsch like tasseled lamps on refurbished plows and uncomfortable chairs with picturesquely torn upholstery.The only thing that made us feel welcome was the cuisine, which offered finely seasoned salad with tasty duck's breast, succulent rabbit fillet with mild asparagus salad, salty cream of asparagus soup with salmon, cream of prawn soup, braised lamb haunch with a concentrated sauce and tender and succulent fillet tips of beef.The service is correct and unobtrusive. The wine list emphasizes mediocre regional wines, but also offers some renowned French names. Anybody want to pay 1,200 DM for a 1982 Château Lafite-Rothschild?

GEISENHEIM Hessen

Rüdesheim 3

GUTSSCHÄNKE SCHLOSS JOHANNISBERG 14/20

65366. Johannisberg
(0 67 22) 85 38, Fax 73 92

Closed Monday in November, December and March, Tuesday in January, February. Tables d'hôte: 50, à la carte: 33/68, No Credit Cards

For tourists, a visit to this imposing manorial estate high above the Rhine, with its beautiful view of the Rheingau, is a must. In the restaurant, Dieter Biesler doesn't pamper his customers with pompous cuisine; instead, he serves well-cooked, honest meals. The menu is small, with only 14 dishes, plus one regional speciality and an interesting daily fixed-price menu.If you are lucky and Dieter Biesler has just picked some figs in his castle garden, you might get them with duck liver terrine. On our last visit, he prepared a gratin of sole with zucchini, chanterelles in cream, and exquisite lamb cutlets, excellent herring salad, a savory house pâté, sausages with sauerkraut, and a hearty ragout of lamb with potato gratin. There are wines from the famous Schloss Johannisberg and the sparkling "Fürst Metternich" wines from the Mumm estate. Wines by the glass and by the bottle are relatively low-priced.

GELNHAUSEN Hessen

Frankfurt 42 - Fulda 62

SCHIESSHAUS 13/20

5 km southwest in Ortsteil Meerholz
63571, Schießhausstr. 10
(0 60 51) 6 69 29, Fax 6 60 97 res.

 P

Closed Wednesday, 1—14 January, 2 weeks during the Hessen summer school holiday. Tables d'hôte: 35L, 55/77D, à la carte: 38/61

Surrounded by woods and meadows on a hill overlooking Gelnhausen, this hunting lodge built in 1831 offers familiar hospitality in its comfortable dining rooms, a winter garden and an outdoor terrace. The dishes Peter Lefèvre prepared go with the homey atmosphere of the place. We had honest, consistent country cooking, plain and savory. Besides saddle of lamb coated with herbs, and venison with red cabbage and spaetzle, the kitchen offers classic haute cuisine such as foie gras with grapes in port-wine sauce.The service is circumspect and discreet. The wine list offers good Italian, Spanish, French and German wines at attractive prices. The red wines by the glass are better than the whites.

GERA Thüringen

Erfurt 81 - Chemnitz 52

ELSTERTAL IN HOTEL GERA 10/20

07545, Heinrichstr. 30
(03 65) 69 30, Fax 2 34 49 res.

P

Tables d'hôte: 26/35, à la carte: 25/73

The young ladies who look after the customers here are especially nice. Little more can be said in praise of this spacious restaurant. The wine list has become even smaller than it was, although some (unfamiliar) vintages can still be had at an acceptable price. Although we smiled at the idea of having "our Easter menu" offered in summer, we failed to see the humor in undressed lamb's lettuce with underdone scallops, lamb saddle with frozen vegetables and a rubbery chocolate mousse. A new chef is supposed to take over soon, so let's keep our fingers crossed.

HOTEL GERA

07545, Heinrichstr. 30
(03 65) 69 30, Fax 2 34 49

P

303 rooms, **S** 195/250, **D** 270/290,
APP 380/450, **1/2P** +30, **P** +60

The spacious, modern lobby houses a piano bar and a pleasant reception area, and leads to beautifully equipped rooms, suites and apartments. The rooms have been renovated and offer all modern amenities. One wing of the hotel is reserved for non-smokers. Opulent breakfast. The Café Heidecker has a spacious outdoor terrace. Nightclub and bar with dancing.

GEROLSBACH Bayern

Schrobenhausen 10

GASTHAUS BENEDIKT BREITNER 11/20

85302, Probsteistr. 7
(0 84 45) 2 08

P

Closed Tuesday. Tables d'hôte: 25/35, à la carte: 15/62

In this historic priory, guests sit at tables around an immense tiled stove in winter or outside under a venerable chestnut tree in summer. The prices are reasonable, the service is friendly and the menu offers good value for the price: beautiful big trout prepared six different ways, lovely mushrooms and prime game in season, roast veal with spaetzle and duck's breast with black raspberry and mustard sauce.The respectable wines by the glass, as well as some bottles from Germany and France, are incredibly low-priced.

GIESSEN Hessen

Marburg 30 - Frankfurt 67

DA MICHELE 12/20

35390, Grünberger Str. 4
(06 41) 2 32 26, res.

P

Closed Sunday, closed for lunch Monday.Tables d'hôte: 43/87D, à la carte: 27/67

If Michele Liut isn't in his kitchen, we miss the proverbial salt in the soup. Giessen's best restaurant—a clever bistro with Italian specialties—rises and falls on the strength of its owner, who radiates a southern spirit sadly lacking in the rest of the kitchen and service staff.Order the special dishes—for example, fish on Thursday, Wednesday and Friday—and you'll really get something good. The nondescript pasta on the menu was uninteresting compared to the cannelloni offered as a daily special. Neither the desserts nor the wine list gave cause for complaint.

STEINSGARTEN

35390, Hein-Heckroth-Str. 20
(06 41) 3 89 90, Fax 3 89 92 00

P

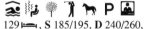

129, **S** 185/195, **D** 240/260, **APP** 320

Closed 22 December through 8 January

It's not often that one can find a quiet hotel located in the center of town with its own access road to the autobahn. This hotel is your best choice in Giessen. Modern convention center, solarium, restaurant.

GIFHORN Niedersachsen

Braunschweig 30 - Celle 44

GOURMET-RESTAURANT RAUCH 13/20

38518, Stadtteil Winkel
Kellerberg 1
(0 53 71) 5 17 82

Closed Monday. Tables d'hôte: 39L, 65/85D, à la carte: 44/78

With a change in style and quality, this restaurant has done itself a favor. There are still some gaps in the wine list, but at least it's become more international. The cuisine is ambitious. We had lasagna with spinach and slightly dry crayfish, lovely green salad with quail's breast and oranges and a slightly overdone but still tender rack of lamb with a wildly assorted heap of mixed vegetables.

GLASHÜTTEN Hessen

Königstein 6 - Frankfurt 30

SCHÜTZENHOF 17/20

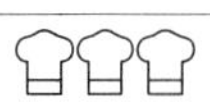

61479, Ortsteil Schloßborn
Langstr. 13
(0 61 74) 6 10 74, Fax 96 40 12 res.

P

Closed for lunch Sunday, closed Monday, Closed for lunch Tuesday and Wednesday, closed 4 weeks in spring. Tables d'hôte: 105, à la carte: 60/102, No Credit Cards

It is always a wonderful experience to eat in this restaurant. We started with a sensational appetizer of scallops prepared in three different ways. Seldom have we tasted anything as perfect! Also superb were spaghetti with chanterelles à la crème and a delicately dressed salad of avocado and artichoke with pigeon. The gazpacho served here has nothing in common with the rustic Andalusian original, but is an elegant savory tomato soup. The best thing that can happen to a bass is to be baked in a salt crust here and be served in an flavorful sauce with truffles. The fantastic desserts are served in a parade of different plates.The comprehensive choice of wines is outstanding. You can always follow connoisseur Lothar Mohr's advice in choosing the right wines.

GLONN Bayern

München 30 - Rosenheim 33

HERMANNSDORFER SCHWEINSBRÄU 15/20

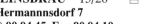

85625, Hermannnsdorf 7
(0 80 93) 90 94 45, Fax 90 94 10

Closed Monday, Tuesday, first week in January, à la carte: 36/67

This restaurant is about 30 kilometers from Munich and is always worth the trip. The two owners have cooked their way to the top in Munich and manage this country restaurant with its simpler cooking on the side. The interior of the restaurant is light and airy.In the kitchen, only ecologically grown produce from the Hermannsdorf farm is used, and the meat is raised on the meadows and pastures of the restaurant's estate. The cheese, butter and bread is homemade, and even the beer is brewed here! The small but respectable choice of wines comes from ecological wine growers. As a result, everything here tastes better than average and makes you feel healthy, too. We appreciated the clear oxtail soup with noodles and the green lentil soup with bacon, and the artistically arranged red beets with fried brook trout and endive salad. We loved the surprising whole-wheat liver ravioli with fresh herbs. Fruit from the farm makes great desserts. The service is attentive and obliging.

GLOTTERTAL Bad.-Württ.

Denzlingen 5 - Freiburg 16

GASTHAUS ZUM ADLER 12/20

79286, Talstr. 11
(0 76 84) 10 81/1, Fax 10 83

Closed Tuesday. Tables d'hôte: 35/69, à la carte: 28/68

The typical Black Forest facade, comfortable dining rooms and garden behind the house make this restaurant attractive and popular. But where the quality of the cuisine is concerned, it is in for a crash landing if it doesn't pull up fast. The dishes, usually served by waitresses in a great hurry, don't taste any more remarkable than in any other normal *gasthof.* At least the anglerfish in orange and pepper sauce and the roast lamb were of respectable quality.

HIRSCHEN 13/20

79286, Rathausweg 2
(0 76 84) 8 10, Fax 17 13 res.

Closed Monday. Tables d'hôte: 68/110, à la carte: 48/90

Serving high-quality food at 50 tables is seldom easy. It is difficult to meet the demands of gourmet palates while feeding crowds with big appetites. The Hirschen offers many different dishes to a wide range of diners and tries hard not to serve anything less than good cooking. Families who take grandma out to Sunday dinner are as at home here as the professor from Freiburg or the young man seeking to impress his girlfriend. They all appreciate the comfortable Black Forest atmosphere and hospitality. An experienced kitchen brigade gave us lamb's lettuce with pink sea bream, lovely bouillabaisse, salmon roulade in champagne sauce, calf's tongue and figs in port-wine sauce.We recommend the regional wines, like those from the Roter Bur vineyard.

HIRSCHEN

79286, Rathausweg 2
(0 76 84) 8 10, Fax 17 13

P

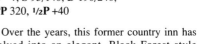

54 beds, **S** 95/140, **D** 190/240, **APP** 320, **½P** +40

Over the years, this former country inn has evolved into an elegant, Black Forest-style hotel. The rooms are modern and tastefully furnished. Bar and restaurant.

GLÜCKSTADT Schl.-Holst.

Itzehoe 20 - Elmshorn 22

RATSKELLER 12/20

25348, Am Markt 4
(0 41 24) 24 64, Fax 41 54 res.

Tables d'hôte: 45/53, à la carte: 27/61

The owner has picked a winner in her new chef, Thomas Brast, who may be able to repair the somewhat damaged reputation of the Ratskeller. Besides offering the traditional herring in different variations, Brast tries his hand at refined regional cuisine, so ask the competent service staff for special suggestions that are not on the menu. We had excellent plaice with fresh shrimps and succulent codfish with a light sauce of herbs and mustard. The comprehensive wine list even includes famous names from Bordeaux and Burgundy.

GÖHREN-LEBBIN MV

Malchow 8 - Waren 18

HOTEL SCHLOSS BLÜCHER 14/20

17213, Göhrin-Lennin
(03 99 32) 1 75, Fax 1 79 99

P

Tables d'hôte: 40/75, à la carte: 33/78

A stylish ambience, lots of fine stucco work, floral glass art on the windows and decorative Art Nouveau chairs keep the large dining halls from being intimidating and create a charming and elegantly comfortable ambience. The beautiful interior, together with the marvelous cuisine, make this the best restaurant in this part of the country. In addition to a small menu, the kitchen offers one three-course prix-fixe meal and a few daily specials. Our delicious cream of spinach soup with shrimps was expertly prepared, salmon and anglerfish with ratatouille excellently fried and the praline parfait with rum sauce and mango slices exquisitely arranged. The service isn't a positive element of the picture yet: the waitresses were too rushed and stiffly serious. The good choice of wines includes reasonably priced bottles from Germany, Italy and France.

HOTEL SCHLOSS BLÜCHER

17213, Göhrin-Lennin
(03 99 32) 1 75, Fax 1 79 99

41, **S** 80/185, **D** 100/265,
APP 350/375, **1/2P** +40, **P** +80

Count Ludwig von Blücher built this little castle near the Müritz National Park for his guests in 1830. In July 1990, it was made over into a hotel, and soon it will be the focal point of an exclusive complex with a golf course and tennis courts, yachting harbor and polo field. Some rooms and suites have already been exquisitely renovated to make guests feel like lords of the manor. The cellar of the castle has a bar and a library.

GOTHA Thüringen

Erfurt 25 - Eisenach 32

SCHLOSSHOTEL REINHARDSBRUNN

14 km southwest in 99894 Friedrichroda
(0 36 23) 42 53/4, Fax 42 51

54, **S** 55/210, **D** 70/320,
1/2P +25, **P** +45

This castle, built in 1828 and situated in a marvelous park with a pond, has been a hotel since 1961 and was recently renovated. It is so quiet here and the air is so clean that you can sleep with the windows open. Pleasant convention rooms. Restaurant. Breakfast: 17.50 DM.

GRAAL-MÜRITZ MV

Rostock 20

GRAND HOTEL

18181, Waldstr.
(03 82 06) 7 98 00, Fax 2 27

P

70, **S** 95/125, **D** 130/165,
APP 155/330, **1/2P** +30, **P** +55

The best hotel of this traditional seashore spa is located directly behind a dune. A variety of recreational facilities compensates for the somewhat drab exterior. Physiotherapy, beauty farm, hairdresser, skittle alley, bar, restaurant.

GRABOW MV

Schwerin 41

SCHLACHTERBÖRSE 12/20

19300, Marktstr. 12
(03 87 56) 24 36

Butcher Manfred Gollnik has established a restaurant in his beautiful old house facing the medieval marketplace of this lovely little town. He serves cabbage roulades, generously proportioned steaks, homemade aspics and regional soups, all prepared from locally raised beef, veal and pork. The wine list is meager, but there's draft beer as well.

GRAINAU — Bayern

Garmisch-Partenkirchen 5

ALPENHOF

82491, Alpspitzstr. 34
(0 88 21) 80 71, Fax 8 16 80
P
36, S 95/170, **D** 240/360

This house, surrounded by a large park, could have come right out of a picture book about Bavaria. The rooms are cozy and comfortable. The idyllic Grainau region offers cross-country and downhill skiing. The Zugspitzbahn (train to the Zugspitze) is five minutes away.

GASTHOF HÖHENRAIN 12/20

82491, Eibseestr. 1
(0 88 21) 88 88, Fax 8 27 20
A la carte: 17/52

We discovered this gem on our way to the lake. Inconspicuous from the outside and rustic and plain inside, it has a kitchen full of surprises. Heartily Bavarian in style were such dishes as soup with pancake strips and liver dumplings, succulent pork roast with potato dumplings and red cabbage, and sauerbraten with bread dumplings. Gourmets will appreciate the pike-perch fillet, saddle of rabbit, poached fillet of ox, calf's kidneys in mustard sauce and delicate stuffed quail.The respectable wine list offers good wines by the glass and well-chosen French, Italian, German and Spanish wines at uncommonly reasonable prices. The service is young, quick and circumspect.

GREIFSWALD — MV

Stralsund 31 - Anklam 37

EUROPA HOTEL

17491, Hans-Beimler-Str. 1-3
(0 38 34) 80 10, Fax 80 11 00
P
55, **S** 160/225, **D** 230/265,
1/2P +25, **P** +45

This new and comfortable hotel has elegantly decorated rooms. The Galloway restaurant features meat grilled on rock lava and fish. Ample breakfast buffet.

GREVENBROICH — NRW

Düsseldorf 30 - Köln 31

ZUR TRAUBE 19.5/20

41515, Bahnstr. 47
(0 21 81) 6 87 67, Fax 6 11 22 res.
P
Closed Sunday, Monday, 20 December through 20 January, 10-18 April, 18 July through 1 August. Tables d'hôte: 72/92L, 148/178D, à la carte: 73/183

Kaufmann's Traube is one of the best restaurants in the world. Everything that can be said in praise of the deceptively simple elegance of its dining room, the unparalleled choice of wines, liqueurs and Champagnes and the charmingly perfect service has been said before. As a result, we are forced to repeat ourselves. Everything harmonizes, and the cuisine is unique in its straightforward simplicity. At first sight, the food seems modest and unpretentious, a bit like chef Dieter Kaufmann himself, who doesn't jet around the world to advertise himself like many of his colleagues. You won't see him on television or on a billboard because he is where he thinks he belongs—behind the range of his own kitchen in Grevenbroich. Two of the standards we always love to order are sturgeon parfait and a sort of layer cake consisting of foie-gras parfait and mousse and pastry. This has been copied often, but never equaled. Firm consistency and enchanting lightness are not contradictions in Kaufmann's cuisine. Nobody can prepare fish better than he can; his bass with chard and chanterelles was perfect. So were the venison and the fantastic truffled pigeon breast. The zucchini flower stuffed with prawns and scallops in pink champagne was a feast for the eyes and an unforgettable experience for the senses! Kaumann's restaurant can easily compete with the top French restaurants in the choice of cheeses in different stages of ripeness. Even after seven or eight courses, we rose from the table feeling lighthearted and carefree—and speechless with delight.

ZUR TRAUBE

41515, Bahnstr. 47
(0 21 81) 6 87 67, Fax 6 11 22
P
6, **S** 190/340, **D** 290/350,
APP 420/490,
Closed 10—18 April, 18 July through 1 August

This hotel offers modern rooms with every amenity. The rooms are named after varieties of grapes. The "Silvaner" room, for instance, has a charm of its own—like bubbly Champagne. Luxurious marble bathrooms. Opulent breakfast.

GRÖMITZ Schl.-Holst.

Neustadt 12 - Oldenburg 20

LA MAREE IN HOTEL PINGUIN 14/20

23743, Chr.-Westphal-Str. 52
(0 45 62) 98 27, Fax 1717 res.

Closed for lunch, closed Monday, 10 January through 15 March. Tables d'hôte: 75/130, à la carte: 42/78, No Credit Cards

New furniture and a lovely decor have created a lively and harmonious ambience in this little gem of a restaurant. Chef Ernst Fischer has shown impressive consistency and developed finesse over the years. On the menu we found attractive prix-fixe suggestions rounded off with a few daily specials à la carte. We liked his regional cuisine best: lovely and light sturgeon parfait with savory Riesling zabaglione, delicately hearty saddle of young wild boar with green string beans and chanterelles and an aromatic parfait of elderberry blossoms and sorbet of Cavaillon melon (15/20!) Agreeable and attentive service. Some Italian and Californian wines have been added to the wine list.

GRONAU NRW

Enschede 9 - Münster 53

HEIDEHOF 14/20

4 km west of Ortsteil Epe
48599, Amtsvenn 1
(0 25 65) 13 30, Fax 30 73

Closed for lunch Saturday, closed Monday, 14 February through 28 May, 14—30 October.Tables d'hôte: 30/40L, 60/99D, à la carte: 39/76. Tables d'hôte with wine: 45/99

When we discovered Theo Lammer's restaurant 11 years ago, most of his customers came from nearby Gronau. Today, his clientele is international—his best frequent customers cross over the border from the Netherlands. This country restaurant with its thatched roof has added on a tastefully furnished and elegantly decorated conservatory as an additional dining room. The service has not kept up with the pace of the growing restaurant, and when all the tables are occupied, sometimes slips up when serving delicious sardines with lemon and olive sauce, tender quail's breast with finely seasoned balsamic vinegar, and juicy entrecôte with wonderfully crispy fried potatoes. Lammer's fish dishes are outstanding. We enjoyed our shish kebab of scampi and anglerfish served with flavorful vegetables.

GRÖNENBACH Bayern

Memmingen 15 - Kempten 25

BADISCHE WEINSTUBE 13/20

87730, Marktplatz 8
(0 83 34) 5 05, Fax 63 90 res.

Tables d'hôte: 39/119, à la carte: 27/57. Tables d'hôte with wine: 39/119

This tastefully decorated rustic restaurant with its great tiled stove, located far from the madding crowd in Grönenbach, is worth a visit. After the cold potato soup with fishy shrimps failed to convince us, our spirits revived at a breast of guinea fowl marinated in lemongrass and served with chanterelle risotto. We would have liked a little more champagne vinegar with our duck-liver pralines and salad. The menu, offering mostly regional dishes, seems a bit too comprehensive. The fish creations are interesting, but why stuff potato ravioli with caviar?The choice of wines is delightfully large, with an ample supply of wines by the glass. Burgundy, Alsace and the Loire are dominant —and, of course, wines from Baden.

GROSSKARLBACH Rhl.-Pf.

Frankenthal 5 - Worms 17

KARLBACHER 13/20

67229, Hauptstr. 57
(0 62 38) 37 37, res.

Closed Monday, Tuesday. Tables d'hôte: 65/105, à la carte: 52/78

Under new management, this beautiful old half-timbered building with a vaulted dining room and comfortable cellar is finally getting a cuisine to match its ambience. Whether the cuisine is as unforgettable as the house advertises is debatable, but we were satisfied with the down-to-earth cooking. The tuna parfait was a bit too light, but the cold potato soup was creamy and the chanterelle salad with king prawns delicious, as was the lamb fillet with green beans.

REST. GEBR. MEURER 12/20

67229, Hauptstr. 67
(0 62 38) 6 78, Fax 10 07

 P

Closed for lunch every day except Sunday (Brunch). Tables d'hôte: 55/88, à la carte: 28/75. Tables d'hôte with wine: 88

This restaurant has the nicest terrace by far, which lets us (at least in summer) forget some of the shortcomings of the cuisine. The extensive and beautiful park-like grounds (and the chickens and dogs that populate them) distracted us from our food. We had chervil soup consisting of cream and dry salmon pieces, boring green salad, overdone lamb and sour rhubarb mousse with strawberries nobody could have called fresh. Highlights were delicious asparagus with pike-perch and orange cream, tasty asparagus salad with sweetbreads and classic marbled mousses. The staff changes frequently, but the wine list still emphasizes regional wines from the Mittelhaardt.

GÜGLINGEN Bad.-Württ.

Heilbronn 18 - Stutttgart 44

HERZOGSKELTER 12/20

74363, Deutscher Hof 1
(0 71 35) 17 70, Fax 1 77 77

P

Closed 2 weeks at the beginning of August. Tables d'hôte: 45/55L, 90/110D, à la carte: 35/85

What ever happened to the perfect service and the high level of cooking here? We were served very traditional dishes prepared without competence or charm. A lot of oil and heavy sauces characterize the "nouvelle cuisine" of the Herzogskelter. One plus: the many Zabergäu wines from the nearby wine region and some international vintages are reasonably priced.

GÜSTROW MV

Teterow 25 - Schwerin 60

ERBGROSSHERZOG IN HOTEL STADT GÜSTROW 12/20

18273, Am Markt 2-3
(0 38 43) 48 41, Fax 6 20 00

A la carte: 25/54

The gourmets in Güstrow may heave a sigh of relief: at last a culinary high spot to enliven the drab gastronomic monotony of this town! But they would do well not to rejoice too soon. The cuisine of this stylish modern restaurant with designer chairs and opulent flower arrangements is very promising, but the ambitious kitchen staff can't (as yet) carry through on its ideas. The comprehensive menu includes Swedish specialties such as smoked reindeer ham, snow chicken and flat bread; some regional recipes typical of Mecklenburg; and many international dishes. The service ranges from attentive to unobtrusive to unmotivated. The choice of wines is surprisingly large and offers a good variety of wines by the glass.

STADT GÜSTROW

18273, Am Markt 2-3
(0 38 43) 48 41, Fax 6 20 00

70 rooms, **S** 110/155, **D** 160/210, **½P** +20, **P** +35

This historic hotel offers comfortable modern rooms. The lobby is used as an art gallery.

GÜTERSLOH NRW

Bielefeld 17 - Dortmund 80

PARKHOTEL 13/20

33330, Kirchstr. 27
(0 52 41) 87 70, Fax 87 74 00 res.

P

Tables d'hôte: 32/44L, 74/130D, à la carte: 44/78. Tables d'hôte with wine: 98

During the long time it took for the staff to notice our arrival, we had ample opportunity to admire every fine detail of the wood decor and the immense Tiffany skylight. The chef didn't like us any more than his staff did. Our fish and shrimp tart tasted just fishy, and the tomato consommé with cheese quenelles and chervil lacked flavor. The Westphalian pike-perch fillet wrapped in cabbage leaf with lentils wasn't bad, but annoyingly bony. The vinegar lacking on the salad with quail's breast was splashed too liberally over the marinated salmon with asparagus salad. Bitter chocolate sorbet and dry apricot tortellini made us glad the meal was over. The standard choice of wines helped us more than the uncoordinated service did.

SCHIFFCHEN 15/20

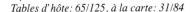

33330, Eickhoffstr. 1
(0 52 41) 1 50 35, Fax 1 34 97 res.

Tables d'hôte: 65/125, à la carte: 31/84

We've resigned ourselves to the cute doll's-house ambience of the Schiffchen. Perhaps the once-inventive (and slightly erratic) cook Johannes Meyer has resigned, too. We missed the highlights we were used to and noticed a lack of motivation, even though most dishes were still first-class. Meyer's cuisine and his second toque have both lost their balance. An appetizer of scallops with black truffle slices can only be worthy if the scallops are perfectly done and the truffles have flavor. A salad with croutons and bacon drowned in cream and fried potatoes with strips of veal had one merit: they filled our stomachs for 22 DM. Meyer was up to his old fantastic form with a pike-perch fillet with sauerkraut in Riesling sauce, whereas our breast of pheasant glazed with sherry was unremarkable. The wine list is getting a little too expensive, but the choice of half bottles is as large as ever. Pleasant service with occasional lapses.

STADT GÜTERSLOH

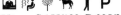

33330, Kökerstr. 23. 1
(0 52 41) 17 11, Fax 1 34 97

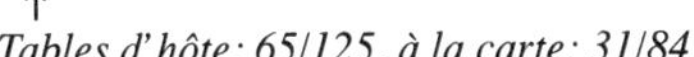

55, **S** 155/180, **D** 205/245

This hotel doesn't fit any usual standard, but offers genuine Frisian tea and homemade marmalade for breakfast (19 DM), as well as personal service and conference rooms. Pleasant, comfortable rooms.

GULDENTAL Rh.-Pfalz.

Langenlohnsheim 4 - Bingen 12

KAISERHOF 14/20

55452, Haupstr. 2
(0 67 07) 87 46, Fax 17 82

P

Closed Tuesday. Tables d'hôte: 62, à la carte: 28/57, No Credit Cards

The cuisine at the Kaiserhof has taken a turn for the better. Markus Buchholz has refined plain German cooking and raised it to a much higher level. He still serves classic dishes to satisfy regular customers. We recommend the light and delicious terrine of duck's breast with sugar peas, iced cream-of-cucumber soup, lovely sweetbreads with Burgundy sauce and carrots, and white chocolate parfait with strawberries. The Kaiserhof's own wines are offered at moderate prices. Kerstin Buchholz's service is always pleasant and attentive.

GUMMERSBACH NRW

Olpe 22 -Köln 55

HEEDT

1.5 km north in
51647 G.-Windhagen
Windhagen 2-6/by the B256 motorway
(0 22 61) 6 50 21, Fax 2 81 61

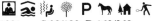

P

130, **S** 98/180, **D** 160/260,
APP 300/360, ½**P** +20, **P** +30

This farmhouse with a lovely half-timbered facade has been ingeniously enlarged, and is now a comfortable rustic hotel in a large park on the edge of a forest. The well-appointed apartments and suites with large bathrooms are relatively reasonable in price. Sports facilities. New conference rooms. There is a restored Baroque chapel for religious services.

DIE MÜHLENHELLE 14/20

7 km south in Dieringhausen
51645, Hohler Str. 1
(0 22 61) 7 50 97, Fax 7 24 01 res.

Closed for dinner Sunday, closed Monday, first week in January, 3 weeks in August/September. Tables d'hôte: 79/128, à la carte: 49/87

Busloads of gourmets haven't discovered this restaurant yet, so the cuisine includes culinary compositions more cautious than bold. The restaurant in this almost 300-year-old house decorated with modern paintings serves its regular customers familiar dishes with a subtle flair that bespeaks careful and expert craftsmanship in the kitchen. We had wonderful white tomato jelly, carpaccio of calf's tongue and haunch in warm tomato vinaigrette, *tafelspitz* millefeuille with delicate mustard sauce, turbot with sliced kohlrabi accompanied by a vegetable composition of beans with fresh asparagus and potato and horseradish sauce (a taste sensation!), pike-perch coated with potato on ratatouille, guinea fowl sausages with foie gras sauce and desserts with lots of fresh berries. We only wish this charming restaurant had a few more diners. Anton Eggel's expertly stocked wine cellar makes his wine suggestions with prix-fixe meals worth following. He also offers comfortable rooms for guests to stay the night.

GUTACH/ELZTAL Bad.-Württ.

Waldkirch 4 - Freiburg 15

STOLLEN 12/20

79261, Ortsteil Bleibach
Am Stollen 2
(0 76 85) 2 07, Fax 15 50 res.

Closed Tuesday, closed for lunch Wednesday, closed 10 days in January. Tables d'hôte: 45L, 45/99D, à la carte: 37/71

This prettily decorated jewel of a hotel makes its guests feel at home in romantic rooms, a festive banquet hall, a rustic *gaststube* and an elegant restaurant. The Stollen cuisine has a pronounced Swiss accent. Some of chef Walter Jehli's strong points are indubitably his *Zürcher Geschnetzeltes* (a ragout of thinly sliced veal) and his *rösti*. The Swiss have a tradition of generous helpings, and most of the portions here are immense. The stuffed breast of poularde served as an appetizer would have been a main course anywhere else. The excellent turbot came in puff pastry with spinach, and the lamb medallions were crisply fried and seasoned with thyme. Wantzenau squab and salmon with cèpes complete the picture of opulent, rich cooking. Sorry, we forgot the large dessert platter with a generous helping of sorbets and parfaits with whipped cream. The wine list is good and the service is well-trained.

STOLLEN

79261, Ortsteil Bleibach
Am Stollen 2
(0 76 85) 2 07, Fax 15 50

10 rooms, **S** 110/130, **D** 160/220, **APP** 300/350, **½P** +45, **P** +85
Closed 10 days in January

The romance of this hotel lies in its idyllic surroundings and the appropriate ambience inside. Elegantly furnished rooms.

HÄUSERN Baden-Württemberg

Waldshut 19-Freiburg 58

ADLER

79838, St.-Fridolin-Str. 15
(0 76 72) 41 70, Fax 41 71 50 res.

Closed Monday and Tuesday, closed mid-November through mid-December. Tables d'hôte: 70/130, à la carte: 33/82

Winfried Zumkeller does not compromise. He cooks grande cuisine, and his menu is dictated by his excellent talent for shopping for the best. He still offers regional dishes, but everything he cooks caters to the demands of a gourmet palate. Headcheese *en tortue* and sliced calf's liver is still served, but Zumkeller's clientele likes sweetbreads and foie gras, quail salad, fried goose and salmon mousse. Vegetable side dishes are a complement here and not just a decoration. The historic dining rooms in this idyllic restaurant create a luxurious and comfortable ambience. The service is especially polite, and the international wine list leaves nothing to desire.

ADLER

79838, St.-Fridolin-Str. 15
(0 76 72) 41 70, Fax 41 71 50

44 rooms, **S** 95/160, **D** 144/266, **APP** 188/380, **½P** +36
Closed Monday and Tuesday, closed mid-November through mid-December. Tables d'hôte: 70/130, à la carte: 33/82

This is a comfortable hotel with a homey atmosphere. The rooms are spacious and com-

fortably furnished. Very good service. Beautiful tennis courts at the edge of the forest. Guided hiking tours.

HAGEN Nordrhein-Westf.

Dortmund 25-Düsseldorf 65

ROSSINI IN HOTEL DAHLER SCHWEIZ 12/20

8 km southeast, Ortsteil Dahl
58091, Am Hemker Bach 12
(0 23 37) 10 84/5, Fax 10 87 res.

Closed Thursday. Tables d'hôte: 58/69, à la carte: 31/56. Tables d'hôte with wine: 85

Bruno Perissinotto's customers are not attracted only by the idyllic location of his Italian restaurant and hotel in a traditional old stone house, but also by his cooking. He serves well-prepared German-Italian dishes, with homemade noodles. If his pasta was always as good as his blue (colored with poppyseeds) tagliarini with pesto and Parmesan, he would deserve a toque. But while he offers fresh fish, carefully seasoned sauces and vegetables al dente, he also serves up sloppily arranged salads, tasteless marinades, flaccid fowl and factory-made ice cream. The wine list includes Italian and other vintage, and the prices range from affordable to astronomical. If you're willing to pay the price, you can have high-quality wines by the glass.

HAGNAU Baden-Württ.

Meersburg 3-Immenstadt 7

KUPFERKANNE IN HOTEL ERBGUTH'S LANDHAUS 15/20

88709, Neugartenstr. 39
(0 75 32) 62 02, Fax 69 97

Closed for dinner Sunday, closed Monday, closed 4 January through 28 February, 20—26 December. Tables d'hôte: 45/120 L, 68/130 D, à la carte: 42/82

The hosts are so charmingly hospitable here that the excellent cuisine seems almost like an extra thrown in. After a lovely appetizer of marinated salmon with caviar, we enjoyed such deceptively simple dishes as cream of lobster soup with scampi, fish fillet with squid sauce, veal medallions with a shiitake mushroom sauce, and rhubarb soup with strawberries and marzipan ice cream. Everything was prepared with a light, expert hand and was artistically arranged on the plates. The fabulous sauces and delicious soups were undisputed highlights, whereas the trout was a bit overdone and the meat a little stringy. Holger Erbguth takes over in the kitchen every so often to help out when a cook is needed. He stands for consistent, moderately experimental cuisine that doesn't deny its regional roots. The good-humored maître d'hôtel touts the regional wines but also offers French and Italian bottles. The charming owners, alas, are selling the place in 1995.

ERBGUTH'S VILLA AM SEE

88709, Neugartenstr. 39
(0 75 32) 62 02, Fax 69 97

6 rooms, **S** 200/250, **D** 240/390, **APP** 400/480

This luxurious villa on a lakeshore offers rooms with all the modern amenities. If you book far ahead, you might get one of the south-facing apartments or the bridal suite. The lake is only 200 meters away. Hotel guests are automatically members of the golf club here. Solarium. Good breakfast buffet. The villa is also being sold 1995 along with the restaurant.

HAIGER Hessen

Siegen 25-Geißen 50

LANDHAUS MÜHLENHOF 13/20

35708, Ortsteil Offdilln
Mühlenhof 1
(0 27 74) 24 52, Fax 5 19 93 res.

Closed Monday and Tuesday, closed 1 week in August. Tables d'hôte: 41/60L, 65 D, à la carte: 36/68

Claudia and André Hohe not only deserve a toque but also a medal for courage. Rarely do the Hohes cook for a full house, but they haven't (yet) given up trying to offer fine cuisine at moderate prices. There is no flashy experimental cooking here; self-taught, talented André Hohe has continuously improved his classic dishes. We didn't find much to rave about, but none of his dishes disappointed us. We had tasty salmon variations—marinated, fried and as tartare—with well-dressed salads, good sweetbreads with green beans and puréed celery root, sole fried (too long) in butter, and a somewhat dry saddle of rabbit. Pleasant service and adequate wine list.

HAIGERLOCH Bad.-Württ.

Hechingen 15-Horb 18

SCHWANEN 16/20

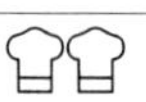

72401, Marktplatz 5
(0 74 74) 75 75, Fax 75 76 res.

 P

Closed Monday, closed for lunch Tuesday. Tables d'hôte: 59/76 L, 96/142 D, à la carte: 55/101

The Dier family feels at home in Haigerloch, and their customers feel at home in their beautiful, historic *Gasthaus*. We enjoyed Bernhard Dier's delicately marinated salmon terrine with asparagus salad, nicely balanced cream soup with cherry tomatoes and chives, superb pigeon breast with a fantastic sauce and glazed Belgian endive leaves, and tender fried fillet of anglerfish with saffron and fried potato quenelles, young onions and spinach tortellini. We were impressed by an imposing quail suprême with kohlrabi gratin and gnocchi, and nearly went crazy over our dessert: 10 assorted sweets, ranging from white chocolate ice cream with caramel mousse and mango and cassis sherbet to pear strudel and wonderful puréed berries! Fine petits fours were offered with coffee, along with a little thank-you from our chef—an assortment of cakes.The service staff was perfect and was able to give sound advice in choosing both food and wine.The wine list includes the best (moderately priced) German wines and many wines by the glass.

HALLE Sachsen-Anhalt

Leipzig 26 - Göttingen 169

HOTEL GARNI BK

06110, Pfännerhöhe 44
(03 45) 2 43 86 , Fax 2 84 07

 P

30 rooms, **S** 60/120, **D** 100/120, **APP** 300/320
No Credit Cards

This house is an alternative to the overcrowded Hotel Stadt Halle two minutes away and an example of successful restoration in a rundown part of town. Breakfast: 12 DM.

MÖNCHSHOF 13/20

06108, Talamtstr. 6
(03 45) 2 17 26

P

Closed Sunday. Tables d'hôte: 19L, 25D, à la carte: 17/40

This restaurant on a prominent street corner has been redecorated, but the menu lists just as many dishes as before. Customers find everything from brook trout to sheatfish (a type of catfish) and from Angus rumpsteak to venison fillet here. Less quantity would probably result in better quality, but all dishes are prepared with solid know-how, and if you can stomach the immense portions, you'll enjoy the low-priced food here. We had carefully prepared honeydew melon with ham and Calvados sauce, nicely done salmon fillet with wild rice, crispy pork roast with sauerkraut, and apple tarts and berry soup like Grandma used to make. The choice of wines is outstanding and the service competent and well-informed.

SCHWEIZER HOF 11/20

06108, Waisenhausring 15
(03 45) 50 30 68, Fax 2 63 92

Closed for dinner Sunday, closed for lunch Monday. Tables d'hôte: 35L, 45/60D, à la carte: 28/47

This restaurant, with its postmodern decor, also serves as the reception area for hotel guests. The kitchen offers rich, heavy cuisine with some highlights: rabbit leg, duck's breast and lamb, smoked salmon with Savoy cabbage. The desserts make it easy for those on a diet to say no. A few respectable wines by the glass are offered.

SCHWEIZER HOF

06108, Waisenhausring 15
(03 45) 50 30 68, Fax 2 63 92

18 rooms, **S** 145/170, **D** 195/240, **½P** +20, **P** +35

This centrally located hotel has plain, functionally furnished rooms.

STADT HALLE

06009, Riebeckplatz 17
(03 45) 5 10 10, Fax 5 10 17 77

346 rooms, **S** 225/325, **D** 294/398, **APP** 350/460, **½P** +40, **P** +68

The rooms in this concrete building have been modernized. Massage, solarium, hairdresser and beauty treatments are supposed to follow in 1995. Nightclub.

ZUM KLEINEN SANDBERG 13/20

06108, Kleiner Sandberg 5
(03 45) 7 70 02 69, Fax 7 70 02 69 res.

Tables d'hôte: 22/40, à la carte: 15/45

In the middle of a rundown quarter of town, there stands a precious little 17th-century half-timbered house that is home to a restaurant and a small hotel. The dining room is bright and rustically comfortable. The cuisine doesn't undertake any fancy escapades but offers regional dishes from Baden, like a hearty lentil stew with wieners and homemade spaetzle, or savory Swabian ravioli with potato salad. Black-forest trout and apple tarts with vanilla ice cream are highlights here. Small but good choice of wines from Baden, France and Saale-Unstrut.

HAMBURG

Bremen 119-Hannover 155-Flensburg 160

ANNA 13/20

20354, City
Bleichenbrüke [E4]
(0 40) 36 70 14
Closed Saturday, Sunday, à la carte: 33/64

When it opened a few years ago, this amusing bistro with its terrace on a pontoon in the water was applauded as a novelty in Hamburg. Attractive dishes with a touch of Asia or Tuscany drew crowds of customers and so did the cheerful service crew. But on our last visit, instead of more creativity we found stagnation and a creeping boredom, perhaps because in the meantime, the cuisine has left Asia and Italy and become what is nonchalantly called international. The cook doesn't want to call attention to himself (or to his cuisine): his dishes are strangely unfocused. The honey and ginger sauce with chicken breast was tasteless, the cherries marinated in red wine that accompanied our liver were just red, and the fish sauces were at best nondescript. The atmosphere is pleasant, though, and lots of customers still throng to Anna's for lunch.

ANNA E SEBASTIANO 17/20

20251, Eppendorf
Lehmweg 30
(0 40) 4 22 25 95, Fax 4 20 80 08 res.
Closed for lunch, closed Sunday, Monday, 24 December through 20 January, 3 weeks during the HH summer school holiday. Tables d'hôte: 110, à la carte: 63/88

The most expensive Italian restaurant in Hamburg is also its best. Anna in her kitchen and Sebastiano in his dining room are self-ordained prophets of Milan's great cook Gualtiero Marchesi. They have made their restaurant into a temple for gourmets. Instead of the typical folklorish decor, you'll find a cool, styled interior with designer furniture fit for the Museum of Modern Art in New York. Because Anna performs solo in the kitchen without a large staff, customers have a choice of only two main courses per table. This means that all dishes can be prepared on the spot. Anna's creations display a seemingly effortless elegance; everything is beautifully arranged, and nothing is artificially decorated. Her first courses and entremets are fabulous, and her risottos famous. Whether you order liver, suckling lamb, kid or sturgeon, Anna will make something special out of it. Sebastiano supervises an attractive service brigade and is recognized as a wine expert. The prices on the wine list are limited only by the sky.

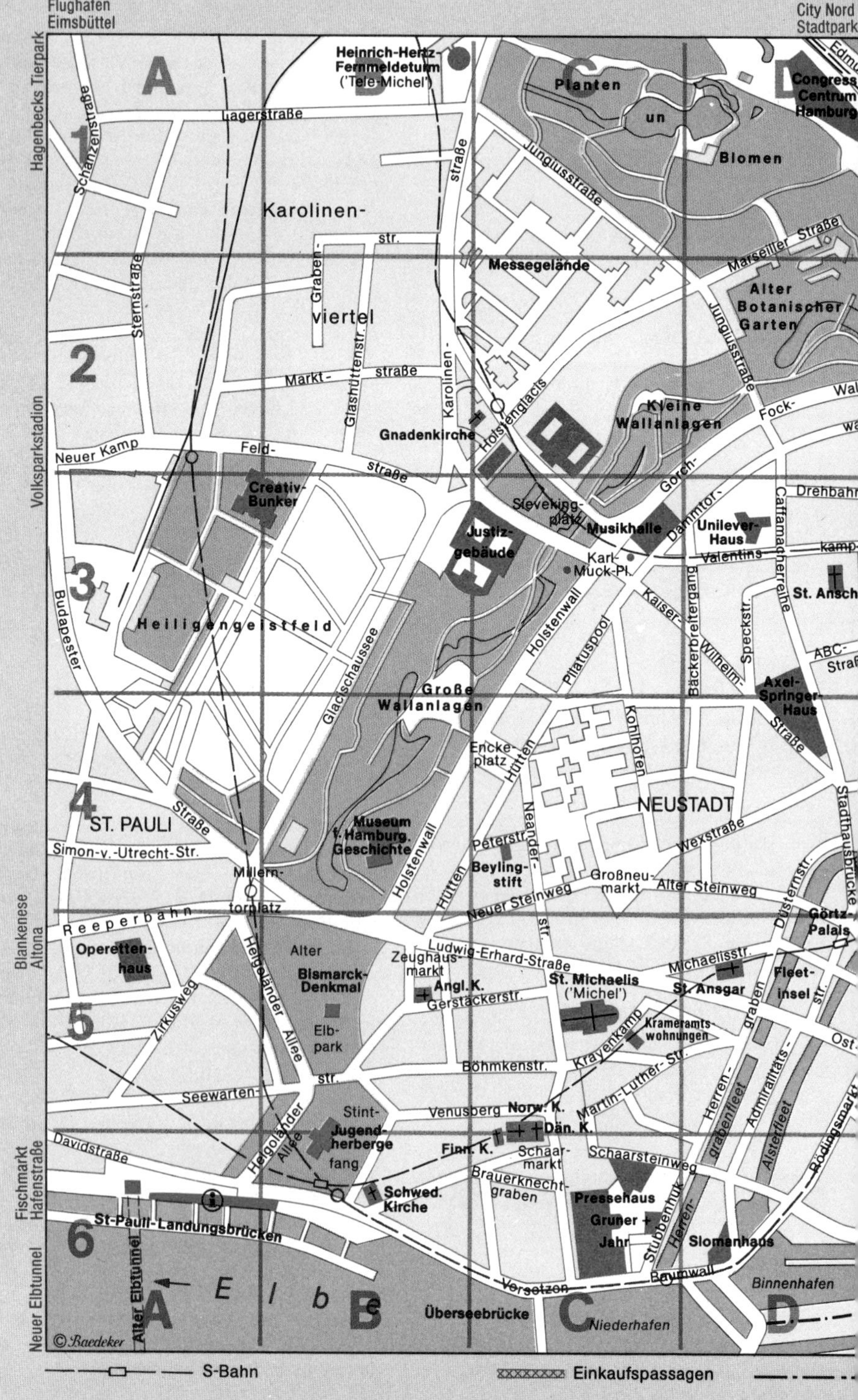

Flughafen Eimsbüttel
City Nord Stadtpark
Hagenbecks Tierpark
Volksparkstadion
Blankenese Altona
Fischmarkt Hafenstraße
Neuer Elbtunnel
Heinrich-Hertz-Fernmeldeturm ('Tele-Michel')
Planten un Blomen
Congress Centrum Hamburg
Karolinenviertel
Messegelände
Alter Botanischer Garten
Kleine Wallanlagen
Gnadenkirche
Creativ-Bunker
Justizgebäude
Musikhalle
Unilever-Haus
Heiligengeistfeld
Große Wallanlagen
Axel-Springer-Haus
NEUSTADT
ST. PAULI
Museum f. Hamburg. Geschichte
Beylingstift
Operettenhaus
Alter Bismarck-Denkmal
Elbpark
Angl. K.
St. Michaelis ('Michel')
St. Ansgar
Görtz-Palais
Fleetinsel
Krameramtswohnungen
Norw. K.
Dän. K.
Finn. K.
Jugendherberge
Schwed. Kirche
Pressehaus
Gruner + Jahr
Slomanhaus
St.-Pauli-Landungsbrücken
Alter Elbtunnel
Elbe
Überseebrücke
Niederhafen
Binnenhafen
© Baedeker
S-Bahn
Einkaufspassagen

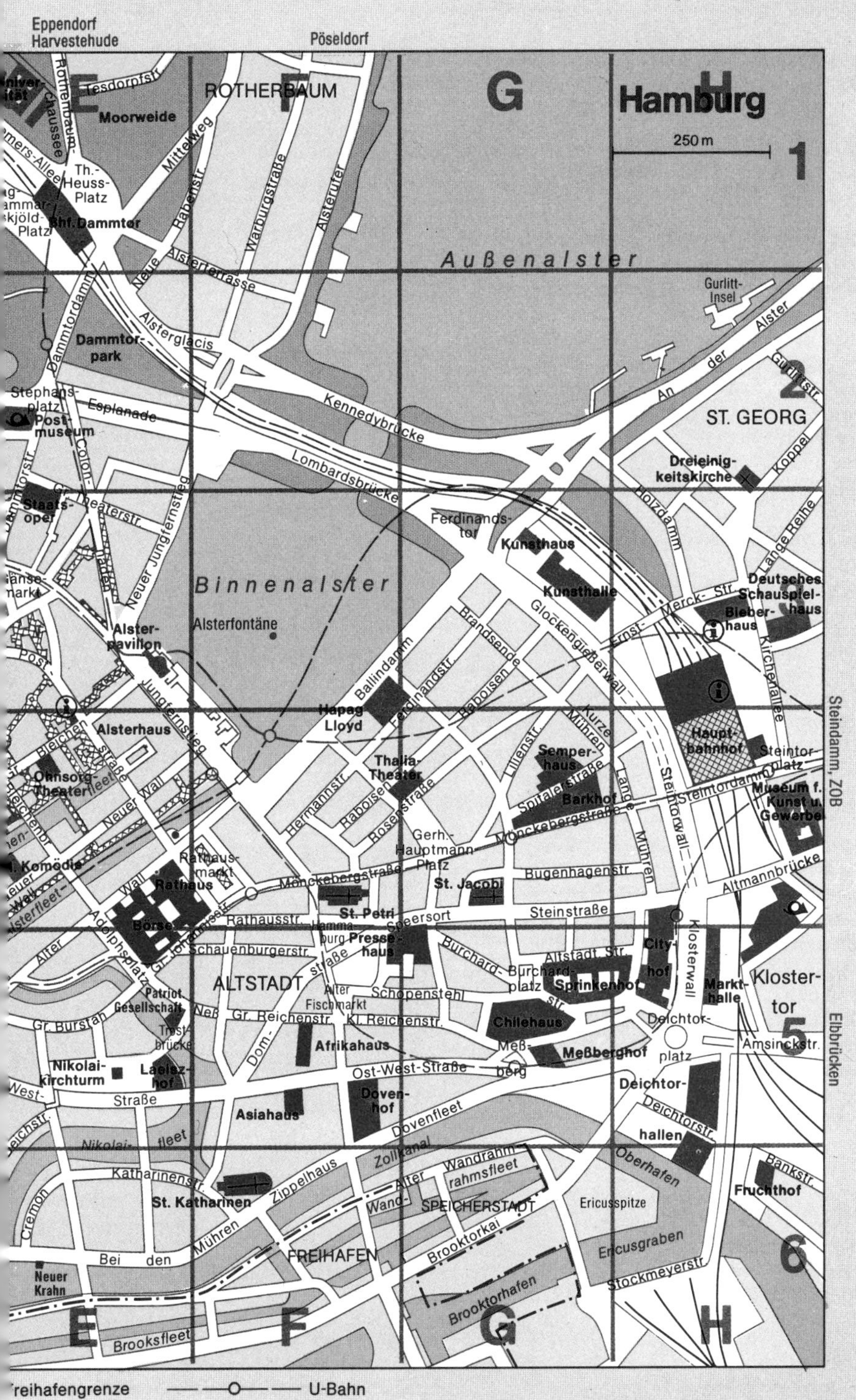

Eppendorf
Harvestehude
Pöseldorf
ROTHERBAUM
E
F
G
H
Hamburg
250 m
1
2
5
6
Moorweide
Tesdorpfstr.
Rothenbaum-Chaussee
Th.-Heuss-Platz
Bhf. Dammtor
Mittelweg
Rabenstr.
Warburgstraße
Alsterufer
Außenalster
Neue Alsterterrasse
Alsterglacis
Dammtordamm
Dammtorpark
Gurlitt-Insel
An der Alster
Gurlittstr.
ST. GEORG
Kennedybrücke
Stephansplatz
Esplanade
Postmuseum
Lombardsbrücke
Dreieinigkeitskirche
Koppel
Holzdamm
Staatsoper
Gr. Theaterstr.
Colonnaden
Neuer Jungfernstieg
Ferdinandstor
Kunsthaus
Lange Reihe
Binnenalster
Kunsthalle
Deutsches Schauspielhaus
Ernst-Merck-Str.
Bieberhaus
Alsterfontäne
Glockengießerwall
Brandsende
Alsterpavillon
Ballindamm
Ferdinandstr.
Raboisen
Kirchenallee
Jungfernstieg
Hapag Lloyd
Kurze Mühren
Alsterhaus
Hauptbahnhof
Steindamm, ZOB
Lilienstr.
Semperhaus
Steintorplatz
Bleichenstraße
Ohnsorg-Theater
Alsterfleet
Thalia-Theater
Spitalerstraße
Steintordamm
Museum f. Kunst u. Gewerbe
Neuer Wall
Hermannstr.
Rosenstraße
Barkhof
Lange Mühren
Steintorwall
Mönckebergstraße
Gerh.-Hauptmann-Platz
Rathausmarkt
Komödie
Rathaus
Bugenhagenstr.
Altmannbrücke
St. Jacobi
Steinstraße
St. Petri
Rathausstr.
Speersort
Börse
Hammaburg
Pressehaus
Adolphsplatz
Schauenburgerstr.
Burchardstr.
City-hof
Klosterwall
Altstadt Str.
Burchardplatz
ALTSTADT
Alter Fischmarkt
Schopenstehl
Sprinkenhof
Markthalle
Klostertor
Patriot. Gesellschaft
Gr. Reichenstr.
Kl. Reichenstr.
Elbbrücken
Gr. Burstah
Trostbrücke
Chilehaus
Deichtorplatz
Amsinckstr.
Domstraße
Afrikahaus
Meßberg
Meßberghof
Nikolaikirchturm
Laeiszhof
Ost-West-Straße
Deichtorhallen
Dovenhof
Deichtorstr.
Asiahaus
Dovenfleet
Nikolaifleet
Zollkanal
Oberhafen
Katharinenstr.
Alter Wandrahm
Wandrahmsfleet
Bankstr.
St. Katharinen
Zippelhaus
SPEICHERSTADT
Ericusspitze
Fruchthof
Cremon
Brooktorkai
Ericusgraben
Bei den Mühren
FREIHAFEN
Stockmeyerstr.
Neuer Krahn
Brooktorhafen
Brooksfleet
Freihafengrenze
U-Bahn

ATLANTIC-RESTAURANT 11/20

20099, Ander Alster 72/79 [H2]
(0 40) 2 88 88 60, Fax 2 24 71 29 res.

Closed for lunch. Tables d'hôte: 79D, à la carte: 62/104

The view of the Alster is beautiful from here, and the decor is luxurious. The cuisine has improved since the last time we visited. We found one dish we could enjoy: lamb ribs with a savory sauce of fresh herbs. The first courses were elaborate, as usual, but not much else can be said about them. The main courses were expensive and boring, and the desserts opulent and heavy. The service is attentive and helpful, and the wine list just wonderful.

L'AUBERGE FRANÇAISE 12/20

20146, Rotherbaum
Rutschbahn 34
(0 40) 4 10 25 32, Fax 4 10 58 57 res.

Closed for lunch Saturday, closed Sunday, 20 December through 8 January. Tables d'hôte: 65L, 95D, à la carte: 45/93

What is Hamburg without its star French chef? Jacques Lemercier's inn is a shrine to French cuisine. Unfortunately, Lemercier seems to take himself for a monument and seldom deigns to serve the customers of his well-frequented restaurant. Instead, blasé French waiters dart to and fro between the tables, serve the appetizer, hand over the menu and then disappear for a long time. The highly praised cuisine seems to have lost its fine touch. The alcoholic lobster soup was heavy and almost as salty as the stuffed artichoke hearts that followed. The fresh anglerfish with garlic and saffron sauce was prepared with much less than loving care, and the duckling in sweet and sour sauce just tasted fatty.

BISTRO ÖSTERREICH 13/20

20251, Eppendorf
Martinistr. 11
(0 40) 4 60 48 30, Fax 47 24 13 res.

Closed Sunday, Monday. A la carte: 34/70. Tables d'hôte with wine: 70

Hidden between pizzerias and Chinese shops, we found the Bistro Österreich, an Austrian oasis decorated with pictures of modern Austrian heroes (Arnold Schwarzenegger?). Roasted blood pudding with fried potatoes, juicy and tender Wiener schnitzel with potato salad, and pike-perch fricassee with finely balanced horseradish sauce were all very enjoyable. The heavy desserts, however, were not good examples of Austrian cooking.The service is sometimes charmingly snobbish, sometimes carelessly impudent. The wines were brilliant and the different kinds of coffee fantastic.

BRAHMS -STUBEN 13/20

20249, Eppendorf
Ludolfstr. 43
(0 40) 47 87 17 res.

Closed Monday. Tables d'hôte: 48L, 68D, à la carte: 38/81

Behind the creaking door of the little red brick house just opposite the church is the cozy Brahms-Stuben restaurant. The subtle lighting, wooden ceiling and framed Brahms lullaby suggest peace and quiet. You should not come here if you are in a hurry—although there are only 10 tables, there is often only a single waitress, who never loses her smile.Chef René Lucht sticks to Hanseatic traditions, but sometimes experiments with dishes like scampi tempura. Pleasing dishes included Tyrolean bacon with salad and an interesting (if sticky) vinaigrette of figs and mustard, crispy duckling with Savoy cabbage, and tender lamb ribs with a delicate crust. Fine desserts concluded the meal. The wine list lacks character; you won't find any great vintages here.

CALLA 16/20

20459, City
Heiligengeistbrücke 4 [D5]
(0 40) 36 80 60, Fax 36 80 67 77

Closed Sunday, Monday, 6 weeks during the summer. Tables d'hôte: 45/79, à la carte: 40/ 73

Most of the restaurants in Hamburg are overrated. The Calla is one of the few that are, in the contrary, underestimated. We admit that the interior takes a bit of getting used to, but

Alfred Schreiber serves cuisine with an Asian flair that is unequaled in Hamburg. A lot of cooks list sushi and tempura along with the traditional cabbage roulade on their menus in the hopes of picking up more trendy customers. Alfred Schreiber is as far removed from these colleagues as a racing driver from a cyclist. Having worked in Thai kitchens, he really knows how to use a wok and is an expert in Asian seasoning. With sensibility and taste, he manages to combine the best of East and West on his plates. His prix-fixe menus are a steal, and his fish dishes cost much less than his first courses, a good example for other cooks to follow. Because of this, you can sample more dishes, like anglerfish with orange and ginger sauce, lobster with chili and coriander, or gurnard with warm papaya and tomato salad and curried mayonnaise.

LE CANARD 19/20

22763, Altona
Elbchaussee 139
(0 40) 8 80 50 57/8, Fax 47 24 13 res.

P

Closed Sunday. Tables d'hôte: 50/115L, 135/189D, à la carte: 60/126. Tables d'hôte with wine: 115

Thanks to good business sense on the part of its owners, Le Canard has remained untouched by the recession and hasn't had to lower its high standards one iota. This lovely restaurant, housed in the half rotunda of a modern building on the prestigious Elbchaussee, is furnished with light-colored wood and has a coolly styled interior without plush or superfluous pomp. Josef Viehhauser, an angular Austrian with a wooden smile, comes out of his kitchen to welcome customers and advise. Viehhauser offers four prix-fixe menus at noon: a seven- and a five-course meal, a lunch with wine and a businessman's lunch served in 40 minutes. Viehhauser's kitchen still prepares superb fish, and his pike-perch with lobster risotto has been often copied but never equaled. His first courses were clever and ingenious: herring in Riesling jelly, duck *labskaus* with fried quail's egg, and scallop carpaccio with truffled lamb's lettuce. His lobster perfumed with anise and his tournedos Rossini were grandiose. If you want to enjoy the best Viehhauser has to offer, just order a bottle of wine and ask him to cook something to go with it.

CÖLLN'S AUSTERNSTUBEN 17/20

20457, AltstadtBrodschagen 1-5 [F5]
(0 40) 32 60 59, Fax 32 60 59 res.

Closed Saturday and Sunday 1 January through 31 August, closed for lunch Saturday and Sunday 1 September through 31 December. Tables d'hôte: 88/146, à la carte: 57/101

Cölln's Austernstuben is one of the first and finest addresses for gourmet dining. It all started in 1760 with a little oyster and fish shop. In 1833 some customers couldn't wait to go home to eat and ate their oysters while still standing in the shop. Thirty years later, the firm opened a small restaurant in the basement. Those were the days when Cölln caught fish (mostly sturgeon) in Astrachan and sold half of all the oysters consumed in Germany, and when bankers and stockbrokers met in the restaurant's small rooms to make business deals (or celebrate them). In addition to oysters, caviar and lobster, the customers ate Cölln's steak with fried potatoes. The Cölln dynasty came to an end in 1990, and the restaurant has since been renovated and reopened. More than a thousand old Art Nouveau tiles gleam brightly in the original dining rooms (Bismarck ate here!), which still suggest the old spirit of discretion and Hanseatic understatement. There is no false modesty about the menu, however, which has raised the plain fare of this one-time snack bar to the level of haute cuisine. The ambitious Wolfgang Grobauer is one of the most talented cooks in Hamburg. He serves his fish with unusual side dishes (for instance, fillet of sole with green string beans in red wine) and his sauces are always finely balanced and never jarring. The fish portions are more generous than the vegetables that go with them. Like those bankers back in 1860, today's customers can still order Cölln's steak, but now it has been turned into a exquisite fillet of Husum beef à la Johann Cölln!

DOMINIQUE 13/20

20355, Karl-Muck-Platz 11 [E3]
(0 40) 34 45 11 res.

Closed for lunch, closed Sunday. Tables d'hôte: 60/62, à la carte: 47/68

From the writing on the windows ("Vin en pichet—Biere à la pression"), it is not hard to guess that Dominique Lemercier serves French cuisine. His food is of good quality and is sometimes even ingenious. The cream of prawn soup seasoned with cognac was as finely balanced as the baked goat cheese with polenta. We recommend the anglerfish fillet with puréed watercress, the chicken leg with lemongrass sauce and the opulent (if highly alcoholic) sherbet of mascarpone on puréed raspberries.Madame Lemercier serves her customers with pleasant attention to their wishes.

DON CAMILLO E PEPPONE 12/20
22179, Bramfeld
Im Soll 50
(0 40) 6 42 90 21

Closed Monday. Tables d'hôte: 48/78, à la carte: 36/66

Like those two pugnacious characters from a popular Italian novel, Sergio Camerini is fighting for a place in Hamburg's gourmet scene. He didn't win this time. Even though his menu is small, some dishes were unavailable even though we were his first customers of the evening. The nice but confused waitress brought us an assortment of good, if not original, first courses. The pike-perch was salty, the tips of beef stringy and the desserts disappointing. The wine list proudly presents Tignanello and Sassicaia and keeps mum about their price. The waiter will whisper it in your ear...

LA FAYETTE 12/20
22085, Uhlenhorst
Zimmerstr. 30
(0 40) 22 56 30, Fax 22 56 30

P

Closed Sunday. Tables d'hôte: 80, à la carte: 44/75

White walls and striking red upholstery have chased the dust of ages out of this restaurant and let in some fresh air. Customers eat well here when there are enough of them to keep the chef busy in the kitchen. If only a few tables are occupied, the chef would rather spin yarns with his customers than cook for them. If he does get around to cooking, you might have salad with rabbit fillets and raspberry vinaigrette and walnut oil, neutral-tasting California spring roll with sweet-and-sour sauce, nice gurnard fillet with a strangely unfinished crab sauce and spinach, or good saddle of lamb with overdone side dishes. The service is friendly and the wine list respectable.

FISCHEREIHAFEN-RESTAURANT 16/20
20767, Altona
Große Elbstr. 143
(0 40) 38 18 16, Fax 3 89 39 21 res.

P

A la carte: 37/104

Owner Rüdiger Kowalke is a Jaguar driver, a golf player and a prominent figure in Hamburg society. As such, he does the honors in this pointedly exclusive establishment. The Fischereihafen-Restaurant is different from other Hamburg restaurants in that it is traditional, spacious and formal. The well-known regular customers get tables in front, while tourists are led to the rear of the restaurant. Wolf-Dieter Klunker is one of the best cooks in Hamburg. His choice of dishes ranges from simple herring to exquisite Asian creations, and the prices range from stiff to astronomical. As far as the specialties of the house are concerned, Klunker can't be beaten. His generous helping of turbot is beyond compare, and his Fischereihafen platter with assorted fresh fish is fantastic (both 69 Deutsche marks). And you can still order a tasty herring for 18 Deutsche marks or a typical Hamburg meal for 58 Deutsche marks.

FISCHKÜCHE 14/20 
20459, City
Kajen 12 [D5]
(0 40) 36 56 31 res.

Closed Saturday, Sunday and holidays, à la carte: 32/60

The recipe for this successful fish bistro isn't unusual, but it's seldom carried out with such perfection: a cheerful decor, pretty ladies-in-waiting, and a small menu consisting of five first courses and five main courses. The cooks don't crave attention and cook honest, plain dishes without sensation. The customers, mostly businesspeople out for lunch or dinner, like it that way. They want fresh codfish, pike-perch or three kinds of herring. And they like it when the blond, attractive Karin Brahm calls them by name and treats them like VIPs. It helps them forget the high prices for champagne and wines by the glass. On nice summer days, customers sit outside and try to ignore the exhaust fumes of the busy traffic flowing by.

FLIC FLAC 14/20

22587, Blankenese
Blankeneser Landstr. 27
(0 40) 86 53 45, Fax 8 66 36 77 res.

P

Closed for lunch, closed Monday, à la carte: 40/76, No Credit Cards

This restaurant in Blankenese is about a 40 minute drive from the city's center, but it draws enough customers from Hamburg to be included in its culinary scene. Years ago, this was an opulent flower shop with excellent food. Meanwhile, the floral arrangements have become more discreet to make room for a few more tables. New on the menu is a unique prix-fixe that caters to the wishes of those who want to taste everything. Two mini-dishes are served with every course: for example, a colorful summer salad with fried scampi and beef carpaccio, or fried chanterelles in cream with herbs and a potato pancake with crème fraîche, followed by a tiny pizza with salmon and a few stuffed cherry tomatoes. Cynics have been known to say that one plate would have been enough for everything! But the customers seem to find this bombardment with china amusing. Besides, there are the attractive à la carte dishes to choose from. They're tasty and savory and—even if it's tempura or sushi—reassuringly German.

FONTENAY GRILL IN HOTEL INTER-CONTINENTAL 10/20

20354, Harvestehude
Fontenay 10 [F1]
(0 40) 41 41 50, Fax 41 41 51 82

P

286, **S** 275/460, **D** 325/510,
Closed for lunch every day except Sunday. Tables d'hôte: 85/109, à la carte: 57/104

Of the three hotel giants in Hamburg, this one wins the prize for the worst cooking. The view of the Alster river from the ninth floor restaurant is breathtaking,.but does not make up for the inferior cuisine.The wine list has a wide choice of high-priced wines. The service is casual.

LE FRANÇIEN 13/20

22303, Winterhude
Grasweg 70
(0 40) 2 70 50 49

Closed for lunch Saturday, closed Sunday. Tables d'hôte: 54/59L, 85/110D, à la carte: 52/87

The soft evening light transforms this establishment into a French country restaurant with homey wooden tables, a warm apricot-colored ceiling and landscape paintings. The ambience is as French as the cuisine. We had flavorful lobster soup with scampi, excellent pigeon in a light garlic sauce with tasty vegetables, and flawless anglerfish with chanterelles, potatoes, zucchini and asparagus. For dessert, there was wonderful fruit in raspberry sauce and a baked apple in Calvados. Everything was hearty but refined, well-seasoned but delicate. If the portions are too large, Madame Quint will serve half. We only found one hair in this good soup: there is just one high-quality Bordeaux on the wine list.

IL GABBIANO 12/20

20251, Eppendorf
Eppendorfer Landstr. 145
(0 40) 4 80 21 59, Fax 4 80 79 21 res.

Closed for lunch Saturday, Closed Sunday, closed month of July. Tables d'hôte: 78, à la carte: 36/62

This former haven of excellent Italian cuisine isn't a retreat for gourmets any more. In an attempt to hold on to its regular customers, the Gabbiano has sadly neglected its cooking. The appetizer, an oily mustard dip, almost took our appetite away, and soggy green asparagus covered with stale Parmesan cheese didn't revive it. The veal fillet alone was edible, though the Gorgonzola sauce killed the little taste it had. The wine list is still grand and features Italian wines at reasonable prices.

IL GIARDINO 12/20

22999, Winterhide
Ulmenstr. 19
(0 40) 47 01 47, Fax 47 22 72 res.

P

Closed for lunch. Tables d'hôte: 59/69, à la carte: 42/74

This is a restaurant for people who are on the lookout for trends rather than high-quality cuisine. The convivial atmosphere and the lovely garden are good-enough reasons for regular customers to come here, but the Italian dishes available at extravagant prices at Il Giardino can be had at nearly any other Italian restaurant, most of which would be unlikely to charge 50 Deutsche marks for the cheapest Pinot Grigio!

HAERLIN IN HOTEL VIER JAHRESZEITEN 12/20

20356, Neuer Jungfernsteig 9-14 [E3]
(0 40) 3 49 40, Fax 3 49 46 02 res.

Closed for lunch Saturday, closed Sunday. Tables d'hôte: 58/72L, 108/144D, à la carte: 56/103

Three words sum up the restaurant in Hamburg's most famous hotel: grandiose, expensive and boring. The menu lists culinary antiquities, and the dishes are classics without imagination. But you don't go to the Haerlin for the food but for the breathtaking ambience: unique Gobelin tapestries on the walls, heavy carpets, precious wooden chairs and tables, the very finest porcelain, an obliging pianist and perfect service. A more refined and distinguished restaurant cannot be found in Hamburg. The wine list, with its gigantic choice of vintages and cosmic prices, will also take your breath away.

HORIZONT 13/20

22765, Altona
Karkortsteig 4
(0 40) 3 89 33 36

Closed Sunday. Tables d'hôte: 30/60D, à la carte: 30/60

This restaurant, which was the first to offer ecologically correct food in Hamburg, has outgrown its old image. There is hardly a trace of the old wheat-germ days left. The decor is modern, with warm tones of red. Windows offer customers a look into the kitchen from the restaurant. We has a delicious first course of delicately smoked salmon with crispy potato cakes and a perfectly balanced honey-and-mustard sauce, followed by wonderful plaice with potato salad, and a great saddle of lamb with al dente vegetables. The desserts are made with the ingredients of the season. The wine list needs improvement.

HOTEL ABTEI 15/20

20149, Harvestehude
Abteistr. 14
(0 40) 44 95 95 , Fax 44 98 20 res.

Closed for lunch, closed Sunday, Monday, 1—18 January. Tables d'hôte: 70/150, à la carte: 62/89

This is the smallest and finest restaurant in the city. Fritz and Petra Lay, Merry Old England buffs, set only five tables in their cultivated and elegant English country-style dining room. An aperitif is served in an antiques-furnished parlor, and customers choose their meal from the menu there before they sit down in the dining room. Four or five first courses and a six-course prix-fixe were offered. The cuisine was classic: expensive fish with saffron or caviar sauce, fowl and fillets with orthodox side dishes. Everything was prepared with great care and precision, and nothing was cheap.

LANDHAUS DILL 12/20

22763, Altona
Elbchaussee 94
(0 40) 3 90 50 77, Fax 3 90 09 75 res.

P

Tables d'hôte: 78, à la carte: 37/77

This restaurant has moved out of its beautiful country inn into a new building with all the charm of a laundromat. Volkmar Preis, also owner of the Il Giardino, hasn't quite decided whether to keep to the former elegant country-inn style or to tone down his cuisine. Obviously, he thinks refined regional cooking is a way out of this dilemma. People who mistake chaos for genius may like it here. We had a savory fried blood pudding with onion rings, and fine but flat lobster salad ostentatiously prepared at our table. The wine list has retained the extravagant prices of the former Landhaus, but the service staff has adapted itself to the new surroundings with increasing nonchalance.

LANDHAUS SCHERRER 18/20

22763, Altona
Elbchaussee 130
(0 40) 8 80 13 25, 8 80 10 11,
Fax 8 80 62 60 res.

P

Closed Sunday. Tables d'hôte: 60L, 159/186D, à la carte: 62/124

This beautiful house right on the Elbchaussee is Hamburg's oldest and most famous gourmet restaurant. A remarkable concession to modern tastes (and purses) is the new bistro, with its cheerfully comfortable ambience, a marked contrast to the stately main restaurant and its crystal chandeliers. If the restaurant is a Wagnerien opera, the bistro is a waltz. The bistro menu is a sort of summary of the magnificent restaurant menu, with its regional touches, hints of Italy and echoes of Asia. Wehmann cooks with true Hanseatic understatement. A simple, savory sausage with cabbage and roasted onions turns into a delicate dish with strong flavors, expertly seasoned and highly aesthetic. In short, grande cuisine.Many gourmet cooks are much more imaginative when they write their menus than when they prepare their dishes in the kitchen, but Wehmann goes in the opposite direction, using simple names for first-class cuisine. Pike-perch with watercress, oxtongue salad with vinaigrette, or fried veal kidneys with spinach all surpassed our expectations. The service is lively, brisk and very competent. The difference between the restaurant and the bistro lies mainly in details of the decorating scheme, not in the quality of the food. The bistro prices are comparable to what you would find in first-class establishments, whereas those in the restaurant are simply beyond the pale.

LE MOUILLAGE 12/20

20095, Depenau 3 (Chilehaus A)
(0 40) 32 71 71 res.

P

Closed Sunday. Tables d'hôte: 30/45L 30/99D, à la carte: 36/62. Tables d'hôte with wine: 66

Pastel landscapes on the walls, pink cloths on the tables and empty seats in the evenings characterize this restaurant in the middle of Hamburg's business district. The first course of dark bread and shrimp with honey and dill sauce, and the dessert – parfaits of walnut, chocolate, grape and Calvados—were the high—lights of an otherwise unremarkable meal. The wine list offers young, little-known wines.

MÜHLENKAMPER FÄHRHAUS 12/20

22085, Uhlenhorst
Hans-Henny-Jahnn-Weg 1
(0 40) 2 20 69 34, 2 20 73 90,
Fax 2 20 69 32 res.

P

Closed for lunch Saturday, closed Sunday, à la carte: 32/90

A visit to the Mühlenkamper Fährhaus, with its gentlemen's club ambience, is like a trip into the past. Time has stood still here. The waiters serve their customers with discreet British charm, and the comprehensive wine list offers a choice of wines from all renowned wine regions of Europe. The prices are British, too: a 1976 Château Lafitte sells for 365 Deutsche marks. Even the cuisine is true to style. The duck liver terrine was more rustic than elegant, the fish soup watery and the beef Stroganoff stringy. The Argentinian beef was good, and the desserts a bit too sweet but sometimes refreshing.

NEVSKY—DAS BISTRO IM KONTORHAUS 13/20

20095, City
Domstr. 17-21 [F4]
(0 40) 33 90 51, Fax 33 90 52 res.

A la carte: 28/64. Tables d'hôte with wine: 30/60

This isn't Holger Urmersbach's first restaurant. In addition to Hamburg's Ratsweinkeller and Cölln's Austernkeller, he also runs a successful restaurant in Moscow and is refurbishing the restaurant of the world-famous Bolshoi Theater there. His tastefully designed bistro offers Russian cuisine that's been on a diet: lighter, fresher and better-looking. The menu sounds typically Russian, with pelmeni, borscht and blinis, but is purely a masquerade for not-very-authentic but decorative cooking. The products used are of high quality, however, and Hamburg's fish obviously harmonize well with Russian recipes.

PETER LEMBCKE 12/20
20099, Holzdamm 49 [H3]
(0 40) 24 32 90 , 24 51 30,
Fax 2 80 41 23 res.
Closed for lunch Saturday, closed Sunday. Tables d'hôte: 57L. 78D, à la carte: 35/96

The cuisine of this restaurant plods along old, well-worn paths without looking either to the right or left. Time-tested products prepared without motivation result in pure boredom. For excitement, we suggest the chef take a look at the prices of his competition. Who's paying 71 DM for turbot or a 110 DM for 56 grams of caviar anymore? And that's not all—the side dishes all cost extra! There isn't a more expensive restaurant in Germany. But we'd gladly pay the extra five marks for those memorable fried potatoes again!

PETIT DÉLICE 13/20
20354, Große Bleichen 21 [E4}
(0 40) 34 34 70
Closed Sunday and holidays, à la carte: 25/57, No Credit Cards

This little restaurant is located among the elegant boutiques in the Galleria. We sampled specialties like carpaccio of red beets and marinated vegetables, sashimi, savory cod with spinach, lamb shoulder with green beans, and venison noisettes with creamed kohlrabi. The Petit Délice's main attractions, though, are its central location, nice interior design and the terrace facing the water.

PLAT DU JOUR
LE BISTRO DE JACQUES
LEMERCIER 14/20
20095, City
Dornbuschstr. 4 [F5]
(0 40) 32 14 14, Fax 4 10 58 57 res.
Closed 23 December through 6 January. Tables d'hôte: 37L, 49D, à la carte: 28/55

Jacques Lemercier, the grand master of classic French cuisine in Hamburg, shows his young colleagues what a bistro can and should be. His new establishment facing that sober Hamburg institution, Cölln's Austernkeller, exhibits genuine Parisian flair, with its upholstered banquettes and mirrored walls. Madame Lemercier supervises her expert French service brigade (and charmingly tries to maneuver customers into the back rooms when all tables are reserved by 1 P.M.). The menu features classic French cooking, often designated *"à la grandmère."* The daily specials offered here are not a sign of a modest new cuisine, but a continuation of beloved traditions. We had a savory leg of lamb and rabbit with a choice of *sauce béarnaise* or garlic sauce *provençal.* Pasta is served as if it were a French invention.

LE RELAIS DE FRANCE 12/20
22397, Duvenstedt
Poppenbütteler Chaussee 3
(0 40) 6 07 07 50 res.
P
Closed Sunday, closed for lunch Monday, à la carte: 49/99

From the many Jaguars and Rolls Royces in the parking lot, jewel-laden customers drift into the restaurant. But the fact that it attracts all that money does not mean that this restaurant offers cosmopolitan flair and exclusive comfort. The kitchen is grandiose, but oh so slow. The cream of asparagus soup was heavy with butter and too salty. Fresh tagliatelle with truffles and shiitake mushrooms promised more than they delivered. Everything tasted like everything else. The turbot with spinach was drowned in champagne sauce, and the lamb in a pepper crust tasted like the fat it was fried in. The service staff could use a little training in a French restaurant.

IL RISTORANTE 15/20
20354, Große Bleichen 16 [E4]
(0 40) 34 33 35 , Fax 34 57 48 res.
Tables d'hôte: 55L, 85D, à la carte: 43/82

In spite of its name, you won't get classic Italian cuisine here. Uwe Witzke offers cuisine with a Mediterranean touch, but won't bind himself in culinary chains. You'll find the finest pasta in Hamburg on the menu, as well as decidedly un-Italian creations like herring variations with pumpernickel or scampi fried in a wok with vegetables and sesame seeds. This is a favorite rendezvous for shoppers who have worked up an appetite while spending money in boutiques. The restaurant is a little worn around the edges, but admirably covers it up with opulent floral arrangements and clever lighting. The service staff is usually good-humored, and the atmosphere has a summery southern flair. By the way, Witzke makes the best desserts in Hamburg.

RIVE 12/20
22767, AltonaVan-der-Smissen-Str. 1
(0 40) 3 80 59 19, Fax 3 89 47 75

Tables d'hôte: 40, à la carte: 28/72

The youngest brainchild of Hamburg's successful gastronomer Alice von Skepsgardh (Il Ristorante, Ventana) is especially popular with the young media and news-agency set. The view of the Elbe from here and of interesting people in here is unbeatable. The menu offers popular bistro dishes, ranging from Caesar's salad to fried fish, as well as Hanseatic classics like grilled salmon, cod with mustard sauce and pike-perch covered with sauerkraut. Asian influences are obvious in such dishes as Saigon scampi with sprouts. Customers don't expect haute cuisine here, but they appreciate the exotic accents.

SALIBA 11/20
20259, Eimsbüttel
Osterstr. 10/Eppendorfer Weg
(0 40) 33 19 56, Fax 33 19 59 res.
Closed Monday. Tables d'hôte: 69, à la carte: 50/78

The Saliba reminds us of an Oriental bazaar. The small dining room is crammed full of tables, so that hurried customers and harried waiters continuously bang against chairs or bump into tables. We had an outstanding "mazza," a plate of 16 different first courses: parsley salad, tsatsiki, green pepper dishes, eggplant and chick-pea dips, beef tartare, spinach, vegetarian hamburgers, and much more.The rest was pure boredom.The wine list includes the highly praised Château Musar from Lebanon.

TAFELHAUS 16/20
22525, Altona
Holstenkamp 71
(0 40) 89 27 60, Fax 8 99 33 24 res.
 **P**
Closed for lunch Saturday, closed Sunday, Monday, closed 3 weeks in January and July. Tables d'hôte: 58L, 95D, à la carte: 56/82, No Credit Cards

This restaurant on a desolate street corner of Altona has a good reputation in Hamburg. It offers quality cuisine without the pomp and prices of the big gourmet temples. Christian Rach, who can cook for about 50 customers in this rebuilt streetcar station, ranks just after the very best of Hamburg. His culinary creations are a feast for the eye and the palate—there are just too few of them. The Tafelhaus is almost always fully booked in the evenings (every reservation is verified a few hours before) and is proud of its many regular customers. It offers a minimalist menu, consisting of two fish and two meat courses, plus three first courses. A menu of four courses costs 95 Deutsche marks and of six courses 115 DM. The à la carte choice is neither bigger nor cheaper. The cucumber soup we had was a bit too spicy, but still delicate, and the turbot wrapped in leaves of Savoy cabbage was worth a rating of 18/20. While the venison with gnocchi was rather mediocre, the anglerfish was exquisite. If the choice of dishes were a little better and the service more professional, this could be one of Hamburg's best gourmet addresses.

TAO 15/20
20354, City
Poststr. 37 [E4]
(0 40) 34 02 30
Tables d'hôte: 25/45, à la carte: 22/52

This restaurant's biggest problem is its practically invisible location. Only small gold letters on a curtained window indicate that it is a place to eat. A larger notice wasn't allowed on the facade of this historic building, which houses the most beautiful, unusual and elegant Chinese restaurant in Germany. The silver, china and glassware are of the finest quality, and even the chopsticks are first-class and lie on little jade rests. The interior design is also luxurious, with marble, lacquered furniture, toned-down colors and chic refinement. All this creates an exclusive ambience. The menu has grown to include a variety of dim sum and egg rolls, a spicy ginger lobster and three low-priced prix-fixe lunches that are a steal at 25 to 45 (for seven courses) DM. The food was artistically arranged and was a feast for the eye as well as for the palate. The only drawback: when the charming owners are at their (more lucrative) fast-food restaurant, the service quickly becomes disorganized and loses its good humor.

VENTANA 13/20

20146, Harvestehude
Grindelhof 77
(0 40) 45 65 88, Fax 48 17 19 res.

Closed for lunch Saturday, closed Sunday.Tables d'hôte: 40L, 79/98D, à la carte: 40/78

When this restaurant opened in 1985, it was the first Italian-Chinese- French-Japanese restaurant with Californian godparents in Hamburg. Nowhere else (except in Los Angeles) is East-meets-West cuisine celebrated so perfectly. Spago's pizza (with crème fraîche, smoked salmon and caviar) is the most expensive in town. The classics of 10 years ago are still served today—wok-fried vegetable strips, sushi and sashimi, curried shrimp and noodles, and duck glazed with honey—but they're just as good as ever. Daily specials are offered for customers who don't like repetition. All dishes are cooked to a turn, even the vegetables, and the arrangement of the food always delights Japanese amateur photographers. The same dishes are cheaper if you eat them for lunch instead of dinner.

WA-YO 13/20

22085, Winterhude
Hofweg 75
(0 40) 2 27 11 40, Fax 22 71 14 90 res.
A la carte: 40/92

Its name (East-West) is as simple as its appearance, which might make the high prices surprising. This restaurant is functionally furnished and concentrates on essentials—the food. The dining rooms, though plainly furnished with Japanese windows and wooden tables, have an elegant flair, and customers—many of them Japanese—fill the house almost every evening. The cuisine is traditional and good. The sushi chef behind the bar prepares 20 different kinds of the dainty and exquisite delicacies with true expertise, and Japanese waitresses provide faultless service.

ZEIK 14/20

20144, Harvesthude
Oberstr. 14a
(0 40) 4 20 40 14, Fax 4 20 40 16

P

A la carte: 28/56, No Credit Cards

This young bistro with its (chic?) open-plan office layout is an offshoot of the Petit Délice. The interior decorator must have given up before he finished. A gray curtain ineffectively serves as a partition, and the lighting divides the restaurant into a light and a dark half. Customers can also sit on a little grass plot behind the house and admire the facades of neighboring high-rise buildings. Since the chef stays away often, the service brigade lacks leadership. The international menu has grown to include almost everything from herring to sashimi, lasagna, veal, Chinese soup and Italian pot-au-feu, as well as some plain bistro-style German fare.

ZUM ALTEN RATHAUS 13/20

20457, Börsenbrücke 10 [E5]
(0 40) 36 75 70 , Fax 37 30 93 res.

P

Closed for lunch Saturday, closed Sunday and holidays. Tables d'hôte: 40L, 80D, à la carte: 39/90

We hope the new owners can catapult the cuisine of this traditional restaurant in the heart of the city to new culinary heights. Until that happens, however, some hindrances have to be moved out of the way, including the nonchalant, sometimes negligent service. Outside of that, eating here was sheer pleasure. We enjoyed a wonderfully light shrimp cocktail with piquant sauce, exquisite zucchini mousse with scallops, and lovely cream of vegetable soup. Our fillet of lamb was a little too soft, but the ratatouille accompanying it was pleasantly savory and not cooked to pieces, and the fillet of beef with hot enoki sauce and shoestring potatoes was delicious. The ice-cream pizza took our breath away.

The choice of wines by the glass is superb, and if you don't want to order one of the great, expensive Bordeaux, you'll find something good at a lower price.

ZUM WATKORN 15/20

22417, Langenhorn
Tangstedter Landstr. 230
(0 40) 5 20 37 97, Fax 47 24 13 res.

Closed Monday. Tables d'hôte: 69/93, à la carte: 43/78

Is a distinguished, elegant ambience absolutely necessary to the enjoyment of top-quality cuisine? Those who answer no will like the Wattkorn. This inconspicuous little thatched cottage north of Hamburg is a gourmet hideaway. A stuffed wood grouse and antlers on the walls, simple wooden stools and rustic tablecloths might not seem to be the appropriate setting for excellent cooking, but this is exactly what is celebrated here. The terrine of chanterelles with chicken breast was delicately light, lemon sole with kohlrabi perfect, peppered grilled salmon with spinach and diced potatoes just delicious. We found the suckling pig cutlet with lentils and dumplings especially flavorful, mocha mousse with grapefruit and melon light and fluffy, and peaches poached in white wine with fresh raspberries enchanting. The wines are fairly priced. Children are welcome. If you want to sit in the beautiful garden, you must reserve far in advance.

HOTELS

AIRPORT HOTEL

22415, Flughafenstr. 47
(0 40) 53 10 20, Fax 53 10 22 22

158 rooms, **S** 230/295, **D** 275/340

Flight delays tick away on the monitors in the lobby, allowing passengers to sit at the bar for another half-hour before taking the free shuttle to the airport some 600 meters away. Hamburg's airport hotel is bright, cheerful and attractive. Conference and fitness centers and a gallery with exhibitions of internationally known artists. Restaurant. Breakfast: 14-22 DM.

ALSTERKRUG HOTEL

22297, Alsterdorf
Alsterkrugchaussee 277
(0 40) 51 30 30, Fax 51 30 34 03

P

79 rooms, **S** 199, **D** 227/245,
APP 239/288

This good hotel is located halfway between the airport, Eppendorf and Hamburg-North and has a curious little turret on top of its two stories. Ambitious restaurant. A canoe and a few bicycles are available for sightseeing along the Alster. Skittle alley, fitness center, solarium.

ATLANTIC HOTEL KEMPINSKI HAMBURG

20099, Ander Alster 72 [H2]
(0 40) 2 88 80, Fax 24 71 29

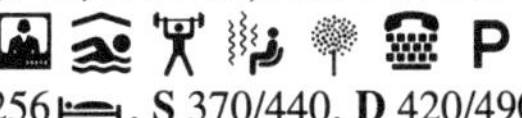

256 rooms, **S** 370/440, **D** 420/490,
APP 700/1700

This is a typical example of a first-class chain that has to justify its high prices by offering extensive service (400 employees). The pompous edifice built in more splendid times was refurbished in 1989 for its 80th birthday and offers everything money can buy. 24-hour room service. Breakfast: 29 DM.

AUSSEN ALSTER HOTEL

20099, Schmilinskystr. 11 [H2]
(0 40) 24 15 57, Fax 2 80 32 31

27 rooms, **S** 185/210, **D** 275/310
Closed 24-27 December

It calls itself Hamburg's smallest luxury hotel, but the boast in no way diminishes its individuality and personal atmosphere. The 27 rooms with bathrooms are modern. The breakfast rooms and the lobby, with its fireplace bar, look like the reception room of an advertising agency. The hotel is centrally located but quiet. The only problem is parking in the one-way street. Bicycles and the hotel's own sailing yacht are available free of charge.

ELYSÉE

20148, Harvesthude
Rothenbauschaussee 10
(0 40) 41 41 20, Fax 41 41 27 33

305, **S** 270/330, **D** 310/370,
APP 450/700

This hotel is one of the most popular in Hamburg. All day (and half the night) long, there's something going on in the lobby, with its tropical garden surrounding the Bourbon Street Bar. Sometimes there is live music, too. There is no concierge to regulate the mingling of house guests and chance visitors. The rooms (some with balconies or bay windows) are pleasantly styled and have air-conditioning and marble bathrooms. Health club on one entire floor, library, restaurants. Breakfast: 19 DM.

FÜRST BISMARCK MÜHLE

26 km east
in 21521 Aumühle
Mülenweg 3
(0 41 04) 20 28, Fax 12 00

7, **S** 120, **D** 190

From 1350 to 1959, grain was milled in this half-timbered building. Then Princess AnnMari established a hotel-restaurant here, furnishing it with Bismarck family heirlooms. The rooms underneath the slanting roof are comfortable and afford an idyllic view. When not overrun by holidaymakers on weekends, the hotel is quiet.

GARDEN

20148, Pöseldorf
Magdalenenstr. 60
(0 40) 41 40 40 , Fax 4 14 04 20

60, **S** 180/300, **D** 280/400,
APP 450/1200

This old villa on the Alster is frequented by people from radio, television, advertising and the press, whose offices are all in the neighborhood. The rooms are comfortable and individually furnished. Opulent breakfast: 14-20 DM.

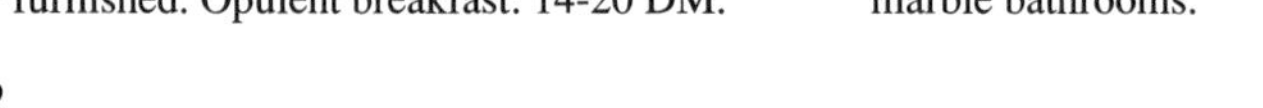

HAMBURG RENAISSANCE

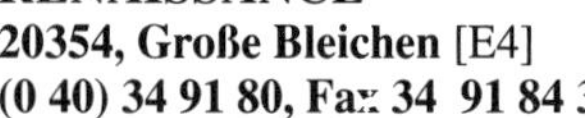

20354, Große Bleichen [E4]
(0 40) 34 91 80, Fax 34 91 84 31

207, **S** 285/335, **D** 335/385,
APP 580/1950, **½P** +49

Even if it doesn't look like it, this is one of Hamburg's new luxury hotels. It is housed in a lovely old brick building, which has become part of a popular and attractive shopping mall in the center of Hamburg. The rooms are comfortably furnished. Massage, fitness facilities, saunas, restaurant. Breakfast: 27.50 DM.

HANSEATIC

22299, Sierichstr. 150
(0 40) 48 57 72, Fax 48 57 73

13, **S** 230/255, **D** 300/375,
APP 300/450

A former patrician villa now houses Hamburg's smallest elegant guesthouse. Landlord Wolfgang Schüler seems to be omnipresent and is always ready to lend a capable and friendly hand. His personal touch is evident everywhere, from the marble steps at the entrance to the tastefully furnished rooms. True Hanseatic understatement: there is no sign on the front of the hotel. Sumptuous breakfast: 27.50 DM.

HOTEL ABTEI

20149, Harvestehude
Abteistr. 14
(0 40) 44 29 05, Fax 44 98 20

12, **S** 250/280, **D** 350/450,
APP 450
Closed 1—18 January

This refurbished patrician house in a fashionable residential area is an alternative to big, often impersonal hotels. The charming rooms have stuccoed ceilings, English antiques and marble bathrooms.

INTER-CONTINENTAL 

20354, Harvestehude
Fontenay 10 [F1]
(0 40) 4 14 15 10, Fax 41 41 51 86

286, **S** 275/460, **D** 325/510,
APP 650/1400

This unlovely concrete building has hidden qualities: an extravagantly styled interior, 24-hour room service, Lufthansa check-in, free bike rental, jogging suits and shoes, massage, solarium and restaurants.If you don't want to spend an evening in your room, but don't want to leave the house, you can enjoy yourself in the casino on the ninth floor. Breakfast: 29 DM.

MADISON

20459, Neustadt
Schaarsteinweg 4 [C6]
(0 40) 37 66 60, Fax 37 66 61 37

165, **S** 190/210, **D** 240/290,
APP 390

If you like unconventional hotels, you'll like this one. It opened in 1994 and is located a few steps away from the main piers. Regular guests report that the rooms are getting smaller and the prices higher. The restaurant satisfies those who don't mind dishes that look and taste as if they're prepared far in advance. The rooms are pleasant and the service still training. A modern health club is located nearby. Breakfast: 19 DM.

PREM

20099, An der Alster 9 [H2]
(0 40) 24 17 26, Fax 2 80 38 51

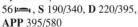

56, **S** 190/340, **D** 220/395,
APP 395/580

Like the Adlon, the Ritz and the Negresco, the Prem is named after its founder, Rudolf Prem, an Austrian hotelier and art collector. The new management has tried to restore some of its former splendor. Valuable antiques abound. Rooms in front face a noisy street and afford a view of the Alster; at the back, there is a quiet garden. Breakfast: 29.50 DM.

SAS HOTEL HAMBURG PLAZA

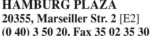

20355, Marseiller Str. 2 [E2]
(0 40) 3 50 20, Fax 35 02 35 30

560, **S** 280/360, **D** 330/410,
APP 500/1200

The Plaza, which has been taken over by SAS, rises more than a hundred meters above the famous "Planten und Blomen" garden surrounding it. The Royal Club floors offers extensive services. The hotel also has a floor for nonsmokers and a business service center. If you don't have a room at the top of the building, you can still enjoy the skyline of Hamburg from the disco "Top of the Town" on the 26th floor. Two restaurants. Conference guests appreciate being close to the Hamburg Congress Center. Breakfast: 17-27 DM.

STEIGENBERGER HAMBURG 

20459, City
Heiligengeistbrüke 4 [D5]
(0 40) 36 80 60, Fax 36 80 67 77

234, **S** 275/335, **D** 325/385,
APP 530/1250

With its red stone facade, Hamburg's newest grand hotel fits into the traditional ensemble. Inside, the hotel is cool, clean and functional, but the combination of marble, granite and precious wood gives it an attractive flair. The rooms have extra-long beds; some suites even have their own sauna. Bistro-café, bar, modern conference technology. The hotel has its own pier for excursions on the Alster and to the harbor. Breakfast: 18-29 DM.

VIER JAHRZEITEN 

20356, Neuer Jungfernsteig 9-14 [E3]
(0 40) 3 49 40, Fax 3 49 46 02

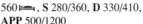

170, **S** 375/455, **D** 465/595,
APP 750/1600

This is a "grand hotel" in the best sense of the word and an institution in Hamburg. A guest is not merely a number here. At first the Hanseatic understatement with which luxury and modern technology are presented leaves one a little breathless, but the loving care that went into the assembling and arranging of valuable antiques, carpets, lovely old wood and costly paintings is apparent throughout. The service is so maddeningly perfect that one is tempted to take advantage of it even when it isn't needed. Breakfast: 34.50 DM.

HAMMELBURG Bayern

Kissingen 18-Schweinfurt 29

HOTEL NEUMÜHLE 15/20

6km west
in 97797 Wartmannsroth
Neumühle 54
(0 97 32) 80 30, Fax 8 03 79 res.

Tables d'hôte: 49L, 49/93D, à la carte: 39/60, No Credit Cards

This restaurant in a spacious gabled room with a fireplace and antique paintings has a congenial atmosphere, and customers quickly feel at home. The cuisine is creative but does not adulterate regional recipes. We especially liked the turbot with mushrooms, bacon and potatoes, and we also enjoyed exquisite quail galantine with puréed rose hips and salad with walnuts, delicious sorrel soup with ham biscuits, John Dory and king prawns with zucchini slices seasoned with saffron, veal schnitzel with white wine sauce and good cheese. Heavenly cinnamon parfait in a plum soup rounded off our meal.The service is correct, competent and pleasant, and the wine list features Franconian wines as well as French and Italian vintages and wines from overseas at prices connoisseurs appreciate.

HOTEL NEUMÜHLE 

6km west
in 97797 Wartmannsroth
Neumühle 54
(0 97 32) 80 30, Fax 8 03 79 res.

28, **S** 150, **D** 220/260,
APP 280/400
No Credit Cards

This lovingly restored historic dwelling is the perfect setting for the unusually decorated rooms and comfortable maisonettes that create an ideal hotel atmosphere. The rooms all have a personal touch and are furnished with precious antiques. The focal point of the lovely courtyard with an old well is an ancient chestnut tree. Breakfast: 20 DM.

SEPP HALBRITTER'S LANDGASTAHUS 16/20 

6 km west in 97797
Wartmannsroth
Hauptstr. 4
(0 97 37) 8 90, Fax 89 40 res.

Closed for dinner, closed Monday, Tuesday, closed mid-January through mid-February. Tables d'hôte: 125/150, à la carte: 54/98

We loved the charming atmosphere of this beautiful country inn. The service wasn't just pretty and charming but competent as well, and Max Matreux, who has taken over the kitchen, served a fireworks of fantastic taste sensations. The appetizer was an explosion of flavors: oyster parfait with onion confit, followed by a grandiose pigeon terrine that melted in our mouths and wonderful autumn salads. The sheatfish (a type of catfish) was precisely poached in a broth of horseradish and vegetables, and the venison consommé with cèpes ravioli had a fabulous flavor. After terrific lamb from the salt meadows with a ragout of green and yellow beans, ratatouille and zucchini tarts, expertly ripened cheese and peach and plum ragout with almond ice cream ended our culinary experience.The wine list is grandiose and includes half bottles, champagne and a small choice of wines by the glass.

SEPP HALBRITTER'S LANDGASTAHUS 

6 km west in 97797
Wartmannsroth
Hauptstr. 4
(0 97 37) 8 90, Fax 89 40

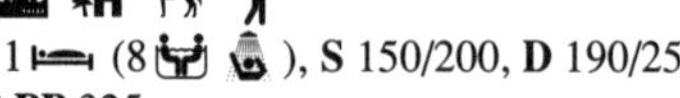

11 (8), **S** 150/200, **D** 190/250,
APP 325
Closed mid-January through mid-February

This country inn located near the autobahn exits to Hammelburg and Kissingen offers romantic comfort behind the rustic, geranium-garlanded half-timbered walls. Modern amenities, innovative styling and almost extravagant spaciousness.The hotel arranges special activities: live jazz, hunting, fireworks and more. Breakfast: 25 DM.

HANNOVER Niedersachsen

Bremen 125 - Hamburg 155 - Berlin 282 - Frankfurt/Main 350

ADELE

30159, Sophienstr. 6 [C4]
(05 11) 32 59 73

P

Tables d'hôte: 75/85, à la carte: 30/70

The restaurant named after the owner's grandmother is a pleasant place to eat and drink. The wines are choice and moderately priced and the cuisine, though still finding its way, will be worth a rating of 14/20 if the quality remains consistent. We had wafer-thin sliced sturgeon with orange and coriander sauce as an appetizer, followed by more flavorful than delicate duck-liver parfait with perfectly dressed salads. Seasonal soup and an entremet of king prawns with asparagus noodles and hearty lobster sauce left just enough room for an excellent *tafelspitz* of veal with wonderful vegetables and passable potatoes. The desserts were, in comparison, very plain.

L'ADRESSE IN THE MARITIM GRAND HOTEL 12/20

30159, Friedrichswall 11 [B5]
(05 11) 3 67 70, Fax 32 51 95 res.

Closed Sunday, closed during the NRW summer school holiday. Tables d'hôte: 48L, 85D, à la carte: 40/83

Since the Maritim chain took over the Hannoveranian Interconti, the cuisine has become much less cheerful. The menu has only à la carte dishes, and the prices have risen. The foie gras with salad was terrifically expensive and, even though tender, tasted as if it were breaded. The plaice could have done with a little less flour, and the turbot with salmon and lobster sauce tasted like a typical hotel-kitchen dish - that is, simply boring. The saddle of venison was tender but tasteless (did it come frozen from New Zealand?). Chef Norbert Classen can do a whole lot better!

ALTE MÜHLE

30559, Stadtteil Kirchrode
Hermann-Löns-Park 3
(05 11) 55 94 80, Fax 55 26 80 res.

Closed Tuesday. Tables d'hôte: 24/46L, à la carte: 40/75

Although a typical restaurant for holidaymakers, the Alte Mühle still attempts to keep a certain standard of quality cuisine. In the dining room of this renovated half-timbered house, crystal chandeliers and waiters in tail coats create an elegant ambience, but neither the menu nor the cuisine justified our high expectations. The choice of wines was small. The lovely garden under old trees, however, was a perfect setting for a romantic evening.

BAKKARAT IN THE MASCHSEE CASINO 15/20

30169, Arthur-Menge-Ufer 3 [B6]
(05 11) 8 40 57, Fax 88 75 33 res.

Closed for lunch Saturday, closed Sunday, Monday. Tables d'hôte: 49L, 59/128D, à la carte: 56/105

Ever since Jürgen Richter took over the kitchen here, the lights of this gourmet restaurant have been shining more brightly than ever. After a Nordic appetizer of Sylt oyster, Büsum shrimp and vegetable terrine, we had excellent lobster with crawfish and caviar, followed by harmonious sole and turbot with spinach. Everything deserves two toques except perhaps the desserts, which are a bit lame in comparison to the rest. The view of the Maschsee from here is beautiful. The service is excellent, the wine list is adequate and there is live piano music.

BENTHER BERG 13/20

10 km southwest on the B65,
in 30952 Ronnenberg-Benthe
Vogelsangstr. 18
(05 11) 6 40 60, Fax 64 06 50 res.

Closed for dinner Sunday. Tables d'hôte: 40/63L, 79105D, à la carte: 44/89

Everything is respectable here, from the correctly dressed service staff to the furniture, the

Hannover

500 m

A B C D
1 2 3 4 5 6

Jakobistraße
Voßstr.
Kriegerstr.
Podbielskistr.
Lister Platz
Markusk.
Lukask.
Vahrenwalder Str.
Voßstr.
Kriegerstr.
Bonifatiusplatz
Kopernikusstr.
Engelbosteler Damm
St. Marien
Marschnerstr.
Weidendamm
Raiffeisenstr.
Schützenstr.
Am Welfenplatz
Welfenplatz
Celler Straße
Lister Meile
Bödekerstr.
Hohenzollernstr.
Eilenriede
Wedekindstr.
Kl. Pfahlstr.
Flüggestr.
OSTSTADT
Hamburger Allee
Sedanstraße
Fundstr.
Arndtstr.
Christusk.
Nikolaistr.
Herschelstr.
Hallerstr.
Friesenstraße
Dreifalt.-K.
Bödekerstr.
Schloßwender Str.
Postkamp
Körnerstr.
Celler Str.
Fernmeldeturm
Andreas-Hermes-Platz
Raschplatzhochstr.
Eichstr.
Hohenzollernstr.
Conti-Hochhaus
Otto-Brenner-Str.
Brüderstr.
Odeonstr.
Lister Meile
Raschplatz
ZOB
Volgersweg
Berliner Allee
Hochsch. f. Musik u. Theater
Anzeiger-Hochh.
Lange Laube
Kurt-Schumacher-Str.
Am Steintor
Hauptbahnhof
Ernst-August-Pl.
Königstr.
Ellernstr.
Brühlstraße
Schillerstr.
Bahnhofstr.
Georgstr.
Am Marstall
Goethestraße
Kröpcke
Rathenaustr.
Am Schiffgraben
St. Elisabeth
Leisewitzstr.
MITTE
Knochenhauerstr.
Schmiedestr.
Osterstr.
Opernhaus
Prinzenstr.
Lavesstr.
Kestnerstraße
Goetheplatz
Kreuzk.
Hist. Mus.
Ballhof
Am Hohen Ufer
Leibnizufer
St. Clemens
Neust. K.
Neustädter Str.
Markt
Altes Rathaus
Kramerstr.
Karmarschstr.
Marktstr.
Georgstr.
Warmbüchenstr.
Dieterichsstr.
Berliner Allee
Calenberger Str.
Landtag
Leineschloß
Aegidienk.
Arnswaldtstr.
Marienstraße
Ref. K.
Lavesallee
Adolfstr.
Friedrichswall
Leine
Aegidientorplatz
Sallstraße
Rautenstr.
Gustav-Bratke-Allee
Waterlooplatz
Waterloosäule
Kestner-Museum
Trammpl.
Rathaus
Theater
Jungfernplan
Große Barlinge
Hildesheimer
Landesbibl.
Am Schützenplatz
Culemannstr.
Maschteich
Am Maschpark
Langensalzastr.
Maschstr.
Birkenstr.
Regierung
Waterloostr.
Landesmuseum
SÜDSTADT
Schlägerstr.
Nazarethk.
Sallstraße
Lavesallee
Schützenplatz
Sprengel-Museum
Auf dem Emmerberge
Meterstr.
Krausenstr.
Beuermannstr.
Ihme
Arthur-Menge-Ufer
Rudolf-v.-Bennigsen-Ufer
Wiesenstraße
Paulusk.
St. Heinrich
Spielbank
Seufzerallee
Bürgerm.-Fink-Str.
Bandelstr.
NDR
Niedersachsen-Stadion
Maschsee
Alte Döhrener Str.
Straße
Geibelstr.
© Baedeker

U-Bahn

Herrenhausen, Welfenschloß, TU
Zoo
Stadthalle
Hannover-Messe

many traditional German names on the wine list and the style of cooking. The prices have also risen to a respectable height. The traditional lobster menu (with salads, au gratin and stewed in turnip broth) seems less attractive when you've just eaten a very firm lobster thermidor à la carte. Meat and vegetables were often overdone, and the fish could have used a finer hand —and a little more of the chef's attention. The morels in cream sauce were, however, very good, and the mousse with fresh fruit excellent.There is a nice view from the Benther Berg. With better cooking and lower prices, this restaurant would have good prospects, too.

BENTHER BERG

10 km southwest on the B65,
in 30952 Ronnenberg-Benthe
Vogelsangstr. 18
(05 11) 6 40 60, Fax 64 06 50 res.

  P

70, **S** 135/185, **D** 180/240,
1/2P +40, **P** +60

This quiet hotel, surrounded by extensive gardens and forest, is situated on the outskirts of Benthe. Its three wings include the "Altes Haus," with spacious and elegantly furnished rooms and apartments; the "Neues Haus," with more functionally equipped rooms; and the "Landhaus," facing a park with old trees. Breakfast buffet.

BERGGASTAHUS NIEDERSACHSEN

In 30989 Gehrden
Gehrdener Berg
(0 51 08) 31 01, Fax 20 31 res.

  P

Closed for lunch Wednesday through Friday, closed Monday, Tuesday. Tables d'hôte: 38/78, à la carte: 33/68, No Credit Cards

When city folks from Hannover make an excursion, they like to take to the hills—perhaps because there are so few of them around here. They climb the Benther Berg and the facing hill, where this restaurant draws throngs of tourists on nice weekends. The cuisine is so-so, but the atmosphere in this comfortable, pretty half-timbered house with its beautiful terrace is so congenial that we like eating here. In any case, customers can be sure of generous portions and low prices.

LE CHALET 15/20

30161, Isernhagener Str. 21 [B1]
(05 11) 31 95 88 res.

Closed Monday. Tables d'hôte: 69/99, à la carte: 51/91, No Credit Cards

He's back! After a long absence, the legendary William Le Mevel from Brittany has taken over the kitchen here again. He has a new cuisine that uses less cream, much to our delight, and Mevel now cooks fresh, light meals. And they can look like this: a wonderfully savory terrine of *tafelspitz* with caper sauce and straw potatoes, followed by absolutely fresh scallops in tangy orange butter, turbot with ginger and lime sauce, tender lamb with (purely decorative) vegetables, almond jelly with pears and pear sauce, or crepes filled with mango sherbet. Reception and service are charmingly personal; the wine list is good and getting better.

CLICHY 13/20

30161, Weißekreuzstr. 31 [C3]
(05 11) 3 24 47, Fax 31 82 83

Closed for lunch Saturday, closed Sunday. Tables d'hôte: 45L 65/129D, à la carte: 51/89. Tables d'hôte with wine: 65

Does the future belong to the past? Almost all gourmet cooks now back away from the old standbys of lobster, caviar and foie gras, but Ekkehard Reimann still swears by them. He has also retained the Clichy's original "roaring '70s" decor, with a lot of tassels and second-hand furniture. After tasteless chicken aspic, the fried duck foie gras was perfect and the lobster almost so. The brook trout was a little soft, and the fillet of beef was accompanied by over-cooked but tasty vegetables. The potato gratins are as wonderfully creamy and delicious as they were years ago. Ekkehard Reimann's customers like the good wine list, the attentive service, the ambience and the maestro's tour of the tables.

GALLO NERO 15/20

30655, Stadtteil Groß Buchholz
Gr. Buchholzer Kirchweg 72B
(05 11) 5 46 34 34, Fax 32 28 59 res.

Closed Sunday, first week in January, last 3 weeks of the Neidersachsen summer school holiday. Tables d'hôte: 70/85, à la carte: 38/75

The gallo nero (black cock) is crowing louder and louder, and he has every reason to call attention to himself. This restaurant was designed with loving care, a lot of money and much more taste. The dining room of the frame house is just splendid.The cuisine, prepared by German cooks, has developed its own character. Ingenious combinations (fish in rhubarb sauce, duck ragout with olives) are part of the repertoire, as are equally original but simpler creations. à la carte dishes are as inexpensive as fixed-price menus, which owner Biaggio Tropeano loves to put together. After toasted white bread with olive oil and tomatoes, a meal might look like this: a wonderfully dressed salad, astonishing wine soup with tender salmon and ravioli filled with eggplant and ricotta, sea bream fillet with orange fennel sauce, shrimp with rhubarb and crispy potato chips, flavorful and tender lamb, and, finally, a crepe with fresh fruit. The service is flawless, and Tropeano makes his customers feel like personal friends. The choice of Italian wines is without rival, and the prices are astoundingly modest.

GASTWIRTSCHAFT WICHMANN 13/20
30519, Stadtteil Bothfeld
Hildesheimer Str. 230
(05 11) 83 16 71

A la carte: 31/70

With a more comprehensive and imaginative menu and some new prix-fixe suggestions, the Wichmann is on its way up. The ambience was always the main attraction here, but now the cuisine is trying its best to come up to par. A picturesque mountain of salad with marinated salmon was called a first course although it was as generous as a main course. We tried headcheese in two variations. Accompanied by sole with curry, it seemed unexciting and flat, but with half a lobster and lovely artichoke hearts, it was a taste sensation! The price was a little short of sensational, too: more than 60 DM!The wines are also expensive, but the ostentatious wine folio offers many wines by the glass as well as half bottles. The service is professionally attentive.

GATTOPARDO 14/20
30159, Hainhölzer Str. 1 [A2]
(05 11) 1 43 75, Fax 31 82 83

Closed for lunch. Tables d'hôte: 45/84, à la carte: 35/59, Tables d'hôte wih wine: 50

A full house does not necessarily mean the chef cooks well. But it is true in this case. Gattopardo's kitchen staff has fully earned its toque. The choice of dishes is small but well-chosen and includes those Italian favorites carpaccio and vitello tonnato (excellent with tomato). It is apparently a trans-Alpine custom to announce the entire menu (in almost one breath) as the chef's suggestion for the evening—is this a test of the customer's memory? But we enjoyed the recommended anglerfish with asparagus, light and savory guinea fowl with run-of-the-mill side dishes, lovely salad with rabbit livers, and delicious ravioli with tomato sauce, followed by pannacotta with ice cream. The service is amiable and the choice of wines agreeable.

HINDENBURG KLASSIK 12/20
30175, Gneisenaustr. 55 [C4]
(05 11) 85 85 88, Fax 81 92 13 res.

Closed for lunch Saturday, closed Sunday.Tables d'hôte: 45/65L, 60/90D, à la carte: 49/84

Hannover "society" patronizes the Hindenburg Klassik and is always charmingly welcomed by the Italian owners. Mario Grappolini and Pierino Viero like to talk to their customers, interpret and comment on the dishes on the menu, and give absolutely sound advice as to which wine to order. By the way, this is one of the few restaurants where you can order any of the wines by the glass—they're extraordinarily good. The salmon carpaccio here was fishy, and the duck liver was fried to a turn and served with a sloppily dressed salad. The sturgeon had a nice consistency and the fillet of beef was tender; both came with the same side dishes.

DIE INSEL
30519, Rudolf-von-Bennigsen-Ufer 81
(05 11) 83 12 14

P

A la carte: 47/61, No Credit Cards

The Insel (which means "island") is a complex consisting of a bar, restaurant, café, beach bistro, banquet rooms and beer garden. The restaurant offering fine cuisine is on the first floor. The menu is modest (no prix-fixe) and so is the wine list, but the quality of the food and wine here is good. Our first course was opulent: on a few leaves of lettuce we found marinated salmon, squab leg with apple and pineapple pieces, king prawns, a little quail's egg and other delicacies. The sole was perfectly cooked and served in lovely Riesling sauce, and our duck with Savoy cabbage was delicious. We'll give owner Norbert Schuh a little more time before we rate him, but we can say one thing already: this island is a nice place to drop anchor.

KASTENS LUISENHOF

30159, Luisenstr. 1-3 [B4]
(05 11) 3 04 40, Fax 3 04 48 07

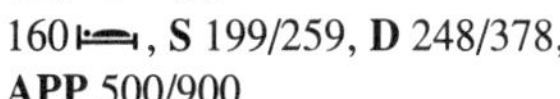

160, **S** 199/259, **D** 248/378, **APP** 500/900

Hannover's oldest hotel, within easy walking distance of the train station and the shopping area of town, is rich in tradition. This family heirloom (since 1856) is furnished with antiques. Restaurant and grill. Ample breakfast buffet.

DAS KÖRBCHEN 13/20

30159, Körnerstr. 3 [B4]
(05 11) 1 31 82 96 res.

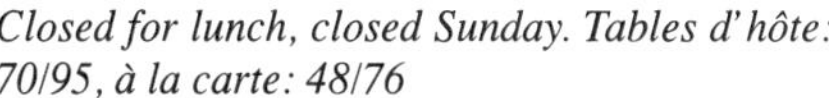

Closed for lunch, closed Sunday. Tables d'hôte: 70/95, à la carte: 48/76

Owner Wolfgang Prost does his best to make his customers feel at home in his restaurant. Pretty pastel drawings on the wall, elegantly set tables and a large choice of liqueurs make a good impression. The prices on the wine list, though, are not as reasonable as those on the menu. With a dash of herbs and a touch of color, Prost tries to make his dishes more exciting, but they remain rather nondescript. Our meal began with a leek soufflé that could have used more salt and less cream, continued with a fish course of fresh salmon, red mullet and scallops, followed by sautéed quails and poached saddle of lamb. Everything was tender, fresh, nicely prepared—and yawningly unexciting.

LANDHAUS AMMANN 15/20

30173, Hildesheimer Str. 185 [C6]
(05 11) 83 08 18 , Fax 8 43 77 49 res.

 P

Tables d'hôte: 125/165D, à la carte: 55/106

The most impressive things about this grand establishment are the wine list and its prices. The wines (even the Bordeaux and most Burgundys) are surprisingly inexpensive, whereas the prices on the menu are out of proportion to the quality of the food served. Sometimes the cuisine is not as well-balanced and dependable as it should be. The typical gourmet menu starts with an appetizer of venison terrine, followed by tender lobster with pink grapefruit and avocado, clear oxtail soup and sweetbreads with a tired sauce, nice melon soup, lovely lamb with vegetables, good cheese and dessert. The service can be a bit negligent. We missed a capable sommelier to help us with our choice of wines. The wine list offers champagne galore.

LANDHAUS AMMANN

30173, Hildesheimer Str. 185 [C6]
(05 11) 83 08 18 , Fax 8 43 77 49

  P

15, **S** 220/290, **D** 290/330, **APP** 320/520

This luxurious mansion makes a hospitable impression. The individually decorated rooms, apartments and suites have all the modern amenities. Commendable conference rooms, winter garden and café, bar. Breakfast (à la carte): 25 DM.

MARITIM AIRPORT

30669, Langenhagen
Flughafenstr. 5
(05 11) 9 73 70, Fax 9 73 75 90

Tables d'hôte:59/89, à la carte: 38/78

The lobby of this new concrete hotel at the airport is something to see: it is several floors high, and glass elevators glide silently up and down its facade. The hotel's bistro offers attractive cuisine, livened up by daily or weekly specials: nice soups, standard fish and meat courses, acceptable desserts. The wine list is tiny, but the prices soar: a half-liter of Pellegrino for 12 DM indicates a luxury we didn't find.

MARITIM GRAND HOTEL

30159, Friedrichswall 11 [B5]
(05 11) 3 67 70, Fax 32 51 95

285, **S** 255/495, **D** 296/5446,
APP 345/1300, **1/2P** +40, **P** +80

This former Inter-Continental hotel in the heart of the city was completely renovated in 1992. Several restaurants, pub, bar, discotheque, 24-hour room service. Hairdresser and cosmetician. Breakfast: 26 DM.

MARITIM STADTHOTEL

30169, Hildesheimer Str. 34-40
(05 11) 9 89 40, Fax 9 89 49 01

293, **S** 245/429, **D** 298/588,
APP 680/980, **1/2P** +40, **P** +70

This hotel provides every modern comfort and quick access to the city and the convention centers. Rooms, studios and suites are all cleverly divided into living, working and sleeping areas and have spacious bathrooms. During fairs and conventions, prices are higher. Solarium, fitness facilities, restaurant, bar, café. Breakfast buffet.

NEUE ZEITEN 12/20

31063, Jakobistr. 24
(05 11) 39 24 47, Fax 3 36 05 09 res.

Closed Sunday, Monday, 24 December through 4 January. Tables d'hôte: 52/59, à la carte: 41/61, No Credit Cards

Times are changing. This restaurant is not as unreliable as it was in the past, but the kitchen is still good for some surprises. The beautiful ambience, cool reception and long waits between courses have not changed at all, but the wine list is larger. Prices are still low. We had tender rabbit livers with Belgian endives, red beet soup with fennel and limp shrimp, juicy sea trout, nice saddle of lamb and a variety of desserts. The sauces are generally heavy and filling, but seldom inspired and well-balanced.

OPUS 1

30159, Georgstr. 35 [B4]
(05 11) 32 43 43 , Fax 32 43 43 res.

P

Tables d'hôte: 28L, 50D, à la carte: 24/59

This little restaurant on the top floor of the Mövenpick complex next to the opera is mentioned in this guide not because of its exceptional cuisine—the cooking here is just average —but there are few other restaurants with such a large choice of low-priced American wines, some of which are even served by the glass. We keep coming back to drink our way through the brave new world.

LA PROVENCE

30459, Stadtteil Ricklingen
Beekestr. 95
(05 11) 41 30 30, fax 42 73 47 res.

Closed for lunch, closed Monday, Tuesday. Tables d'hôte: 52/115, à la carte: 39/71, No Credit Cards

Ricklingen, a country suburb of Hannover, has become really chic. Old farmhouses have become luxurious villas, and modesty is passé. La Provence fits in with the new surroundings. Outside, it is a beautiful ensemble of large framework buildings with old chestnut trees. Inside, glowing candles, dark mirrors, daring floral arrangements and a fireplace remind one of the '70s in France (as nostalgic Germans see it today). Confusing? The menu lists as many dishes as that of a Chinese restaurant, including such creative combinations as saddle of lamb with fruit and fruit sherbet, potato gratin and melon. The price is high for this kind of originality. The service is unconventional and really nice. Children are welcome here. And when the soft spring air blows lightly through Ricklingen, you could not find a prettier place to sit outside. And you won't mind the mediocre cuisine at all.

ROTHER'S RESTAURANT 13/20 
30655, Gottfr.-Keller-Str. 28-30
(05 11) 6 96 66 65, Fax 6 96 57 35 res.
 P
Tables d'hôte: 20/45L, 49/79D, à la carte: 28/63, No Credit Cards

Rother's place on the drab Podbielskistrasse doesn't look like a gourmet restaurant. And customers who are brave enough to enter still doubt it when they're inside this typical suburban café. The service is familiar, the menu a little confusing, and the wine list meager, but cook Harry Rother gave us reason enough to hope for better things. We got them: wonderful vegetable terrine was followed by marinated salmon with a delicious potato pancake and a great fillet of Angus beef with terrific fried potatoes, zucchini and savory shallot sauce.

SCHWEIZERHOF 
30175, Hinüberstr. 6 [C4]
(05 11) 3 49 50, Fax 3 49 51 23
  P
200, **S** 230/295, **D** 280/345, **APP** 450/750

This hotel, built in 1983, has a central location in a quiet side street right behind the train station. The spacious rooms and suites with balconies, terraces and bay windows are furnished in an unconventionally modern style. The hotel has an imposing hall for Versailles-style festivities. Breakfast buffet: 19 Deutsche marks.

STERN'S RESTAURANT IN HOTEL GEORGENHOF 18/20 
30167, Stadtteil Herrenhausen
Herrenhäuser Kirchweg 20
(05 11) 70 22 44, Fax 70 85 59
 P
Tables d'hôte: 36/60L, 199/169D, à la carte: 65/111

There is no doubt about it, Heinrich Stern is the best cook in this part of Germany. His cuisine is light and savory. The fancy "layer cake" of eels was enchantingly mild, his foie-gras terrine with a lovely salad fantastic, and the quail nice and juicy. The scallops, with their unbelievably intense Tuscan sauce, were simply sensational. Even the lobster was magnificent. The buttermilk sherbet with orange juice was nothing short of excellent, and the venison was outstanding. It was all too good to be true, and we braced ourselves for at least one disappointment, but it never came. Desserts are exquisite and the choice of cheeses grand (even if the cheese was a bit cold). The seasonal menu deserved the 18/20 rating, too; it included an asparagus terrine, cream of asparagus soup with salmon quenelles, asparagus with anglerfish, fresh goat cheese with fig-mustard and cherries. The ambience is flawless, and the wine list would be too if the prices were lower and the choice wider. The advice given on the wines is competent, however. On warm evenings, customers can dine on the terrace.

TITUS 13/20 
30519, Stadtteil Döhren
Wiebergstr. 98
(05 11) 83 55 24 , Fax 8 38 65 38 res.
 P
Closed Sunday. Tables d'hôte: 38L, 79/99D, à la carte: 44/101

Dieter Gruber previously cooked under the famous Heinrich Stern in Hannover's Georgenhof. Now he has transported some of that cuisine to Döhren. The menu is small, but everything we tried was of high quality, including red cabbage salad, sea trout, quails (not young ones), and a tasty salad with sheep's cheese. The service is good.

WEIN WOLF 15/20 
30159, Rathenaustr. 2
(05 11) 32 07 88
P
A la carte: 45/63.

After Joachim Stern gave up his gourmet temple in the suburbs, he took over this rustic *weinstube* in the center of town. Wein Wolf is an institution in Hannover, but it has never been an attractive address for gourmets. Thanks to the pleasure Stern takes in good cooking, however, the restaurant is slowly gaining merit. We had marinated and smoked Irish salmon with lamb's lettuce, hot smoked salmon with kohlrabi noodles and a hearty orange sauce, blood pudding and liver sausage, legs of guinea fowl with morel sauce, and stuffed oxtail braised in red wine sauce. The desserts here include standards ranging from parfait to mousse. The wine list is flawless. There is no prix-fixe listed, but the waiters can help with suggestions.

HARSEWINKEL NRW

Gütersloh 7 - Bielefeld 29

POPPENBORG 16/20

33428, Brockhägerstr. 9
(0 52 47) 22 41, Fax 17 21 res.

Closed Wednesday, 1 week at Easter and 1 week in autumn. Tables d'hôte: 49/124

Heinrich Poppenborg remains true to his style and is one of the best cooks in eastern Westphalia. We enjoyed delicately seasoned tartare with potatoes, piquant Bouillabaisse salad with crawfish and salmon, hearty potato salad with turbot, and exquisitely done salmon in pasta dough. The classically prepared Bresse duckling, served in two courses, was just as excellent as the pigeon breast with white beans and fully deserved both toques.Anne Poppenborg manages a charming and competent service staff. You can trust her counsel in the choice of wines. The wine list offers excellent dry white wines, as well as a few lovely sweet and fruity German Rieslings and many vintages from Bordeaux and Burgundy.

POPPENBORG

33428, Brockhägerstr. 9
(0 52 47) 22 41, Fax 17 21

18, **S** 60/80, **D** 130/140
Closed 1 week at Easter and 1 week in autumn

The six very comfortable rooms overlooking the garden are highly recommended; those facing the street are only for those who don't mind noise. Complimentary fresh fruit and mineral water.

HATTINGEN NRW

Bochum 12 - Wuppertal 24

LANDGASTHAUS HUXEL 14/20

9 km south in Niederelfringhausen
45529, Felderbachstr. 9
(0 20 52) 64 15 res.

Closed Monday, Tuesday, 2 weeks in February. Tables d'hôte: 55L, 105D, à la carte: 43/85

The dining room of this country inn, decorated with antique clocks, old musical instruments and other curiosities, is a strange little museum. But elegantly set tables and a nostalgic atmosphere create the right setting for high-quality cuisine. Werner Westphal's cooking is reassuringly up-to-date. He prepares trout raised in the ponds in back of the house in 10 different ways, and cooks many other good things, too. After an enticing appetizer, we enjoyed our trout and salmon terrine and scallop praliné. In addition to a small prix-fixe, a large "surprise menu" and his trout variations, Westphal offers everything from foie gras to lamb rack à la carte. His exquisite pot-au-feu with turbot, anglerfish, salmon and scallops in Riesling cream was finely balanced, and his veal medallions with truffled butter sauce, asparagus and cèpes first class. The service is charming, and the poetic wine list makes interesting reading.

HEIDELBERG BW

Karlsruhe 57 - Darmstadt 58

HIRSCHGASSE

69120, Hirschgasse 3
(0 62 21) 45 40, Fax 45 41 11

20, **S** 245/295, **D** 245/295,
APP 295/550
Closed 24 December through 31 January

Germany's oldest students' inn, facing Heidelberg's castle, exudes a romantic flair and offers rooms decorated with Laura Ashley fabrics. Breakfast: 25 DM.

KURFÜRSTENSTUBE IN HOTEL EUROPÄISCHER HOF 13/20

69117, Friedrich-Ebert-Anlage 1
(0 62 21) 51 50, Fax 51 55 55

P

Tables d'hôte: 84, à la carte: 55/89

This restaurant exudes overall good spirits. The comfortable, cozy atmosphere is topped by perfect service and a surprisingly comprehensive wine list with fairly priced wines.The Kurfürstenstube's new chef offers a more ambitious cuisine. We honored the attempt and tried a scallop salad that was more of a treat for the eye than for our palates. The variations of salmon were fresh, but the caviar wasn't. The consommé with marrow quenelles had too much salt, whereas the ravioli in it could have used some more. The mashed potatoes and sauerkraut that came with the stuffed guinea hen was more flavorful than the bird itself.

DER EUROPÄISCHER HOF

69117, Friedrich-Ebert-Anlage 1
(0 62 21) 51 50, Fax 51 55 55

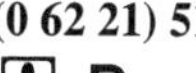

135, **S** 299/339, **D** 390/450,
APP 500/750, **½P** +58/77, **P** +116/154

Heidelberg's grandest hotel has maintained an elegantly comfortable ambience throughout its 130-year history. The courtyard has a lovely garden. Restaurant. Breakfast: 29 DM

PRINZHOTEL HEIDELBERG

69120, Neuenheimer Landstr. 5
(0 62 21) 4 03 20, Fax 4 03 21 96

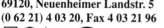

48, **S** 195/245, **D** 225/295,
APP 295/350

A nicely renovated, pleasant hotel in the Art Nouveau style. If you want a quiet room with a view, ask for numbers 303, 307, 308, 310, 312, 313 or 314. The hotel offers the use of Germany's largest indoor whirlpool, a steam bath with waterfall, a solarium and a lot of marble. Breakfast buffet: 25 DM.

SIMPLICISSIMUS 14/20

69117, Ingrimstr. 16
(0 62 21) 18 33 36, Fax 1819 80

Closed for lunch, closed Tuesday, week at Carnival, 2 weeks at the end of July through the middle of August. Tables d'hôte: 60/120, à la carte: 51/86

The name and the decor of this restaurant eschew fancy Heidelberg romanticism and embrace clearly defined bistro simplicity. Simple does not necessarily mean good, however. Our fillet of beef was tough and overdone, and many dishes that should have been hot were served lukewarm. Chef Lummer has not lost his touch, however. We had respectable lasagna with seafood and tarragon sauce, a nicely dressed salad with an expertly prepared duck breast, and a superb cheese strudel with berries for dessert. Thanks to a lovely baby chicken, wonderfully fresh pike-perch, stuffed sole roulade and seafood salad, we have a pleasant memory of another enjoyable evening. The very large choice of wines (by the glass as well as by the bottle) and pleasant service are characteristic of this restaurant.

ZUR HERRENMÜHLE 13/20

69117, Hauptstr. 237/9
(0 62 21) 1 29 09, Fax 2 20 33

P

Closed for lunch, closed Sunday, 1—16. Tables d'hôte: 85/115, à la carte: 53/89

Beneath the castle of Heidelberg near the Neckar river, we found the romantic Herrenmühle. Constructed in the 17th century, the building was renovated in the 1980s and turned into a restaurant.After a pleasant reception, we followed our waiter's suggestions and tried well-balanced fresh salads with marinated turbot carpaccio, anglerfish gratin with basil butter and tomato confit and rice, arugula salad and lightly fried sweetbreads with balsamic vinegar, and, finally, nut crepe with Grappa zabaglione, grapes and homemade nut ice cream. The wine list offers a cross-section of local and international vintages.

Some establishments change their closing times without warning. It is always wise to check in advance.

HEIDENHEIM Baden-Württ.

Aalen 23 - Ulm 43

WEINSTUBE ZUM PFAUEN 14/20

89518, Schloßstr. 26
(0 73 21) 4 52 95 res.

Closed for lunch Saturday, closed Sunday, closed for lunch Monday, closed 1—10 January, 1—14 August. Tables d'hôte: 68/95, à la carte: 36/66, No Credit Cards

Evelin-Maria Scherff takes special pains to make sure her customers feel at home in her restaurant. She is a born hostess and an expert on wines you can trust. In the kitchen, chef Ingo Scherff like to experiment—much to the delight of his customers, who can try light new creations, interesting sauces and daring but successful combinations. We enjoyed venison consommé with chanterelles and ravioli, rounded off with apples, strawberries and cranberries; excellently prepared anglerfish medallions with pesto crust; deliciously light apricot ravioli with vanilla sauce, plum ice cream and steamed grapes; and strawberries, raspberries, and red currants in their own sauce. The comprehensive, international wine list offers low priced half-bottles and excellent wines by the glass.

HEILBRONN

Stuttgartt 50 - Karlsruhe 68

BEICHTSTUHL 12/20

74072, Fischergasse 9
(0 71 31) 8 95 86, Fax 62 73 94 res.

Closed for lunch Saturday, closed Sunday. Tables d'hôte: 75/98, à la carte: 43/81

This little pub with its nice waitresses is comfortable and cozy, but we were not too happy about the cold bread served with stale butter and the sour Swabian salad with dry rabbit terrine, and we hunted vainly for the champagne sauce that our fish was supposed to be served in. But we liked the buttermilk parfait with herbs and the tender schnitzel of venison in cream sauce with mushrooms. The wine list is surprisingly well-stocked with moderately priced international vintages and commendable wines by the glass.

HEILBRONNER WINZERSTÜBLE 13/20

74072, Ludwig-Pfau-Str. 14
(0 71 31) 8 40 42, Fax 96 24 32

Closed for lunch Saturday, closed Sunday and holidays. Tables d'hôte: 50/99, à la carte: 38/63. Tables d'hôte with wine: 99

The restaurant has been redecorated, but the ambience still has a few snags here and there. Peter Wagner's cuisine is honest and imaginative, although somewhat traditional. The potato ravioli with a savory sauce was delicious, and the sauerkraut soup with fried scallops was flavorful but mild and mellow. The turbot and salmon with wine and saffron sauce, served with fennel, were nicely fried, and the leg of suckling lamb was very good. Honey parfait and vanilla mousse were prettily garnished with tropical fruit.Gabriele Wagner guarantees perfect, pleasant service and bravely undertakes sommelier duties. Landlord Robert Drauz's wines are on the wine list, as well as French and Italian vintages at very reasonable prices. The choice of wines by the glass is ample.

INSEL-HOTEL

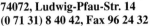

74072, Friedrich-Ebert-Brücke
(0 71 31) 63 00, Fax 62 60 60

120, **S** 148/198, **D** 198/268,
APP 320/440, **½P** +38, **P** +76

The peaceful setting of this small family-run hotel on an island in the Neckar river is unique. The rooms are lovely but not soundproof. A good number of conference rooms, one of which even has a roof garden. Two restaurants, dance bar with a band, café, solarium.

PARK-VILLA

74074, Gutenbergstr. 30
(0 71 31) 9 57 00, Fax 95 70 20

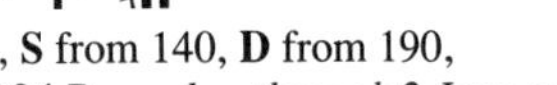

25, **S** from 140, **D** from 190,
Closed 24 December through 2 January

This historic mansion offers individually styled and colorful rooms in a quiet residential area of town.

HEILIGENBERG BW

Überlingen 20 - Sigmaringen 38

BERGHOTEL BAADER 17/20 

88633, Salemer Str. 5
(0 75 54) 3 03 , 81 91, Fax 81 92 res.

Closed Tuesday. Tables d'hôte: 45/65L, 105/135D, à la carte: 37/77

Clemens Baader has never followed new cooking trends just because they're modern. Using his native dialect, he tries to make grande cuisine less imposing on his menu. Along with the cute names for his dishes, Baader offers two types of cooking: on one side he lists fine cuisine, on the other refined regional dishes. There was not much difference between them in terms of price or quality. Three prix-fixe menus offered at noon include a choice of both; one of them even lets you test Baader's talent for less than 50 DM. From the fine cuisine menu, we tasted lobster aspic with chive cream and salad, bass with leaf spinach with pepperoni sauce, and fillet of beef coated with marrow in a truffled sauce. From the regional dishes, we selected *tafelspitz* salad with foie gras, perch with mushroom tart and white Burgundy sauce, veal saddle in puréed tomatoes with potato soufflé and asparagus à la crème. The two separate cuisines seem mere coquetry, so we didn't even try to decide which side our appetizer—exquisite rabbit leg marinated in fine olive oil—came from. The poularde breast with foie gras, salad of green asparagus and truffled potato noodles was a sublimely flavorful composition! After all this, we didn't mind that the house pastry was a little nondescript. We found the nice but incompetent service much more irritating.

HEILIGKREUZSTEINACH

Heidelberg 21

GOLDENER PFLUG 13/20

3 km north in Eiterbach
69253, Ortsstr. 40
(0 62 20) 85 09, Fax 74 80 res.

Closed Monday, Tuesday, closed for lunch from Wednesday throgh Friday. Tables d'hôte: 75/130, à la carte: 64/93

The Goldener Pflug really offers its customers something special: a sensational wine list that wine lovers can spend hours studying.But while the Hess brothers have invested much love and care in stocking their wine cellar, their cooking seems to have become purely incidental. After an appetizer of salmon tartare, we had chicken with shallots and red wine confit, pike-perch with an unidentifiable sauce, saddle of lamb with risotto and a heavy sauce, and hollowed-out pineapple stuffed with (guess what?) pineapple. The service, at least, is simple and friendly.

HEIMBACH Nordrh.-Westf.

Schleiden 18 - Düren 22

LANDHAUS WEBER 12/20

52396, Hasenfeld
Schwammenaueler Str. 8
(0 24 46) 2 22

Closed Tuesday, Wednesday, 2 weeks in February, 1 week in September. Tables d'hôte: 35L, 75D, à la carte: 38/69, No Credit Cards

This country inn in the middle of nowhere is surrounded by a picturesque forest and tries to create an ambience that is compatible with refined cuisine. A small prix-fixe is offered at noon, and à la carte dinners are served from 6:30 p.m. to 8:30 p.m. From the vegetable stew down to the farmyard chicken straight out of the oven, customers can count on fresh products and competent cooking. We liked our prawns and sea trout with well-seasoned salads and the fried breast of poularde with a light, tasty parsley sauce. We were surprised at the wine list our charming hostess brought: it contained a comprehensive, intelligent choice of wines from Germany, Italy and France, all moderately priced!

HEITERSHEIM Bad.-Württ.

Müllheim 10 - Freiburg 20

KRONE 13/20

79423, Hauptstr. 7
(0 76 34) 28 11, Fax 45 88

Closed for lunch Tuesday and Wednesday. Tables d'hôte: 29L, 55/85D, à la carte: 26/75

This traditional *gasthof* has divided its dining hall into four small, comfortable rooms and fixed up the vaulted cellar, called "Anno 1777" after the date it was built. The great variety of dishes on the menu belongs to the category of refined bourgeois cooking, with prices to match. Main courses don't exceed 40 DM, and the six-course prix-fixe for gourmets costs 80 DM (and convinces many city people from Freiburg and Basel to make an excursion to Heitersheim).We had warm asparagus salad with king prawns, followed by vegetable consommé with gorgonzola ravioli, salmon soufflé with two sauces, and lovely saddle of wild boar with lentils and delicate dumplings. The choice of cheese was adequate, and the desserts wonderful. The wine list features regional wines, with some French and Italians.

HEMER Nordrh.-Westf.

Iserlohn 6 - Menden 6

HAUS WINTERHOF 12/20

58675, Stephanopel 30
(0 23 72) 89 81, Fax 8 19 25 res.

 P

Closed Tuesday, first week in January, 14 days in August. Tables d'hôte: 38/75, à la carte: 33/71

Haus Winterhof, with its terrace and garden near a lake, is especially nice in summer. The cuisine is by and large not as heavy as the massive upholstery here. Most dishes are prepared as Grandma used to make them, including fried blood pudding with onions, beans with bacon and sausage, and *tafelspitz* with horseradish and spinach beets. You can also order the gourmet prix-fixe and enjoy salmon in puff pastry or duck's breast in mustard velouté. If you're watching your weight, avoid the "Sundwiger Schwan," a gigantic puff pastry with cream - order berries instead. The service is friendly, and the wine list offers 15 good wines by the glass.

HERBORN Hessen

Gießen 39 - Limburg 50

LE BISTRO IN THE SCHLOSS-HOTEL 12/20

35745, Scloßstr. 4
(0 27 72) 70 60, Fax 4 01 11

 P

à la carte: 36/65

Herborn's Schloss-Hotel remains unscathed by recession and trends. Le Bistro offers solid, down-to-earth cooking and concentrates more on satisfying regular customers than tickling gourmets' palates. Most customers enjoy steaks and salads in the bistro, but you can order seasonal specialties as well. We found our fillet of lamb in its soggy crust a little tough, but we liked the delicious variations of herring, good asparagus cream soup, and noodles with scampi in tomato sauce. The bistro's wine list is small, and the service is attentive.

SCHLOSS-HOTEL

35745, Scloßstr. 4
(0 27 72) 70 60, Fax 70 66 30

70, **S** 135/165, **D** 195/215, **APP** 250

When Karl Hartmann first inspected this bankrupt hotel in 1957, he found a cow tied to the front door. Today, expensive cars park in front of the enlarged complex in the picturesque old part of town. This comfortable bourgeois house is the best hotel in Herborn.

HOHE SCHULE 13/20

35745, Schulhofstr. 5
(0 27 72) 28 15, Fax 4 32 12 res.

Closed Monday. Tables d'hôte: 45/60L, 50/75D, à la carte: 30/66

Under new ownership, the Hohe Schule, in the heart of the picturesque Old Town, is on its way up. This restaurant, completely renovated along with the hotel, doesn't try to be a formal gourmet temple, just a comfortable place to take friends to drink a glass of wine and get something to eat. Hans Hees is capable of more than he's showing in Herborn. With standard dishes ranging from poularde breast to scampi to lamb fillet, however, he is catering to the taste of his satisfied customers. All dishes are fresh and light, well-seasoned and cooked just right.The service is pleasant and obliging. Try the four-course prix-fixe.

DAS LANDHAUS 14/20

35745, Döringweg 1
(0 27 72) 31 31

 P

Closed for lunch, closed Sunday, Monday. Tables d'hôte: 79

There's no place in Herborn where you can sit in lovelier surroundings—and feel lonelier.

Only a few people find their way to this elegant country restaurant; most of them drive down from the nearby autobahn. Maybe the elegant ambience keeps regular customers from the region away, though the staff takes pains to be pleasant and not formal. It can't be the relatively modest prices, either: 79 DM for a four-course prix-fixe of this quality isn't too much to ask. Perfectionist Juliane Cloos-Rech offers only this one prix-fixe with a few alternatives, using the best, freshest products. We had veal carpaccio with tuna sauce, marinated salmon with crème fraîche and green salads, king prawns in champagne butter, duck's breast with creamed Savoy cabbage and plum sauce, and, finally, sweet curds with fruit. There are a number of fine bottles in the wine cellar.

RESTAURANT THEISS 13/20

35745, Westerwaldstr. 2
(0 27 72) 22 08 res.

Closed for lunch every day except Sunday. Tables d'hôte: 45/84, à la carte: 33/65

This little restaurant is usually full of locals. Martin Theiss serves plain, refined fare, and thanks to his continuous and dependable performance in the kitchen, we have yet to taste a dish we didn't like. He earned his first toque with this kind of prix-fixe: calf's liver with sherry vinegar as an appetizer, followed by shrimp salad, potato soup, fish with saffron noodles, and (unimpressive) lamb fillet with good side dishes. The service is pleasant, and the wine list is improving.

HERFORD NRW

Bielefeld 15 - Osnabrück 58

TÖNSINGS KOHLENKRUG 15/20

32051, Ortsteil Eickum
Diebrockerstr. 316
(0 52 21) 3 28 36, Fax 3 38 83

Closed for lunch Saturday, closed Tuesday. Tables d'hôte: 24/34L, 44/140D, à la carte: 42/72

His champagne and mustard soup was delectable, and we couldn't find any flaws in Bernd Tönsing's cuisine. His salads and vinaigrettes, fish and meat main courses are wonderfully cooked and presented, which is why we gave him a second toque. Eikam isn't the prettiest spot on the map, and the ambience of Tönsing's Kohlenkrug isn't particularly compatible with fine dining and wining, but at least the service is in keeping with the wonderful cuisine. The cellar offers bottles from the best vineyards in Germany, France and Italy.

HERLESHAUSEN Hessen

Bad Hersfeld 49 - Kassel 73

HOHENHAUS 15/20

37293, Ortsteil Holzhausen
8 km northwest via Nesselröden
(0 56 54) 6 80, Fax 13 03 res.

Tables d'hôte: 55L, 130D, à la carte: 58/99

Sitting on the terrace of this beautiful estate, everything tastes twice as good. We loved the cream soup with crawfish and caviar, the excellent quail galantine, fried foie gras in yeast dough and formidable lobster ravioli in lovely, light Sauterne sauce. The John Dory fillet with fresh green beans and morels was delightful, and the veal fillet stuffed with saddle of rabbit on steamed Belgian endives and the baked champagne cream soup with kiwi slices and a delicate sauce outstanding. Günther Haderecker has compiled his wine list with special attention to detail. He chooses his wines from the best German and French wine-growing regions and sells them at acceptable and sometimes really low prices.The service is pleasant and amiable.

HOHENHAUS

37293, Ortsteil Holzhausen
8 km northwest via Nesselröden
(0 56 54) 6 80, Fax 13 03

P

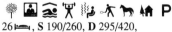

26, **S** 190/260, **D** 295/420,
1/2P +55, **P** +85

This former coach house has been rebuilt with a fine eye for style and detail. Guests enjoy the peaceful countryside, the tennis courts, the media center in the conference room, social events in the hotel's salon, or simply relax in front of a fire and forget they're in a hotel. Solarium, table tennis. Breakfast: 30 DM.

BAD HERRENALB — BW

Baden-Baden 22 - Pforzheim 30

MÖNCHS POSTHOTEL 

76328, Dobler Str. 2
(0 70 83) 74 40 , Fax 74 41 22

P

35, **S** 125/220, **D** 170/370,
APP 350/520, **1/2P** +45

From the outside a 19th-century chalet, this hotel offers charmingly individual rooms inside. The quiet rooms toward the back of the house face a wonderful park. The rooms have been renovated and enlarged. Spacious suites and studios, as well as conference rooms with modern technology. Elegant dining rooms, sunny breakfast room and bar.

LAMM 14/20 

76332, Ortsteil Rotensol
Mönchstr, 31
(0 70 83) 9 24 40, Fax 92 44 44 res.

Closed Monday, 2 weeks in January. Tables d'hôte: 28/34L, 65/75D. à la carte: 21/77

The Schwemmle family is putting a lot of time and energy into its beautiful country restaurant and hotel. The newly decorated rustic dining room is delightful, and the view of the valley just magnificent. Their efforts show in the improved cuisine. We had tender but crispy fried quail with sugar peas, mango, mushrooms and quail's egg; perfectly poached pike-perch in a light carrot butter; flavorful seafood soup with scampi; saddle of lamb with a delicate sauce and ratatouille, garlic and potatoes; and a delicious apple tart with Calvados and ice cream. If you like Swabian cooking, try the lamb's lettuce with bacon and croutons, green spelt soup, pike dumplings or Swabian sauerbraten.The wine cellar is stocked with first-class vintages that are a bargain at these low prices! A superb choice of wines by the glass is offered. The service has also improved and is now more competent.

HERRSCHING — Bayern

Starnberg 17

ANDECHSER HOF

82211, Zun Landungssteg 1
(0 81 52) 30 81, Fax 57 61

A la carte: 16/49

When summers are sunny and hot, we'd like to move to this beer garden and stay here. In addition to the famous Andechs beer (and some decent wines by the glass), we enjoyed creamed mushrooms with bread dumplings, brook trout, succulent pork roast, roast chamois and a Bavarian sauerbraten. Even when it gets cold, we would still be willing to drive out to the Ammersee and eat Bavarian specialities in this comfortable little *gaststube*.

BAD HERSFELD — Hessen

Alsfeld 37 - Fulda 45

WENZEL

36251, Nachtigallenstr. 3
(0 66 21) 9 22 00, Fax 5 11 16

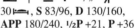

30, **S** 83/96, **D** 130/160,
APP 180/240, **1/2P** +21, **P** +36

There are only two alternatives for visitors to the Bad Hersfeld festival who wish to stay near the ruins of the monastery: Stern or Wenzel. On Wenzel's café terrace you can stare at the stars sitting at the table next to yours. Warning: rooms for July and August must be reserved in March. Restaurant.

ZUM STERN 12/20

36251, Linggplatz 11
(0 66 21) 18 90, Fax 18 92 60 res.

Closed for lunch Friday, closed 2-20 January. Tables d'hôte: 19/32L, 5/90D, à la carte: 37/73

For those who do not insist on fancy dishes like scallops with black noodles or saddle of lamb with pumpkin crust at lunchtime, we recommend eating here at noon. The cuisine is simpler but still good and is less expensive than in the evening. The drawbacks are that lunch customers have to get their own salad and first course at buffets and must put up with a somewhat listless and lazy service crew. An excellent cream of salmon soup, perfectly balanced and delicately seasoned with sorrel, was the highlight of our meal. Why can't Stern's kitchen always cook like this?

ZUM STERN

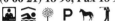

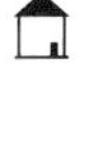

36251, Linggplatz 11
(0 66 21) 18 90, Fax 18 92 60

P

45, **S** 100/145, **D** 200/220,
½P +40, **P** +68

The romantic Stern has been the leading hotel in this city for over 500 years. Festival guests book their rooms at least a quarter of a year in advance. The double rooms in the old building are spacious and comfortable, the singles in the new wing functionally appointed.

HERXHEIM Rheinland-Pfalz

Landau 10 - Karlsruhe 27

ZUR KRONE IN THE HOTEL ZUR KRONE 17/20

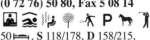

76863, Ortsteil Hayna
Hauptstr. 62-64
(0 72 76) 5 08 10, Fax 5 08 14 res.

 P

Closed for lunch, closed Monday, Tuesday, 14 days at the beginnig of January, end of July through mid-August. Tables d'hôte: 115/149, à la carte: 68/96

When customers pay high prices, they deserve high quality and imaginative variety. True to this maxim, the cuisine at the Krone is characterized by opulence and perfection in every detail. The appetizers—a potpourri of terrines, tarts and soufflés—shame the first courses. Our variations of foie gras and quail were delicate compositions with extravagant details. We just couldn't eat slowly enough to enjoy all the taste sensations! Karl Kuntz's roulade of salmon fillet and pike-perch soufflé poached in a black lasagna noodles was a perfectly harmonious creation worth a rating of 18/20. His venison saddle in salt crust was perfectly done. The classic goat-cheese terrine and the fruit variations are almost standards in the prix-fixes offered here. The perfection we found in the cuisine is curiously absent in the understaffed service team. The wine list needs to be revised. Quite a few vintages listed are out of stock.

PFÄLZER STUBEN IN THE HOTEL ZUR KRONE 15/20

76863, Ortsteil Hayna
Hauptstr. 62-64
(0 72 76) 5 08 10, Fax 5 08 14 res.

 P

Closed Monday, Tuesday, 14 days at the beginnig of January, end of July through mid-August, à la carte: 31/68

This rustic restaurant also run by Karl Kuntz in the Hotel Zur Krone serves better food than most gourmet temples. The menu, however, offers simpler dishes at lower prices. The regional accents are strong and are especially obvious in succulent rumpsteak with onions. Chef Kuntz doesn't confine his creativity to regional recipes, however. We had green asparagus mousse, smoked salmon, a wonderful carpaccio of beef and anglerfish, a mixed mountain of salad (that somehow didn't belong here), an artistically composed soufflé of brill with noodles, anglerfish piccata, mild perch from Lake Victoria, and, finally, rhubarb prepared in seven different ways. The wine list features regional wines from the Pfalz, and the service is in keeping with the high standard of the house.

HOTEL ZUR KRONE

76863, Ortsteil Hayna
Hauptstr. 62-64
(0 72 76) 50 80, Fax 5 08 14

P 

50, **S** 118/178, **D** 158/215,
APP 200/245, **½P** +40, **P** +79

This country inn offers its customers comfortable beds in modern, tastefully furnished rooms. Pub, solarium. Very good convention facilities.

HERZOGENAURACH Bayern

Erlangen 13 - Nürnberg 22

GASTHAUS GLASS 14/20

91074, Marktplatz 10
(0 91 32) 32 72, 37 11, Fax 7 57 87

Closed for lunch Saturday, closed Monday, 14—20 February, end of August through early September. Tables d'hôte: 40/60, à la carte: 34/64

"German wine with German food" is the motto of the Galster family, and around it they have developed their own expressive cuisine. Their style of cooking incorporates regional influences from all over Germany, as well as decided touches of haute cuisine. You may get home-smoked ham of venison, wonderful Swabian-style ravioli filled with pork, an exquisitely marinated Asian-style duck's breast or a sensationally well balanced fennel consommé with seafood. The main courses are hearty and savory; examples are delicious roasted chicken or turbot with curried rice. This is not a cuisine of finely polished nuances but of clear, flavorful accents. The wines offered here come from the best German wine growers.

MONDIAL IN THE HOTEL HERZOGSPARK 11/20

91074, Beethovenstr. 6
(0 91 32) 77 80, Fax 4 04 30

P

Closed Sunday. Tables d'hôte: 78D, à la carte: 49/85

The posh Hotel Herzogspark has three restaurants. The Weinstube offers snacks to go with wine, the Stüberl's menu features Bavarian and Franconian specialties, and the grand restaurant Mondial cosmopolitan gourmet cuisine. We had high expectations for chef Dieter Schiffer, and the house brochure promised even more: concentration on essentials, for instance, and fresh produce of the season. Instead, we found nothing more than the usual high-priced gourmet dishes (foie gras, truffles, fillets of various meats, fine gourmet fish) with a touch of (regional?) herbs. The beautiful, expert presentation of the dishes turned out to be pure showmanship. Pretty salads were sour, vegetables overdone, meat and fish well-cooked but incredibly boring. The wine list is mediocre, and its only claim to fame the fact that wines from the most faraway regions are offered. Only the service is really what the brochure promises: unobtrusive.

HILCHENBACH NRW

Siegen 19 - Olpe 28

SIEBELNHOF 15/20

57271, Siebelnhofstr. 47
(0 27 33) 8 94 30, res.

P

Closed for lunch Saturday, 2 weeks during the NRW summer school holiday. Tables d'hôte: 65L, 90/145D, à la carte: 46/89

Owner Erich W. Steuber is a pioneer of refined regional cuisine in Germany. He has continuously raised his standards, and we thought that this would go on forever. But his ingenuity seems to have reached a climax: chef Wolfgang Schäfer serves new combinations of well-tried ingredients in the (sometimes closed) upscale restaurant Chesa and in the Ginsburg-Stuben, which we usually prefer. A menu with more than 60 dishes to choose from is a bit overwhelming until you realize that duck, steak, venison, herring, calf's liver, noodles, etc. are each served in five versions. Steuber cannot live on gourmets alone, and he is taking the consequences. He concentrates on his catering service, and his menu includes such simple fare as the traditional regional *Krüstchen* (a schnitzel with fried egg, fried potatoes and salad). For gourmet palates, there is delicately fried cod in savory mustard seed sauce or fillet of pork in cream sauce with pike-perch and green beans. His duck is wonderful and his homemade terrines and pâté terrific.The service and the wine list were both commendable.

SIEBELNHOF

57271, Siebelnhofstr. 47
(0 27 33) 8 94 30

P

25, **S** 140/190, **D** 240/290, **APP** 300/380, **1/2P** +45, **P** +55

Closed 2 weeks during the NRW summer school holiday

The hotel has been a family business for over 460 years and offers functional, sometimes tastefully decorated rooms and apartments. The hotel is quiet, the lobby spacious. Breakfast: 24 Deutsche marks. Facilities for non-smokers.

HILDESHEIM Niedersachsen

Hannover 30 - Göttingen 90

FORTE HOTEL

31134, Markt 4
(0 51 21) 30 00, Fax 30 04 44

109, **S** 200/425, **D** 260/485,
1/2P +25, **P** +50

This modern hotel with a renovated facade is located on the medieval marketplace in the heart of town. Large rooms, suites and rooms for the disabled are decorated in an English style and provided with all modern amenities. Well-equipped conference rooms. Fitness facilities, clubhouse-bar, restaurant.

KUPFERSCHMIEDE 13/20

31139, Ortsteil Ochtersum
Steinberg 6
(0 51 21) 26 30 25, Fax 26 30 70 res.

 P

Closed Sunday, Monday. Tables d'hôte: 44/92, à la carte: 34/85

Signs now show the way to the Kupferschmiede on the street leading from Ochtersum. The service here was always on a very high level and so was the wine list (many half-bottles and a good choice of wines by the glass). Now, the cuisine has improved, too, and makes a visit worthwhile. The menu is much larger than it was. We found a vegetarian meal this time, with such enticing items as kohlrabi gratin and sugar peas in zabaglione with balsamic vinegar, spinach and wild rice. The clear calf's tail soup with vegetables was excellent, as was the Canadian lobster with two outstanding sauces and fresh vegetables. The dishes could have done with a little more attention to detail, though. The potatoes were tasteless, the fish somewhat overdone, and the desserts unimaginative. In summer, we like to sit on the wonderful terrace under old trees.

HIMMELPFORTEN Nieders.

Stade 10 - Cuxhaven 62

KAMPHOF

21707, Hauptstr. 28
(0 41 44) 33 31,

Closed Monday, à la carte: 35/75

Rainer Wolter, celebrated as Hamburg's best hotel cook, has taken over the kitchen of the Kamphof. With toned-down blues and greens, wooden furniture and a red-tiled floor, the owner makes an effort to create a pleasant ambience, and the service staff tries hard to be efficient. The appetizer and the desserts convinced us that Wolter can cook if he has a mind to. The potato dumplings with chanterelles and bacon in parsley cream were an enticing start, and plum compote with plum ice cream and a Grand-Marnier parfait a delicious ending. The wine list includes great German names and even a bottle of Haut Brion.

HINDELANG Bayern

Sonthofen 8 - Pfronten 32

ALPENHOTEL

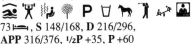

87541, Ortsteil Oberjoch
Am Prinzenwald 3
(0 83 24) 70 90, Fax 70 92 00

P

73, **S** 148/168, **D** 216/296,
APP 316/376, **1/2P** +35, **P** +60

This new, extravagantly decorated hotel is one of the best the Allgäu has to offer. The impressive entrance hall and elegant salons set the tone in this spa and sports hotel. The comfortably furnished rooms with balconies have spacious baths. Numerous chic boutiques and a health club inside as well as attractive cross-country skiing paths and alpine ski-lifts are complemented by a spa-clinic that belongs to the hotel. The restaurant doesn't come up to standard, but the breakfast buffet is opulent.

GRADERS GASTHOF AM BUCHL 13/20

10 km north in Unterjoch
87541, Obergschwend 10
(0 83 24) 71 66, Fax 75 09

 P

Closed Tuesday, beginning of November through mid-December. Tables d'hôte: 35/120, à la carte: 20/68, No Credit Cards

This restaurant in an unobtrusive mountain cottage serves carefully prepared, refined yet hearty fare. We liked our veal saddle with figs and cassis sauce, and an immense, flawlessly prepared fillet of beef in a nest of leeks and chanterelles with creamed potatoes. Game and lamb are of good quality here, and the desserts are unexciting but good. Reasonable prices and a fine choice of wine—the toque fits.

OBERE MÜHLE 12/20

87541, Bad Oberdorf
Ostrachstr. 40
(0 83 24) 28 57, Fax 86 35 res.

Closed for lunch, closed Tuesday, à la carte: 25/62, No Credit Cards

Typical regional dishes are served at scoured wooden tables here, including suckling pig fresh from the oven with bread dumplings, venison from the nearby forest, and a savory rack of lamb. This rustic old farmhouse is delightfully Bavarian (it is a tourist attraction), but the kitchen sometimes slips up. Our fish soup à la Marseille was cooked to death, salads were insipid and the melted butter on our unexciting *Schlupfkrapfen* was burnt. Knowing that the butter was homemade didn't help much. Charming waitresses wear dirndl skirts. Moderately priced wines are bottled right from the wooden casks.

PRINZ-LUITPOLD-BAD

87541, Ortsteil Bad Oberdorf
(0 83 24) 89 00, Fax 89 03 79

102, **S** 109/163, **D** 248/330,
1/2P +20, **P** +30
No Credit Cards

An air of rustic nobility pervades the rooms of this spa-hotel, known for its historically documented hot springs. Lovely view of the mountains from the balconies of the rooms facing south in the new wing. Several of the impressive large halls have been imported intact from Lanrick Castle in Scotland. Use of spa waters and tennis courts is included in the price.

HINTERZARTEN Baden-Württ.

Freiburg 25 - Donaueschingen 41

PARKHOTEL ADLER

79854, Adlerplatz 3
(0 76 52) 12 70, Fax 12 771 7

78, **S** 155/275, **D** 290/460,
APP 420/1200, **1/2P** +62, **P** +95

This first-rate family-run hotel is one of the best in Europe. VIPs have always frequented this elegant establishment: the list begins with Marie Antoinette and includes emperors, kings, sheikhs and television stars. The hotel complex is located on the outskirts of Hinterzarten and consists of the old main building, a restaurant and a new addition called "Adler Residence," all maintained in an elegant Black Forest style. They are surrounded by a large park with deer, a duck pond and riding stables. Indoor swimming pool, conference rooms with modern technology. Restaurants.

HÖCHST IM ODENW. Hessen

Erbach 17 - Dieburg 17

ZUR KRONE 15/20

64739, Hetschbach
Rondellstr. 20
(0 61 63) 22 78, Fax 8 15 72

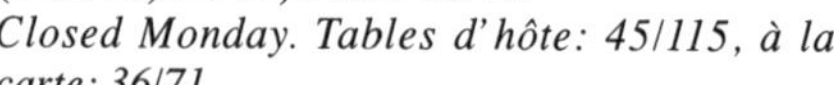

Closed Monday. Tables d'hôte: 45/115, à la carte: 36/71

Don't confuse this restaurant with the one next door. There you'll get "Hawaii toast," here you'll be surprised at the fine gourmet cuisine. Even if you make a mistake, it won't take long to find out if you're in the right place. After a promising appetizer of rabbit aspic with chanterelle vinaigrette, we had unbelievably savory leg of lamb fried with thyme and served with a flavorful garlic and herb sauce, delightful fennel cream soup with salmon quenelles, succulent guinea chicken with noodle gratin, and potato ravioli with glazed sweetbreads and chanterelles. The taste of our delicious turbot was accented by a crust of red onions and complemented by ginger soufflé and puréed peas. Superb goat cheese dumplings with peach compote concluded our memorable meal. There is a special menu for vegetarians.The prices are astoundingly moderate, and the wine list offers treasures seldom seen anywhere else, such as vintages from the Château Simone, at sometimes low prices. Diners can choose among 35 wines by the glass as well. The service is attentive and obliging. The food and wine are reason enough to celebrate here, and there are some rooms for those who want to stay the night.

HÖVELHOF NRW

Paderborn 14 - Bielefeld 29

GASTHOF BRINK 15/20

33161, Allee 38
(0 52 57) 32 23 res.

Closed for lunch, Closed Monday, July. Tables d'hôte: 89, à la carte: 33/75, No Credit Cards

When you see the sloppy-looking menu, you'll probably want to leave right away. A better choice is to hand the menu back to the waiter and trust blindly to the recommendations of Hermann Brink. With enthusiastic eloquence, he will tell you what his wife and son are cooking up in the kitchen. They follow classic French cuisine and prepare terrific terrines, anglerfish, lobster and scallops, as well as stupendous desserts like raspberry sherbet with honeyed cream. You can taste the freshness and high quality of the produce used in the kitchen, as well as the harmony and precision that make each dish a wonderful culinary experience. If you're looking for a hair in the soup, chew on some underdone sugar peas. It will serve you right! Sorry, you will have to ask for the menu again, after all, to choose one of the many fine wines. Hermann Brink sells his best vintages for a song. There are pretty guest rooms here if you want to stay the night.

HOFHEIM Hessen

Mainz 20 - Frankfurt 21

VÖLKER'S 13/20

65719,Ortsteil Diedenbergen
Marxheimer Str. 4
(0 61 91) 30 65

Closed for lunch Saturday, closed Wednesday, 1 weeks at the beginning of January. Tables d'hôte: 38/45L, 85/125D, à la carte: 47/92

Plain, unpretentious furniture and shirt-sleeved waiters hint at a typical schnitzel *gasthaus* rather than a gourmet restaurant, but the prices definitely belong to the latter category. The fish was succulent and the lamb flawless, but the kitchen couldn't cook to match the high prices. We want a little more imagination for our money, and we don't want the same side dishes with different courses. We can't escape the feeling that hiding behind all this is someone who could fry great potatoes if he didn't feel compelled to cook haute cuisine. The service doesn't inspire customers to stay longer than they have to, and the wines by the glass taste a little flat, whereas nice bottles are available at appropriate prices.

HOHENSTEIN Hessen

Bad Schwalbach 9

OBERMÜHLE

65329, Ortsteil Hennethal
Im Schneidertal 4
(0 61 20) 33 80, Fax 33 80

Closed Thursday, month of October. Tables d'hôte: 35, à la carte: 21/43, No Credit Cards

Meat - pork, beef and rack of lamb - is the main thing here, grilled over a fire and served in generous portions. Nobody asks for fine sauces or delicate vegetables. While you're waiting, you can assuage your hunger with herring, salmon with dill cream or potato soup. The small choice of wines ranges in price from 25 to 85 DM and includes a dozen good wines by the glass.

HOHWACHT Schleswig-Holst.

Oldenburg 20 - Plön 25

GENUESER SCHIFF 13/20

24321, Seestr. 18
(0 43 81) 75 33, Fax 58 02

Closed for lunch, closed Tuesday, November, January/February. Tables d'hôte: 54/59, à la carte: 39/68

This little restaurant is part of a romantic ensemble housing holiday apartments, hotel, bistro, and a beach café. Chef Rainer Freund surprised us with a prix-fixe that changes daily. We had marinated slices of veal saddle and green asparagus mousse as appetizer, tender and succulent turbot with basil and tomatoes, lovely fried pigeon with a mousse of carrots and peas and wafer-thin potato slices, and a poached peach covered with white chocolate and cassis sauce.

The wine list has improved and now satisfies even fastidious customers. The service is polite and very obliging.

PARKRESTAURANT IN THE HOTEL HOHE WACHT 12/20

24321, An der Steilküste/Kurpark
(0 43 81) 9 00 80, Fax 90 08 88

 P

Tables d'hôte: 28L, 75D, à la carte: 36/71./ Tables d'hôte with wine: 40/78, No Credit Cards

The cuisine here isn't in keeping with the elegant floral ambience of the restaurant. The pleasantly small menu offers regional dishes that could surely be better prepared by a motivated kitchen staff. Apart from a delicious asparagus mousse with smoked anglerfish and watercress sauce, the dishes we ate ranged from simply flavorless to outright dubious. The wine list is adequate, and the service staff makes an effort.

HOTEL HOHE WACHT

24321, An der Steilküste/Kurpark
(0 43 81) 9 00 80, Fax 90 08 88

90, **S** 160/230, **D** 220/320,
APP 230/450, **1/2P** +40, **P** +65
No Credit Cards

The new hotel and apartment complex run by the Anders family is located in the middle of the spa gardens, only a few minutes away from the beach. The rooms are elegantly and comfortably furnished. Fitness center, solarium. Swimming pool with sea water and sailing nearby.

HOLZMINDEN Niedersachsen

Göttingen 60 - Hannover 95

HELLERS KRUG 14/20

37603, Altendorfer Str. 19
(0 55 31) 21 15, Fax 21 15 res.

Closed for lunch Saturday, closed Sunday. Tables d'hôte: 55L, 87D, à la carte: 46/79

Diners here sometimes get a whiff of the nearby scent factory, but the the aromas from the kitchen soon drown out the competition. The menu has grown larger (some dishes have strong seasonal accents) but hardly more creative. After a pretty mini-carpaccio we had dry duck foie gras and overdone duck breast with a respectable salad. The asparagus soup with salmon was perfect, whereas the fish potpourri was hopelessly overdone. We enjoyed our fresh, savory saddle of venison, and even more our dessert of strawberry gratin. The wine list is so-so.

PENSION CORVEYBLICK 15/20

37603, Corveyblick 15
(0 55 31) 6 11 94 res.

P

Closed Monday, 2—12 January, Tables d'hôte: 55/130, à la carte: 59/130. Tables d'hôte with wine: 59/130, No Credit Cards

In this out-of-the-way place, the owners have courageously invested time and money in the improvement of the cuisine, wine cellar and ambience. The Kasten family's youthful cordiality made us feel welcome, and the appetizer they served was as generous as a first course. The flower buds and herbs were both pretty and flavorful, and the German "truffle" found in the woods by a specially trained French (!) dog were more than an original trifle. We liked the watercress salad with delicate kohlrabi carpaccio and the quail with fine sherry sauce. The comprehensive (and growing) wine list offers a wonderful choice of wines by the glass.

SCHLOSS BEVERN 15/20

5 km norteast on B64
in 37639 BevernScholß 1
(055 31) 87 73 res.

Closed Monday, closed for lunch Tuesday, closed 2 weeks in February and August. Tables d'hôte: 52/90, à la carte: 39/75

On the ruins of an ancient citadel, Statius von Möchhausen built this castle on the Weser river in 1603. Today, it is considered a gem of Renaissance architecture. After the castle was renovated in the 1960s, a restaurant was established in one of its four beautiful wings. The grandiose ambience and costly decorating scheme, flawless service and outstanding choice of wines would be a good excuse for exorbitant prices anywhere else, but here both food and drink are extraordinarily low-priced. Kobinger's cuisine is getting better every year. He is especially good with fish. The salmon slice and the shish kebab of salmon, mushrooms, and dried tomatoes on a savory bed of spinach leaves were fantastic. We loved the chicken breast filled with shrimps and served with artichokes. The salads were great and consisted of more than just a few leaves. The half portions are very generous, and the cheeses and desserts are also excellent.

HOMBURG Saarland

Saarbrücken 32 - Kaiserslautern 37

LE CONNAISSEUR IN THE HOTEL STADT HOMBURG 13/20

66424, Ringstr. 80
(0 68 41) 13 31, Fax 6 49 94

Closed for lunch Saturday, closed Friday. Tables d'hôte: 36/69, à la carte: 27/62

Colorful Tiffany lamps light up the cuisine served in this rustic restaurant: delicate kohlrabi soup with shrimp, fillet of cod with mild and creamy champagne sauce, well-seasoned with lots of chives, nicely fried breast of poularde with creamy and savory tarragon sauce, fresh mango slices with lovely elderberry sorbet, garnished with red fruit purée. The service is friendly, and the wine cellar adequately stocked.

SCHWEIZERSTUBEN 13/20

66424, Kaiserstr. 70-74
(0 68 41) 14 11, Fax 6 80 38

Closed for lunch Saturday, closed Sunday. Tables d'hôte: 45/68L, 75/115D, à la carte: 42/76

A cook should always have a successor who is ready to step in his shoes. Since Markus Schneider left the Schweizerstuben, the high standard of the cuisine has gone way down. The pike-perch and salmon duo looked nice, but the salmon tasted a bit aged and the sauce had too much salt. Salt was also the only seasoning we tasted in the brown sauce served with the succulent duck's breast, and the choice of unimaginative desserts is meager. The service was too quick to let us take a deep breath between courses and too slow to serve our coffee while it was hot. The two separate wine lists included an enticing, moderately priced choice of Burgundys (many Romanée Contis) and Bordeaux (premier cru), and well-aged and fine vintages and white wines from Germany, France and Switzerland. Some examples: a 1986 Château de Fuissé for 75 DM, a 1980 Condrieu for 70 DM, a 1983 Grillet for 180 DM, and a 1949 Chambertin for 980 DM. The formerly large choice of half bottles has grown smaller.

SCHWEIZERSTUBEN-HEIKE BÖTTLER

66424, Kaiserstr. 70-74
(0 68 41) 14 11, Fax 6 80 38

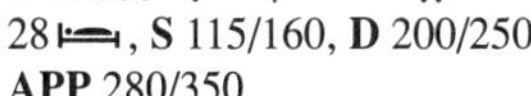

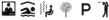

28, **S** 115/160, **D** 200/250, **APP** 280/350

The rooms toward the back of this carefully renovated hotel are quiet, as are the ones facing the street if you close the soundproofed windows. Ample, delicious breakfast buffet.

BAD HOMBURG Hessen

Frankfurt 18 - Wiesbaden 45

ASSMANNS RESTAURANT 13/20

61348, Kisseleffstr. 27
(0 61 71) 2 47 10, Fax 2 91 85 res.

Closed for lunch Wednesday. Tables d'hôte: 49L, 94D, à la carte: 62/102

You won't find a nicer place to eat in summer than on the shady terrace of Assmann's restaurant. The catering service and beer garden belong to the family business, and the place itself is divided into a bistro and a beautifully decorated restaurant. The difference is less apparent where the prices are concerned. A thickly breaded veal schnitzel with pale fried potatoes at 38 DM is a bit steep, to say the least. While the leg of lamb must have been from a remarkable skinny animal, we liked the crispy and succulent farmyard duck, and the foie gras was a definite highlight. The soups are made for those who like light cuisine: we would have liked them better with more substance and flavor. Sometimes more care is taken with the design of the food than with its ingredients or preparation. The wine list offers sufficient good French and German wines, but the red wines by the glass are served much too warm. The service is cheerful and competent.

OBERLE'S 14/20

61348, Obergasse 1
(0 61 71) 2 46 62, Fax 2 46 62 res.

Closed for lunch Saturday, closed Monday. Tables d'hôte: 76/115, à la carte: 57/94

We could hardly decipher the tightly written menu here, but the appetizer, foie-gras mousse and fresh bread, soothed our annoyance. The first course—smoked goose breast filled with foie gras—was just as delicate and lightly portioned. Fresh, succulent rabbit was prepared to perfection and served with just a tiny portion of mushroom risotto. We missed the light, sensitive hand that created the finely seasoned salad dressing in those dishes with too obvious Asian accents. Fish and meat main courses show careful preparation of good products, and the Swabian side dishes are appreciated by the Hessian clientele. The vegetable garnishes are more decorative than anything else.If you can read the small print on the wine list, you will discover some interesting wines. The red wines by the glass are served too warm, and the staff could give better advice.

SÄNGERS RESTAURANT 12/20

61348, Kaiser-Friedrich-Promenade 85
(0 61 71) 2 44 25, Fax 4 42 84 res.

P

Closed for lunch Saturday and Monday, closed Sunday. Tables d'hôte: 55.95L, 165D, à la carte: 60/103

In this nicely furnished restaurant that looks like a private living room, diners' conversations seldom rise above a whisper, that is, until Klaus Sänger comes in and swaggers from one table to the next, greeting his customers. The sauces here lack in finesse, and the salmon we had was either flat or fatty, the turbot overcooked and insipid, and the crayfish stringy. Truffled baked risotto turned out to be an oversized crispy egg roll with a few soggy rice kernels inside. The fried foie gras and the delicious goose drippings saved us from eating the table in desperation. The food doesn't justify the high prices. The wines are expensive, too.

WALLHALLA 13/20

61348, Wallstr. 6
(0 61 71) 2 93 05, Fax 2 93 05 res.

Closed for lunch Saturday, closed Sunday. Tables d'hôte: 28L, 60D, à la carte: 43/69

Cheerful restaurants with ingenious cuisine are scarce, but identical twin brothers Stefan and Armin Bauer have found their own way. They have turned a smoky pub into a lovely restaurant with a nonchalant flair and ambitious cuisine. Some dishes may still be far from perfection, but the Bauers are on the right path. We liked the imaginative mustard cream soup with potato dumplings and the delicious anglerfish coated with dried tomatoes and basil. Tender rabbit with asparagus mousse, *rösti* and sugar peas was a fresh, cheerful composition, as was the marinated sea trout with avocado mousse. One of the twins cooks and the other supervises the service; they often change places without anyone noticing. The small wine list offers an adequate choice at reasonable prices, including some wines by the glass.

ZUM WASSERWEIBCHEN

61348, Am Mühlberg 57
(0 61 71) 2 98 78; after 5 p.m.: 30 25 53, Fax 30 50 93 res.

Closed for lunch, closed Saturday, holidays, during the Hessen summer school holiday, à la carte: 24/55

With its congenial atmosphere and good, plain fare, this typical pub in the old part of town has always been one of our favorite places. Our last visit was disappointing, however. The food wasn't prepared with the usual care, and the unpleasant service didn't inspire us to stay.

BAD HONNEF NRW

Bonn 18 - Neuwied 35

CAESAREO 13/20

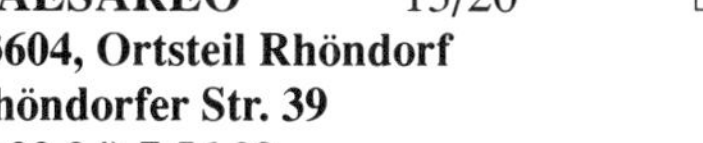

53604, Ortsteil Rhöndorf
Rhöndorfer Str. 39
(0 22 24) 7 56 39 res.

Closed Monday. Tables d'hôte: 80, à la carte: 34/72

This modern little gabled house behind a chapel is always full of regular customers. The cuisine's Mediterranean flair attracts politicians, journalists, artists or just people who are hungry and thirsty. We enjoyed sweetbreads with artichokes, tuna carpaccio with fresh salad, mozzarella with tomatoes and basil, grilled bass sprinkled with olive oil, and tasty rabbit and lamb saddles. And if you want to try an ostrich schnitzel with Italian flair, it's on the menu.Some good wines aren't on the wine list.

DAS KLEINE RESTAURANT 12/20

53604, Hauptstr. 16a
(0 22 24) 44 50 res.

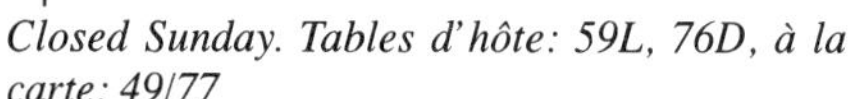

Closed Sunday. Tables d'hôte: 59L, 76D, à la carte: 49/77

This restaurant is small and comfortable, and has tastefully decorated tables and a lovely terrace. The menu is small, too, and offers only a few dishes made of fresh products. Chips, crackers and peanuts gave us an initial scare, but we recovered quickly: a foie gras galantine with figs and a lovely salad helped, as did a delicious venison ham with cèpes. Our pike-perch fillet harmonized well with its lobster sauce. The service is friendly, and the wine list a little skimpy.

HORBRUCH Rheinland-Pfalz

Bernkastel 19 - Kim 26

HISTORISCHE SCHLOSSMÜHLE 12/20

55483, southwest of the village
(0 65 43) 40 41, Fax 31 78 res.

 P

Closed for lunch every day except Sunday, closed Monday. Tables d'hôte: 70L, 95D, à la carte: 40/72

This restaurant is small and comfortable, and has tastefully decorated tables and a lovely terrace. The menu is small, too, and offers only a few dishes made of fresh products. Chips, crackers and peanuts gave us an initial scare, but we recovered quickly: a foie gras galantine with figs and a lovely salad helped, as did a delicious venison ham with cèpes. Our pike-perch fillet harmonized well with its lobster sauce. The service is friendly, and the wine list a little skimpy.

HISTORISCHE SCHLOSSMÜHLE

55483, southwest of the village
(0 65 43) 40 41, Fax 31 78

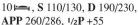

 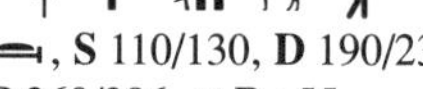

10, **S** 110/130, **D** 190/230,
APP 260/286, **1/2P** +55

This old mill was originally located at the foot of the castle in Kirn, but has been rebuilt, stone by stone, in Horbruch. The rooms are comfortable and reminiscent of bygone days. The quiet, idyllic surroundings are inviting, as is the ample breakfast buffet.

HÜNSTETTEN Hessen

Limburg 20 - Wiesbaden 27

ROSI'S RESTAURANT 15/20

65510, Ortsteil Bechtheim
Am Birnbusch 17
(0 64 38) 21 26, Fax 7 24 23 res.

 P

Closed Tuesday, closed for lunch Wednesday, closed January, during the Hessen summer school holiday. Tables d'hôte: 65.50, à la carte: 23/65, No Credit Cards

Rosi's sensational four-course surprise prix-fixe now costs 65.50 DM—and is still cheaper than many a main course in other gourmet restaurants. This restaurant offers good value for little money, with a pleasant ambience thrown in. Our avocado salad with marinated sea trout had finely balanced piquant seasoning, and the mussels were served in an unbelievably flavorful dill broth. The herring with crisp potato pancakes was so superb that we just ignored the somewhat old green beans. Rosi is Bavarian and proud of it, so you're bound to get bread dumplings with at least one course. But we like Bavaria this way—light, fluffy and fantastic, with delightful sauces. Saddles of lamb and venison and prime rib of beef are expertly done classics. Fish is one of Rosi's strong points. Gurnard with lemon butter, warm fish salad and fried coalfish with asparagus butter were excellent. The wines are low-priced, and Rosi always has a few special bottles set aside, but you can also have fine draft beer.

IDSTEIN Hessen

Wiesbaden 16 - Frankfurt 28

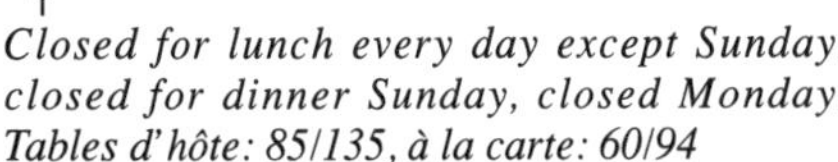

HÖERHOF 15/20

65510, Obergasse 26
(0 61 26) 5 00 26, Fax 50 02 26 res.

Closed for lunch every day except Sunday, closed for dinner Sunday, closed Monday. Tables d'hôte: 85/135, à la carte: 60/94

This beautiful little château is a true gem of German hospitality. With its choice antiques and modern accents, the historic building has a cheerful yet distinguished ambience. The cobblestoned courtyard is the ideal setting for a savory snack, the *gutsstube* for bistro-like meals and the restaurant one floor up for elegant dining. The house cuisine limits its creativity to classic dishes. Our foie gras with morels was perfect, and fillet of ox coated with leeks and served with gratin and vegetables superb. The pike tasted a little weary, and the chervil sauce with it lacked flavor. Desserts were amusing and the cheese nicely ripe. The wine list needs improvement. Some more Italians would round out its profile. The emphasis is on German and Swiss wines. The service is discreet and competent.

HÖERHOF

65510, Obergasse 26
(0 61 26) 5 00 26, Fax 50 02 26

14 rooms, **S** 240/340, **D** 240/290, **APP** 340/440

With its turrets and crown, The Höerhof looks like a miniature château. The Renaissance building with four carefully restored wings is an exclusive country hotel on the outskirts of the Old Town. Centrally located but quiet, the hotel offers modern, comfortable rooms, with historic ambience and functional decor creating an interesting contrast. Of the 14 rooms, we liked number 3 best because it looks like a little cottage.

ILLERTISSEN Bayern

Ulm 24 - Memmingen 30

DORNWEILER HOF 14/20

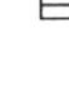

89257, Ortsteil Dornweiler
Dietenheimer Str. 91
(0 73 03) 27 81, Fax 78 11 res.

P

Closed Tuesday, 2 weeks in January, à la carte: 24/62

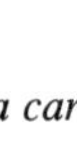
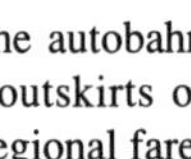

This *gasthof* not far from the autobahn is located on the wooded outskirts of Illertissen and offers good regional fare. Hans Steinhart does more than just prepare delicious Swabian specialities like ravioli filled with quail. His slightly garlicky king prawns with lentil sprouts and wild rice had us clamoring for a second helping. Guests can either eat outside on the terrace or under dark wooden beams in the little dining rooms. The menu offers a prix-fixe for 24.60 DM and a variety of dishes à la carte—lamb noisettes with kohlrabi or veal medallions with morel cream sauce—at moderate prices.

WEISSES ROSS 14/20

92278, Am Kirchberg 1
(0 96 66) 2 23, 12 33, Fax 2 84 res.

P

Closed Monday. Tables d'hôte: 40/85, à la carte: 17/60

The wizard Hans Nägerl Jr. has apparently reached his limit. His restaurant is well-frequented, and the convention business is thriving. Gourmets come because they like Nägerl's refined regional cuisine, and other customers appreciate the simple, low-priced dishes he offers. This double-track cuisine has its problems. When we wanted to test his gourmet cooking, we were served routinely seasoned, imprecise and unbalanced dishes from the first course to the dessert. The creative slivered asparagus with pigeon breast was sloppily prepared, and the ravioli in salty venison consommé tasted like cardboard. The (overdone) black spaghettini with slivered green asparagus and (not fresh, overcooked) fried shrimps made Nägerl's dilemma plain: his ideas are ingenious, but he cannot follow through on them. We do not think Nägerl is leaving the gourmet stage yet, but it is difficult to rate his two types of cooking: Bavarian rustic and gourmet. The wine list has grown and is decently priced. The service is amiable and attentive.

ILMENAU — Thüringen

Erfurt 40 - Coburg 70

BERG-UND JAGDHOTEL GABELBACH 13/20

98693, Waldstr. 23a
(0 36 77) 5 66, Fax 31 06

Tables d'hôte: 18/27L, 29/32D, à la carte: 19/46

The restaurant, situated in the beautiful Thuringian forest, has a pleasant ambience, a small choice of French and German wines, and friendly, quick service. The tomato consommé with excellent ham dumplings and vegetable julienne was delicious. The delicate fish ragout in white wine and dill was fantastic, and so was the roast of venison that came in a magnificent sauce with excellent dumplings and red cabbage. The choice of desserts is meager and unimaginative, even when decorated with a little plastic trophy in the middle of the plate!

BERG- UND JAGDHOTEL GABELBACH

98693, Waldstr. 23a
(0 36 77) 5 66, Fax 31 06

86 rooms, **S** 80/155, **D** 140/230,
APP 200/270, **½P** +30, **P** +50

A more beautiful setting for a hotel just isn't possible. Not even the thickest fog spoils this lovely landscape in the Thuringian forest. The rooms are simply appointed with new, though not very pretty, furniture. The bathrooms don't always come up to modern standards. Fitness facilities, solarium, skittle alley.

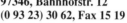

IPHOFEN — Bayern

Kitzingen 5 - Würzburg 28

ZEHNTKELLER

97346, Bahnhofstr. 12
(0 93 23) 30 62, Fax 15 19

43 rooms, **S** 110/150, **D** 140/220
Closed 10-30 January

The rooms in the new guest house of the 400-year-old Zehntkeller are furnished in especially good taste. Some beautiful antiques. Restaurant.

ZUR IPHÖFER KAMMER 14/20

97346, Marktplatz 24
(0 93 23) 69 07 res.
43 rooms, **S** 110/150, **D** 140/220
Closed Monday, Tuesday, 2 weeks in February, 3 weeks in July/August. Tables d'hôte: 58L, 80D, à la carte: 40/70

Arnold Bode cooks for a small but faithful fan club that likes his simple, down-to-earth good cooking. He pays more attention to creating a tasteful harmony of fresh regional produce than to setting off gastronomic fireworks. Demanding gourmets may find his presentation too modest. Everything he serves looks unassuming. Examples are a plain but delicious headcheese with asparagus salad, and marinated salmon with salad as first courses, and saddle of venison or stuffed kid as an excellent main course. Everything is accompanied by perfectly prepared vegetables. The wine list offers mostly regional wines, and prices (while not as modest as the food prices) are correct. The service is unobtrusive. By the way, the quality of the cooking is somewhat uneven when the Bode family is on summer vacation.

ISERLOHN Nordrhein-Westfalen

Hagen 18 - Dortmund 26

PUNTINO IN THE HOTEL KORTH 12/20

58636, In der Calle 4-7
(0 23 71) 4 65 56, Fax 4 49 44 res.

 P

Closed Sunday, Monday, 18 July through 15 August. Tables d'hôte: 75, à la carte: 44/90, Tables d'hôte with wine: 75/140

The original restaurant in the Hotel Korth offers a high standard of plain bourgeois fare with classic lobster, ox tongue and steak dishes. Now it has strong competition from Puntino, an Italian restaurant that has opened up under the same roof. The beautifully decorated dining room of the best *ristorante* in town is full of eye-catchers: turquoise beams, pastel upholstery, flowered china, old clocks and Impressionist paintings. Chef and service are charming, but not all of the dozen dishes offered on the small menu are prepared with fresh products. We pitied the poor, rubbery (frozen?) anglerfish and put away the toque we were ready to award for excellent pasta and delicious beef tartare prepared at our table. Next time, perhaps we'll have better luck with baked turbot or guinea fowl in leaves of Savoy cabbage. With only 14 passable Italian wines, the restaurant doesn't do justice to its customers.

ISERNHAGEN Niedersachsen

Hannover 15

HOPFENSPEICHER 14/20

in Ortsteil Kirchner Bauernschaft
30916, Dorfstr. 16
(0 51 39) 9 76 09 res.

 P

Closed for lunch, closed Monday, 2 weeks in January. Tables d'hôte: 89/120. à la carte: 48/92

The meadow behind the house is a wonderful place to spend a summer evening. The service was amiable and the kitchen deserved praise for an appetizer of melon, strawberries and Parma ham, followed by a tasty salad (flooded with vinaigrette) with prawns or foie gras, delicious fennel with turbot and a wonderful fish ravioli.The wine list and choice of liqueurs were good.

ISMANING Bayern

München 14 - Erding 19

GASTHOF ZUR MÜHLE 11/20

85737, Kirchplatz 5
(0 89) 96 09 30, Fax 96 09 31 10 res.

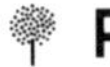 P

Tables d'hôte: 45, à la carte: 23/58

The original restaurant in the Hotel Korth offers a high standard of plain bourgeois fare with classic lobster, ox tongue and steak dishes. Now it has strong competition from Puntino, an Italian restaurant that has opened up under the same roof. The beautifully decorated dining room of the best *ristorante* in town is full of eye-catchers: turquoise beams, pastel upholstery, flowered china, old clocks and Impressionist paintings. Chef and service are charming, but not all of the dozen dishes offered on the small menu are prepared with fresh products. We pitied the poor, rubbery (frozen?) anglerfish and put away the toque we were ready to award for excellent pasta and delicious beef tartare prepared at our table. Next time, perhaps we'll have better luck with baked turbot or guinea fowl in leaves of Savoy cabbage. With only 14 passable Italian wines, the restaurant doesn't do justice to its customers.

ITZEHOE Schleswig-Holstein

Rendsburg 43 - Hamburg 56

GUT KLEVE 14/20

9 km north in 25554 Kleve
Hauptstr. 35
(0 48 23) 86 85, Fax 68 48

 P

Closed for lunch Wednesday through Friday, closed Monday, Tuesday, 15 January through 15 February. Tables d'hôte: 65/80, à la carte: 37/72

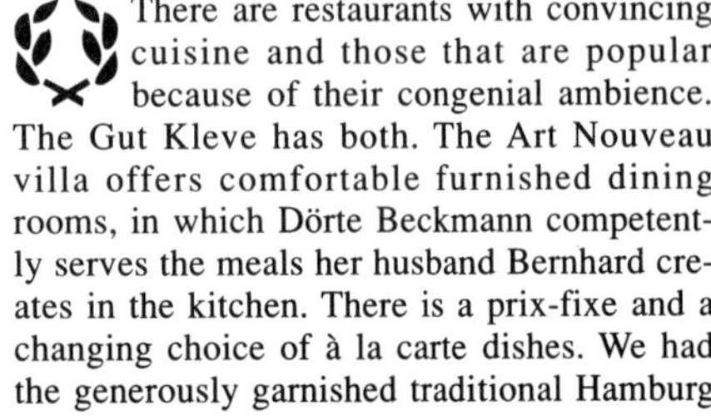

There are restaurants with convincing cuisine and those that are popular because of their congenial ambience. The Gut Kleve has both. The Art Nouveau villa offers comfortable furnished dining rooms, in which Dörte Beckmann competently serves the meals her husband Bernhard creates in the kitchen. There is a prix-fixe and a changing choice of à la carte dishes. We had the generously garnished traditional Hamburg eel soup, perfectly done pike-perch fillet with lentils, and succulent Bresse pigeon with truffled noodles. Every course is an appetizer for the next one. And we succumbed to the tempting mango tart with mocha ice cream. The wine list includes good wines by the glass at reasonable prices.

ORANGERIE IN THE SCHOSS HEILIGENSTEDTEN 12/20

25524, Schloßstr. 13
(0 48 21) 8 73 35/7, Fax 8 73 38 res.

Closed January. Tables d'hôte: 40/75, à la carte: 40/75

Modern accommodations don't jar with the historic facade of this château ensemble. The dining room decorated in black and white has everything that is good and expensive: lacquered chairs, fireplace with comfortable designer sofas facing it, wooden ceiling and beautifully set tables. A lot of plants and some screens partition the dining hall for 80 diners into more intimate sections. The ambience, however, is more fascinating than the cuisine. We had stringy cream of leek soup, overdone hare medallions with tasty nut cream sauce and rutabaga cakes, and bony but otherwise delicious fish fillet. The service staff obviously thinks ordinary is better than perfect. The wine list offers good wines by the bottle and the glass at moderate prices.

HOTEL JARDIN IN THE SCHOSS HEILIGENSTEDTEN

25524, Schloßstr. 13
(0 48 21) 8 73 35/7, Fax 8 73 38

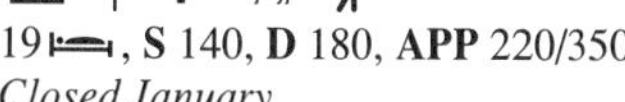

19, **S** 140, **D** 180, **APP** 220/350
Closed January

This exclusive little hotel is located in the Baroque towers of the castle Heiligenstedten. All rooms are decorated in black and white and are elegantly and individually furnished. The house even has a Rolls-Royce with chauffeur and a horse-drawn coach on hand.

JENA Thüringen

Weimar 21 - Gera 22

HOTEL SCHWARZER BÄR 14/20

07743, Lutherplatz 2
(0 36 41) 2 25 43/4, Fax 2 36 91

Tables d'hôte: 25/45, à la carte: 17/45

To our great surprise, the Osburg family has managed to keep its traditionally modest prices in this well-kept, historical restaurant. How do they do it? Everything is perfect here: nicely decorated dining rooms, banquet rooms, cuisine, wine cellar and service. Chef Eckhardt Kirsche earned his toque with an aromatic cream of tomato soup, complete with savory cheese croutons and basil strips, trout roulade with a masterly cream sauce, magnificent saddle of ox, and delicious walnut-nougat parfait with fresh strawberry and vanilla sauce.

HOTEL SCHWARZER BÄR

07743, Lutherplatz 2
(0 36 41) 2 25 43/4, Fax 2 36 91

66, **S** 95/125, **D** 180/200,
APP 280, **½P** +25, **P** +45

This traditional hotel was first heard of in 1498. Some of its prominent guests were Martin Luther, Goethe and Bismarck. Under its new owner, the hotel has been completely renovated. There are just a few parking places in front of the house, and they are almost always occupied.

STEIGENBERGER MAXX HOTEL 12/20

07747, Stauffenbergstr. 59
(0 36 41) 30 00, Fax 30 08 88

A la carte: 20/50

The view from the winter garden over the idyllic Thuringian landscape is stupendous. Inside, guests find American decor of the 1930s to 1950s. The restaurant offers a small menu with so-called Texan and Mexican cuisine: savory consommé with mushrooms and vegetables, lobster thermidor, steak and champagne sorbet. The cuisine is about as Tex-Mex as a hot dog. The wine list offers eight wines by the glass and 20 bottles, but most guests prefer beer to wash down the hot sauces.

STEIGENBERGER MAXX HOTEL

07747, Stauffenbergstr. 59
(0 36 41) 30 00, Fax 30 08 88

  P

246, **S** 180, **D** 235, **APP** 360

The rooms of this hotel located just five minutes from the inner city are decorated with American flair. They're not very spacious but are adequate. Fitness center and many conference facilities.

JEVER Niedersachsen

Wilhelmshaven 20 - Aurich 32

ALTE APOTHEKE 15/20

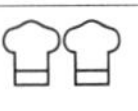

26441, Apothekerstr. 1
(0 44 61) 40 88, Fax 7 38 57

Closed Monday, 2 weeks at the end of January/beginning of Febraury. Tables d'hôte: 35L, 58D, à la carte: 31/68

This extremely pleasant restaurant is situated in a 500-year-old house in a narrow alley of the historic Old Town of Jever, not far from the postmodern towers of the well-known brewery. We found charmingly unobtrusive service here, surprisingly reasonable prices and, above all, good cooking. The Riesling jelly with seafood and salad looked as captivating as it tasted. The cream soup with fresh North Sea shrimp was delicious, but the same shrimps au gratin with fresh bass threatened to overwhelm the exquisitely delicate sauce that went with them. The turbot and halibut medallions with lobster crème, shoestring potatoes and chard in champagne sauce were flawless. Those with truly enormous appetites are welcome to have a second helping of every main course. The menu includes some interesting game. The wine list has an astounding variety of regional wines at reasonable prices.

JORK

Buxtuhude 9 - Stade 20 - Hamburg 21

HERBSTPRINZ

21635, Osterjork 76
(0 41 62) 74 03, fax 57 29 res.

Closed Monday, 2 weeks around the beginning of January. Tables d'hôte: 30/75, à la carte: 27/72, No Credit Cards

This spacious 300-year-old farmhouse with rooms furnished in a turn-of-the-century style is a favorite excursion destination of Hamburg city folks. The best thing to order here is the *Hochzeitssuppe*, a stew that was traditionally served at weddings. You can order Altländer duck ahead of time and enjoy it whole and crisply fried. Although about two dozen wines are offered, most guests drink beer. By the way, the name of the restaurant doesn't have anything to do with aged royalty: Herbstprinz (autumn prince) is the name of a regionally grown apple.

JÜTERBOG Brandenburg

Berlin 72

ALTE FÖRSTEREI 14/20

5 km north in
14913 Kloster Zinna
Markt 7
(033 72) 46 50, Fax 46 52 22 res.

A la carte: 25/45

Behind the historic walls of the old forester's house, the dining rooms have been lovingly decorated with antique accessories, farm implements and old furniture in different styles. You can even sit quite comfortably in the former stable. The large but hard-to-read menu is placed on an easel at your table. If you have good eyesight, you'll order quiche lorraine, succulent leg of lamb, or tender cutlets of young wild boar with a sauerkraut-stuffed potato. Fish sauces are prepared with a light, expert hand to accompany pike quenelles and salmon steak. The desserts are imaginative, and the wine list wisely stocked. Every bottle can be ordered by the glass as well.

ALTE FÖRSTEREI

5 km north in
14913 Kloster Zinna
Markt 7
(033 72) 46 50, Fax 46 52 22

20, **S** 95/105, **D** 135/165, **APP** 195/260

The door leading into this whitewashed, half-timbered building is a precious antique and reminds one (like the entrance to the restaurant) of the Prussian king Frederick the Great. This is where the famous monarch welcomed his visitors; today guests can enjoy the atmosphere of a country inn here. The rooms are romantic but comfortable and are furnished with antiques. The bathrooms are individually decorated and have modern equipment. Breakfast: 13 DM.

PICCO 12/20

14913, Schloßstr. 87
(033 72) 46 60, Fax 46 61 62

P

A la carte: 13/49

This stylish corner house on the edge of the Schlosspark can't help being an eye-catcher. Its mighty stone tower reminds of medieval times, when a stone wall protected the town. Large windows and an extravagant color scheme characterize the interior of the hotel restaurant, whereas the ambience of the adjacent Schlossschänke is more rustic and comfortable, with the charm of a Berlin pub. Sadly enough, however, the appropriately hearty food can't be ordered here—apart from a lonesome cabbage roulade with a savory bacon sauce and homemade potato pancakes with smoked salmon.

JUIST Niedersachsen

Cars must park north of the seawall as automobiles are not permitted on Juist Island. Call the shipping company (0 49 35) 5 87 for assistance with crossing and garages.

ACHTERDIEK 15/20

26561, Wilhelmstr. 36
(0 49 35) 80 40, Fax 17 54

Closed Monday, November through March. Tables d'hôte: 96, à la carte: 48/78, No Credit Cards

The first surprise was finding gourmet cooking of such high quality on a Frisian island in the far northwestern corner of Germany. The second surprise: this is a hotel restaurant! The kitchen offers regional specialties and a great choice of seafood, and knows how to prepare them. The proof was in the flawlessly fried, flavorful medallion of anglerfish with ratatouille. We also enjoyed a terrific salad with lobster, and shrimps grilled with homemade noodles or salad with mustard-seed dressing. We can also recommend the saddle of veal in morel cream sauce with garden vegetables, the Frisian lamb from the salt meadows, and the Barbary duck. The wine list is wonderful, and the service is calm and collected, even when the house is full. Remember to park your car on the Norddeich, because driving is prohibited in the city.

ACHTERDIEK

26561, Wilhelmstr. 36
(0 49 35) 80 40, Fax 17 54

48, **S** 105/203, **D** 242/406, **APP** 326/540

Closed 2 November through 20 December, No Credit Cards

Directly behind the southernmost promenade stands this modest building with its large garden. A fire is almost always burning in the open hearth of the main hall. The sunny restaurant for hotel guests opens onto a lovely winter garden facing the sea.

KAISERSLAUTERN RP

Saarbrücken 71 - Karlsruhe 89

ALTE POST 13/20

67655, Mainzer Tor 3
(06 31) 6 43 71,

Closed for lunch Saturday, closed Sunday, 1—6 January, 24 July through 8 August. Tables d'hôte: 54L, 62/85D, à la carte: 41/79

This is a subdued, elegantly decorated restaurant with classic cuisine. Customers get good value for their money in dishes like the perfectly done quail's breasts with excellent homemade noodles. Our perch from Lake Victoria with potatoes and herbs was heavy, rich and filling. The wine cellar is stocked with many wines from Italy and the German Pfalz.

Other wines are carelessly presented. The service is quiet and competent.

DORINT HOTEL KAISERSLAUTERN

67663, St.-Quentin-Ring 1
(06 31) 2 01 50, Fax 1 48 09

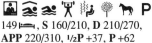

P

149 rooms, **S** 160/210, **D** 210/270, **APP** 220/310, **½P** +37, **P** +62

This modern, relatively quiet hotel, located on the outskirts of town and on the edge of the Pfälzer forest, is the best in Kaiserslautern. Pub, bar and sports center.

1A

67655, Pirmasenser Str. 1a
(06 31) 6 30 59, Fax 9 21 04

Tables d'hôte: 49D, à la carte: 24/43, No Credit Cards

Uwe Schwarz, Kaiserslautern's inventive gastronome, has opened another popular restaurant in the pedestrian district of town. Having passed through a postmodern ice-cream parlor that draws crowds of people during the day, we came to a plain white dining room with nicely laid tables. Saffron noodles, beef carpaccio, salmon and pike-perch quenelles in a nest of pasta, a little lobster and lots of ice cream are served from morning till 10:30 p.m.

UWE'S TOMATE 15/20

67655, Schillerplatz 4
(06 31) 9 34 06, Fax 69 61 87

Closed Sunday, Monday, 3 weeks in September.Tables d'hôte: 85/100, à la carte: 42/79

The nonchalant, cheerful bistro atmosphere of this fine restaurant has done away with most snobbery about gourmet dining in Kaiserslautern. Light cuisine, uncomplicated snacks and the casual way the menu is written on the wall makes this "tomato" an appetizer for the courses to follow. Creativity has obviously taken a break, however: we've had artichoke dip with our appetizer for a few years now. The marinated salmon was of store-bought quality, and the duck liver terrine tasted coarse and bitter. The succulent sweetbreads, however, were as excellent as always, as were the fresh shrimp salad and a daring composition of headcheese and prawns - creative, light and prepared with expertise. Bringing headcheese, garlic, seaweed, artichoke hearts, fine vegetables and prawns harmoniously together in a butter sauce of red wine and shallots is a triumph. The service is flawless, but the wine list doesn't come up to the high standard of the restaurant, especially when shelf-warmers past their prime are served by the glass.

KALLSTADT Rheinland-Pfalz

Neustadt/Weinstr. 18 - Mannheim 26

WEINCASTELL ZUM WEISSEN ROSS 13/20

67169, Weinstr. 80-82
(0 63 22) 50 33, Fax 86 40

P

Closed Monday, Tuesday 4 weeks in January/February, 1 week in July/August, Tables d'hôte: 40/140, à la carte: 51/83. Tables d'hôte with wine: 140

This typical *gaststube* in a pretty corner house is proud of its warm hospitality and classic cuisine, influenced by refined regional recipes. We had flavorful, succulent lamb cutlets in puff pastry and a wonderful sweetbread terrine. Calf's liver with spinach and dumplings was satisfying, as was the trout parfait. Our marinated salmon tasted soapy, the oxtail soup lacked flavor and chocolate ravioli just looked pretty. The haphazardly arranged wine list includes mostly wines from the owner's renowned estate, with only a skimpy choice of red wines.

KAMP-LINTFORT NRW

Wesel 19-Duisburg 23

HAUS PÖTTERS 13/20

47475, Weseler Str. 362/B 58
(0 28 02) 40 29, Fax 8 06 13

P

Closed for lunch, closed Monday, 1—10 January, 4 weeks during the NRW summer school holiday. Tables d'hôte: 65, à la carte: 31/62

To draw gourmet diners, a restaurant off the main road has to offer more than a large parking lot. Many people between Dortmund and Cologne who appreciate fine cooking frequent Haus Pötters, with its comfortable, cozy ambience, cordial service, and well-stocked wine cellar.Uwe Lemke has come back from his vegetarian health trip and is at home once more in his classic cuisine. With great enjoyment, we tried quail salad with rosemary and perfectly prepared sturgeon with asparagus tips and spinach. Redfish with beet spinach and fillet of beef with grated horseradish were grand in their simplicity.The wines are offered at surprisingly low prices—wines by the glass for 7 and 8 DM and bottles from Germany, Italy and France from 26 DM and up.

KANDERN Baden-Württ.

Mülheim 16 - Freiburg 55

VILLA UMBACH 13/20

78400, Ortsteil Riedlingen
Bahnhofstraße
(0 76 26) 88 00, Fax 88 48 res.

Closed Tuesday, Closed for lunch Wednesday, 1 week at Shrove Tuesday. Tables d'hôte: 38L, 69D, à la carte: 43/66. Tables d'hôte with wine: 98, No Credit Cards

You can't miss this prominent Art Nouveau villa on a hill to your right as you enter Kandern. A landscaped park surrounds the villa, and a garden terrace adds to the attractions of the restaurant within. While Martina Adamik is responsible for the distinguished, elegant ambience, Frank Adamik celebrates international cuisine in his kitchen. Prices have bowed to the general recession, and special diet platters are offered. Our lovely asparagus salad with prawns was followed by wonderful anglerfish with saffron sauce, wild rice and spinach. After a deliciously delicate herb soup, we had excellent saddle of lamb and exquisite caramel parfait with mascarpone. The choice wines from the region were moderately priced.

The prices quoted in this guide are those whick we were given by the restaurants and hotels concerned. Increases in prices are beyond our control.

KARLSRUHE Baden-Württ.

Stuttgart 82 - Frankfurt 140

LA GIOCONDA 13/20

76133, Akademiestr. 26
(07 21) 2 55 40 res.

Closed Sunday and holidays, 1—8 January, 23 July through 6 August. Tables d'hôte: 20/30L, 50/120D, à la carte: 44/78. Tables d'hôte with wine: 30/120

Mario Parente's restaurant offers a reserved kind of Italian hospitality and good Mediterranean cuisine. At last he has found a cook who does his best to realize the boss's ideas. The cuisine is not yet very refined, but the portions are larger and the house is fuller. We had wonderfully fresh seafood salad, arugula salad with truffled cheese, homemade gnocchi with basil tomatoes, a simple but delicious sea bream with butter and lemon, and an unadorned fillet of ox. The desserts, however, are definitely not highlights of Italian cooking. The cheese could use some attention, too. Good espresso, lovely grappa, and a relatively modest bill concluded our meal.

HASEN 13/20

76131, Gerwigstr. 47
(07 21) 61 50 76, Fax 62 11 01 res.

Closed Saturday, Sunday 23 December through 7 January, 10 July through 22 August. Tables d'hôte: 50L, 85/110D, à la carte: 38/85, No Credit Cards

A little more verve and a lot less mediocrity would do wonders for this restaurant. The avocado cream soup with salmon quenelles had decidedly too much cream, and the orange butter on the salad with (really fresh!) lobster and scallops was a little on the tangy side. The anglerfish in potato crust was overdone and salty, which didn't matter much since the chive sauce killed the taste anyway. Quite nice, though, were oxtail with fresh chanterelles and entrecôte, and the beef Stroganoff. It is not a bad idea to do without cheese and dessert to avoid any further interminable waits between courses. You won't miss much.

OBERLÄNDER WEINSTUBE 16/20

76133, Akademiestr. 7
(07 21) 2 50 66, Fax 2 11 57

Closed Sunday. Tables d'hôte: 55/95L, 80/150D, à la carte: 48/98

The Oberländer Weinstube, with its comfortable, relaxed ambience, its gigantic, low-priced wine list and the fine cuisine of Austria's Günter Buchmann, is the best restaurant in Karlsruhe. In addition to two fixed-price menus, Buchmann offers three "surprise menus"—regional, "fishy" and seasonal. The courses are a well-kept secret until they are served. We had a delicious rabbit terrine with vegetables, excellent trout parfait with lobster, delicately prepared kid livers with green and white asparagus, and correctly poached fillet of beef. Another time we had fine mushroom risotto with fried pigeon, fresh pikeperch (fried so carefully that it seemed positively dietetic), and beautiful plum ice cream with cake. One word about the desserts: they are all lovely but in no way light.The service shows some lapses, especially when the owner is away tasting new wines in neighboring Alsace. His wine list is exceptionally good.

RAMADA RENAISSANCE HOTEL

76131, Mendelssohnplatz
(07 21) 3 71 70, Fax 37 71 56

215, **S** 215/280, **D** 265/330,
APP 450/1000, **½P** +35, **P** +65

Dark Veronese marble dominates the extravagantly spacious lobby. The rooms are somewhat small but functional and comfortable. Bar and two restaurants. Hairdresser, beauty treatments, fitness center, solarium, massage. Breakfast: 26 DM.

RESTAURANT NAGEL'S KRANZ 12/20

76149, Stadtteil Neureut
Neureuter Hauptstr. 210
(07 21) 70 57 42 res.

P

Closed for lunch Saturday, closed Sunday, Closed for lunch Monday, closed 1—10 January, 2 weeks during the Baden-Württ. summer school holiday. A la carte: 45/84, No Credit Cards.

Wolfgang Nagel is supposed to be a great cook, but it is not always obvious. Sometimes, he's just not in the mood. The lobster (low quality) with hollandaise sauce and the warm asparagus salad and sprouts with sour vinaigrette were so disappointing that we practically rejoiced over a barely respectable saddle of lamb and a flat-tasting duck breast. The wine list has some rare wines at really low prices, but those who prefer white wine by the glass have a choice between dry and demi sec!

SCHLOSSHOTEL

76137, Bahnhofplatz 2
(07 21) 3 50 40, Fax 3 50 44 13

P

96, **S** 155/185, **D** 235,
APP 220/270, **½P** +35, **P** +55

The lobby of this renowned hotel seems a little cold, but the rooms are comfortable and spacious. Modernization hasn't destroyed the ambience here. The Schwarzwaldstube restaurant is on the rustic side, while the Résidence is an elegant place for fine dining. Balls are sometimes held in the mirrored hall. Fitness center. Bar until 3 a.m. Breakfast: 18 DM.

TRATTORIA TOSCANA 12/20

76133, Blumenstr. 19
(07 21) 2 06 28, res.

Tables d'hôte: 28/35L, 90/105D, à la carte: 40/82

Padrine Salvatore is very friendly and sometimes likes to affectionately stroke his favorite ladies' arms. They don't seem to mind, but be forewarned! We thought our first course of antipasti belonged to the repertoire of a pizzeria rather than a trattoria, but we liked our excellent sea bream. The sole swam in an ocean of butter, while the fish in a salty crust of dough tasted fairly dry (we've had it better, though). The vegetables were limp and not very fresh.

UNTER DEN LINDEN 12/20

76185, Kaierallee 71
(07 21) 84 91 55 res.

P

Tables d'hôte: 79/155, à la carte: 50/82

This restaurant has nothing to do with the famous Prussian boulevard in Berlin. Phlegmatic comfort reigns here. The service staff makes an effort, the prices are relatively reasonable and the wine list is promising, but what kind of a first course is "little frivolities"? Even the waiter didn't know, and we didn't dare to find out. The ambience is determinedly high class and stiffly elegant—but no fish knives are available.The cocktail of asparagus and shrimps was a hit 20 years ago. The turbot *"au four"* tasted fried. The shrimp in green olive sauce and ratatouille were satisfactory, but the choice and freshness of the cheese did not engender high spirits. We are sorry to see Vedran Bobanovic's ambitions gone awry, and we are taking away his toque.

ZUM LÖWEN 13/20

12 km south in 76344
Eggenstein Hauptstr. 51
(07 21) 78 72 01, Fax 78 83 34 res.

Closed for lunch Saturday, closed Sunday. Tables d'hôte: 100/140D, à la carte: 40/84

Here you can count on honest regional cooking of dependable quality without frills or pretension. We were fully satisfied with our marinated wild salmon with excellent mustard-dill sauce, savory truffled parfait of foie gras, venison noisettes with cassis sauce and cèpes, veal fillet with pesto, kohlrabi noodles and spinach gnocchi.If the dining room is too crowded and noisy, there are also tables in the better-ventilated room next to it - but you risk being forgotten by the waitress. The remarkable wine list offers French, Italian and regional vintages at reasonable prices.

ZUM OCHSEN 15/20

76227, Pfinzstr. 64
(07 21) 94 38 60, Fax 9 43 86 43 res.

Closed Monday, closed for lunch Tuesday Tables d'hôte: 52L, 98/130D, à la carte: 51/99

The verbose, loud and temperamental Monsieur Jollit "sells" you with great enthusiasm the courses of the meal he puts together, and you feel truly honored by all the attention. Then he puts on the same show at a neighboring table. Madame Jollit's cooking shows both German and French influences. We enjoyed the egg roll with scallops, noodles and celery, a wonderful cream of prawn soup, fresh red mullet fillet, a rustically prepared leg of goose, fried goat cheese and delicious ice cream.We saw four tables share one wine cooler, so customers ought watch the label when the wine is being poured. The wine cellar is well-stocked with expensive wines.

KASSEL Hessen

Hannover 164 - Frankfurt 200

LA FRASCA 14/20

34117, Jordanstr. 11
(05 61) 1 44 94 res.

Closed for lunch, closed Sunday. Tables d'hôte: 50/120, à la carte: 40/71, No Credit Cards

La Frasca is an old address for gourmet dining in Kassel but is just as youthful and spirited as ever. Gisela Levorato's cuisine is still first class. Try as we might, we could not find a flaw. Everything was perfect, from the trout mousse to capon with capers and raisins, and homemade licorice ice cream. Signora Gisela served delectable gnocchi with goat cheese sauce and flavorful slices of lamb saddle, and saddle of lamb with lamb shoulder, surrounded by zucchini stuffing in a sauce of red wine and cèpes (for large appetites only). If you like fish, you will love the tagliatelle with squid and bean sauce or the stewed bass with mushrooms and fried polenta. Those who are watching their weight should order half portions. Signore Eli's selection of wines (many by the glass) and grappa is as good as his wife's cooking.

RESTAURANT PARK SCHÖNFELD 12/20

34121, Bosestr. 13
(05 61) 2 20 50, Fax 2 75 51 res.

Closed Monday. Tables d'hôte:36L, 65/90D, à la carte: 39/80

This is without a doubt the most beautiful restaurant in Kassel, a unique example of classicism at its best. Two imposing stairways lead down from the entry to the dining room, whose modern decor harmonizes well with the castle's historic architecture. You can also dine on a beautiful terrace. Things have improved since our last visit, but Hermann Krasenbrink still has not cut down his immense repertoire. Instead of keeping to a few choice ingredients and preparing them with exactitude and refinement, he wants to show all of his tricks all of the time. This means that he sometimes has to improvise: his aspic of *tafelspitz* contained a lot more vegetables than meat, the poached beef carpaccio with leek noodles was accompanied by tasteless truffles (and no truffle vinaigrette), and the grappa mousse with (gritty) cappuccino parfait tasted like alcoholic whipped cream. His nicely presented turbot in a crepe with lobster mousseline was worth a rating of 14/20.

SCHLOSSHOTEL WILHELMSHÖHE 

34131, AmSchloßpark 8
(05 61) 3 08 80, Fax 3 08 84 28

100 rooms, **S** 170/175, **D** 220/230,
APP 280/290, **½P** +35, **P** +60

The castle itself is famous for its art gallery and its mountain park. The hotel is not housed in the palace, but in a separate building beside it. The rooms and lounges are tastefully elegant. The amenities include restaurant, bar, café, two sun terraces, pub and four skittle alleys. Breakfast: 18 DM.

KAUFBEUREN Bayern

Landsberg/Lech 30 - Kempten 35

NEUE POST 13/20 

7km south
in 87640 Biessenhofen
Füssener Str. 17
(0 83 42) 9 37 50, Fax 93 75 32 res.

Closed Monday. Tables d'hôte: 39/145, à la carte: 38/103. Tables d'hôte with wine: 49

The legendary Bavarian King Louis II used to stop here on his way to the castle Neuschwanstein. Let's hope he ate better. Everything we tried here disappointed us. Cooking times and temperatures were more or less ignored, as was the use of quality products. A few good bottles of wine from the formidable cellar helped us get over the first shock, but if the cooking doesn't improve to its former standards soon, we'll have to withdraw the other toque, too.

NEUE POST 

7km south
in 87640 Biessenhofen
Füssener Str. 17
(0 83 42) 9 37 50, Fax 93 75 32

20 rooms, **S** 85/130, **D** 130/180,
APP 150/250, **½P** +40, **P** +60

The functional hotel building, painted egg-yolk yellow, is more tasteful inside. The rooms are comfortable, quiet and nicely decorated. Various opportunities for recreation are offered: art exhibitions, cooking lessons, fishing, parachuting, paragliding, ice skating, ice hockey, horseback riding.

KELKHEIM Hessen

Frankfurt 20 - Wiesbaden 26

LE DUC IN THE SCHLOSSHOTEL RETTERSHOF 14/20 

5km northwest
in 65779 Kelkheim-Fischbach
near the B 455 motorway
(0 61 74) 2 90 90, Fax 2 53 52 res.

Tables d'hôte: 48L, 89/119D, à la carte: 52/82

Kelkheim's idyllic little castle in the countryside provides a perfect break from the hectic city. Cars are parked away from the castle, so the romantic, intimate ambience on the beautiful terrace can be enjoyed undisturbed. Inside, the restaurant is elegant and comfortable.The kitchen serves dependable, good-quality cooking that is somewhat lacking in inspiration. The fillets of sole in leek sauce were flawlessly prepared, and the garlic sauce with the saddle of rabbit was very flavorful, but the rabbit itself was a little underdone. We enjoyed the cheese dumplings with rhubarb compôte and strawberry sherbet. The ravioli with cottage cheese filling gave us an idea of how good the cuisine can be. But was it worth 23 Deutsche marks? The wine cellar has been stocked by a collector and has rare and precious wines galore, but we would prefer a larger choice of wines of average good quality. There are sufficient wines by the glass to choose from. The service is calm and attentive.

KELTERN Baden-Württemberg

Pforzheim 10 - Ettlingen 17

GOLDENER OCHSEN 14/20

75210, Ortsteil Ellmendingen
Durlacher Str. 8
(0 72 36) 81 42 , Fax 71 08

Closed for dinner Sunday, closed Thursday, Friday, February though the beginning of March, 25 July through 18 August. Tables d'hôte: 40L, 65D, à la carte: 25/60, No Credit Cards

Hermann Augenstein is over 75 but has not retired yet. And we were glad to hear it. While waiting for a qualified successor, he and his wife still prepare wonderful meals in the kitchen of the Goldener Ochsen. This time, his famous duck liver terrine in Cumberland sauce was served with a julienne of apples and vegetables, mushroom slices, orange fillets and quail's egg. We also enjoyed fine perch fillet with pike quenelles in champagne sauce, good consommé with sautéed sweetbreads, and perfectly done saddle of venison in mushroom sauce with spaetzle. Brigitte Augenstein is not only responsible for perfect service but for the desserts as well. She arranges beautiful dishes like the flavorful orange parfait with tropical fruit.The choice of wines is small but interesting and moderately priced. The first-class guest rooms here are inviting.

KEMPFELD Rheinl.-Pfalz

Morbach 10 - Idar-Oberstein 12

GOURMET IM HUNSRÜCKER FASS 13/20

55758, Hauptstr. 70
(0 67 86) 70 01, Fax 70 03

Closed Tuesday, 9 January through 4 February. Tables d'hôte: 60L, 60/120D, à la carte: 47/81

The Schwenk family manages a country hotel with a rustic restaurant that is well-established in Kempfeld. The refined cooking of son Alexander draws gourmets and visiting diamond merchants from nearby Idar-Oberstein (where precious stones are cut and refined). The quality vacillates somewhat, but time and time again we have been surprised by the first-class dishes he creates. The crispily fried but succulent quail with fresh salad and an aromatic sauce made a terrific first course. We also liked the anglerfish with turnips and potatoes, and bass ragout with curry and cherries. The veal fillet wrapped in Italian ham was a little salty. After a while, we got used to having almost all the dishes garnished with some sort of fruit. Desserts are Alexander Schwenk's strongest point, and the light and fruity raspberry and champagne soup was worth two toques! The service is pleasant and helpful. The usual wines are available, including many from Mosel and Nahe.

KEMPTEN Bayern

Memmingen 41 - Bad Wörishofen 67

FÜRSTENHOF

87435, Rathausplatz 8
(08 31) 2 53 60, Fax 2 53 61 20

75 rooms, **S** 115/145, **D** 170/225,
APP 280/350, **½P** +24, **P** +48

Just a few steps from the Rathaus in the center of town, this hotel was first mentioned in 1187. The crowned heads of the Hohenstaufens and Hapsburgs head the list of guests here and are responsible for the name of the hotel, "counts' court." In 1600, the Fürstenhof was rebuilt in the Italian style. It was renovated in 1971 to house this traditionally fine hotel. The best rooms still have some of the charm and extravagance of these bygone days, and the others are adequately equipped. Ample breakfast buffet.

M & M 14/20

87435, Mozartstr. 8
(08 31) 2 63 69, res.

Closed for lunch Saturday and Sunday, closed Monday. Tables d'hôte: 68/98, à la carte: 48/78

A new name, a livelier menu, and success should come knocking at your door. That's what Margret and Michael Mayer (the M & M of the name) thought, and it seems to have worked. With light, fresh and uncomplicated dishes, they cater to the tastes of customers who just want a delicious salad with salmon or shrimps, or some fettuccine with flavorful chanterelles for lunch. In summer, meals are served in the shady garden; bad weather chases customers indoors to the elegant ambience of the dining room. High-quality food, a well-stocked cellar with great French wines, good wines by the glass and moderate prices—that's what a bistro should be. If you're still not convinced, try the fantastic veal roast with chives and a whiff of cloves.

KERNEN/REMSTAL BW

Waiblingen 6 - Stuttgart 19

OCHSEN 13/20

71394, Ortsteil StettenKirchstr. 15
(0 71 51) 2 40 15, Fax 4 71 03 res.

P

Closed Wednesday, 3 weeks in July/August. Tables d'hôte: 54/125, à la carte: 31/83

It's fun to watch the Schlegel family run its big traditional restaurant. There is not a hitch anywhere! The seven dining rooms are usually full, but there is always time for a little chat with the customers. The food is good and the helpings enormous. We sampled salad with fried quail and marinated foie gras, soup of calf's brains with basil, fried bass with leeks in saffron garlic sauce, veal tongue in a delicate chive sauce, and ice-cream soufflé with a delicious raspberry purée. Swabian specialties are also available.It takes some time to study the comprehensive wine list. The prices are moderate.

KERPEN Nordrh.-Westf.

Düren 15 - Köln 20

SCHLOSS LOERSFELD 15/20

50171, Schloß Loersfeld
(0 22 73) 5 77 55, Fax 5 74 66 res.

 P

Closed Sunday, Monday, first 2 weeks in January, 3 weeks during the NRW summer school holiday. Tables d'hôte: 75L, 105D, à la carte: 56/92, No Credit Cards

You don't have to be an aristocrat to dine in the most beautiful castle on the river Erft. Anyone who's willing to pay high prices for classic grande cuisine is welcome to the baroque splendor of this distinguished restaurant. The six-course prix-fixe costs less than 100 DM and may include fried prawns with buttermilk terrine, leek consommé, bass in a wreath of zucchini slices, fillet Wellington, cheese and chocolate variations.The chef showed a more unique profile and has extended his culinary imagination to embrace such creations as crayfish with saffron barley and Nantua sauce (bechamel with crayfish butter), swordfish with ratatouille, sweetbreads with vegetable ravioli and chervil sauce, and cheese soufflé with shallot confit.With his brilliant talent, Bellefontaine could attain a rating of 17/20 quite easily—if he avoided those little mistakes that make him less than a great cook. Nobody deserves a fish terrine that isn't fresh or a mediocre parsnip soup, stringy lobster, overdone rice or bony sea bream. The service is amiable, and the wine cellar gives connoisseurs of French red wines reason for ecstasy. The prices are moderate, and the choice of good half bottles more than adequate.

LA SOPRESSA 12/20

50170, Ortsteil Sindorf
Erftstr. 124-126
(0 22 73) 5 13 90

P

Closed for lunch Saturday, closed Monday, à la carte: 32/63

This drab little house at a busy street crossing looks more like a truck stop than a gourmet restaurant. But we were surprised at the excellent performance ex-pizza maker Roberto della Rovere gives in the kitchen. His professional, high-class cuisine and his wine cellar (as well as the penetrating background music) are pointedly Italian, even though the decor is more like a run-of-the-mill German *gasthaus*. The liberally garnished fish soup had too much tomato in it, the lovely gnocchi in gorgonzola could have used some sage to be really classy, and the strawberries with our tiramisù were tasteless, but we loved the lamb cutlets prepared in the very best Mediterranean tradition.

KIEL Schleswig-Holstein

Flensburg 90 - Hamburg 95

BECKMANN'S GASTHOF 13/20

in 24239 Achterwehr
Dorfstr. 16
(0 43 40) 3 51

P

Closed Monday. Tables d'hôte: 45/68, à la carte: 37/67

The well-frequented *gasthof* with a rustic ambience is quickly developing into a good address for gourmets. At noon, Klaus Ismer and son Oliver offer fresh, down-to-earth food with a strong regional accent. In addition to a few classic dishes, in the evening customers can choose between a three-course hotel prix-fixe and a four-course gourmet meal. The emphasis is on fresh fish from nearby farms or local fishermen. We liked our fried pike-perch with noodles in a mussel broth. Perfectly done John Dory with cabbage strips and beans, and the excellent squab with rosemary, corn cakes and salad showed that son Oliver combines traditional cuisine with new ideas. Original desserts, like pumpernickel mousse with rhubarb and blackthorn sorbet, were exciting. The service is motivated, but not always well-informed. Slowly but surely, the reasonably priced wine list is growing larger and finer.

CLAUDIO'S RISTORANTE ALLA SCALA 13/20

24114, Königsweg 46
(04 31) 67 68 67 res.

 P

Closed for lunch, closed Sunday, 3 weeks during the Schl.-Holst. summer school holiday. Tables d'hôte: 65/130, à la carte: 55/82

Behind an unobtrusive facade, this little restaurant offers excellent Italian cooking. Original paintings, romantic lighting, extravagant floral arrangements and Claudio's cordial reception make this a place customers quickly feel at home in. Claudio advises customers himself and often offers dishes not on the menu. Regular customers like the daily changing four-course prix-fixe. Ours included succulent anglerfish medallions with delicious risotto, lamb cutlets with fried sage, and zabaglione with strawberries. The wine list is unique and includes only Italian wines. Personal, attentive service.

DAMPERHOF 15/20

24103, Damperhofstr. 5
(04 31) 9 23 24 res.

Closed for lunch, closed Sunday, Monday, 4 weeks during the Schles.-Holst. summer school holiday. Tables d'hôte: 80, No Credit Cards

Jan Marxen and Jochen Strehler can congratulate themselves. Their courageous idea of offering only one four-course prix-fixe every evening is accepted without complaint. It also explains why customers have to reserve a table a week in advance. A nonchalant, relaxed atmosphere and the finest silver and china create the perfect setting for the unadulterated, ingenious regional cuisine of Jochen Strehler, who made few mistakes on our recent visits. Excellent terrine of rabbit saddle, soup of Jerusalem artichokes garnished with spinach and cod, succulent venison with red beet noodles and Brussels sprouts were remarkable dishes that we'll remember for a long time. The service is attentive, personal and obliging. There is one thing we don't understand: why is the wine list only shown on request?

HOTEL BIRKE

24109, Martenshofweg 8
(04 31) 5 33 10, Fax 5 33 13 33

P

64, **S** 135/250, **D** 170/250,
APP 190/290, **½P** 28/32, **P** +50/55

Located on the rural outskirts of Kiel yet only five minutes' drive from the ferry port and the center of town, this hotel is quieter and cheaper than its urban rivals. Fitness center, solarium, jogging in the nearby woods. Breakfast buffet.

HOTEL WIKING

24114, Schützenwall 1-3
(04 31) 67 30 51, Fax 67 30 54

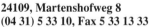

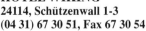

42, **S** 105/140, **D** 160/195,
½P +26, **P** +49

This is a friendly hotel with modern rooms, ideally located on the approach to the Hamburg autobahn and only two minutes' drive from the ferry or the city. Solarium.

KIELER YACHTCLUB 

24105, Hindenburgufer 70
(04 31) 8 50 55, Fax 8 50 39

61 rooms, **S** 175/245, **D** 240/295,
APP 315, **½P** +45,

Formerly the Imperial Yacht Club, this hotel has preserved its exclusive aura. The modern, spacious rooms afford a lovely view of the bay and the yacht marina. Fish dishes feature prominently on the menu of the hotel's restaurant. Bar.

MARITIM-BELLEVUE 12/20

24105, Bismarckallee 2
(04 31) 3 89 40, Fax 33 84 90

Tables d'hôte: 38/40, à la carte: 37/68

Hotel kitchens seldom attain quality high enough to draw gourmets, but this is a notable exception. Pains are taken to buy fresh products, prepare them carefully and present them attractively. The kitchen is on the way to a higher rating with succulent quail stuffed with veal and pistachios, salmon ragout with black noodles, and refreshing champagne soup with marinated berries. The dishes offered on the menu should be changed more often and could use some more creativity. The simple wine glasses spoil the enjoyment of many a nice bottle. Friendly, agreeable service.

NOI DUE 12/20

24103, Fleethörn 25
(04 31) 9 22 27

P

Closed Sunday. Tables d'hôte: 48/80, à la carte: 38/70

A favorite rendezvous for dinner as well as for those who only want to chat and drink, this little restaurant offers a small menu and two prix-fixe meals. Some classics are always to be found: carrot soup with scallops, cucumber soup with shrimp, or lamb saddle with rosemary. Our perfectly fried veal saddle was infinitely more interesting, largely due to an excellent lemon-balm and thyme sauce that accompanied it. The repetitive side dishes of vegetables and potato gratin could use some inspiration, or at least a change.The wine list offers some bottles from renowned estates but could still be improved. Quick, friendly service.

PARKHOTEL KIELER KAUFMANN 

24105, Niemannsweg 102
(04 31) 8 81 10, Fax 8 81 11 35

47 rooms, **S** 179/20, **D** 220/270,
APP 290/320

Kieler's commercial fraternity maintains a venerable turn-of-the-century mansion as its club. Adjoining it is this modern hotel surrounded by the club's grounds. The keynote of the interior is comfort and elegance, and the furniture consists largely of antiques. The breakfast buffet is ample. Commendable restaurant.

QUAM

24105, Düppelstr. 60
(04 31) 8 51 95, Fax 80 24 48

P

Tables d'hôte: 44, à la carte: 30/59, No Credit Cards

People come here to see and be seen. The spacious dining room creates a congenial atmosphere for relaxed conversation. Customers like the fresh seasonal salads with slices of duck's breast, and the nicely done steak or fillet with tasty vegetables. The service is admirably relaxed but quick and competent. The wine list, which offers everything that is good in Italy, is one of the restaurant's highlights. The choice of French wines and more than 20 wines by the glass show that an expert is buying here.

RESTAURANT IM SCHLOSS 11/20

24103, Wall 80/at Oslokai
(04 31) 9 11 55 res.

P

Closed for dinner Sunday, closed for lunch Monday. Tables d'hôte: 38/95, à la carte: 39/84

You'll find it difficult to get a table during the week here. This place hasn't yet heard that there's been a recession. Customers enjoy a marvelous view of the harbor from the window and can rubberneck at the local bigwigs who eat here. The cuisine has its ups and downs. While our duck's breast with prawns and salad dressed with balsamic vinegar were flawlessly done, the breasts of guinea chicken tasted more like turkey. The market vegetables were probably from the deep freeze, and desserts had too much sugar. At least the wine list came up to the advertised high standard of the place. The service was quick and obliging.

SEPTEMBER 15/20

24113, Alte Lübecker Ch. 27
(04 31) 68 06 10, Fax 68 88 30 res.

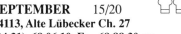

Closed for lunch, closed Sunday, 23—30 December, 15 July through 15 August. A la carte: 44/70. Tables d'hôte with wine: 67/84, No Credit Cards

This restaurant, with its ambitious owner and his talented chef, are on the way to the top of the list of northern Germany's elite restaurants. Instead of a large à la carte choice, customers are offered two moderately priced prix-fixes (four and six courses) that include wine and a few alternatives. Some of the highlights: quail's breast with braised Belgian endives and excellent Sauternes sauce, sturgeon fillet with red beets and lamb's lettuce, stuffed calf's kidneys with cassis sauce and chanterelles, homemade tagliatelle with foie-gras sauce and Périgord truffles, and stuffed leg of rabbit wrapped in Savoy cabbage with a coriander sauce. Chef Wiendieck is famous for his flavorful, unadulterated sauces, each one a masterpiece of creativity and perfection. The excellent service is personal, and the wine list is constantly improving.

STEIGENBERGER AVANCE CONTI-HANSA

24103, Schloßgarten 7
(04 31) 5 11 50, Fax 5 11 54 44

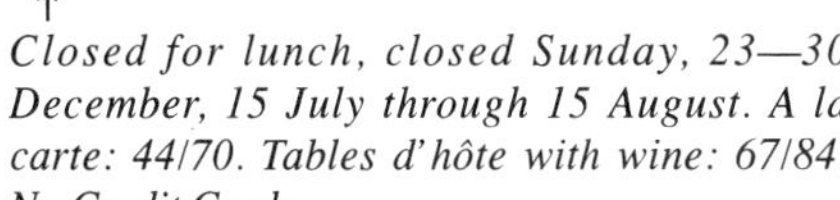

167 rooms, **S** 215/245, **D** 260/310, **APP** 540, 1/2**P** +38, **P** +72

This modern, attractively designed hotel enjoys an ideal location: close to the port, the train station and the autobahn access roads, it is also just a few minutes away from the pedestrian zone in town. The decor is pleasant and modern, and the rooms afford a view of the harbor or of a park. Bar, fitness center, solarium, hairdresser, restaurants. Breakfast room.

WALDESRUH 13/20

24109, Martenshofweg 2
(04 31) 52 00 01, Fax 52 00 02 res.

P

Closed for lunch, Tables d'hôte: 36L, 62/85L, à la carte: 50/90. Tables d'hôte with wine: 60/85

The idyllic location of the Waldesruh on the edge of a forest isn't the only reason for its popularity. With clever specials (lobster week, for instance) and activities (concerts and cabarets), owner Norbert Dünne attracts plenty of regular customers. The formerly comprehensive menu has been cut down to offer only a few good dishes. After having tried a delicious rabbit potpourri, warm lobster salad, lovely lamb rack with tomato and olive sauce, and succulent veal medallions with sautéed sugar peas, we had to award a toque. Sauces could be more flavorful and creative, however. The service is relaxed and personal. The wine list offers a well-balanced choice of international wines and wines from German regions.

KIRCHDORF Bayern

Wasserburg 14 - München 52

CHRISTIANS RESTAURANT IN THE GASTHOF GRAINER 14/20

83527, Dorfstr. 1
(0 80 72) 85 10, Fax 33 04 res.

P

Closed for lunch every day except Sunday, closed Monday, Tuesday. Tables d'hôte:78

A young, ambitious cook has taken over the kitchen of this little village *gasthof*. Christian Grainer serves only three to five-course meals, cooks only seasonal produce and prefers that his customers reserve a few days in advance. His high-class cuisine and low prices are worth a detour. Our wonderful dinner began with an appetizer of duck liver aspic with a salad of cucumbers and radishes, followed by salad with fresh shrimp, mild pesto and potato pancakes with salmon. We loved the consommé with strips of rabbit saddle and poached quail's egg, sole with salad and asparagus and the poularde with mushroom cream sauce. Well-prepared pear variations concluded our meal. The wine cellar is stocked with 140 vintages (the emphasis is on Austria, Burgundy and Bordeaux) and offers an unusual choice of half bottles and magnums.

KIRCHHEIM/TECK BW

Sturttgart 32 - Ulm 55

LANDGASTOF AM KÖNIGSWEG 16/20

4km east in Ohmden
Karlstr.1/Hauptstr. 58
(0 70 23) 20 41, Fax 82 66

 P

Closed for lunch Saturday, closed Monday, closed for lunch Tuesday. Tables d'hôte: 52/129, à la carte: 38/92

The ambitious Fritz Richter went to France to recruit the new kitchen staff for his beautiful country restaurant. His cuisine is creative and accomplished. We enjoyed lobster and sweetbreads with an excellent port sauce as an appetizer, followed by a duck foie gras duo (marinated raw and perfumed with red currants in red wine), lovely lobster ragout in red wine with green asparagus, perfectly done John Dory, and oysters covered with ginger confit with a light pepper cream sauce, tarragon sherbet as an aid to digestion between courses, followed by tender and flavorful lamb cutlets, and, finally, millefeuilles with red berry mousse and rhubarb purée. Coffee was accompanied by a fresh apple tart with cassis sauce.The accomplished French service staff helps Fritz Richter advise and wait on his customers. The choice of wines is international, the vintages exclusive and the prices reasonable. For overnight stays, we can recommend the agreeably furnished guest rooms.

KIRKEL Saarland

Saarbrücken 24 - Kaiserslautern 49

RESSMANN'S RESTAURANT 15/20

66459, Ortsteil Neuhäusel
Kaiserstr. 87
(0 68 49) 2 72, Fax 61 60

 P

Closed for lunch Saturday, closed Tuesday, 1 week at Lent. Tables d'hôte: 45L, 82/110D, à la carte: 42/73

Günther Ressmann and his kitchen staff are professionals in the best sense of the word. Many ingenious creations are cleverly seasoned and served with decorative flair. Our pike-perch and salmon terrine was light and lovely with its mild cream sauce and salmon caviar, and the salmon cubes with a finely dressed and exquisitely garnished lamb's lettuce were perfectly marinated. We liked the paprika consommé with sweetbread ravioli and the excellent duck's breast with caramelized red cabbage and a delicately seasoned orange sauce with red pepper. Our wine zabaglione decorated with marinated strawberries was heavenly. The service is praiseworthy, the background music merely irritating. The wine list should be revised; too many bottles are out of stock, with other vintages substituted. The choice of Bordeaux and Burgundys is excellent. The 1936 Mouton Rothschild sold for 380 DM, 1976 Aloxe-Corton for 148 and 1982 Rayne-Vigneau for 125 DM.

RÜTZELERIE GEISS 15/20

66459, Blieskasteler Str. 25
(0 68 49) 13 81

Closed Sunday, Monday. Tables d'hôte: 58/118, à la carte: 43/85

The decor of this rebuilt farmer's cottage shows a love of detail that's also apparent in the preparation of the food here. Dark wooden beams, small windows, antique furniture and church pews, historic china and paintings create a comfortably nostalgic ambience. Rudi Geiss pays so much careful attention to fine details in his kitchen that the exquisite garnishes sometimes distract from the main ingredients. A lovely caramelized quail was accompanied by a green salad decorated with strips of Belgian endives and duck, slices of cherry tomatoes, peaches,figs, kiwis, grapes and nuts. The light, creamy curry sauce harmonized with the perfectly done catfish, accompanied by a large variety of vegetables. The wine list offers some good German bottles, in addition to young French vintages and some wines from Italy and Austria at acceptable prices. Competent, very attentive service.

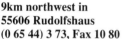

KIRN Rheinland-Pfalz

Idar-Oberstein 16 - Bad Kreuznach 33

FORELLENHOF REINHARTSMÜHLE 13/20

9km northwest in
55606 Rudolfshaus
(0 65 44) 3 73, Fax 10 80

 P

Closed Monday, beginning January through the end of February. Tables d'hôte: 35/95, à la carte: 34/70

We're always off to a good start when we eat Weckmüller's delicious first courses. This time we had tasty ravioli stuffed with blood pudding with exquisitely dressed lamb's lettuce, and a superb smoked fillet of beef marinated in chestnut vinaigrette. The thick, rich cream of cèpes soup was a filler we didn't need, but the flavorful essence of tomatoes with fish ravioli and the classic (and always tasty) trout quenelles in Riesling sauce were true highlights of a fine seasonal and regional cuisine. The service is prompt and unobtrusive. The wine list now offers Nahe wines from the best estates and some good Moselles at moderate prices.

KYRBURG 12/20

55606, An der Burgruine
(0 65 44) 65 44, Fax 59 34

 P

A la carte: 38/74

There is a lovely view of Kirn from up here, and we feel at home in the tastefully decorated sentry house of this former medieval citadel. On our last visit, we appreciated the cuisine as well. We liked the fresh, mildly dressed gourmet salad garnished with many little delicacies, and, apart from a dull jellied sweet wine that accompanied it, the duck's liver was delicious. The tender, succulent lamb saddle with rosemary, beans and unexciting potatoes was excellent. The ratatouille and risotto with the anglerfish were scrumptious, whereas the fish tasted mostly of garlic.The service is pleasant and competent. If you confine yourself to regional wines, you might make a catch. Owner Horst Kroll, by the way, is one of world's top collectors of old whiskeys; he sometimes organizes tastings.

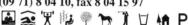

BAD KISSINGEN Bayern

Schweinfurt 24 - Würzburg 50

KURHAUSHOTEL

97688, Am Kurgarten 3
(09 71) 8 04 10, fax 8 04 15 97

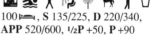

  P

100 rooms, **S** 135/225, **D** 220/340,
APP 520/600, **1/2P** +50, **P** +90

The hotel located in the park of the spa is an island of calm. Rooms and salons have been redecorated. Personal service is a characteristic of this hotel. Don't hesitate to ask the waiter to bring you a glass of spa water from the nearby pump room instead of the usual mineral water. It will help digest the fabulous breakfast from the buffet. The hotel's amenities include a beauty farm, sanatorium, fitness center and restaurant.

LAUDENSACKS PARKHOTEL 14/20

97688, Kurhausstr. 28
(09 71) 7 22 40, Fax 72 24 44

 P

Closed for lunch from Monday to Wednesday, closed for lunch Friday, closed end of December through January. Tables d'hôte: 44/54L, 48/98D, à la carte: 38/80

Light-colored furniture, colorful floral decorations and elegantly laid tables create an attractive ambience.Chef Hermann Laudensack advises his customers personally. We followed his recommendations and had good turbot consommé garnished with impressive sweetbread ravioli and sliced cèpes, overdone sea bream with weak lobster sauce, marinated zucchini slices and overcooked wild rice, squab with a lovely sauce and grilled onions, puréed celery and sunflower crepes, followed by red currant sherbet with a delicate honey and champagne sauce and a baby pineapple that lacked flavor.The service is somewhat shy and quiet but correct.

LAUDENSACKS PARKHOTEL

97688, Kurhausstr. 28
(09 71) 7 22 40, Fax 72 24 44

19 rooms, **S** 120/130, **D** 210/240,
APP 290, **1/2P** +45
Closed end of December through January

This hotel built in 1901 has been lavishly and tastefully modernized and has its own sun lawn and direct access to the spa facilities as well as the tennis courts, a beauty farm, and (within easy reach) a golf course.

TANNECK

97672, Altenbergweg 6
(09 71) 7 16 00, Fax 6 86 14

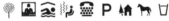

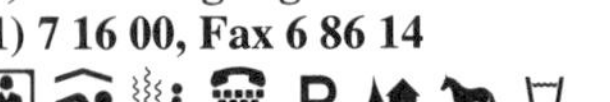

46 rooms, **S** 80/130, **D** 160/240,
APP 270, **1/2P** +30, **P** +60
Closed 1 January through 15 February, No Credit Cards

Most of the hotels in Bad Kissingen try to serve several purposes at the same time. Tanneck, for instance, is a sanatorium, beauty farm and hotel in one. The rooms are quiet and comfortable and the lovely swimming pool well-equipped. The service is attentive.

KLAUSDORF Brandenburg

Zossen 9 - Luckenwalde 19

IMPERATOR 13/20

15838, Zossener Str. 76
(03 37 03) 9 90, Fax 9 92 35

Tables d'hôte: 25/35, à la carte: 22/50

Nothing but the location reminds Berliners of an old pub on the lakeshore that used to be a popular summer excursion destination. The new building—an eye-catcher that manages to harmonize with the landscape it inhabits—is the best gourmet address in the region. Wild fowl on the menu turned out to be pheasant, partridge and wild duck with excellent chanterelles, tastefully arranged on a silver platter. The sauces are all served on the side and are prepared with almost unequaled expertise. Fish dishes are imaginative, like the "smoked salmon of the region," which turned out to be a meltingly delicate fillet of mirror carp. We had fresh pike-perch, eel and redfish caught in the Mellensee, fried in butter and seasoned with fresh herbs from the garden. The desserts need improvement and so does the service. Good choice of wines. Behind its blue and white facade, the Imperator also offers elegantly furnished suites and rooms equipped with every modern amenity. The baths have whirlpools. Sauna, surfing lessons, excursion programs.

KLEINWALSERTAL

Austrian territory linked economically to Germany. The German mark is legal tender. Identity cards/passports required.
Oberstdorf 10 - Stuttgart 200

ALMHOF RUPP 13/20

In 87567 Riezlern
Walserstr. 83
(0 83 29) 50 04, Fax 32 73

P

Closed for lunch, closed 22 April through 15 May, 2 November through 18 December. Tables d'hôte: 35/55, à la carte: 26/60, No Credit Cards

This restaurant is mostly frequented by the Almhof's guests, so don't be surprised if the kitchen stops serving dessert at 9 p.m. We enjoyed pork roast with onions, tasty fried potatoes and beans, as well as salmon soufflé with homemade noodles. The sorrel soup with salmon quenelles was a bit thick. The menu offers a variety of dishes that are attractive for passing tourists, including a vegetarian prix-fixe, many smaller portions and a well-raided salad buffet.

ALMHOF RUPP

in 87567 Riezlern
Walserstr. 83
(0 83 29) 50 04, Fax 32 73

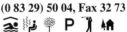

30 rooms, **S** 110/180, **D** 150/320,
1/2P +25

Closed 22 April through 15 May, 2 November through 17 December. No Credit Cards

Located close to the main road and directly beside the open-air swimming pool and ski lifts, this hotel is nevertheless extremely quiet. Its rooms, furnished in a rustic Alpine style, are very comfortable. The amenities include sports and spa facilities and special recreation programs for guests.

IFEN-HOTEL 15/20
in 87568 Hirschegg
Oberseitestr. 6
(0 83 29) 5 07 10, Fax 34 75
P

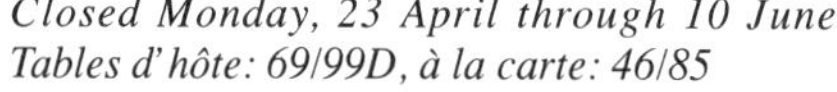

Closed Monday, 23 April through 10 June. Tables d'hôte: 69/99D, à la carte: 46/85

Old-fashioned style characterizes this traditional hotel, as creativity and perfection characterize the cuisine of its restaurant. We like to remember our wonderful warm carpaccio of venison fillet with a salad of fresh chanterelles, lovely parfait of duck liver in port wine jelly with warm grapes, and a suprême of Barbary duck. Chef Martin Jäger is an expert at refined regional cuisine, but also courts natural, fresh ingredients and wholesome recipes. The service is attentive, and the wine list offers high quality.

IFEN-HOTEL
in 87568 Hirschegg
Oberseitestr. 6
(0 83 29) 5 07 10, Fax 34 75
P

62, **S** 145/215, **D** 290/450,
APP 450/560, **1/2P** +55, **P** +80
Closed 23 April through 10 June

This is a Grand Hotel in the true sense of the term: exclusive and sumptuously comfortable at the same time. The rooms (some of them are more like suites) are very comfortable in an old-fashioned way, as are the lounges. Indoor swimming pool, solarium, massages, beauty farm, balneological center, billiard room. Breakfast till noon. Top restaurant for hotel guests only.

KLETTGAU Baden-Württemberg

Waldshut 19 - Schaffhausen 22

LANDGASTHOF MANGE 13/20

4km south in Ortsteil Grießen
79771, Kirchstr. 2
(0 77 42) 54 17 res.
P

Closed Monday, Tuesday, last 2 weeks in August. Tables d'hôte: 35L, 80D, à la carte: 22/64

Previously rather forlorn-looking, the building is now one of the architectural gems of this little village. The restaurant has been refurbished in a postmodern style with everything that's elegant. Paul Maier offers rich, classic dishes made with a lot of cream. We expected more taste from our salmon ravioli with Parmesan cheese and basil, but what little flavor there was succumbed to a liberal dose of crème fraîche. Sweetbreads, fillet of veal and a savory gratin of fine fish were all smothered in creamy white sauces. The side dishes didn't have a chance. The chef's (cream-free) consommés, fresh salads and lovely orange soup with crispy parfait were excellent. The wine list emphasizes German, French and Italian wines. The service is pleasant but needs more self-confidence.

KLEVE Nordrhein-Westfalen

Emmerich 10 - Kalkar 12

CORDES 12/20
47533, Tiergartenstr. 50
(0 28 21) 1 76 40

P

Closed Monday, Tuesday, closed for lunch Wednesday through Saturday. Tables d'hôte: 50/60, à la carte: 41/66, No Credit Cards

This restaurant, located in a classic villa with crystal chandeliers, stuccoed ceilings and red velvet hangings, has a peaceful, comfortable ambience. Brigitte and Jürgen Cordes serve what Kleve's gourmets like: nouvelle cuisine, but not too new. This is uncomplicated, filling and not overly expensive food, presented in familiar atmosphere. Our anglerfish medallions with endive salad, chives and red lentils fought the good fight but lost against an overwhelmingly sour vinaigrette. Our saddle of rabbit was a more positive experience, flavorful and tender, with a lovely basil sauce. Whether ragout of snails, pike-perch fried in sesame seeds, lamb fillet or yogurt mousse, none of the dishes swept us off our feet, but none were complete failures. The international wine list offers something for every taste and 10 wines by the glass, but no half bottles.

LOHENGRIN IN THE HOTEL CLEVE 11/20

47533, Tichelstr. 11

(0 28 21) 71 70, Fax 71 71 00

P

Closed for lunch, closed Sunday. Tables d'hôte: 57, à la carte: 34/78, Tables d'hôte with wine: 57/115

No prices are listed on the menu here; customers put together their own three-, four- or five-course prix-fixe meals from the choice offered. Even gourmets with big appetites should be able to order a good meal for around 100 DM, if they're satisfied with one or two wines by the glass. After a correctly fried sole fillet with insipid caviar sauce as an appetizer, we had a nicely done John Dory with a confused mass of squid noodles, colorful vegetables and crayfish. Lohengrin's chef, we deduced from that, isn't a cook but an artist. Total flops are rare, but the kitchen keeps writing fine prose in its menu, loads platters generously with exchangeable victuals and leaves no lasting impression, not even a bad one. The wine is kept at the right temperature in wine chests, but there are no half-bottles.

KLINGENBERG Bayern

Mittenberg 12 - Aschaffenburg 25

WINZERSTÜBCHEN 17/20

63911, Bergwerkstr. 8

(0 93 72) 26 50, Fax 29 77 res.

Closed for lunch Wednesday through Friday, closed Monday, Tuesday, 2 weeks in August. Tables d'hôte: 79/125, à la carte: 59/96

This is not just a restaurant but an art gallery as well. Displays of unusual artifacts—from cutlery sculptures to ingenious goldsmith's work—add to the dining experience here. The last time we ate at the restaurant, the table centerpiece was a collection of earrings under glass! The true gems, however, are served by Ingo Holland, who never tires of creating new and thrilling taste sensations. His dishes are light and sensual experiences: a tomato aspic with smoked salmon vinaigrette for instance, or a strudel of sprouts with poppyseed, yogurt sauce and lukewarm salmon cubes. We were entranced by smoked pork cheeks with lentil salad and roasted beef cheeks with beans. The iced melon soup, however, did not go very well with lobster, which was a little too firm. On the other hand, the poularde was incredibly tender and juicy, the hyssop noodles had verve, and the morels were handpicked. The fried foie gras with grapes and moscato zabaglione is one of our all-time favorites. The highlight of our last meal was an ingenious dessert creation—gratin of white peaches with berries and Périgord truffle ice cream! The subtle nutty flavor of the truffles was sublime. The wine list is always good for surprises and puts the emphasis on German and French vintages. The home-grown wines by the glass are of good quality. Susanne Holland's service is pleasant and competent. The neighboring Schankstube serves the same dishes in simpler forms. Guest rooms are available.

KLÜTZ Meckl.-Vorp.

Wismar 22 - Lübeck 25

KLÜTZER MÜHLE 11/20

23948, An der Mühle

(03 88 25) 5 53, fax 5 53

 **P**

Tables d'hôte: 35L, 65D, à la carte: 18/62. Tables d'hôte with wine: 30/40

The new owner has brought fresh impetus to this strikingly handsome place. The restaurant has been thoroughly modernized, and a young and motivated service staff takes pains to please the customers. The quality of the cuisine hasn't kept pace with the many improvements, though, and the kitchen still serves unremarkable regional and international dishes. The modest choice of wines includes two Californians by the glass, but no adequate selection from German wineries.

KNITTELSHEIM Rheinl.-Pfalz

Landau 12 - Karlsruhe 24

ISENHOF 12/20

76879, Hauptstr. 15a
(0 63 48) 57 00, Fax 59 17 res.

 P

Tables d'hôte: 60/70, à la carte: 41/79. Tables d'hôte with wine: 80/140

Many of the half-timbered houses in Knittelsheim have been spruced up to create romantic ensembles. One of these is the Isenhof, where Peter Steverding makes the most of his talent preparing meat dishes à point. Entrecôte, fillet or tournedos of Angus beef are his forte, and his customers' best bet. He also offers some more or less successful fish dishes and an immense dessert platter at an incredibly low price. We recommend ordering the regional wines from the Pfalz, but there are some good French and Italian wines as well.

KOBLENZ Rheinl.-Pfalz

Bonn 55 - Mainz 88

LOUP DE MER 13/20

56068, Neustadt12/Schloßrondell
(02 61) 1 61 38 res.

  P

Closed for lunch Saturday, closed July. Tables d'hôte: 65L, 90D, à la carte: 29/88

This is the place for people who like fish. The choice is large and encompasses (almost) everything that swims in salt or fresh water and a lot of crustaceans and caviar besides. Whether you order pike-perch, bass, red snapper, turbot, swordfish from the Arctic or plaice from Hamburg with shrimp, everything is prepared fresh in the kitchen in front of the customers, in the form salad or soup, poached, fried or baked, with light sauces and vegetables. If you don't like fish, there's steak and duck's breast, too. The desserts are unremarkable, and the choice of wines meager.

STRESEMANN 12/20

56068, Rheinzollstr. 8
(02 61) 1 54 64, Fax 16 05 53 res.

P

Closed Tuesday, closed Monday from October through Easter, 1—22 January, à la carte: 26/68

On weekends, you don't stand a chance of getting a table without a reservation. The popularity of this restaurant is partly due to its low prices and unpretentious, friendly service. Regular customers like this and know what's best without looking at the menu. The cuisine is plain but good and the portions served are immense. They come to eat sauerbraten, blood pudding and opulent salads, as well as pork with Gorgonzola sauce and fish. The desserts are cold and fruity. The wine list is adequate, considering that most of the customers drink beer.

KOCHEL Bayern

Bad Tölz 24 - München 70

RABENKOPF 13/20 

5km northeast in Ried
82431, Kocheler Str. 23
(0 88 57) 2 08, Fax 91 67 res.

 P

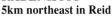

Closed Thursday, 15 January through 20 February, 15—30 October. Tables d'hôte: 25L, 58D, à la carte: 22/57. Tables d'hôte with wine: 24/96

The well-drafted Budweiser beer goes well with the Austrian cuisine served here. To enjoy them, however, it is a good idea to reserve a table as Jörg Slaschek, whose cooking is more despotically monarchical than aristocratically refined, draws a full house. We enjoyed enormously the red-hot tripe soup and the strongly seasoned chicken soup with noodles, and appreciated the tender venison ham and the Topinky foie gras pâté. Slaschek's roulade of Savoy cabbage can also be recommended. Everything is served in grand portions, including the Znaim beef roulade, all sorts of game, Budapest fish goulash or Walchensee trout. After that, the maestro offers desserts rich in calories.The wine list is modest.

RABENKOPF 

5km northeast in Reid
82431, Kochler Str. 23
(0 88 57) 2 08, Fax 91 67

 P 

18, **S** 48/68, **D** 96/136,
1/2P +25, **P** +40

Closed 15 January through 20 February, 15—30 October

Kochel once lay on the ancient pilgrims' route from Germany to Rome, and it looks back on centuries of hospitality offered to weary travelers. The hotel fosters this tradition and pampers its guests with every conceivable amenity. In summer, guests can use the hotel's own boats on the nearby lake, and in winter, Rabenkopf has its own ski lift and ski instructors. The rooms are charming and the service is friendly. Breakfast: 13 DM.

KÖLN Nordrhein-Westfalen

Düsseldorf 47 - Aachen 70 - Frankfurt 200

L'ACCENTO 12/20

50676, Kämmergasse 18 [B4]
(02 21) 24 72 38 res.

P

Closed for lunch Saturday, closed Sunday, à la carte: 36/59, No Credit Cards

This little Italian restaurant has low prices and a lot of customers. An unpretentious but tasteful decor and a cheerful and communicative service staff create a congenial ambience. Franco Medaina's cuisine is full of suspense: nondescript dishes alternate with those that deserve standing ovations. You never know what you're going to get. In any case, don't miss the superb calamari stuffed with fish. The pasta was well-seasoned but not homemade and the vegetable antipasti delicious, but the lamb saddle tough and stringy. The desserts are always good. The modest choice of wines offers no highlights, and the wines by the glass are best ignored.

ALFREDO 13/20

50667, Tunisstr. 3 [B3]
(02 21) 2 57 73 80 res.

Closed Saturday and Sunday. Tables d'hôte: 95, à la carte: 60/85

Carelessness has become the exception rather than the rule at Alfredo's. We still can't understand why some people consider this restaurant the best Italian in Cologne, but we do admit to having experienced some taste sensations here: salad with scallops or crayfish, warm bass carpaccio with julienned vegetables or bass with cèpes, sole, sea bream, fillet of veal with tarragon, and marinated rabbit saddle with rosemary. Customers who can or want to pay relatively high prices can get a good bottle of wine. Half-bottles are rare, and the wines by the glass are at best mediocre. Tables are placed economically close together, but the friendly service staff makes up for this lack of comfort.

AMBIANCE AM DOM IN THE HOTEL EXCELSIOR ERNST 15/20

50667, Trankgasse 1-5 [C2]
(02 21) 2 58 20 92 res.

Closed Saturday, Sunday last 3 weeks of the NRW summer school holiday. Tables d'hôte: 60L, 105D, à la carte: 55/97

Over the last few years, this restaurant has been at the very top in Cologne. Since then, misfortune has struck: the star cook has left and the restaurant had to move to another location. Owner Johannes Kokjé calls this a new beginning with his ambitious chef Jürgen Flocke. Our high rating is a mark of confidence and the result of positive first impressions: *tafelspitz* tart with caramelized sauerkraut and horseradish sauce, quail's breast with chanterelles, pike-perch covered with potatoes in beurre blanc, fried pigeon with apple and honey sauce, and sweets ranging from pear mousse to plum variations. Other variations tasted more like leftovers. The Ambiance is true to classic cuisine à la Escoffier; Jürgen Flocke has yet to develop his own style. The decor in this new restaurant in the Hotel Excelsior is a necessary compromise between Baroque buoyancy and a dark and airless cellar dining room. Johannes Kokjé makes up for it with personal charm and discreet service. The wine list, we hope, will soon be as formidable as it once was. We'd like a few more German and Italian wines, some more half bottles and more wines by the glass under 20 DM.

ATELIER AM DOM IN THE DOM-HOTEL 12/20

50667, Domkloster 2a [C3]
(02 21) 2 02 40, Fax 2 02 44 44

P

Tables d'hôte: 59L, 98D, à la carte: 48/96

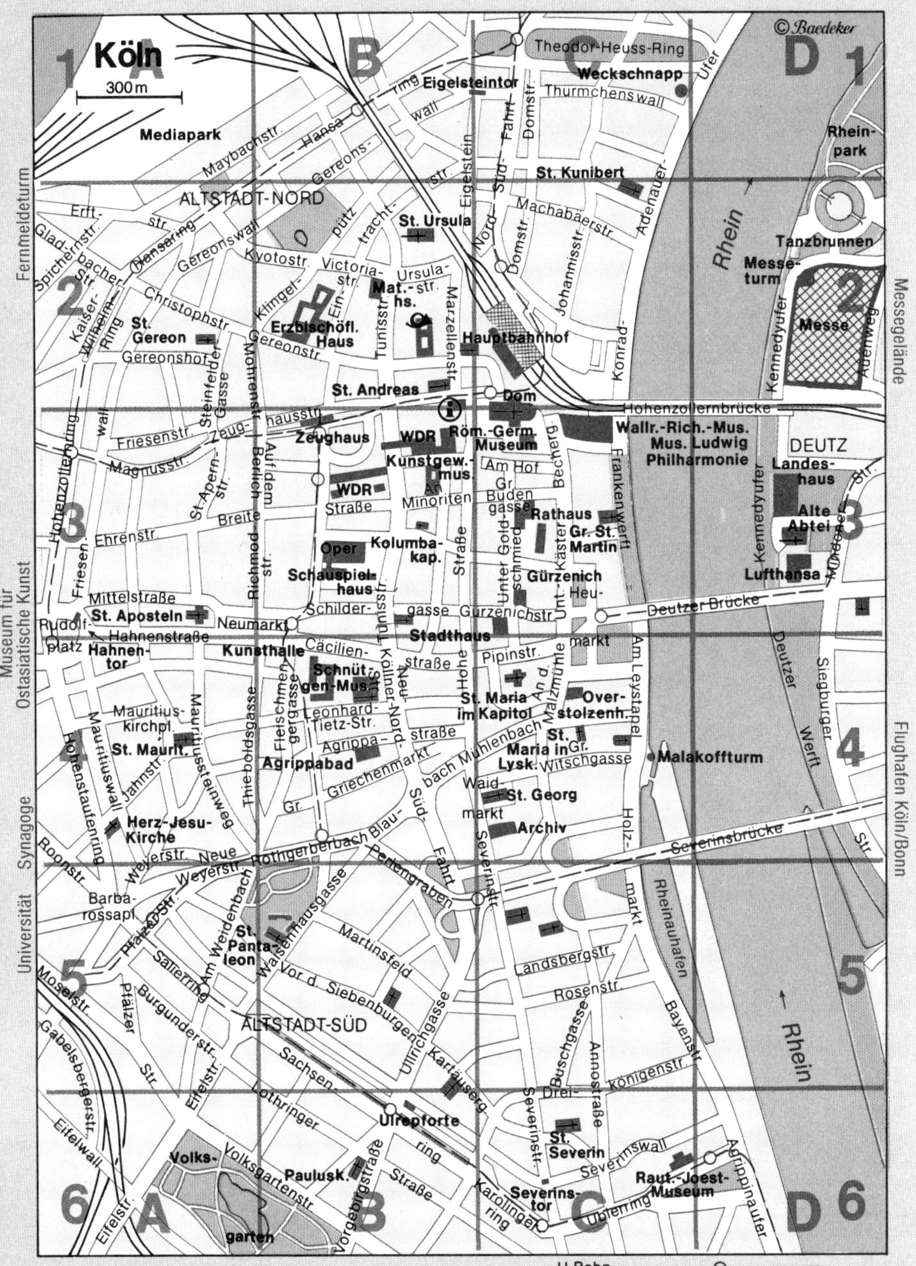
Köln
300 m
© Baedeker
Mediapark
ALTSTADT-NORD
Theodor-Heuss-Ring
Eigelsteintor
Weckschnapp
St. Kunibert
Rheinpark
Tanzbrunnen
Messeturm
Messe
St. Ursula
Mat.-hs.
Erzbischöfl. Haus
St. Gereon
Hauptbahnhof
St. Andreas
Dom
Hohenzollernbrücke
Zeughaus
WDR
Röm.-Germ. Museum
Wallr.-Rich.-Mus.
Mus. Ludwig
Philharmonie
DEUTZ
Landeshaus
Alte Abtei
Lufthansa
Kunstgew.-mus.
Rathaus
Gr. St. Martin
Oper
Kolumbakap.
Schauspielhaus
Gürzenich
St. Aposteln
Neumarkt
Hahnentor
Kunsthalle
Stadthaus
Deutzer Brücke
Schnütgen-Mus.
St. Maria im Kapitol
Overstolzenh.
St. Maurit.
Agrippabad
St. Maria in Lysk.
Malakoffturm
St. Georg
Archiv
Herz-Jesu-Kirche
Severinsbrücke
St. Pantaleon
ALTSTADT-SÜD
Rheinauhafen
Rhein
Ulrepforte
St. Severin
Volksgarten
Paulusk.
Severinstor
Raut.-Joest-Museum
Fernmeldeturm
Museum für Ostasiatische Kunst
Synagoge
Universität
Messegelände
Flughafen Köln/Bonn
U-Bahn

This bistro with winter garden, terrace and bar and a view of the famous cathedral has developed into a popular meeting place. Customers sit on cane chairs under palm trees and try to enjoy the wavering quality of the cuisine here. We would have liked our sweetbreads with lobster and our saddle of suckling kid much better if they had been served warmer (and not warmed up). The pastry was excellent. The prices, however, were far above bistro level. We've heard rumors of a wonderful wine list, but we didn't want to bother the quick young waiters (who had enough trouble with the service as it was) and were satisfied with the dozen good wines by the glass offered on the menu.

BASILIKUM 12/20

50676, Am Weidenbach 33
(02 21) 32 35 55

Closed for lunch every day except Sunday, closed for dinner Sunday, closed Monday, month of August. A la carte: 38/64, No Credit Cards

There should be more restaurants like this, without pretension but with good, plain food that is no worse than that served in some expensive gourmet temples. The secret of Basilikum's success is simple indeed: Margret Juchem cooks everything with loving care and with a sure sense of good taste. Fresh bread and butter with olives makes a nice appetizer for the tasty à la carte dishes or the big prix-fixe to follow. We liked cream of potato soup with marjoram, classic gnocchi with gorgonzola and sage, and semolina with cherry brandy parfait so much that we managed to overlook (almost) the soggy anglerfish and tasteless duck's breast. The service is pleasant and the wine list adequate.

BIER-ESEL

50667, Breite Stre. 114 [A3]
(02 21) 2 57 60 90, Fax 2 57 62 85 res.

A la carte: 18/59

We like to visit this place between September and March, because nowhere else do we get such fantastic mussels. We like them best steamed in their shells in a broth of white wine and served with black bread and butter. You eat them with your hands, using an empty shell as pincers. For those who don't likc mussels, the kitchen offers regional specialities and fish. If the house is full, everything takes a little longer, but it's worth waiting for.

BITZERHOF 12/20

50997, Stdtteil Immendorf
Immendorfer Hauptstr. 21
(0 22 36) 6 19 21, Fax 6 29 87

P

Tables d'hôte: 55L, 80D, à la carte: 34/65

This picturesque country inn is a haven in the midst of the chemical industry complexes that surround it. In addition to the usual schnitzel, beef tips and duck's breast, vegetarian dishes and natural cuisine are offered here. Basmati rice and vegetable strudel, millet cannelloni and lentil cookies tasted much better than the unexciting sweetbreads or lobster ragout. For 65 DM customers can choose their own five-course vegetarian prix-fixe. With a full house, service and kitchen soon reach their limits, but the comprehensive wine list offers some good Bordeaux and ecologically grown wines.

BIZIM 14/20

50668, Weidengasse 47-49 [B1]
(02 21) 13 15 81 res.

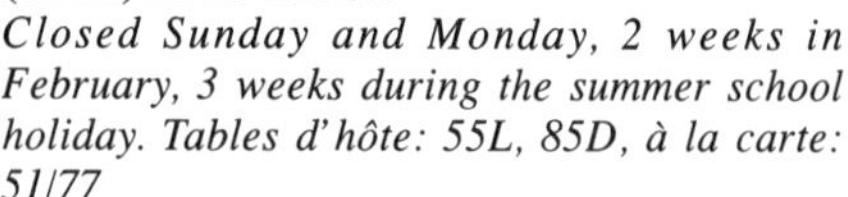

Closed Sunday and Monday, 2 weeks in February, 3 weeks during the summer school holiday. Tables d'hôte: 55L, 85D, à la carte: 51/77

Cologne's Turkish showpiece has become more and more successful—and less and less Turkish. When Enis Akisik invented his *"nouvelle cuisine à la turque,"* we gladly gave him a toque. But we hesitate to give him another one, because we can't tell where the Bizim is going and if it is going to get there. The cuisine's entire repertoire is moving far away from its Turkish origins. We were impressed with Akisik's creative red bean stew with scampi and sole and with his ragout of lamb hearts with lamb kidneys and deep-fried celery. And we devoured his rabbit livers with walnut vinaigrette and his lamb saddle in a crust of hazelnuts with lemongrass sauce. Compared with the fish and meat creations, the desserts were banal. We hope that at least the wine list remains uncompromisingly Turkish. If you're not up on Turkish wines, the owner's charming wife will help. Most main courses cost more than 40 DM, but smaller portions are also available.

BOSPORUS 12/20

50668, Weidengasse 36 [B1]
(02 21) 12 52 65 res.

Tables d'hôte: 55/75, à la carte: 30/58

If the Bizim is too expensive or too Westernized for you, just go across the street to the Bosporus, Little Turkey's oldest restaurant. You may not be able to avoid an Oriental evening with belly dancing, but you'll always find authentic Turkish cuisine that is fresh and tasty. The restaurant has an elegant ambience and was decorated by the owner, who was originally an architect. The prix-fixe shows customers what Turkish cooking is all about: at a "farmer's table" or a "sultan's table," different specialties are served. At lunchtime, customers get a prix-fixe for the price of a main course in the evening.

BRENNER'SCHER HOF 12/20

50858, Stadtteil Junkersdorf
Wilhelm-v.-Capitaine-Str. 15-17
(02 21) 9 48 60 00, Fax 94 86 00 10

 P

Closed for lunch every day except Sunday. Tables d'hôte: 39L, 84D, à la carte: 43/78, Tables d'hôte with wine: 39/140, No Credit Cards

With the best gastronomic intentions and an ambitious public relations campaign, the exclusive Brenner'scher Hof opened a few years ago in a historic country manor house built in 1754. The striking decorating scheme and some curiosities about the cuisine convinced us that our hosts were architects and aesthetes rather than gastronomes. Since then, however, they've learned a few things. Their wine cellar is exceptionally well-stocked, and the cuisine is in traditional and (too?) safe hands. Chef Peter Bahn doesn't like surprises or experiments, so he cooks classic standards. But that is not why he didn't get a toque this time. Even (and especially!) unexciting cuisine has to be perfectly prepared and can't allow serious lapses. Our cream of mussels soup was very tasty—after we removed the last shell and stirred the skin away! Experimental cuisine reached its apex with a turbot steamed with lemongrass, curiously decorated with a stalk of green asparagus. The service is pleasant.

DELFTER HAUS 11/20

50667, Frankenwerft 27
Buttermarkt 42 [C3]
(02 21) 2 57 40 44

A la carte: 38/79

This building on the way from the Frankenwerft to the Buttermarkt is a historic gem. The original facade, with its battlements facing the river, was built late in the 15th century, and the picturesque gabled front about 200 years later. Rustic meals are served in the vaulted cellar, and the floor above offers a more elegant ambience but not the matching cuisine. The food was hearty and filling, just a little above the average quality found in Old Town restaurants. The anglerfish with champagne and mustard sauce, and the hearty aspics of suckling pig and smoked duck with fried potatoes and sauce tartare were commendable. The ambitious wine list offers wonderful choices, with sometimes even a French catch.

GOLDENER PFLUG 18/20

51109, Stadtteil Merhein
Olpener Str. 421/B 55
(02 21) 89 55 09 res.

Closed for lunch Saturday, closed Sunday and holidays. Tables d'hôte: 59L, 110D, à la carte: 88/153

After many excursions to Asia and Italy and the regions of Germany, some gourmets pine for truffled soup, lobster beurre blanc or Nantaise duck—they want to rediscover Escoffier's classic cuisine. With a little nostalgia and a lot of admiration, we praise Cologne's Goldener Pflug, where this kind of cooking is practiced more perfectly than anywhere else in the country. Cook Herbert Schönberger doesn't deserve his three toques just because he revels in the past, but because of the contrasting dishes he serves. Our flavorful lobster seasoned with 10 exciting spices was exquisitely exotic. Nevertheless, we refuse to be ashamed of our liking for blood pudding in puff pastry with red cabbage purée. Fried foie gras with apple slices and port wine sauce was as superb as a delicious scampi salad with green asparagus. The bass coated with mushrooms and accompanied by a savory sauce of olives and herbs, and the rabbit saddle with hearty rosemary flavor swept us off our feet. Ask for rack of lamb with garlic, fried potatoes and beans, and maybe Madame Robertz will put in on the menu instead of suggesting this hearty dish in a whisper.The desserts are truly traditional—and could use a little creative impetus. The lunchtime prix-fixe is as sensationally low-priced as ever and the best way to try Schönberner's cuisine without growing poor. We're not happy about the small choice of wines, but the wines by the glass are affordable. The service is charming, relaxed and highly professional.

LE GOURMET 13/20

50939, Stadtteil Klettenberg
Gottesweg 129
(02 21) 41 00 29, (02 28) 48 07 88 res.

P

Closed for lunch every day except Sunday, closed Monday. Tables d'hôte: 64/99, à la carte: 49/86, No Credit Cards

Customers who enter in a rush may fall into the lobster pool here. But far from feeling cramped in this tiny dining room, customers like the nostalgic charm, which makes up for a want of comfort. Wolfgang Schäfer is a perfectionist in his kitchen, and Hermann Walt's service is flawless. Classic dishes free from experimentation are served here, and we like it because the products are fresh and the cooking is perfect. Lack of creative ambition bothers us only when we find identical salads in two courses and the same appetizer we've had for years. We liked what we tried, though: scampi with noodles, fresh cèpes fried in thyme butter, lovely baked sole, venison fillet with a gingerbread sauce and excellent Brussels sprouts. The wine list offers everything from Brouilly by the glass to a noble La Romanée-St.-Vivant.

GRAND DUC 13/20

50968, Stadtteil Marienburg
Bonner Str. 471
(02 21) 37 37 25, Fax 38 37 16 res.

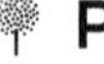 P

Closed for lunch Saturday, closed Sunday. Tables d'hôte: 49L, 78/125D, à la carte: 52/87

Without its palm trees and winter garden, the ambience could be called countrified French, a perfect setting for the hearty cuisine of the Alsatian Bernard Grandis. We liked what we saw and even more what we ate: duck's breast fried with honey and thyme, Scottish salmon with red wine sauce, lovely champagne risotto with cèpes and sweetbreads, and delicious sole fillet with a crust of oranges and curried sauce. Leave a little space for one of the marvelous desserts. The wine list may have a strong French accent, but it isn't chauvinistic: a dozen good wines by the glass are also offered.

GRANDE MILANO 14/20

50674, Hohenstaufenring 29-37 [A4]
(02 21) 24 21 21, Fax 24 48 46 res.

P

A la carte: 44/79

This former academic cooks the best Italian food in Cologne. He aims for the highest quality, and he usually reaches his goal. His warm scallops with truffled sauce laced with Collio Picolit and served on leaves of Savoy cabbage was worth a rating of 16/20. Just as perfect: homemade tagliatelle with cèpes, lamb fillets flavored with garlic and rosemary with a discreetly tangy sauce of balsamic vinegar, cognac and Marsala, and the delicious panna cotta. The fish dishes were highlights. The service has become more professional in quality, and the wine list promises enjoyment. Besides choice Italians like Sassicaia and Tignanello, a few noble French red wines as well as some good half bottles have been added. The elegant ambience is in keeping with the outstanding cuisine. The less chic bistro Pinot di Pinot next door has a more informal ambience.

GRAUGANS IN THE HYATT REGENCY 15/20

50679, Stadtteil Deutz
Kennedy-Ufer 2a [D3]
(02 21) 8 28 17 75, Fax 8 28 13 70 res.

Closed for lunch Saturday and Sunday. Tables d'hôte: 56L, 115/135D, à la carte: 60/92

This gray goose (Graugans) is extremely colorful and should have been called the Peking Duck. Since 1988, the kitchen of this restaurant in the Hyatt Regency Hotel has been experimenting with Asian cuisine. The exotic dishes aren't always served as flawlessly as they should be. Sometimes a tempura isn't crispy enough and tastes more overbearing than subtle. The menu needs a lot of explanation, which usually confuses more than it clarifies. Our advice is not to guess—just enjoy a carpaccio-like dish of swordfish with lamb's lettuce, ginger and sesame sauce. From the sautéed pigeon breast with shiitake mushrooms to anglerfish tempura with papaya salad and (altogether too) discreet chili cream sauce, everything was flawlessly prepared and beautifully presented. The desserts are cheerful and floral, and the wine list international.

HANSE-STUBE IN THE HOTEL EXCELSIOR ERNST 12/20

50667, Domplatz [C2]
(02 21) 27 01, Fax 13 51 50 res.

Closed Monday. Tables d'hôte: 50L, 85D, à la carte: 52/109

True Hanseatic discretion is a treat. After we spent a few hours in this restaurant, we felt completely relaxed and comfortable. No rushing waiters, no obnoxious, self-important customers, no irritating background music, no overheard conversations and no cigarette smoke from neighboring tables disturbed our quiet enjoyment in this truly distinguished restaurant. Some might suspect the cuisine isn't the main reason we like to come here, and they wouldn't be far from wrong. Wolfgang Nestler stands for honest craftsmanship and solid bourgeois fare, appropriately refined to match the elegant ambience. The braised leg of hare in Burgundy was pure enjoyment, and everything from lobster soup to chestnut cream was at least good.

HAUS SCHOLZEN

50823, Stadtteil Neu-Ehrenfeld
Venloer Str. 236
(02 21) 51 59 19

Closed Monday, Tuesday, à la carte: 21/58

Most evenings, this plain *gasthof* has a full house. People don't just come to have a beer, but to eat hearty meals. What do they like? Kale with bacon and sausage, homemade aspics, fillet of herring, potato pancakes, salmon with cognac cream, and everything else made of beef and pork. All this is not worth a special trip for gourmets, but if your expectations aren't too high, you'll like the old-fashioned, friendly atmosphere here. Not all the wines are dry, but the house brandies are good.

HAUS TÖLLER

50676, Weyerstr. 96 [A4]
(02 21) 21 40 86

Closed for lunch, closed Sunday. A la carte: 18/43, No Credit Cards

Cologne's finest *bierstube* doesn't serve home-brewed beer anymore, but its cuisine makes a visit to this historic brewery worthwhile. The waiters, called *"köbes"* in these pubs, aren't as roughly familiar here as they can be elsewhere, and the food is carefully prepared. Order marinated kidneys or liver on Tuesday, potato pancakes on Friday, and bean soup, aspic and beefsteak Monday through Saturday.

ISENBURG 14/20

51067, Stadtteil Holweide
Johann-Bensberg-Str. 49
(02 21) 69 59 09, Fax 69 87 03 res.

Closed for lunch Saturday, closed Sunday, Monday, mid-July through mid-August. Tables d'hôte: 69/95, à la carte: 52/89. Tables d'hôte with wine: 69

The culinary performance in the dining hall hung with precious tapestries is so perfect that this romantic castle on the water can expect its second toque soon. The small menu offers about a dozen different dishes. The produce was fresh and the dishes were creative even if they sounded relatively ordinary, like terrine of hare with pistachios, duck rillette with crispy pieces of fried mushrooms, salad with crayfish and fried artichokes, and (highlight of the season!) sturgeon with celery and lamb rack with lavender sauce. Owner Günter Blindert even generously opened his private wine cellar: a 1964 Chevrey Chambertin for 210 DM was a steal. An exemplary service staff also served lower-priced standard wines from France and Germany.

DAS KLEINE STAPELHÄUSCHEN

50667, Fischmarkt 1-3 [C3]
(02 21) 2 57 78 62/3, Fax 2 57 42 32

Closed 20 December through 14 January. Tables d'hôte: 35L, à la carte: 33/76

Don't confuse this little Stapelhäuschen with the large Stapelhaus on the Rhine promenade just a few meters away. You can eat there, too, but only in the smaller Stapelhaus can you experience the charming ambience of a typical tall, narrow gabled townhouse in Cologne. Restaurant and hotel in one, this house built in 1235 offers bourgeois cooking for hungry customers. The food isn't always prepared on the spot, and the products aren't always fresh, since a lot of tourists are also being fed here. But the choice of wines is fabulous. The voluminous wine list gives a comprehensive review of the German art of winemaking during the past 50 years, from a 1937 Rheingau Trockenbeerenauslese (sweet and fruity aperitif or dessert wine) to the modern dry wines drawn from the barrel. Most wines are affordable.

LE MOISSONIER 16/20

50670, Krefelder Str. 25 [B1]
(02 21) 72 94 79, Fax 7 32 54 61 res.

Closed Sunday, Monday, Christmas through the beginning of January, 4 weeks in summer, à la carte: 44/70, No Credit Cards

The success of this astonishing restaurant rankles the lazy competition. Le Moissonnier is almost always full, and customers who want to eat here on a weekend have to reserve a table two weeks ahead. The authentic Art Nouveau setting is the perfect background for the creative cuisine that leaves traditional bistro repertoire far behind. The atmosphere is relaxed, the service quick and the prices low. Cook Eric Menchon borrows from French and Italian cuisine as well as from Grandma's recipes and creates stupendous dishes that take your breath away. Wonderful risotto, for instance, was seasoned with white truffled oil, which gave it a subtle garlic flavor. The terrific scallops we tried got their temperament from the red paprika compôte marinated in mint. The grilled sea bream tasted fresh from the ocean, and our duck's breast with thyme zabaglione was superb. The cheapest dessert was the best: don't ever turn down a delicious *tarte du jour* here. Bottles of wine under 80 DM are also served by the glass.

PÄFFGEN

50670, Friesenstr. 64-66 [A3]
(02 21) 13 54 61

A la carte: 13/32, No Credit Cards

This pub serves its own beer brewed in back of the house, just as it has been for the last hundred years. The customers come from all walks of life and enjoy the tasty beer at scrubbed wooden tables. We don't want to complain about the food here, but your best bets are the Cologne specialities—*halven hahn"* (half a chicken), *flönz* (blood pudding), or potato pancakes after 5 p.m. (only in winter). In summer, customers have to order something to eat in the beer garden with its lovely chestnut trees.

PAN E VIN 11/20

50667, Heumarkt 75 [A5]
(02 21) 2 58 11 63, Fax 72 80 97

P

Closed Monday (except during the Fair). Tables d'hôte: 42/98, à la carte: 42/82. Tables d'hôte with wine: 88

Our rating is an average, because the cuisine has its ups and downs. Sometimes, lunchtime or Sunday customers are in luck: when Rino Casati personally motivates his crew, they are very capable and creative. But if you can neither see nor hear the maestro, you can be sure the standard drops. In that case, order something from the antipasti or dessert buffets, a glass of wine to go with it, and put all thoughts of a complete meal far behind you. We didn't, and we got what we deserved: salad without dressing, unremarkable pasta, deplorable rack of lamb in soggy olive crust, and insipid vegetables.

PAUL'S RESTAURANT 12/20

50733, Stadtteil Nippes
Bülowstr. 2
(02 21) 76 68 39, Fax 7 39 03 54
Closed for lunch, closed Monday. A la carte: 38/69

With prices well under 40 DM, the talented young Christoph Paul is trying to keep the clientele that used to have beer and pork roast here before he took over this pub. He kept most of the plain, old-fashioned furniture, and the only thing that shows ambition is the menu: sturgeon parfait with two kinds of caviar, lobster with mango sauce, breast of poularde with gnocchi and apple and Calvados sauce, and mint parfait with chocolate all sounded enticing and were served in an appetizing manner. But the portions were too large to be elegant. Even a traditional clientele deserves more finesse! The choice of wines was astonishing for a restaurant of this size: many bottles of international renown, aged Bordeaux vintages, and enough good wines by the glass. The service could be improved.

PULCINELLA 13/20

50677, Sachsenring 3 [B6]
(02 21) 32 16 73,
Closed Sunday. Tables d'hôte: 140, à la carte: 45/75

This good restaurant has changed owners—and we weren't sorry. The cuisine of the former owner had grown tired, and the new owner carries on where Eros Lini left off. The interior decoration hasn't changed except for the addition of some Pulcinella dolls that justify the new name. High-quality products are a prerequisite for good cuisine here, so the kitchen limits itself to a few absolutely fresh dishes prepared on the spot. There's no menu or wine list. The new owner gets the appropriate bottle from the wine chest, and the dishes are chalked on the wall. We weren't half surprised: from the finely seasoned antipasti to an intense zabaglione, the new cook has a fine hand with flavors. Gnocchi and ravioli were first class.

PUR-NATUR À LA CARTE 12/20

50676, Jahnstr. 26 [A4]
(02 21) 24 72 20
Closed for lunch, closed Monday. Tables d'hôte: 49/79, à la carte: 33/65, No Credit Cards

Vegetarians are welcome here, if they don't mind seeing other customers consuming scampi, halibut, or venison saddle at the next table. As far as is possible, the kitchen prepares only ecologically grown and raised products. Even the beverage list emphasizes natural beers and wines. Everything is prepared before the eyes of the customers in the glassed-in kitchen, and the dishes served are very filling. The opulent Savoy cabbage soufflé, for instance, was served with smoked tofu in pastry, morel sauce and potato gratin. In addition to tempura, Heinz Gierse's strong points are his excellent soups, like the delicious curried soup with perch and dill yogurt. The desserts are still sadly nondescript.

REMISE 13/20

50933, Stadtteil Müngersdorf
Wendelinstr. 48
(02 21) 49 18 81, Fax 49 18 81 res.
P
Closed for lunch Saturday, closed Sunday. Tables d'hôte: 60/70L, 90/125D, à la carte: 52/92

A visit here can be lovely, especially on a weekend or in the evening. When we were here, the eloquent maître d'hôtel managed convince all his customers to order the same prix-fixe. No wonder the kitchen is able to do its best! We also tested the Remise at noon and on weekdays, however, when the chef seemed to have gotten up on the wrong side of the bed. The aged turbot we had was just as bad as the owner's manners. The only thing we liked was the wine sauce that went with it and the fabulous soups. Other dishes we tried still justified the toque. The professional service and a large (but by no means cheap) choice of wines do much toward attracting customers. The romantic ambience with picturesque fireplace and candlelight does the rest.

RESTAURANT BADO LA POÊLE D'OR 15/20

50667, Komödienstr. 50-52 [B2]
(02 21) 13 41 00
Closed Sunday, closed for lunch Monday, closed 23 December through 4 January. Tables d'hôte: 28/45L, 68/149D, à la carte: 38/94. Tables d'hôte with wine: 92

Jean-Claude Bado has freshened up the decor of his restaurant without changing its style and - with charm and low prices - is attracting more relaxed, informal customers who seem to have come from the bistro next door. The menu promises new taste sensations: We ate with enthusiasm cream of onion soup, Orientally seasoned lobster salad, pike-perch with smoked salmon in pastry crust, lamb noisettes with zucchini, and a duet of hare and rabbit fillets in two kinds of sauces. The tender fried sturgeon was well-served by a caviar sauce, and the foamy cherry brandy zabaglione with our pineapple soufflé was just superb! Wine buffs enjoy trying rare bottles (some are even affordable!) from the famous cellar and are satisfied with cheese and bread.

RINO CASATI 13/20

50668, Ebertplatz 3-5 [B2]
(02 21) 72 11 08, 72 74 98, Fax 72 80 97 res.

Closed Sunday (except during the Fair). Tables d'hôte: 48L, 115D, à la carte: 59/96, Tables d'hôte with wine: 100

A shadow seems to have been cast on Casati's fine, popular restaurant. We missed Rino on our last visits, and felt sorry for the talented young sommelier who had to manage alone with a sheepish-looking (and acting) service crew. We've decided not to withdraw the toque in view of the black noodles with (salty) lobster sauce, the venison noisettes with (insipid) Savoy cabbage, and the (formerly more imposing) desserts. The rest was embarrassing enough: greasy game terrine, tasteless lobster terrine with dry salad, and overdone bass with an overly concentrated red wine sauce.

RÔTISSERIE ZUM KRIELER DOM 13/20

50935, Stadtteil Lindenthal
Bachemer Str. 233
(02 21) 43 29 43 res.
Closed for lunch Saturday, closed Tuesday, closed for lunch Wednesday. Tables d'hôte: 63/100, à la carte: 44/82

Regular customers enter this old-fashioned steakhouse as naturally as they'd step into their own dining rooms. A charming French service staff and the hospitable hostess make customers feel at home (even if they had to reserve their table far ahead). If the chef has shopped well, fish and shellfish are commendable: lobster, scampi with mango and garlic sauce, or sole fried in butter were delicious and worth an encore. The soups are a must here. Some of the desserts, like the iced *baumkuchen,* are interesting.

LA SOCIÉTÉ 14/20

50674, Kyffhäuser Str. 53 [A5]
(02 21) 23 24 64, Fax 21 04 51
Closed for lunch. Tables d'hôte: 77/115, à la carte: 48/79, Tables d'hôte with wine: 100

The wine list with 600 different vintages is the main attraction of this claustrophobically small restaurant. But the cuisine has no reason to hide behind the choice wines. The dishes are incomparably light, finely balanced and perfectly portioned. The discreetly seasoned and slightly sweet snail ragout in puff pastry and the super succulent lamb rack with shallots and braised sauerkraut were worth more than a rating of 14/20. The salmon and plaice, and the braised pigeon with glazed chestnuts were clever compositions, and tomato mousse and red beet soup, and the catfish in saffron pasta were delightful!

TAPABO 12/20

50674, Kyffhäuserstr. 44 [A5]
(02 21) 24 45 03, Fax 21 04 51

Closed for lunch, closed Tuesday. Tables d'hôte: 55, à la carte: 34/60

Tapabo is literally the "little brother" of the Société across the street: Peter Hesseler's younger brother Harald cooks in the kitchen of the Tapabo. The tasty family cuisine is less expensive here and, if they want, customers can choose from the Société's wine list. The sauces in this bistro-type restaurant are always a little richer and more filling and the flavors less subtle. Cooking times and temperatures aren't always observed with the same care as at the Société. The ambience, though, is inviting, and "little brother" has a stucco ceiling with a crystal chandelier and the Société doesn't—so there!

DIE TOMATE 12/20

50674, Aachener Str. 11 [western A3]
(02 21) 25 29 62, Fax 25 25 46
Closed for lunch Saturday, à la carte: 33/68

This restaurant is a bit shrill and loud and has a colorful clientele to match who don't mind waiting for a place to sit. In spite of, or maybe because of, the hubbub, we enjoyed seafood ravioli with leaf spinach and bouillabaisse sauce. And if customers don't want to eat the veal carpaccio again, they can order hearty kale with smoked sausages. The wines by the glass are good, but our dry white wine was too warm.

UFER-GALERIE 11/20

50996, Stadtteil Rodenkirchen
Uferstr. 16
(02 21) 39 38 63, Fax 39 38 63 res.

 P

Closed for lunch Saturday, closed Monday. Tables d'hôte: 55/90, à la carte: 49/73, No Credit Cards

Compared with the local competition, the Ufer-Galerie is the best place you can eat in this part of Cologne. On the other hand, those who experienced the promising cuisine shortly after the restaurant opened are bound to be disappointed. The fantastic saddle of lamb we tasted then and the mediocre piece of meat we were served on our last visit were worlds apart. Our tip: wait for a warm day, reserve a table on the terrace, avoid the mushrooms in cream and the pigeon in truffled sauce,ask instead if the fish is fresh and, if it is, order it.

VINTAGE

50672, Pfeilstr. 31-35 [A3]
(02 21) 2 58 29 18, Fax 2 58 28 37
Closed for lunch Sunday, à la carte: 26/54

The Vintage is a wine store, wine academy and wine restaurant. The choice of international wines is impressive and reasonably priced. Claudia Stern, our sommelier of the year 1991, arranges wine seminars and tastings. The kitchen offers a substantial foundation for private or official tastings, with dishes like cream of squash soup, fried king prawns with celery, pike-perch with red beets, or lamb haunch with Burgundy sauce—everything fairly well done. From noon to midnight, customers can sample the two dozen wines offered by the glass or empty one bottle after another. The service is amiably competent and the ambience functional.

LA VITA 13/20

50672, Magnusstr. 3/Kreishaus-Galerie
(02 21) 2 57 04 51, Fax 25 48 96 res.

Tables d'hôte: 49L, 85D, à la carte: 58/96

Everybody loves Salvatore—and so do we. With natural charm and cheerful joie de vivre, he's attracted a loyal clientele. His cuisine doesn't distract customers from his bonhomie, and maybe that's just the way it should be. Nobody comes here solely because of the food, but we - dutybound—ignored the congenial atmosphere and looked for hairs in the soup. We found enough: our fish soup was a vegetable consommé with fish leftovers, and our risotto with spinach and Gorgonzola was soupy and insipid. But if the Roman cook has one of his good days, he'll surprise you with wonderful ravioli in sage butter, delicious turbot with Pinot Grigio, and fabulous beef fillet with Barolo.

D'R WACKES 12/20

50672, Bennesisstr. 59 [A3]
(02 21) 2 57 34 56 res.
Closed for lunch, closed Sunday. Tables d'hôte: 42, à la carte: 31/53, No Credit Cards

This restaurant is like a colorful dab of folklore in drab surroundings. The Alsatian cuisine is more than just good. We had savory salads and soups, snails by the dozen, garlicky *bibeleskäs* (cream cheese) with potatoes, poularde in Riesling, and Colmar cheesecake. But the cook (wearing a turban!) was also familiar with Mediterranean cuisine: he served us cassoulet with goose and a flavorful orange parfait. A choice of 14 (mostly Alsatian) wines by the glass.

WAGNERS 13/20

50667, Neumarkt-Passage 18a
(02 21) 2 57 71 10, 2 57 71 50

P

Closed Sunday and holidays, à la carte: 34/61

A snack bar with a toque? The fact that Jürgen Wagner calls his noble snack bar a restaurant didn't convince us, and neither did the fact that customers were served at tables. But one look at the appetizing antipasti buffet, a second one at the cooks behind the kitchen counter, and a third at the promising menu, and we ordered more than pasta and oysters. We had delicious bouillabaisse and fish terrine, tasty rabbit saddle with white beans, savory hare saddle with red currants, and afterwards light mousses and creams. All dishes were well prepared, light and tasty. The small choice of wines by the glass and by the bottle was intelligent. One drawback of this restaurant in a shopping area: soon after the shops close, Wagner has to turn out his lights.

WEINHAUS IM WALFISCH 11/20

50667, Salzgasse 13 [C3]
(02 21) 2 57 78 09, Fax 2 58 08 61 res.

Closed for lunch Saturday, closed Sunday and holidays, 24 December through 6 January. Tables d'hôte: 65/120D, à la carte: 49/88

The stuffed baby turbot with warm grapefruit salad reminded us of a creative leftover recipe: a colorful heap of indifferent fruit and a soggy salmon terrine with a just a little bit of turbot (well, it was a baby, after all) with an "instant" sauce. Haddock with mustard butter, venison saddle, and three kind of fillets satisfy tourists, and even we didn't have much to criticize about chanterelle consommé with morel quenelles, and breast of pheasant with grapes and red wine sauce. Because all of the courses were portioned so generously, the pastries didn't have to try very hard. There is a well-stocked cellar, and the service is familiar and nonchalant.

WIPPENBEKK 12/20

50937, Stadtteil Sülz
Sülzbergstrl 193
(02 21) 41 82 60

50678, Südstadt
Ubierring 35
(02 21) 3 31 94 02

P

A la carte: 24/53

The myth about these two "in" restaurants with the same name is that the second Wippenbekk in Sülz attracts more "ordinary" people, and the original on the Ubierring drawing the beautiful people with trendsetting ambitions. We don't see much difference: both cool and functionally styled restaurants are filled with everyone from nature freaks to successful businesspeople, from well-behaved regular customers to shrill, silly social butterflies. What really surprised us was the incredibly good quality of the cooking and the unbelievably low prices. In addition to the pasta and salads usually offered in bistros, we found extravagant dishes on the menu, such as tasty gurnard fillet with a lemon and caper sauce, great *tafelspitz* (for 17 DM!) and codfish poached in Chardonnay.

ZUM OFFENEN KAMIN

50823, Stadtteil Neu-Ehrenfeld
Eichendorffstr. 25
(02 21) 55 68 78, Fax 5 50 24 25 res.

Closed Sunday, Monday, last 3 weeks during the NRW summer school holiday. Tables d'hôte: 48/65L, 110/135D, à la carte: 54/106

In reaction to the recession, this restaurant has toned down its ingenious cuisine to a level that attracts more customers than a few gourmets. The front room has now become a bistro, and the gourmet restaurant has been banished to the modernized back room. Even if we don't want to rate his accomplishments so soon, the new French cook deserves a toque, although his dishes are more classic than imaginative. But the products are good, and the food is prepared with great care. We had carpaccio with Parmesan cheese, headcheese salad with warm raspberry vinaigrette, anglerfish medallions with paprika sauce, leg of duck with orange sauce, and blueberry pancakes with homemade vanilla ice cream. More than half of the 500 wines (lowered prices!) stocked in the cellar are French, and at least a dozen are served by the glass.

ZUR TANT' 14/20

51143, Stadtteil Porz
Rheinbergstr. 49
(02 21) 8 18 83, Fax 8 73 27 res.

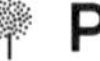 P

Closed Thursday, 13—28 February. Tables d'hôte: 52/65L, 95/125D, à la carte: 52/102

This is the tragedy of a true pioneer: the Austrian Franz Hütter created the foundations for today's ambitious young gourmet cooks 20 years ago when cooking nouvelle cuisine in Porz was a daring act.Now, many of his more careful colleagues have passed him on their way to the top, whereas Hütter's cuisine, in keeping with a phlegmatic service staff and sedate and somber furniture, stagnates at its noble high level. The culinary repertoire knows neither risk nor flamboyant experiments, but instead is satisfied with swimming in the backwaters of new trends. Duck's breast with ginger and honey sauce was delicious and expertly prepared, but not exactly an imaginative highlight, and neither was the equally excellent turbot filled with mango and served with green curry sauce. The side dishes—spinach quenelles, polenta strudel, kohlrabi noodles and millet soufflé—saved the cuisine from being totally unexciting. Desserts have a strong Austrian accent, as does the wine list.

HOTELS

ATRIUM RHEINHOTEL

50996, Stadtteil Rodenkirchen
Karlstr. 2-12
(02 21) 39 30 45, Fax 39 40 54

66, **S** 128/298, **D** 148/438,
APP 198/698, **1/2P** +20, **P** +45

The redecorated Atrium-Rheinhotel has a quiet location, an elegant lounge, draft beer at the bar, and bike rentals (free) for excursions along the Rhine. Breakfast: 25 DM.

BREMER

50931, Stadtteil Lindenthal
Dürener Str. 225
(02 21) 40 50 13, Fax 40 20 34

70, **S** 100/165, **D** 135/215
Closed 23 December through 2 January, 13—17 April

One wing of this modern, functional hotel still awaits modernization. Originally decorated pub, solarium, breakfast buffet.

CONSUL

50668, Belfortstr. 9 [C1]
(02 21) 7 72 10, Fax 7 72 12 59

120, **S** 190/310, **D** 230/350,
APP 450, **1/2P** +30, **P** +60
Closed 23—26 December

This hotel is situated at a safe distance from the bustle of the city center. The rooms are spacious and quiet and are functionally but comfortably furnished. Restaurant. Breakfast: 20 DM.

DOM-HOTEL

50667, Domkloster 2a [C3]
(02 21) 2 02 40, Fax 2 02 44 44

125, **S** 300/410, **D** 530/710,
APP 1300/1400, **1/2P** +92, **P** +162

This is one of Europe's great traditional hotels, located opposite the famous cathedral on the edge of a quiet pedestrian area. The hotel offers a sophisticated lobby, bar and two restaurants. Breakfast buffet: 30 DM.

DORINT KONGRESS-HOTEL

50557, Helenenstr. 14 [A3]
(02 21) 22 80, Fax 2 28 13 01

290, **S** 285/490, **D** 325/530,
APP 490/1200

This former Inter-Continental Hotel offers spacious rooms, all modern conveniences, excellent swimming pool, solarium, massage, bar, restaurant. Breakfast buffet: 28 DM.

EXCELSIOR ERNST

50667, Domplatz [C2]
(02 21) 27 01, Fax 13 51 50

160, **S** 340/450, **D** 450/650,
APP 700/1200

In the heart of the city, facing the cathedral, stands the most luxurious of Cologne's hotels. It offers opulent lounges and restaurants, spacious and elegantly furnished air-conditioned rooms (occasionally noisy), a good breakfast buffet and a commendable fitness center.

HOTEL IM WASSERTURM 

50676, Kaygasse 2 [B4]
(02 21) 2 00 80, Fax 2 00 88 88

90, **S** 390/490, **D** 490/590,
APP 590/1200,

Europe's largest water tower was rebuilt at tremendous expense and transformed into this spectacular hotel, whose striking interior was designed by Andrée Putman. Instead of lights there are walls of shredded glass for diffuse lighting, and there are sandstone instead of marble washstands in the bathrooms. Some of the furniture has rounded edges. Conference rooms, helicopter port, limousine rental with chauffeur, 24-hour room service, babysitter, secretarial service. Restaurant. Breakfast: 29 DM.

HYATT REGENCY 

50679, Stadtteil Deutz
Kennedy-Ufer 2a [D3]
(02 21) 8 28 12 34, Fax 8 28 13 70

307, **S** 295/695, **D** 335/735,
APP 980/2900

Hyatt's first hotel in Germany is proof of the fact that chain hotels can be charming. The lobby, with its 15-foot waterfall, offers a fine view of the cathedral, the old part of town and the Rhine river. This panorama, most impressive when the sun is setting behind the cathedral, is shared by the lounge-restaurant, the Graugans restaurant and many of the spacious rooms and (sometimes enormous) suites. VIP service on the top floor. Attractive fitness club. The parking situation in front of the house is problematic, so reserve a place in the hotel garage. Super-breakfast: 26 DM.

LYSKIRCHEN 

50676, Filzengraben 26-32 [C4]
(02 21) 2 09 70, Fax 2 09 77 18

94, **S** 175/261, **D** 199/340,
Closed 24—26 December

This likable and familiar hotel in the heart of Cologne near the Rhine offers such amenities as a solarium and skittle alley, a pub and two restaurants. Some rooms are furnished in a rustic style, some have an English accent, but all are nicely renovated. Good breakfast buffet.

SPIEGEL 

51147, Stadtteil Porz-Grengel
Hermann-Löns-Str. 122
(02 22 03) 6 10 46/7, Fax 69 56 53

27, **S** 95/190, **D** 140/300

This small, homey hotel located on the outskirts of the forest in Porz looks like a snug little cottage in a fine residential area of town. The service is amiable, the breakfast buffet ample. Even though it's close to the airport, the hotel is relatively quiet because of its soundproofed windows.

VIKTORIA 

50669, Worringer Str. 23
(02 21) 72 04 76, Fax 72 70 67

47, **S** 175/285, **D** 245/420,
APP 295/460
Closed 23 December through 2 January

This hotel has plenty of individual charm and modern comfort. Most of the rooms have a view of the Rhine river.

KÖNIGSBACH-STEIN BW

Pforzheim 10 - Karlsruhe 23

EUROPÄISCHER HOF 13/20 

75203, Steiner Str. 100
(0 72 32) 10 05, Fax 46 97 res.

Closed for lunch Saturday, closed for dinner Sunday, closed Monday, 26 February through 12 March, 7—27 August. Tables d'hôte: 57L, 72D, à la carte: 45/74

This is pure country living: you can't order after 9 p.m., and most customers pay their bill at 10 and go to bed. The helpings are country-style, too, meaning gigantic, with innumerable side dishes and sauces in enormous tureens. The waitresses do not stint on second helpings, either. In spite of all this, the cooking is mostly very good, and sometimes even refined (at moderate prices!). A huge salad is served with each main course.We were satisfied with fresh asparagus and king prawns with lobster sauce. The salad of fresh lobster with green asparagus was just heavenly. The asparagus terrine with smoked salmon was nicely tender and savory, and the veal medallions with lobster, watercress sauce and noodles were wonderful. Both kitchen and service work at such a high speed that you hardly have time to take a deep breath between courses. We suspect that a lot of food is prepared in advance. The wine list is (in part) very moderately priced.

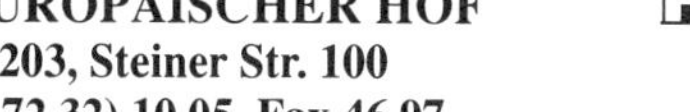

EUROPÄISCHER HOF

75203, Steiner Str. 100
(0 72 32) 10 05, Fax 46 97

 P

20, S 95, **D** 160

Closed 26 February through 12 March, 7—27 August

This hotel is furnished like a country estate, which means that it is comfortable and has plenty of woodwork throughout. The Mast family is almost overpoweringly charming and remains unruffled even when business reaches a peak. The breakfast buffet here is a nice way to start the day.

KÖNIGSLUTTER Niedersachsen

Helmstedt 15 - Braunschweig 22

LA TREVISE IN THE HOTEL KÖNIGSHOF 12/20

38154, Braunschweiger Str. 21a
(0 53 53) 50 30, Fax 50 32 44 res.

 P

Closed for lunch, closed Sunday, Monday, 4 weeks during the VW-Werks holiday. Tables d'hôte: 69/129, à la carte: 49/99

The service in this gourmet restaurant is as self-confident as the high prices on the menu. Supermarket background music, impossible cheap plastic chairs on the terrace, and a choleric cook in the kitchen don't exactly create a congenial atmosphere. We had sole with raw cucumber, firm lobster with badly prepared salads swimming in dressing, a sea bream that wasn't fresh, tiny venison medallions, flat-tasting raspberries with factory-made praline ice cream. The service was good and so was the wine list.

KÖNIGSTEIN/TAUNUS Hessen

Frankfurt 23 - Wiesbaden 28

SONNENHOF 14/20

61462, Falkensteiner Str. 7-9
(0 61 74) 2 90 80, Fax 29 08 75 res.

 P

Tables d'hôte: 30/35L, 69/98D, à la carte: 39/76

This restaurant is located in the Rothschilds' former summer residence in an enchanting park. From the terrace, there is a wonderful view of the Taunus and even of Frankfurt. The Sonnenhof cuisine is aimed at a conservative clientele, and they stick to standard classic dishes. The fried anglerfish fillet with lime butter was first-rate and not expensive. The careful attention to side dishes deserves special praise: we had delicately savory spinach with garlic, flavorful chanterelles and a fantastic potato soufflé. We also enjoyed the stuffed loin of venison with fresh mushrooms, Savoy cabbage, spaetzle and baked apple and were enthusiastic about our tender poularde breast. The dish called "Allerlei" of rhubarb turned out to be a nice combination of mousses and compôtes. All this was had at very moderate prices. Where else can you order a high-quality meal for 30 Deutsche marks? The wine list emphasizes wines by the glass from the Rheingau. The service was sometimes a little disorganized.

SONNENHOF

61462, Falkensteiner Str. 7-9
(0 61 74) 2 90 80, Fax 29 08 75

 P

45, **S** 150/180, **D** 180/290, **1/2P** +40, **P** +65

Surrounded by an extensive natural park, this enchanting hotel guarantees a relaxing stay. The nicest room is in the old building (number 15) and has a large terrace with a great view. Not all of the rooms have balconies or terraces. The rooms in the modern annex hidden behind trees are somewhat less charming, but are closer to the swimming pool, sauna and solarium.

KÖNIGSWINTER Nordrh.-Westf.

Bad Honnef 4 - Bonn 11

GASTHAUS SUTORIUS 13/20

53639, Ortsteil Stieldorf
Oelinghovener Str. 7
(0 22 44) 47 49, Fax 47 49 res.

Closed for lunch every day except Sunday, closed Monday, 14 days in January, 4 weeks in September. Tables d'hôte: 78/105, à la carte: 44/82

This *gasthaus* located across from the church here has been a family property for the last hundred years or more. Personal, charming service makes customers feel at home. The cuisine is neither pretentious nor flamboyant, but practices simple cooking with first-class, fresh ingredients. The menu changes often, depending on what is available at the market. We had red cabbage soup with sole, scallop ragout and morels with black ravioli. Having unwrapped it from a leaf of tough beet spinach, we found the turbot just delightful. The choice of desserts is adequate.

KOHLBERG Bad.-Württ.

Neuffen 3 - Reutlingen 14

BEIM SCHULTES 13/20

72664, Nueffener Str. 1
(0 70 25) 24 27, Fax 45 46 res.

Closed Monday. Tables d'hôte: 65/69, à la carte: 32/60

A cheerful outdoor café in front of the restaurant is occupied by an enthusiastic clientele on nice summer days. We tried assorted first courses and found the dried Italian hams with melon and smoked salmon much better than the shrimp salad. They were followed by excellent fillet of lamb with ratatouille, strawberry sherbet with pistachios, and mousse au chocolat with orange slices.

KONSTANZ Bad.-Württ.

Winterthur (CH) 30 - Stuttgart 190

GASTHAUS ZUM RÖSSLE 13/20

78467, Stadtteil Wollmatingen
Radolfzeller Str. 19a
(0 75 31) 7 81 15 res.

Closed Tuesday and Wednesday, Closed for lunch Thursday and Friday, closed June through September, à la carte: 32/64

The ninth generation of Stadelhofers are carrying on the family tradition in the restaurant built in 1784. Don't be fooled by special platters for old folks and children, low prices and a large menu. Quality and freshness are the rule here. Our grilled turbot, firm and succulent, with a light and flavorful basil sauce and delicious parsley potatoes was outstanding. Regional dishes are prepared with expertise as well: fish from Lake Constance, boiled beef, calf's liver and superb tripe salad. We can also recommend crispy duck with Armagnac plums or a fillet of beef with green pepper. Homemade sorbets concluded our meal. The choice of about 20 wines by the bottle and by the glass included many regional wines and some from France. The hotel is being rebuilt and is closed from June to September 1995.

PINOCCHIO 11/20

78462, Untere Laube 47
(0 75 31) 1 57 77 res.

Closed for lunch Wednesday and Thursday, closed 3 weeks in June/July. Tables d'hôte: 35/65, à la carte: 26/58

Maurizio Canestrini knows exactly what Germans want: pizza and pasta, scampi and squid, and such an immense menu that each member of an office party could order something different. We didn't feel much like reading a book, so we trusted to the owner's recommendations. We were irritated by sloppily boned fish, sour vegetables and terrible lamb with fragments of artichoke fricassee and soggy Brussels sprouts (in spring!). The enticing "surprise mascarpone" turned out to be tiramisù, but the salami ravioli with white beans was superb. The wine list was comprehensive, the wines by the glass mediocre and the collection of grappas remarkable. If Canestrini likes you, you might get a table in a historic vaulted cellar where you can see part of the medieval town wall.

SEEHOTEL SIBER 16/20

78464, Seestr. 25
(0 75 31) 6 30 44, Fax 6 48 13 res.

Tables d'hôte: 55L, 110/180D, à la carte: 40/105

For some people, Siber's is the best address on Lake Constance. As far as we are concerned, Siber's may be one of the best, but is certainly the most expensive restaurant here. The Arcadian terrace, fine silverware and choice china create an elegant but not always congenial atmosphere when customers have to wait interminably long times for their food. Wine list, appetizer and first course took a good hour to find their way to our table! In spite of all that, Siber's attempts to earn a third toque may be successful in the near future. His classics are expertly prepared and exquisitely seasoned, such as bouillabaisse and Barbary duck with Beaujolais sauce or a duet of bass and red mullet with young garlic, eggplant and ratatouille crème. There was a nice variety of prix-fixes to choose from, but the kitchen wasn't particularly flexible about à la carte dishes. We liked truffled salad of venison fillet and duck liver with dandelion greens, arugula and barley, and a fresh and lightly souffléed lobster wrapped in a tender strudel (even though we had to bite on some hard lobster shells). The service was haphazard, and the wine list ill-kept: too many of the wines were "out of stock."

SEEHOTEL SIBER

78464, Seestr. 25
(0 75 31) 6 30 44, Fax 6 48 13

12 rooms, **S** 270/390,
APP 590, **1/2P** +75, **P** +120

This fine late-Victorian villa has a lovely terrace overlooking Lake Constance. The rooms are spacious and well-furnished. Ask for rooms 3 or 7, which have balconies overlooking the lake. There is a disco in the basement whose music will appeal to most age groups. A word of warning: do not confuse this hotel with the adjacent Parkhotel. Breakfast à la carte: 35-50 DM.

STEIGENBERGER INSELHOTEL

78462, Auf der Insel 1
(0 75 31) 12 50, Fax 2 64 02

103 rooms, **S** 195/235, **D** 300/390,
APP 550/700, **1/2P** +60

Housed in a 13th-century Dominican priory, this hotel is as comfortable and lavishly appointed as its prices suggest. What a pleasant change to come across a spacious bathroom! Book a room with view of the lake. Restaurant.

KONZ Rheinl.-Pfalz

Trier 6 - Saarburg 13

SCHEID 16/20

2.5 km west
in 54332 Wasserliesch
Reinigerstr. 48
(0 65 01) 1 39 58, Fax 1 39 59

Closed for lunch every day except Sunday, closed Monday, 14 days at Carnival. Tables d'hôte: 98/115, à la carte: 51/97

At first sight, customers are perplexed: such an unobtrusive building can't possibly house a gourmet restaurant! A second look at the inviting menu reassures them. We enjoyed wonderfully mild marinated salmon, foie gras marinated in sweet Eiswein and served with fresh apple slices in cream, very tasty asparagus with caviar sauce, anglerfish and basil tomatoes, venison fillet with a fabulous sauce, and a simple but good dessert of strawberries with champagne zabaglione and vanilla ice cream. The wine list is legendary. Scheidt offers as many champagnes as other restaurants offer wines. No one else is as well-stocked with wines from Moselle, Saar and Ruwer and aged vintages. His choice of Bordeaux is excellent. Wines in half bottles or by the glass can be asked for: usually Scheid opens a bottle, and customers drink as much as they want from it.

SCHEID

2.5 km west
in 54332 Wasserliesch
Reinigerstr. 48
(0 65 01) 1 39 58, Fax 1 39 59

P

12, **S** 55/75, **D** 75/120
Closed 14 days during Carnival

Until the son of the house took over the restaurant, the hotel was the main attraction. Its guests were drawn by the high standards of comfort in the hotel's few rooms. If one dined in the restaurant, it was only for the sake of convenience. Today the reverse is true: connoisseurs, friends and regular customers come because of the restaurant.

KRAIBURG Bayern

Mühldorf 11 - Wasserburg 30

HARDTHAUS 13/20

84559, Marktplatz 31
(0 86 38) 7 30 67, Fax 7 30 68 res.

P

Closed Tuesday. Tables d'hôte: 40L, 63/79D, à la carte: 24/55, No Credit Cards

A tasty combination of regional cooking and modern cuisine attracts many customers to this new restaurant and its vaulted cellar. We liked calf's tongue with lentils and mustard cream, carpaccio of smoked goose breast with strawberry salad, green salad with a succulent duck's breast, well-seasoned lamb aspic and wild fowl consommé. Wonderful catfish, delicious fillet of beef, sweet and spicy marinated rabbit ragout and tender veal fillet with morels and fine pasta were further highlights. The wine list offers a nice assortment of wines by the glass and the bottle at surprisingly moderate prices. The service is pleasant and circumspect.

KRANZBERG Bayern

Freising 10 - München 35

FISCHERWIRT 13/20

85402, Obere Dorfstr. 19
(0 81 66) 78 88 res.

 P

Closed for lunch every day except Sunday, closed Monday, Tuesday, à la carte: 34/54, No Credit Cards

This pretty country restaurant, with its whitewashed walls and domed ceiling, is situated in a 14th-century building right in the middle of town. The attentive service works flawlessly, and the small menu changes often. Light cuisine is the rule here. We liked the flavorful consommé with julienne, spaghetti with lime sauce and shrimps, stuffed leg of guinea fowl with tender kohlrabi and sugar peas, perfectly done pike-perch with rice, spinach and a well-seasoned cucumber side dish. Try the glazed calf's liver, the venison ragout or the loin of lamb with rosemary, the famous apple tarts and "rote Grütze" (a cold soup of fresh berries). Count on the hostess to recommend the right wine to go with the meal.

KREFELD Nordrh.-Westf.

Duisburg 20 - Düsseldorf 26

LE CROCODILE 13/20

47800, Uerdinger Str. 336
(0 21 51) 50 01 10

Closed for lunch Sunday, closed Monday.Tables d'hôte: 68D, à la carte: 37/67

Good food at low prices served in the relaxed atmosphere of a nice bistro draws a lot of customers. Almost everybody likes fresh products prepared without complications and served in a beautiful Art Nouveau house. We enjoyed new herring with a salad of potatoes and beans, a light ham aspic that harmonized perfectly with fresh asparagus tips in vinaigrette and crème fraîche. The modest desserts, like the cheese strudel with strawberries, were just great. Many wines by the glass are offered and some noble bottles.

GASTHOF KORFF (ZUM KÖNIGSHOF) 13/20

47807, Kölner Str. 256
(0 21 51) 31 17 89 res.

 P

Closed for lunch Saturday, closed Sunday. Tables d'hôte: 44/99, à la carte: 38/76

Not only the locals like the rustic, comfortable ambience of this 200-year-old post station with its agreeable (and sometimes a little too jovial) service staff. The cuisine offers a wide variety of intelligent creations, all prepared fresh with good products. Low-priced bistro-type meals are offered at noon. We enjoyed asparagus with delicate potato crepes, poached catfish with asparagus yogurt, and succulent Guinea chicken leg with elderberry sauce. If customers don't like the desserts recommended with the prix-fixe, they choose from a list full of good things. Nice choice of German and French wines.

KOPERPOT 13/20

47799, Rheinstr. 30
(0 21 51) 61 48 14 res.

Closed for dinner Sunday, closed Monday.
Tables d'hôte: 84L, 92/112, à la carte: 40/81

With its immense bar and beautiful old tiles, this gourmet pub is inviting. The kitchen buys high-quality products, but the cooking isn't consistently good. Our fresh chanterelles were finely seasoned and served in a light and creamy sauce. Our ox-tongue salad was also perfectly seasoned with capers, although the meat was a little soft. The sauces with fish were too salty and the asparagus overdone. An interesting composition: salmon filled with black olives and accompanied by an excellent ratatouille. The wine list includes a good choice of half bottles and wines by the glass.

PARKHOTEL KREFELDER HOF

47800, Uerdinger Str. 245
(0 21 51) 58 40, Fax 5 84 35

P

150, **S** from 190, **D** from 260, **APP** from 550, **1/2P** +40, **P** +80

This hotel combines two valuable assets: it's located near the city yet set in the absolute quiet of a wonderful park with old trees. The rooms of the Krefelder Hof are all inviting and comfortable, and some antiques here and there give them a tasteful personal touch. Amenities include a pub, café and bar. Breakfast: 20 DM. For golfers who want to put in some practice, there's a pitching and putting course.

RESTAURANT IM PARK IN THE PARKHOTEL KREFELDER HOF 14/20

47800, Uerdinger Str. 245
(0 21 51) 58 40, Fax 5 84 35 res.

P

Tables d'hôte: 45/60, à la carte: 29/79

The extensive grounds of this hotel keep the noise of a busy nearby thoroughfare at a respectable distance. The rebuilt and renovated restaurant is an elegant, quiet oasis where customers can enjoy good cooking.The kitchen concentrates on preparing products of the highest quality instead of buying a lot of luxury foods. The prix-fixe meals are clearly structured and low-priced. Some dishes were amazingly simple, like tagliatelle with summer truffles, Belgian endive salad with grapefruit and sautéed chicken livers, as well as the unsurpassed champagne soup with lobster. Our turbot fillet with pink caviar sauce was just as impressive and appetizing as the diced fillet of beef with light morel cream sauce and leaf spinach. Like all desserts here, the crème caramel with orange salad was prepared with loving attention to fine detail. The wine list is adequate.

BAD KREUZNACH RP

Mainz 45 - Kaiserlautern 55

IM GÜTCHEN 13/20

55545, Hüffelsheimer Str. 1
(06 71) 4 26 26, Fax 4 26 26 res.

Closed for lunch Saturday, closed Tuesday.
Tables d'hôte: 42/45L, 72/95D, à la carte: 53/78

In the most beautiful restaurant of this spa resort, the Gütchen's new cook Jan Treutle takes pains to cook as well as the high-class ambience warrants. Combining duck liver and beef tongue to make a millefeuille was an interesting idea, but because of the different consistencies not a complete success. We liked the fresh Mediterranean crustaceans with lovely salads much better. Treutle's fortes are his strongly seasoned and concentrated sauces, especially noticeable with almost overdone lamb saddle with savory olive crust, and breast of poularde penetratingly seasoned with mint leaves. The truffled noodles, fresh summer vegetables and potato tortillas were delicious. The service is a little too quick and could be more discreet. The wine list includes the best wines from the Nahe at moderate prices.

INSEL-STUBEN 12/20
55542, Kurhausstr. 10
(06 71) 83 79 90, Fax 8 37 99 55

P

Tables d'hôte: 35/40, à la carte: 28/65

If Anton Dötzer's successor keeps this up, he can count on a toque next time. Joachim Altmayer's succulent and tasty roast beef, asparagus tips with delicious scampi, lovely halibut in light champagne sauce, and tender lamb saddle with a delicate, not dominating crust of herbs were proof enough that the young cook has talent. Instead of first courses, the menu offers tasty little dishes à la carte. The prices have grown much more attractive, too. The wine list includes renowned wines from the Nahe at reasonable prices. The service is circumspect and pleasant.

LANDHAUS LE PASSÉ
3 km north in 55559 Bretzenheim
Naheweinstr.
(06 71) 4 61 68, Fax 4 55 60

P

Closed Tuesday, à la carte: 30/60

This country restaurant is one of the nicest places in this part of the country. Rita and Louis Szijarto, who run an antique shop on the premises, have rebuilt their barn and opened a pretty restaurant. Son Oliver serves delicious first courses, including a savory Alsatian pizza called "*Flammkuchen*" and a nice choice of sausage and cheese on a so-called Swiss platter. As main courses, we recommend the baby chicken and fillet of lamb. The wine list offers many choice wines of the region (Nahe), some at moderate prices. In spite of early-morning traffic on the main thoroughfare of this village, the two beautifully furnished guest rooms are worth recommending.

METZLERS GASTHOF 15/20
2 km southeast
in 55546 Hackenheim
Hauptstr. 69
(06 71) 6 53 12 res.

Closed for dinner Sunday, closed Monday, 3 weeks during the Rheinl.-Pfalz summer school holiday. Tables d'hôte: 65/108, à la carte: 44/76

Even though their recently opened *Weinstube* (see below) serving bistro fare is an immense success, Bernhard and Petra Metzler promise to continue cooking in their original gourmet restaurant. We enjoyed the crepe with salmon and a striking lime sauce, fried foie gras, perfectly done prawns with pesto and a mousse of peppers, and breast of poularde in pastry crust with foie gras (although the truffled sauce was a bit oily). The roasted rabbit with puréed potatoes and olives was all right. We find Bernhard Metzler's sauces too alcoholic when he primes them with aquavit, grappa and whiskey. And if leeks are served as a side dish for four different dishes again, we will have to confiscate our second toque.The wine list is getting better and more comprehensive. The best wines of the region can be ordered, as well as Italian and French red wines. The charming and resolute Petra Metzler supervises the service.

METZLERS WEINSTUBE 
2 km southeast
in 55546 Hackenheim
Hauptstr. 69
(06 71) 6 53 12

Closed Monday, à la carte: 21/50, No Credit Cards

This little *Weinstube* with bistro-type fare was opened two years ago and has become very popular. Reservations are necessary. Regional specialities are served with imagination and flair, and good regional wines can be had by the glass.

PONTE VECCHIO 12/20
55543, Viktoriastr. 6
(06 71) 4 22 33, Fax 4 35 89 res.

P

Closed Monday. Tables d'hôte: 45L, 60/85D, à la carte: 29/60, Tables d'hôte with wine: 45/85

Marco Troncana, formerly chef of the Gütchen, has discovered his love for Italy. The Ponte Vecchio is by no means a gourmet temple, and maybe that's why this colorful and not exactly tastefully decorated Italian restaurant is always full of customers. Swiss-born Troncana offers Italian cuisine with verve and (sometimes too much) creativity. Besides the usual antipasti, lamb and calf's liver, which range from nicely done to absolutely fantastic, Troncana also offers interesting oddities, like strawberry crème with green asparagus coated with chocolate or asparagus sorbet in an almond basket.We missed Nahe wines on the list; the red wines are served much too warm.

STEIGENBERGER AVANCE KURHAUS

55543, Kurhausstr. 28
(06 71) 20 61, Fax 3 54 77

108, **S** 149/189, **D** 230/280,
APP 440/480, **½P** +43, **P** +80

This extensive and stately hotel complex dominates the center of the spa resort and is located on the banks of the Nahe river. The hotel has direct access to the spa facilities. The rooms are (excepting some wall beds and their mattresses) comfortable, but not exceptional. The bathrooms seem somewhat antique. Health club, beauty farm, pub, café and bar.

KRONBERG/TAUNUS Hessen

Bad Homburg 11 - Frankfurt 15

GOLDENE KUGEL 15/20

61476, Mauerstr. 14
(0 61 73) 47 36 25, Fax 24 30 res.

Closed Sunday, Monday, 2 weeks in December/ January. Tables d'hôte: 58/98, à la carte: 50/81

In the center of the Old Town with its narrow alleys and cobblestone streets, one of Frankfurt's star cooks has opened a gourmet restaurant in an imposing 17th-century half-timbered building. Obviously, the move from the big city to the small town has agreed with Edmund Teusch: his cuisine is light and cheerful. His pike-perch with puréed sauerkraut and paprika zabaglione, anglerfish medallions and fish soup, and succulent Nantaise duck from the oven were excellent, and the variations of foie gras perfect. The strawberry dumplings we had as dessert were somewhat underdone, but nevertheless gave us an idea of how good they could have been. The whole meal tasted as though someone were actually having fun cooking for us! That's more than we can say for the hasty service. Besides renowned French and Italian wines, the wine list offers German wines and includes six wines by the glass and draft beer.

SCHLOSSHOTEL KRONBERG

61476, Hainstr. 25
(0 61 73) 7 01 01, Fax 70 12 67

58, **S** 335/385, **D** 465/655,
APP 895/1850

The hotel enjoys a quiet location and has its own golf course on the grounds. The rooms are fitted with every modern convenience, but if you can't do without a whirlpool or sauna on the premises, you'll barely be consoled by the thought that this nostalgic building with its many antiques was once the residence of the emperor's widow. Restaurant. Breakfast: 28 DM.

KÜHLUNGSBORN MV

Rostock 33 - Wismar 42

BORGHOLM IN THE TRAVEL CHARME HOTEL ARENDSEE 13/20

18225, Straße des Friedens 30
(03 82 93) 4 46, Fax 66 45

Tables d'hôte: 25, à la carte: 26/52

The cuisine of this restaurant decorated in true Scandinavian style is surely the best on this coast of the Baltic sea. Moderately priced regional and international dishes are prepared with care and creativity. Our terrine of salted and smoked herring with pike-perch was very tasty, but the salad served with it could have used a vinaigrette. You can't get the regional fish stew, *Kühlungsborner Fischtopf,* any better than here. The fresh cod fillet poached in a broth of vegetable roots was delicious. The service is quick and professional, and the choice of wines is getting better and better.

TRAVEL CHARME HOTEL ARENDSEE

18225, Straße des Friedens 30
(03 82 93) 4 46, Fax 66 45

66, **S** 165/175, **D** 185/195,
APP 230/260, **½P** +25, **P** +45

This family-run hotel on the shore has been rebuilt to preserve its asymmetrical structure, with a single turret on the southeastern gabled front. The rooms are exclusively furnished.

BRONSHÖVER MÖHL 12/20

18225, An der Mühle 3
(03 82 93) 9 37 res.

P

Closed for lunch every day except Sunday, closed for dinner Sunday and closed Monday from October through April, à la carte: 24/53

Kurt Giese's rustic, comfortable restaurant in a picturesque old mill house has the same unchanging international menu the year round. Nevertheless, the savory, well-garnished fish soup with tomatoes, marinated lamb cutlets with tomato slices, and Baltic salmon with leeks were perfect. Pleasant service and a respectable choice of French and German wines rounded off our positive impression.

HOTEL AM STRAND 11/20

18225, Straße des Friedens 16
(03 82 93) 66 11, Fax 5 71

P

A la carte: 23/68

A lovely winter garden with white cane chairs has made this restaurant much more attractive. A shame, though, that the cuisine hasn't been renovated to match this new ambience. The choice of international dishes on the menu is dull. Apparently the kitchen thinks so, too, and doesn't even try to prepare anything with care. We had imperfectly carved salmon, a nondescript fish soup, and either overdone or almost raw vegetables. The service competed with the kitchen and seemed unmotivated and impersonal. The wine list wasn't convincing, either.

HOTEL AM STRAND

18225, Straße des Friedens 16
(03 82 93) 66 11, Fax 5 71

 P

40, **S** 90/130, **D** 140/180,
½P +20

This little family-run hotel, just a few meters away from the beach, has been renovated. The rooms are spacious and comfortably furnished. Restaurant and bar.

HOTEL SCHLOSS AM MEER

18225, Tannenstr. 8
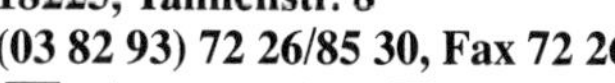
(03 82 93) 72 26/85 30, Fax 72 26

27, **S** 80/95, **D** 120/190
Closed 1 January through 28 February

Ostensibly, no other hotel on Germany's coast lies so close to the beach as this one. We didn't measure it, but this stately mansion really is close to the beach. Every winter, the hotel closes down and undergoes intensive renovation.

RESIDENZE WALDKRONE 11/20

18225, Tannenstr. 4
(03 82 93) 5 96

P

A la carte: 28/56

This kitchen of this restaurant, with its stylish decor and circumspect and polite service, obviously cooks well only in season. On our last visit, we just found boring international dishes that weren't even well-prepared.

RESIDENCE WALDKRONE 

18225, Tannenstr. 4
(03 82 93) 5 96

P

21, **S** 130/165, **D** 175/200,
APP 225/350, **½P** +25, **P** +50

The hotel complex built in 1906 has been completely renovated in the original style. The exclusive rooms and suites are comfortably furnished and almost all have balconies, some with a view of the sea. Excellent breakfast buffet.

SCHWERINER HOF 

18225, Straße des Friedens 46
(03 82 93) 66 96, 1 22 06/7, Fax 1 22 08

27, **S** 90/185, **D** 120/220,
APP 140/285

This family-run hotel on the shore has been rebuilt to preserve its asymmetrical structure, with a single turret on the southeastern gabled front. The rooms are exclusively furnished.

KUPPENHEIM BW

Rastatt 5 - Baden-Baden 12

KREUZ-STÜBL 14/20

76456, Ortsteil Oberndorf
Hauptstr. 41
(0 72 25) 7 56 23, Fax 7 93 78 res.

 P

Closed Sunday, Monday, 2 weeks at the end of the Bad.-Württ. summer school holiday. Tables d'hôte: 35/78, à la carte: 28/67

If you want to eat well, but do not want to patronize Raub's gourmet temple, you can order a meal at its (humbler) dependence, the Kreuz-Stübl. Regional cuisine is refined yet down-to-earth (especially in terms of prices). We were happy to find that fish courses can be ordered as half-portions. On nice summer days, meals are served in the garden. The repertoire includes chicken breast and livers, brook trout with green asparagus and turmeric sauce, perfectly done beef saddle with artichokes and shiitake mushrooms, and roulade of fresh fish with cabbage.The wine list includes vintages from all the major regions in Baden and from neighboring French regions. Wines by the glass are good and moderately priced.

RAUB'S RESTAURANT 17/20

76456, Ortsteil Oberndorf
Hauptstr. 41
(0 72 25) 7 56 23, Fax 7 93 78 res.

 P

Closed Sunday, Monday, 2 weeks at the end of the Bad.-Württ. summer school holiday. Tables d'hôte: 85/163, à la carte: 59/107

With becoming modesty and without putting on airs, Wolfgang Raub has a good time cooking and is open to new ideas and ingenious combinations of carefully prepared products.We had to be careful not to eat too much of the wonderful breads and rolls served with every course (generous helpings each time). We loved our appetizer, a gazpacho that would have served just as well as a first course. The John Dory, subtly and exquisitely seasoned and served with a nest of grated potatoes, had a distinct Asiatic touch. It was followed by a more classically prepared sole with lobster mousse. The olive quenelles with perfectly done saddle of lamb were spectacular, and the accompanying side dishes (green asparagus and eggplant) simply great. Foie gras with port zabaglione and glazed strawberries, as well as the sweetbread tortellini, were well worth a round of applause. Marvellous desserts concludes the meal.The service is friendly and (sometimes too) familiar. The wine list and its prices are in keeping with the high performance of the kitchen.

BAD LAASPHE NRW

Marburg 40 - Siegen 41

L'ECOLE 16/20

57334, Ortsteil Hesselbach
Hesselbacher Str. 23
(0 27 52) 53 42 res.

 P

Closed for lunch Saturday, closed Monday, Tuesday, January. Tables d'hôte: 110/140, à la carte: 54/98

Michael Debus is trying hard for his third toque. Even with his new team, Debus maintains his old style, which is extremely refined, light haute cuisine without daring or extravagance of any kind. Nearly everything is perfect, but we would like to see a little more variety. The similarity in preparation and indistinct taste sensations do not warrant a higher rating. It must be taken into account, however, that Debus's restaurant has a problematic location. He can't live on gourmets alone in Bad Laasphe. An excerpt from the menu should give anyone an appetite to visit Hesselbach: variations of foie gras, cream of prawn soup with ginger and tarragon, poached fillet of beef with parsley sauce and truffled ravioli, red mullet and squid in curry sauce, and lime soufflé with lemongrass sauce.The service staff is well-trained, and the wine list magnificent.

JAGDHOF GLASHÜTTE 14/20

17 km west in Glashütte
57334, Glasshütter Str. 20
(0 27 54) 39 90, Fax 39 92 22 res.

P

Tables d'hôte: 58/98L, 85/139D, à la carte: 31/87

The Jagdhof had a big party in 1994 to celebrate the 10th anniversary of this gem of a restaurant and the 40th birthday of its owner, Edmund Dornhöfer. Our high rating isn't meant as a birthday present, however, and it is not meant for the Jagdhof Stuben (where 95 percent of the customers go), but for the cuisine of the promising little gourmet restaurant. A young, motivated kitchen team offers only one delicious prix-fixe. We had marvelous marinated apple with blood pudding and millet salad, lovely halibut wrapped in a rice leaf and served with warm leek salad, a superb millefeuille of veal fillet and sweetbreads, and duck's breast with Asian vegetables. The spirited service team is charming and competent. But why are the wines so expensive? 15.80 DM for a glass of wine is just too much!

JAGDHOF GLASHÜTTE

17 km west in Glashütte
57334, Glasshütter Str. 20
(0 27 54) 39 90, Fax 39 92 22

30 beds, **S** 188/235, **D** 350/390,
1/2P +50, **P** +100

This first-class hotel is as nice and personal as a family-run boarding house. The hotel isn't too big for people to feel at home in. A rustic, countrified ambience, good cuisine, and many modern amenities such as indoor swimming pool, boutique, cocktail bar and skittle alley, as well as many recreation programs make this an attractive place to spend a few days. Guests can book elegantly furnished rooms, beautiful apartments or luxurious royal apartments with gallery, tiled stove and marble bathroom. Opulent breakfast for guests of all three categories and relatively low prices.

LADBERGEN NRW

Münster 27 - Osnabrück 32

ROLINCK'S ALTE MÜHLE 15/20

49549, Mühlenstr. 17
(0 54 85) 14 84 res.

 P

Closed for lunch every day except Sunday, closed Tuesday, 14 days in the NRW summer school holiday. Tables d'hôte: 80/105, à la carte: 53/89

On our last visit, we were almost the only customers here—and we enjoyed it! The hostess, who is often stressed when the restaurant is busy, was charming, relaxed and good-humored. She recommended special dishes and served them with nonchalant, professional perfection. They included delicate lobster medallions with superb marinated salads, excellent truffled foie gras parfait with slices of mango and avocado, and tender and succulent quail's breast with port wine sauce. But chef Tücher shouldn't neglect his side dishes as much as he does. Cold broccoli, almost-raw vegetables and soggy potato gratin aren't fitting company for exquisite sole roulade with minced pike and outstanding saddle of lamb with Provençal herbs. His desserts could also be more sublime than mousse au chocolat or ice cream with fruit, that is, if he wants another toque. The wine list is (slowly) improving.

LAHNSTEIN Rheinl.-Pfalz

Koblenz 7 - Limburg 53

HISTOR. WIRTHAUS AN DER LAHN 15/20

56112, Lahnstr. 8
(0 26 21) 72 70 res.

 P

Closed Monday, the week of Lent, 2 weeks in August/September. Tables d'hôte: 69/98D, à la carte: 41/69

The Lahn river flooded the restaurant 1993 but didn't wash away any of the antiques or the rustic, homey atmosphere. It didn't harm the cuisine, either. With verve and vehemence, the kitchen serves food that makes our mouths water. The foie gras has always been good here, but last time it was even better, with a perfect consistency and a fabulous caramelized sauce. Another terrific taste sensation was the venison saddle in red currant sauce with spaetzle. The quail were not only delicious, they were also—thanks to a thoughtful cook—expertly boned. All sauces were highly flavorful and had a perfect consistency. The kitchen team even manages to give new impetus to time-tried standards like maties herring and paella with turbot, salmon, shrimp and crayfish. All desserts have class. The wine list, however, can't match the quality of the cuisine. The service is discreet and polite.

LAHR Baden-Württemberg

Offenburg 18 - Freiburg 54

ADLER 12/20

77933, Ortsteil Reichenbach
Reichenbacher Hauptstr. 18
(0 78 21) 70 35, Fax 70 33

 **P**

Closed Tuesday, 1 week over Lent. Tables d'hôte: 40/98, à la carte: 25/72

We have the impression that the chef is never here when we are. The food we had last time should not have left a respectable kitchen. Three menus are offered—with everything on them from fried liver to lobster and company (which probably obscured the contours of the cuisine). We hope Otto Fehrenbach finds his way back to quality food to go with his already excellent service, good wine list and elegant restaurant with a new hotel wing.

LAMPERTHEIM Hessen

Mannheim 15 - Darmstadt 42

WALDSCHLÖSSL 16/20

68623, Luisenstr. 2a
(0 62 06) 5 12 21, Fax 1 26 30 res.

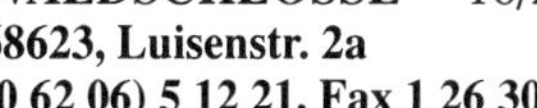

 **P**

Closed for lunch Saturday, closed Sunday, Monday, 1 week during Lent. Tables d'hôte: 85/135, à la carte: 54/96

The converted Waldschlössl is the most important address for gourmets between Mannheim and Frankfurt. It is saved from being too grandiose and stiff by Christel Adelfinger's unaffected friendliness toward her guests and her skill at making them feel comfortably at home.The kitchen is ambitious, but the prices remain affordable. The farmyard duckling, served in two versions, was a dream and deserved a rating of 18/20. The cook, on the other hand, apparently was not paying attention when he prepared the first course—the pigeon was badly carved and not of the best quality. A pale foie gras terrine prevented the awarding of a third toque, but we will not forget the magnificent selection of cheese. The pastry was perfect as usual and also deserved a rating of 18/20.The unobtrusive, pleasant service staff is always available when needed.The Adelfingers were considered trendsetters because they have two separate wine lists, one for reds, the other for whites. But maybe there's a simpler reason: one wine list (with 550 different wines) would have been too heavy!

LANDAU Rheinl.-Pfalz

Speyer 28 - Pimasens 45

LANDHAUS HERRENBERG

76829, Lindenbergstr. 72
(0 63 41) 6 02 05, Fax 6 07 09

 **P**

Closed for lunch, closed Tuesday. Tables d'hôte: 49/95, à la carte: 40/77. Tables d'hôte with wine: 95/145

After an investment of time and money, the Lergenmüller family has built a new hotel with *weinstube* and restaurant, the latter glassed-in like a wintergarten, decorated with a profusion of green plants and furnished with cane furniture. The menu promises more than the kitchen delivers. The cuisine is decent, but no more. We had a tasty vegetable dip as appetizer, quail served suspiciously quickly (probably prepared beforehand), sour green salad with herbs, and lovely trout fillet with good asparagus. The cook obviously likes his vegetables almost raw, but we don't. The wines are mostly from the Lergenmüller estate, and most bottles can be had by the glass as well. Wines from other estates have big-city prices.

PROVENÇAL 12/20

76829, Queichh. Hauptstr.
(0 63 41) 5 05 57, Fax 5 07 11 res.

P

Closed Monday, 3 weeks during the Rheinl.-Pfalz summer school holiday. Tables d'hôte: 35L, 73D, à la carte: 38/76

Is this really the best address for gourmets and connoisseurs as the restaurant claims? We are not out to prove it, but we did like the good, simple fare we were served. The dining room is small and nicely if modestly furnished. Siegfried Höppler cooks with a French accent. His savory (but not too firm) celery terrine with mushrooms and snail ragout with not entirely appropriate red wine were tasty. The leek soup with quail's eggs could have used less cream and more leeks, and the fish Provençal less butter. The wine list has some good but not too expensive regional wines. Apart from that, there are some unpleasant surprises, like a Mouton Cadet blanc de blancs for an exorbitant 70 Deutsche marks. Cornelia Höppler serves correctly but without much enthusiasm.

LANDSHUT Bayern

Regensburg 66 - München 70

FÜRSTENHOF 15/20

84034, Stethaimerstr. 3
(08 71) 9 25 50, Fax 8 90 42 res.

 P

Closed Sunday. Tables d'hôte: 98D, à la carte: 46/81

Behind its light yellow gabled front, the historic Fürstenhof houses two comfortable, cozy restaurants: a bistro-café and a stylish gourmet restaurant. The owner Hertha Sellmair creates a pleasantly familiar atmosphere, and if you've got something special to celebrate, she'll make your dinner an occasion. We don't hesitate to praise André Greul's light cuisine, especially his vegetarian and his small prix-fixe menus. Choosing something à la carte can be a problem here: everything is highly commendable and worth trying. Try the clear tomato consommé with salmon and light sage quenelles, terrific salad with venison sausages, marinated beef, lightly smoked angler with champagne sauce, and delicious turbot filled with chanterelles, as well as succulent breast of poularde with polenta. For dessert, we had tasty compositions like apricot ice-cream cake with a sauce of mocha and Drambuie. The comprehensive international wine list includes a nice choice of wines by the glass and is moderately priced.

FÜRSTENHOF

84034, Stethaimerstr. 3
(08 71) 9 25 50, Fax 8 90 42

P

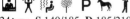

24, **S** 140/185, **D** 185/210,
1/2P +47, **P** +95

This hotel offers a pleasant lobby and tastefully furnished rooms as well as spacious rooms for non-smokers under the roof. Ample breakfast buffet: 24 DM.

KRAUSLER-FEINE SPEISEN IN THE BERGCAFÉ 15/20

15km northeast in
84100 Niederaichbach
Georg-Baumeister-Str. 25
(0 87 02) 22 85, Fax 35 30 res.

 P

Closed Monday, Tuesday. Tables d'hôte: 48/125L, 98/125D, à la carte: 46/84

Krausler's kitchen is prone to accidents. The salmon terrine as appetizer was tasteless, while the shallot soup, quail potpourri, roulade and lobster cooked in court bouillon were interesting. The shrimp lacked flavor and were underdone, but the chanterelles that went with them were terrific. A ragout of anglerfish and lobster was flawless and the pigeon breast tender, but the soufflé served with it much too thick. The Nantaise duckling and the lamb ribs gratin were far better. As dessert we recommend the pear tart and a Benedictine ice-cream cake with fruit.The choice of wines by the glass is not overwhelming, but the prices are. There is a good variety of wines by the bottle, however, especially from Bordeaux and Burgundy. The service is satisfactory.

LANGENARGEN BW

Friedrichshafen 10 - Bregenz 24

HOTEL ADLER 15/20

88085, Oberdorfer Str. 11
(0 75 43) 30 90

P

Closed for dinner Sunday, closed Monday, closed for lunch Tuesday. Tables d'hôte: 65/110, à la carte: 50/85

There's no reason to deny Rudolf Karr his second toque. Unmolested by the crowds of tourists that throng the nearby lakeshore, Karr keeps both feet on the ground and prepares his own (extravagant) grande cuisine. He has as much fun in the kitchen as Irene Karr has furnishing and redecorating the elegant dining room of the gourmet restaurant or the more rustic Adler-Stuben. But while the interior decorating schemes are often playful and witty, Rudolf Karr's cooking sticks to the basics: the products. He avoids fancy frills and concentrates on impeccably harmonious compositions like salmon terrine covered with salmon, lobster medallions with avocado and asparagus salad, finely dressed with lemon, fried bass with superb chervil and thyme sauce, and a duet of rabbit saddle and sweetbreads in morel cream sauce. The pastry alone deserves a higher rating! Order the grand dessert variations and just eat your way through. Without exaggeration, Rudolf Karr is a brilliant cook of classic cuisine. Surprises are strictly limited to the grand wine list.Comfortable hotel rooms.

HOTEL LÖWEN 

88085, Obere Seestr. 4
(0 75 43) 30 10, Fax 3 01 51

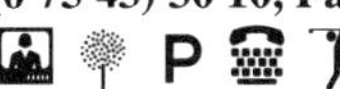

27 rooms, **S** 125/185, **D** 170/240
Closed 3 January through 28 February

The quiet rooms here are spacious, and those overlooking the lake have balconies. Bicycles and a boat can be rented. Friendly, helpful service. Restaurant.

LEHNITZ — Brandenburg

Oranienburg 5 - Berlin 8

GUT LEHNITZ 12/20

16565, Am Gutsplatz 1
(0 33 01) 80 15 19 res.

Closed Monday. Tables d'hôte: 35.54, à la carte: 21/53

The facade of the yellow Classic manor house shines brightly, and in the elegant restaurant, flawlessly performing waitresses serve good, simple fare: succulent turkey roasts, pork cutlets with herbs, well-seasoned goulash of lamb with apples, and cherries flambée on vanilla ice cream. There is a small but good choice of wines.

LEIMEN — Baden-Württ

Heidelberg 7

BADISCHE WEINSTUBE JÄGERLUST

69181, Rohrbacher Str. 101
(0 62 24) 7 72 07, Fax 7 83 63 res.

Closed for lunch, closed Saturday, Sunday, Monday, Christmas through mid-January, mid-August through the beginning of September, à la carte: 27/62, No Credit Cards

This business does not need any outside help. Most evenings, there is standing room only, and if you get a seat you cannot count on having a table to yourself. The down-to-earth cuisine is plain and without frills of any kind. We have seldom tasted such delicious potato salad and meatballs!The sole, a strongly seasoned entrecôte, and a perfect veal roast with first-class spaetzle were all very good. This *weinstube* offers mostly its own wines by the glass at very moderate prices. The service is attentive and quick.

LEINSWEILER — Rheinl.-Pfalz

Landau 9 - Bad Bergzbern 10

ZEHNTKELLER

76829, Weinstr. 5
(0 63 45) 30 75

Closed Tuesday, à la carte: 27/33, No Credit Cards

We can't decide whether we'd rather sit in front of the cozy stove in winter or outside in the cobblestoned courtyard or in the rebuilt barn in summer. The customers here like to eat what Mom (a German Mom, that is) used to cook. An that is exactly what the owner's mother prepares: hearty regional specialities like meat dumplings, excellent fried potatoes, chestnut mousse and cheese dumplings. The comfortable, rustic ambience of this century-old estate and the respectable wines of the region make this an appealing destination for an excursion.

LEIPZIG — Sachsen

Halle 26 - Dresden 125 - Berlin 179

APELS GARTEN 12/20

04109, Kolonnadenstr. 2 [A4]
(03 41) 28 50 93 res.

Closed for dinner Sunday. Tables d'hôte: 33/42, à la carte: 22/50

A pioneer of good cooking stands behind the stove in this restaurant. We'd appreciate him even more if he had the courage to serve even finer cuisine. That means not coloring his really good poularde aspic or serving canned vegetables with his excellent beef roulade. Unassuming desserts like Saxon cheese dumplings were flawless. Nice terrace and a good choice of wines.

AUERBACHS KELLER

04109, Mädlerpassage [C3]
(03 41) 2 16 1040, Fax 2 16 10 49 res.

A la carte: 26/65

Auerbach's Keller, named after a scene in Goethe's "Faust," is a must for cultural reasons. Apart from that, we like the beer served in the cellar. The cuisine wouldn't attract gourmets: pork haunch, beef roast in Burgundy, and venison medallions are by no means prepared on the spot, but you'll get good value for little money at noon, when a pleasant service staff serves generous helpings of plain, filling German fare.

BRÜHL IN THE HOTEL INTER-CONTINENTAL 11/20

04105, Gerberstr. 15 [B1]
(03 41) 98 80, Fax 9 88 12 29 res.
P

Tables d'hôte: 40L, 65D, à la carte: 31/67

The dining hall is still spacious and generously appointed, the tables elegantly laid, and the view from the windows as marvelous as before, but the customers are few and far between. This is the only really refined, quiet dining in room in Leipzig, but it's also the loneliest. Jazz brunches and business lunches don't help much. The service crew takes pains to please customers, but the wine list has grown smaller, and the cuisine is insignificant. Some things are still excellent, like the celery consommé we had with shrimp and tomatoes, and the stuffed king prawns with red beans.

YAMATO IN THE HOTEL INTER-CONTINENTAL 12/20

04105, Gerberstr. 15 [B1]
(03 41) 9 8810 88

Closed Sunday. Tables d'hôte:50/95, à la carte: 40/75

This is a highlight in Leipzig's drab gourmet scene. Both dining rooms are pleasantly furnished, one with a sushi bar. The emphasis is on sashimi and sushi offered à la carte or combined as *"moriawase"*. There is also tempura and miso soup. The other restaurants in the Hotel Interconti, the Milano and the Arabeske, are now closed, but we are lucky to have this one as a replacement.

INTER-CONTINENTAL LEIPZIG

04105, Gerberstr. 15 [B1]
(03 41) 98 80, Fax 9 88 12 29

 P

447 rooms, **S** 290/440, **D** 320/440,
APP 550/1500, **1/2P** +64, **P** +99

This is an ideal hotel for businesspeople visiting Leipzig's fairs and conventions. The rooms in the 27-story building were recently modernized. Book one of the rooms facing south, and you'll have a view of the whole city. Translation service, physiotherapy, hairdresser, beauty farm, bowling, jogging path, boutiques. Breakfast: 19-29 DM.

CITY/GALERIE IN THE HOTEL ASTORIA 11/20

04109, Willy-Brandt-Platz 2 [C1]
(03 41) 7 22 20, Fax 7 22 47 47
P

Tables d'hôte: 35/80, à la carte: 25/59

These two restaurants are run side by side in the Astoria Hotel near Leipzig's train station. Since the Maritim chain has taken over, you never know which of them will be open, the City, with its waiting-room atmosphere, or the Galerie, with its slightly musty elegance. The accomplishments of the respective kitchens are on the same level, namely hotel standard. In addition to the usual hotel fare, though, some regional specialities are served. There is well-trained hotel service in both restaurants and a respectable choice of wines.

ASTORIA

04109, Willy-Brandt-Platz 2 [C1]
(03 41) 7 22 20, Fax 7 22 47 47/9
P

323 rooms, **S** 185/249, **D** 250/336,
1/2P +40, **P** +68

The refurbished (Maritim) hotel is centrally located near the historic train station and offers comfortable rooms, a fitness center, massage, solarium and beautiful salons. The restaurants are unexciting, with the exception of the City, where you can admire a wonderful mural.

ERDENER TREPPCHEN

04109, Neumarkt 26 [B4]
(03 41) 20 95 60, 20 95 75

A la carte: 20/36

There are other wine pubs in Leipzig, but this is the most centrally located and also one of the best. From 11 a.m. to midnight, the kitchen offers everything from fish to pork and grilled sausage, all sorts of ragouts with tomatoes and green beans, or just soup or salad. This is the perfect place for a late breakfast or a meal after the cabaret. The international choice of wines is attractive.

GOSENSCHENKE OHNE BEDENKEN

04155 Stadtteil Gohlis
Menckestr 5
(03 41) 5 57 34, Fax 28 66 00

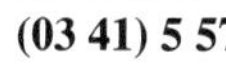

Closed for lunch. Tables d'hôte: 25/30, à la carte: 16/30

The "Gose" in this restaurant's name is an alarmingly yellow brew with a thin, sour taste that has only a fleeting resemblance to beer. Doubts about the wholesomeness of this beverage must have led to the second part of the name, "ohne Bedenken" (have no fear), which is how a waiter calmed nervous customers during the Roaring Twenties. Those who want to drink Gose without fear today often add a little Kümmel-schnaps. Apart from that, this wonderful old pub/restaurant, whose beer garden is well-frequented on nice summer days, serves simple fare at ridiculously low prices.

HOTEL DEUTSCHLAND

04109, Augustusplatz 5/6 [D4]
(03 41) 2 14 60, Fax 28 91 65

283 rooms, **S** 190/235, **D** 260/335, **APP** 330/400, **1/2P** +25, **P** +50

Having undergone complete renovation, this small hotel in the vicinity of Gewandhaus and the university is a low-priced alternative to the bigger hotels. The rather small rooms are functionally equipped. Nice hotel bar. Restaurant.

S'NOCKERL 11/20

04109. Elsterstr. 35 [A4]
(03 41) 9 80 01

Closed for lunch, closed Sunday, à la carte: 16/43, No Credit Cards

This comfortable, plainly furnished restaurant offers typically Austrian specialities, such as good *tafelspitz* (made with prime boiled beef) with roast potatoes and a sauce of apples and horseradish, Viennese baked chicken, *kaiserschmarren* (sweet raisin omelet), and cheese dumplings. The Viennese schnitzel, however, isn't typical: it's made with pork instead of veal! There is a nice choice of Austrian wines, but hardly any wines by the glass.

PAULANER PALAIS

04109, Klostergasse 3-5 [B3]
(03 41) 9 60 00 00, Fax 2 11 72 89 res.

A la carte: 18/54

This Bavarian food emporium includes a few restaurants, garden terrace, café, bar, banquet rooms, a catering service and, to top it all off, the proud and unbelievable slogan, "Individuality is our strong point." The whole complex is well-frequented , and there is something for every taste and appetite, from pretzels and beer to *tafelspitz,* lamb and pike-perch fillet in garlic butter. The Saxon sauerbraten and the chicken fricassee in Noilly Prat won't satisfy gourmets but will make ordinary hungry wayfarers happy.

RATSKELLER PLAGWITZ

04229, Stadtteil Plagwitz
Weißenfelser Str. 10
(03 41) 4 79 60 35, Fax 4 79 60 55

Tables d'hôte: 25/35D, à la carte: 20/45

Leipzig's best, most popular pubs are in the suburbs. This Ratskeller was one of the first, with a comfortable, typical beer cellar atmosphere. Customers who want to eat here don't have to be rich, but they have to be very hungry. The hearty, savory *wurstsuppe* is a steal. After that, try ham hocks with potato dumplings, pork marinated in beer, or the lighter halibut with spinach, or chicken fricassee.

STADTPFEIFFER 12/20

04109, Augustusplatz 8 [C4]
(03 41) 28 64 94, Fax 2 11 35 94 res.

Closed Sunday. Tables d'hôte: 39/72, à la carte: 32/66

The Stadtpfeiffer in the famous Gewandhaus is admittedly the best restaurant in Leipzig. That doesn't say much, since the competition isn't particularly strong. The kitchen can't cope with the crowds of customers that come here, and it's no wonder dishes can't be prepared on the spot when tables have to be reset two or three times every evening. The kitchen does its best with beef consommé or leg of poularde with Burgundy sauce, Leipziger Allerlei and mashed potatoes, and has no time to vary the low-priced prix-fixe meals. We liked fried turbot, lamb ham with lentil salad and unexciting but good desserts like vanilla parfait with dates and raspberry sauce.Very good choice of wines by the bottle and by the glass and pleasant service.

LEMBRUCH Niedersachsen

Osnabrück 42 - Bremen 77

LANDHAUS GÖTKER 17/20

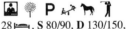

49459, Tiemanns Hof 1
(0 54 47) 12 57, Fax 10 57 res.

Closed Monday, closed for lunch Tuesday, 2—17 January, 10 days during the Nieders. autumn school holiday. Tables d'hôte: 59/90, à la carte: 60/98

The welcoming reception is as charming and personal as the overall ambience of this lovely country inn. There's nothing exaggerated or forced about this inn; everything is fine, and people feel at home here. Friedrich Eickhoff serves the "house cuisine" perfectly. He arranges the food to look like a work of art. The opulent appetizer consisted of potato and sauerkraut *rösti* with salad and fried smoked beef, followed by a heavenly terrine with pike and eel, an exquisite mussel ravioli, and superb pike-perch with cèpes. Our venison noisettes in a pumpernickel and thyme crust was sensational, partly because of the many "extras" served with it: truffled Savoy cabbage, red cabbage, celery mousse and a sauce we gladly would have eaten with a spoon on its own. Perfectly ripened cheese preceded a fantastic dessert: peach mousse millefeuilles, and peach slices and plums in a delicate crepe. Coffee and pastries were a perfect conclusion to the meal. The service is perfect, and the regal wine list offers 420 wines, including some nicely aged and moderately priced vintages and an outstanding choice of wines by the glass.

TIEMANN'S HOTEL

in 49448 Lemförde-Stemshorn
An der Brücke 26
(0 54 43) 5 38, Fax 28 09

28, **S** 80/90, **D** 130/150,
1/2P +18, **P** +35

Closed 10 days during the Easter holiday, 2 weeks in August

This architectural gem is only four miles down the road from Landhaus Götker. Its friendly hospitality and lovely surroundings make up for missing amenities like swimming pool, sauna and fitness center.

LEONBERG Baden-Württ.

Stuttgart 20 - Pforzheim 33

SCHLOSS HÖFINGEN 18/20

71229, Am Schoßberg 17
(0 71 52) 2 10 49, Fax 2 81 41 res.

P

Closed Sunday, Monday, 4 weeks during the Bad.-Württ. summer school holiday. Tables d'hôte: 54L, 138D, à la carte: 52/89

At Schloss Höfingen you're in for a sumptuous gourmet experience. The Feckl family has been running this restaurant for 10 years now. Franz Feckl has cooked his way to the top, and Manuela

Fleckl is responsible for the comfort of her guests. Examples of the impressive cuisine here are an appetizer of salmon and smoked eel tartare topped with caviar, and, as a first course, a platter with green asparagus, lamb's lettuce, foie gras mousse, fried goose liver, breast of guinea fowl and sweetbreads, as well as pigeon consommé. The variations of king prawn with a delicate sauce and ratatouille timbale was superb, and the turbot with lobster carpaccio and red wine butter in a spinach ring with champagne sauce enticed us with just a touch of tarragon. The best parts of a suckling lamb were served as a fillet with Parma ham and Parmesan, a fillet in its own sauce, a cutlet with pesto, and kidneys with onion confit. It was stupendous, as were the desserts. The Swabian specialties deserve the same high rating: warm headcheese with sweet and sour vegetables, roast beef with onions, and oxtail ragout in wine sauce.The grand wine list offers international vintages, and Manuela Feckl's recommendations always harmonize in the best way possible with the food. Prices are moderate.

SCHLOSS HÖFINGEN 
71229, Am Schoßberg 17
(0 71 52) 2 10 49, Fax 2 81 41

 P

9 rooms, **S** 95, **D** 140

Closed 3-4 weeks during the Bad.-Württ. summer school holiday

Rebuilt in the 16th century, this palace has been a hotel since 1970. From its cozy, comfortable rooms, there is a marvelous view of the valley. Medieval hall for dinner parties and conferences. Nice breakfast buffet.

LEVERKUSEN — NRW

Köln 16 - Dusseldorf 33

GALLO NERO 13/20
51379, Stadtteil Opladen
Altstadtstr. 4-6
(0 21 71) 4 79 44

Tables d'hôte: 53/83, à la carte: 36/70

Renato Fendi's thriving ice-cream parlors and pizzerias have made this little gourmet palazzo possible. Effective lighting, comfortable niches and lovely cane chairs create an attractive setting, and the choice of Italian wines at moderate prices was conducive to our enjoyment of the carefully prepared and attractively presented cuisine. There's more than enough pasta and pizza, but the daily prix-fixe suggestions satisfied gourmets: game terrine, carpaccio with arugula, grilled salmon and anglerfish, turbot with orange and saffron sauce, and lamb saddle. Our excellent *osso bucco alla Toscana* was served with black olives in a light, unobtrusive tomato and paprika sauce and accompanied by an outstanding potato and vegetable gratin. Other highlights were spaghetti with fresh lobster (though we needed a magnifying glass to find the lobster) and generous helpings of delicious standard desserts.

BAD LIEBENZELL — BW

Calw 7 - Pforzheim 20

KRONEN-HOTEL 11/20
75378, Badweg 7
(0 70 52) 40 90, Fax 40 94 20

Tables d'hôte: 65/103, à la carte: 38/89

The menu offers only a small variety of dishes. Our prix-fixe consisted of a piece of mediocre dry salmon as an appetizer, fine carpaccio with hardly any vinaigrette, oil or Parmesan, insignificant beef consommé, and noncommittal trout. Another time we tried venison medallions with a morel sauce that lacked flavor. Low-priced wines and friendly service.

KRONEN-HOTEL 
75378, Badweg 7
(0 70 52) 40 90, Fax 40 94 20

43 rooms, **S** 117/155, **D** 208/276

No Credit Cards

This extravagant, elegant spa and holiday hotel located on the bank of the Nagold has spacious, comfortable rooms and a new swimming pool. Restaurant.

WALDHOTEL POST 16/20 
75378, Hölderlinstr. 1
(0 70 52) 40 70, Fax 4 07 90

 P

Closed January. Tables d'hôte: 42/98L, 55/110D, à la carte: 47/102

This restaurant is not easy to find. Start at the Kurhaus and drive toward Stuttgart until you reach Kaffeehof. Only a very small sign at the curb indicates that you have found this lovely hotel restaurant surrounded by woods, which has a marvelous view of the city and citadel. The food here is excellent. The Krieg family let their chef Stefan Fehse develop his own distinctive style, and he is cooking his way slowly but surely to the top.We enjoyed marinated trout from the nearby brook with its own caviar, poached John Dory wrapped in leeks and served on sugar-pea salad, lobster ravioli with green asparagus and a fabulous sauce, lamb ribs with pine-kernel crust and broccoli, taleggio (a soft Italian cheese) with a ragout of figs in port, and a magnificent dessert. The wine cellar offers appropriate wines at reasonable prices. The service is competent and friendly

---

WALDHOTEL POST

75378, Hölderlinstr. 1
(0 70 52) 40 70, Fax 4 07 90

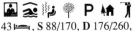

43 rooms, **S** 88/170, **D** 176/260,
½P +33, **P** +54
Closed January

Bad Liebenzell's most comfortable hotel is located on high ground on the outskirts of town and offers a remarkable view of Liebenzell. Spa, park and bathing facilities are within easy reach. Solarium, massage, beauty farm.

LINDAU Bayern

Ravensburg 33 - Augsburg 160

BAD SCHACHEN

88131, Ortsteil Schachen
Bad Schachen 1-6
(0 83 82) 50 11, Fax 2 53 90

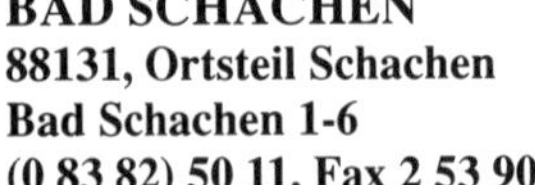

129 rooms, **S** 177/293, **D** 288/282
Closed October through April

Grand Hotel atmosphere in the middle of a park. Customers can choose between rooms facing the park or the lake. Both are quiet. Spa baths and beauty farm. Breakfast in the morning sun with a view over lake and park provides a pleasant start for the day. Restaurant..

BAYERISCHER HOF

88131, Seepromenade
(0 83 82) 50 55, Fax 50 54

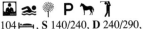

104 rooms, **S** 140/240, **D** 240/290,
APP 700/750, **½P** +58, **P** +116
Closed 1 November through 31 March

This is a true holiday hotel, from the elegantly furnished rooms and spacious bathrooms to the band concerts around the corner. The rooms in back are quieter, but don't have such a breathtaking view of Lake Constance and the Swiss Alps in the distance. Swimming pool, conference rooms with modern technology, restaurants and bar.

HOYERBERG SCHLÖSSLE 16/20

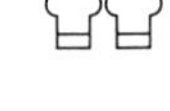

88131, Ortsteil Hoyren
Hoyerbergstr. 64
(0 83 82) 2 52 95, Fax 18 37 res.

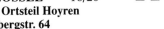

Closed Monday, closed for lunch Tuesday, closed February. Tables d'hôte: 98/158, à la carte: 59/101

After we've sung the praises of the stupendous view from this enchanting Art Nouveau restaurant, we'll continue our concert by lauding Friedbert Lang's cuisine. He presents dishes as artistic masterpieces, with each course arranged on different china and looking almost too exquisite to eat. He was originally a dedicated pastry maker, and Lang's aesthetic creations sometimes remind us of his sweet temptations even when they are main courses. His delicate roulade of salmon and sturgeon, fanned out in wafer-thin slices, seemed like a composition of pink and white marzipan. Pike-perch fillet in bread crust and fried anglerfish with leeks and paprika cream were delicious and perfectly done. The exquisite lentil ravioli were arranged like pretty petits fours with morel cream sauce. But Lang's imagination doesn't go much beyond visual finesse. If he wants to keep his toques, he'll have to pay more attention to quality. Instead of the promised lobster medallions, we found tiny morsels of lobster in our tomato essence, and a rabbit saddle tasted suspiciously like battery chicken. Excellent service and an imposing wine list are in keeping with the good reputation of the Schlössle.

PICOLIT 12/20
88131, Ludwigstr.7
(0 83 82) 2 37 28 res.
Closed Sunday, à la carte: 36/67. Tables d'hôte with wine: 49/69

Adriano Baldi's kitchen in this pretty, historic building in the old part of town commits itself to high-quality cuisine. Customers are welcomed with an appetizer (we had a fine vegetable terrine with foie gras) and all the pasta is homemade. The daily changing prix-fixe suggestions were low-priced and included ravioli stuffed with duck and served in rosemary sauce. The main courses à la carte cost less than 40 DM. The menu was small and indicated fresh products. Nothing extraordinary, but we liked our flavorful tomato essence. Sauces lacked a little refinement, and fish and meat correct seasoning. The small choice of wines includes German and Italian bottles.

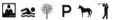

REUTEMANN
88131, Seepromenade
(0 83 82) 50 55, Fax 50 54

64, **S** 120/200, **D** 195/330,
1/2P +45, **P** +90

This elegant, spacious hotel is furnished like the Hotel Bayerischer Hof next door, which has the same owner. Yachting school nearby. Heated swimming pool.

SCHACHENER HOF 14/20
88131, Ortsteil Schachen
Schachener Str. 76
(0 83 82) 31 16, Fax 54 95

Closed for lunch every day except Sunday, closed Tuesday, Wednesday, 2 January through 8 February, 2—8 November. Tables d'hôte: 45/85, à la carte: 39/75

The stream of tourists on their way to the Hoyerberg passes by the quiet rural village of Schachern, and Thomas and Brigitte Kraus don't miss them. It would be a mistake to underestimate the amiable owner of the Schachener Hof, however. His cuisine is neither extravagant nor costly, and he prepares only high-quality (not always the most expensive) products and invests even everyday ingredients with a little glamour. The last time we ate here, the theme seemed to be rabbit: we liked kidney, fillet and aspic bedded on avocados, asparagus and leeks. His maties herring tartare was as delicious as the salmon slice in anchovy crust. Kraus' regional prix-fixe—smoked whitefish soup, roast beef and rhubarb cake in generous helpings—was a steal. Finely balanced sauces were highlights, including the caviar sauce served with the brook char or the slightly tangy hollandaise with fillet of beef. An unusual, tasty banana mousse and the choice wines from the respectably stocked cellar added to our enjoyment. The service is charming and friendly.

STOCKENWEILER 13/20
10km northeast in 88138
Stockenweiler/near the B12 motorway
(0 83 82) 2 43 res.

P

Closed for lunch, closed Thursday, 2 weeks in January and in June. Tables d'hôte: 90, à la carte: 53/85

Although this is a new beginning for him, Anton Lanz has returned to his old (bad) habits in the kitchen. Our terrific veal carpaccio with fried shrimp was drowned in soupy, salty tarragon butter sauce, and (overdone) turbot Provençal was "enriched" with cream and accompanied by asparagus dressed in an even more superfluous hollandaise. Our wonderful venison medallions stuffed with exquisite foie gras lost all their culinary charm in an ocean of morel sauce (consisting mostly of cream), and the "Champagne vinaigrette" with poppyseed mousse was discouraging. Top-quality produce and a few spurts of genius aren't substitutes for careful cooking and subtle seasoning. The competent, motivated service did its best to put us in a good mood again. We found enough French and Italian wines on the wine list, but only a few mediocre German wines and just three wines by the glass.

VILLINO 16/20
88131, Hoyerberg 34
(0 83 82) 50 22, Fax 64 40 res.

Closed for lunch, closed Monday, 3 weeks in January. Tables d'hôte: 82, à la carte: 63/84

Halfway up the Hoyerberg, Reiner Fischer has realized his Italian dream. Three years ago he bought the Villino, rebuilt and extended it until he was ready to start cooking. The kitchen of this intimate restaurant is tiny, but perfect organization prevents the cooks from treading on each other's toes. Sonja Fischer's service was professional and charming and she kept smiling even in the midst of the hectic bustle. We smiled back, because Reiner Fischer's cooking was reason enough to be happy here. His grilled scampi, pesto spaghettini, garlic tomatoes, duet of stuffed squid and scampi with tomato sauce, cannelloni with ricotta, and Taleggio cheese with potato strips soaked in grappa let him get close to authentic Italian cuisine. Fischer is an expert in cooking times and temperatures and showed a fine hand for herbs and seasoning. His anglerfish and lobster fried with cardamom, and leg of lamb with garlic were proof enough of that. The desserts were less transalpine and more German but, in any case, enticing. The wine list included vintages from France and Italy as well as the regions of Germany and other countries.

VILLINO

88131, Hoyerberg 34
(0 83 82) 50 22, Fax 64 40

12, **S** 140/200, **D** 220/260, **APP** 280/320

Closed 3 weeks in January

Very Italian, light, bright and flowery, this house is a relief for those tired of staying in anonymous palace hotels.

LINGEN Niedersachsen

Nordhorn 20 - Rheine 31

ALTES FORSTHAUS BECK 17/20

49809, Georgstr. 22
(05 91) 37 98 res.

Closed for lunch, closed Monday, first 3 weeks in January. Tables d'hôte: 59/139D, à la carte: 55/89

This old forester's house has left its last vestige of homely rusticity far behind. The elegant, manor-like exterior is the perfect complement for tasteful, artistic interior decoration we didn't expect in this part of the country. Bravo!We also salute Lothar Beck for trying to educate the competition: he gives courses in gourmet cooking. The third toque is our mark of esteem for Beck's cooking. His cuisine is imaginative, characterized by fresh regional produce and careful, light preparation. Beck doesn't compromise in shopping for the best ingredients, and he keeps both feet firmly yet creatively on the ground. Our last words are in praise of Erika Beck's charming service and her fantastic wine cellar.

LÖF Rheinl.-Pfalz

Koblenz 23 - Cochem 23

WEINHAUS GRIES 13/20

56332, Ortsteil Kattenes
Moselufer 14
(0 26 05) 6 46, Fax 16 43 res.

P 

Closed last 3 weeks in January. Tables d'hôte: 49L, 78/98D, à la carte: 39/72

The Moselle river flows quietly past the Weinhaus Gries, with its romantic view of Thurant castle and the vineyards. The interior of the Café Plüsch is plushy and comfortable, and you can enjoy your coffee and cake while looking at the artistic efforts of local painters. The new team cheerfully served herring with mango on pumpernickel and buttermilk terrine with marinated salmon. The fish ragout with a pastry crust looked a little sad on black plates, but the coq au vin cooked in Moselle Riesling was excellent. The tender, delicately seasoned fillet of venison was served in red Moselle wine with chanterelles, Teltow turnips and dumplings, and was followed by a dessert of mango and strawberries with the respective mousses. Norbert Hardenberg offers wines (by the glass, too) from the best Moselle vineyards.

LÖHNBERG Hessen

Limburg 16 - Wetzlar 23

ZUR KRONE 12/20

35792, Obertorstr. 1
(0 64 71) 60 70, Fax 6 21 07 res.

 P

Closed for lunch Wednesday and Friday. Tables d'hôte: 25/55L, 55/89D, à la carte: 24/60, No Credit Cards

This family-run hotel with its mighty tower is a landmark for tourists visiting nearby Weilstadt, a lovely Baroque town. The Schlosser family call this a gourmet restaurant, but friends of fine dining shouldn't take this too literally. Customers can expect good or better simple bourgeois fare, but not much refinement. Taking this into account, we were not disappointed. After a nondescript salad, we had good cream of broccoli soup, halibut coated with mushrooms with well-prepared vegetables, and veal steak with green asparagus and soggy *rösti*. The crème caramel tasted like yesterday's leftovers.

LÖNINGEN Niedersachsen

Cloppenburg 25 - Lingen 42

LE CHA CHA CHA 12/20

49624, Langenstr. 53
(0 54 32) 39 58, Fax 44 03 res.

Closed Monday. Tables d'hôte: 42/69, à la carte: 36/59

A dancing school in the same building explains this restaurant's odd name. Customers have a lot of room and privacy at spaciously placed tables. We found the fish soup with saffron lacking in flavor and superfluously enriched with vegetables and cream. Instead of the promised saffron sauce, our pike-perch in potato crust was served with an excellent basil sauce. We didn't mind the change as much as the cold dishes the food came on. Quail's breast with fried oyster mushrooms was tasty but could have used more seasoning. Throughout the whole meal, the kitchen offered a dispassionate cuisine, as if the cook didn't really care. His desserts, however, reached an imaginative climax with strawberries, marzipan sauce and vanilla ice cream. The service is friendly, and the wine list contains many wines that are "out of stock." Dancing school probably makes customers very thirsty.

LÖRRACH Bad.-Württ.

Basel (CH) 10 - Karlsruhe 200

INZLINGER WASSERSCHLOSS 15/20

6km southeast in 79594 Inzlingen
Riehenstr. 5
(0 76 21) 4 70 57, Fax 1 35 33 res.

Closed Tuesday, Wednesday, mid-July through the beginning of August. Tables d'hôte:59L, 105D, 145, à la carte: 57/96

Sepp Beha isn't the world's greatest experimental cook and is something of a perfectionist, but when he comes out of his shell, he creates marvelous compositions. Our lasagna turned out to be a rare delicacy: four or five tiny al dente pasta plates colored and arranged like the Italian flag, accompanied by scallops, lobster and trout caviar and served with a lovely white-wine sauce. The other dishes are fine, too, like beef carpaccio with truffles and Parmesan, delicious Bresse pigeon with saffron rice, a hearty grilled codfish, veal cutlet, entrecôte and suckling lamb. Pear strudel with vanilla sauce was an appropriate dessert. The variety isn't as great as in other places, but the quality is very good. What Beha recommends is better than the choice on the menu. The customers, mostly Swiss, don't mind paying high prices for the unique surroundings in a castle on the water. The service is personalized, and the wine list has grown to encompass more French and Italian wines.

VILLA ELBEN

79539, Hünerbergweg 26
(0 76 21) 20 66, 8 47 66, Fax 4 32

34 rooms, **S** 105/120, **D** 140/160

A modern new building has been added to this lovely Art Nouveau villa located in a large, quiet park on the outskirts of Lörrach. All the rooms have balconies and a nice view of the park. This comfortable hotel is just the right thing if you like quiet and a touch of nostalgia.

ZUM KRANZ 12/20

79540, Basler Str. 90
(0 76 21) 8 90 83, Fax 1 48 43 res.

Closed Sunday, Monday. Tables d'hôte: 40L, 45D, à la carte: 25/75

Standards are not rising, but they aren't going down, either. This popular restaurant remains true to its tried-and-true recipe: respectable quality for a reasonable price. Günter Rosskopf's talents really come to the fore when he cooks prearranged festive dinners. At noon he offers a variety of plain, simple dishes, all well-prepared, from the *rösti* and liver to fine fish. The sweetbreads with our salad tasted deep-fried. Oxtail soup, grilled halibut with lovely hollandaise and crème caramel were good. The summer terrace is lovely, and the service attentive.

LOHMAR Nordrh.-Westf.

Bonn 15 - Köln 25

HAUS AM BERG 12/20

53797, Ortsteil Honrath
Zum Kammerberg 22-24
(0 22 06) 22 38, Fax 17 86 res.

 P

Closed for lunch Saturday, closed Sunday. Tables d'hôte: 65L, 75/110D, à la carte: 48/80

This little place is hidden between Lohmar and Overath and you may be half-starved by the time you get there. Maybe that explains why the portions are so immense. The charming German-Belgian couple who own the restaurant want to do things differently than the competition. A small menu disguised as a letter, a handwritten wine list, and a countrified ambience with antiques and elegantly laid tables make customers feel at home. A sunny terrace, delicious nut bread, tasty appetizers, and the pleasant anticipation of being able to spend the night here as well make this a gem of country hospitality in the vicinity of the big cities on the Rhine. We would have preferred a less copious but more delicate and disciplined cuisine. The first-class sweetbreads with spinach didn't need mozzarella, and our perfectly fried turbot would have tasted better without a heavy, rich gratin and beans wrapped in bacon. After a heavy bombardment with countless calories we were surprised at a light dessert platter that was more than just a treat for the eye.

LONGUICH Rheinl.-Pfalz

Trier 13 - Wittlich 25

RESTAURANT ROBERT 13/20

54340, Auf der Festung
(0 65 02) 49 20, Fax 63 13 res.

Closed for dinner Sunday, closed Monday, 3 weeks during the Rh.-Pf. summer school holiday. Tables d'hôte: 48/95, à la carte: 32/83

This restaurant is located in a stately house in the middle of town. With its dark furniture and discreet decor, the dining room has a tasteful, modern ambience. Mrs. Robert supervises the quiet but ever-present service staff, while Joachim Robert's domain is the kitchen. Creative fish dishes are his strong point, and they are simply excellent, without frills or flourish. His salad of shrimps and salmon was served much too cold, but the meat pâté seasoned with wine was perfect. We were hardly satisfied with an overdone saddle of lamb with a salty sauce. The almond soufflé with Amaretto and white chocolate mousse, however, was a final highlight of the meal. The wine list offers many regional wines that can also be ordered by the glass. Specialties of the house are the large selection of grappas and fruity Longuich liqueurs.

LUDWIGSBURG BW

Stuttgart 17 - Heilbronn 38

ALTE SONNE 12/20

71634, Bei der kath. Kirche 3
(0 71 41) 92 52 31/2, Fax 90 26 35 res.

P

Closed Tuesday, 8—24 January. Tables d'hôte: 50/65, 90/120D, à la carte: 35/81, Tables d'hôte with wine: 150

The old sun (Alte Sonne) is polished and shines brightly, especially the modernized kitchen we could see through the glass door. The renovated restaurant seemed a little more austere and not as comfortably cozy as before: the obvious elegance still needs a personal touch. We had rabbit leg with (barely warm) mushroom tartare, vegetable *gugl-hupf* with thin slices of smoked duck's breast, dark and bitter soup of king prawns, and perfectly grilled salmon with a delicious asparagus ragout. The trilogy of sweetbreads, tongue and headcheese in a white wine sauce with soggy noodles was disappointing, the roast beef with onions was overdone, and breast and leg of duck were tough.

BUGATTI IN THE SCHLOSSHOTEL MONREPOS 14/20

71634, Im Schloßpark
(0 71 41) 30 20, Fax 30 22 00 res.

P

Closed for lunch, closed Sunday, 1—8 January. Tables d'hôte: 70, à la carte: 45/78

The appetizer of scampi, scampi terrine, cherry tomato stuffed with caviar and white bread with tomato, olive oil, garlic and basil was an opulent welcome. The shrimp salad with fresh mint leaves was tasty, and the antipasti with salmon, San Daniele ham and dried beef were delicious. We were enraptured by the mousses of salmon, avocado and anglerfish that accompanied a little salad of scallops, and found nothing to criticize in the game consommé with *panzarotti* (deep-fried ravioli with three kinds of cheese), fresh pea soup with shrimp, or savory carrot soup with champagne. Stuffed duckling with balsamic vinegar and glazed grapes, figs and puréed chestnuts, and the lamb ribs in a crust of cèpes with rosemary and potato gratin are highly commendable. We were a little disappointed with the fish potpourri because the sauce was too salty and the risotto too dry, but the fish fried with rosemary was superb. Some desserts were a bit too sweet. The limited wine list offers Italian wines from Alto Adige to Sicily, and the prices are in keeping with the cultivated ambience.

SCHLOSSHOTEL MONREPOS

71634, Im Schloßpark
(0 71 41) 30 20, Fax 30 22 00

81, **S** 160/260, **D** 200/340, **APP** 380/520, **½P** +35, **P** +70 *Closed 24 December through 8 January*

"Repos" means more a respite from travel than quiet rest here. Guests who sleep in rooms facing west can't help but hear the busy autobahn nearby. Otherwise the rooms are comfortable and for the most part elegantly furnished. The indoor pool leads to the garden outside. Nearby golf course.

LE CARAT 15/20

71636, Schwieberdinger Str. 60
(0 71 41) 4 76 00, Fax 47 60 60

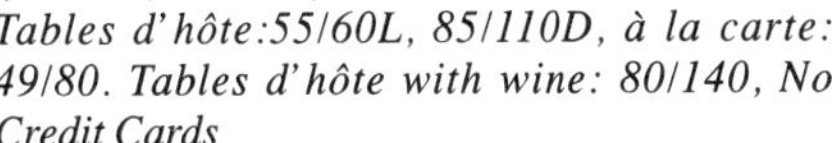

Tables d'hôte:55/60L, 85/110D, à la carte: 49/80. Tables d'hôte with wine: 80/140, No Credit Cards

After you've taken the elevator up to the fifth floor, you'll be enchanted by the spacious dining room with a lovely bar and French windows. This layout looks expensive but by no means posh or pompous. A sommelier offered choice wines from a well-stocked cellar at moderate prices, and the talented chef served delicate tomato mousse with wine jelly and sour cream, warm salmon carpaccio with a dressing of tomato and basil, and excellent red mullet with asparagus and spinach accompanied by tasty Beaujolais sauce. Our veal fillet was unexciting and didn't harmonize with its vegetable risotto, but the pigeon we had was superb, as was our dessert: marbled cheese soufflé with brandy-laced pear.

LUDWIGSLUST Meckl.-Vorp.

Perleberg 35 - Schwerin 36

PARK-HOTEL

19288, Kanalstr. 19
(0 38 74) 2 20 15, Fax 2 01 56

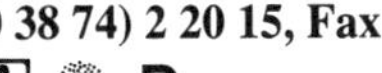

19, **S** 70/90, **D** 100/120

The lovely landscaped park of the Ludwigslust palace is the largest in Mecklenburg and is a popular tourist excursion. The house brochure of the nice-looking Park-Hotel promises much more than it delivers. The hotel is a bit noisy, but passably furnished. The prices are too high for what is offered here. Restaurant.

REST. FRITZ REUTER IN HOTEL ERBPRINZ 13/20

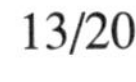 

19288, Schweriner Str. 38
(0 38 74) 4 71 74, Fax 2 91 60

Tables d'hôte: 45, à la carte: 24/50

We were pleasantly stunned on our most recent visit to this restaurant. The place had undergone a sensational change: no more floury sauces, standard East German fare, canned vegetables, ghastly salad garnishes, burnt steaks or fake oak furniture. Instead, we enjoyed a savory beef consommé, delicious chicken breast with basil sauce and green noodles, and a fruit salad. The growing wine list offers good names at low prices. Attentive and pleasant service.

HOTEL ERBPRINZ

19288, Schweriner Str. 38
(0 38 74) 4 71 74, Fax 2 91 60

P

36, **S** 135/185, **D** 210/230, **APP** 280/380, **½P** +25, **P** +50

This castle in Ludwigslust and the extensive park don't have to be viewed in a hurry any more. We recommend a stay in this new hotel with international standards and a tasteful interior. The service is excellent. The hotel is connected to a shopping mall with hairdresser, beauty farm, doctors, stores. Breakfast: 15 DM.

STADT HAMBURG 11/20

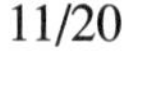

19288, Letzte Str. 4-6
(0 38 74) 41 50, Fax 2 30 57

à la carte: 13/36, No Credit Cards

A tastefully redecorated dining room with wooden paneling is the right place for hungry guests. And they have to be hungry to tackle the enormous portions that are served here, where quantity is more important than quality. The service is very friendly. We recommend that you order Lübzer beer rather than the wines offered.

HOTEL STADT HAMBURG

19288, Letze Str. 4-6
(0 38 74) 41 50, Fax 2 30 57

33 (23), S 40/85, **D** 60/130
No Credit Cards

If you want to spend some time visiting the remarkable Ludwigslust Palace, we recommend a stay at the Hotel Stadt Hamburg. The rooms in the old building have been tastefully renovated; those in the new wing are cheaper but smaller.

LÜBBENAU Brandenburg

Cottbus 32 - Berlin 94

SCHLOSS LÜBBENAU

03222, Clara-Zetkin-Str. 8
(0 35 42) 87 30, Fax 87 36 66

53 (41), **S** 119/150, **D** 200/270,
APP 290, **½P** +35, **P** +60

This palace offers modern, comfortable rooms in its east wing. The management obviously couldn't wait to finish the planned renovation, with new whirlpools, saunas and tennis courts, before raising the prices. The hotel has a quiet location and a marvelous view of the park.

LÜBECK Schleswig-Holstein

Hamburg 65 - Kiel 79

HOTEL KAISERHOF

23560, Kronsforder Allee 11-13
(04 51) 79 10 11, Fax 79 50 83

65, **S** 135/180, **D** 180/225,
APP 240/390

These two renovated mansions house a modern hotel with all conveniences. The rooms are nicely furnished.

DAS KLEINE RESTAURANT 13/20

23552, An der Untertrave 39
(04 51) 70 59 59, Fax 70 59 59 res.

Closed for lunch, closed Sunday. Tables d'hôte: 50, à la carte: 39/75

Gourmets in Lübeck throng to this stylishly rustic little restaurant. They all want to try the incredibly low-priced, weekly changing prix-fixe consisting of 10 small courses. We had marinated salmon, fish ravioli, white bean and mussel salad, pork fillet with spinach and gorgonzola sauce, roast beef roulade with Burgundy sauce, and lime cream with puréed raspberries, to mention just a few dishes. The style of the cuisine is hearty and savory, but the food is finely prepared, tasty, and beautifully arranged. Besides the prix-fixe, there's also salmon with puff pastry or saddle of lamb with paprika and thyme sauce à la carte. The wine list emphasizes German and French vintages and offers a good choice of wines by the glass. The service is competent and charming.

MÖVENPICK

23554, Beim Holstentor
(04 51) 1 50 40, Fax 1 50 41 11

197, **S** 160/205, **D** 200/245,
APP 250/330, **½P** +27, **P** +50/54

This hotel, built in the 1950s, is located within sight of the Holstentor. Air-conditioned conference rooms. Restaurant. Breakfast buffet: 21 DM.

RIST. ROBERTO ROSSI 11/20

23552, Mühlenstr. 9
(04 51) 7 07 09 08, Fax 70 45 39 res.

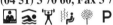

Closed Sunday, January. Tables d'hôte: 42/75, à la carte: 34/66

Some things that come out of Rossi's kitchen are really good, like his succulent anglerfish medallions with cèpes and venison medallions with steamed Belgian endives and Marsala sauce. But the kitchen staff slips up time and time again, especially in the seasoning of main courses: oyster mushrooms and rabbit fillet lost the battle against a domineering pepper sauce, and the duck fillet that came with the lentil soup was overdone. Attentive service and some finds on the wine list make the cooking easier to bear.

SCANDIC CROWN HOTEL

23568, Travemünder Allee 3
(04 51) 3 70 60, Fax 3 70 66 66

 P

159, **S** 160/230, **D** 160/305, **APP** 495, **1/2P** +35, **P** +70

Scandinavian hospitality, attractive ambience, first-class service and comfort characterize this new hotel near the center of town. The rooms are air-conditioned and offer all the modern amenities. Conference center, solarium, fitness club, bar, restaurants. Breakfast: 25 DM.

SCHABBELHAUS 11/20

23552, Mengstr. 48-50
(04 51) 7 29 11, Fax 7 59 51

Closed Monday. Tables d'hôte: 35L, 55D, à la carte: 40/73. Tables d'hôte with wine (for 2): 111.11

We couldn't help our sour faces on our last visit: somebody in the kitchen had a soft spot for vinegar. Penetratingly sour marinated crayfish were accompanied by almost equally tangy rutabaga parfait. The shrimp ragout in strudel was a treat for the eye, but we should have kept looking at it: the strudel hid but a few glassy shrimp accompanied by a vinegary lentil side dish. The wine list emphasizes great French wines, but we would have liked some new discoveries as well. The service is correct.

SCHIFFERGESELLSCHAFT 11/20

23552, Breite Str. 2
(04 51) 7 67 76, Fax 7 32 79 res.

Closed Monday, à la carte: 26/69, No Credit Cards.

Most tourists visit the traditional *gasthaus* in this historic building with an imposing gabled front that dates to 1535. Kitchen and service are constantly stressed-out, so don't expect culinary perfection. We've had better scampi cream soup with salmon crepes, and our mackerel fillet with salmon mousse, sauerkraut and Savoy cabbage was a haphazard and unharmonious combination. The lamb with green beans, however, was good, and the strawberry and rhubarb gratin with cherry and pumpernickel parfait consoled us. The choice of French and German wines is adequate.

SENATOR HOTEL

23554, Willy-Brandt-Allee 6
(04 51) 14 20, Fax 1 42 22 22

 P

226, **S** 175/255, **D** 225/296, **APP** 450/800, **1/2P** +35, **P** +70

The architecture of this hotel, centrally located on the peninsula between Holsten harbor and the city moat, is a fascinating contrast to that of the historic old part of town facing the Trave. Breakfast: 22 DM.

ÜBER DEN WOLKEN IN THE MARITIM HOTEL 14/20

23570, Stadtteil Travemünde
Trelleborgallee 2
(04 51) 89 20 35, Fax 7 44 39 res.

P

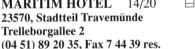

Closed for lunch, closed Sunday, 3 weeks in January. Tables d'hôte: 98, à la carte: 69/105

The change of chefs hasn't hurt the Maritim's restaurant at all. We would also welcome a change from the traditional classic cuisine to something more imaginative, and we would like to see more attention paid to sauces, which could be lighter and more flavorful. But we like eating here, especially the pigeon with marinated oyster mushrooms or venison saddle with Chinese cabbage. The panoramic view from the 35th floor, discreet live music and perfect service make a visit worthwhile. Ask for new wines not yet on the well-stocked list and you might be in for some surprises.

WULLENWEVER 16/20

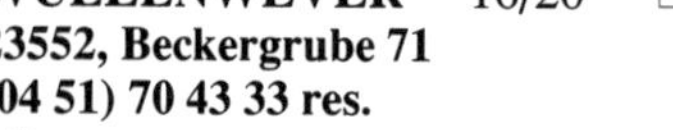

23552, Beckergrube 71
(04 51) 70 43 33 res.

Closed for lunch Saturday, closed Sunday, Monday. Tables d'hôte: 35L, 78/98D, à la carte: 40/86

Roy Petermann's dilemma isn't unusual for cooks of his talent and caliber: sometimes he prepares dishes for a full house, and other times he twiddles his thumbs in an empty restaurant. Because he can't calculate in advance his customers' appetites or their visits to his restaurant, some slips in his cuisine are almost unavoidable. The last spoonfuls of his clear oxtail consommé and ingenious ravioli stuffed with beef fillet were a little salty, and our anglerfish fried in basil didn't seem to be absolutely fresh. With a more succulent pigeon, the heavenly foie gras sauce would have been better appreciated. But the highlights prevailed: subtly seasoned vegetable salad with sole and coriander, wonderfully fresh scallops with leeks and dreamy vanilla and Sauternes butter, and extravagant and excellent noodles seasoned with Asian spices and served with succulent lobster. The service is excellent and well-informed. The wine list is improving steadily and now also offers an interesting choice of medium-priced wines.

LÜDENSCHEID NRW

Hagen 28 - Gummersbach 32

PETERSILIE 17/20

58511, Loher Str. 19
(0 23 51) 8 32 31, Fax 86 18 73 res.

P

Closed Sunday, Monday, 1st through mid-January. Tables d'hôte: 35/45L, 82/140D, à la carte: 55/89

This twig of "Petersilie" (parsley) has grown magnificently. Its lovely aroma draws guests from the big cities on the Rhine as well as from the Sauerland. A visit to the white manor house on a hilltop is enough to satisfy most gourmet fantasies. The cuisine is simple but refined and creative. Mediterranean and regional influences add character to Salzmann's cooking. The prices are fair, and the kitchen respects the individual wishes of its customers. We chose our favorites from three separate meal suggestions: shrimp wrapped in won-ton, smoked salmon tart, gazpacho with sautéed scampi, followed by oxtail aspic with balsamic vinegar. A fantastic highlight was the fried fillet of John Dory with artichokes, olives and basil—haute cuisine can be this simple. We loved the steamed fillet of sea trout with turnips, the roulade of baby chicken with kohlrabi, and the colorful stew with lamb from the salt meadows. With his almost unequalled sauces, Manfred Salzmann creates a lasting impression. Pastries and desserts are of high quality as well. There is also a bistro-style *Tafelstübchen,* where you can have good but simpler lunches and dinners.The wine cellar is well-stocked and offers a sufficient number of half-bottles.

LÜNEN Nordrh.-Westf.

Dortmund 15 -Münster 48

SCHLOSS SCHWANSBELL 15/20

44532, Schwansbeller Weg 32
(0 23 06) 20 68 10, Fax 2 34 54 res.

 **P**

Closed for lunch Saturday and Sunday, closed Monday. Tables d'hôte: 49L, 58/96D, à la carte: 52/75, No Credit Cards

Lünen's bureaucrats have taken over the castle, which now houses the municipal government. Franz Lauter, cook, poet and painter, has to be satisfied with an outbuilding, but he has decorated his restaurant in a truly aristocratic manner. With his rakish hat, artistic beard and Silesian dialect, he seems more like the legendary mountain ogre Rübezahl than the would-be lord of this castle. Lauter makes an event out of eating. His menu is lyrical, and the artistic counterparts of his culinary creations decorate his dining room. To represent his delicious "salad tower of Babel" he built a tower of old cooking utensils with a magic-lantern peep show inside. He is also an artist in his kitchen, especially when he leads the way into "vegetarian paradise" with delicately tangy vegetable aspics and light and savory tofu terrines. But we were just as entranced by his ravioli with blood pudding filling. The culinary trip into the deep sea was not nearly as exciting, however. The pike-perch did not take to his bed of rhubarb and oranges and neither did we. We liked the painting of veal roulade with okra and mozzarella much better than the real thing. Terrific desserts saved Lauter's second toque from falling down, and his fantastic pastries deserved nothing but the highest praise.The comprehensive wine list with its grand choice of wines by the glass leaves nothing to be desired, except perhaps a few more of the best Bordeaux. The youthful service has its weak points and should be better informed about the stock in the wine cellar.

MAGDEBURG SAH

Braunschweig 70 - Berlin 112

GOETHESTRASSE 

39108, Goethestr. 49
(03 91) 34 47 77, 3 29 87, Fax 3 35 77

 P

30 rooms, **S** 105/165, **D** 155/225,
APP 205/330, **½P** +22, **P** +47

This well-cared for hotel offers comfortable rooms, salons, a conference center, restaurant and bar. The service is very friendly and the breakfast buffet more than ample.

MARITIM HOTEL MAGDEBURG 

39104, Otto-von-Guericke-Str. 87
(03 91) 5 94 90, Fax 5 94 99 90

S 229/389, **D** 258,
APP 488/568, **½P** +40, **P** +70
Re-opening 6 April 1995

This hotel was torn down in November 1993, and the new building should open April 1, 1995, with the above-mentioned prices. Breakfast: 22 DM.

DIE SAISON IN HOTEL HERRENKRUG 13/20 

39114, Herrenkrugstr. 194
(03 91) 8 50 80

P

Tables d'hôte: 15/54, à la carte: 23/68

This big, beautiful Art Nouveau dining hall on the ground floor of the Hotel Herrenkrug offers a distinguished ambience for noble dining. Lother Winter serves a cuisine that strives to match. We had first-class home-smoked salmon with mustard and dill dip, hare with ravioli, perfectly poached pike-perch with herbs, and a duet of pink, succulent beef and overdone, dry pork fillet with Calvados and pepper sauce. The potato cakes and vegetables with the fillets tasted suspiciously deep-fried. More attention to details and fresher products would make high-class cuisine out of what is merely good cooking. Even when the house is full, the admirable service remains pleasant, cheerful and competent, and takes time to advise. The good choice of international wines includes the best vintages from famous wineries at incredibly low prices as well as many good wines by the glass and half-bottles.

HERRENKRUG 

39114, Herrenkrugstr. 194
(03 91) 8 50 80,

P

159 rooms, **S** 225/285, **D** 265/325,
APP 450/570,

It cost 6.5 million DM to rebuild this ruined house. The hotel now has a large, beautiful lobby with a piano bar and luxuriously furnished rooms and suites with large desks, as well as hookups for fax machines and computers. Almost all rooms afford a lovely view of the grounds. Conference rooms, health center, fitness facilities.

SAVARIN 12/20

39104, Breiter Weg 226
(03 91) 34 47 10, Fax 3 01 87 res.
Closed Sunday, 15 July—15 August. Tables d'hôte: 38/65L, 40/120D, à la carte: 15/54. Tables d'hôte with wine: 70

Highlights of our meal here were fresh steamed salmon (nice, but not sensational), excellent venison medallions with mushroom cream sauce, and sweet pancakes with strawberries and whipped cream. Most side dishes were a disappointment.The service staff in this comfortable little restaurant is always friendly and competent. The great wine list offers a good number of international vintages at affordable prices and a large choice of wines by the glass.

MAINTAL Hessen

Hanau 10 - Frankfurt 13

HESSLER 18/20 

63477, Ortsteil Dörnigheim
Am Bootshafen 4
(0 61 81) 4 30 30, Fax 43 03 33

P

Closed Sunday, Monday, 3 weeks in July. Tables d'hôte: 48L, 90D, à la carte: 66/101

Creative Doris Hessler never gets tired of trying out new ideas. Maybe that's why her capable kitchen team is still highly motivated, even though the Hesslers have been cooking here for 25 years. Our enterprising *patronne* has fallen in love again. This time, her liaison with exotic cuisines created exiting new taste sensations. Her marinated saddle of lamb with pronounced Arabic seasoning, lentils and dates let us experience the flavors of 1,001 nights. Anglerfish medallions with coconut rice and peanut sauce were seasoned with spicy Thai finesse, and fried prawns wrapped in a wonton and served with foamy ginger sauce were a treat for a gourmet's palate.In spite of her love for Asia, Doris Hessler has not let culinary elements from the Far East take over her cuisine. Far from having left the path of the healthy cuisine she favors, she's given it new impetus: wheat pancakes as an appetizer, whole wheat noodles as a side dish, a terrine of yogurt and herbs with seafood and watercress salad and, as always, a lovely salad of sprouts and flowers. Regional dishes are particularly light here (green sauce with quail and quail's egg) and seasonal creations especially flavorful, like lasagna with fresh mushrooms from the nearby woods. Lamb from the dike meadows in a crust of pesto and saddle of mountain goat in a gingerbread coating were delicious, but we found the desserts far from spectacular and not always even good. The steadily growing wine list is orgiastic, and an Italian sommelier advises with competence and charm.Many guests who in the past would have liked to order another bottle from the formidable cellar will be glad to hear about the six hotel rooms decorated in Art Deco style above the restaurant. Opulent breakfast. Rooms cost from 160 to 225 DM.

MAINZ Rheinland-Pfalz

Frankfurt 40 - Kaiserslautern 78

DREI LILIEN 12/20

55116, Ballplatz 2
(0 61 31) 22 50 68, Fax 23 77 23 res.

P

Closed Sunday, Monday. Tables d'hôte: 39/50L, 50/115D, à la carte: 39/87

Chef Hans Joachim Stuhlmiller is completely taken up with his catering service. Photos, newspaper articles and advertisements on the restaurant's walls document his success outside of his own premises: his chic and rich clientele in Mainz like this service, which promises to "cook anything you want."The house cuisine isn't any less creative than Stuhlmiller's catering operation. Nut oil on our delicious salmon and scallop carpaccio may have been original, but imagination took precedence over good taste. Our fish terrine looked and tasted wonderful—until we got to the "centerpiece," a raw, rubbery piece of sole. The strongly flavored olive crust smothered the delicate perch from Lake Victoria underneath it. The veal kidneys with bread dumplings looked and tasted like the Sunday dinner Mom used to make. The desserts are tasty if you don't pay close attention to details like lumps in the orange sherbet. The service is quick and capable. The 210 DM for a 1980 Château La Lagune isn't a mistake on the wine list, but a joke.

L'ECHALOTE 12/20

55116, Bahnhofsplatz 6
(0 61 31) 61 43 31, Fax 67 28 06

P

Closed Sunday. Tables d'hôte: 89/120, à la carte: 54/90

Like a salesman praising the vacuum cleaner he wants you to buy, voluble maître d' Günter Bornheimer advises his customers (whether they like it or not) and pushes his cuisine. Since his talented chef, Michael Knöll, left the kitchen, this seems to be necessary. We were satisfied with pigeon salad with young onions and almond sauce, an unremarkable carpaccio of scallops and salmon, good fried ray wing and a bulky beef fillet in Burgundy sauce with delicious sweetbreads. But our duck's breast and lamb medallions with Parma ham and sage and boring potato gratin were no highlight. A whole carrot in a vegetable side dish gave us an indication of just how motivated and enthusiastic the kitchen crew was! Our anglerfish swam in a soupy sauce that was called Riesling crème, and the chocolate sauce for desserts was much too sweet. Günter Bornheimer, at least, is convinced of the high quality of his cuisine and charges exorbitant prices. The wine list includes more than a few bottles past their prime; the German Burgundy the maître d' recommended had definitely seen better days.

GÄNSTHALER'S KUCHLMASTEREI 12/20

55116, Stadtteil Finthen
Kurmainzstr. 35
(0 61 31) 47 42 75, Fax 47 92 13 res.

 P

Tables d'hôte: 58/68L, 62/75D, à la carte: 36/75

The run on the Kuchlmasterei hasn't abated, even though the cuisine has come to a standstill. Diners like the unpretentious and relaxed atmosphere in these pleasant dining rooms. Some of the decorative bric-a-brac is highly original, but the choice of dishes is much less imaginative—especially since Karl Gänsthaler has withdrawn some of his good and hearty regional specialties from the menu. The *tafelspitz,* however, was tender and delicious, even if the somewhat pungent horseradish spoiled our pleasure. Fillets of veal and beef were tasty and accompanied by a light, lovely cognac sauce, whereas the market vegetables turned out to be just the usual garnish. Lamb's lettuce with potato dressing and smoked goose breast slices were much more exciting than the pancakes with jam for dessert. The wine list has lost much of its attraction since the best Austrian wineries are no longer listed. The service is correct and decisive.

DER HALBE MOND 13/20

55116, Stadtteil Kastel
in der Witz 12
(0 61 31) 2 39 13, Fax 64 58 res.

P

Closed for lunch, closed Sunday and holidays, beginning through mid-January. Tables d'hôte: 65, à la carte: 40/69

This restaurant, whose name means "half moon," is one of the highlights of the Mainz gourmet scene. We've always liked the simple, elegant decor and the idyllic beer garden, and we have appreciated the obliging and unobtrusive service here. At our last visit, the kitchen won us over too. We awarded our toque for a light champagne cream soup with young onions, perfectly done prawns with good saffron sauce, colorful salads with excellent vinaigrette, and tender veal fillet with aromatic gorgonzola sauce. Our duck's breast with Asian vegetables was tasty, whereas the saddle of lamb encrusted with herbs wasn't as tender as it should have been.The wine list has grown and now includes (besides wines from the Rheingau) other German regions, Italy and France. Connoisseurs can find a deal once in a while, since the wines are priced as moderately as the dishes on the menu.

MEISSNER'S RESTAURANT IN LEININGER HOF 12/20

55116, Weintorstr. 6
(0 61 31) 22 84 84, Fax 23 45 41 res.

Closed for lunch, closed Sunday. Tables d'hôte: 65/95, à la carte: 40/75

Maître Meissner is one of those chefs who have to "try and try again" to finally make the grade. The ambience, at least, is perfect: a vaulted, elegantly furnished cellar in the middle of the Old Town. The cuisine is good, though far from perfect, with lots of ups and downs. Our small king prawns weren't absolutely fresh, but—as if this would make up for it—overdone, whereas the vinaigrette on the salad was finely balanced. We were also satisfied with glazed chicken slivers on summer salads. Our fish potpourri consisted of succulent salmon, good pike-perch and tough lobster. The rabbit in Calvados sauce could have been juicier.The service needs more self confidence—and more information from the kitchen, so simple questions can be answered without having to ask the chef first. The wine list is more informative, but the Bordeaux are still too expensive. We're not going to spend 138 DM for a second-best wine from Château Palmer!

RHEINGRILL IN THE MAINZ HILTON 13/20

55116, Rheinstr. 68
(0 61 31) 24 51 29, Fax 24 55 89
Closed Monday, Tuesday, July/August. Tables d'hôte: 44L, 60D, à la carte: 50/87. Tables d'hôte with wine: 43/69

This restaurant, with its subtle indirect lighting, domed ceiling, exquisite china, fine Christofle silver and a marvelous view of the majestic Rhine, is something palatial. The obsequious headwaiter, who can always amuse guests (or royalty?) with a charming little anecdote, also fits perfectly into the picture of a gourmet temple. And the cuisine does its best. We had delicate, delicious foie gras with nondescript rabbit aspic, excellent turbot with flavorful truffled vinaigrette and tasty paprika essence with potatoes. The main courses weren't quite as good: nicely fried venison medallions and somewhat pale and flat-tasting pheasant with delicious leeks and potatoes. The sorbets with puréed fruit were good, but nothing special.The headwaiter here is an institution: charming, professional and always human. The wine list should be revised. Apparently this is an area where the restaurant wants to save money. More often than not, bottles are out of stock, and there's not a choice of wines by the glass on the menu. Half bottles are also scarce. The cheap glasses might have been bought at a Woolworth's sale.

MAINZ HILTON

55116, Rheinstr. 68
(0 61 31) 24 51 29, Fax 24 55 89
P
433, **S** 260/380, **D** 260/430,
APP 1300/1600, **½P** +70, **P** +113

The original hotel and the new building across the street are connected by a covered walkway. The former is located on the Rhine and boasts its own landing for passenger boats; the latter has an attractive bar, restaurant, lobby lounge and modern conference facilities. If you want a view of the river, ask for a room in the original building. The hotel has direct access to the casino. Breakfast: 19-26 DM.

MANNHEIM Baden-Württ.

Heidelberg 15 - Karlsruhe 70

BLASS 14/20

68165, Friedrichsplatz 12
(06 21) 44 80 04, Fax 40 49 99 res.
Closed for lunch Saturday, closed Sunday, 2—20 August. Tables d'hôte: 70/80L, 90/110D, à la carte: 56/89

Its elegant ambience makes this restaurant one of the two best in Mannheim. The maître d'hôtel, however, in contrast to his sedate surroundings, can be nonchalant and casual. At our last visit he loudly entertained old friends at a neighboring table and left us at the mercy of a nice young waitress. The excellent meal made us forget the maître d'hôtel, however. We enjoyed cream of potato soup, salmon roulade filled with scampi and fried in thyme with leek strips, a superb entrecôte with shiitake mushrooms, and a wonderful variety of desserts. The wines are well-chosen but somewhat high-priced.

DA GIANNI 18/20

68161, R7, 34
(06 21) 2 03 26 res.
P
Closed Monday, 3 weeks following the end of July. Tables d'hôte: 98L,148D, à la carte: 67/104

Gianni's is not just an institution in Mannheim, but is also one of the best Italian restaurants in Germany. Situated centrally near the Rosengarten and the famous water tower, it is as functional and elegant as a restaurant of this class should be. Wolfgang Staudenmaier brought Gianni's cuisine to the top. From time to time, we hear rumors that he is leaving and setting up his own business. We hope he stays, not only because we like his cooking, but also because he has enough leeway here to experiment with all types of regional Italian cuisine and does not have to bother about anything but his kitchen.Staudenmaier is a whiz with fish and crustaceans. Be sure to try his daily menu suggestions. We went into raptures over the ravioli filled with truffled oxtail stuffing and home-baked olive bread with all of the fish first courses. His appetizer (sardines, ham, John Dory with flaked potatoes) is a work of art, the chicken consommé delicate, and bass in salt crust just fantastic. All of the side dishes are absolutely fresh and perfectly done. Staudenmaier's duckling and pigeon are as good as his fish, and while the desserts are not quite up to par, the pastry is much better than it was. Only the best Italian wines are served, but be careful when ordering older vintages, since the Italian wines do not always age well.

DOBLER'S RESTAURANT L'EPI D'OR 15/20 
68159, H7, 3
(06 21) 1 43 97 res.

P

Closed for lunch Saturday, closed Sunday, closed for lunch Monday, closed 2 weeks at the end of July and 2 weeks after Christmas. Tables d'hôte: 38/128L, 108/132D, à la carte: 56/91

Dobler has his own recession-beating recipe: he lends a hand in his own kitchen. His repertoire includes pigeon breast, foie gras or lobster as first course, and turbot, John Dory, duck's breast, rabbit legs or loin of lamb as main courses. Businesspeople in a hurry often lunch here, paying 38 DM for a two-course meal. We chose pigeon breast with sesame seeds served with dandelions, John Dory with green asparagus, and ribs of suckling lamb with shallots and tiny potatoes. With a full house and Dobler alone in the kitchen, sometimes there is no time for the meat juices to settle. We forgave him readily as we tasted our superb dessert of exquisitely stuffed dates with homemade coconut ice and coffee sauce. The choice of cheeses is as perfect as the petits fours with coffee. Pastel colors contribute to a cheerful ambience, with very pleasant service. The comprehensive wine list is moderately priced.

GRISSINI 13/20
68161, M3/6
(06 21) 1 56 57 24 res.

Closed for lunch Saturday, closed Sunday, 22 December through 3 January, 3 weeks in August. Tables d'hôte: 28L, à la carte: 46/74

Menu and wine list here are rather mediocre, but Gianfranco Melideo's friendly and expansive welcome makes the atmosphere buoyantly Italian. The tartare of head-cheese in pastry as appetizer was outstanding, and we were pleasantly surprised by the first course platter, which offered such delicacies as salmon tartare, beef carpaccio and duck's breast. We liked the fennel cream soup with salmon strips, but found the consommé with poached fillet of beef humdrum. The lamb ribs in potato crust were much better. The service is pleasant and unobtrusive, and the friendly way Melideo says good bye makes you want to come again.

JÄGERLUST 13/20 
68199, Stadtteil Neckarau
Friedrichstr. 90
(06 21) 85 22 35, Fax 85 64 11 res.

Closed for lunch Saturday, closed Sunday, Monday, end of August/mid-Spetember. Tables d'hôte: 65L, 120D, à la carte: 50/93

It has a rather unattractive location in the industrial part of town, but the Jägerlust is still a good place to eat, especially on summer days when its wonderful orchard attracts plenty of customers. Our meal began with a delicate galantine of foie gras with vegetable fettucine, followed by passable lasagna with pike-perch, salmon with chervil sauce, and Barbary duck with Savoy cabbage and cognac sauce. The sauces are in general a little on the thick side, and the desserts are so-so. The service is satisfactory. The comprehensive wine list offers sufficient half-bottles and wines by the glass at reasonable prices.

KOPENHAGEN 12/20
68165, Friedrichsring 2a
(06 21) 1 48 70 res.

P

Closed Sunday. Tables d'hôte: 107, à la carte: 41/107

The Kopenhagen is supposed to be a historic institution in Mannheim. So far, so good. Well-dressed waiters led us to tables set much too close together and served a flavorful asparagus soup with shrimp. The recommended fresh kid liver (not on the menu) was tough, and the accompanying salad drowned in liver sauce on the same plate. King prawns from Martinique fried with garlic in olive oil and served with tomato noodles and lamb's lettuce sounded interesting, but the prawns and noodles were overdone.

MARITIM PARKHOTEL
68165, Friedrichsplatz 2
(06 21) 1 58 80, Fax 1 58 88 00

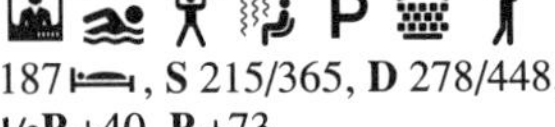

187, **S** 215/365, **D** 278/448,
1/2P +40, **P** +73

Mannheim's most elegant hotel stands directly opposite the Rosengarten convention center. The stylishly renovated neo-Renaissance hotel, built in 1901, offers spacious rooms and soundproofed windows. Restaurant and pub.

STEIGENBERGER AVANCE MANNHEIMER HOF
68165, Augustaanlage 4-8
(06 21) 4 00 50, Fax 4 00 51 90

155, **S** 195/245, **D** 260/340,
APP 340/380, **1/2P** +40, **P** +75

The spacious lobby of this functionally styled hotel, which is close to the Rosengarten convention center, is impressive. The house offers all modern amenities. The rooms range from comfortable to Spartan, so you'd better specify what you want when you book. Restaurants, bar. Excellent service and hospitality.

MARBURG Hessen
Gießen 30 - Korbach 60

DAS KLEINE RESTAURANT 13/20
35037, Barfürßertor 25
(0 64 21) 2 22 93, Fax 5 14 95 res.

P

Tables d'hôte: 45/68, à la carte: 37/58

This little restaurant can finally don a big toque! This chic bistro is the best place to eat in Marburg. None of the dishes failed entirely, but some had small failings. Intrinsically boring pike quenelles didn't become more exciting just because the chef poured lobster sauce over them, and an "essence of pink mushrooms" was (at best!) food for thought. Smoked salmon wasn't the ideal accompaniment for mushrooms in crepes, either, and the combination of squab with king prawns was, if anything, dubious. The products, though, were all of high quality and their preparation nice and light, finely balanced and exquisitely seasoned. Main courses could be had for about 30 DM, and were often worth much more – for instance our anglerfish in paprika sauce with ricotta ravioli and fillet of ox with creamed leeks. We suspect the wine list to be merely camouflage. The owner, who supervises the service, likes to recommend drinkable wines himself.

MARKTHEIDENFELD Bayern
Würzburg 30 - Aschaffenburg 45

HOTEL ANKER
97821, Obertorstr. 6-8
(0 93 91) 6 00 40, Fax 60 04 77

P

39, **S** 98/140, **D** 160/210,
APP 295/450,

The quietest rooms are those in the new building overlooking the attractive courtyard. Old-fashioned hospitality is more important here than modern fads. The amenities include stable facilities for horses, babysitter, playground, beauty treatment and free bike rental. Wine tastings in the 400-year-old cellars can be arranged.

MAYEN Rheinland-Pfalz
Koblenz 29

GOURMET-RESTAURANT WAGNER 15/20
56727, Markt 10
(0 26 51) 28 61, Fax 7 69 80 res.

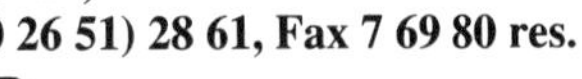

P

Closed Monday, Tuesday. Tables d'hôte: 45/98, à la carte: 39/76

This restaurant takes great pains to satisfy its guests—with great success. Jupp Wagner cooks his regional products just right, the menu is small and seasonal accents strong. He even found some new ways to prepare and present asparagus, including a *guglhupf* of asparagus mousse, deep-fried and baked, as soup, or the way we've always had it. There was nothing exciting or disappointing about our cod in potato coating, duck out of the oven with dumplings and cheese gratin with rhubarb. When the outdoor theater festival begins in summer, the cuisine becomes dramatic; chef Wagner adjusts the themes of his prix-fixe meals accordingly. The choice of wines is time-tested, and there's always an appropriate wine by the glass.

MEERBUSCH NRW

Neuß 8 - Düsseldorf 10

GSCHWIND 13/20

40670, Ortsteil Osterath
Hochstr. 29
(0 21 59) 24 53, Fax 24 22 res.

Closed for lunch Saturday and Sunday, closed Monday, 20 February through 2 March, August.Tables d'hôte: 59/89D, à la carte: 33/74

The young and talented cook Andreas Gschwind is particularly lucky: his father (not a gastronome) opened a new restaurant, installed him as chef and took over as his son's manager and maître d'. Gschwind Senior never tires of singing his son's praises, but since Junior follows through with appropriate performance in the kitchen, we don't hesitate to award a toque. The great talent his father sees in him has yet to be developed, however. Our white truffled soup was worth all of 13/20, and with a little more flavor would have been rated higher. The lobster sauce with excellent fresh scallops was obviously made in too great a hurry. But we've seldom had salmon as good as this, and the finely balanced Chablis sauce with it was superb! The choice of wines emphasizes French bottles, and even offers some good French wines by the glass.

MEERSBURG Baden-Württ.

Friedrichshafen 10 - Überlingen 14

BÄREN

88709, Marktplatz 11
(0 75 32) 4 32 20, Fax 43 22 44

 P

17 rooms, **S** 80/85, **D** 130/150

Closed 1 January through 10 March, 15 November through 31 December. No Credit Cards

Guests feel at home in this lovingly restored house, which was built in the 14th century, and usually don't mind the cramped bathrooms. Restaurant.

3 STUBEN 17/20

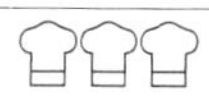

88709, Kirchstr. 7
(0 75 32) 60 19, 16 57, Fax 13 67 res.

Closed for lunch every day except Sunday. Tables d'hôte: 58/65L, 98/110D, à la carte: 52/89

Restless Stefan Marquard always has to cook up something new to maintain his high standard. The menu offers a variable prix-fixe meal in all three little dining rooms, and a choice of alternative à la carte courses as well as hearty regional dishes. While the regional fare is plainer and sounds simpler, however, it's far from rustic and is cooked and arranged as delicately as the finest cuisine.Whether we ordered oxtail, breast of veal, kidneys or tripe, poularde with *aceto balsamico* or turbot with prawns, saffron sauce and caramelized cabbage, all dishes were finely and delicately balanced, perfect down to the last detail and presented without frills or flamboyance. Sometimes the deceptive simplicity was provoking, however. The aspic of salmon with asparagus turned out to be jellied essence of mildly marinated fish, and one highlight of the meal wasn't even mentioned on the menu, namely the heavenly apple and rosemary mousse that came with it. Marquard not only served grand gnocchi with his exquisitely fried pike-perch, but also added a ragout of tomato and headcheese, and he stuffed our lamb haunch with sweetbreads and liver, serving them together with Albenga artichokes on superb polenta. The 18/20 rating is definitely within reach next time.The wine cellar, excellently stocked with French, Italian and German wines, still offers only a few half bottles and even fewer wines by the glass. The service is engaging, charming and pleasantly competent.

HOTEL 3 STUBEN

88709, Kirchstr. 7
(0 75 32) 60 19, 16 57, Fax 13 67

25 rooms, **S** 130/150, **D** 210/250,
1/2P +45,

After extensive renovation, this hotel reopened in 1990. Its rooms are elegantly and comfortably furnished.

VILLA BELLEVUE

88709, Am Rosenhag 5
(0 75 32) 97 70, Fax 13 67

P

11 (10), **S** 100/130, **D** 200/210, **APP** 230
Closed 1 November through 15 April

This hotel is more like a private villa, and offers a panoramic view of the lake and the Swiss Alps. Comfortable and elegant, all the rooms face south and have balconies or terraces. The center of town and beach are only a few minutes away.

WINZERSTUBE ZUM BECHER 12/20

88709, Höllgasse 4
(0 75 32) 90 09, Fax 16 99

Closed Monday, closed for lunch Tuesday, closed mid-December through mid-January. Tables d'hôte: 65L, 98D, à la carte: 28/77

It was in this picturesque house (one of the oldest buildings in Meersburg) that the fire started that practically wiped out the town nearly 400 years ago. After the inferno, this street was called "Höllgasse" or "Zur Höll" (Hell's Alley). At least, that's how the story is told in these rustically comfortable dining rooms. The Benz family offers two menus: one with rustic and regional cooking, the other with fine cuisine. Traditional roasts and fish from the nearby lake compete with scampi, lobster and Barbary duck. This double track isn't always problem-free, but it seems to work here. We enjoyed mousse of smoked sea trout in jellied Riesling, a creamy snail soup and good headcheese with mustard sauce, broccoli and excellent *rösti*. After this, the ambitious pastry was a letdown. The service is quick, and most of the regional wines on offer are made by the house.

MEININGEN Thüringen

Eisenach 51 - Bad Kissingen 57

SCHLOSS LANDSBERG

98617, Landsberger Str. 150
(0 36 93) 23 52, Fax 23 53

  P

21, **S** 170/350, **D** 210/360, **APP** 400/450, **1/2P** +40, **P** +70

This palace was built 150 years ago in the neo-Gothic style to house ducal art treasures, and has been a hotel since 1978. The rooms have recently been redecorated, but have kept their original woodwork. Restaurant. Breakfast: 18 DM.

MEISSEN Sachsen

Dresden 20 - Leipzig 87

DIE VILLA IN PANNONIA PARKHOTEL 13/20

01662, Hafenstr. 27-31
(0 35 21) 7 22 50, Fax 72 29 04

P

Tables d'hôte: 30/65, à la carte: 24/52

The view of the summer terrace, garden, Elbe river and Meissen's castle is fabulous. The restaurant has an elegant, timeless and attractive ambience, cheerful young service and a moderately priced international wine list. Some highlights of the repertoire on our last visit: beef carpaccio with excellent olive-oil vinaigrette, regional potato soup with bacon and croutons, a fish pot-au-feu, venison ragout (a little dry) with red cabbage, and iced chocolate terrine with fresh fruit.

PANNONIA PARKHOTEL

01662, Hafenstr. 27-31
(0 35 21) 7 22 50, Fax 72 29 04

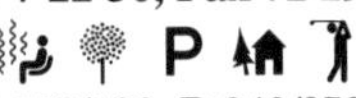

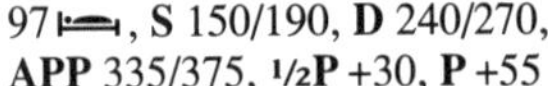

97, **S** 150/190, **D** 240/270, **APP** 335/375, **1/2P** +30, **P** +55

This unusual new hotel castle, villa and historic monument rolled into one has a unique flair and an excellent ambience. Most rooms are elegantly furnished and afford a lovely view of the Elbe river and Meissen, complete with castle and cathedral. Restaurant, bar, terrace and garden.

VINCENZ RICHTER 14/20

01662, An der Frauenkirche 12
(0 35 21) 45 32 85, Fax 45 37 63 res.

Closed for lunch, closed Sunday, Monday, 2—30 January. Tables d'hôte: 39L, 47D, à la carte: 26/51

Eating in Vinzenz Richter's historic *Weinstube* and drinking a glass of his own

Meissner Müller-Thurgau puts us into a good mood. The dining rooms and the pretty courtyard are almost always crowded with customers who are more interested in the Weinstube as a museum than as a restaurant. We had an excellent smoked goose breast with salads, hearty and savory consommé, salted tongue with cabbage, a gigantic turkey steak with cheese, and the housedessert specialty, wine crème with Riesling and grapes. The service staff is always pleasant and works quickly, so there is usually time for a chat and sound advice. Owner Gottfried Herrlich likes to praise his own wines and readily arranges wine tastings for his customers. They are worth it every time, since his wine list offers the best of every German region—at incredibly low prices.

MENGERSKIRCHEN Hessen

Weilburg 12 - Herborn 22

DIE LANDENTE 13/20

35794, Klosterstr. 9
(0 64 76) 29 24

P

Closed Monday. Tables d'hôte: 86, à la carte: 36/77

The competition has nothing good to say about dining in this beautiful villa. The food is mediocre, the prices exorbitant and the show they put on flamboyant but nothing else—so say envious observers. We went to visit to see if this were all true, and then came back because we liked it. Incidentally, so do a lot of other people. The Landente is "in," so reserve a table, especially on weekends. A nice evening is more important to most diners than an exquisite gourmet dinner, so they order popular dishes and get good value for their money: steaks, duck's breast, saddle of lamb or exotic pike-perch with an Asian touch—either in a hearty, regional style or classic and refined. We liked our fish terrine, salads with guinea chicken and quail, game consommé, pike-perch with zucchini in champagne sauce and veal fillet with leeks. Notorious grumblers might find the desserts nondescript and miss a wine list. The service recommends a few drinkable French and Italian wines. Ask for prices first, or you may be unpleasantly surprised when the bill comes.

BAD MERGENTHEIM BW

Würzburg 54 - Heilbronn 74

ZIRBELSTUBEN IN HOTEL VICTORIA 16/20

97980, Poststr. 2-4
(0 79 31) 59 30, Fax 59 35 00 res.

Closed Sunday and holidays, Monday. Tables d'hôte: 86, à la carte: 37/82

This elegant restaurant has a relaxing and agreeably spacious dining room decorated with metropolitan flair. The kitchen's originality and creativity have given way to a more down-to-earth cuisine. Only the best products are used, prepared as carefully as possible. The regional cuisine occasionally has a touch of Asia, as in, for instance, tuna marinated in soy sauce and ginger, and a Hohenlohe chicken out of the oven. The classic French cuisine, on the other hand, has a strong Italian accent. Even the traditional roast goose with dumplings has found a place on the menu. Whatever you order, everything is finely balanced and well-seasoned. The comprehensive wine list includes well-known rare vintages, as well as Otto Geisel's little "discoveries." All are moderately priced. The excellent, attentive service is professional and sincerely cordial.

HOTEL VICTORIA

97980, Poststr. 2-4
(0 79 31) 59 30, Fax 59 35 00

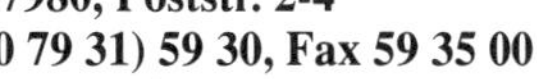

73, **S** 143/179, **D** 184/280, **APP** 380, **1/2P** +45, **P** +90

This hotel has changed from being a typical spa with diet food to a lavish country hotel for holiday guests. It combines the flair of a grand old hotel with the appealing atmosphere of a family-run guesthouse. The renovated rooms have soundproofed windows, balconies and comfortable furniture. Several restaurants ranging from elegant to rustic are supplemented by a piano bar.

Some establishments change their closing times without warning. It is always wise to check in advance.

METZINGEN Baden-Württ.

Reutlingen 8 - Nürtingen 14

KRONE 15/20

5 km north in 72658 Bempflingen
Brunnenweg 40
(0 71 23) 3 10 83, Fax 3 59 85 res.

 P

Closed Sunday and holidays, Monday, 24 December through 10 January, 23 July through 10 August. Tables d'hôte: 38/40L, 60/100D, à la carte: 38/100, No Credit Cards

Walking through the flower garden into the restaurant in the evening light, we had reason to expect a pleasant evening. The dining rooms here are comfortable, almost elegant, and the tables nicely set. We had high hopes for Werner Veit's cuisine, and he didn't disappoint us. He served little culinary works of art, such as seafood ragout with grape risotto, white asparagus mousse with perfectly fried foie gras and apple slices, a flavorful consommé of tomatoes with turbot and basil, pigeon breasts with fresh figs, fillet of beef with a fine Burgundy sauce served with corn, and a gratin of fruit ratatouille with iced sour cream. The portions were a bit too opulent, and the service a little too quick to be elegant. We hardly had time to take a deep breath between courses.Marianne Veit's service staff is especially friendly, however. The large wine list offers a goodly number of wines by the glass.

MITTENWALD Bayern

Garmisch 18 - Innsbruck 30

ARNSPITZE 15/20

82481, Innsbrucker Str. 68
(0 88 23) 24 25 res.

 P

Closed Tuesday, closed for lunch Wednesday, closed April except for Easter, 25 October through 19 December. Tables d'hôte: 39L, 79D, à la carte:36/68

In a town overrun by tourists who want to see the famous violin makers and experience the typical German "sauerbraten" mentality, Mittenwald chef Herbert Wipfelder has remained true to himself with his high-quality, original cuisine. We had an exquisite consommé of anglerfish and sole, an intensely savory apple and foie gras tart, and tender sweetbreads with unusually delicate fried morels. Wipfelder prepared his sheatfish (a type of catfish) in a new way: he fried it very carefully and served it with a light lemon butter and lemon slices, sugar peas, zucchini and asparagus. The saddle of rabbit was served with an excellent strudel with lovely foie gras, Burgundy sauce, and tender kohlrabi in a nest of spinach. The sherbets were first class, but we also liked the mint parfait with chocolate zabaglione and Wipfelder's "classic," the *guglhupf* (a cake made with raisins and almonds) parfait. The wine list, with its nice choice of German, French and Austrian wines, has grown, but the prices are as moderate as ever. The service is perfect.

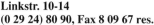

MÖHNESEE Nordrhein-Westfalen

Soest 11 - Arnsberg 15

HAUS DELECKE 13/20

59519, Ortsteil Delecke
Linkstr. 10-14
(0 29 24) 80 90, Fax 8 09 67 res.

 P

Closed January. Tables d'hôte: 45/110, à la carte: 52/80

There is probably not a nicer place to eat or to celebrate in this region than in this elegant but unpretentious restaurant by the Möhnesee. That said, however, you must not expect a culinary revelation with every dish you order.You can put together your own meal here; the menu offers only suggestions. Customers supply their own creativity since it is lacking in the kitchen. Chef Abraham guarantees reliable, if only average, good quality. Some dishes were really good, however, including a flavorful tomato consommé, succulent and finely seasoned lamb cutlets with a light, sweet sauce, and a veal fillet so tender that it melted in our mouths. We would like to see more half bottles and better German wines by the glass offered here.

HOTEL HAUS DELECKE 

59519, Ortsteil Delecke
Linkstr. 10-14
(0 29 24) 80 90, Fax 8 09 67

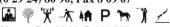

39, **S** 110/190, **D** 200/270,
APP 290, **1/2P** +38, **P** +75
Closed January

The extensive resources of a well-known industrial concern were necessary to restore this once-dilapidated hotel to its prewar grandeur. The large terrace looks out over the lake. Sports and fitness facilities. Polite and friendly service.

MÖLLN Schleswig-Holstein

Lübeck 29 - Hamburg 56

RATSKELLER 12/20

23879, Am Markt 12
(0 45 42) 83 55 75, Fax 8 66 57 res.

Closed Tuesday, 2—16 January. Tables d'hôte: 45/90, à la carte: 27/59, No Credit Cards

Udo Sonntag has established his beautiful restaurant in the cellar of the historic city hall, built in 1373 directly across from the Eulenspiegel museum. The low-priced regional cuisine of this postmodern restaurant has strong Mediterranean accents. Our pike-perch fillet fried in olive oil with herbs and salads was perfect, calf's liver with sage tender and expertly done, and potpourri of fish from the Lauenburg lakes with smoked eel sauce deliciously delicate. The attentive, unobtrusive service matches the elegant style of the house. The choice of mostly French wines has been enlarged by 20 rare vintages (which sell for between 180 and 1,200 DM). Some more German wines should be added.

MÖMBRIS Bayern

Aschaffenburg 12 - Alzenau 12

ÖLMÜHLE 17/20

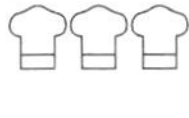

63776, Im Markthof 2
(0 60 29) 80 01/3, Fax 80 12 res.

Closed for lunch Saturday, closed Sunday, 1—20 August. Tables d'hôte: 69L, 130D, à la carte: 40/85

Just a few kilometers from the Frankfurt-Würzburg autobahn exit Hösbach/Mömbris lies the pretty little town of Mömbris, where the first-class restaurant Ölmühle is located. It is worth not only a detour, but also a special trip. Continuity characterizes the expert cuisine of André Kuhar and his brother. We have yet to see a lapse or a snag in any of the dishes that leave the Kuhar kitchen. The unique salad tower with smoked salmon and horseradish vinaigrette has often been copied, but never equaled. The tomato consommé with cheese ravioli was unbelievably flavorful. The Kuhar brothers only offer it when they can get the best San Marzano tomatoes from the foot of Mount Vesuvius! One of the best fish dishes we have ever eaten is the turbot fillet in wine cream we had here, and if we had our pick of main courses, we would choose duckling with marjoram dumplings and fillet of venison saddle in thyme sauce. The service is youthful, cheerful and well-trained. The wine list is adequate.

MÖNCHENGLADBACH NRW

Krefeld 22 - Düsseldorf 30

DOHRENDORF 13/20

41238, Zoppenbroich 87
(0 21 66) 18 74 64

P

A la carte: 49/85

This country *gasthof* used to serve plain and substantial German fare. But since Christian Dohrendorf took over the kitchen, this has become a well-known address for gourmets. Ripe avocado filled with lobster and served with dill dressing, or salad Landaise with fried lamb fillet, béarnaise sauce and fresh vegetables are generously portioned first courses. Dohrendorf's salmon, anglerfish and pike-perch, well-seasoned, fried and served with lobster zabaglione, convinced us of his talents just as much as his grilled steak with pepper sauce. Only the desserts are still of mediocre quality. French wines are offered, but most diners here drink beer.

MIKE'S BISTRO 12/20

41061, Weiher Str. 51
(0 21 66) 1 25 40

Closed for lunch Saturday, closed Sunday, Monday, à la carte: 36/71, No Credit Cards

Wooden tables with paper napkins, a menu written on the wall and an appetizer buffet describes the nonchalant atmosphere of this popular bistro. Mike's dishes aren't eye-catchers but are nice looking; his cooking isn't spectacular but tasty, like our crepes filled with rolled marinated herring, angler with seaweed, salmon in orange and pepper sauce and the lamb fillet in Savoy cabbage. We loved our excellent grappa parfait.

MOERS Nordrhein-Westfalen

Duisburg 13 - Krefeld 18

KURLBAUM 11/20

47441, Burgstr. 7
(0 28 41) 2 72 00

Closed for lunch Saturday and Sunday, closed Tuesday. Tables d'hôte: 56/90, à la carte: 51/77

This restaurant is easy to find: just look for a pink piglet over a door in the old part of town. The dining room is modern and tastefully decorated with opulent flower arrangements. Discreet and perfect waiters offered an intelligent, fairly priced choice of wines, 15 of them by the glass. The beautiful ambience was obviously motivating, and the cuisine showed promise—that is, when the kitchen limited itself to what it does best. Champagne and vodka sorbet didn't belong among the highlights, and neither did an overdone lamb or an unappetizing fowl terrine. We liked the delicious seafood chowder, though, as well as our poularde breast stuffed with avocados and foie gras and a poppyseed parfait with port-wine plums.

WILDENTE IN WELLINGS HOTEL ZUR LINDE 12/20

6 km north in Stadtteil Repelen
47445, An der Linde 2
(0 28 41) 7 30 61, Fax 7 12 59 res.

 P

Tables d'hôte: 55/110, à la carte: 37/88

This stone country house facing the church in Repelen would make a lovely picture postcard. The dining rooms are prettily furnished, and the linden-tree-shaded courtyard is quiet and peaceful. Unfortunately, if you want to sit outside in the Graftschafter Biergarten, you are restricted to a very small menu. The restaurant's menu has a greater variety of dishes (tender rabbit livers, breast of guinea fowl or wild duckling) to offer, but we prefer to stay outside and order herring tartare or the respectably done roasted rabbit leg. The wine list is offered both inside and in the beer garden.

MORITZBURG Sachsen

Dresden 6

SCHLOSSALLEE & REITERSTUBEN 13/20

01468, Schloßallee 35
(03 52 07) 7 83,

 P

Tables d'hôte: 26/45, à la carte: 22/48

The Schlossallee welcomes diners in pleasant surroundings with large French windows, whereas the Reiterstuben in the comfortable cellar restaurant underneath offers a more rustic and homely ambience. Saxon cuisine is served here with an international touch, for example nicely marinated carpaccio, perfectly fried pike-perch fillet with dill sauce and tomato rice, pork noisettes spiked with garlic and served with absolutely fresh market vegetables, and homemade coconut crème with raspberry sauce and peach frozen yogurt. Once in a while guests can even order foal-meat sauerbraten, goulash or roulades. There's also a little boarding house with a sauna and solarium.

MÜHLHEIM/MAIN Hessen

Hanau 7 - Frankfurt 8

WAITZ 12/20

5 km southeast in Lämmerspiel
63165, Bischof-Ketteler-Str. 26
(0 61 08) 60 60, Fax 60 64 88 res.

 P

Closed for lunch Saturday, closed for dinner Sunday, closed 27 December through 10 January.Tables d'hôte: 75/138, à la carte: 44/81

In a big city with a lot of competition, this restaurant wouldn't stand a chance. Here, surrounded by dull beer pubs and schnitzel bistros, this country inn is the undisputed cream of the crop. Indeed, the service is way above average: good-humored, quick and very attentive. But the food brings one back to banal realities. Five appetizers—spoonfuls of foie gras on an apple slice, snail with curry sauce, smoked goose breast, shrimp with tomato purée and salmon strips - sounded nice, but were no more than conventional party hors d'œuvres. The curried chicken was pale and drab rather than spicy, and the risotto sticky. We got nondescript hotel cuisine, no matter how poetically the menu praised the courses. The wine list offers a lot of good things, especially from Germany. The red wines by the glass are served too warm, though, and the Champagne isn't handled correctly, either.

HOTEL WAITZ

5 km southeast in Lämmerspiel
63165, Bischof-Ketteler-Str. 26
(0 61 08) 60 60, Fax 60 64 88

75 beds, **S** 165/185, **D** 230,
APP 300/380
Closed 27 December through 10 January

A little hotel that offers personalized attention. Breakfast: 20 DM.

MÜLHEIM/RUHR NRW

Oberhausen 7 - Duisburg 10

ALTES ZOLLHAUS 14/20

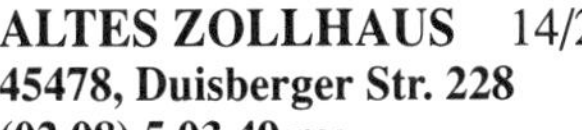

45478, Duisberger Str. 228

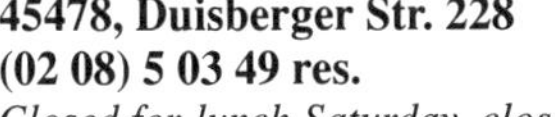

(02 08) 5 03 49 res.
Closed for lunch Saturday, closed Monday, à la carte: 39/70, No Credit Cards

Centuries ago, this building on the road to Duisburg was a toll house for travelers. Today, we gladly pay our "toll" to eat here. We liked the two comfortably furnished dining rooms with prettily laid tables, and we have nothing but applause for the kitchen. We had nicely done fish prepared with a regional accent, including bass and striped mullet with leeks, and anglerfish and king prawns with basil. The ham mousse with asparagus salad and the savory saddle of rabbit with morel cream sauce and homemade spaetzle were just as delicious as the caramelized pineapple mousse and the fantastic rum savarin with cherry ragout and chocolate parfait.Karola Möllecken provided cordial, competent service and moderately priced wines from France and Germany.

AM KAMIN 12/20

45473, Striepens Weg 62
(02 08) 76 00 36, Fax 76 07 69 res.

Closed for lunch Saturday. Tables d'hôte: 49/98, à la carte: 43/74

If you didn't know you were two minutes away from an autobahn exit in the highly industrialized Ruhr valley, you'd think you were in the thick of the woods in the gingerbread house of Hansel and Gretel. The dining rooms of this rustic restaurant protected by old beech trees are pretty and old-fashioned, and the tables beside the open fireplace seem to be part of a romantic dream. The quality of the cuisine is respectable, but chef Henric Monning is still finding his way. There is a surprise menu and vegetarian dishes. The service under the auspices of Heike Nöthel-Stöckmann is pleasant and uncomplicated.

LA BELLE ÉPOQUE 14/20

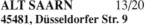

45479, Mühlenberg 12
(02 08) 42 64 50

Closed for lunch Saturday, closed Sunday, Monday. Tables d'hôte: 85, à la carte: 45/70, No Credit Cards

Right across from the city hall in Mülheim are the Art Nouveau dining rooms that Peter von Füssy has furnished with the appropriate antiques and floral arrangements.The quality of the cuisine is dependable here, especially where fish is concerned. La Belle Époque preserves tradition and serves the same dishes year after year. We would prefer a few more inventive dishes like the sweetbreads with warm sugar peas. The service is personable, and there is a good choice of wines, with some nice (but in no way cheap) wines by the glass.

HENZEK'S RESTAURANT ALT SAARN 13/20

45481, Düsseldorfer Str. 9
(02 08) 48 84 59, Fax 48 64 53

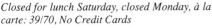

Closed Thursday, closed for lunch Friday and Saturday. Tables d'hôte: 60, à la carte: 33/69, No Credit Cards

Ever eat in a doll's house? Try this new address in this part of Mühlheim. The dining room has wooden beams and is colorfully and playfully furnished. In back of the house there's a patio under shady trees. The cuisine goes easy on luxury products and doesn't serve superfluous or extravagant side dishes. Instead, we had so-called "plain" dishes of a quality we'd like to find more often, for instance roast beef with fried potatoes, savory seafood cream soup with shrimps and grilled saddle of lamb with rice and basil sauce. Our ginger parfait with chocolate mousse was a fireworks of flavor. The choice of wines is excellent, moderately priced and includes half bottles and wines by the glass.

SCHLOSS STYRUM

45476, Moritzstr. 102
(02 08) 77 90 42

Closed for lunch Monday through Saturday, à la carte: 22/42

This little castle doesn't look very aristocratic—more like a lovely manor house in the middle of a park, near an old water tower. The kitchen serves nothing very exciting: a few soups, baked camembert with red currants, and (for 22.90 DM) the "King Arthur" gourmet platter, including pork and beef medallions, baked potato, green salad and so on. The drinks, served by the young students who work here, aren't anything to write home about, either. But the unique ambience in this fabulous beer garden with its lovely view of a pond with water lilies is worth a visit.

MÜLLHEIM Baden-Württ.

Badenweiler 6 - Freiburg 30

ALTE POST 14/20

79379, near the B3 motorway
(0 76 31) 55 22, Fax 1 55 24 res.

P

Closed Sunday, closed for lunch Monday. Tables d'hôte: 35/52L, 56/95D, à la carte: 38/77

Whatever Heimer Mack cooks and serves is delicious and good for you at the same time. He's been awarded many prizes for his ecologically run hotel. Lots of wood in the hotel rooms and old wooden paneling with extremely bad lighting in his restaurant help create a comfortable and natural atmosphere. Heiner Mack's cuisine isn't as polished as that of his competitors, but it might be a little more natural and closer to the original products prepared, for example, his wild boar noisettes coated with herbs, poularde galantine with asparagus salad, and lentil terrine with salad. Speaking of which, every salad is fortified with sprouts and wheat germ, something we like sometimes but not always. We also liked our sorrel soup, salmon with noodles, saddle of veal with spaetzle and yogurt with sorbet and fresh fruit. The only thing you need here is patience. The service staff does its best. The wine list is international.

MÜNCHEN Bayern

Augsburg 67 - Garmisch-Partenkirchen 87
Salzburg 130 - Nürnberg 165

ACQUARELLO 16/20

81677, Bohenhausen
Mühlbaurstr. 36
(0 89) 4 70 48 48 , Fax 47 64 64 res.

Closed for lunch Sunday. Tables d'hôte: 41L, 125D, à la carte: 54/84

Giuseppe Culoso, the famous "Pippo," used to cook here until Walter Sacchetti, Valerio Scopel (Al Pino, Spago) and Mario Gamba took over. The spacious interior is dominated by two gigantic pastel paintings (in shades of blue) done by the same artist who decorated Witzigman's. But the new owners are not just redecorating Pippo's; they want to start new trends, not follow old ones. Mario Gamba thinks before he cooks and consequently avoids routine. He serves *pasta e fagioli*—a simple dish—only if he found some particularly nice beans at the market that morning. Apart from cooking only with absolutely fresh products, Gamba likes the traditional soups of his native country, such as iced cucumber soup with just a whiff of garlic and some scampi. Other delicious cold dishes were his sole salad with chanterelles, and calamaretti with piquant marinated tomatoes. Beautifully dressed salads came with every first course. Pasta was perfectly al dente and the sauces fresh and finely balanced. Fresh fish was simple and served without frills. Gamba's rabbit ragout was a superb masterpiece of delicate flavors. Without a doubt, the Acquarello is the best Italian restaurant in Munich.

AL PINO 16/20

81479, Solln
Frans-Hals-Str. 3
(0 89) 79 98 85, 79 98 72

P

Closed for lunch Saturday, closed Monday. Tables d'hôte: 40L, 76D, à la carte: 79/70. Tables d'hôte with wine: 40

Solln, a suburb of Munich, is a little out of the way for some, but more and more gourmets are finding their way to the largest of the three restaurants owned by that successful gastronomic duo Sacchetti and Scopel. The restaurant's homey ambience boasts thick carpets, comfortable benches and the atmosphere of a private club. The menu offers well-known classics as well as specialties from Valerio Scopel's northern Italian home, such as deliciously light *cotechino* (a cooked sausage) with lentils. In addition to various types of pasta, Al Pino is also famous for its fish. You will have to ask for it as it is not on the menu. The highlight of our meal was fillet of bass with tomato and fennel cream. The desserts were not exciting, but they were refreshing. The wine list is overwhelming, but you can trust to the recommendations of the capable service staff.

AUBERGINE 17/20

80333, Maximiliansplatz 5 [D3]
(0 89) 59 81 71/2, Fax 5 50 43 53 res.

Closed Sunday, closed for lunch Monday. Tables d'hôte: 140/198, à la carte: 70/125

Patrik Jaros is the best sous-chef he's ever had, says Eckart Witzigmann. Jaros's repertoire seemed like a grand culinary opera: carpaccio of red beets with Sevruga caviar and poached quail's eggs, Brittany lobster with Asiatically seasoned sugar peas, sautéed Bresse pigeon with cèpes, and nougat parfait with honey and chocolate. These four courses cost 204 DM—and were worth maybe 140 DM if Chef Witzigmann wasn't watching. We consoled ourselves by looking at the trompe l'œil wall paintings and ordering one of the treasures in the wine cellar.As soon as star partner Witzigmann was there to advise the new owner, however, the splendid cuisine deserved the highest praise. The decision wasn't easy: should it be 19.5/20 for Witzigmann or 15/20 for Jaros, because his lobster was too soft and his combination of cèpes, chanterelles and tomatoes abstruse? We compromised and gave a rating of 17/20.

BISTRO TERRINE 16/20

80799, Schwabing [E1]
Amalienstr. 89 (Amalien-Passage)
(0 89) 28 17 80, Fax 2 80 93 16 res.

Closed for lunch Saturday, closed Sunday, closed for lunch Monday, closed first week in January. Tables d'hôte: 43L, 85D, à la carte: 47/74. Tables d'hôte with wine: 115

This bistro is hidden in a corner of the Amalienpassage. Some may not like the decor of basket chairs, hanging lamps and Parisian bistro mirrors, but what counts here is the kitchen. The prices are high, but not too high for the quality. Chef Werner Licht cooks his way through French cuisine with a love of detail and without a lot of flashy showmanship. We were favorably impressed with his tender sweetbreads, expertly prepared bass with horseradish and tarragon sauce, and savory venison cutlets in red wine, all accompanied by lovely, creative side dishes. Licht's sauces are unequaled, especially his delicately balanced sauce with oranges, ginger and Calvados. In spite of its excellence, there is still room for improvement in the cuisine.The service is without flaw, and the wine list is impressive.

BOETTNER 13/20

80333, Theatinerstr. 8 [E4]
(0 89)22 12 10 res.

Closed for dinner Saturday, closed Sunday and holidays, à la carte: 66/129

Boettner's restaurant is renowned in Munich; everybody who's chic or rich or important in politics or culture goes there to see and be seen. We went there to eat, and had crayfish with rice and dill sauce, a sole literally smothered with mayonnaise, duck's breast swimming in stiffly rich hollandaise, and stringy veal fillet with pasty truffled sauce and overdone noodles. We were merciful and gave Boettner's a bonus for being one of Munich's institutions.

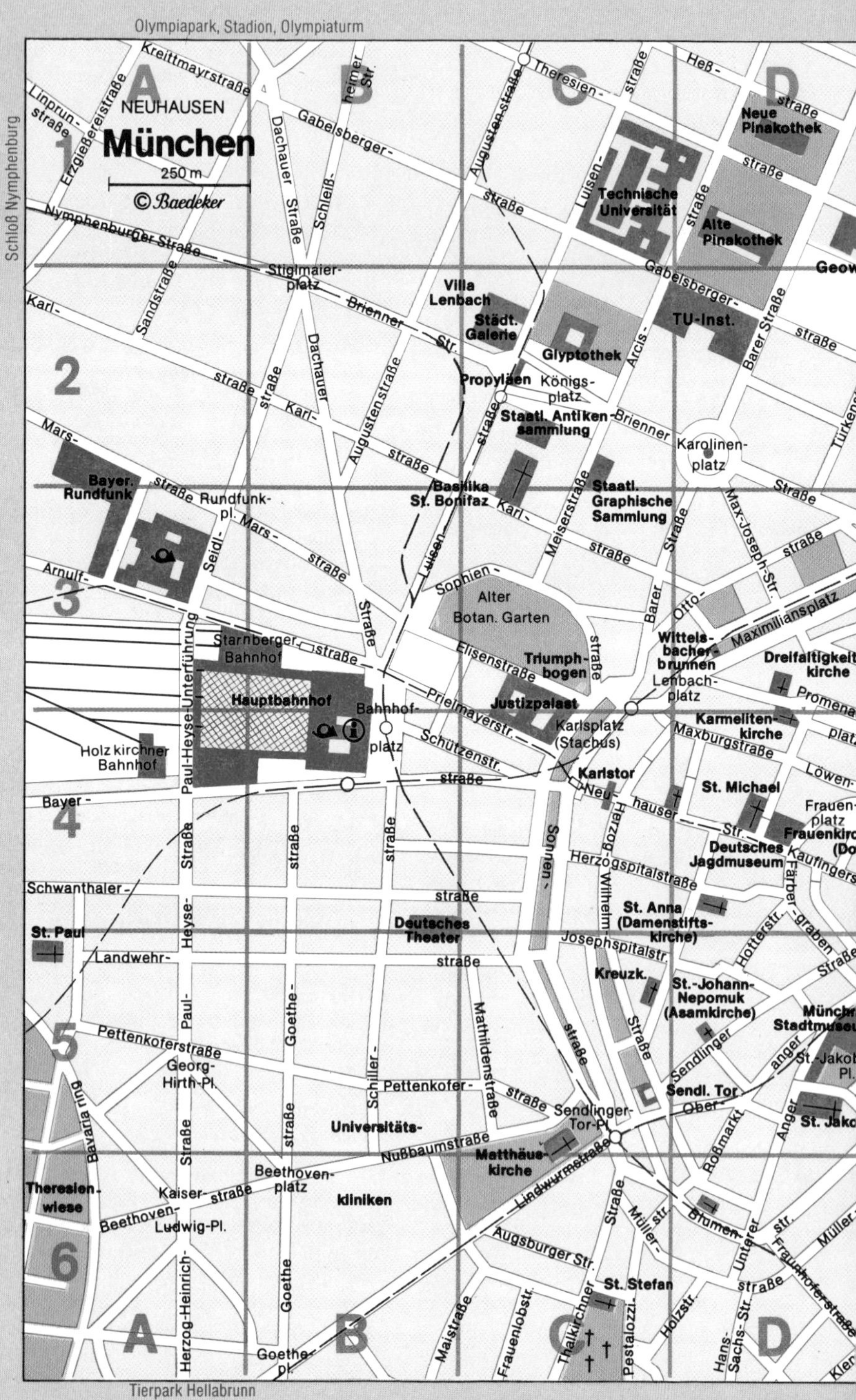

Olympiapark, Stadion, Olympiaturm
Schloß Nymphenburg
Tierpark Hellabrunn
NEUHAUSEN
München
250 m
© Baedeker
A
B
C
D
1
2
3
4
5
6
Kreittmayrstraße
Linprunstraße
Erzgießereistraße
Dachauer Straße
Schleißheimer Str.
Gabelsberger-
Augustenstraße
Theresien-
Luisen-
Heß-
Neue Pinakothek
Technische Universität
Alte Pinakothek
Nymphenburger Straße
Stiglmaierplatz
Sandstraße
Karl-
Brienner Str.
Villa Lenbach
Städt. Galerie
Glyptothek
TU-Inst.
Arcis-
Barer Straße
Propyläen
Königsplatz
Staatl. Antikensammlung
Brienner
Karolinenplatz
Türkenstr.
Mars-
Bayer. Rundfunk
Rundfunk-pl.
Basilika St. Bonifaz
Staatl. Graphische Sammlung
Meiserstraße
Max-Joseph-Str.
Arnulf-
Seidl-
Sophien-
Alter Botan. Garten
Otto-
Maximiliansplatz
Starnberger Bahnhof
Elisenstraße
Triumphbogen
Wittelsbacherbrunnen
Dreifaltigkeitskirche
Lenbachplatz
Paul-Heyse-Unterführung
Hauptbahnhof
Bahnhofplatz
Prielmayerstr.
Justizpalast
Promenadeplatz
Karlsplatz (Stachus)
Karmelitenkirche
Maxburgstraße
Holzkirchner Bahnhof
Schützenstr.
Karlstor
Löwen-
Bayer-
Neuhauser Str.
St. Michael
Frauenplatz
Frauenkirche (Dom)
Deutsches Jagdmuseum
Kaufingerstr.
Herzogspitalstraße
Herzog-Wilhelm-Str.
Sonnenstraße
Schwanthaler-
St. Anna (Damenstiftskirche)
Färbergraben
St. Paul
Deutsches Theater
Josephspitalstr.
Hotterstr.
Landwehr-
Kreuzk.
St.-Johann-Nepomuk (Asamkirche)
Münchner Stadtmuseum
Goethe-
Mathildenstraße
Pettenkoferstraße
Georg-Hirth-Pl.
Sendlinger-
St.-Jakob-Pl.
Schiller-
Pettenkofer-
Sendl. Tor
Ober-anger
Bavariaring
Sendlinger-Tor-Pl.
St. Jakob
Universitätskliniken
Nußbaumstraße
Matthäuskirche
Roßmarkt
Theresienwiese
Beethovenplatz
Lindwurmstraße
Kaiser-Ludwig-Pl.
Beethoven-
Müller-str.
Blumen-
Unterer Anger
Augsburger Str.
Fraunhoferstraße
Heinrich-Herzog-
St. Stefan
Thalkirchner
Pestalozzi-
Holzstr.
Hans-Sachs-Str.
Maistraße
Frauenlobstr.
Goethe-pl.

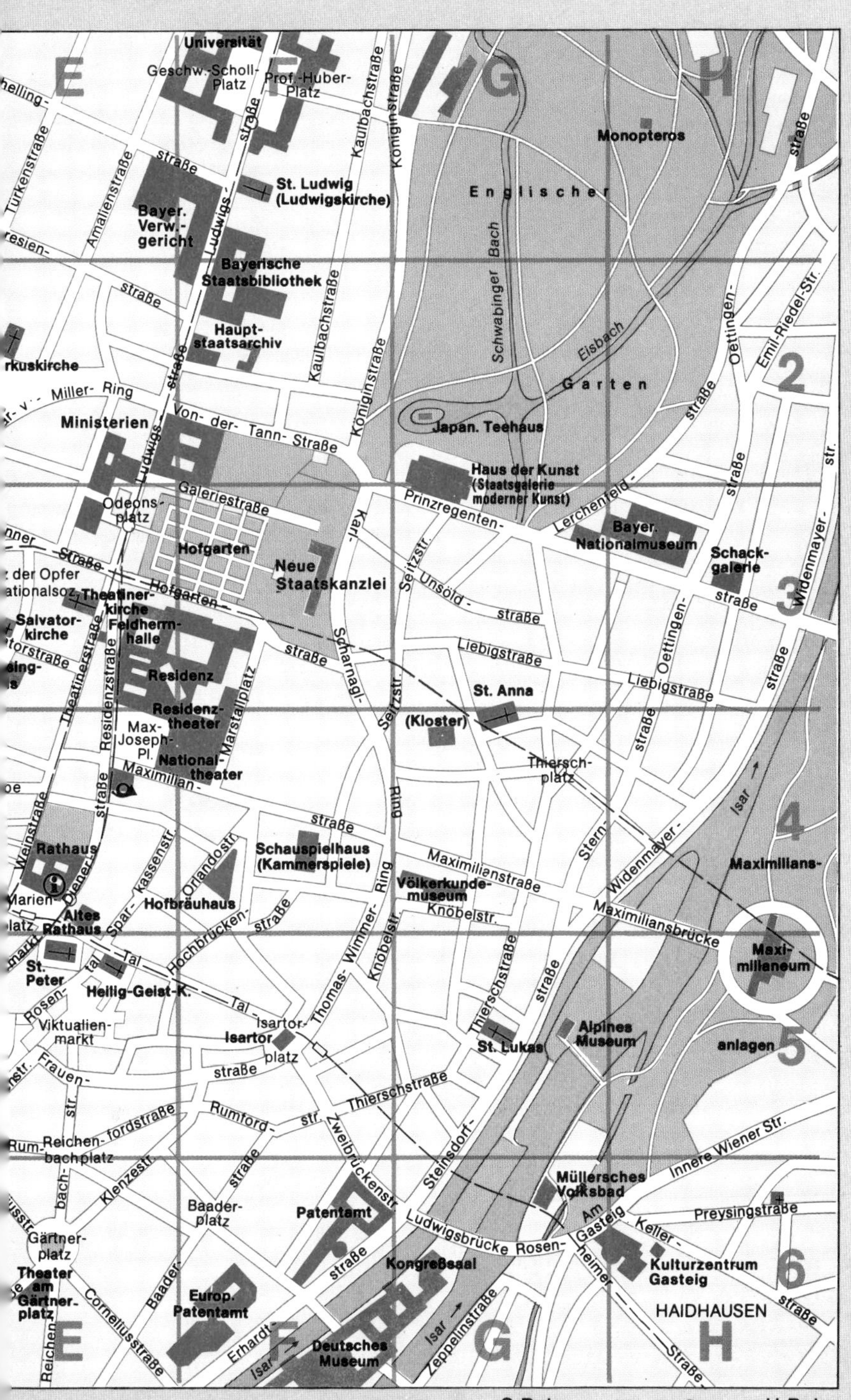

Universität
Geschw.-Scholl-Platz
Prof.-Huber-Platz
Monopteros
St. Ludwig (Ludwigskirche)
Englischer Garten
Bayer. Verw.-gericht
Bayerische Staatsbibliothek
Schwabinger Bach
Eisbach
Haupt-staatsarchiv
Ministerien
Japan. Teehaus
Haus der Kunst (Staatsgalerie moderner Kunst)
Odeonsplatz
Hofgarten
Neue Staatskanzlei
Bayer. Nationalmuseum
Schack-galerie
Theatiner-kirche
Feldherrn-halle
Salvator-kirche
Residenz
Residenz-theater
Max-Joseph-Pl.
National-theater
St. Anna
(Kloster)
Thierschplatz
Rathaus
Schauspielhaus (Kammerspiele)
Völkerkunde-museum
Maximilians-anlagen
Hofbräuhaus
Altes Rathaus
Marienplatz
St. Peter
Heilig-Geist-K.
Maxi-milianeum
Viktualien-markt
Isartor
Isartorplatz
St. Lukas
Alpines Museum
Müllersches Volksbad
Gärtner-platz
Theater am Gärtner-platz
Patentamt
Kongreßsaal
Kulturzentrum Gasteig
Europ. Patentamt
Deutsches Museum
HAIDHAUSEN
Baader-platz
Isar
S-Bahn
U-Bahn

BOGENHAUSER HOF 13/20

81675, Bogenhausen
Ismaninger Str. 85
(0 89) 98 55 86, Fax 9 81 02 21 res.

Closed Sunday and holidays, Christmas through 6 January. Tables d'hôte: 96, à la carte: 41/87

This idyllic place in Munich caters to all appetites and all tastes. You can order everything from blood pudding to scampi, potato soup, lobster bisque, rabbit navarin, and almond butter with your pike-perch. There are usually enough of the local bigwigs present to occupy the best tables, and the cellar offers choice wines. If we had to give a rating just for ambience, Ilse Kuttin would deserve 19.5/20. Her garden is heavenly on summer evenings!

DAS KLEINE RESTAURANT IN GATHAUS BÖSWIRTH 13/20

81249, Stadtteil Langwied
Waidachanger 9
(0 89) 8 64 41 63, Fax 8 64 38 57 res.

Closed Sunday, Monday, 3 weeks in January. Tables d'hôte: 85/125D, à la carte: 32/56

The quality of the cuisine here has declined. On our last visit, the kitchen did not deliver what the menu promised. The Beuscherl ravioli with a sauce of herbs made our mouths water, but mysteriously dark strips of calf's lung in a tasteless, dry-edged dough with a watery sauce was rather upsetting. We felt misled, if not actually swindled. Still, Böswirth's special tomato consommé was just as fresh and good as ever; his celery gratin was an original and harmonious accompaniment to a flawlessly done lamb fillet; and the slightly sweetened chestnut purée for dessert soothed our jaded palate. The service is pleasant but not always competent, the wines much too expensive, and the garden outside noisy because of the nearby autobahn.

FORSTHAUS WÖRNBRUNN 12/20

in 82031 Grünwald
Wörnbrunn 1
(0 89) 6 41 82 80, Fax 6 41 39 68 res.

Tables d'hôte: 43/119D, à la carte: 27/63

Munich city dwellers like to make Sunday excursions to the Forsthaus. The kitchen serves appropriate dishes whether diners come in lederhosen or in the latest style. A tip for newcomers: order only dishes that need as little "help" from the kitchen as possible, and enjoy them in one of the three dining rooms or outside in the beer garden.

FRANZISKANER

80333, City
Perusastr. 5/Residenstr. 9 [E4]
(0 89) 2 31 81 20, Fax 23 18 12 24 res.

A la carte: 23/69

The Franziskaner is far from being a gourmet temple, and doesn't even try to be one. So we enjoyed the traditional Munich white sausages with sweet mustard (the best in Munich) and a lot of other Bavarian specialties in a full house as usual.

GALLERIA 16/20

80331, Ledererstr. 2 [E4]
(0 89) 29 79 95, 2 91 36 53 res.

Closed Sunday, 1—10 January, 1—15 August. Tables d'hôte: 48L, 78D, à la carte: 50/72

Modern art on the walls and modern Italy on our plates and in our glasses—ambience and cuisine are both equally imposing. Peter Lodes's cuisine is lightly prepared, flavorfully seasoned and colorfully presented. With great enjoyment we tried carpaccio of marinated hake, scampi with pesto lasagna, fried guinea chicken with lavender *jus* (an old Medici recipe!), potato gnocchi with vegetables, veal haunch braised in red wine and onions, succulent rack of rabbit with steamed Savoy cabbage, and pear in red wine with nougat parfait. One of Lodes's colorful compositions: white John Dory with black olive slivers, light yellow lemon sauce and tender green broccoli. The service has class, and the wine cellar is well-stocked with products from choice wineries.

GARDEN-RESTAURANT 15/20

80333, Promenadeplatz 2-6 [D3]
(0 89) 2 12 00, Fax 2 12 09 06

Tables d'hôte: 50L, 89/128 D, à la carte: 51/98

Chef Pierre Pfister likes to call himself *maître* and autograph every menu in his Garden Restaurant. He also likes extravagant cuisine, and served us dishes like sliced calf's liver and a bouchée with sweetbread and chanterelles as well as mashed potatoes. He put his anglerfish (to sleep?) on a bed of puréed ratatouille, and served Mediterranean-style spaghetti with generous pieces of anglerfish, red mullet and king prawns instead of the usual mussels and shrimps. Obviously, Maître Pierre wants to recall the ancient times of opulent Roman feasting. The service in the spacious dining rooms and in the garden is very attentive and pleasant. Children are welcome here. The wines are overpriced.

GASTHAUS GLOCKENBACH 18/20

80337, Kapuzinerstr. 29/ Ecke Maistr.

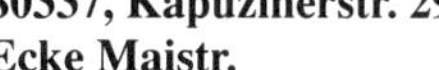

(0 89) 53 40 43, Fax 53 40 43 res.

Closed Sunday, Monday. Tables d'hôte: 70L, 85/125D, à la carte: 40/98

We try to be economical in handing out points and toques to deserving restaurants, yet year after year we give the Gasthaus Glockenbach a higher rating . Karl Ederer in the kitchen and Michel Dupuis in the wine cellar are an unbeatable duo, and they have made this our favorite restaurant. The wine expert Dupuis always finds the perfect wine to accompany each course (and it is not necessarily something noble from Bordeaux or Burgundy). He also offers first-class German wines. Ederer is a brilliant cook who works only with the very best ingredients produced in Germany. He does not have to go far to shop, since most of his produce comes from ecologically run farms east of Munich (where Ederer also runs his Schweinsbräu, a restaurant with private brewery). We loved the superb lobster with ravioli and the fried pike-perch, blood pudding and liver sausage, as well as the tangy passion-fruit parfait. The discreetly decorated restaurant in Munich's Glockenbach quarter has kept its comfortable flair in spite of its high rating. You will not find pomp or vanity here, just excellent cooking, wonderful wines, and kind, attentive service.

GEISEL'S VINOTHEK

80335, Schützenstr. 11 [B4]

(0 89) 55 13 70 40, Fax 55 13 71 21

Tables d'hôte: 38/45, à la carte: 24/57

You can have a wonderful San Daniele ham and a choice of more than 400 wines here from 10 in the morning to 1 a.m. The wine is served in specially designed glasses. The ever-changing menu offers dishes from the nearby Hubertus to go with the wine. You can either have just a glass of wine and a bite to eat, or celebrate with a rare bottle.

LE GOURMET 18/20

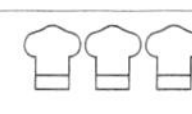

80333, Hartmannstr. 8 [D4]

(0 89) 2 12 09 58, Fax 2 90 41 72

Closed Sunday, Monday. Tables d'hôte: 68L, 158D, à la carte: 56/118

The culinary fireworks are over, but Le Gourmet still pampers its customers with the very best cooking. Otto Koch, who runs a number of other establishments as well as this restaurant, cooks with less spectacular accents, but still has an unmistakable creativity. We had exquisite veal fillet stuffed with foie gras, superb ravioli stuffed with lobster and mushrooms in a refreshing watercress sauce, and subtly truffled fillet of Charolais beef. The desserts were as sublime as always. Just try the croquant parfait—it tastes much more exciting than it sounds! Koch does not chase after trends; he just prepares his classic dishes with loving care. The choice of wines is as top-notch as the cellar of Koch's wine store.

GRÜN TAL

81925, Bogenhausen

(0 89) 98 09 84, Fax 98 18 67 res.

P

A la carte: 19/70

This is the most popular beer garden in Munich, well-frequented by those who like to be seen but don't get excited about it anymore. Nobody comes here just to dine elegantly under old chestnut trees, but if the kitchen has one of its good days you can order a respectable meal worthy of a toque. The service ranges from in-training to well-trained.

HALALI 15/20

80539, Schönfwldstr. 22 [F2]
(0 89) 28 59 09, Fax 28 27 86

Closed for lunch Saturday, closed Sunday, 14 days in August. Tables d'hôte: 34L, 85D, à la carte: 35/73

The cuisine here is not as radically rustic as the restaurant looks. Some dishes (marinated tuna with tangy lime vinaigrette or strips of Barbary duck with mushrooms and lamb's lettuce) point in the right direction, namely a light and tasty cuisine. Other dishes, however, are smothered in fat and cream, like the rather boring venison terrine that was supposed to be pepped up by its heavy cranberry cream. The menu offers game in many variations, and the best dishes are those without many frills. The fish dishes were far from light, and the kitchen would not serve a simple sea bream without a gratin of scallops on the side, and insisted on dressing up turbot with a cèpes crust. We resigned ourselves to heavy opulence, and ordered oxtail stuffed with everything from sweetbreads to bacon (why not scallops gratin?), persuaded at last that such restaurants also have a right to exist. The desserts are no less opulent, but the strawberry rosette with rhubarb cream was, at least, refreshing.The wine list offers a classic choice of French wines, prosaic German vintages and an eccentric assortment of Italians. The service is flawless.

HILTON-GRILL 14/20

80538, Schwabing
Am Tucherpark 7
(0 89) 3 84 50, Fax 38 45 18 45

Closed for lunch Saturday, closed Monday, 2—16 January, end of July through mid-August

There's no chain hotel in Germany with a restaurant that has as congenial an atmosphere as the Hilton Grill in Munich. The cuisine is doing its best to match, often with a creativity that is long passé. Who needs two sauces to go with herring, what's a quail egg doing on lobster tartare and who wants truffled squash? Chef Urbansky cooks with such expertise that he doesn't really need all these fancy, superfluous gimmicks. Without the frills, and with a sensible conception instead, he'd be worth two toques any time. Maybe then he'd also lower the high wine prices.

HUBERTUS 14/20

80335, Schützenstr. 11 [B4]
(0 89) 55 13 71 42, Fax 55 13 71 21

P

Closed 1—8 January. Tables d'hôte: 45/110, à la carte: 52/87

This tasteful, cultivated and comfortable restaurant deserves a more original, splendid or at least interesting cuisine. The Königshof, Hubertus's big brother, seems to take the best products and leave the rest here. The owner, the Königshof chef and the Hubertus cook should get together to raise the level of this restaurant. Until then, excellent service and rare wines must console us.

HUNSINGERS BOUILLABAISSE 15/20

80331, Falkenturmstr. 10 [E4]
(0 89) 29 79 09, Fax 36 10 15 14

Closed Sunday, closed for lunch Monday.Tables d'hôte: 39L, 99D, à la carte: 38/80

In most restaurants, waiters come close to nervous breakdowns if you express special wishes. At Hunsingers, it is normal procedure not only to choose the kind of fish you want but how you want it done and what you want to go with it. We like to pick and choose, but it reminds us a little of these notorious breakfast buffets in hotels.In any case, we were glad to find a (small) menu as well. We chose a feuilleté with scallops and asparagus, and tail of spiny lobster with typical Thai seasoning. Both were delicious. We do not understand, however, why Hunsinger has to bury the fine taste of his sea bream under mounds of potato gratin!Those who do not like fish can choose among such delicacies as smoked saddle of lamb, asparagus consommé and ravioli stuffed with sweetbreads with truffled sauce. Hunsinger's wine list contains many French vintages, a few Italian wines, and an increasing number of German wines. The service is attentive and discreet.

KÄFER'S AM HOFGARTEN

80539, Odeonsplatz [E3]
(0 89) 2 90 75 30

Käfer's most recent bistro coup: in this rebuilt original Parisian bistro, almost 250 places can be laid inside and nearly 600 outside. Starting in 1995, the restaurant abandons gourmet cuisine in favor of bistro fare, and offers delicate little snacks from early morning to late at night, like the famous Käfer-burger and sandwich specials.

KÄFER-SCHÄNKE 15/20

81675, Bogenhausen
Prinzregentenstr. 73
(0 89) 4 16 82 47, Fax 4 16 86 23 res.

P

Closed Sunday. Tables d'hôte:47L, 80/160D, à la carte: 42/100

Michael Käfer's restaurant right above his famous delicatessen has been an "in" place for Munich's smart set for years. The building is a beautiful historic monument and a tourist attraction. Among the many spacious rooms you can choose the ambience you prefer, ranging from bright and functional to dusky, rustic and comfortable. The kitchen cooks everything that is good and expensive, but prefers Mediterranean dishes. In addition to the grand choice of seafood from his own tanks, Käfer offers unusual imports, like butterfly fish from New Zealand or black grouper from Singapore. Those who are allergic to edible status symbols can order a simple baked chicken. With all this variety, there is bound to be some disappointment. A few daring sauces turned out to be merely adventurous.

DER KATZLMACHER 14/20

80539, Schwabing
Kaulbachstr. 48 [F1]
(0 89) 34 81 29, Fax 33 33 60 res.

Closed Sunday, Monday, Bayern Whitsun holiday. Tables d'hôte: 45L, 75D, à la carte: 37/68

This popular Italian restaurant is on its way up. It does not try to create gourmet ambience with a pompous decor, and we think North Italian cooking tastes better in a relaxed atmosphere, anyway. We enjoyed unusually tender rabbit with bacon and black olives, and an excellent grilled sole. If the dishes were a little more creative, Katzlmacher would deserve a higher rating. The choice of first courses is confined to the classic vitello tonnato, Parma ham with melon, salmon carpaccio with arugula, and a somewhat oily platter of various antipasti.The service staff is quick and dependable, and sometimes entertaining, whether the customers want to be entertained or not.The choice of wines from the Friaul region is impressive.

KAY'S BISTRO 13/20

80469, Utzschneiderstr. 1 [E5]
(0 89) 2 60 35 84, Fax 2 60 55 26 res.

P

Closed for lunch, à la carte: 55/78

The magnificent murals created for this restaurant are more decorative than artistic. You can imagine yourself at the carnival in Rio or in the lagoons of Venice without stepping out of Kay's bistro. We felt like we were on the stage of a musical comedy. People come here to look and to be looked at, but it is possible to eat here as well. If, by chance, you order the respectable lamb rack with potato gratin instead of the overdone red mullet, you might even like it here.

KÖNIGSHOF 17/20

80335, Karlsplatz 25 (Stachus)
(0 89) 55 13 60, Fax 55 13 61 13

P

Tables d'hôte: 118/145D, à la carte: 59/113

People do not eat at this restaurant, they dine. Instead of trying to create sensational dishes, the kitchen of the conservative Königshof serves fine, honest, solid cuisine. The creative menu is changed often and offers opulent, ingenious compositions. We liked our potpourri of lobster, prawns and crawfish seasoned with tarragon and served with melon, and found the red mullet fillet with fennel salad just wonderful. The fried foie gras in apple-raisin sauce and the tender calf's kidneys with thyme sauce were masterpieces of aromatic harmony. The strawlike mushrooms with the otherwise excellent venison carpaccio were a gaffe, but the warm raspberry tarts with cinnamon-vanilla mousseline were as exquisite as the strawberry strudel with apricot purée! Hotel owner Carl Geisel has reason enough to be proud of his wine list, and the service is famous for its discreet attention that doesn't miss a thing.

MARK'S IN THE RAFAEL HOTEL 13/20 

80331, Neuturmstr. 1 [F4]
(0 89) 29 09 80, Fax 22 25 39

P

Tables d'hôte: 55L, 95D, à la carte: 51/86

The Rafael (see p. 277) is one of the few luxury hotels in the world without an appropriate restaurant. The only attraction here is the low-priced lunches. On the other hand, guests who don't want to leave the hotel can eat here. Neither the menu nor the courses are promising; the only thing exciting is the bill. A shame, because the service is good. A toque, we hope, will motivate the chef.

MASSIMILIANO 16/20

81669, Haidhausen
Rablstr. 5
(0 89) 4 48 44 77

P

Closed for lunch Saturday, à la carte: 42/99

Up until now only a restaurant for insiders and connoisseurs, this wonderful little place needs only a little marketing and public-relations work to become one of the great Italian eateries in Munich. Kurt Gasser in the kitchen and Gesumino Pireddu were both institutions at Witzigmann's Aubergine before he had to give it up. Their new restaurant is pretentiously decorated, and needs a little more comfort and charm to make customers feel at home. The cuisine is a combination of Aubergine standards, Mediterranean influences and modern down-to-earth bourgeois cooking. A prix-fixe menu can look like this: carpaccio of celery and red beets, sea bream done in foil, Viennese schnitzel or delicious Bresse chicken, and chestnut crème with gingerbread ice cream. All salads were absolutely fresh, the sauces savory and the vegetables tasty. The service was as perfect as in the Aubergine, and the choice wines are worth a toast to an auspicious beginning and a great future.

We are always interested to hear about your discoveries, and to receive your comments on ours. Please feel free to write to us, stating your opinions clearly.

NÜRNBERGER BRATWURSTGLÖCKL

80331, Frauenplatz 9 [E4]
(0 89) 22 03 85, 29 52 64,
Fax 2 90 47 36 res.

Closed 24 and 25 December, New Year's Eve and New Year's Day, à la carte: 19/41, No Credit Cards

Some people stand in line to get a table in this smoky, black-domed cellar just to eat equally smoky black meat. While they wait, they have a beer outside the door. Grumpy waitresses squeeze persistent fans and tourists together at wooden tables and feed them beer, fried sausages, and (the best bet) *Surhaxl* (pickled pork haunch) with potatoes and sauerkraut, but most Bavarians stay outside. We would rather meet our friends outside at ten in the morning and have some pretzels with our beer.

OSTERIA ITALIANA 12/20

80799, Schwabing
Schellingstr. 62
(0 89) 2 72 07 17, Fax 2 73 10 32 res.

Closed Sunday, closed for lunch Monday, à la carte: 45/70

Osteria, the oldest Italian restaurant in Germany, will soon celebrate its 100th anniversary. One dubious claim to fame: Hitler liked to eat here. We hope the Osteria has found a workable concept for its cuisine by the time the big birthday party is celebrated. In the past few years, the Osteria seems to have been having an identity crisis: is it an Italian restaurant with a Bavarian touch, a Bavarian restaurant with Italian verve, or simply a restaurant with high prices? In the meantime, the Osteria has returned to cooking good old middle-of-the road cuisine, dependable, but unexciting, with lobster spaghetti and beef carpaccio, tagliatelle with chanterelles and nonchalantly fried anglerfish and veal medallions. The service is snobbishly grumpy, and the wine list so-so.

RISTORANTE BEI GRAZIA 15/20

80805 SchwabingUngererstr. 161
(0 89) 36 69 31 res.

Closed Saturday, Sunday, à la carte: 36/64

We just can't have enough of these friendly little Italian restaurants with excellent cuisine. But the more of them we do have, the more we find to criticize. Let's face it, competition is strong, and, without becoming too strict with Grazia, we don't want our plates garnished with (the perpetual!) tasteless rosettes of broccoli, two carrot strips and a tablespoon of watery spinach. Apart from this irritating excuse for vegetables, we were as satisfied as most of the customers here. We had piquantly prepared lasagna—and were captivated by its excellent quality. Our anglerfish fillet with mushrooms and chicken stuffed with arugula were superb (and, for once, came without the irritating broccoli, carrot, spinach trio!) The service is pleasant and personal, and the wine list makes impressive reading.

SCHUMANN'S 

80539, Maximilianstr. 36 [F4]
(0 89) 22 90 60, Fax 2 28 56 88

Closed Saturday, à la carte: 15/26, No Credit Cards

Schumann's, named after its famous bon vivant owner, is a place full of joie de vivre. Diners here enjoy a great variety of cocktails, fruit brandies and champagne. The kitchen feeds the cheerfully hungry multitudes with pastrami, a plat du jour, Bavarian meatballs and roast beef with fried potatoes. If you still feel as if you're not sharing in the general excitement, you can at least read up on it—in one of the three "insider" books Schumann has written about Munich's nightlife.

SCHWARZWÄLDER 15/20

80333, Hartmannstr. 8 [D4]
(0 89) 2 12 09 79, Fax 2 90 41 72

Closed Sunday. Tables d'hôte: 24L, 68D, à la carte: 24/72

Otto Koch is finally drawing a line between his elegant and extravagant Le Gourmet restaurant upstairs and his more populist Schwarzwälder on the ground floor. Those who liked eating Le Gourmet dishes at cheaper Schwarzwälder prices will be disappointed, but the old customers are glad to find unadulterated plain fare on the menu. Apart from an overdone salmon soufflé and a dry fillet of beef, we had only good experiences. We liked simple dishes like bread dumplings with chanterelles, lamb's lettuce with bacon and croutons, and tender Viennese schnitzel just as much as the more extravagant duck confit with salads or tripe and morels in champagne. The service is pleasant.

BISTRO SCHWARZWÄLDER 13/20 

80333, Hartmannstr. 8 [D4]
(0 89) 2 12 09 79, Fax 2 90 41 72

Closed Sunday. Tables d'hôte: 24, à la carte: 18/54

Nothing like a real Parisian bistro, this restaurant is more like an annex to the Schwarzwälder next door. After the last theater curtain has come down, the fun begins in Otto Koch's (Schwarzwälder, Le Gourmet) third culinary playground. In a relaxed and uncomplicated ambience, the kitchen offers daily changing snacks and meals, like meatballs with potato salad or fried vegetables. Really hungry guests may even choose dishes from the Schwarzwälder menu. In any case, it's worthwhile to try some of the wines.

SPAGO 15/20

80799, Schwabing
Neureutherstr. 15/Ecke Arcisstr.
(0 89) 2 71 24 06, Fax 2 78 04 42 res.

Closed for lunch Saturday and Sunday. Tables d'hôte: 39L, 69D, à la carte: 41/73

This is the third and smallest restaurant run by the Italian duo Sacchetti/Scopel (Al Pino, Acquarello). What exactly makes this an "in" restaurant we haven't yet discovered. Maybe it's the beautiful garden, where you could eat on summer evenings if the chairs weren't so excruciatingly uncomfortable. But Spago's regular customers don't seem to mind, and even accept the sometimes horrendous prices. We remember fondly the carpaccios of salmon, tuna and swordfish. In addition to the menu, the kitchen offers daily specials, and the waiters can recommend specialties like sea bream stuffed with spinach, a creative counterpoint to the usually purist cuisine. The products used are fresh and of good quality, and are sometimes even combined and prepared ingeniously, like the homemade *ripiena* (stuffed pasta). Once you've tried the ravioli filled with turbot or the tortellini with sweetbread or chanterelles, you'll eat nothing but pasta here.

STRAUBINGER HOF 12/20

80331, Blumenstr. 5 [E5]
(0 89) 2 60 84 44, Fax 2 60 89 17 res.

Closed for dinner Saturday, closed Sunday, à la carte: 18/46

The Straubinger Hof close to the Viktualienmarkt is the best (and only) place in Munich to try truly typical Bavarian food. Soup with strips of pancake, calf's lung hash with bread dumplings, sausage with warm potato salad, a wonderfully succulent pork roast with a crispy crust, or the famous *weisswürste*. On nice summer days you can sit in a little biergarten, which is usually as closely packed with customers as the two dining rooms inside. But the waitresses always manage to squeeze in just a few more.

TANTRIS 19.5/20

80805, Schwabing
Johann-Ficte-Str. 7
(0 89) 36 20 61/2, Fax 3 61 84 69 res.

P

Closed Sunday and holidays, Monday, 1—9 January. Tables d'hôte: 98/148L, 188/212D, à la carte: 68/140

What is Hans Haas's secret? He doesn't have one. His cooking is perfectly aboveboard, astonishingly simple and deceptively plain. He isn't a magician, and he hasn't just waved a magic wand to get the highest rating of all the restaurants in Germany. He works, or rather cooks, for it. He fries some sardines, adds two drops of sesame seed oil and puts them on a salad of fresh sprouts—voilà! Or he bones a tender quail, grills foie gras terrine on hot coals and serves them with a bunch of young beans. No tricks, no rabbits out of hats. With an apparent lack of effort, Haas always manages to make something special out of ordinary ingredients. His exquisite cuisine has its roots in his native region, the Tyrolean mountains. And this is why his cooking—in spite of it flights of fancy—remains so solidly down-to-earth. Old traditions are preserved in two wonderful pot-au-feu variations, one with seafood and lobster, the other with suckling lamb. Courageous ingenuity is displayed in the turbot with asparagus and chervil sauce, bass with tomato sauce and ravioli, and the especially harmonious composition of breast of Bresse pigeon with artichoke hearts.Semolina dumplings with strawberry ragout, and cheese soufflé with rhubarb and strawberries have a distinct Tyrolean touch. In keeping with the wishes of his customers, Haas serves two desserts with the evening meal.If the black and orange decorating scheme of the restaurant bothers you, visit Tantris on a sunny day, when you can eat in the beautiful garden. The service is perfect, inside and outside.

TRADER VIC'S 12/20

80333, Promenadeplatz 2-6 [D3]
(0 89) 2 12 00, Fax 2 12 09 06

P

Tables d'hôte: 64/74, à la carte: 33/80

The cellar restaurant with its Polynesian theme is almost always full. We're probably the only ones who notice that dishes are less than subtly seasoned and the products used of less than high quality. The food is served charmingly—sometimes quickly, sometimes slowly, frequently too hot and often too cold. The dishes don't taste as exquisitely extravagant as they sound on the menu: prawns mimosa, almond duck, cosmos tidbits (spareribs) or fish from a Chinese oven.

LA VIGNA 16/20

81927, Stadtteil Englschalking
Wilhelm-Dieß-Weg 2/
Engleschalkinger Str.
(0 89) 93 14 16 res.

P

Closed Saturday, 1 week at the beginning of January, 1 week at Whitsun. Tables d'hôte: 45L, 78D, à la carte: 36/67

Very few good restaurants are located in the heart of Munich. Still fewer can be found in historic buildings or on the glamorous boulevards. The trend these days seems to be to open restaurants in otherwise unremarkable suburbs. Englschalking is a good example. Gourmets don't mind the drive to the comfortable, deceptively simply furnished restaurant. Two Italians from the southern tip of the boot have made this the best-known insider tip in Munich. The recipe sounds simple: take first-class ingredients, prepare them according to an uncompromisingly high standard and avoid flashy frills as much as possible. We loved the simple but superb bean soup, which was prepared with the best Borlotti beans and the finest olive oil from Sassicaia, and the delicious nettle soup. The scallops on a bed of potatoes and the truffled polenta were a little grander. The desserts are wonderful but more complicated; deep-fried ravioli with rhubarb, for instance, or a little apricot soufflé with pudding. The wine list could be improved, but offers some rare vintages. The friendly, competent service staff can tell you just why they're so rare.

WEINHAUS NEUNER 13/20

80331, Herzogspitalstr. 8 [C4]
(0 89) 2 60 39 54 res.

Closed Sunday, 14 days in August. Tables d'hôte: 34L, 55/85D, à la carte: 23/61

The Weinhaus Neuner tries to combine simple regional cooking with haute cuisine, but neither one is very convincing. The ravioli stuffed with duck with cèpe consommé was an ingenious idea, but the consommé tasted artificial and the duck was overdone. The attempt to refine regional cooking wasn't very successful, either. The *tafelspitz* could have used more horseradish and less cream, and the spaetzle that accompanied the venison goulash reminded us of mini-pancakes. But we also had an excellent carpaccio with truffles, superb lamb rack in thyme crust, and heavenly Grand Marnier crème. The service was really nice, and the wine list is comprehensive.

ZUM DÜRNBRÄU

80331, Dürnbräugasse 2 [E5]
(0 89) 22 21 95, Fax 22 14 17 res.

Tables d'hôte: 15L, 30/50D, à la carte: 22/69

This little restaurant in a quiet corner of Munich's pedestrian zone offers rustic Bavarian cooking for refined urbanites. It offers typical dishes found in every good Bavarian country *gasthof*. If rustic cuisine doesn't appeal to you, try the really good Wiener schnitzel or the *tafelspitz* with horseradish sauce. In any case, the Dürnbräu is a nice alternative to the big beer halls around the Marienplatz, and it even has a little garden in front. The service is friendly and swift.

HOTELS

BAYERISCHER HOF

80333, Promenadeplatz 2-6 [D3]
(0 89) 2 12 00, Fax 2 12 09 06

428, **S** 280/350, **D** 380/510,
APP 730/1050

The Bayerischer Hof is a city within a city: it offers 428 individually styled and furnished rooms and suites, three restaurants, a nightclub, theater, artistically redecorated salons, shops and a swimming pool with terrace on the roof. The regular guests feel at home here, but newcomers must make the best of this confusing and amusing cosmopolis with sometimes impersonal service.

EXCELSIOR

80335, Schützenstr. 11 [B4]
(0 89) 55 13 70, Fax 55 13 71 21

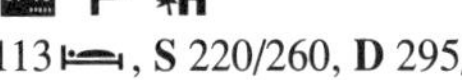

113, **S** 220/260, **D** 295/325,
APP 400/480

A gem close to the railway station, this hotel offers attractively renovated, quiet rooms ranging from refined to luxurious with old-fashioned flair and a relaxing atmosphere. Breakfast: 25 DM.

GÄSTEHAUS ENGLISCHER GARTEN

80802, Schwabing
Liebergesellstr. 8
(0 89) 39 20 34/6, Fax 39 12 33

27, **S** 138/158, **D** 152/168,
No Credit Cards

The days when this tranquil hotel was an insider tip are long gone. Today, you can't be too early to reserve one of the 27 rooms. But it's worth the trouble: there isn't a nicer and cheaper place to stay in Munich. Breakfast: 16 DM.

KÖNIGSHOF

80335, Karlsplatz 25 (Stachus)
(0 89) 55 13 60, Fax 55 13 61 13

103, **S** 295, **D** 370/395,
APP 520/995

The noble Königshof is located in the heart of Munich, but is still easily reached by car (large garage). The soundproofed rooms were luxuriously modernized by Count Pilati. Nine enchanting suites, elegant halls and a fashionable bar make a stay here an experience.

LEOPOLD

80804, Schwabing
Leopoldstr. 119
(0 89) 36 70 61, Fax 36 04 31 50

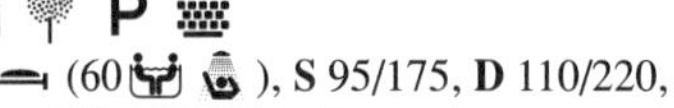

80 (60), **S** 95/175, **D** 110/220,
Closed 22—31 December

With an address on the famous Leopoldstrasse, the hotel is located farther north, on the outskirts of Schwabing. The comfortable rooms facing the courtyard are quiet and the atmosphere is more relaxed than in most large hotels.

MÜNCHEN PARK HILTON

80538, Bogenhausen
Am Tucherpark 7
(0 89) 3 84 50, Fax 38 45 18 45

477, **S** 295/450, **D** 360/515,
APP 800/1600

The Munich Hilton can't deny being one of an international chain, but it does its best to make you forget it. Its proximity to the Englischer Garten, the friendly service and the excellent restaurant all help. The rooms comply with high international standards; the hotel offers two whole floors of apartments and a shuttle service to the airport and city. Free jogging, golf and tennis equipment. Beauty farm and the largest convention center in town. Breakfast buffet: 33 DM.

PALACE

81675. Bogenhausen
Trogerstr. 21
(0 89) 4 70 50 91, Fax 4 70 50 90

P

71, **S** 230/425, **D** 320/520,
APP 450/1500

The directors and interior decorators have taken great pains to enhance the anonymous luxury typical of most new hotels with individual nuances. Sauna with roof terrace. The service can be a bit negligent. Breakfast: 24 DM

PLATZL HOTEL

80331, Platzl 1 [E/F1]
(0 89) 23 70 30, Fax 23 70 38 00

P

167, **S** 210/275, **D** 280/398,
APP 450

In the middle of the historic old city, the Platzl features marble in the lobby and fine woodwork in its rooms furnished in the traditional (somewhat functional) Munich style. Whirlpools and fitness facilities help guests relax. Roof terrace and restaurant under vaulted arches in the cellar.

PREYSING

81667, Haidhausen
Preysingstr. 1 [H6]
(0 89) 48 10 11, Fax 4 47 09 98

P

76, **S** 160/260, **D** 298,
APP 375/540
Closed 23 December through 6 January

The greatest advantage of this medium-sized, hospitable hotel is its proximity to the new Philharmonic concert hall, the German Museum, the Isar meadows and the new "in" quarter of town, Haidhausen, which is almost as popular as Schwabing.

PRINZREGENT

81675, Bogenhausen
Ismaniger Str. 42-44
(0 89) 41 60 50, Fax 41 60 54 66

P

66, **S** 220, **D** 300/330

The discreetly rustic decor of the rooms, with a lot of woodwork, may not enthrall every guest, but it's a change from the uniform look of most international hotels. It's just a few minutes' walk to the center of the city. Attentive service.

RAFAEL

80331, Neuturmstr. 1 [F4]
(0 89) 29 09 80, Fax 22 25 39

73, **S** 390/540, **D** 490/690,
APP 690/2000

The Rafael is Munich's top address for luxury. Each room and suite has individual charm and is provided with several telephones and computer hookups. Many bathrooms are as spacious as the bedrooms. Heated pool and roof terrace.

SHERATON HOTEL & TOWERS

81925, Bogenhausen
Arabellastr. 6
(0 89) 9 26 40, Fax 91 68 77

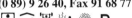

637, **S** 255/450, **D** 255/490,
APP 950/1800

Easy to reach from both airport and autobahn but inconveniently connected to the center of the city, this hotel is the right choice for those who thrive in the hectic atmosphere and perfect but impersonal service of a mammoth hotel. Fitness center, nightclub. Breakfast: 20—32 DM.

SPLENDID

80538, Maximilianstr. 54 [G4]
(0 89) 29 66 06, Fax 2 91 31 76

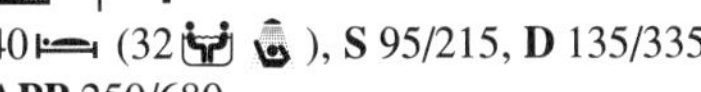

40 (32), **S** 95/215, **D** 135/335,
APP 250/680

This somewhat small hotel in the residential quarter of Lehel offers individually decorated rooms, excellent service, a splendid location and perversely enough—reasonable prices.

VIER JAHRESZEITEN KEMPINSKI

80539, Maximilianstr. 17 [F4]
(0 89) 23 03 90, Fax 23 03 96 93

322, **S** 395/660, **D** 465/730,
APP 1180/1620

The appointment of the rooms in this large establishment is sometimes flawless and sometimes surprisingly amiss; it wouldn't hurt to inquire about details when booking. The usually pleasant service can become less than friendly when under the strain of large conventions. Lufthansa service desk, pool on the roof. Breakfast: 23—31 DM.

MÜNSTER NRW

Osnabrück 57 - Düsseldorf 130

BAKENHOF 12/20

4 km west 48161, Stadtteil Gievenbeck
Roxeler Str. 376
(02 51) 86 15 06

P

Closed Monday, Tuesday, 2 weeks in February, 3 weeks in July/August. Tables d'hôte: 32L, 69D, à la carte: 33/71

The comfortable and quaint ambience inside harmonizes well with the typical romantic brick exterior. Italian and French accents compete with one another to make some dishes seem almost too clichéd: snail ragout with garlic and mushrooms in Pernod, fish with champagne sauce and tender *escaloppa romana* with a garlic and herb sauce. Apparently, the cook has a weakness for garlic and buckets of cream. Our brill with flat-tasting pike sauce let us down, and with a sallow duck's breast with sesame crust and sweet plum sauce, the cuisine hit rock bottom. The passably stocked wine list offers good value for money.

DAVERT-JAGDHAUS 15/20

48163, Stadtteil Amelsbüren
Wiemannstr. 4
(0 25 01) 5 80 58 res.

Closed Monday, Tuesday, 4 weeks during the NRW summer school holiday, 10 days at Christmas/New Year. Tables d'hôte: 60L, 105D, à la carte: 49/85

The always hurried but nevertheless pleasant service here functions as precisely as clockwork. We hadn't even ordered our drinks before a nimble helper welcomed us with an appetizer (salmon terrine with kohlrabi mousse). Guests who want to dine in a leisurely fashion had better inform the quick service staff; otherwise courses are served at top speed. Apart from some sour sauces and a pasty potato pancake with lovely mild herring, we enjoyed everything we tried here: tender sweetbreads with ragout of chanterelles, delicate anglerfish navarin and shrimp in saffron sauce, and quail's breast with chanterelles and noodles. The wine cellar is well-stocked, especially with the best German and French wines.

GASTSTÄTTE RENFERT HÖLT'NE SLUSE

48159, Max-Clemens-Kanal 303
(02 51) 21 64 40

Closed Monday, 24 December through 2 January, 1 August through 4 September, à la carte: 13/21, No Credit Cards

This is one of the most original restaurants in the Münsterland and well worth an excursion. The place is named after a lock *(sluse)* in the Max-Clemens canal, which was demolished in 1853. The fare is simple, plain and good. Wilhelm Renfert and his sister Sophia serve fresh bread with smoked Westphalian ham or pancakes with bacon by the fireplace in their rustic, stone-flagged dining room. Dark beer and Münsterländer schnaps are served with meals.

HOTEL CENTRAL

48143, Aegidiistr. 1
(02 51) 51 01 50, Fax 5 10 15 50

25 beds, **S** 150/225, **D** 185/225, **APP** 255/325

Closed 20 December through 6 January

A charming small hotel with lovely rooms designed in a postmodern style. Rooms 30 and 31 are particularly nice.

KAFFEEHAUS MAIKOTTEN

48155, Maikottenweg 208
(02 51) 3 10 95, Fax 31 67 15

Closed Monday, January, à la carte: 21/56

This café with conservatory, biergarten and rustic pub in the green belt of Münster draws many cyclists and weekend visitors. In the summer, you can picnic in the biergarten. Smoked Westphalian ham is a specialty here, as well as home-baked bread and a grand variety of freshly prepared salads. The house's own wines can be ordered by the glass.

KLEINES RESTAURANT IN OERSCHEN HOF 13/20

48143, Königsstr. 42
(02 51) 4 20 61, Fax 0 25 82 70 15

Closed Sunday, Monday, late January through mid-February, beginning through mid-August. Tables d'hôte: 30L, 60D, à la carte: 33/67. Tables d'hôte with wine: 30, No Credit Cards

This is surely one of the prettiest little restaurants in town. The cuisine has recuperated from the previous slump and offered us some delectable dishes on our last visit. We enjoyed delicious lamb tongue with salad and ripe avocados with pine nuts and a delicate sauce. Our fish soup tasted of southern oceans and summer, and the braid of sole and salmon with noodles and the tender rack of lamb with parsley crust would have deserved a rating of 14/20 if it hadn't been for a somewhat bitter rosemary sauce served with lamb and a flat-tasting herb sauce with asparagus and scampi.The small wine list sports high prices.

KRAUTKRÄMER 16/20

6 km southStadtteil Hiltrup
48165, Hiltruper See 173
(0 25 01) 80 50, Fax 80 51 04 res.

Closed 23—26 December. Tables d'hôte: 55L, 69/110D, à la carte: 50/92

In spite of a variety of changing chefs, the cuisine of the Krautkrämer has maintained its high standards. On our last visit to this distinguished-looking three-gabled house on the lake in Hiltrup, Stefan Schau served a wonderful salad of headcheese and calf's tongue in champagne vinegar, an exquisite lobster in lemongrass sauce, and a delicately boiled fillet of beef with horseradish sauce. The service is as excellent as it ever was. The choice of wines has been reduced from more than 1,000 to (merely?) 850. The restaurant's kitchen now also cooks for the previously independent bistro in the basement. Here you can order first courses from a Mediterranean buffet and other delicious little snacks till midnight. You can choose from wines by the glass or from the excellent wine list of the restaurant upstairs.

WALDHOTEL KRAUTKRÄMER

6 km south, Stadtteil Hiltrup
48165, Hiltruper See 173
(0 25 01) 80 50, Fax 80 51 04

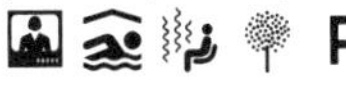 

70 ⊢, **S** 170/250, **D** 250/290,
APP 400/600, **1/2P** +60, **P** +105
Closed 23-26 December

This beautifully situated hotel on the shore of Lake Hiltrup offers a high standard of comfort and relaxation in its rooms and suites. Recreational facilities include swimming in the lake, tennis and fishing.

MAURITZHOF

48143, Eisenbahnstr. 15-17
(02 51) 4 17 20, Fax 4 66 86

39 ⊢, **S** 185/280, **D** 235/330,
APP 380, **1/2P** +50, **P** +80

This hotel of consequence, located on the green promenade near the Old Town, offers individually furnished, comfortable and spacious rooms. Every detail is a harmonious part of the modern decorating scheme. Breakfast: 19 DM.

PARKHOTEL SCHLOSS HOHENFELD

6.5 km west towards Versmold
in Stadtteil Roxel48161,
Dingbänger Weg 400-402
(0 25 34) 80 80 , Fax 71 14

89 ⊢, **S** 170/185, **D** 215/230,
1/2P +35, **P** +70

Completely rebuilt, this former palace offers a wide variety of activities, from bicycling to getting married in the historic chapel. Convention center and swimming pool, sauna, skittle alleys and sunbathing. Ambitious restaurant.

PINKUS MÜLLER

48143, Kreuzstr. 4-10
(02 51) 4 51 51/2, Fax 5 71 36 res.

Closed Sunday, à la carte: 20/57, No Credit Cards

With regret, we've seen this traditional institution, a one-time bulwark of hearty and savory Westphalian cooking, succumb to the taste of mass tourism. In memoriam of one of our favorite haunts we recall excellent aspic with fried potatoes and Müller's superb veal ragout. This time, we couldn't possibly enjoy a dry fried sausage, a soggy heap of Savoy cabbage with potatoes and hard rather than crispy pork haunch. Only our outstanding pork shoulder on black bread and a true-blue waitress reminded us of former good times.

SCHLOSS WILKINGHEGE 15/20

48159, Steinfurter Str. 374 (B54)
(02 51) 21 30 45, Fax 21 28 98 res.

Tables d'hôte: 81L, 98D, à la carte: 55/94. Tables d'hôte with wine: 97/122

The lovely castle on the water with stucco ceilings and silk tapestries was always Münster's most elegant address for weddings and receptions. But Lubert Winneken wasn't satisfied with that. Today, Schloss Wilkinghege is one of the best restaurants in the entire region. We appreciate the way chef Martin Löffler prepares every one of his dishes without unnecessary flourish. His lobster with tender scallops was wonderfully succulent, the terrine of smoked fish with eel sauce simply brilliant, the fillet of venison with a sauce of grapes and honey of sensationally good quality, and the tournedos with a concentrated sauce magnificent. The choice of cheeses could be better. The service is attentive and is supported from time to time by Lubert Winneken himself. Sufficient wines by the glass are offered, and the wine list now includes the best German wine-growers, as well as good red wines from Bordeaux, Burgundy and Tuscany.

SCHLOSS WILKINGHEGE

48159, Steinfurter Str. 374 (B54)
(02 51) 21 30 45, Fax 21 28 98

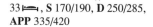

33, **S** 170/190, **D** 250/285,
APP 335/420

Outside the city gates of Münster, this idyllic castle rests on foundations dating back to the 14th century. Lovely stucco ceilings, precious paintings and old etchings are reminders of the splendid furnishings of past centuries. The modern rooms offer every amenity.

VILLA MEDICI 14/20

48145, Ostmarkstr. 15
(02 51) 3 42 18, Fax 39 30 94

Closed Sunday, Monday, 2 weeks each in summer and winter. Tables d'hôte: 79D, à la carte: 46/73

In our favorite Italian restaurant in Münster, we appreciate the pleasant and discreet service and the softly played arias from the loudspeakers. Our appetizer platter was generously heaped with vitello tonnato, aromatic lamb carpaccio, lobster claw with *sauce americaine*, salads, delicious salmon, seafood salad, melon and ham, for all of 23.50 DM! We enjoyed delicate noodle pralines stuffed with turbot, salmon marinated in oranges with Japanese watercress, and excellent zucchini flowers filled with minced veal with a light tomato sauce. The highlight of our meal was bass with a mild pepper sauce and leaf spinach. Only the sweet sauce with our saltimbocca of calf's liver and a dry trout fillet with a sour artichoke and tomato concassé made our confidence in the kitchen's prowess waver somewhat. The desserts made up for it, though.The comprehensive Italian wine list offered an adequate choice for every course.

WEIN-UND AUSTERNKELLER

48143, Bogenstr. 9
(02 51) 4 49 44, Fax 5 67 66

P

Closed for dinner, closed Sunday, Monday. Tables d'hôte: 42, à la carte: 30/44

Klaus Friedrich Helmrich's little cellar bistro is decorated with wine cases, corkscrews and all sorts of accessories. The solid food here includes herring with pumpernickel, fresh goat cheese with capers, tomatoes with basil, fried lamb sausages with vegetables à la Provence, and, last but not least, oysters from Sylt or Brittany. The bistro is only open when the adjacent delicatessen is, so the few available seats are much sought-after toward closing time and on Saturday afternoons. The wines by the glass are terrific, and sometimes there is an opportunity to try some great Bordeaux brought back by Helmrich from an auction at Christie's in London: 1975 Beychevelle, 1976 Brane-Cantenac and 1979 L'Evangeline sold for 18 DM a glass. The late breakfast here is fantastic and cheap.

MÜNSTERTAL Bad.-Württ.

Freiburg 25 - Basel 65

SCHMIDT'S GASTHOF ZUM LÖWEN 12/20

79244, Wasen 54
(0 76 36) 5 42, Fax 7 79 19

P

Closed Tuesday, Wednesday, mid-January through Lent. Tables d'hôte: 48/84, à la carte: 35/82, No Credit Cards

Abundance and opulence are the dominating principles of this cuisine, which offers six prix-fixe meals, each with the same appetizer platter and different main courses. The appetizer consists of a mountain of foie gras, salmon, ham, terrines, quail eggs and sometimes even an oyster when in season. Needless to say, Ekkehard Schmidt is popu-

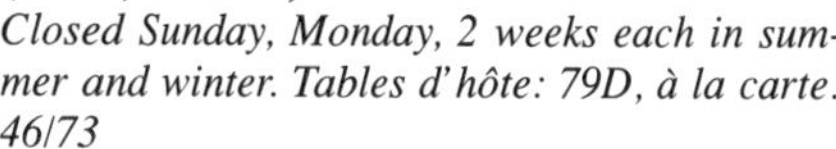

lar with hungry guests who like to eat well and copiously. His traditional German duck is a best-seller here, and so is pigeon and ox combined in a pot-au-feu. Pleasant service and great choice of wines from Baden and Franconia.

SPIELWEG 14/20
Obermünstertal
79244, Spielweg 61
(0 76 36) 70 90, Fax 7 09 66

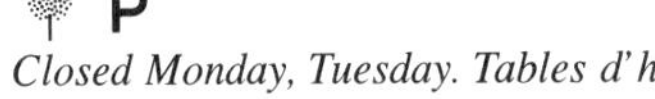

Closed Monday, Tuesday. Tables d'hôte: 75/98, à la carte: 59/104

The star of German haute cuisine, Eckhard Witzigmann, felt at home here when he visited his former apprentice Hansjörg Fuchs. We didn't. We missed that kind of personal hospitality that simply has to go with fine cooking. Nevertheless, the ambience is comfortable and snug, the wine list offers the best regional wines and the kitchen gives proof of its fine cuisine. We enjoyed the hearty regional fare usually served to house guests—everything from trout to blood pudding (delicious!). The foie gras terrine was a little fatty and alcoholic around the edges. The wild boar aspic gave us an appetite for more of the same thing, but, strangely enough, the wild boar didn't turn up anywhere else on the menu. A noodle dish with fresh John Dory was exquisite and perfectly balanced, however, and the main courses were delightful. We especially liked the marrow quenelles that came with the fillet of beef gratin. The *tafelspitz*, on the other hand, was a little overdone, and the horseradish sauce that came with it much too creamy. The dessert of cheese with fruit was a perfect conclusion of our meal, and we loved the little piece of cake served with coffee.

SPIELWEG
Obermünstertal
79244, Spielweg 61
(0 76 36) 70 90, Fax 7 09 66

P

40, **S** 150/180, **D** 190/380,
APP 370/540, **½P** +70

In a narrow valley at the foot of the Black Forest, this massive historic building has been completely renovated. The various buildings of the extensive complex are all connected by passageways and galleries. The hospitable atmosphere has a personal touch. The rooms are of different sizes and the nicest are in the new "Soonhalde." The service is good and breakfast ample.

MURNAU Bayern

Weilheim 20 - Garmisch 25

ALPENHOF MURNAU 15/20
82418, Ramsachstr. 8
(0 88 41) 49 10 , Fax 54 38 res.

P

Tables d'hôte: 49/135, à la carte: 52/93

Opulent portions and high-quality food justify the somewhat lowered, but still high prices here. Chef Karl Johann Hamberger served light, fluffy celery mousse with sorrel and tender rabbit livers with a savory Burgundy sauce. Lovely fillet of pike-perch was accompanied by crispy potato slices and the perfectly done John Dory by Champagne sauce. Guinea fowl in sesame-seed crust, Barbary duck with asparagus, veal piccata, and succulent saddle of suckling lamb were highlights of our meal. The wonderful desserts deserve as much praise as the impressive wine list, with its regional wines and noble vintages from Burgundy and Bordeaux. The service is circumspect, obliging, and pleasant.

ALPENHOF MURNAU
82418, Ramsachstr. 8
(0 88 41) 49 10, Fax 54 38

P

43, **S** 75/140, **D** 140/350,
APP 400/450, **½P** +65, **P** +130

The Alpenhof is located in almost untouched natural surroundings. The clear, unobstructed view of the Alpine foothills and the peak of the Wetterstein makes a stay here worthwhile. The courtyard is full of flowers, and the reception rooms are attractive. Most of the rustically decorated rooms have balconies. Extensive grounds with heated outdoor pool. Breakfast: 30 DM.

NACKENHEIM Rheinl.-Pfalz

Oppenheim 9 - Mainz 12

GUNDERLOCH 13/20

55299, Karl-Gunderloch-Platz 1
(0 61 35) 23 41

P

Closed for lunch every day except Sunday, closed Monday, Tuesday, à la carte: 23/47

The Austrian-born Hans-Werner Verdonik had cooked himself to the top of the ranks in Mainz in his Palais Rosella, but to the bottom of his financial resources. In this country inn not far from Mainz, he shows that he can prepare less extravagant dishes with the same expertise he exhibits in his fine cuisine. After a somewhat unexciting smoked ham with nut bread, we had a delicious regional version of *vitello tonnato:* fried veal with good tuna sauce and bean salad. Verdonik's pork roast in Riesling with potato salad was excellent, and his saddle of lamb with a crust of herbs succulent and tender. Like many Austrian cooks, Verdonik is an outstanding pastrymaker, and his *topfenschmarrn* (sweet curds) was heavenly. The service is refreshingly competent and even advises against dishes on the menu if the ingredients are not absolutely fresh and perfect. The wine list includes mostly excellent wines from the Gunderloch winery. The facade could use a coat of paint.

NAGOLD Bad-Württ.

Tübingen 35 - Freudenstadt 40

ELES 14/20

72202, Neuwiesenweg 44
(0 74 52) 54 85 res.

 P

Closed for lunch, closed Sunday. Tables d'hôte: 75, à la carte: 39/72, No Credit Cards

With its modern decor, conspicuously placed lamps, paintings for sale on the walls, colorful ceiling, and old wooden chairs and tables, the ambience created by Wolfgang ("Eles") Kaupp is hard to classify. We followed Kaupp's suggestions for our meal and were not disappointed. We enjoyed a savory potato soup, a delicious salad with a tartare of bacon dumplings and perfectly done quail, as well as an exquisitely prepared turbot fried with ginger and shallots. Although the venison could have been tastier, it was still very good served with peppered red-wine sauce, red beet spaetzle, chestnuts and Savoy-cabbage dumplings. Kaupp's one-man kitchen put on a perfect show. Kudos for his white-chocolate parfait with vanilla cream and cassis figs! Kaupp has stocked choice German, French and Italian wines at moderate prices. If the weather permits, reserve your table in the garden on the bank of the Nagold.

POST

72202, Bahnhofstr. 3-4
(0 74 52) 40 48, Fax 40 40

P

23 rooms, **S** 84/104, **D** 142/180

Closed 20 December through 8 January

This beautiful 400-year-old half-timbered house located in the center of town is the best and, in fact, the only large hotel in Nagold. Some of the comfortably equipped rooms are furnished with antiques.

NAURATH (WALD) Rheinl.-Pfalz

Trittenheim 7 - Hermeskeil 14 - Trier 20

LANDHAUS ST. URBAN 16/20

54426, Büdlicherbrück 1
(0 65 09) 9 14 00, Fax 9 14 00

Tables d'hôte: 54/64L, 82/102, à la carte: 54/81

Harald Rüssel has not let early success go to his head. Instead, this intelligent young man has polished and refined his cuisine. The aspic of mildly smoked brook trout with pesto was wonderful, as were the prawns in rice leaves with asparagus risotto and sauce bourride, and the crispy fried pike-perch with eggplant tortellini. Another standout was the headcheese and calf's tail with summer truffles and fresh goat-cheese strudel. Harald Rüssel's cuisine seems close to perfection, but this chef has yet to reach his limits. The wine list has grown and includes more French red wines and white wines from the Moselle. Ruth Rüssel supervises the impeccable service. Modern guest rooms are available.

BAD NENNDORF Nieders.

Hannover 30 - Bielefeld 82

LA FORGE IN SCHMIEDEGASTHAUS GEHRKE 17/20

4 km west in Ortsteil Riepen
31542, Riepener Str. 21
(0 57 25) 50 55, Fax 72 82 res.

Closed for lunch, closed Monday, Tuesday, 2 weeks in January, 3 weeks during the Nieders. summer school holiday. Tables d'hôte: 89/125, à la carte: 62/109

Here, gourmets experience the high art of cooking. The Gehrke brothers have transformed this plain village *gasthof* into a mecca for gourmets in northern Germany. The cuisine has developed its own original and inimitable style, thanks to its regional emphasis and unceasing creativity, and the chef's exactitude in buying and preparing high-quality products. The result is dishes that not only look, but also taste delectable. Appetizers included a heavenly trout mousse with eel and a delicious terrine of young wild boar. The rolled sole fillets and the pigeon breast stuffed with foie gras were memorable. Ernst-August Gehrke is at his best when he serves refined regional cuisine: a salad of suckling pig with marjoram vinaigrette, pike-perch and eel strudel with cabbage and turnips, a mountain of pancakes with mushrooms and rabbit. These all sound much simpler than they taste. Mr. Gehrke is a perfectionist. We have never tasted a better suckling kid, and his desserts are fantastic. Andreas Gehrke mirrors his brother's accomplishments with impeccable service and attention to his guests. It is almost always possible to have the wines of your choice by the glass.

NEUBRANDENBURG MV

Greifswald 148 - Berlin 162

BONJOUR 12/20

17033, Kleiststr. 9
(03 95) 5 66 64 91, Fax 5 66 64 92

Closed for lunch Sunday, Tables d'hôte: 40/50, à la carte: 26/87. Tables d'hôte with wine: 45/70

Most visitors have a long and arduous search behind them before they find this hidden little bistro-restaurant. A comprehensive menu with an emphasis on French cuisine rewards hungry searchers. Crab claws with salad and grilled John Dory with cucumber and cream sauce tasted as delectable as they sounded, but some dishes couldn't deliver what the menu promised—like our dry quail's breast with salad. Some prices demonstrated unwarranted self-confidence in the cuisine's quality, for instance, a grilled spiny lobster tail for 65 DM! The service is correct, obliging and attentive. The choice of German, French and Italian wines could be improved.

LA MANDRIA IN HOTEL VIER TORE 13/20

17033, Treptower Str. 1
(03 95) 5 58 60, Fax 5 84 10 15

P

Tables d'hôte: 25/69, à la carte: 24/55

In the course of this hotel's complete renovation the restaurant has also been refurbished. So has the cuisine, which on our last visit managed to cover all the latest trends in one menu. Italian influences (*vitello tonnato* and pasta) are just as obvious as Asian (exotically seasoned poularde breast in sesame crust) and regional (duck's breast stuffed with baked plums and dumplings) recipes. All dishes are prepared with care and mostly without flaws, but the cuisine has yet to find its own distinctive style.

HOTEL VIER TORE

17033, Treptower Str. 1
(03 95) 5 58 60, Fax 5 84 10 15

190, **S** 175/195, **D** 205/225, **APP** 280/350, **½P** 25/30, **P** +45/50

This nondescript hotel with its large lobbies and restaurants still hasn't rid itself of that drab Eastern German atmosphere, but some rooms have been stylishly renovated. Café-bar and bar.

BAD NEUENAHR Rheinl.Pfalz

Bonn 30 - Koblenz 57

REST. BROGSITTER 14/20

53474, Ortsteil Walporzheim
Walporzheimer Str. 134/B 267
(0 26 41) 9 77 50, Fax 97 75 25 res.

Tables d'hôte: 50L, 73D, à la carte: 42/91. Tables d'hôte with wine: 125

At the foot of the Ahr Valley, this restaurant attracts gourmets and a number of guests who like the exclusive ambience. Sometimes gourmets have to share the dining rooms with avid (and loud) conversationalists or cigar and pipe smokers. After a creamy asparagus mousse and a small salad with quail's breast and squab in Madeira, we enjoyed a wonderful sheatfish with leaf spinach and watercress mousse. Our veal steak took a bit of chewing, but the nice presentation did its best to make it worth the 46 DM we had to pay for it. Apple tart and raspberries with rhubarb and mascarpone were delicious conclusions to our meal. The choice of wines, especially regional Ahr wines, is great.

STEIGENBERGER

53474, Kurgartenstr. 1
(0 26 41) 94 10, Fax 70 01

236 rooms, **S** 180/206, **D** 286/320, **APP** 370/880, **½P** +45, **P** +70

This is a mixture of a modern spa and an old-fashioned grand hotel. The public areas are elegant. There's a bar, Viennese café, cosmetic studio, casino and restaurant. Ample breakfast buffet.

STEINHEUERS REST. ZUR ALTEN POST 17/20

53474, Stadtteil Heppingen
Landskroner Str. 110
(0 26 41) 70 11, Fax 70 13 res.

Closed Tuesday, closed for lunch Wednesday, closed 3 weeks in July/August. Tables d'hôte: 95L, 115/149, à la carte: 67/107

Hans Stefan Steinheuer is a quiet, unobtrusive cook who nevertheless dominates the Ahr region with an absolute commitment to first-class cuisine. He's ambitious and ingenious, using only the freshest and best products. None of his dishes are flamboyant, but all are strikingly effective, like prawns with tempura, variations of calf's liver and foie gras, sorrel soup, oxtail consommé, sheatfish with apple and horseradish sauce, and rabbit in mustard sauce.The service is agreeable and offers a choice of 400 wines from the well-stocked cellar, including the very best vintages from the Ahr. Beautifully appointed rooms offer all modern amenities. Bed and breakfast: 140 to 200 DM.

NEU-ISENBURG Hessen

Frankfurt 7 - Darmstadt 17

WESSINGER AM WALD

63263, Alicestr. 2
(0 61 02) 80 80, Fax 80 82 80

Closed Monday. Tables d'hôte: 33/45, à la carte: 29/71

The Wessinger family is enterprising and ambitious. In addition to a hotel, they run a sweet shop, and they have now opened a new restaurant that offers international cuisine and renowned wines. But the new decor hasn't turned this simple *gasthaus* into a gourmet restaurant. An obviously overworked service team has to fight its way through tables and chairs set too close together; some mishaps, like overturned bottles, are excused with rustic charm. But no amount of charm can excuse the food we were served. The red snapper medallions had lost their taste in a sesame coat, our saddle of veal had seen better days, and the chanterelle sauce had a suspiciously tangy edge. The only highlights were the succulent sheatfish and the fried potatoes. More care and attention to detail were invested in the desserts. We liked our red berries with vanilla sauce and ice cream and tea parfait with rum mousse. The same goes for an incredible variety of delicious tarts and cakes.

NEULEININGEN Rheinl.-Pfalz

Bad Dürkheim 8 - Worms 7

ALTE PFARREY 13/20

67271, Untergasse 54
(0 63 50) 8 60 66, Fax 8 60 60 res.

Closed Monday, closed for lunch Tuesday, closed 1 week in January, 2 weeks in July/August. Tables d'hôte: 38/125, à la carte: 40/86

In the pretty and romantic town of Neuleiningen, Utz and Susanne Ueberschaer have made their particular dream come true by opening their own restaurant and hotel. The pleasant new dining room is located in a conservatory, which has been added to the old house. The service is excellent.The aromatic and savory venison and lamb cutlets, as well as the salmon with honey and mustard sauce and sesame seeds, convinced us that Utz Ueberschaer has definitely earned his toque. Although the lamb's lettuce with beef and herbs was slightly wilted and the leg of suckling lamb rather insipid, an opulent helping of chocolate mousse and sherbet more than made up for these lapses. The wine list has apparently been compiled by a connoisseur of regional and French wines who has made some discoveries in other countries as well.

ALTE PFARREY

67271, Untergasse 54
(0 63 50) 8 60 66, Fax 8 60 60

10, **S** 105/140, **D** 160/190

This carefully restored Gothic house offers exquisitely furnished rooms decorated in Bavarian country Baroque style with luxurious bathrooms. Friendly hospitality in a pleasant ambience.

LIZ'STUBEN 13/20

67271, Am Goldberg 2
(0 63 59) 53 41 res.

Closed for lunch, closed Sunday, Monday, 2 weeks in January, 3—4 weeks in June/July. Tables d'hôte: 89/98, No Credit Cards

The Gissels have been running their private restaurant for 13 years now. From the outside, you cannot tell that it is a restaurant. Inside, it has the charm of a pretty living room, and Maître Gissel is your attentive (and only) waiter. Reservations are a must.The Gissels like Italy and Italian cooking, and they offer an entire dinner for 89 Deutsche marks, consisting of four or five small first courses, entremets, main course and dessert. On the whole, some dishes could use a little more typically Italian seasoning. The cuisine is relatively simple. We started with tomato with mozzarella and basil, fried quail's egg, artistically stuffed zucchini blossoms, and spaghettini with pesto, followed by fried quail on a mainly decorative salad. We enjoyed our iced melon soup, as well as the creative combination of anglerfish with *salsa verde* and red-beet carpaccio with a light vinaigrette. The fillet of beef Piemonte with balsamic vinegar was superb. The wine list is concise and concentrates on Italian vintages.

NEUMÜNSTER Schl.-Holst.

Keil 32 - Hamburg 66

AM KAMIN 13/20

24534, Probstener 13
(0 43 21) 4 28 53, Fax 4 29 19 res.

P

Closed for lunch Saturday, closed Sunday. Tables d'hôte: 55/98, à la carte: 40/74

The chef of the Kamin has correctly read the signs of the times and offers a choice of four prix-fixe menus. We liked his finely balanced lentil cream soup with champagne and his rolled sole strudel with Riesling from his gourmet prix-fixe meal. His desserts were pretty to look at but didn't tickle our palates. A comfortable fire, rustic furniture and paintings by local artists on the walls create the perfect ambience for a relaxing evening. The service is pleasant and attentive, and the wine list, though doubtful in quality, has grown in variety.

NEUNKIRCHEN Bayern

Nürnberg 25 - Bamberg 40

KLOSTERHOF 14/20

91077, Inner Markt 7
(0 91 34) 15 85 res.

Closed for dinner Sunday, closed Monday, 1 week in February, 3 weeks after mid-August. Tables d'hôte: 70/90, à la carte: 38/72

The Klosterhof in Neunkirchen is one of the most dependable addresses for gourmet dining in this region. Safe from experimental cuisine, guests in the dusky, comfortable Franconian dining rooms enjoy dependable, if somewhat uninspired, cooking. Armin Kohlmann prepares his dishes expertly, and whatever he cooks tastes good. His light touch gives aromas a better chance to develop. Neunkirchen is asparagus country, and you will find a variety of asparagus dishes on the menu when the vegetable is in season.

Fish is always fresh and well-prepared, although the seasoning could use a little verve. Meat courses are savory and simply served.The service is attentive, personal and pleasant. The wine list is carefully compiled but somewhat limited. When the weather permits, guests can dine on the terrace.

NEUNKIRCHEN Saarland

Homburg 15 - Saarbrücken 23

HOSTELLERIE BACHER 18/20

66539, Ortsteil Kohlhof
Limbacher Str. 2
(0 68 21) 3 13 14 res.

Closed Sunday, Monday, first 3 weeks during the Saarland summer school holiday. Tables d'hôte: 52/98L, 72/140D, à la carte: 43/100

Eating at Margarethe Bacher's is always a culinary experience. This modest cook creates amazing taste sensations, perfect down to the last detail. A light and tender oyster parfait with a sweet-and-sour tomato sauce started our meal, and was followed by delicious ravioli filled with fresh salmon in a savory potato soup laced with white wine. Grilled turbot, sweet-and-sour tomato ragout with green olives, well-seasoned leaf spinach and a creamy, delicate potato sauce with chives resulted in a harmonious concert of strikingly different flavors. Our excellent main course was another perfect combination: tender quail stuffed with liver with a slightly sweet dark sauce and Savoy cabbage. An exquisite dessert—white chocolate mousse with poppyseeds, vanilla ice cream laced with orange liqueur, rhubarb purée and warm cake filled with nuts and chocolate - rounded off a memorable meal.The service is pleasant and competent. The wine list includes bottles from the best wineries of the major German regions as well as French and Italian wines. The mostly young vintages are drinkable, and a small choice of rare vintages is also offered, among them many Bordeaux from the 1980s. The choice of wines by the glass is interesting (including Potensac, Médoc) and the half-bottles are worth a try.

NEURUPPIN Brandenburg

Potsdam 78 - Rostock 155

HOTEL GILDENHALL

5 km northeast in
16827, Alt Ruppin
Wuthenower Str. 10
(0 33 91) 7 52 42, Fax 7 52 43

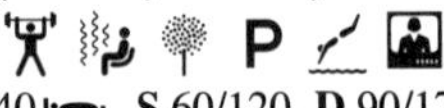

40 rooms, **S** 60/120, **D** 90/170, **1/2P** +18, **P** +30

This idyllic location in an extensive park on the shore of Neuruppin's lake would be a perfect setting for an exclusive hotel. But rooms and salons still exhibit the drab decor of East German designers. You can nonetheless spend a few agreeable days here, row on the beautiful lake, visit Neuruppin or make an excursion to nearby Rheinsberg or the monastery of Chorin.

NEUSS Nordrhein-Westfalen

Düsseldorf 10 - Krefeld 20

HERZOG VON BURGUND 13/20

41460, Erftstr. 88
(0 21 01) 2 35 52 res.

Closed for lunch Saturday and Sunday, closed Thursday, 1 week in February, 2 weeks in September. Tables d'hôte: 59L, 98/110D, à la carte: 52/84. Tables d'hôte with wine: 98/145

The menu here is straightforward, uncomplicated and changes often. We especially like the way Chef Tiefenbacher serves appropriate wines by the glass with his prix-fixe menus, although the waits between courses sometimes left us high and dry for long stretches on end. After a salmon tartare as appetizer and ravioli with crayfish mousse and asparagus salad, we had to wait 45 minutes for our soup. Delicate codfish fillets with creamed sauerkraut, brook trout with spinach and salmon quenelles were satisfactory. The lamb we had was a bit chewy, but it tasted wonderful. Some maniac in the kitchen whittled potatoes into the shape of mushrooms. Terrific Salzburg sweet dumplings are worth the trip here!

NEUSTRELITZ Meckl.-Vorp.

Neubrandenburg 29 - Berlin 133

FASANERIE IN PARKHOTEL 12/20

17235, Karbe-Wagner-Str. 59
(0 39 81) 44 36 00, Fax 44 35 53 res.

P

A la carte: 25/47

In spite of its size, this hotel-restaurant exudes a cheerfully elegant atmosphere with its apricot-colored walls and eye-catching bar. The kitchen struggles with the too-large variety of international dishes offered on the menu. No wonder there's no time to pay attention to fine detail. We liked our generously garnished Spanish fish soup, whereas the seafood with mild curried cream tasted rubbery. There's a small choice of French and German wines by the glass and an incredibly low-priced collection of wines by the bottle (worth improving). Some aged vintages should be drunk quickly. Well-trained, correct and informative service.

PARKHOTEL

17235, Karbe-Wagner-Str. 59
(0 39 81) 44 36 00, Fax 44 35 53

  P

69, **S** 135/146, **D** 187,
½P +17, **P** +37

This new hotel is located on the outskirts of town in the park of the former Fasanerie. The rooms are comfortably and elegantly furnished.

NIDEGGEN NRW

Düren 13 - Euskirchen 25

BURG NIDEGGEN

52385, Kirchgasse 10
(0 24 27) 12 52, Fax 69 79 res.

 P

Closed Monday, à la carte: 31/67

This old citadel erected in the 12th century is a paradise for amateur historians and school groups. Spine-chilling legends are told about this stronghold. Things aren't as spooky in the elegant restaurant, but the way the staff tried to be trendy was touching. The head waiter didn't tire of impressing us with the absolutely fresh cuisine, especially when he had to report one thing or another on the menu was "out." In fact, half of the menu wasn't available, and putting together a meal posed a bit of a problem. The tasteless (probably deep-fried) saddle of venison we eventually got didn't have much in common with the fresh seasonal products advertised. The wine list and service may satisfy day trippers and tourists.

NIEDERSTOTZINGEN BW

Ulm 27 - Augsburg 65

REST. VOGELHERD IN SCHLOSSHOTEL OBERSTOTZINGEN 15/20

89168, Stettener Str. 35-17

(0 73 25) 10 30, Fax 1 03 70 res.

 P

Closed for lunch every day except Sunday and Wednesday, closed Monday, January. Tables d'hôte: 45L, 80D, à la carte: 53/92

The constant turnover of service staff does not seem to have affected the kitchen. Thank goodness. The cuisine maintains its high standards. We enjoyed marbled terrine of pigeon and foie gras in port jelly, surrounded by asparagus salad covered with slivered truffles. We loved the little scallops with saffron sauce, young vegetables and caviar. The roulade of lobster and sole with spinach, served with champagne sauce, was utterly delicious. The highlight of the meal was the lamb *crépinettes* with shallots, fresh beans, tomatoes and potato gratin. There was an impressive selection of whole-milk cheeses, and our dessert—cheese soufflé on iced rhubarb soup with vanilla ice-cream and sliced strawberries—was a delight. Biscuits and pralines, evidently not home-made and disappointing in flavor, were served with coffee.The high prices of the wine list have been reduced. The choice of wines by the glass is sufficient and moderately priced, but champagne is much too expensive.

NÖRDLINGEN/RIES Bayern

Donauwörth 28 - Ulm 82

MEYER'S KELLER 14/20

86720, Marienhöhe 8
(0 90 81) 44 93, Fax 2 49 31 res.

 P

Closed Monday, closed for lunch Tuesday, closed 2 weeks in February. Tables d'hôte: 39/119, à la carte: 41/85

Joachim Kaiser's biggest competitor is himself. A passionate host, he likes to feed the thousands of hungry people who visit his biergarten in the summer. Just as passionately, he likes to prepare gourmet cuisine for a select few. He indulges both passions and wins every time. In addition to the biergarten outside and his pub, he has portioned off a part of his vaulted cellar and created a little restaurant. Here the atmosphere is personal and the bar spacious, and his younger guests can overcome their awe of gourmet dining. Evelin Kaiser's cheerfulness and spontaneity make all her guests feel at home. Kaiser's menu is broad enough to satisfy the tastes of all his guests. He even offers a meal for those who just want to sample refined cuisine for 55 Deutsche marks (including aperitif, wine and coffee). Gourmet veterans, though, should order one of his more extravagant compositions, including salad with pigeon and lentils, lobster soup with a soufflé of red beets, bass with ravioli and various strawberry desserts. All of his (mostly regional) ingredients are of high quality. Sometimes, however, the hectic activity in the beer garden seems to interfere with accurate seasoning and disturbs the harmony of some dishes. We only wish Kaiser would buy his wine with as much discrimination as he does his kitchen products. The wine list is conventional, but not much more.

NÖRTEN-HARDENBERG NS

Göttingen 12 - Hannover 100

NOVALIS IN BURGHOTEL HARDENBERG 14/20

37176, Im Hinterhaus 11a
(0 55 03) 10 47, Fax 16 50 res.

Closed Sunday, 24—26 December, January. Tables d'hôte: 35L, 120D, à la carte: 54/84

Despite the traditional bull's-eye windowpanes and the raftered ceilings that tourists rave about, this restaurant is run in a thoroughly modern way. The cuisine is simple, but it has verve and originality. Reception and service are pleasant, and when the weather permits, you can even sit outside in the courtyard. The prices on the comprehensive wine list are relatively high, compared with those of the menu. As courses of a complete meal, the dishes à la carte can be ordered in smaller portions. Our tasty appetizer, a seafood terrine, was followed by salmon tartare with slivered white asparagus and an exquisite roulade of sole. Almost everything in this restaurant is first-class. The Nantaise duckling, however, was not all we expected it to be (a little dry, but tender and well-seasoned), and the desserts were unexciting.

BURGHOTEL HARDENBERG

37176, In Hinterhaus 11a
(0 55 03) 10 47, Fax 16 50

44, **S** 145/180, **D** 210/220,
APP 250/260, **½P** +42, **P** +62
Closed 24-26 December

Below the ruins of Burg Hardenberg, this quiet hotel offers tastefully decorated, spacious rooms.

NORDENHAM Niedersachsen

Brake 25 - Bremen 69

LANDHAUS TETTENS 14/20

5 km north in Ortsteil Tettens
26954, Am Dorfbrunnen 17
(0 47 31) 3 94 24, Fax 3 17 40

Closed Monday, 13-24 March, 3-14 July. Tables d'hôte: 39/79, à la carte: 30/61, No Credit Cards

The house behind the dike had a thatched roof, reason enough for us to anticipate regional cuisine and northern German hospitality. We got both at incredibly low prices, justified only by the out-of-the-way location of this place. You can get a four-course prix-fixe meal here for less than 60 DM—wine and coffee included! We liked fish ravioli and saffron fish soup, even though the fish could have used more delicate handling and the side dishes more attention to detail. But the locally raised lamb was wonderful. Many dishes were offered only for two, but the friendly service made exceptions without a lot of fuss. The desserts weren't sensational, but the choice of wines (also available by the glass) was good. Nice variety of liqueurs.

NÜRNBERG Bayern

München 165 - Frankfurt 222

ARVE 13/20 

90473, Stadtteil Langwasser
Görlitzer Str. 51
(09 11) 8 92 28 88, Fax 8 92 21 15

P

Closed Sunday, 26 December through 6 January, August. Tables d'hôte: 50L, 70/98D, à la carte: 45/75

This hotel kitchen does more than just feed guests until they are satisfied. The restaurant is located inside one of the ugliest functional buildings of Nürnberg's unattractive satellite town, Langwasser, but it has been serving fine cuisine for years. Besides serving conventions and banquets, the highly motivated cook Jürgen Utsch finds time to prepare more extravagant gourmet meals in his Arve restaurant. The menu offers classic haute cuisine, such as marinated salmon with salad, a variety of cream soups, beef tournedos, saddle of lamb, delicately fried fish and more. These are not enough to draw gourmets from Nürnberg, however. What is astonishing is the perfection that goes into the preparation of all these dishes. The desserts are unimaginative, and the wine list is that of your average hotel restaurant.

BAMMES 15/20

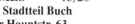

90427, Stadtteil Buch
Bucher Hauptstr. 63
(09 11) 38 13 01/3, Fax 34 63 13 res.

 P

Closed Sunday, Monday. Tables d'hôte: 48L, 95/118, à la carte: 46/91

Karl-Bernd Sperber has not let crises or recessions influence the style or quality of his cooking. True, he does more catering and has lowered his prices, but his restaurant is as well frequented as ever—largely because of his unwavering commitment to high quality. This is Sperber's only extravagance. The Bammes is characterized by uncomplicated and cheerful hospitality, and the guests, not the food, are the center of interest. The cuisine is neither intellectually creative nor particularly ingenious. Chef Vockentänzer offers light, international and perfectly prepared cuisine. The seafood pot-au-feu was refreshingly simple and tasted as grand as fresh fish does when as little as possible is done to it. The red-mullet fillet with asparagus and chive sauce was simply served and tasted fantastic. Admittedly, this kind of purist cooking takes some getting used to, but we loved the pigeon cutlet on wild-mushroom ragout just the way it was—simple and good. With all this perfection, however, creativity hardly stands a chance. The desserts were good but unimaginative. Regional specialities are available. The service is attentive, always busy but relaxed. The Bammes offers a choice of wines as well, but more in the line of duty than pleasure.

ENTENSTUB'N 13/20

90491, Stadtteil Erlenstegen
Günterbühler Str. 145
(09 11) 5 98 04 13, Fax 5 98 05 59 res.

 P

Closed for lunch Saturday, closed Sunday, Monday, 1 week each in January and August. Tables d'hôte: 65L, 89D, à la carte: 50/86. Tables d'hôte with wine: 65/94

Now that all the stuffy bric-a-brac has been thrown out, the historic dining rooms of this idyllic old house in the woods seem light and spacious. The restaurant's menu has been revised as well, and it now contains two whole meals and a half-dozen first courses and main courses. The emphasis is on fish. One meal, for example, consists entirely of fish courses. We had seafood salad with stuffed squid, salmon lasagna, tuna with curry oil, and fried halibut with asparagus. The choice of meat main courses was skimpy. The food sounded exciting, but it fell a little short of our expectations. The seasoning was bland, the flavors had lost their characteristic accents, side dishes were prepared carelessly, and desserts were, on the whole, too sweet. The cuisine needed a little more finesse and a lot more precision. The wine list, appropriately, contains a great number of wines from almost all famous wine-growing regions in the world, but these are of poor vintages and from second-class estates. The attentive and very pleasant service deserves praise.

ESSIGBRÄTLEIN 18/20 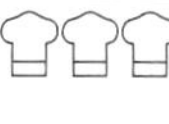

90403, Am Weinmarkt 3
(09 11) 22 51 31 res.

P

Closed for lunch Saturday, closed Sunday, Monday, 2 weeks each in January and August. Tables d'hôte: 68/78L, 98/120, à la carte: 62/92

The "simple cuisine for advanced gourmets" that Andree Köthe advocates makes the oldest restaurant in Nürnberg one of the region's most interesting dining addresses. Precision is the secret of this ambitious young cook, who never tires of presenting new and exciting creations. Andress Köthe is not a man of manneristic flourishes; his tastes run to the pure and simple. His suggestions are just as precise as his cooking: He offers one meal and some alternative à la carte courses. We remember with pleasure the following highlights: a sensational and ingenious combination of fried sardines with sweet and sour cabbage, garnished with roasted pine kernels; king prawns fried in orange oil and served with onions; and a wonderfully fresh turbot, precisely done, arranged on fresh beans dressed with the finest olive oil and thin slices of smoked bacon. This light cuisine reduces gourmet eating to its essentials and creates taste sensations of great finesse. Duck's breast marinated in soy sauce and ginger, fried in the skin and served with wok-fried vegetables and noodles was sensational and simple at the same time. And what was modestly described as "chocolate pudding" in the menu turned out to be sheer poetry: melted bitter chocolate covered with an incredibly light pastry on homemade orange compôte. Unusual and rare wines are fitting company for Andree Köthe's cuisine. His wine list consists of the best regional wines, an excellent choice of *crus bourgeois*, and good California wines at reasonable (but just barely so) prices. The attentive and obliging service provides the right background for a relaxed and comfortable meal.

FUNK 15/20

90471, Breslauer Str. 350
(09 11) 80 48 08, Fax 89 86 59 res.

P

Closed Sunday, Monday, à la carte: 58/96

The neighborhood could not be more inappropriate for a high-class restaurant. Funk's restaurant is located on the top floor of a post-modern industrial complex, which houses his wholesale sanitary-appliance business. The restaurant itself has a cheerful Caribbean touch with lots of palm trees—and empty tables. Although Chef Hermann-Peter Fischer does his best, many gourmets are obviously put off not by his cooking, but by the negative image of this Nürnberg suburb, with its drab apartment houses and industrial districts. The arrogance of the restaurant's management and the exorbitant prices frighten off the rest of the customers. We were irritated by the brusque negative answer we received when we asked whether we could combine the meal suggestions on the menu with à la carte dishes. Funk's hospitality is unusual, to say the least: A uniformed butler pressed the elevator button for us, but we could not get the waiters to refill our glasses at the table. The cuisine is characterized by high technical perfection and originality. Whether it is salad with pigeon, turbot with truffles or *feuilleté* of spiny lobster, the chef's compositions are unusual, sometimes even exaggerated, but always absolutely harmonious. We would have taken greater pleasure in our delicious Bohemian dumpling if Fischer hadn't signed his name on it with powdered cocoa. The Funk's wine cellar stocks the usual repertoire of quality wines at highly imaginative prices.

ROTTNER 14/20

90431, Stadtteil Großreuth
Winterstr. 15
(09 11) 61 20 32, Fax 61 37 59 res.

P

Closed for lunch Saturday, closed Sunday, 24 December through 10 January. Tables d'hôte: 58/92, à la carte: 48/84

The appearance of this country restaurant matches the regional emphasis of its cuisine. The squat and sturdy stone house is opulently adorned with flowers, the shady beer garden (which offers rustic regional fare) is inviting, and the garden behind the house is small and cozy. The dining rooms inside are typically Bavarian, with a lot of wood and large tiled stoves. The service is relaxed, pleasant and competent. Chef Stefan Rottner is a fanatical advocate of refined regional cuisine, and he insists on the freshest produce out of his own neighborhood. Most salads, vegetables and herbs are grown in the restaurant's own garden. Rottner's salads, served with pigeon breast, kid livers or seafood and fresh garden herbs, are all delicious. For the main course, we recommend fish and game dishes. The wonderful side dishes are far more than merely decorative, and the regionally inspired desserts are refined yet hearty. The wine list is a haphazard collection of soaked-off wine labels in plastic folders. Insisting on regional products has its limits: You can't drink a Franconian white or red wine with a savory dish of game.

SCHWARZER ADLER 15/20

90427, Stadtteil Kraftshof
Kraftshofer Hauptstr. 166
(09 11) 30 58 58, Fax 30 58 67 res.

Closed 22 December through 6 January. Tables d'hôte: 49/55L, 95/120D, à la carte: 58/93

Times are changing, but the Schwarzer Adler still serves classic cuisine, complete with the grandeur and formality that used to accompany it. The staff's attitude tends to be bureaucratic (you cannot get here at 9 p.m., for instance, and still expect to get something to eat). This and the high prices may be reasons for gourmets to stay away. Peter Wagners still serves exceptional dishes, such as the delicious stuffed rabbit saddle with barley grain, sensational anglerfish medallions with soybean sprouts, and the fantastic grenadine of veal with morels and sherry sauce. Some main courses are more showy than tasty—for instance, a lobster mousse with tandoori sauce and smoked sturgeon and Jerusalem artichokes. Even if a number of excellent first courses more than make up for these lapses, all of the dishes seem artificial, formal and entirely without verve. The service is pleasant and attentive but as formal as the cuisine. The wine list offers many wines from Franconia, the usual French assortment and trendy Italians.

ZIRBELSTUBE 15/20

90455, Stadtteil Worzeldorf
Friedrich-Overbeck-Str. 1
(09 11) 8 81 55 res.

Closed for lunch, closed Sunday, Monday, 2 weeks in February, 2 weeks in July/August. Tables d'hôte: 89/110, à la carte: 57/94, No Credit Cards

No doubt about it, Rüdiger Bub is an excellent cook. But now that he is alone in the kitchen of his little Zirbelstube, we miss his creativity, his brilliantly balanced seasoning and imaginative presentation. He has reduced the number of tables and offers only one full-course meal. But because he prepares everything from the appetizer to dessert himself, he has no time left over for niceties. Despite this, the Zirbelstuben remains one of the best restaurants in the region. The ingredients are of the highest quality, the dishes perfectly done and extravagantly served, and each course is finely seasoned. All we missed was that dash of fun that makes cuisine enjoyable. The wine list is small, and the wines are cleverly chosen and adequately priced. The service is attentive and makes an effort to be personal. In the summer, you can dine in the garden. This charming hotel also offers eight nicely equipped, quiet guest rooms that deserve a special recommendation.

HOTELS

ALTEA HOTEL CARLTON

90443, Eilgutstr. 13-15
(09 11) 2 00 30, Fax 2 00 35 32

130, **S** 165/265, **D** 245/355,
1/2P +30, **P** +60

The venerable old Carlton, located between the train station and the Maritim Hotel, is now presented in a completely renovated version. The rooms are agreeably but functionally furnished. The house itself is quiet, but in spite of the soundproofed windows you can't help hearing the trains.

ATRIUM

90478, Münchener Str. 25
(09 11) 4 74 80, Fax 4 74 84 20

187, **S** 179/349, **D** 234/498,
APP 590/780, **1/2P** +35, **P** +65

This hotel next to the Meistersinger Hall is surrounded by parks, but still close to public transportation. The rooms are modern and tastefully furnished. Jogging trails, bicycle rental, solarium, Rôtisserie Médoc, bar. Breakfast: 20 DM.

BURGHOTEL 

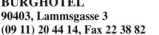

90403, Lammsgasse 3
(09 11) 20 44 14, Fax 22 38 82

46, **S** 118/175, **D** 170/225,
APP 200/275

The traditional hospitality of this rustically furnished hotel is apparently very popular. It's booked up weeks ahead, partly because of the attractive location in the Old Town and the quiet, friendly atmosphere.

DÜRER-HOTEL 

90403, Neutormauer 32
(09 11) 20 80 91, Fax 22 34 58

  P 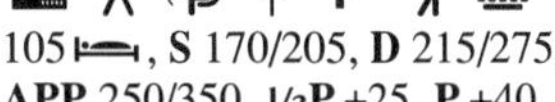

105, **S** 170/205, **D** 215/275,
APP 250/350, **½P** +25, **P** +40

This hotel is located at the foot of the castle and near the Dürer residence. The modern, comfortably furnished rooms are quiet, and the hotel has its own garage. Conference rooms, fitness center, solarium, bistro-bar.

GRAND HOTEL 

90402, Bahnhofstr. 1-3
(09 11) 2 32 20, Fax 2 32 24 44

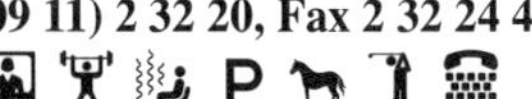 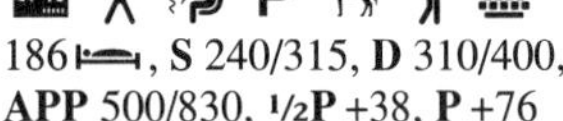

186, **S** 240/315, **D** 310/400,
APP 500/830, **½P** +38, **P** +76

This hotel has been extensively renovated since the Forte group took over. All rooms have soundproofed windows, are individually decorated and have marble bathrooms. Pub, two restaurants. Breakfast: 25 DM.

HOTEL AM JAKOBSMARKT 

90402, Schottengasse 5
(09 11) 24 14 37, Fax 2 28 74

 P

77, **S** 138/154, **D** 194/204,
APP 168/254
Closed 24 December through 6 January

A noncommittal postmodern style combined with the usual functionality characterize the ambience of this hotel—a little sterile perhaps, but spacious and quiet. It's just a few steps to the center of town. Apartments are offered for longer stays. Fitness center, solarium.

HOTEL ARVENA PARK 

90473, Stadtteil Langwasser
Görlitzer Str. 51
(09 11) 8 92 20, Fax 8 92 21 15

P

242, **S** 135/195, **D** 220/2250,
APP 350/800, **½P** +25, **P** +50
Closed 23 December through 6 January

This nondescript concrete building in a suburb of Nürnberg isn't an architectural masterpiece, but the rooms in the large, comfortable hotel are pleasant and well-appointed. Convention center, fitness club, solarium.

MARITIM 

90443, Frauentorgraben 11
(09 11) 2 36 30, Fax 2 36 38 36

 P

316, **S** 213/373, **D** 274/434,
APP 580/1300, **½P** +40, **P** +72

This stylishly decorated house with an extravagant atmosphere is located within easy reach of the pedestrian district and the center of town. Besides a swimming pool with sauna and steam bath, fitness center and solarium, the hotel offers a popular hotel bar, modern conference rooms and a large auditorium. Breakfast: 25 DM.

MERIAN 

90403, Unschlittplatz 7
(09 11) 20 41 94, Fax 22 12 74

21, **S** 130/140, **D** 180/190

Located in the heart of this proud city, the almost 400-year-old building reminds one of the splendor of times gone by. Nostalgia teams up with modern hotel comfort.

NESTOR-HOTEL 

90419, Stadtteil Buch
Bucher Str. 125
(09 11) 3 47 60, Fax 3 47 61 13

74, **S** 152/230, **D** 165/280,
APP 195/330, **½P** +30, **P** +60

The newest hotel in Nürnberg also has the most striking design and ambience. Classic architecture is combined with modern decor. A glassed-in entrance hall has been added to the renovated patrician building, and functional design in strong colors gives the hotel a cool and somewhat artificial atmosphere. The rooms are grandly styled and comfortably furnished. Solarium, restaurant, conference rooms. 15-minute walk to the center of town. Breakfast: 19 DM.

ROMANTIK HOTEL AM JOSEPHSPLATZ

90403, Josephsplatz 30-32
(09 11) 24 11 56, Fax 24 31 65

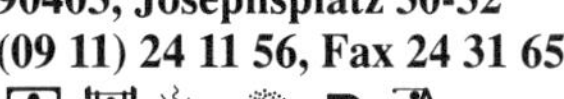

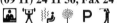

36 , **S** 140/180, **D** 190/250,
APP 180/300
Closed 24 December through 8 January

This hotel, located in the middle of town, has a friendly atmosphere. The surrounding nightlife is a little noisy if your room faces the Josephsplatz.

SCANDIC CROWN HOTEL

90480, Stadtteil Zerzabelhof
Valznerweiherstr. 200
(09 11) 4 02 90, Fax 40 40 67

152 , **S** 225/325, **D** 285/385,
APP 385/495, **½P** +35, **P** +70

This gigantic hotel, opened in 1991, has a fashionable entrance hall and somewhat plainer, comfortable rooms. The Scandic Active Club offers a variety of sports and recreation. The hotel offers air-conditioned and perfectly equipped conference rooms and public transportation to the Nürnberg conventions and fairs. Breakfast: 25 DM.

ZIRBELSTUBE

90455, Stadtteil Worzeldorf
Friedrich-Overbeck-Str. 1
(09 11) 99 88 20, Fax 9 98 82 20

8 , **S** 130/150, **D** 180/220,
Closed 2 weeks in February, 2 weeks in July/August

This romantic, historic building is located on the old Ludwigskanal—just 10 minutes from the autobahn, 7 minutes from the convention center and 15 minutes from the center of town. The hotel offers quiet, comfortably equipped rooms. The idyllic surroundings invite guests to stroll, fish, bicycle and ride.

NÜRTINGEN Baden-Württ.

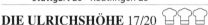

Stuttgart 20 - Reutlingen 25

DIE ULRICHSHÖHE 17/20

3 km northwest in Hardt
72622, Herzog-Ulrich-Str. 14
(0 70 22) 5 23 36, Fax 5 49 40 res.

Closed Sunday, Monday, 3 weeks in January, 2 weeks during the Bad.-Württ. summer school holiday. Tables d'hôte: 112/146, à la carte: 60/114

The ambience is exceptional! From this beautiful, elegantly furnished restaurant, we looked out to a colorful sea of flowers, and we did not dare hope for a cuisine that matched the perfection of the surroundings. But we underestimated Helmut Schulz. The warm salad of veal shank in vinaigrette with capers and a touch of Gruyère cheese was superb. The scallops with bouillabaisse-julienne were delicious, as were the cream of endives soup with sweetbread and the red mullet with sliced zucchini. The savory lamb cutlet with its light crust of paprika was fabulous, and the light cheese soufflé with orange purée on date ice cream just heavenly. You can peruse the wine list just for fun because Annegret Bub-Schilling is on hand to advise you competently on the choice of wines for your meal. From the beautiful terrace, you have a marvelous view of the Neckar valley and the Swabian mountains.

NUSSDORF AM INN Bayern

Rosenheim 17 - Salzburg 88

NUSSDORFER HOF 11/20

83131, Hauptstr. 4
(0 80 34) 75 66, 80 65, Fax 15 32

A la carte: 22/59

We have always felt at home in this typically Bavarian country restaurant, with its painted gables and lovely terrace at the back. We are glad to report that the quality of the cuisine is getting better. We enjoyed the semolina dumplings in our consommé and the succulent duck's breast on salad. The trout from the restaurant's own ponds are always worth an order. The *tafelspitz* and beef were adequate, but the suckling pig was simply tough. The wine list offers a variety of wines by the glass and a respectable choice of wines by the bottle. The service is nonchalant at best. The 13 guest rooms have been renovated with attention to modern comfort, and you can even vacation here with the whole family.

OBERAUDORF Bayern

Kufstein 9 - Rosenheim 25

GASTHAUS WALLER

83080, Urfahrnstr. 10
(0 80 33) 14 73

A la carte: 14/32

In this rustic idyll with beer garden, a pleasant staff brings hearty Bavarian cooking to guests at plain wooden tables. Besides the traditional pork roast and venison, customers can order such healthful alternatives as Savoy cabbage strudel, whole-wheat noodles and ravioli filled with vegetables. Beer goes best with all dishes.

OBERHAUSEN NRW

Essen 12 - Düsseldorf 24

FRINTROP 12/20

46047, Mühlenstr. 116
(02 08) 87 09 75 res.

Closed for lunch Saturday, closed Sunday, 24 December through 3 January. Tables d'hôte: 50L, 74D, 118, à la carte: 37/87. Tables d'hôte with wine: 74/130, No Credit Cards

This pub is located on a village street corner in Dümpten. With its gigantic pillar in the middle of the room and massive oak buffet, it is a monument to the traditional *wirtshaus* ambience, typical of the Ruhr region. In the pub section of the restaurant, you can order tasty little snacks to go with your beer. The so-called back room is the gourmet restaurant, where Hermann Frintrop serves refined cuisine with only a few misses. An excellently done turbot with mustard sauce was followed by a sorry excuse for duck's breast; a tangy mushroom soup with a bitter soufflé of Brussels sprouts was succeeded by a delicious leg of hare. The desserts are recommended. The service is pleasant, and the choice of wines excellent.

HACKBARTH'S REST. 12/20

46047, Im Lipperfeld 44
(02 08) 2 21 88, Fax 8 59 84 19 res.

Closed for lunch Saturday, closed Sunday, 24 December through 8 January. Tables d'hôte: 30L, 48D, 59, à la carte: 24/64

Hackbarth's extraordinary success was short-lived. The imaginative and promising cuisine of this new restaurant in the middle of an industrial section of town has clipped its own wings. Instead of soaring to exciting culinary heights with daring Asian and Italian impressions, it has returned to down-to-earth cooking. *Vitello tonnato*, duck's breast and lentil stew with beef belonged to the repertoire of our last visit. We had refreshing coq au vin, flawless *tafelspitz* and a savory blood-pudding pancake with lamb's lettuce. Our lasagna of duck's liver, asparagus and pumpernickel was very tasty—once we managed the art of eating this artistically arranged creation! The surprise prix-fixe menus are moderately priced, and there's a good choice of wines by the glass.

PARKHOTEL OBERHAUSEN

46119, Teutoburger Str. 156
(02 08) 6 90 20, Fax 6 90 21 58

85, **S** 114/234, **D** 168/278,
APP 258/378, **1/2P** +20, **P** +45
Closed 22 December through 2 January

This modern, functional building is located not far from the autobahn, and offers a solarium, fitness center, skittle alleys and jogging trails in the nearby park. Children up to 12 years of age are free. Opulent breakfast buffet.

OBERKIRCH Bad.-Württ.

Offenburg 16 - Achern 17

ZUR OBEREN LINDE 14/20

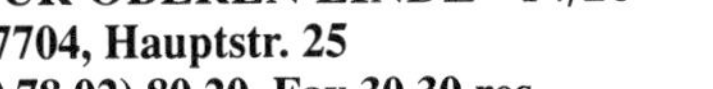

77704, Hauptstr. 25

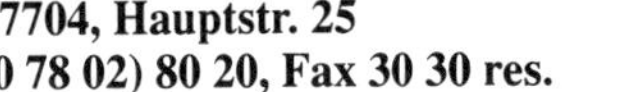

(0 78 02) 80 20, Fax 30 30 res.

 P

Tables d'hôte: 45/95, à la carte: 34/75

Highly professional interior decorators have created a unique ambience in this historic half-timbered building. The cuisine combines high quality, perfection and style with the hospitality of cordial service. We didn't find one single hair in this wonderful soup. Our beef carpaccio with lentils, asparagus with salmon and Black Forest-cured ham, pigeon breast with Savoy cabbage and potato cakes were excellent. They were followed by three delicious kinds of chocolate mousse. Simpler fare isn't any less good, like the Black Forest trout, pig's cheeks or beef the way Grandma used to make it. The wine list offers many regional wines from Baden, but there's also a Bordeaux château wine by the glass.

ZUR OBEREN LINDE

77704, Hauptstr. 25

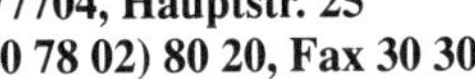

(0 78 02) 80 20, Fax 30 30

37, **S** 130/175, **D** 195/280,
APP 350, **1/2P** +45, **P** +65

The two 17th-century houses that make up this lovely, romantic hotel are historic landmarks in this region. They're located on a main street and are connected by a covered bridge. The new hotel wing, however, is quiet. The rooms are comfortably and individually furnished with all modern amenities; some have four-poster beds. Ample breakfast.

OBERSTAUFEN Bayern

Immenstadt 24 - Kempten 45

ALLGÄU SONNE

87534, Am Stießberg 1

(0 83 86) 70 20, Fax 78 26

169, **S** 140/185, **D** 340/400,
APP 200/300, **1/2P** +30, **P** +50

The facade of this attractive three-story hotel is full of balconies decorated in a charming Alpine style with a lovely view over the Weissach valley and the peaks of the nearby mountains. The rooms are spacious and comfortable. Fitness and beauty programs are offered. The apartments in the adjoining building guarantee peace and quiet. Restaurant.

BAYERISCHER HOF

87534, Hochgratstr. 2

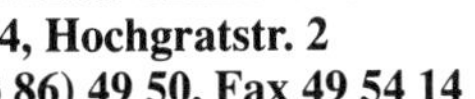

(0 83 86) 49 50, Fax 49 54 14

61, **S** 120/180, **D** 260/390,
APP 450/510

No Credit Cards

The rooms of this renovated hotel are of various sizes, but all are comfortably and tastefully furnished. Restaurant.

KURHOTEL ZUM LÖWEN 17/20

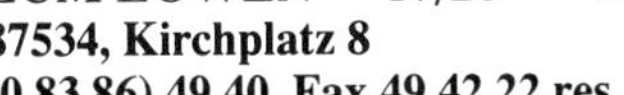

87534, Kirchplatz 8

(0 83 86) 49 40, Fax 49 42 22 res.

P

Closed Wednesday, mid-November through 20 December. Tables d'hôte: 59/108, à la carte: 40/76

The superior quality of Jörg Rasmus's cuisine, with exquisite compositions like veal fillet and anglerfish with two sauces and black noodles, establishes the Kurhotel restaurant as more than a gourmet temple for rich spa guests. This is simply the best place to eat between Lindau and Oberstdorf! Excellent and unobtrusive service, a small but choice menu and an impressive wine list make this restaurant attractive. We enjoyed aspic of *tafelspitz* with a small salad and fried potatoes, delicate herb soup with scallops and wonderful lamb with paprika, rosemary sauce and potato crepes. Everything was just as perfect as our black and white champagne soup, saddle of venison with a gingerbread crust and the house dessert platter.

Remember to reserve your table or your room in advance, and please let the restaurant or hotel know if you cannot honour your reservation.

KURHOTEL ZUM LÖWEN

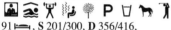

87534, Kirchplatz 8
(0 83 86) 49 40, Fax 49 42 22

30, **S** 155/165, **D** 260/310,
APP 400, **½P** +40, **P** +70
Closed mid-November through 20 December

The lovely facade is one of Oberstaufen's architectural highlights. The rooms are spacious and have balconies overlooking the beautiful Allgäu landscape. Solarium, massage, beauty treatments, sports and spa treatments. Very good breakfast.

PARKHOTEL OBERSTAUFEN

87534, Argenstr. 1
(0 83 86) 70 30, Fax 70 37 04

91, **S** 201/300, **D** 356/416,
APP 446/690, **½P** +20, **P** +40

Located on the edge of the spa park, this house has luxuriously appointed rooms, suites and duplexes and also offers the perfect service that goes with a high hotel standard. Marble floors, columns and statues abound. The restaurant is closed to nonresidents when the hotel is full.

WEISSACHER HOF

87534, Ortsteil Weißach
Mühlenstr. 14
(0 83 86) 70 80, Fax 13 17

36, **S** 132/152, **D** 244/308,
APP 102 per person, **½P** +20, **P** +35
No Credit Cards

This comfortable hotel with spacious rooms and apartments lies in the lovely Weissach valley and has a lively atmosphere. A wide variety of sports and recreation programs is offered, as well as a grotto-like indoor pool.

ZUR ALTEN SALZSTRASSE 14/20

6 km east
in 87534, Wiedemannsdorf
Salzstr. 36
(0 83 86) 6 68
A la carte: 34/70

Richard Hecht serves creative, down-to-earth cuisine in his original country inn not far from the Alpensee. Our bustling host's not always being where he should have been, namely in the kitchen, had immediate effects on the quality of the cooking. Our otherwise delicious watercress soup had too much salt; instead of sprouts we found lentils in our salad; and the almost-perfect duck's breast was nearly drowned in morel sauce. Our carpaccio gratin of Russian sturgeon had an international elan, whereas saddle of suckling lamb with a sauce of tomatoes, herbs and garlic was a regional specialty of the Allgäu. The service is very personal and the wine list leaves almost (again!) nothing to be desired.

OBERSTDORF Bayern

Kempten 40 - München 165

FILSER

87561, Freibergstr. 15
(0 83 22) 70 80, Fax 70 85 30

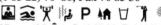

97 (95), **S** 106/139, **D** 212/258,
APP 266/306, **½P** +30, **P** +40
Closed 1 November through 19 December, No Credit Cards

Wrought iron, wood and heavy upholstery create the atmosphere of this hotel in the spa area, in its spacious lobby an in each of the rooms. Schroth and Kneipp cures, guided excursions, sanatorium. Restaurant.

GAISBERG-STUBENIN ALPENKURHOF VOLLMAN 13/20

87561, Ortsteil Tiefenbach
Falkenstr. 15
(0 83 22) 70 20
Closed for lunch every day except Sunday, closed Tuesday, Thursday, à la carte: 38/80

This imposingly ugly hotel block is an affront to the beautiful landscape surrounding it. Guests can best avoid seeing it by going inside, where the lovely view from the windows makes up for the tasteless exterior and quaintly rustic decor of the restaurant. We had delicious Italian onion soup, Savoy cabbage dumplings with a delicate but overdone saddle of venison, and a harmonious combination of Allgäu char with kohlrabi and watercress, Riesling sauce and rice with chanterelles. Italian wines inspired the good wine list, which offers extraordinarily low-priced bottles.

GRÜNS RESTAURANT 16/20

87561, Nebelhornstr. 49
(0 83 22) 24 24 res.

P

Closed Monday, closed for lunch Tuesday, closed 3 weeks following Whitmonday. Tables d'hôte: 56L, 78/110D, à la carte: 35/79, No Credit Cards

We like Grün's dependability and his consistently good cuisine, which is as down-to-earth and unpretentious as he is. His bouillabaisse is always pure enjoyment, and so are his curried noodles with lobster. Grün is an expert on soups and sauces, but his rack of lamb with beans and potato gratin melted in our mouths. All meat comes from choice Allgäu stock, and neighbors often see the chef himself looking for fresh mushrooms. Time after time, we enjoy Grün's delicious cheese dumplings with plums and his heavenly sorbets. The restaurant, in the vicinity of the Nebelhornbahn, is attractive, even though the decor could use a little sprucing up. The service is attentive and personal, and the choice of wines is good.

KUR-UND SPORTHOTEL EXQUISIT

87561, Prinzenstr. 17
(0 83 22) 9 63 30, Fax 96 33 60

42, **S** 90/200, **D** 136/380,
APP 370/420, **1/2P** +30

Closed beginning of November through 18 December

The hotel's name is well-chosen. Even the most fastidious guest will feel at home in these tastefully appointed, spacious rooms (opulent bathrooms) with a view of Oberstdorf's mountains. Solarium, massage, cosmetic treatments, putting green for golfers on the hotel grounds, cross-country skiing opportunities.

MAXIMILIANS REST. 14/20

87561, Freiberstr. 21
(0 83 22) 8 05 15 res.

Closed for lunch every day except Sunday, closed 14 days each in May and November. Tables d'hôte: 45/90, à la carte: 36/79, No Credit Cards

We just had to try the fantastic boned pigeon in hazelnut crust with cassis sauce, our euphoric neighbors at the next table told us. A pity they'd just eaten the last of the birds. We ordered the surprise prix-fixe menu instead and were not disappointed: salads with quail and a whiff of raspberry marinade, tomato essence with vegetable strudel, asparagus with wild boar ham and delicate salmon with leek spaghetti were delicious. Our boned, flavorful and tender saddle of venison with spinach noodles was perfect, and our parfait with brandy, and rhubarb tart with zabaglione ingenious. Even though our Barbary duck's breast was a bit overdone and the homemade ravioli with truffle cream tasted indifferent, the owners from the Rhineland have given new culinary impetus to Oberstdorf's gastronomy. Pleasant Rhine wines.

PARKHOTEL FRANK

87561, Sachsenweg 11
(0 83 22) 70 60, 55 55, Fax 70 62 86

P

68, **S** 132/202, **D** 278/402,
APP 356/458, **1/2P** +20

Closed 1—20 November, No Credit Cards

Even if you can't see a mountain from every window, this rustic, Baroque-style house is one of the most pleasant hotels in Oberstdorf. Most of the comfortable rooms and suites have been divided into living and sleeping areas. Extensive spa and fitness facilities. Restaurant.

---

7 SCHWABEN RESTAURANT 14/20

87561, Pfarrstr. 9
(0 83 22) 38 70

Closed Wednesday. Tables d'hôte: 28L, 58D, à la carte: 25/65

Our compliments to the Gutensohns. They serve Swabian specialities of the highest quality. A Swabian version of sauerbraten called *böf-flamott* is served here with a light sauce and dumplings. The cream of potato soup tasted homemade, and the cheese dumplings were delicious. The stuffed venison schnitzel with rosehip sauce, as well as the leg of mountain goat with red cabbage and bread dumplings, scaled the heights of Swabian perfection. Prices are reasonable.

WIESE

87561, Stillachstr. 4a
(0 83 22) 30 30

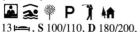

13 rooms, **S** 100/110, **D** 180/200,
APP 205/215
No Credit Cards

A mosaic showing historic facades of Old Hamburg decorates one wall of the indoor swimming pool. The owner was food director on a ship taking holiday guests to Helgoland. The house is full of antiques and Oriental rugs.

OBERTHAL Saarland

St. Wendel 9 - Saarlouis 33

ZUM BLAUEN FUCHS 16/20

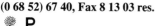

66649, Ortsteil Steinberg
Walhausener Str. 1
(0 68 52) 67 40, Fax 8 13 03 res.

P

Closed for lunch everyday except Sunday, closed Tuesday, 1 week each in February and during the summer. Tables d'hôte: 62/96, à la carte: 52/73

Far away from the main roads, a former village pub has become a gourmet restaurant with a *bierstube* attached. Olaf Bank captivates his guests with imaginative, light, fresh and beautifully presented creations, and his wife Christiane supervises the service with charm and competence. A refreshing yogurt terrine with pieces of smoked fish and sweet arugula salad was a wonderful start, followed by a harmonious combination of fried quail and baked sweetbreads with a slightly sweet cream sauce and warm asparagus salad. Together with a savory sauce gently seasoned with caraway seeds, our sheatfish fillet wrapped in a tasty Savoy cabbage leaf and garnished with king prawn was an unexpected taste sensation. Another highlight of our fantastic meal was succulent and tender saddle of venison served with a winy thyme sauce and prettily arranged potato gnocchi, kohlrabi, shallots and asparagus tips. A fabulous dessert—*kaiserschmarrn* with cassis and yogurt ice cream on wafer-thin meringue and fresh berries—was the grand finale. The wine list offers an adequate choice of regional wines, some Italian and some French wines. A few half bottles are also listed.

OBERWESEL Rheinl.-Pf.

Bingen 20 - Koblenz 40

HISTORISCHE WEINWIRTSCHAFT

55430, Liebfrauenstr. 17
(0 67 44) 81 86 res.

Closed for lunch, closed Tuesday, à la carte: 24/44, No Credit Cards.

The resolute and vigorous Iris Marx had always wanted to run a *weinstube.* Out of the oldest and most completely rundown half-timbered house in town, she's made a jewel of hospitality and fine down-to-earth cooking that draws enthusiastic guests from miles around. Antique furniture and art exhibitions create an attractive ambience, and the menu offers something for every appetite. We liked our ox breast with apple and horseradish sauce, delicate herring and crispy fried potatoes with bacon, onions and rosemary, and we loved our wonderful dumplings with Riesling sauce for dessert. The wines from the Rhine region are especially low-priced and good. Ever try a basil cobbler as an appetizer?

OCHTENDUNG Rheinland-Pfalz

Mayen 13 - Koblenz 17

GUTSHOF AROSA 13/20

56299, Koblenzer Str. 2
(0 26 25) 44 71, Fax 52 61 res.

P

Closed Monday. Tables d'hôte: 42L, 75D, à la carte: 32/69, Tables d'hôte with wine: 42

Simply cooked with a great deal of finesse, but without any sort of showy flamboyance or creative nonsense—such is the cuisine of this comfortable, rustic restaurant decorated with lots of dusty bric-a-brac. We enjoyed sauerkraut soup with blood pudding, mushrooms stuffed with snail ragout and tender king prawns. Sole with prawns steamed in bamboo baskets, vegetables and rice deserved a standing ovation. The regionally inspired dishes were wonderfully flavorful, and the lovely desserts removed the last particle of doubt that the cooking here is far above average. The service is pleasant and the wine list adequate—and even includes some wines by the glass.

ÖHRINGEN Bad.-Württ.

Heilbronn 28 - Stuttgart 66

WALD & SCHLOSSHOTEL FRIEDRICHSRUHE 18/20

74639 Zweiflingen-Friedrichstr.
(0 79 41) 6 08 70, Fax 6 14 68 res.

Tables d'hôte: 135/195, à la carte: 64/133

We'll get rid of our nasty remarks first: if Lother Eiermann copies recipes from other German star cooks in order to be trendy, he should at least prepare them as perfectly as they do. But if he stays within the bounds of classic haute cuisine, nobody can show him up. His guinea hen, for instance, with foie gras sauce, croutons and truffled purėed potatoes or his wild duckling with Chevrey Chambertin sauce and cèpes were superb and deserved the highest praise. Diners should be sure to leave a little room for the fabulous desserts. The ambience is classic and elegant, but not as luxurious as the competition's, whereas the prices are on the same high level. The wine list leaves nothing to be desired.

JÄGERSTUBE 14/20

74639 Zweiflingen-Friedrichstr.
(0 79 41) 6 08 70, Fax 6 14 68
A la carte: 31/70

The Jägerstube, with its comfortable ambience (tiled stove, old hunting implements and antique etchings on the walls), offers a combination of regional dishes, refined plain fare - and a sense of "all's right with the world." Everything was good and relatively low-priced, such as headcheese with potatoes, carpaccio of duck's breast, tripe in vinegar sauce with celery stalks, pigeon with rutabagas and Swabian ice cream *guglhupf*. The agreeable service offers wines by the glass at friendly prices, but will also let you choose from the wine list of the Friedrichsruhe next door.

WALD & SCHLOSSHOTEL FRIEDRICHSRUHE

74639 Zweiflingen-Friedrichstr.
(0 79 41) 6 08 70, Fax 6 14 68

51 rooms, **S** 165/195, **D** 295/390,
APP 490/580

In recent years, Friedrichsruhe has emerged as one of the most beautiful and pleasant country hotels in Germany. Just as in a private house, each room is individually styled. The rooms in the Schloss are larger and furnished with antiques. The modern wing offers comfortable rooms with terraces or balconies and an indoor pool. The former gatehouse also includes a charming apartment decorated in the Laura Ashley style. Perfect service and an 18-hole golf course nearby. You can even enjoy your breakfast at noon.

OELDE Nordrhein-Westfalen

Beckum 10 - Gütersloh 22

ALTES GASTHAUS KREFT 12/20

59302, Eickhoff 25
(0 25 22) 44 22, Fax 8 16 34 res.

Closed for lunch, closed Sunday. Tables d'hôte: 58/85, à la carte: 38/71

The facade of this old farm estate has been lovingly restored, but the inside is an uncomfortable conglomeration of styles and thwarted intentions to create a harmonious ambience. Burkhard Schürmann has cooked better food at strange stoves (Steinhagen's Alte Schmiede) than in his own kitchen. Our turbot was served with a heavy lobster sauce and commercial, not homemade, noodles; scampi with tortellini and basil sauce were slightly aged, as was the red snapper with champagne sauce; and our veal saddle came with Swiss chard that was cooked to shreds. Long waits between courses didn't heighten our enjoyment. The wine list was adequate, but without many surprises.

OESTRICH-WINKEL Hessen

Eltville 7 - Rüdesheim 8

GRAUES HAUS 17/20

65375, Graugasse 10
(0 67 23) 26 19, Fax 18 48 res.

 P

Closed for lunch from Monday through Friday, closed for dinner Tuesday, closed 1 February through 1 March. Tables d'hôte: 75/90L, 85/140D, à la carte: 54/101. Tables d'hôte with wine: 110/170

It was difficult to keep our feet on the ground here. In this restaurant at the foot of great vineyards and with a view of the romantic Rhine, Egbert Engelhardt tries to incorporate some of the lyric atmosphere of the renowned Rheingau in his cuisine. Most aperitifs in other restaurants are dull and unimaginative, but here we enjoyed a sparkling Riesling wine with rhubarb juice. An exquisite appetizer—deep-fried mackerel, goat cheese with cherry tomato, duck and asparagus, Alsatian pizza with cream, ham and onions—promised us still better things to come. We weren't disappointed. Classic and regional dishes are prepared with verve and temperament as well as perfection and expertise. We loved our mousse of smoked salmon and asparagus crepe with a Riesling sauce and a fantastic pike-perch fillet with kohlrabi. Foie gras with honeyed shallots on Savoy cabbage and red mullet with fresh peas were exciting taste sensations. Though we would have hesitated to order the following anywhere else, we confidently tried kid liver with sugar peas and artichokes fried in olive oil with tomatoes and herbs—and were not in the least sorry we did. Engelhard and his team cook with a sure instinct for exact times and temperatures, flavors and seasonings. Our sorbet of sorrel and curds with rhubarb sauce was so fabulous we're going to order bowls of it next time! The pastry was deceptively simple but of the highest class and quality. And the tarts and petits fours with coffee were superb. The service was attentive, competent and cheerful. The extravagant design of the chairs forces guests to assume an exemplary posture.

SCHLOSS VOLLRADS' GUTSAUSSCHANK

65375, Schloß Vollrads
(0 67 23) 52 70, Fax 18 48 res.

 P

Closed Wednesday and Thursday from November through April, 2—31 January. Tables d'hôte: 40L, 60D, à la carte: 22/60, No Credit Cards

We sometimes feel as if we're on an excursion boat when we come here: good weather draws everybody who's traveling in the Rheingau out on deck. The captains in the kitchen were drifting without direction the last time we visited. The pike-perch heaped on a plate was served with a thin brown sauce that wasn't anything like the coriander and tomato sauce we were supposed to get. Marinated mountain cheese turned out to be a couple of cheese slices with marinade hurriedly poured over it. Hearty dishes like bacon pancakes and desserts like elderberry blossom crème were more to our liking, even if the portions were immense. The wine list offers a dozen or so wines by the glass and many passable bottles.

OEVERSEE Schlesw.-Holst.

Flensburg 5

HISTORISCHER KRUG 12/20

24988, next to the B 76
(0 46 30) 94 00, Fax 7 80 res.

 P

Tables d'hôte: 39/84, à la carte: 34/79

In 1994, this pretty thatched cottage celebrated its 475th anniversary as the oldest *gasthaus* in this part of the country. Proud of its history and royally bestowed privileges (purely historical!), the Hansen-Mörcks found the anniversary reason enough to modernize its culinary conception. Instead of trying to impress critics with creative cuisine, the kitchen serves good, down-to-earth country fare at reduced prices. Along with a great variety of dishes à la carte, eight prix-fixe menus are offered, five at midday dinner alone. A reduction here would do the quality and freshness no harm. We liked curried mussel soup, codfish with bacon and Riesling sauce, and braised squab with sherry sauce and homemade noodles.The friendly service staff recommends a well-stocked wine list with understandable pride.

HISTORISCHER KRUG

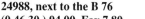

24988, next to the B 76
(0 46 30) 94 00, Fax 7 80

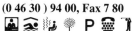

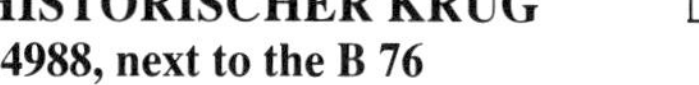
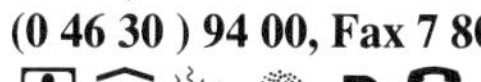

50, **S** 99/119, **D** 149/189,
1/2P +40, **P** +70

This traditional hotel with its typical thatched roof has rooms equipped with modern comforts. Solarium, canoeing excursions, bike rental, fitness center, beauty farm.

BAD OEYNHAUSEN NRW

Osnabrück 60 - Hannover 80

BUCHENHOF

10km north in Bergkirchen
32549, Knicksiek 9
(0 57 31) 38 78 res.

Closed Monday, Tuesday, January. Tables d'hôte: 55/129, à la carte: 52/90

We'd like to see more small, elegant, unpretentious country inns like this one. A latecomer to this profession, Werner Schnabel nonchalantly neglects formality and trendy gimmicks and commits himself and his team to that rare combination of charm and professionalism in kitchen and service we always look for and seldom find. We enjoyed fried bass with potato salad, salmon with asparagus salad and veal fillet stuffed with morels and accompanied by asparagus strudel and a strongly caramelized sauce. Our scallops with wild asparagus and saffron sauce and (10!) peas was outstanding, whereas the pike-perch coated in pumpernickel with sugar peas and lentils lost much of its delicate taste in the mighty crust of bread that covered it. Wonderful fruit, sorbets, mousses, jellies and soups were arranged on an immense dessert platter. The large staff doesn't miss anything, and we appreciated the very pleasant and personally attentive service. The owner prefers French wines but can also recommend some German and Italian bottles as well as excellent wines by the glass.

HAHNENKAMP

32549, Alte Reichsstr. 4
(0 57 31) 7 57 40, Fax 75 74 75

27, **S** 109/149, **D** 149/189,
1/2P +20/40, **P** +40/60

This small and well-cared-for hotel in a 200-year-old frame house surrounded by a park used to be a carriage stop. It's located three kilometers from town and offers rustic, comfortable and spacious accommodations. Restaurant.

HOTEL WITTEKIND

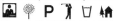

32549, Am Kurpark 10
(0 57 31) 2 10 96 , Fax 31 82

22, **S** 80/120, **D** 155/198,
1/2P +30, **P** +40

A quiet spa with a view of the lovely park. Thermal baths, diets, elegant public areas and a friendly atmosphere. Pub.

OFFENBURG Bad.-Württ.

Freiburg 66 - Karlsruhe 79

TODDY'S 17/20

77652, Hauptstr. 83a
(07 81) 7 77 27, Fax 2 57 25 res.

P

Closed for lunch, closed Sunday. Tables d'hôte: 98/165, à la carte: 74/94, No Credit Cards

The new owner and chef had cooked his last employer up to a rating of 18/20. Now he's striking out on his own—with no small success. We didn't hesitate to give him three toques to start with. Ambrosius welcomed us with an appetizer of jellied lobster gazpacho and potato filled with caviar. Our rabbit tart with marinated cauliflower, very fresh pike-perch with mashed potatoes and red mullet with candied horseradish and red cabbage *jus* deserved applause. The Parmesan in an ingenious cheese dish overpowered the beef fillet cubes that went with it. Delicious petits fours accompanied good espresso. A side entrance to the press building leads down to the unobtrusive restaurant in the cellar. Wine buffs will look askance at the black tablecloths, but the choice and affordable wines more than make up for it.

OLDENBURG Niedersachsen

Bremen 48 - Wilhelmshaven 60

CITY CLUB HOTEL

26123, Europaplatz 4-6
(04 41) 80 80 , Fax 80 81 00

88, **S** 140, **D** 190, **APP** 330

This modern brick house is the best hotel in Oldenburg. The rooms adjoining the elevators are noisy and those near the big assembly hall seem larger, but the bathrooms are all tiny. Solarium, whirlpool, massage.

FISCH-RESTAURANT SEEWOLF 13/20

26121, Alexanderstr. 41
(04 41) 8 65 60

Closed Monday. Tables d'hôte: 28L, 48D, à la carte: 25/61, No Credit Cards

A former gourmet cook has opened an unpretentious little bistro on the outskirts of town. Everything is smaller, more modest and less extravagant here, but quicker and cheaper in the bargain. Guests can leave after an hour, well-satisfied with the food and the prices. For less than 50 DM, for instance, you can order lovely duck parfait with salads and green and white asparagus, fresh and perfectly fried bass with spinach and an excellent horseradish sauce and a (somewhat disappointing) yogurt with fruit sauces. Quick and prompt service, small but choice wine list.

LE JOURNAL 13/20

26122, Wallstr. 13
(04 41) 1 31 28, Fax 88 56 54 res.

Closed Sunday. Tables d'hôte: 38L, 74D, à la carte: 39/67. Tables d'hôte with wine: 74

We like bistros that, like their French models, offer quick and uncomplicated service, good, light cuisine and moderate prices. The Journal meets our expectations.The service is quick, although the warmed bread was served rather late. The soups (such as a cream of tomato with oregano) were excellent, but heaven only knows why the spaghetti with mushrooms and grated walnuts was served as a gratin. Good wines by the glass are available. Smokers are welcome here. This does not conform to the spirit of the times, but it does create that genuine, smoky French-bistro atmosphere.

OSNABRÜCK

Bremen 121 - Hannover 140

HOHENZOLLERN 13/20

49074, Heinrich-Heine-Str. 17
(05 41) 3 31 70, Fax 3 31 73 51

P

Tables d'hôte: 45/55, à la carte: 29/81

The ambience of the Hohenzollern is light, decorative and classic, with a conservative touch. With the sun shining outside and elegant curtains fluttering in a soft breeze, you'll think you're dining in a country manor house. Only the plastic bouquets on the tables brought us back to reality. We found our smoked halibut to be surprisingly tasty, though the lamb's lettuce accompanying it was a bit gritty. Our tomato and basil soup with thin slices of orange zest was first-class, and scampi with garlic cream, mushrooms and black noodles was good. Our steak with onion confit, sugar peas and potato waffles was tough, however. The service is super, and the international wine list comprehensive, with strongly varying prices (some low, some exorbitant) and a large choice of wines by the glass.

HOHENZOLLERN

49074, Heinrich-Heine-Str. 17
(05 41) 3 31 70, Fax 3 31 73 51

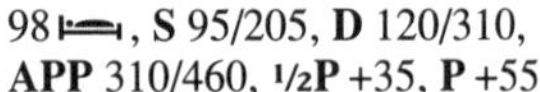

98, **S** 95/205, **D** 120/310,
APP 310/460, **1/2P** +35, **P** +55

The renovated rooms of this hotel are comfortable and tastefully furnished. The management has selected original paintings and not just prints to hang on the walls. Modern pool with sauna and solarium.

OSTERHOLZ-SCHARMBECK

Bremen 26 - Bremerhaven 45

ZUM ALTEN TORFKAHN 13/20

27711, Am Deich 9
(0 47 91) 76 08, Fax 5 96 06

P

Tables d'hôte: 55L, 70/110D, à la carte: 45/81

This is a lovely, comfortable restaurant with attentive service. The Torfkahn kitchen serves traditional dishes of high quality. These include an exquisitely fried pike-perch with turnips (seasoned with curry), a respectable steak with wonderfully prepared chards, and tasty noisettes of lamb. We enjoyed the warm quince with vanilla ice cream. The choice of wines is good.

ZUM ALTEN TORFKAHN 

27711, Am Deich 9
(0 47 91) 76 08, Fax 5 96 06

12 rooms, **S** 100/120, **D** 160/180, **APP** 180/270

Closed 2 weeks during the summer school holiday

Not only restaurant customers get a good night's rest with clean air in quiet surroundings here, but also those who couldn't get a room in Bremen. The rooms are rustically decorated and comfortable. Late breakfast possible.

OSTRACH Bad.-Württ.

Saulgau 14 - Überlingen 29

GASTHOF ZUM HIRSCH 12/20

88356, Hauptstr. 27
(0 75 85) 6 01, 27 74, Fax 31 59

 P

Closed Friday, first week in January through the last week in October. Tables d'hôte: 36, à la carte: 33/61. Tables d'hôte with wine: 42

The preparation of meat dishes is Josef Ermler's forte. No wonder, since he runs a butcher shop on the side. On our last visit, we ate the best roast beef we've ever had, classic and almost rare. We enjoyed tripe in Riesling and tongue and liver in red wine sauce, but found less to admire in an Angus fillet, saddle of veal and Barbary duck's breast we could have just as well had anywhere else. The more Ermler confined himself to regional recipes and regional products, the more satisfied we were. The fish dishes, however, were an exception to this rule: the sheatfish medallions from the nearby lake tasted like deep-fried fish and chips. Game and fresh terrines are other specialties of the Hirsch. With a full house, guests need patience. The small but good choice of wines at low prices helps.

OTTWEILER Saarland

St. Wendel 5 - Saarbrücken 30

EISEL-ZIEGELHÜTTE 14/20

66564, Mühlstr. 15a
(0 68 24) 75 77, Fax 82 14 res.

 P

Closed for dinner Sunday, closed Monday, closed for lunch Tuesday and Friday. Tables d'hôte: 55L, 68D, 115, à la carte: 52/83

The restaurant is located behind the walls of an old corn mill, and the rustic dining rooms with dark wooden beams, painted ceilings and narrow windows have a comfortably medieval ambience. All dishes are hearty and substantial, and the sauces are especially flavorful and savory. Fresh shrimps with a creamy sauce and salad bouquet were followed by excellent salmon with herb sauce, potato and leek soup, and a tender Barbary duck's breast with an exquisite, sweetly seasoned sauce gently laced with balsamic vinegar. Our pineapple sorbet tasted fresh and fruity, and the hazelnut and chocolate parfait with vanilla sauce and fresh berries was delicious.The wine list is well and discriminatingly stocked with German wines of high quality, some Italian and many French wines, an adequate choice of wines by the glass and liqueurs. The wines are moderately priced: a 1988 Chapelle Chambertin for 180 DM and an Ausone for 285 DM.

OVERATH Nordrhein - Westfalen

Köln 11 - Bergisch-Gladbach 13

SÜLZTALERHOF 14/20

7 km northwest in Immekeppel
51491, Lindlarer Str. 83
(0 22 04) 77 46, Fax 7 45 20 res.

 P

Closed Tuesday, closed for lunch Wednesday, closed 1 week in January, 3 weeks in July. Tables d'hôte: 59L, 85/115D, à la carte: 52/90

The Sülztalerhof belongs to the dozen or so well-established good restaurants in this part of the country, and is run by the fourth generation of the same family. Comfortable furniture, pleasant and personal service and good cooking create an ambience of harmony and charm. Josef Selbach tries out new ideas without forgetting his absolute commitment to fresh seasonal products and light cooking. Our borscht, a rustic Russian stew with red beets, tasted as good as it looked. The salads served with meat slices or fish were excellent. Beef roulade in Burgundy with cabbage soufflé and bread dumplings belongs to the countrified cuisine here. Our calf's kidneys in mustard cream sauce with salmon slices was superb, and the fresh figs deep-fried in dough with cinnamon ice cream and vanilla sauce delicately rounded off a hearty meal. The wine list includes an attractive choice of German and French wines; most are also offered by the glass.

PANKER — Schleswig-Holstein

Lütjenburg 5 - Kiel 33

FORSTHAUS HESSENSTEIN 12/20

24321, 3 km west
(0 43 81) 94 16 res.

 P

Closed Monday, Tuesday (during the winter). Tables d'hôte: 140

Peter Marxen demands a lot from his guests. After they've navigated the bumpy road lined with chestnut trees up to the Hessenstein, a seven-course prix-fixe meal staggers customers in the rustic dining room of the Forsthaus. A reduction of courses and one alternative main course were allowed. The choice of wines didn't leave anything to coincidence: the service made only one suggestion, and handed us the wine list only on special request. The prices for food and drink were not listed and had to be asked for! This was the sort of surprise prix-fixe meal we didn't appreciate at all, especially when we got the bill: 140 DM was justified neither by the cooking nor by the products used. The paprika consommé with ravioli was not harmonious, our bass with oversalted fennel was soggy, and the saddle of veal was overdone. Some dishes (and our white wine, too) were lukewarm. The service is generally motivated, but what can they do when complaints are parked in the kitchen and don't provoke a single reaction?

PASSAU — Bayern

Regensburg 117 - München 186

PASSAUER WOLF 13/20

94032, Rindermarkt 6
(08 51) 3 40 46, Fax 3 67 57 res.

P

Closed for dinner Sunday. Tables d'hôte: 30L, 68D, à la carte: 29/69

Although the quality of the cuisine wavers sometimes, the Passauer Wolf remains a recommended address. The sweetbreads in the nettle soup had the consistency of chewing gum, and the amount of cream in the soup could have been used to decorate a cake. The clear calf's tail soup and the fillet of lamb, however, were wonderful. Some of the dishes—such as the roast beef with capers, anchovies and pickles—were reminiscent of Austrian cooking. We always choose sherbet for dessert here, and this time we enjoyed one made from white and red grapes .Good, moderately priced wines from Austria and Franconia are offered. The service was slightly uncertain, and the staff could have benefited from more training.

WILDER MANN 15/20

94032, Schrottgasse 2/Rathauspl.
(08 51) 3 50 71, Fax 3 17 12 res.

Tables d'hôte: 89/119, à la carte: 32/70

The service is disciplined and professional, and the cuisine both dependable and imaginative. The first courses are particularly interesting. These include an aspic of suckling pig with horseradish, a tender breast of wild pigeon with sautéed mushrooms, and potato lasagna with deliciously fresh scampi and scallops. The fillet of pike-perch, fresh out of the Danube, is perfectly prepared, and the basil sauce is as finely balanced as all the sauces here. Cooked calf's tongue with cauliflower and olive sauce is an exciting but harmonious combination. The baked suckling kid with peas in cream is simply sensational, as is the stuffed leg of rabbit with carrots and leeks. For dessert, we had strawberries and oranges with mascarpone.The wine list offers a pleasing assortment of regional wines, choice Italian wines, fine vintages from Burgundy and the Bordelais, as well as a great number of excellent Austrian wines.

WILDER MANN

94032, Schrottgasse 2/Rathauspl.
(08 51) 3 50 71, Fax 3 17 12

53, **S** 60, **D** 100/160,
APP 200/270

Four patrician houses dating from Gothic, Renaissance and Baroque times have been combined to create this modern and comfortable hotel complex without destroying their original characters. The restaurant and roof terrace afford a wonderful view of the Danube and the Old Town. The rooms are of cool rustic elegance and, if they face the garden, quiet. Breakfast buffet: 15 DM. The hotel also houses a glass museum and a remarkable collection of old cookbooks.

PEGNITZ Bayern

Bayreuth 26 b- Nürnberg 54

PFLAUMS POSTHOTEL 12/20

91257, Nürnberger Str. 12-16
(0 92 41) 72 50, Fax 8 04 04 res.

Tables d'hôte: 125/165, à la carte: 50/95

Bread and circus would be the right motto for this gourmet theater. No other restaurant in the region serves its food with such flamboyant showmanship. The experience begins with the opulently decorated dining room, continues with Manager Andreas Pflaum's star attitude and climaxes in the claims of the gourmet menu. Alas, the curtain falls here. Where was the highly praised lightness of the salads, aspics and mushrooms? We looked in vain for the promised flavors of the vinaigrettes, buttery cream sauces and tasteless vegetables. The main courses were not much better. We suspect that the dry, tough kid, pigeon and duck were prepared beforehand and warmed up before serving. We had better luck with the freshly fried meat, and our venison medallions were nicely done. The best thing for dessert was the flavorful homegrown fruit. The wine list, with its much-too-expensive wines, reflects the Pflaums' conceit. The prices in the adjacent Posthalterstube are more humane.

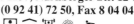

PFLAUMS POSTHOTEL

91257, Nürnberger Str. 12-16
(0 92 41) 72 50, Fax 8 04 04

P

50, **S** 150/290, **D** 190/445,
APP 445/1500, **1/2P** +115

The front of the Posthotel presents an attractive half-timbered facade. A peek around the next corner reveals a modern building with high-tech equipment. The rooms and suites offer various degrees of comfort, from the simplest to the noble "Lohengrin" suite. High-tech beds and Wagner videos in the whirlpool set the tone of the house. Superlative facilities for conference and convention guests.

PERL Saarland

Saarburg 20 - Merzig 25

SCHLOSS BERG 14/20

9 km north in Perl-Nennig
66706, Schloßhof 7
(0 68 66) 7 90, Fax 7 91 00

Closed Tuesday. Tables d'hôte: 65L, 85/136D, à la carte: 54/100

Surrounded by lovely Moselle vineyards, Schloss Berg, built in the 12th century, houses a restaurant within its noble walls. Discreet lighting, warm colors, elegantly set tables and choice porcelain give today's bourgeoisie a taste of aristocratic luxury. The prices are aristocratic as well. Franz Karner's cuisine is highly decorative and refined. We enjoyed the artistically arranged and tasty salmon terrine with fresh celery and carrot salad; the fresh anglerfish medallions with crispy potato and vegetable crust (although the saffron sauce was rather bland); the saddle of kid with savory onion crust, served with a superb, mild caramelized garlic sauce; and choice desserts with ripe fruit. The service was pleasant and attentive although slightly condescending. The wine list offers an impressive choice of wines from the best estates of all major German wine-growing regions, French and Austrian white wines, and red wines from the Rhône, Burgundy, the Bordelais and Italy. There is a sufficient selection of half bottles and fine liqueurs.

SCHLOSS BERG

9 km north in Perl-Nennig
66706, Schloßhof 7
(0 68 66) 7 90, Fax 7 91 00

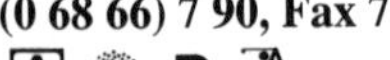

17 rooms, **S** 220/320, **D** 330/430,
APP 490/590

Rooms and suites are furnished with considerable splendor and elegance. The hotel has its own casino and a helicopter port. If these don't interest you, look for the *gasthaus* Die Scheune with wine cellar and bar.

PERLEBERG — Meckl.-Vorp.

Berlin 135 - Hamburg 150

HENNINGS HOF

19384, just 3 km west
via Quitzower Str.
(0 38 76) 25 84 , 50 31, Fax 50 35

23 rooms, **S** 80/135, **D** 100/160,
APP 210, **1/2P** +23, **P** +43

This old farmhouse at the city gates with its barns and stables has been turned into a modern hotel, convention and sports center. The comfortably appointed rooms are absolutely quiet (except for a lustily crowing rooster). Breakfast: 15 DM.

PETERSHAGEN — NRW

Minden 15 - Bremen 91

SCHLOSS PETERSHAGEN 12/20

32469, Schloßstr. 5-7
(0 57 07) 3 46, Fax 23 73

Tables d'hôte: 35L, 58/120D, à la carte: 34/70

After having climbed up the circular staircase of this more than 700-year-old castle, guests can enjoy a splendid view of the Weser landscape from the restaurant. The dining room combines a romantic ambience with timeless elegance. Guests have to be a little romantic themselves in order to enjoy the cuisine here. Our gourmet prix-fixe menu began (better late than never) with (banal) white bread and cream cheese, followed by a light mousse with salad and slightly spotty avocados, a nice leek broth with pieces of prawns, an almost insipid anglerfish fillet with oversalted *rösti* and tough "tender saddle of lamb" with eggplant and potato gratin. The portions were mighty, perhaps to make up for the lack of quality, but we would have preferred a little more finesse, flavor and seasoning. The service is peasant and attentive. The wine list is well-stocked, but the wines by the glass are more expensive than the champagne.

SCHLOSS PETERSHAGEN

32469, Schloßstr. 5-7
(0 57 07) 3 46, Fax 23 73

12 rooms, **S** 150/180, **D** 220/250,
APP 350, **1/2P** +40

This elegant castle and former bishop's residence is an idyll on the banks of the Weser. The comfortably furnished rooms provide every modern amenity. The hotel offers many sports and recreation facilities, and the historic palace kitchen with its fireplace and well is a perfect setting for medieval-style banquets. Opulent breakfast buffet.

PFAFFENWEILER — BW

Bad Krozingen 5 - Freiburg 15

HISTORISCHES GASTHAUS ZUR STUBE 16/20

79292, Weinstr. 39
(0 76 64) 62 25, Fax 6 16 24 res.

Closed Sunday, Monday. Tables d'hôte: 59L, 98/135D, à la carte: 59/97

In his gourmet temple for an elite clientele, Friedrich Zehner makes no compromises. In spite of the recession, fewer guests and smaller expense accounts, he personally guarantees high quality. His excursions into Asian cuisine have led to new taste sensations, for example, his Korean duck lightly glazed with honey and seasoned with a whiff of aniseed.Some memorable highlights of our meal were lobster doughnuts with green asparagus, asparagus soup with diced salmon, superb turbot with herb sauce and thin noodles, breast of Bresse pigeon with *pommes dauphines,* and finally a poppyseed parfait with cake. The large wine list is for snobs who want to order Lebanese or South African wines while in Baden. The Bierkeller pub one floor down is Zehner's answer to the recession. Everybody meets in this bistro and eats a plateful of good things for 18 DM.

PFALZGRAFENWEILER

Freudenstadt 16 - Stuttgart 80

SCHWANEN 14/20 

7 km west
in Ortsteil Kälberbronn
72285, Große Tannenstr. 10
(0 74 45) 18 80, Fax 1 88 99 res.

Closed mid-November through mid-December. Tables d'hôte: 38, à la carte: 25/65

The tables are elegantly set, the ambience tasteful, the service pleasant without trying to be competent, too, and the wine list is excellent. We were welcomed with fresh leek tart and had to ask for bread and butter. Bread we got, butter we didn't. But then we had one pleasant surprise after the other: well-done headcheese, flavorful Swabian brain soup, excellent warm chanterelle salad, perfectly fried turbot with a flavorful crayfish sauce, well-fried duck's breast and praline parfait with spicy oranges.

SCHWANEN 

7 km west
in Ortsteil Kälberbronn
72285, Große Tannenstr. 10
(0 74 45) 18 80, Fax 1 88 99

56 rooms, **S** 100/130, **D** 190/220,
APP 290, **½P** +30, **P** +36

Closed mid-November through mid-December

In the 1970s, a spacious new building was annexed to this 250-year-old house on the edge of the forest, in which the holiday visitor finds all the comfort he desires. In spite of its size (there are two more buildings in the garden), this hotel has retained the personal atmosphere that makes a stay here so pleasant. Medicinal baths, beauty farm, solarium, fitness center, skittle alleys, restaurant with diet menus. The cross-country skiing trail begins at the door.

WALDSÄGMÜHLE 12/20

7 km west in
72285, Ortsteil Kälberbronnon
the road to Durrweiler
(0 74 45) 8 51 50, Fax 67 50 res.

Closed for dinner Sunday, closed Monday, beginning of January through the beginning of February, 2 weeks in July/August. Tables d'hôte: 22L, 35D, à la carte: 29/76

Out of the high season, visitors find this restaurant a little gloomy. We tried a typical prix-fixe menu: Swabian ravioli in cream sauce, two slices of goose liver with delicious port wine sauce and poached pear slices, creamy and flat sorrel soup with tasty pike quenelles, overdone anglerfish medallions with a fine sherry sauce, excellent saddle of lamb with good herb sauce and nicely garnished sorbets. The international wine list is moderately priced.

PFINZTAL Bad.-Württ.

Karlsruhe 12 - Pforzheim 20

VILLA HAMMERSCHMIEDE 15/20

76327, Ortsteil Söllingen
Hauptstr. 162
(0 72 40) 60 10, Fax 6 01 60 res.

Tables d'hôte: 55/65L, 85/95D, à la carte: 49/92

Between Karlsruhe and Pforzheim, we discovered a new gourmet paradise. The restaurant's exclusive, elegant atmosphere led us to expect high prices, but we were pleasantly surprised. Nothing on the menu was exorbitantly expensive. We tried the fried sole as well as a whole fried bass with fresh herbs, olives, tomatoes and vegetables; both dishes were conservatively but perfectly prepared. We also liked the saddle of suckling pig with cabbage and bread dumplings, a whole duck carved at our table and the stuffed saddle of rabbit. Whatever you eat, leave room for the delectable and unforgettable *Schwarzwälder Kirschtorte*. Discreet hospitality characterizes the Villa Hammerschmiede, but the service could be more attentive to details. We should mention that there is a terrace for nice days—and that the wine list needs to be revised (soon!) and stocked by an expert.

VILLA HAMMERSCHMIEDE

76327, Ortsteil Söllingen
Hauptstr. 162
(0 72 40) 60 10 , Fax 6 01 60

26, **S** 148/248, **D** 198/298, **APP** 448/498

This a small but exclusive gem of a hotel, located on extensive grounds and hidden behind old trees. Each room is spacious and has elegant, unique furniture as well as as a marble bathroom. Library and fitness center. Breakfast: 20 DM.

PFORZHEIM BW

Karlesruhe 35 - Stuttgart 50

BABETT'S ZUNFTSTUBE 12/20

75172, Poststr. 8
(0 72 31) 35 86 12 res.

Closed Sunday, à la carte: 30/75, No Credit Cards

You'll need to reserve a table in this popular little restaurant. Numerous antiques and bric-a-brac create a quaint, old-fashioned atmosphere. The menu promised us fresh lobster, and ten minutes after ordering it, we were served a cheap, precooked import. The Swabian ravioli in (not homemade) beef broth were good, but the boiled beef with horseradish sauce was much better. The service is adequate, as is the small regional wine list.

GALA IN PARKHOTEL 15/20

75175, Deimlingstr. 36
(0 72 31) 16 15 00, Fax 16 16 90

Closed for lunch Saturday, closed Sunday, during the NRW summer school holiday. Tables d'hôte: 75/105, à la carte: 42/68

If you're expecting nothing but refined hotel cuisine here, get ready for a pleasant surprise. In this tastefully decorated restaurant, absolutely fresh products are exquisitely prepared, and unusual combinations and creativity guarantee cuisine with verve and refinement. Jan van Geest is cooking his way to the top. The service may take more time to get there, although it's always friendly.Just looking at the menu is appetizing. We ordered an airy mousse of smoked salmon with cucumber sauce, which reminded us vaguely of *tsatsiki*; asparagus salad with scampi and a touch of Italy; fillet of beef with chards and a whiff of lovage; salmon with basil and orange fennel; and finally, a sherbet of red wine and apples. Everything was high class. We had only a few criticisms. The wine list and cellar need to be revised and restocked, and the piano player in the hotel bar needn't compete with the background music in the restaurant.

PARKHOTEL

75175, Deimlingstr. 36
(0 72 31) 16 15 00, Fax 16 16 90

144, **S** 160/195, **D** 250, **APP** 280/540

This posh hotel is located beside the city hall and the theater on the shore of the Enz, right in the center of town, and offers comfortable rooms and suites. Extravagant beauty farm, modern conference center with a wonderful view of the town and the nearby Black Forest. Piano bar.

GASTHAUS SEEHAUS

75175, Tiefenbronner Str. 201
(0 72 31) 65 11 85

Closed Monday

No expense was spared in renovating this old forester's house, and the Pforzheimers can congratulate themselves on a new restaurant with a pleasant beer garden. Besides daily specials (calf's liver, Swabian ravioli and boiled beef) the menu offers ox-tongue salad, tripe, delicious lentils with sausage, onion roast and a few cold dishes. The service is friendly and guests enjoy Brauhaus beer.

MARITIM 

75177, Hohenstaufenstr. 6
(0 72 31) 3 79 20, Fax 3 79 21 44

148, **S** 189/279, **D** 248/344,
APP 420, **1/2P** +40, **P** +70

Near the station, this hotel presents the largest exhibition of jewelry in Germany. Restaurants.

PYRAMIDE 12/20

75179, Dietlingerstr. 25
(0 72 31) 4 17 54 res.

Closed Monday. Tables d'hôte: 49/69L, 69/89D, à la carte: 51/69

Beate and Andreas Wolf's new restaurant is full of surprises. Its redecoration is still only a plan, and many things seem provisional and sometimes unprofessional. But the promising cuisine more than makes up for little lapses, as does the personal and almost intimate hospitality—on cool evenings in the garden, for instance, they bring blankets for your legs! We had a refreshing consommé of asparagus with scampi, light salmon and anglerfish terrine with dill cream and salad, delicately fried foie gras with almonds, delicious anglerfish piccata, veal fillet with shiitake noodles, strawberry carpaccio with strawberry mousse, and delicious petits fours with our coffee.

SILBERBURG 15/20 

75179, Dietlinger Str. 27
(0 72 31) 4 11 59, Fax 4 11 59 res.

P

Closed Monday, closed for lunch Tuesday, closed mid-July through mid-August. Tables d'hôte: 68, à la carte: 35/76. Tables d'hôte with wine: 78

The residents of Pforzheim like Silberburg, so Gilbert Noesser often has a full house. The simple decor is plain rather than elegant, but this may be why nobody's afraid to eat here. The Alsatian Noesser combines regional cooking with masterly technique. We had an interesting ginger soup with shrimp, a slightly boring headcheese with salad bouquet, fried anglerfish with roasted fennel and an excellent fillet of veal with savory truffled sauce. In short, Noesser is the most dependable address for excellent cooking in Pforzheim.The wine list offers a satisfactory choice of mainly French vintages. Noesser's Alsatian wife has a simple recipe for making guests feel at home—friendliness.

PFRONTEN Bayern

Füssen 12 - Kempten 30

BAVARIA

87459, Kienbergstr. 62
(0 83 63) 90 20, Fax 68 15

P

50, **S** 110/10, **D** 220/300,
APP 140/190 per person, **1/2P** +30

Far away from the road, with a marvelous view of the mountains, this hotel's gleaming blue-and-white facade is a landmark in this part of the country. The rooms, studios and luxury apartments offer a high standard of comfort. Many opportunities for hiking and climbing, and both downhill and cross-country skiing are offered.

BERGHOTEL SCHLOSSANGER ALP 12/20

87459, Ortsteil Obermeilingen
Am Schloßanger 1
(0 83 63) 3 81 , 60 86

P

A la carte: 38/69

This mountain hotel more than 1,000 meters above Pfronten and surrounded by meadows and forests offers solid, plain fare that's decidedly above average. The well-worn menu offered lovely game, like venison noisettes in juniper sauce, and regional delicacies like stuffed pork in beer sauce. We also enjoyed a fried pike-perch with Savoy cabbage and mushrooms. We missed the announced herb crust around our lamb fillets, and our iced cucumber and buttermilk lacked flavor. There were three vegetarian dishes to choose from, and a large variety of wines by the glass. Last but not least, the prices are low.

ST. MAGNUSZIMMER IN GASTHAUS KRONE 16/20

87459, Pfronten-Dorf
Tiroler Str. 29
(0 83 63) 60 76, Fax 61 64 res.

Closed for lunch, closed Sunday, Monday, 1—21 August. Tables d'hôte: 108/128, à la carte: 45/80

This is where gourmets stop being gentlemen: they talk about what they've enjoyed. After our last visit, we have to sing the praises of cook Romeo Hofer, who's the best in this part of the Allgäu. We loved our creamy herb soup with salmon cannelloni and shoestring potatoes, a wonderful pigeon cutlet with lentils, noodles and baked plums, lamb with lobster in paprika butter and anglerfish with shrimp and curried sauce, basmati rice and mango. The beef aspic wasn't that terrific, but—after all that—we didn't mind. Guests can choose between the more rustic *gaststube* with its tiled stove and more regional cooking and the elegant and expensive Magnus room.

GASTHAUS KRONE

87459, Pfronten-Dorf
Tiroler Str. 29
(0 83 63) 60 76, Fax 61 64

32 rooms, **S** 115, **D** 160/200,
APP 360, **½P** +37, **P** +74

When the Gasthaus Krone calls itself a fine hotel, it doesn't exaggerate. The modern, elegant lobby leads to similarly modern, elegant rooms with parquet floors, beautiful rugs and comfortable furniture. The rooms all afford a view of the lovely green meadows and of the farmyard next door. Breakfast is served in a sunny pavilion. Conference rooms with modern technology.

PFUNGSTADT Hessen

Darmstadt 4 - Ludwigshafen 60

V.M. 1 15/20

64319, Borngasse 16
(0 61 57) 8 54 40, Fax 53 72 20 res.

Closed for lunch Saturday and Monday, closed Sunday, 2 weeks each preceding Easter and following mid-September. Tables d'hôte: 40L, 48D, 85, à la carte: 33/72

This restaurant is totally unpretentious, making it easy for customers to concentrate on the delights of the kitchen and wine cellar. The light, cheerful cuisine has a playful Italian touch. We enjoyed little squids stuffed with eggplant and served with garlic and basil sauce, rabbit terrine with olive sauce, anglerfish saltimbocca with lemon and sage, and a perfect leg of suckling lamb. The fresh, well-seasoned gurnard with gnocchi was interesting—and terrific. The daily specialities attract many customers. Prices are relatively moderate, the service is attentive but discreet, and the wine list has a definite Italian preference. Grappa and wines by the glass are well chosen.

PINNEBERG Schl.-Holst.

Hamburg 17 - Kiel 88

ZUR LANDDROSTEI 12/20

25421, Dingstätte 23
(0 41 01) 20 77 72 res.

Closed Monday. Tables d'hôte: 40L, 65D, à la carte: 36/66

In four picturesquely angular rooms in the cellar of the historic Landdrostei, Inken and Peter Löffler have opened a stylishly rustic restaurant. The menu includes regional specialties as well as international dishes, all well-prepared, generously portioned and moderately priced. We recommend lightly fried salmon tartare, oxtail sausage with flavorful red wine sauce and apple compôte with raspberry sorbet. A professional staff offers a good choice of wines by the glass at moderate prices, but the wine list could be improved to include more and better bottles.

PLAU Meckl.-Vorp.

Pritzwalk 35 - Rostock 85

PARKHOTEL KLÜSCHENBERG

19395, Klüschenberg 14
(03 87 35) 3 71, 25 14, Fax 3 71

50 rooms, **S** 105/145, **D** 139/175,
APP 190, **½P** +25, **P** +50

After complete renovation, the hotel offers pleasant, comfortable rooms, a conference center with modern facilities, solarium, bike rental, sports facilities and a playground. Opportunities for sailing, yachting, hunting and fishing. Breakfast: 15 DM.

SEEBLICK IN SEEHOTEL 13/20

19395, Hermann-Niemann-Str. 6
(03 87 35) 5 68, Fax 22 79

Tables d'hôte: 20/40, à la carte: 17/47

From the winter garden guests can enjoy an unobstructed view of the lovely lake—and also regional specialties from a comprehensive menu. Don't miss the fresh whitefish fried in butter if it's offered on the menu. There is also all sorts of game from the nearby forests, like leg of wild boar with red cabbage and apples or venison steak with red currant cream. Whatever you order here will be hearty and savory, with attention given to natural flavors and generous helpings. The service is pleasant and uncomplicated, and the choice of wines adequate.

SEEHOTEL PLAU AM SEE

19395, Hermann-Niemann-Str. 6
(03 87 35) 5 68, Fax 22 79

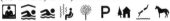

94, **S** 98/129, **D** 158/178, **APP** 198, **1/2P** +27, **P** +54

This small hotel and its neighboring château with 45 new rooms is located on the lakeshore and surrounded by fields and woods, an ideal setting for nature lovers and water sports. Modern, tastefully appointed rooms, conference rooms, bar.

PLAUE Brandenburg

Brandenburg 9 - Genthin 13

LINDENHOF 12/20

14774, Chausseestr. 21
(0 33 81) 40 35 10, Fax 40 24 95

Tables d'hôte: 35/45, à la carte: 24/61. Tables d'hôte with wine: 48

This lovely Art Nouveau villa painted in tasteful shades of green stands out among its drab gray neighbors. The restaurant combines turn-of-the-century charm with modern country style: upholstered benches and a cherrywood bar harmonize with stained glass windows and Tiffany lampshades. The kitchen prepares good bourgeois fare with a regional touch. We had pike-perch and crayfish from the Havel river and eel and pike from the Plauer See. Our pike roulade was served with a creamy Noilly-Prat sauce, and tender salmon roulade stuffed with pike with saffron sauce was accompanied by overcooked spinach. The venison roast with hearty port wine sauce and creamed Brussels sprouts was succulent and tasty. The menu seems endless and the desserts boring. Friendly service, well-stocked wine cellar.

PLIEZHAUSEN Baden-Württ

Tübingen 12 - Nürtingen 14

SCHÖNBUCH 14/20

72124, Lichtensteinstr. 45
(0 71 27) 72 86, Fax 77 10

2 weeks during the Bad.-Württ. summer school holiday. Tables d'hôte: 45/80à la carte: 36/82

This restaurant, with its marvelous panoramic view over the unspoiled nature of Schönbuch, is the perfect setting for excellent cuisine. We had first-class squab galantine with foie gras, delicate jelly made of plums and Marsala and choice salads (in salty marinade), sugar-pea soup with pieces of red mullet, grilled turbot with truffled crust and perfect tournedos with diced potatoes and rutabagas. Our poppyseed soufflé with strawberries and delicious vanilla ice cream was superb. The service is professional and pleasant. The wine list is comprehensive and most wines are (barely) affordable, something we can't say of the exorbitantly priced champagne.

PÖCKING Bayern

Starnberg 5

FORSTHAUS AM SEE 12/20

1.5 km southeast in Possenhofen
82343, Am See 1
(0 81 57) 9 30 10, Fax 42 92 res.

A la carte: 33/81

This is a fabulous place to spend a summer day. You can sit on the terrace and watch the sailboats on the lovely lake Starnberg, or you can sit inside and enjoy the ambience of the comfortably decorated restaurant. The only difficulty here is the food. Apparently, the quality of the food has plummeted along with the prices. Banalities like schnitzel and french fries are served, as is a mediocre anglerfish with asparagus. A pasta dish with sweetbread offered a ray of hope in an otherwise disappointing restaurant.Wines by the glass are expensive, as are the wines by the bottle from Germany, France, Italy and Austria. The selection will satisfy modest expectations.

POTSDAM Brandenburg

Berlin 15 - Brandenburg 38

BAYRISCHES HAUS 13/20

14471, Im Wildpark 1
(03 31) 97 31 92, Fax 97 23 29

P

A la carte: 31/60

The royal summer residence, built in 1847 and located in the middle of hunting grounds, is an architectural gem turned into a romantic and comfortable hotel. Time has stood still in the restaurant and salons, and the kitchen serves down-to-earth cuisine featuring well-known classics. From a creamy soup of herbs fresh from the hotel's garden to a wonderful salad with delicate duck liver parfait, our appetizers were tantalizing promises of the good things to come. Our roulade of pike-perch from the Havel river filled with light pike stuffing was served with a chive cream sauce, and fresh trout, carp and pike went into a fine fish stew with vegetables and white wine. Savory sauces accompanied leg of lamb, pork medallions and saddle of venison, all perfectly prepared. The service was deferential and pleasantly professional. The international choice of wines was impressive, and even included the interesting but rare Werderaner Wachtelberg. We just don't understand why the finest china and lovely silver cutlery, exquisite bouquets and candles on our table deserved only paper napkins.

BAYRISCHES HAUS

14471, Im Wildpark 1
(03 31) 97 31 92, Fax 97 23 29

24 rooms, **S** 115, **D** 195,
APP 340/490

The game preserve in Potsdam is the perfect setting for this hotel, built in a typically Alpine style. The rooms are equipped with modern amenities. Large terrace, bowling alley. Hunting trips can be arranged.

KLEINES SCHLOSS 12/20

14482, Im Park Babelsberg
(03 31) 7 51 56

A la carte: 33/63

Far from the bustle of Potsdam, this historic little restaurant with its turrets and towers is hidden away in the Babelsberg park. A crown prince used to live here, as well as ladies of the emperor's court. Today, moderately priced plain German fare is served in three intimate dining rooms. It took a while, but the kitchen (eventually) surprised us with lamb fried just right, chicken breast with a creamy cheese stuffing, cabbage roulades with cumin and tender redfish fillet with a savory sauce. Our potato soup tasted like mealy stew, but the apple strudel fresh from the oven consoled us. The small choice of wines needs to be enlarged.

RESIDENCE HOTEL POTSDAM

14478, Saarmunder Str. 60
(03 31) 8 83 00, Fax 87 20 06

P

240 rooms, **S** 90/275, **D** 110/310,
APP 490, **½P** +25, **P** +50

Businesspeople frequent this hotel for conventions and congresses. The hall, which seats 588 people, must be reserved far ahead. The 15 smaller conference and seminar rooms can be booked. Rooms and suites are adequately renovated.

LE SANSSOUCI IN HOTEL MERCURE POTSDAM 12/20

14467, Lange Brücke
(03 31) 46 31, Fax 29 34 96

P

Tables d'hôte: 30, à la carte: 29/58

Previously two mediocre restaurants, the new Le Sanssouci has an elegant Art Nouveau style. The incredibly spacious dining room is now more comfortable, thanks to partitions and little niches, and modern art prints decorate the walls. The cuisine, too, has developed character and style. The menu offered classics such as salmon carpaccio, Argentine steak with savory Burgundy sauce and a piquant stuffed breast of poularde. The regional dishes vary with the season. We had fried fillet of hare with lamb's lettuce and a wonderful raspberry vinaigrette; Brandenburgian potato cream with croutons; poached pike-perch from the Havel, served with spinach; and white chocolate mousse with Kirsch and warm honey. The service is unobtrusive and correct, but the wine list could use some standouts.

MERCURE POTSDAM

14467, Lange Brücke
(03 31) 46 31, Fax 29 34 96

 P

211, **S** 175/260, **D** 205/290,
1/2P +25, **P** +50

Recent cosmetic improvements to the facade haven't improved the drab exterior. The little rooms are comfortable, equipped according to international standards and afford a lovely view of the old city. The new apartments and suites are more spacious and elegant. The service is especially obliging. Sightseeing boats have a pier in front of the hotel, and the center of town is only a few minutes away on foot.

SCHLOSSHOTEL CECILIENHOF

14469, Neuer Garten
(03 31) 3 70 50, Fax 29 24 98

42, **S** 130/230, **D** 250/350,
APP 500, **1/2P** +45,

This is where Truman, Churchill and Stalin met in 1945 to discuss the future of Germany. Since then, this former Prussian palace, which also houses a museum of the Potsdam Conference, has been modernized into a comfortable hotel. The rooms are plainly furnished, but some suites meet the highest standards.

PRIEN — Bayern

Rosenheim 23 - Traunstein 35

LE PETIT RESTAURANT MÜHLBERGER 14/20

83209, Bernauer Str. 40
(0 80 51) 37 96, Fax 6 29 20 res.

P

Closed Tuesday, closed for lunch Wednesday, closed 2 weeks in late July. Tables d'hôte: 46L, 90/120D, à la carte: 61/93

If you're driving from the autobahn into Prien, Le Petit is worth a visit. Inside this unappealing bungalow, the cuisine is dependable and good—not particularly low-priced, but fresh, light and full of ideas.The very good three-course lunch special isn't expensive. On our last visit, we had salad, cream of asparagus soup, poached plaice with champagne sauce, and sliced veal in cream with morels, kohlrabi and noodles. Dessert was pear strudel with vanilla ice cream. Highlights à la carte were the rabbit consommé, rabbit livers and sweetbreads with asparagus, Barbary duck with bay-leaf sauce, chocolate-ginger cake with marzipan and figs, and rhubarb soup with strawberries and cheese dumplings.The wine list was obviously compiled by a connoisseur. In addition to good German vintages, it offers unknown wines from Austria, good Californians, South African wines, nice Alsatians, and noble wines from Burgundy and the Bordelais. The staff is competent and perfectly trained.

YACHTHOTEL CHIEMSEE

83209, Harrasser Str. 49
(0 80 51) 69 60, Fax 51 71

102, **S** 175/245, **D** 230/300,
APP 330/460, **1/2P** +45, **P** +80

This is one of the most beautiful hotels in the region. The rooms are tastefully equipped, and the house has a terrace with a view of the lake and the Alps as well as a yacht for 24 passengers. Modern conference facilities. Restaurant.

PULHEIM Nordrh.-Westf.

Grevenbruch 13 - Köln 16

IL PARADISO 13/20

6 km southwest in Dansweiler
50259, Zehnthofstr. 26
(0 22 34) 8 46 13, res.

 P

Tables d'hôte: 59L, 79/85D, à la carte: 32/75, No Credit Cards

If this comfortable *gasthof* is a culinary paradise, then owner Sahbi Moussa is its bird of paradise. Part Tunisian, part Italian, the owner is a professional who comes from Cologne's glittering gourmet world a few kilometers away. The so-called beautiful people don't make up the clientele here, but Sahbi's Paradiso offers good food for people who like to eat well. If he chases some demons (careless preparation and banal dishes) out of his kitchen, he'll surely keep his toque. Our parsley mousse was much too creamy, our gourmet salad with skinny quail banal and parfait of berries evidently a failure. And why serve factory-made noodles when the chef can make pasta even better than some Italians? His homemade lobster ravioli was first-class. The highlights of our meal were excellent red mullet fillets with lobster mousse, rabbit, lamb with mustard sauce and light clouds of praline and marzipan mousse. The service is very agreeable. The wine list is intelligently stocked and includes an adequate choice of half-bottles and wines by the glass.

QUEDLINBURG Sachsen-Anh.

Goslar 59 - Halle 75

MOTEL QUEDLINBURG

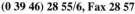

06484, Wipertistr. 9
(0 39 46) 28 55/6, Fax 28 57

48 rooms, **S** 95, **D** 125,
1/2P +20, **P** +40

This typical motel building is located near the center of town at the foot of the castle. The quiet rooms are small and modern, but plainly furnished. Restaurant, breakfast buffet and many rooms with three beds.

QUERN Schleswig-Holstein

Flensburg 22 - Kiel 70

LANDHAUS SCHÜTT 14/20

24972, 4 km north in Nübelfeld
(0 46 32) 3 18, Fax 17 62 res.

Closed Monday, closed for lunch Tuesday, 9—30 January, 3—17 July. Tables d'hôte: 68/108, à la carte: 43/75

If this comfortable *gasthof* is a culinary paradise, then owner Sahbi Moussa is its bird of paradise. Part Tunisian, part Italian, the owner is a professional who comes from Cologne's glittering gourmet world a few kilometers away. The so-called beautiful people don't make up the clientele here, but Sahbi's Paradiso offers good food for people who like to eat well. If he chases some demons (careless preparation and banal dishes) out of his kitchen, he'll surely keep his toque. Our parsley mousse was much too creamy, our gourmet salad with skinny quail banal and parfait of berries evidently a failure. And why serve factory-made noodles when the chef can make pasta even better than some Italians? His homemade lobster ravioli was first-class. The highlights of our meal were excellent red mullet fillets with lobster mousse, rabbit, lamb with mustard sauce and light clouds of praline and marzipan mousse. The service is very agreeable. The wine list is intelligently stocked and includes an adequate choice of half-bottles and wines by the glass.

QUICKBRON Schl.-Holst.

Hamburg 23 - Kiel 76

JAGDHAUS WALDFRIEDEN 14/20

3 km north near the B4 motorway
25451, Kieler Str. 84
(0 41 06) 37 71, Fax 6 91 96 res.

 P

Closed for lunch Monday. Tables d'hôte: 38L, 58/98D, à la carte: 50/88

Pure hospitality is practiced in this noble villa on the outskirts of town—not only by a discreet and attentive service team, but aslo by the motivated kitchen. A full house can lead to carelessness, however.

Our sautéed calf's kidneys with a delicate and ingenious olive sauce and gnocchi were too firm, and the skin of our striped mullet was more than just crispy. But the codfish strudel with discreet horseradish sauce was excellent, and homemade linguine with succulent salmon and black salsify just fabulous. The attractive choice of wines is moderately priced. We're just sorry the excellent Austrian wines have been taken off the wine list because of lack of demand. Instead, some high-quality wines by the glass have been added.

JAGDHAUS WALDFRIEDEN

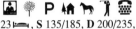

3 km north near the B4 motorway
25451, Kieler Str. 84
(0 41 06) 37 71, Fax 6 91 96

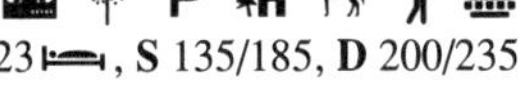

23 rooms, **S** 135/185, **D** 200/235,
1/2P +48, **P** +58

A Hamburg shipowner built this hunting lodge in the middle of a 16-hectare park at the turn of the century. The rooms of this modernized and rebuilt house are inviting and comfortable.

RADOLFZELL Bad.-Württ.

Singen 11 - Konstanz 20

GOTTFRIED 13/20

4 km southwest in 78345 Moos
Böhringer Str. 1
(0 77 32) 41 61, Fax 5 25 02 res.

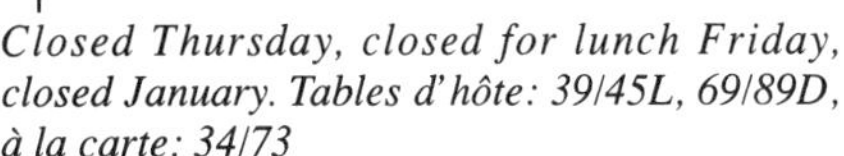

Closed Thursday, closed for lunch Friday, closed January. Tables d'hôte: 39/45L, 69/89D, à la carte: 34/73

The only reason our toque still sits firmly on Gottfried's head is the wonderful fish we had here. Beef aspic and rack of lamb, rhubarb terrine and lumpy ice cream were catastrophic flops. But freshly caught fish from nearby Lake Constance was brilliantly prepared. Our pike fried in sage butter and served on a bed of leeks would have been perfect if adequately boned. Owner Klaus Neidhart tried to keep an eye on the kitchen and the service (who served their dishes with anything from a professional grin to downright sulkiness) at the same time. The choice of wines (served in handsome glasses) is excellent.

RAMMENAU Sachsen

Bischofswerda 4 - Dresden 25

SCHLOSS RAMMENAU 12/20

01877 Rammenau
(0 35 94) 70 30 65, Fax 70 31 60 res.

Closed Monday, January through March. Tables d'hôte: 25/45, à la carte: 29/76

The ambience of this restaurant is just as splendid and elegant as in the rest of this Baroque castle-cum-museum, especially when a master of ceremonies precedes guests into the bird room, garden hall, the blue salon or the hunting salon. A miscellaneous menu brings one down to earth again: fried eggs with ham and fried potatoes, a *Schlachtplatte* with freshly slaughtered pork, potato soup and a roast of wild boar are offered, as well as foie gras galantine, oysters, sweetbreads, châteaubriand and fish from the region and from overseas. The performance of the kitchen varies, and so does the service. Dry hare terrine, tinny tasting (canned?) artichoke hearts, lumpy cream of asparagus and rubbery pike-perch fillet led us to our compromise of 12.5/20. The beauty of the castle doesn't make up for everything.

BAD RAPPENAU BW

Heilbronn 15 - Karlsruhe 70

SCHLOSS HEINSHEIM

6 km northeast in Heinsheim
74906, Gundelsheimer Str. 36
(0 72 64) 10 45, Fax 42 08

42 rooms, **S** 120/170, **D** 140/260,
APP 480, **1/2P** +55, **P** +80
Closed 19 December through 2 February

With a lot of hard work, the present owner has converted this Baroque castle into an elegant country hotel. From its quiet, idyllic setting in the middle of an old park, guests can view the wonderful Neckar valley. Restaurant complex with attractive rooms for smaller festivities.

RASTATT Bad.-Württ.

Baden-Baden 14 - Karlsruhe 22

MAXIMILIAN 14/20 

76437, Lochfeldstr. 30
(0 72 22) 98 97 69 res.

P

Closed for lunch Saturday, closed Sunday. Tables d'hôte: 68/110, à la carte: 38/78

Somebody's rich uncle must be at the bottom of this new and impressive restaurant in an industrial section of Rastatt, for which no expense has been spared. A talented interior decorator (with carte blanche?) has created a modern yet comfortable ambience. Siegfried Egner has worked with some of the best chefs in Germany and cooks true to recipe. His suckling kid, gently braised and with a naturally flavorful sauce, was worth a rating of 17/20. His appetizers (a lot of salmon) were masterpieces, even though some seemed to have been from the day before. Daily specials were recommended by the headwaiter. The main courses didn't rise above average, like a souffléed turbot with herbs and champagne sauce and a cordon bleu with excellent spaetzle.The staff celebrates its own importance with a sometimes pompous, sometimes nonchalant attention to its guests. The wine list offers a choice of German, French and many Italian wines at acceptable prices, although why a 1981 Mouton Rothschild costs so much more than one from 1979 we couldn't imagine, much less taste.

RASTEDE Niedersachsen

Oldenburg 11 - Wilhelmshaven 45

DAS WEISSE HAUS 15/20

26180, Südender Str. 1
(0 44 02) 32 42 res.

Closed Thursday, 10 days each in February and August. Tables d'hôte: 32/48L, 39/82D, à la carte: 29/71, No Credit Cards

With highly professional and yet personal hospitality, this restaurant satisfies a wide range of guests. Gourmets from the big cities nearby and local diners from neighboring villages find the Weisse Haus equally attractive. Customers who just want to eat a main course are as welcome as those who enjoy a gourmet prix-fixe meal. Appetizer highlights were pike-perch in a pesto crust with heavenly saffron sauce and green asparagus and, for those who like to eat light, a finely balanced and seasoned salad with sprouts. Kindermann's bouillabaisse was savory and hearty, and his meaty main courses were delicious: saddle of lamb rolled in cabbage and fillet of ox with morels. Our mousse of Valrhona chocolate was superb! The wine list was expertly stocked, and even included high-quality wines by the glass. Guests who want to take advantage of the low-priced wines can stay overnight in one of three rooms and enjoy a very good breakfast, served from 9 a.m. to 1 p.m.

RAUENBERG Baden-Württ.

Wiesloch 4 - Heidelberg 20

MARTINS GUTE STUBE IN WINZERHOF 16/20

69231, Bahnhofstr. 6-8
(0 62 22) 95 23 53, Fax 95 23 50 res.

 P

Closed for lunch, closed Sunday, Monday, January, during the Bad.-Württ. summer school holiday. Tables d'hôte: 75/125, à la carte: 50/104

Martin's parlor is cozy and comfortable—perhaps too cozy for some customers, who may not enjoy sitting so close to their neighbors at the next table. Jürgen Menges is a first-class cook, and his wife guarantees excellent service. Menges enchanted us with tender pigeon breast, delicately smoked with a touch of thyme; delicious foie gras with grated and fried potatoes; perfectly done anglerfish; and a classic Barbary duck, served with two sauces—the breast with rosehip sauce, the legs with one made from vinegar and shallots. Menges' desserts are always superb, especially the cheese gratin with almond ice cream or the buttered potato ravioli with plum sauce and mango sherbet. This is one of the best restaurants in the Kraichgau.

RAVENSBURG Bad.-Württ.

Friedrichshafen 20 - Ulm 86

KRONE 16/20 

4 km southeast in
88281 Schlier
Eibeschstr. 2
(0 75 29) 12 92, Fax 31 13 res.

 P

Closed Tuesday, Wednesday. Tables d'hôte: 79/109, à la carte: 47/85

The Schlierer Krone doesn't practice the most innovative of cuisines, and the chef doesn't hesitate to serve classic bourgeois dishes. But he also served the most wonderful herb-coated saddle of lamb we've ever tasted. Georg Müller turns this almost compulsory (and boring) dish, which belongs to the standard repertoire of gourmet restaurants, into a sensation: his composition of different fresh herbs makes his crusts superb. Müller, a successful businessman who took over his parents' rundown restaurant relatively late in life and revived it to a beacon of gourmet hospitality, had his eagle eyes on both kitchen and service. From the warm bun filled with ham that started off a prix-fixe meal to a striking and spicy savarin with coconut parfait and vanilla cream, we enjoyed everything. Insider tips: tripe soup laced with balsamic vinegar, headcheese aspic, fish terrine, pike quenelles in Riesling sauce, sea trout coated with leeks and game when in season.

REBLEUTEHAUS 14/20

88212, Schulgasse 15
(07 51) 1 52 00, 3 61 20, Fax 3 61 21 00

Closed for lunch, à la carte: 31/64. Tables d'hôte with wine: 55

The Rebleutehaus isn't a cheaper version of the highly rated gourmet restaurant Waldhorn, but once in a while we notice the maestro's touch in the food served in Bouley's bistro. In an imposing late-Gothic dining hall, we had green asparagus soup with tarragon, red mullet with cucumbers, and veal schnitzel with pesto and tomato spaghetti, and appreciated the flavorful yet simple way most dishes were prepared. We've never tasted better shrimp aspic with dill potatoes or more delicious mustard sauce with our leg of suckling pig. The portions weren't as overwhelming as they used to be, so we treated ourselves to an iced nut cake with cggnog and pineapple for dessert. The service was attentive and the wine list offered a good choice of wines by the bottle and by the glass.

WALDHORN 19/20

88212, Marienplatz 15
(07 51) 3 61 20, Fax 3 61 21 00 res.

P

Closed Sunday, Monday. Tables d'hôte: 54L, 134D, à la carte: 71/107

As always, we expected either a sensation or a drama in Bouley's Waldhorn—and neither occurred. His cuisine is as steadily excellent and as consistently creative as always. We doubt if his usually full house is enough to motivate him to create the highest-quality cuisine. On our last visit, we noticed many who ordered just one course or a soup and enjoyed the good wines by the glass offered here (besides many interesting and not merely exorbitantly priced bottles). At any rate, we didn't scrimp on a grand prix-fixe meal, a masterpiece of a culinary East-meets-West dialogue that included iced tuna and sole sashimi with prawn tart, sheatfish fillet encrusted with shrimps and served with Swiss chard and sambal and trassi sauce, and veal *tafelspitz* with tuna ravioli and olives. Our seven-course meal consisted of many crustaceans, two courses with veal and insipid truffles in kohlrabi butter with fresh noodles and sweetbreads. Everything was served with impressive flamboyance. The highlights of our meal were quail stuffed with foie gras and morels, smoked saddle of rabbit with scallops and bok choy (chinese white cabbage), piquant Spanish-style stuffed saddle of veal with tarragon and sherry sauce and a terrine of passion fruit and puréed raspberries.

WALDHORN

88212, Marienplatz 15
(07 51) 3 61 20, Fax 3 61 21 00

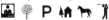

38, **S** 115/158, **D** 158/230,
APP 225/280, **1/2P** +45

The Bouleys now operate two hotels: the romantic Waldhorn hotel and a more modern hotel in the Schulgasse. The rooms are comfortable, chic and cozy. Conference facilities with modern technology. Weekly and weekend rates. Pool, spa park, sauna and tennis courts nearby. Breakfast buffet: 22 DM.

RECKLINGSHAUSEN NRW

Bochum 15 - Essen 30

LANDHAUS SCHERRER 12/20

45659, Stadtteil Bockholt
Bockholter Str. 385
(0 23 61) 2 27 20, Fax 2 19 04 res.

Closed for lunch Saturday, closed for dinner Sunday, closed Monday. Tables d'hôte: 35L, 55/95D, à la carte: 36/79

Where Bockholt's village children used to quake before their teachers, they now come to brunch with their parents. This former schoolhouse has been transformed into a portly old country mansion with a nostalgic charm.The restaurant has a wine cellar as well as a wine book, not just a list that explains what's in it. The restaurant also has a kitchen, where the owner cooks when he isn't busy in his wine cellar. He turns out such curiosities as tomato carpaccio with fillet of lamb and a surprisingly delicious avocado cream with caramel sauce. We enjoyed the venison terrine, red snapper with saffron butter and fillet of pork in flaky pastry. The highlights of Scherrer's cuisine are his fantastic soups, always served with fitting ceremony.

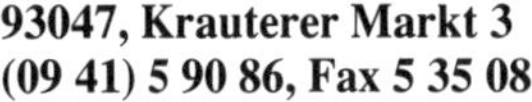

REGENSBURG Bayern

Nürnberg 100 - München 120

BISCHOFSHOF

93047, Krauterer Markt 3
(09 41) 5 90 86, Fax 5 35 08

54 rooms, **S** 110/170, **D** 180/230,
APP 260/310
Closed 23—25 December

Attractive house in the center of town. The rooms overlook a courtyard or a quiet little road to the Danube. Ample breakfast buffet. Restaurant.

HISTORISCHES ECK 16/20

93047, Watmarkt 6
(09 41) 5 89 20, Fax 56 29 69 res.
Closed Sunday, Monday, 7—14 January, 25 August through 7 September. Tables d'hôte: 52/90L, 90/120D, à la carte: 50/89

With much respect for historic architecture, Rüdiger Forst and Stefan Memmer have transformed the ground floor of a turreted patrician house in the old part of town into a small but refined restaurant. Vetter's cuisine is classical, yet it remains relaxed and creative. Rather than offering expensive, extravagant dishes that only a few customers can afford, he offers pleasant surprises on his menu. Excellent products and ingredients are skillfully prepared in an extraordinary way or unusually seasoned. Whether he serves sheatfish with asparagus or with sauerkraut, headcheese or lamb's tongue, pigeon or duck, everything harmonizes perfectly. Some of his combinations create new and exciting taste sensations; these include turbot, red beets and horseradish; anglerfish with marinated kohlrabi and vegetable vinaigrette; and ravioli with calf's tail stuffing, tomatoes and leeks. For those with a sweet tooth, we recommend the warm desserts.The wine cellar is stocked with an interesting selection of Austrian, French and Italian wines, although the ingenious cuisine deserves a more inspiring wine list. Stefan Memmer serves his guests by paying attention to their wishes, and he offers wines by the glass with dessert.

KARMELITEN

93047, Dachauplatz 1
(09 41) 5 43 08/9, 5 46 58, Fax 56 17 51

71 rooms, **S** 80/150, **D** 120/200,
APP 120/220, **1/2P** +25/35
Closed 18 December through 15 January.

This hotel's foundations—which can be viewed in the cellar—date back to Roman times. In its present form, the hotel is about 150 years old, although it has been remodeled over the years to offer modern comforts. The original staircase is particularly lovely, and so is the spacious lobby. The rooms over the inner courtyard are the quietest.

KREUTZER 14/20

93047, Badstr. 54
Am Oberen Wöhrd
(09 41) 8 87 11, Fax 8 88 48 res.

Tables d'hôte: 62/95, à la carte: 37/81

Detlev Schmidkunz's restaurant lies on the shore of the Danube. The walk from the historic part of the city to the so-called Obere Wöhrd is romantic, setting the mood for an evening at Kreutzer's. On the ground floor of this large, respectable town mansion, the former salons with their stucco ceilings and paneled walls have been turned into small, comfortable dining rooms. When the weather permits, customers can also dine behind the house, in the midst of lovely hydrangea bushes, or in front of the house, on a terrace with a view of the Danube. The menu has a distinct regional touch. Among the highlights of this refined but down-to-earth cuisine are veal, country duck and blood pudding served with potatoes and dark ale sauce. The chef doesn't ignore international trends altogether. His Swabian ravioli are filled with scampi, and Bohemian truffles add just the right accent to a tender fillet of beef. We just wish that Schmidkunz's imagination would extend to his sauces, which tend to be similar and rather sweet, and to his side dishes (cabbage and asparagus are served with a number of courses). Superb desserts are Schmidkunz's strong point. His exquisite strawberry dumplings, for instance, were as light as clouds.The wine list doesn't satisfy high expectations. Aside from a few interesting wine growers, various nondescript producers offer their wines here. The service is extremely capable, if only because the staff manages to suggest passable wines out of this repertoire.

PARK-HOTEL MAXIMILIAN

93047, Maximilianstr. 28
(09 41) 5 68 50, Fax 5 29 42

52, **S** 160/238, **D** 210/288, **APP** 350/450, **1/2P** +40, **P** +80

This stylish luxury hotel is the most striking private neo-rococo structure in Bavaria. The rooms leave nothing to be desired, and the prices are affordable. The conference center offers modern technology in historic halls. Restaurant.

REICHELSHEIM Hessen

Michelstadt 15 - Bensheim 25

RESAURANT TREUSCH IN SCHWANEN 14/20

64385, Rathausplatz 2
(0 61 64) 22 26, Fax 8 09 res.

 P

Closed Thursday, closed for lunch Friday, closed 3 weeks in February, 2 weeks at the beginning of September. Tables d'hôte: 30/120, à la carte: 32/82. Tables d'hôte with wine: 80/180

Armin Treusch is full of good ideas. The emphasis he puts on regional cooking lets us enjoy tasty recipes from the Odenwald, especially during the weeks in September and October, when he offers potato specialties. We loved our *Ebbelwoi Hinkelche* (succulent chicken breast stuffed with cheese and served with cider sauce), fried pike-perch, leg of lamb with mushrooms and exciting desserts such as plums in red wine with almond ice cream. The moderately priced wine list is stocked with the best wines from Germany and excellent regional wines (like those from the Simon-Bürkle winery). The more rustic Johann's Stube next door also offers good value for the money.

REICHENAU Bad.-Württ.

Konstanz 10

HOTEL SEESCHAU 12/20

78479, An der Schiffslände 8
(0 75 34) 2 57, Fax 72 64

P

Tables d'hôte: 30/40, à la carte: 24/60. Tables d'hôte with wine: 40/110

After a complete renovation, the two dining rooms have been decorated in an elegant country style with a cheerful, colorful Mediterranean ambience. From our table we could look through a large window and see the cooks at work in the kitchen (and the French vacuum-packed duck breasts). The menu offers everything fastidious tourists appreciate. We liked the fish dishes best, especially the variations of fresh fish in three courses. The quality of the cuisine ranged from a passable cream of potato soup to perfectly fried fish fillet with a light and savory chive sauce, and an insignificant poularde breast with overdone noodles and weak sherry sauce. The highly flavorful parfait of honey vinegar and orange blossoms was an interesting taste sensation. The service and the choice of wines were adequate.

BAD REICHENHALL Bayern

Salzburg 18 - Berchtesgaden 18

HOFWIRT 12/20

83435, Salzburger Str. 21
(0 86 51) 9 83 80, Fax 98 38 36

Closed Monday, 15 January through 15 February, à la carte: 22/47, No Credit Cards

The era of heavy sauces has passed, and a refined regional cuisine has taken over. We now feel more at home than ever in this cozy, rustic restaurant, which offers a wonderful biergarten and a pleasant terrace-café. We enjoyed the trout, pork roast with crispy crust, venison goulash and delicious vegetable strudel. The apple tarts, sweet pancakes and homemade cakes were delectable. The prices on the wine list remain moderate. Wines by the glass as well as by the bottle from Germany, Austria and Italy are available.

HOFWIRT

83435, Salzburger Str. 21
(0 86 51) 9 83 80, Fax 98 38 36

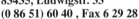

20, **S** 70/80, **D** 120/140,
½P +25, **P** +45
Closed 15 January through 15 February, No Credit Cards

This quiet hotel isn't far from the spa park, and its rooms are tastefully refurbished, spacious and comfortable. Terrace and lawn for sunbathing.

KURHOTEL LUISENBAD

83435, Ludwigstr. 33
(0 86 51) 60 40 , Fax 6 29 28

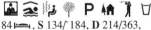

84, **S** 134/184, **D** 214/363,
APP 370/455, **½P** +42, **P** +64

The hotel has its own spa and resident doctor, beauty farm and excursion program. Extensive garden, elegant restaurant, bar and winter garden.

SCHWEIZER STUBEN IN KIRSCHBERG-SCHLÖSSL 15/20

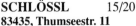

83435, Thumseestr. 11
(0 86 51) 27 60 res.

Closed Wednesday. Tables d'hôte: 38L, 70D, 92, à la carte: 34/74

The picturesque Baroque castle in Kirchberg on the Salach houses the oldest restaurant serving fine cuisine in Bad Reichenhall. The atmosphere is elegant, and the service is prompt, dependable and competent. A tasty appetizer of turkey wings with potato salad was followed by headcheese and sweetbreads with excellent asparagus salad, lobster terrine with salads and a wonderfully delicate cream of lobster soup. The Brittany lobster with shrimp was delicious, and the pike-perch fillet with potato slices perfect. The saddle of rabbit with basil sauce was a highlight of our meal, as were the lovely calf's kidneys with basmati rice and the capon with polenta. The exquisite cheese dumplings with strawberries or cassis parfait were memorable desserts. The wine list offers a good choice at reasonable prices.

STEIGENBERGER AXELMANNSTEIN

83435, Salzburger Str. 2-6
(0 86 51) 77 70, Fax 59 32

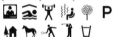

151, **S** 175/275, **D** 255/490,
APP 490/970, **½P** +58, **P** +88

This is one of the unsinkable flagships of the Steigenberger chain. The hotel is surrounded by an extensive park and guarantees peace and quiet. The rooms are furnished in a rustic style and have large bathrooms and pretty balconies. The hotel offers the full range of spa and medical facilities, an indoor pool, solarium and beauty farm. Restaurant, elegant bar.

ZUM SEEWIRT AM THUMSEE 14/20

83435, Am Thumsee 1
(0 86 51) 6 12 92, Fax 6 32 00 res.

Closed Tuesday. Tables d'hôte: 59, à la carte: 31/64, No Credit Cards

A few kilometers past Reichenhall (direction Schneizlreuth), you'll find the idyllic Thumsee. Located on the shores of this quiet lake, the restaurant with terraces looks especially inviting. We liked the tastefully decorated dining rooms, where the talented young cook Helmut Valentin, together with his young, motivated crew, serves specialties such as delicious asparagus soup with smoked fish, scampi in rice leaves, crisp and succulent Barbary duck, excellent Thumsee trout, and tasty veal fillet with morels and noodles. The wine list is still growing, but it already offers some nice young wines.

REICHERTSHEIM Bayern

Mühldorf 16 - Wasserburg 21

RAMPL-BRÄU

84437, Bräustr. 15
(0 80 73) 20 67
A la carte: 12/26

In the midst of tiny Reichertsheim stands this small private brewery, which makes excellent beer. This is the perfect beverage to accompany everything served in the little *gaststube* or in the biergarten outside. Hot meals are served only at lunch; the kitchen offers cold dishes in the afternoon and evening. The hearty, honest fare consists of tasty regional meat dishes, always freshly prepared. We enjoyed the delicious liver-dumpling soup, beef roast, Wiener schnitzel, stuffed veal roast, chicken and fillet of pork. Side dishes included generous helpings of vegetables, salads and spaetzle. The service is friendly and resolute.

REMSHALDEN Bad.-Württ.

Schorndorf 8 - Waiblingen 8

GASTHOF ZUM LAMM 12/20

73630, Ortsteil Hebsack
Winterbacher Str. 1
(0 71 51) 4 50 61, Fax 4 54 10 res.

Closed for lunch Saturday, closed for dinner Sunday, closed Monday, 2 weeks during the Bad.-Württ. summer school holiday. Tables d'hôte: 49/79D, à la carte: 23/67

Appreciated by many Swabians and extremely popular with tourists on weekends, this *gasthof* with its pretty old sign is located within sight of lovely vineyards and unlovely industrial complexes. We tried the surprise prix-fixe menu (on a weekday) and had dry sweetbread mousse with Sauternes jelly and terribly cut salads, delicate and savory tomato soup with cheese dumplings, salty anglerfish medallions with overdone and unpeeled peppers, tough loin of venison in a delicious sauce, tasty orange sherbet with plum compôte, and two rather insipid parfaits. The choice of wines was small but low-priced, and included a good many wines by the glass.

RENNEROD Rheinl.-Pfalz

Limburg 28 - Siegen 42

THOMAS RÖTTGER 14/20

56477, Hauptstr. 50
(0 26 64) 10 75, Fax 9 04 53 res.

P

Closed for dinner Sunday, closed Monday, 2 weeks during the Rh.-Pf. summer school holiday. Tables d'hôte: 35/49L, 58/98D, à la carte: 40/80

We liked this restaurant before, but we like it even better now. The Röttgers have finally gotten rid of all the rustic ballast. They've redecorated the little dining room and created a modern, light and pleasant ambience, which even the remaining leaded glass windows and a wooden bench cannot mar. With only two apprentices to help him in the kitchen, Thomas Röttger takes a lot of trouble to serve fine cuisine. His fine preparation of different kinds of game deserves two toques. We had, for example, a marvelous saddle of roe deer in walnut crust with elderberry sauce, apple gratin and spaetzle. But stuffing sole with salmon, pike and scallops is overdoing it. Röttger concluded his meals with clever and creative desserts.The selection of wines is reasonable, and the service is polite, attentive and correct.

REUTLINGEN Baden-Württ.

Stuttgart 40 - Ulm 88

VINOTHEK EN VILLE

72764, Oberamteistr. 27
(0 71 21) 33 02 90

The former half-timbered stable, built in the 15th century, is now a wine shop. Hans Villforth, a successful businessman who's made a profession out of his hobby, offers his thirsty, knowledgeable clientele everything from agreeable regional wines to excellent Bordeaux vintages. The choice of 160 bottles can either be bought to take home or (for a 12 DM cover charge) enjoyed here. Besides that, there are 30 wines by the glass to choose from, as well as Prosecco and champagne. Spontaneously created little dishes are served, like Alsatian cream pizza or scallopini with white wine sauce.

RIETBERG NRW

Rheda-Wiedenbrück 9 - Paderborn 27

DOMSCHENKE 13/20

7 km south in Mastholte
33397, Lippstädter Str. 1
(0 29 44) 3 18, Fax 69 31 res.

P

Closed for lunch Saturday, closed Tuesday. Tables d'hôte: 35L, 72D, à la carte: 50/83. Tables d'hôte with wine: 72/125, No Credit Cards

Is a kitchen overtaxed when it serves the hungry multitudes in front and the gourmets in the back room at the same time? In any case, the impressive variety offered on the gourmet menu needs a bigger or better kitchen brigade to carry through with good cooking. The quality of the cuisine, which offers everything from the classic to the trendy, ranges from 12 to 15/20. The choice of wines is good and the service agreeable.

RÖSRATH Nordrhein-Westfalen

Siegburg 12 - Köln 19

KLOSTERMÜHLE 13/20

51503, Zum EulenbroicherAuel 15
(0 22 05) 47 58

Closed Monday, Tuesday, 2 weeks at the beginning of January, 4 weeks during the NRW summer school holiday. Tables d'hôte: 45/95L, 75/135D, à la carte: 48/78

Fish is served here in soup bowls and swimming in sauce. That's the way François Mitterrand likes his fish, too, a wise gourmet assured us. Whatever the French president's taste may be, we awarded our toque for an excellent prix-fixe meal like this: salad with duck's breast fried in honey and thyme, pike-perch sausages with Riesling sauce, vegetable julienne and leaf spinach, apple sherbet with cider, lamb medallion with vegetables and gratin, and strawberry and rhubarb strudel with fruit and sherbet. We could have ordered an additional course and cheese and still not paid more than 100 DM for our meal! Guests choose the fresh fish they like and make their own suggestions as to the preparation and side dishes—something we'd rather see offered on a menu. The choice of French wines is grand, and even high-quality wines are affordable. There's also no lack of half-bottles. We would have liked to sink into a bed after we'd spent an enjoyable evening here.

ROSENBERG Bad-Württ.

Aalen 30 - Ansbach 65

LANDGASTHOF ADLER 17/20

73494, Ellwanger Str. 15
(0 79 67) 5 13 res.

P

Closed Thursday, Friday, January, 2 weeks during the Bad.-Württ. summer school holiday. Tables d'hôte: 48L, 120D, à la carte: 25/84, No Credit Cards

With each of the 19 well-worn steps we were that much closer to gourmet enjoyment. We liked the grand hall with antique country furniture, the many liqueur bottles and the opulent flower arrangements. The exquisite creations of the kitchen astonished us. Customers order fried bass with salad, black bread soup with fried foie gras, artichoke noodles with a yellow and red pimento sauce garnished with thyme and rosemary, tripe with morels and sage, and roasted sheatfish with mushrooms, black olives and fried potatoes. We had wonderful pigeon breast with truffles and kohlrabi, a fabulous choice of cheese and rhubarb variations, including lovely light mousse and salad with vanilla ice cream and strawberries. In addition to fine cuisine, Josef Bauer also offers regional delicacies. The service is perfect, and the wine list leaves nothing to be desired.

LANDGASTHOF ADLER

73494, Ellwanger Str. 15
(0 79 67) 5 13,

16, **S** 75, **D** 120/140,
APP 180/230
Closed January, 2 weeks during the Bad.-Württ. summer school holiday, No Credit Cards

Surrounded by the lovely Ellwang mountains, this little country hotel built in 1717 stands in the middle of town. The rooms are quiet and furnished with antique cupboards and modern beds. Individual breakfast. Rothenburg, Dinkelsbühl and Neresheim are no more than 50 kilometers away.

ROSENHEIM — Bayern

München 65 - Salzburg 77

MAXIMILIAN'S 13/20

83024, Hofmillerstr. 9
(0 80 31) 8 61 97

Tables d'hôte: 59, à la carte: 37/68

This new restaurant is located in a quiet, green residential area outside of Rosenheim. In his nicely decorated dining room or on his lovely terrace, the ambitious owner serves a strikingly good garlic cream soup, baby turbot with basil butter and bass from Lake Victoria with herb cream, a well-done rabbit cordon bleu, and a crispy fried duck's breast with red currants. The highly flavorful peach in foil with vanilla ice cream is a must! The wine list includes some good wines from Germany and a nice choice of Italian and French wines at moderate prices.

ROSTOCK — Meckl.-Vorp.

Stralsund 74 - Lübeck 113

ELBOTEL

18069, Fritz-Triddelfitz-Weg 2
(03 81) 8 08 80, Fax 8 08 87 08

98, **S** 98/165, **D** 145/195,
APP 165/235

This new hotel offers spacious, modern rooms and is located about three kilometers from the city.

MALMÖ IN HOTEL WARNOW 11/20

18055, Lange Str. 40
(03 81) 4 59 70, Fax 4 59 78 00

Tables d'hôte: 45/55, à la carte: 23/55

Seriously good cooking is offered only in the main restaurant. The international repertoire includes saddle of veal, tournedos, Barbary duck's breast and salmon medallions with run-of-the-mill side dishes. We missed creativity and precision. The service is anything from pleasant and motivated to slightly arrogant. We can only praise the interesting choice of wines.

HOTEL WARNOW

18055, Lange Str. 40
(03 81) 4 59 70, Fax 4 59 78 00

345, **S** 175/230, **D** 240/270,
APP 440/540, **½P** +25, **P** +50

The best hotel in Rostock stands in the middle of town. All rooms have been completely refurbished. Two suites have all the modern technology for business conferences. Restaurants, bar.

MECKLENBURGER HOF 12/20

18055, August-Bebel-Str. 111
(03 81) 4 92 23 01, Fax 4 92 23 03

P

Tables d'hôte: 32/40, à la carte: 16/36

As a regional fish restaurant, the Mecklenburger Hof was, is and will continue to be successful and popular. The cuisine is stunning in its simplicity. Its motto: take fresh fish, prepare it carefully and well, and charge low prices. Highlights were poached carp with melted butter, fried halibut fillet with red beans, and pike fillet stuffed with grated cheese. The motivated service staff works well in a full house - and enjoys itself. The choice of wines is surprisingly good, especially of wines by the glass.

SIEBEN TÜRME IN HOTEL NORDLAND 13/20

18055, Steinstr. 7
(03 81) 4 92 37 06

P

A la carte: 24/52

The best kitchen in Rostock still has a superfluously large menu, but correctly prepared food and good product quality show that an ambitious staff is at work. Our fish and seafood terrine was very tasty, pike-perch fillet with butter sauce and fresh vegetables nicely fried, and assorted fresh market fish perfectly cooked. The elegant ambience was the perfect setting for a cuisine that wants to go places.The service was seriously professional, but a better knowledge of wines wouldn't hurt. The choice of wines by the bottle was adequate and moderately priced, but the wines by the glass should definitely be improved.

NORDLAND

18055, Steinstr. 7
(03 81) 4 92 22 85, Fax 4 92 37 06

40 beds, **S** 185, **D** 270,
APP 345/405

This exclusive little hotel in the middle of the city offers its guests comfortably elegant rooms and modern conference facilities. Bar.

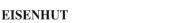

ROTHENBURG/TAUBER Bayern

Feuchtwangen 26 - Würzburg 60

EISENHUT

91541, Herrngasse 3-7
(0 98 61) 70 50, Fax 7 05 45

80 beds, **S** 155/225, **D** 195/380,
APP 520/640, **1/2P** +60, **P** +120
No Credit Cards

In a town famous for its medieval architecture, four patrician houses dating back to the Middle Ages have been combined to form this hotel. The designers were not always successful in creating a contemporary interior within such venerable masonry. The rooms are luxuriously furnished, though, and most bathtubs are made of white marble. The rooms in back afford a nice view of the valley below.

LANDGASTHOF LEBERT 13/20

10 km northeast
in 91635, Windelsbach
Schloßstr. 8
(0 98 67) 6 71, Fax 7 53 res.

Closed for lunch Monday, closed Thursday. Tables d'hôte: 50/80, à la carte:21/68. Tables d'hôte with wine: 48/60, No Credit Cards

"Friendly, fresh, and familiar" is the slogan of this hotel restaurant in the countryside. Appropriately, the cuisine is hearty and down-to-earth rather than refined and fussy. The helpings are big, the ambience is simple and rustic, and the table settings are rather Spartan, but the service is so pleasant and personal you'll feel at home immediately. (The gourmet who demands fine table silver and crystal glasses won't feel at ease here, however.) Everything served was fresh, and most products and ingredients were grown and raised in this region. Manfred Leber's cuisine definitely emphasizes regional recipes, and he peps them up with an Italian flair. Some hearty dishes, however, avoid all claim to fine cooking.The menu and wine list have moderate "country prices," and the choice of wines seems in accordance with the simple tastes of the guests.

ROTTACH-EGERN Bayern

Miesbach 21 - Bad Tölz 22

BACHMAIR AM SEE

83700, Seestr. 47
(0 80 22) 27 20, Fax 27 27 90 res.

Tables d'hôte: 48/66, à la carte: 34/64

This rundown gourmet restaurant finally closed its doors in March 1994. By 1995 it´s supposed to reopen and offer international gourmet cuisine in the main restaurant and regional specialties in the Bayerische Stuben one floor above.

BACHMAIR AM SEE HOTEL

83700, Seestr. 47
(0 80 22) 27 20, Fax 27 27 90

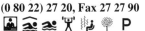

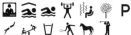

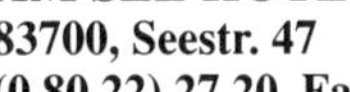

314 beds, **S** (including 1/2P) 200/325,
D (including 1/2P) 340/510,
APP 530/2000

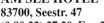

This hotel is a city-within-a-city and still manages to remain attractive. The facilities include a nightclub with top entertainers, bars, shopping arcade, massage, Kneipp treatment, medicinal baths, bowling, boccia ball and yachting. The whole complex is surrounded by a vast, beautiful park. The hotel satisfies even the most fastidious guest.

DICHTERSTUB'N IN PARKHOTEL EGERNER HOF 16/20

83700, Aribostr. 19-21

(0 80 22) 66 60, Fax 66 62 00

Closed for lunch. Tables d'hôte: 88/98, à la carte: 56/84

When we called the Dichterstub'n the best restaurant in the Tegernsee valley, its local competitors complained. In the meantime, the gourmet competition has given up, and Michael Fell maintains the high standards of his cuisine, even though he cooks for the Hubertusstüberl and the 140-bed hotel as well.The only things we missed in the Dichterstub'n were windows. But Fell's artistically arranged plates soon attracted our attention, and we forgot about the missing windows. The home-smoked sturgeon with caviar, lobster consommé with fresh mint leaves, and turbot fillet with tomatoes and roasted diced potatoes tasted as delicious as they looked. The marvelous venison medallions with foie gras, mashed potatoes and Savoy cabbage were superb, as was the chocolate ravioli (albeit a touch too sweet) with honeyed cherries and honey-and-lime ice cream. The wine list is satisfactory but could offer more moderately priced wines. The service is adequate.

HUBERTUSSTÜBERL IN PARKHOTEL EGERNER HOF 13/20

83700, Aribostr. 19-21

(0 80 22) 66 60, Fax 66 62 00

P

Tables d'hôte: 42, à la carte: 32/65

The guests of the Parkhotel are lucky: they only have to walk a few hundred meters to get from the best restaurant to the second best in town. The Hubertusstüberl offers plainer products and lower prices than the extravagant Dichterstub'n, but the dishes are prepared in the same kitchen and under the same chef. Apart from a few classics like veal haunch with potato dumplings or venison ragout with red currants and noodles, the kitchen has refined a few regional dishes: radish carpaccio with beef salad, brook trout encrusted with herbs and served with horseradish mousse, and a mosaic of smoked sheatfish with *rösti*. On the terrace in summer, the kitchen offers a special menu for hungry tourists. Pleasant service.

PARKHOTEL EGERNER HOF

83700, Aribostr. 19-21

(0 80 22) 66 60, Fax 66 62 00

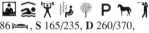

86 rooms, **S** 165/235, **D** 260/370, **APP** 360/510, **1/2P** +45, **P** +65

The owners have invested considerable money and a lot of good taste in this new hotel. The ambience is comfortable without seeming too stylish, and modern without denying its rustic Bavarian character. Attractive restaurants, an indoor pool, tasteful apartments, beauty farm and free garage are points in the hotel's favor. Children are welcome here. The separate convention center doesn´t disturb holiday guests.

WALTER'S HOF IM MALERWINKEL

83700, Seestr. 77

(0 80 22) 27 70, Fax 2 77 54 res.

  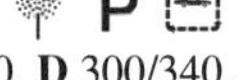

36 rooms, **S** 200/220, **D** 300/340, **APP** 420/480, **1/2P** +40

Countless painters from the Baroque age to the present day have been attracted by this picturesque corner of the lake. This small and exquisite hotel is a welcome change from the huge concrete structures that line the lakeshore. The rooms, suites and duplexes are elegantly furnished, each with its own fireplace and white marble bathtub. Indoor pool and beauty farm.

ROTTWEIL Bad.-Württ.

Tuttlingen 30 - Tübingen 60

VILLA DUTTENHOFER (L'ETOILE) 15/20

78618, Königstr. 1
(07 41) 4 31 05, 4 31 35, Fax 4 15 95 res.

P

Closed for lunch every day except Sunday, closed for dinner Sunday, closed Monday, 14 days after Lent. Tables d'hôte: 85/125, à la carte: 52/87

There's always something new and interesting being done in this beautiful turn-of-the-century villa. Sometimes it's a marvelous new decoration on the spaciously placed tables, or upholstery that matches precious Oriental rugs, or ingeniously placed paintings and sculptures. The wine list has grown to include more than 300 wines, many half bottles and exquisite wines by the glass, all at surprisingly moderate prices. The service has grown even more competent and charming than it was. Chef Bernhard Engler is always good for surprises (which, alas, also included overcooked noodles, too heavily truffled oil and dry anglerfish). Engler's Italian-style spring salad was fantastically flavorful, and his homemade pasta with crayfish and big morels stuffed with salmon soufflé fabulous. After an asparagus soup with scallops and bass, we had fresh char fillets in a champagne and caviar sauce, and fillet of beef stuffed with ham, sweetbreads and foie gras in a terrific truffled red wine sauce. In addition to fresh fruit covered with chocolate and pralines, we had a wonderful crème caramel with chocolate, custard with mango slices and Chianti strawberries, all presented as one perfect work of art.

RUDERSBERG Bad.-Württ.

Schorndorf 8 - Backnang 12

ZUM STERN 14/20

73635, Ortsteil Schlechtbach
Heilbronner Str. 16
(0 71 83) 83 77, Fax 36 77 res.

P

Closed Monday, Tuesday, 2 weeks in January, 3 weeks in August/September. Tables d'hôte: 62/115, à la carte: 28/75.

Anyone who wants to sell haute cuisine in Rudersberg must have a lot of courage. Armin Wiedmann does, and he delights friends and gourmets with lovely dishes and impressive meals in his rustic, comfortable restaurant. The salmon ravioli with diced vegetables and fresh cream was first-class, and the ingenious zucchini carpaccio with grated peccorino (garnished with salad, watercress, tomato, quail's egg and caviar) was simply superb. The fried parrot fish, osso buco of veal shank with wine sauce and the choice of desserts are the best proofs of Wiedmann's creativity and expert craftsmanship. The wine list is not comprehensive, but it is carefully thought out and reasonably priced. The choice of wines by the glass is very good. The service is pleasant and competent, the terrace in the garden quiet and nicely kept.

RÜDESHEIM Hessen

Wiesbaden 25 - Bonn 130

JAGDSCHLOSS NIEDERWALD 14/20

5 km northwest towards Niederwalddenkmal
65385, Auf dem Niederwald 1
(0 67 22) 10 04, Fax 4 79 70 res.

 P

Closed 1 January through 15 February. Tables d'hôte: 46/56L, 68/95D, à la carte: 35/99

During the summer, tourist buses find their up to this restaurant not far from the Niederwald monument high above Rüdesheim. Most guests feel well taken care of. The image and status of the cuisine have improved since Benedikt Freiberger took over the kitchen. The salad variations with fried asparagus, sheatfish and king prawns were good, and our warm pike-perch and eel terrine with spinach and cream sauce (this last seemed to be a running gag throughout our meal) unremarkable. The stuffed pike with lobster sauce, Riesling sauerkraut and (less tasty) potatoes, however, was excellent. After good cream soup with guinea hen and foie gras, we enjoyed nicely done lamb with thyme sauce. We would have rather had two good cheeses from a wagon or a tray than seven mediocre ones on a platter. A few bottles give the nod to French wines, but the rest of the wine list confines itself to (a great choice of) Rheingau wines.

KRONE ASSMANNSHAUSEN 16/20

65385, Assmannshausen
Rheinuferstr. 10
(0 67 22) 40 30, Fax 30 49

Closed 2 January through 24 February. Tables d'hôte: 45/65L, 98/135D, à la carte: 52/101

If we were to award a prize for continuous high-quality cooking, we'd give it to chef Herbert Pucher. Ever since he's been chef of this renowned kitchen (more than 20 years!) we have yet to find a hair in the soup. His cuisine hasn't shown a single weakness—not à la carte, at concerts, wine tastings or family festivities. Without his specific approval, not one single dish leaves his kitchen. He's famous (and feared by his suppliers!) for ruthless discrimination when he shops, and he motivates his kitchen to top performance.The cuisine is classic, not trendy. We had flawlessly prepared and tasty terrines of salmon, turbot and Barbary duck that harmonized perfectly with delicate herb sauce, cucumber salad and plum sauce and apple salad. All-time highlights of the menu were mildly dressed Graved salmon with an exquisite mustard and dill sauce and foie gras with port wine jelly. We enjoyed codfish with sour cream, sauerbraten with rosemary sauce, different lamb dishes and classic saddle of venison in season.The wine list is one of the hobbies of Pucher's partner Ulrich. He's stocked the wine cellar with more than 600 of the best Rheingau vintages and choice French and Italian wines. The list includes 53 red wines from Assmannshausen and many top Bordeaux vintages, among them 21 from Haut Brion and Cheval Blanc.

KRONE ASSMANNSHAUSEN

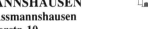

65385, Assmannshausen
Rheinuferstr. 10
(0 67 22) 40 30, Fax 30 49

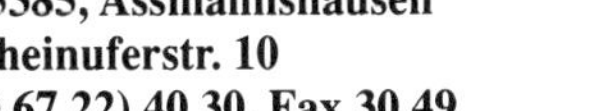

65, **S** 150/280, **D** 220/320,
APP 390/780
Closed 2 January through 24 February,

This must be one of Germany's finest hotels. It offers a degree of thoughtful luxury you'll find hardly anywhere else. Some of the rooms afford a view of the Rhine; some look out over celebrated vineyards. The corner rooms are particularly nice. Breakfast: 22 DM.

RÜDESHEIMER SCHLOSS

65385, Steingasse 10
(0 67 22) 9 05 00, Fax 4 79 60

21, **S** 140/180, **D** 180/260,
APP 260/300, **1/2P** +35, **P** +60
Closed during the Christmas holiday

In this wine *gasthaus* run by one of the most famous wine growers of the region, guests choose from among 330 different Rheingau wines, including a number of rarities. But this isn't the only remarkable thing in this more than 260-year-old castle, where the bishops of Mainz used to collect their taxes. The courtyard is enclosed by a modern hotel that includes 21 elegantly furnished rooms and three impressive suites designed in an avant-garde style. The honeymoon suite is in the historic old bell tower, but the bell tolls only until 10 p.m. Rooms and bathrooms are spacious and the panoramic view from the windows dramatically beautiful. Ample breakfast buffet.

RÜGEN Meckl.-Vorp.

Rostock 125/Cars proceed on the Rügen embankment from Straslund

BINZER HOF 12/20

in 18609 Binz
Lottumstr. 15-17
(03 83 93) 23 26, Fax 23 82

P

A la carte: 23/47

The pleasantly small menu offers only produce from the region, above all fresh fish like succulent, poached pike-perch with chive sauce, salmon with shrimp sauce, and hearty but delicate herring with sliced apple and onion, as well as good game in season. The wine list and the unprofessional service need more attention.

BINZER HOF

in 18609 Binz
Lottumstr. 15-17
(03 83 93) 23 26, Fax 23 82

50, **S** 75/120, **D** 150/190,
APP 200/250, **1/2P** +20, **P** +40

After complete renovation, this is the best hotel in Rügen. Guests feel at home in tastefully furnished rooms and like the quiet location about 50 meters from the promenade. The hotel has its own beach.

CLIFF-HOTEL RÜGEN

in 18586 Sellin
Siedlung am Wald
(03 83 03) 84 84, Fax 84 90

P

242, **S** 120/195, **D** 155/295,
APP 250/475, **½P** +25, **P** +50

The facilities of this modern, spacious hotel complex built in 1978 in lovely surroundings aren't quite up to the newest standards, but it offers a wide variety of amenities, such as massage, table tennis, skittle alley, volleyball, bikes, beach chairs and boats for rent, motor yacht, hairdresser and beauty farm. Restaurants, cafés and bars.

HAUS SCHWANEBECK 12/20

in 18609 Binz
Margarethenstr. 18
(03 83 93) 20 13, Fax 3 17 34

P

Tables d'hôte: 25D, à la carte: 19/53, No Credit Cards

Chef Gunter Preussker has enough self-confidence to claim he's the best cook in Binz. He isn't yet, but we're sure this ambitious cook will soon overcome the few flaws of his cuisine. If, for example, the kitchen would limit its regional menu, it could do without factory-made sauces and ice cream. The generously garnished fish soup could have been more substantial, and the basil sauce with the steamed salmon could have tasted lighter. In spite of some art on display, the large dining room seems a bit cool and functional. Obliging service and adequate wine list.

HOTEL AM STRAND

in 18598 Binz
Strandpromenade 17/18
(03 83 93) 3 50, Fax 23 87

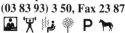

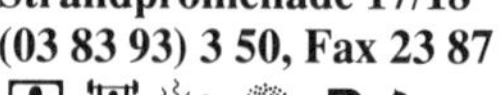

45, **S** 70/90, **D** 100/240,
½P +20
No Credit Cards

This pretty hotel offers a friendly and personal touch, and is located at the southern end of the promenade. All rooms have been redecorated and satisfy high modern standards. Massage, solarium, restaurant.

KLIESOW'S REUSE 12/20

in 18586 Alt-Reddevitz
Dorfstr. 23a
(03 83 08) 21 71, Fax 21 71 res.

P

Closed for lunch from Monday through Friday, closed November and February, à la carte: 29/49

This thatched former barn is well-frequented by gourmets. The genuine old style of regional cooking is as rustic as the comfortable ambience here. Excellent eel dishes (home-smoked), generously garnished cream of fish soup and succulent perch are commendable. The atmosphere calls for draft beer rather than wine. The service is natural and quick.

KÖPI-ECK 11/20

in 18546 Saßnitz
Haupstr. 26
(03 83 92) 2 22 87, 3 30 80, Fax 3 30 35 res.

P

Tables d'hôte: 30L, à la carte: 19/54

It sounds like a mediocre beer pub, but it's actually a seriously good little place to eat – in fact, the best restaurant in Sassnitz. The regular clientele can't help but be bored: the choice of international dishes hasn't varied at all during the past year. The ups and downs of the cuisine irritated us just as it did the last time we were here: the *Rügener Fischpfanne* was overdone, whereas our salmon fillet with creamed fennel garnished with oyster mushrooms was accurately prepared. *Palatschinken* (pancakes with jam) with fruit punch ice cream or genuine *Salzburger Nockerln* (sweet dumplings) are an absolute must here. The service is pleasant and quick enough, but shows little motivation (and neither does the small wine list).

NORDPERD 14/20

in 18582 Göhren
Nordperdstr. 11
(03 83 08) 70, Fax 71 60 res.

P

Closed for lunch, closed 11—24 December. Tables d'hôte: 25L, à la carte: 25/63

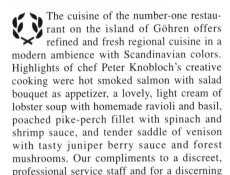

The cuisine of the number-one restaurant on the island of Göhren offers refined and fresh regional cuisine in a modern ambience with Scandinavian colors. Highlights of chef Peter Knobloch's creative cooking were hot smoked salmon with salad bouquet as appetizer, a lovely, light cream of lobster soup with homemade ravioli and basil, poached pike-perch fillet with spinach and shrimp sauce, and tender saddle of venison with tasty juniper berry sauce and forest mushrooms. Our compliments to a discreet, professional service staff and for a discerning choice of wines.

NORDPERD

in 18582 Göhren
Nordperdstr. 11
(03 83 08) 70, Fax 71 60

70, **S** 110/160, **D** 150/240,
APP 200/300, **½P** +25, **P** +50

The most modern and comfortable hotel on the island, designed by Swedish architects, was opened 1990 on the Mönchgut peninsula, which was decreed a nature reserve by the United Nations. Beauty farm, solarium, beach-chair rental, lobby bar, restaurant.

POSEIDON 12/20

in 18609 Binz
Lottumstr. 1
(03 83 93) 26 69, Fax 26 69 res.

Closed November. Tables d'hôte: 35L, 55D, à la carte: 22/57. Tables d'hôte with wine: 35/65

You have to be an incorrigible optimist if you expect to get a table without a reservation, especially in season. The kitchen has cooked so consistently well over a number of years that regular customers throng to this place in summer. There are only eight regional fish dishes to choose from, five game courses and five steak dishes, but everything is freshly prepared, generously portioned and cleverly arranged. Don't miss the *Rügener Fischpfanne* with roasted potatoes or the steamed pike with parsley sauce. Those who want to splurge order lobster with champagne sauce. The service staff keeps a cool head, even if things get hectic. The wine list includes interesting French and German wines at highly adventurous prices.

RESIDENZ RÜGEN

in 18569 TrentVaschvitz 7
(03 83 09) 2 20, Fax 2 29 00

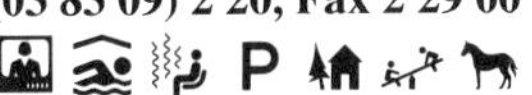

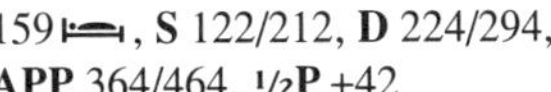

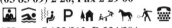

159, **S** 122/212, **D** 224/294,
APP 364/464, **½P** +42

Located on the edge of a natural preserve and about 100 meters from the ocean, this is a nice place to spend a vacation. The country hotel complex offers various creative activities and facilities for relaxation. From breakfast on a cart to romantic excursions by boat on the nearby Lake Bodden, guests are well cared-for. Beauty parlor, library, piano bar. Restaurants.

TRE KRONOR IN SCHWEDISCHEN HOF 12/20

in 18609 Binz
Sonnenstr. 1
(03 83 93) 25 49, 3 23 14, Fax 3 23 15 res.

P

A la carte: 25/64

The fish dishes on the menu sound interesting and ambitious enough to try. We had slices of fine fish with cream sauce on noodles, halibut fillet with saffron sauce and leeks, and cod fillet fried with potatoes and served with tomato sauce. Although the cuisine has improved, the wine list hasn´t kept up. The choice of wines by the bottle and the glass is still too small, whereas the prices have adjusted themselves more quickly to a higher level. The service could be less impersonal.

TRE KRONOR IM SCHWEDISCHEN HOF

in 18609 Binz
Sonnenstr. 1
(03 83 93) 25 49, 3 23 14, Fax 3 23 15

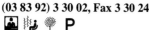

19 rooms, **D** 160/180,
APP 210/350, **½P** +25

The painter Renate Hofmann runs this small private hotel in a quiet side street about three minutes away from the beach. The rooms range from just comfortable to elegant. Art lessons offered. Adequate breakfast.

VILLA AEGIR

in 18546 Saßnitz
Mittelstr. 5
(03 83 92) 3 30 02, Fax 3 30 24

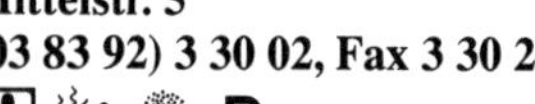

36 rooms, **S** 82/145, **D** 125/185,
APP 195/255

All the rooms of this popular hotel in a turn-of-the-century villa high above the harbor of Sassnitz have been renovated and equipped with spacious white bathrooms. The rooms in the new annex opposite are more elegant and tastefully furnished. The rustic restaurant offers mediocre regional cooking. Café terrace with a view of the Baltic. Adequate breakfast buffet.

SAARBRÜCKEN Saarland

Metz 68 - Mainz 152 - Bonn 200

AUBERGE DÉLICES 15/20

8 km northwest in 66292
Riegelsberg Hizberger Str. 42
(0 68 06) 36 86

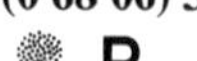

Closed for lunch everyday except Sunday from January through October, closed Thursday, 2 weeks in January, 1 week during the summer. Tables d'hôte: 48/95, à la carte: 45/78

In a rebuilt village pub, the talented, ambitious cook Wolfgang Quack has become serious competition for the established gourmet chefs of the Saarland. One of the most impressive meals we've had here began with an appetizing snail ragout in delicate herb sauce with a tiny brioche, followed by a tasty salmon terrine, and delicious al dente ravioli filled with seafood mousse in curried saffron sauce. Wonderful sautéed veal (meat, sweetbreads, kidneys and liver) in puff pastry was served with a lovely mustard sauce and garnished with vegetables. We enjoyed a dessert of orange gratin with excellent chocolate ice cream. The service was attentive and skillful. The wine list had been improved and included many more wines from Burgundy and Bordeaux (mostly from the 1980s), Alsace, California and Italy. The wines are fairly priced; examples are a 1990 Corton Charlemagne for 150 DM, 1981 Palmer for 158 DM and a 1975 Figeac for 269 DM.

GASTSTÄTTE GEMMEL 12/20

66111, Kappenstr. 2
(06 81) 37 25 25

Closed Monday, à la carte: 30/72

An Alsatian has been running this little bistro-like restaurant in the pedestrian district of Saarbrücken for almost 10 years now. In winter, seafood displayed appetizingly in front of the restaurant attracts customers, and in summer, they can sit outside. The atmosphere is relaxed, and the owner serves customers himself, sometimes speaking French, sometimes German. His handwritten menu offers classics of French cuisine like snails in savory roquefort sauce, delicate headcheese with vinaigrette, and tender rabbit fillet with a tasty, mild mustard sauce. Klein stocks only French wines and offers interesting low-priced wines by the glass.

KUNTZE'S HANDELSHOF 14/20

66117, Wilhelm-Heinrich-Str. 17
(06 81) 5 69 20, Fax 5 84 77 07

P

Closed for lunch Saturday, closed for dinner Sunday, closed Monday, 2 weeks during the Saarland summer school holiday. Tables d'hôte: 45L, 59D, 84, à la carte: 50/92

Gourmets eat well here and don't have to go broke in the process. Jutta Kuntze serves customers amiably, and Peter Kuntze cooks. His specialities: foie gras pâté, fish and crustaceans. A typical meal can start with a fresh beef and vegetable aspic with herb sauce, followed by dandelion salad with slices of rabbit fillet and liver (a little overdone), and a wonderful combination of little crepes filled with smoked salmon and served with a mild, creamy champagne sauce. After tender and succulent braised leg of duck with a finely balanced sauce, we had good strawberry parfait strudel for dessert and an unforgettably delicious apple tart with our coffee. The international wine list offers mostly young and drinkable vintages from excellent wineries, including some from the Saar region, Burgundy and Bordeaux. There is a respectable choice of half bottles and good wines by the glass at fair prices.

PROVENCE IN BAUER HOTEL RODENHOF 11/20

66113, Kalmanstr. 47-51
(06 81) 4 10 20, Fax 4 37 85

P

Tables d'hôte: 42, à la carte: 40/69

The ambience of this renowned restaurant is determinedly elegant, but the cuisine is traditional, and the staff not especially motivated. Our generous portion of salmon and bass (overdone) was served with a flat-tasting champagne sauce. Our lamb fillet, served with overdone mushrooms, vegetables and a brown sauce with specks of fat, was dry. Our white chocolate terrine lacked taste, the white mousse was too rich, and our sorbet of passion fruit was lumpy. The wine list is (still) adequate, but the prices are (already) too high.

RESTAURANT BAYARD— MASION HIRSCH 13/20

66119, Saargemünder Str. 11
(06 81) 5 84 99 49, Fax 5 84 70 11 res.

P

Closed for lunch Saturday, closed Sunday, 2 weeks each in February and August. Tables d'hôte: 33L, 45D, 92, à la carte: 46/98

Most dishes are excellent, but some remain disappointingly mediocre in Lauren Bayard's new restaurant. We enjoyed a fresh fish mousse and a discreetly seasoned pheasant terrine with foie gras and especially delectable salad of celery strips. A lovely, light mushroom soufflé was surrounded by flavorful mushrooms in a creamy crayfish sauce and shrimps. The quail was exquisite: crispy skin, tender and succulent meat, finely seasoned stuffing and delicious sauce—the side dishes were a disappointment, however. Excellent cheese and (too sweet) honey parfait with unremarkable vanilla sauce concluded our meal.The wine list has been improving steadily and includes, besides a number of interesting Alsatian wines, white Burgundy, Moselle and Saar vintages, an attractive choice of red Burgundys (good and very good vintages) and red Bordeaux (mostly young wines of the 1980s). The prices are fair: a 1987 Figeac for 89 DM and a 1985 de Pez for 71 DM, for instance.

RISTORANTE ROMA 12/20

66115, Klausenerstr. 25
(06 81) 4 54 70, Fax 4 17 01 05 res.

P

Tables d'hôte: 49L, 79D, à la carte: 36/71

The cuisine we've praised for its genuine Italian flair in the past has adjusted itself to the typical mediocrity of most Italian restaurants. Our smoked salmon carpaccio with peppery vinaigrette was followed by soggy anglerfish, crystallized lemon sorbet, cassata ice cream that was not fresh, and too-sweet tiramisù. Highlights were excellent ravioli stuffed with spinach, ham, cheese and eggs in a creamy walnut sauce, and flawless fillet of beef with a nondescript brown sauce. The service could have been more motivated. The wine list offers wines from good and excellent wineries in Piedmont and Tuscany. Very good choice of half bottles, wines by the glass and grappa.

SCHLOSS HALBERG 13/20

66121, Auf dem Halberg
(06 81) 6 31 81, Fax 63 86 55 res.

P

Tables d'hôte: 39L, 55D, à la carte: 40/71

Imaginative dishes are served in this highly elegant restaurant. The interior of the historic château has a modern decor. Garden terrace and park are part of the ensemble. We enjoyed tasty foie gras terrine with fresh figs, caramelized pears and corn brioche, delicate pike-perch with cucumber slices and red paprika sauce, succulent saddle of lamb with a savory potato crust, and a flavorful parfait of white nougat. The pastry with our coffee could have been fresher. The service was flawless. The wine list includes an adequate choice of wines by the glass, only a few regional bottles, some from the Loire and Italy, and a barely sufficient number of Bordeaux and Burgundys. More half bottles should be stocked. Some prices: 1987 Gloria, 100 DM; 1986 de Sales, 120 DM; and 1986 Latour (too young to drink), 420 DM.

LA TOURAINE 14/20

66111, Kongreßhalle
(06 81) 4 93 33, Fax 4 90 03 res.

 P

Closed for lunch Saturday, closed Saturday and Sunday during the Saarland summer school holiday. Tables d'hôte: 40/110, à la carte: 39/85

Chef Dominique Schmitt offers delectable traditional French dishes *à la grand-mère:* savory vegetable soup, crispy fried turbot fillet seasoned with black olives and served with a delicious beurre blanc, excellent fillet of rabbit with a finely balanced and slightly sweet sauce, and warm plums in port wine with vanilla ice cream. The desserts could be more imaginative, and the service should allow a little more time to enjoy each course. Other than that, the staff was obliging and charming as well as competent. A new wine list offers (besides a choice of the best German wine regions and some Italians) many wines from Burgundy and still more from Bordeaux: good vintages at reasonable prices. The choice of half bottles is good.

HOTELS

AM TRILLER

66117, Trillerweg 57
(06 81) 58 00 00, Fax 58 00 03

   P

133, **S** 130/185, **D** 205/230,
APP 250/300, **½P** +35, **P** +60

Closed 24 December through 1 January

A venerable survivor of historic Saarbrücken, surrounded by trees and overlooking the river, this hotel is one of the quietest the city has to offer. Lavishly redecorated rooms are wired for fax and modem transmission. Ambitious restaurant, pub, bar and billiards.

HAUS KIWIT

66119, Stadtteil St. Arnual
Theodor-Heuss-Str. 103
(06 81) 85 20 77, Fax 85 20 78

 P

19, **S** 105/150, **D** 150/200

Situated on the outskirts of the city, this hotel is peaceful and quiet. The rooms are comfortably furnished and offer a nice view of Saarbrücken. The spacious restaurant with pub and bar takes the place of a hotel lobby. Café serves lovely pastries. Excellent breakfast.

HOTEL LA RESIDENCE

66111, Faktoreistr. 2
(06 81) 3 88 20, Fax 3 55 70

 P

130, **S** 160/210, **D** 200/250,
APP 300/380, **½P** +30, **P** +60

Located in the center of town close to the convention center, this hotel is clean, tidy and well-run, without offering conspicuous luxury. Ample breakfast.

MERCURE KONGRESS

66111, Hafenstr. 8
(06 81) 3 89 00, Fax 37 22 66

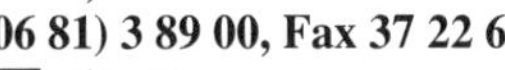  P

150, **S** 145/230, **D** 165/290,
APP 300/450, **½P** +30, **P** +60

Just opposite the convention center, this is Saarbrücken's best, if not its quietest, hotel. The rooms are small but attractively furnished. Rooms with even numbers are quieter.

NOVOTEL

66117, Zinzinger Str. 9
(06 81) 5 86 30, Fax 58 22 42

  P

99, **S** 99/153, **D** 138/186,
½P +25, **P** +50

Although the hotel is conveniently located close to the autobahn and the French border, it is peaceful and quiet. The rooms are furnished according to international hotel standards: the

beds are comfortable and the bathrooms functionally equipped. The service is pleasant and efficient. Children up to 16 years of age are free if they share their parents' room. Restaurant. Breakfast buffet: 18 DM.

PARK HOTEL 

66117, Deutschmühlental 4
(06 81) 5 88 30, Fax 5 30 60

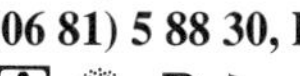

42 beds, **S** 95/120, **D** 125/160,
1/2P +28, **P** +40

The hotel, located on the edge of a beautiful park, offers rooms that range from plain to average. Those facing the park are quieter. The service is obliging and friendly.

SAARBURG — Rheinland-Pfalz

Trier 25 - Saarbrücken 70

SAARBURGER HOF 13/20 

54439, Graf-Siegfried-Str. 37
(0 65 81) 23 58, Fax 21 94

Closed Monday, closed for lunch Tuesday, closed 27 December through 25 January. Tables d'hôte: 56/85, à la carte: 35/64

Ever since Klaus Diewald took over this restaurant three years ago, we've been very satisfied with the pleasant service and the moderately priced and effortlessly good food. The last time we were there, however, we were slightly nonplussed by the fishy-smelling turbot, the lime sherbet drowned in dry Moselle Riesling and the sticky potato pancake served with the lamb fillet. Diewald can surely do better than this. Everything else, however, was of high quality. The highlights of our meal included wonderfully prepared red cabbage; lovely salad with asparagus tips, sweetbreads and foie gras; excellent homemade ravioli; exquisitely prepared lamb fillet; and strawberry gratin with rhubarb.The wine cellar is stocked with young regional wines, but customers can also find old Saar vintages (from as far back as 1921!) . A few of the choice Bordeaux are from the early 1980s.

SAARLOUIS — Saarland

Saarbrücken 25 - Trier 65

ALTES PFARRHAUS BEAUMARAIS 12/20

66740, Hauptstr. 2-6
(0 68 31) 6 08 48, Fax 6 28 98 res.

 P

Closed Sunday. Tables d'hôte: 48/67L, 67/98D, à la carte: 48/88

Brasserie, hotel and a restaurant decorated like a bistro of the 1930s are housed in this old rectory. The menu offers a wide variety of haute cuisine. More salt is one thing the sauces here definitely don't need, but they could use more taste and flavor. Our duck's breast could have been tenderer, and the tomato soup should have tasted more like tomatoes. The saddle of venison, however, was excellent and cooked just right. The dessert we had—Marsala parfait with an unidentifiable red fruit purée—wasn't anything to write home about. The wine list offers a sufficient choice of wines from all the major French wine-growing regions and a few from Germany, as well as good wines by the glass. Impressive liqueurs.

SALACH — Bad.-Württ.

Göppingen 8 - Geislingen 6

BURGRESTAURANT STAUFENECK 15/20 

73084, 2 km east
(0 71 62) 50 28, Fax 4 43 00 res.

 P

Closed Monday, 2 weeks during the Bad.-Württ. summer school holiday. Tables d'hôte: 56/108, à la carte: 40/91

We couldn't wish for more: a lovely view of the Stauferland, creative and delectable cuisine, and excellent wines. We started with an appetizer of homemade sausage, headcheese (in a rice leaf, in strudel pastry and with salad), *tafelspitz* with mustard crust, grilled bass with artichokes and chopped tomatoes, fresh salads with lovely vinaigrette and sliced mushrooms. Then we tried the millefeuille of scallops and truffles, fried sole with diced parsley potatoes and excellent turbot in red wine butter. After roast rabbit livers with caramelized cabbage, chive sauce and kidney salad and a grandiose dessert platter, the chef deserved a standing ovation. Applause, too, for his sister's superb apple cake with our coffee. Straubinger's Swabian specialities are also worth a try. Everything's is topquality in this castle on the mountain.

BAD SALZUFLEN NRW

Bielefeld 33 - Hannover 90

HOKUSPOKUS IN HOTEL ARMINIUS

32105, Ritterstr. 2
(0 52 22) 5 05 04, Fax 7 30 88

Closed Monday, No Credit Cards

Barkeeper Felix Gonzales mixes cocktails like a wizard—with expertise and a lot of charm. This list of good things to drink hasn't found its equal in any of the big cities around here.

ARMINIUS

32105, Ritterstr. 2
(0 52 22) 5 05 04, Fax 7 30 88

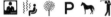

 P

56, **S** 140/180, **D** 200,
APP 300/360, **1/2P** +35, **P** +70

Five houses in the style of the Weser Renaissance make up the most unusual and beautiful hotel in the region. The 500-year-old charm of the houses is successfully combined with modern interior design. Spa and holiday guests are as welcome here as businesspeople, who make good use of the hotel's conference technology. Restaurant.

DIE TRÜFFEL IN HOTEL MARITIM 16/20

32105, Parkstr. 53
(0 52 22) 18 19, Fax 1 59 53 res.

Closed for lunch, closed Sunday, closed Monday, July/August. Tables d'hôte: 58/135, à la carte: 48/86

This light green, elegant dream of a restaurant strikes a rather shrill note in the turn-of-the-century ambience of the staid Maritim Hotel. And the quality of the cuisine is surprising in a place that cannot count on dieting spa guests or local skeptics as customers. Our appetizers, including a trio of crayfish aspic, sweetbread terrine with seaweed, and aspic with foie gras pâté and Bresse pigeon, were excellent starters for a superb meal of the kind that is seldom served in a German hotel-chain restaurant. The quail and foie gras galantine with truffles and salad, duck's hearts with fresh chanterelles, foie gras carpaccio with apple and truffles, and watercress soup with lobster were spectacular highlights of our meal. Creative and modern, though not trendy, were seafood sauté of John Dory, spiny lobster, red mullet with artichoke hearts, lamb saddle with garlic, fennel and couscous, and tender veal cutlets with cumin sauce and gnocchi. Apricot sorbet and yogurt, marinated cherries with pistachio ice cream, puff pastry with marinated strawberries and vanilla ice cream with puréed fruit were the grand finale of a fabulous meal. The service isn't jovial, but is discreet, unobtrusive and competent. The wine list emphasizes French red wines (some rather young) and offers a good number of half bottles and a few exotic wines from all over the world.

MARITIM

32105, Parkstr. 53
(0 52 22) 18 19, Fax 1 59 53

P

208, **S** 198/289, **D** 296/360,
APP from 442, **1/2P** +40, **P** +70

Its location at the edge of one of the most beautiful parks in Germany is an important asset of this hotel. The spacious rooms are equipped with modern amenities. Massage, solarium therapy center and beauty farm. Ample breakfast buffet.

ST. INGBERT Saarland

Saarbrücken 14 - Kaiserslautern 55

LE JARDIN IN HOTEL ALFA

66386, Ortsteil Sengscheid
Zum Ensheimer Gelösch 2
(0 68 94) 8 71 96, Fax 87 01 46 res.

Closed for dinner Sunday, closed Monday, 1—15 January. Tables d'hôte: 49L, 69L, 89, à la carte: 52/89

The dining rooms with their beautifully set tables and the adjoining wintergarten create an elegant ambience. in the summer, customers enjoy their food in the garden at the foot of a sandstone formation popular with sightseers. Fish dishes are Ludwig Braun's speciality. Our pot-au-feu of fine fish with saffron was fabulous, and codfish in potato crust, grouper wrapped in a rice leaf, and bass served in champagne sauce were outstanding (even though we would gladly have done without fried onions!). We liked succulent duck's breast glazed with honey and ginger and a tasty pear custard with creamy wine sauce. The service is pleasant and competent, and the wine list offers 320 choice German and French (mostly Bordeaux) wines at overall reasonable prices. The choice of half bottles is interesting.

HOTEL ALFA 
66386, Ortsteil Sengscheid
Zum Ensheimer Gelösch 2
(0 68 94) 8 71 96, Fax 87 01 46

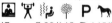

47, **S** 99/145, **D** 145/265

This hotel just two minutes away from the St. Ingbert-West autobahn exit is surrounded by woods. It is an ideal place for business meetings and conventions, but has none of the usual recreational facilities of a hotel complex

ST. PETER Baden-Württ.

Freiburg 18 - Waldburg 21

ZUR SONNE
79271, Zähringer Str. 9
(0 76 60) 2 03, Fax 7 66 res.

Closed Monday, closed for lunch Tuesday except during the summer. Tables d'hôte: 50/130, à la carte: 31/87

This country inn offers good, ambitious cuisine, but we missed that fine, elegant touch that makes great dishes out of merely good food. The Sonne can't be a gourmet temple with all the hikers and tourists that come here to be fed. The tables are elegantly set, the service is motivated, and the waits are long between courses when the house is full. A menu with Black Forest specialities for 10 to 22 DM is offered in the evenings. Noontime meals are often more extravagant, with quiche and shiitake mushrooms, red mullet and squid with artichoke hearts fried in olive oil, good consommé with marrow quenelles, sea trout generously plied with almond butter, fine fish in lobster sauce, and a good leg of lamb with potato soufflé. Our dessert was the best of all: strawberries and elderberry blossoms. The wine list emphasizes regional and French wines.

ST. WENDEL Saarland

Saarbrücken 38 - Kaiserslautern 56

RESTAURANT KUNZ 
66606, Ortsteil Bliesen
Kirchstr. 22
(0 68 54) 8 145, Fax 72 54 res.

P

Closed for lunch Saturday, closed Monday, Tuesday, 2 weeks during the Saarl. summer school holiday. Tables d'hôte: 58L, 78/95, à la carte: 50/86

Klaus and Alexander Kunz aren't afraid of experimenting. Father and son offer ingenious, tasty, attractive creations. They pampered us with an appetizer of cream of celery soup with scampi, followed by spaghettino salad with vegetables and pesto, scallops with potatoes in a creamy tomato sauce with garlic, pike-perch gratin with herbs and a delicate spinach cream sauce, surrounded by sweetened and marinated red shallots. Our saddle of wild hare was superb, and the light and fluffy banana soufflé as dessert fantastic. The service is pleasant, and the well-stocked wine list includes wines from Germany, Italy and France, especially from Bordeaux and Burgundy, at reasonable prices. The choice of half bottles and wines by the glass is adequate.

SASBACHWALDEN BW

Sasbach 3 - Achern 5 - Offenburg 27

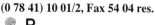

LE JARDIN
IN HOTEL TALMÜHLE 14/20
77887, Talstr. 36
(0 78 41) 10 01/2, Fax 54 04 res.

Closed 15 January through 20 February. Tables d'hôte: 42L, 68D, à la carte: 51/95

It's wonderful to sit on the terrace here and enjoy the extensive park with its old trees and magnolia bushes while listening to the music of a nearby brook. But customers enjoy more than just the idyllic surroundings — chef Gutbert Fallert refines regional recipes to the level of haute cuisine: the ducks, geese, veal and beef are raised in the neighborhood, and the quail and morels are from the Rhine meadows. Some dishes have an international touch, like Angus beef and turbot, but they are offered for gourmets who don't trust regional products in an elegant restaurant. The Badische Stuben have a more rustic ambience. The wine list emphasizes wines from Baden, but also offers a sufficient number of French and some Italian wines.

TALMÜHLE
77887, Talstr. 36
(0 78 41) 10 01/2, Fax 54 04

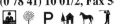

30, **S** 72/123, **D** 162/234,
APP 270, **½P** +38, **P** +60
Closed mid-January through 20 February

A fine two-story hotel in the heart of town. The Fallert family make exemplary hoteliers. The Badische Stuben are a perfect setting for a nightcap.

SAULGAU Baden-Württ.

Ravensburg 30 - Freidrichshafen 50

KLEBER-POST 14/20
88348, Hauptstr. 100
(0 75 81) 30 51, Fax 44 37

  P

Tables d'hôte: 45L, 89D, à la carte: 40/81

Looking toward the future and always keeping an eye on his balance sheet, Andreas Kleber is trying to attract a younger clientele with a bistro-menu that offers small, uncomplicated dishes for little money and a three-course prix-fixe lunch (with a choice of three main dishes). The dishes we tried weren't sensational, but on the whole were good and tasty: sorrel soup with shrimp, a surprising and harmonious ragout of anglerfish, white asparagus and red beans with delicious pancake strips, an excellent Barbary duck's breast, accompanied by a savory lentil sauce and followed by a lemon soufflé tart with fruit. Wonderful choice of wines at reasonable prices.

KLEBER-POST
88348, Hauptstr. 100
(0 75 81) 30 51, Fax 44 37

35, **S** 88/155, **D** 125/240,
APP 380/420, **½P** +45

A former Thurn & Taxis post station, this traditional hotel is improving. The old garages and a part of the main building have made way for a new wing with spacious and generously furnished rooms, suites, attractive lobby, modern conference rooms, fitness center and garage.

SAULHEIM Rheinland-Pfalz

Mainz 18

LA MAISON DE MARIE 13/20
55291, Weedengasse 8
(0 67 32) 33 31, Fax 80 76

 P

Closed Monday, 1—15 January. Tables d'hôte: 39L, 62/105D, à la carte: 52/81

If you want pompous elegance and a flamboyant ambience, you've come to the wrong place. But customers who like cordial hospitality and cheerful and inviting surroundings feel at home here. Most of the dishes we tried were simply good, and most of them were a treat to look at as well. We had an appetizingly presented pigeon terrine with delicious lentil salad, and wonderfully flavorful marinated salmon (with a pink dressing we could have done without). Our fillet of beef was excellent: high quality meat, tasty vegetables and a refined shallot sauce. The breast of poularde was succulent, but the Savoy cabbage with it seemed a little tame in comparison. The service was pleasant and competent. The wine list included many regional wines, but not always the best ones. The best French wines offered are too expensive, but among the plainer ones there are still some drinkable vintages at moderate prices.

SCHÄFTLARN Bayern

Starnberg 11 - München 20

HUBERTUS 13/20
82067, Ortsteil Ebenhausen
Wolfratshauser Str. 53
(0 81 78) 48 51, Fax 33 18 res.

 P

Closed for lunch, closed Sunday and Monday. Tables d'hôte: 65/75D, à la carte: 29/68

We like the comfortable atmosphere of the Hubertus, which is located in the idyllic Isar valley. The service here is obliging, competent and pleasant, but we were surprised by the fluctuating quality of the cooking. On earlier visits, we found nothing to criticize and things really seemed to be looking up for this restaurant. This time, however, we had good consommé spoiled by unskillful seasoning, dry fish, tasteless pancakes, overdone saddle of rabbit, and mango jelly with unripe fruit. We hope this was just a momentary lapse.The wine list offers a good choice of affordable Austrian wines.

SCHENKENZELL Bad.-Württ.

Schramberg 14 - Freundenstadt 24

SONNE 14/20

77773, Reinerzaustr. 13
(0 78 36) 10 41, Fax 10 49 res.

 P

Closed 6—11 January. Tables d'hôte: 30/84, à la carte: 24/73

We love to sit in these spacious dining rooms, waited on by friendly staff and enjoying one of Arnold Dorcas' good, low-priced meals. Our most recent eight-course meal started with an appetizer of salmon tartare. This was followed by a salad of asparagus tips with asparagus parfait and a salad in sherry vinaigrette; crawfish terrine; zucchini blossoms filled with salmon mousse, served with redbeet sauce and tiny courgettes; tender quail with an exquisitely balanced sauce; a perfect roulade of venison saddle with cranberry-horseradish sauce; a good choice of ripened cheese; and fabulous desserts. The different sherbets—apple, cassis, elderberry-bloom and peach—were delightful. A dessert of strawberries, prepared in various ways, was the final highlight of our meal. We also recommend the regional dishes.

SCHERMBECK NRW

Dorsten 8 - Borken 15

LANDHAUS SPICKERMANN 13/20

7 km south in Besten
46514, Kirchhellener Str. 1
(0 23 62) 4 11 32, Fax 4 14 57 res.

 P

Closed Monday. Tables d'hôte: 38L, 74D, à la carte: 31/67

You can congratulate yourself if you manage to find this country restaurant north of the Ruhr valley. It's on a street crossing outside Gahlen, the part of Besten that is a district of Schermbeck, and which lies somewhere in the vicinity of Dorsten. Got it? In any case, gourmets from the Ruhe region seem to find their way to these refined little dining rooms, as do large wedding parties (in the banquet hall) and travelers on bikes (on the lovely terrace). The service does its best, and chef Peter Nicolay serves refined regional cuisine. We had grilled lamb with Swabian potato salad, wild-boar goulash with dumplings and turbot with basil butter. Our lobster with melon, apple slices and basil tasted as delicious as it looked.The choice of wines is surprisingly large.

SCHMALKALDEN Thüringen

Meiningen 22 - Eisenach 36

AUBERGE IN HOTEL HENNEBERGER HAUS 15/20

98574, Notstr.
(0 36 83) 60 40 41, Fax 60 40 46 res.

P

Tables d'hôte: 40/60, à la carte: 33/60

This elegant auberge seems like a well-kept manor house with private salons and a large terrace. Frank Müller served us his meal suggestion of the month: fresh salad with sliced calf's liver and tomatoes, cream of asparagus soup with shrimps, grilled anglerfish and scallops with an excellent saffron-and-Pernod cream sauce, and perfectly done tournedos with morels and noodles. We concluded our meal with an opulent choice of cheeses and strawberry gratin with light pistachio ice cream. By the way, all the dishes on the Auberge menu can be ordered in the adjacent Kornkammer bistro; dishes include roast beef with caraway seeds and Thuringian dumplings, or poached eggs with vegetables, potatoes and cream cheese, each for 14.50 Deutsche marks.The pleasant, competent service staff helps to create an elegant atmosphere. The choice of German and French wines isn't particularly remarkable, but the wines are relatively low-priced.

HENNEBERGER HAUS 
98574, Notstr.
(0 36 83) 60 40 41, Fax 60 40 46

48, **S** 120/160, **D** 180/240,
APP 495, **½P** +20/25, **P** +43/45

Customers have a marvelous view of the Thüringian landscape from up here. Inside the hotel, they enjoy a pleasant reception in an unusually elegant lobby with bar. The rooms are spacious, comfortable and quiet, the bathrooms first class. Fitness center with trainer, nice hiking paths.

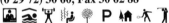

SCHMALLENBERG NRW

Winterberg 28 - Meschede 33

JAGDHAUS WIESE 
57392, Jagdhaus
(0 29 72) 30 60, Fax 30 62 88

66, S 96/180, **D** 175/297,
APP 222/340, **½P** +38, **P** +48
Closed 21 November through 27 December, No Credit Cards

Surrounded by a park in the center of a small village, this hotel guarantees its guests complete peace and quiet. After 6:30 p.m., the hotel belongs to the residents and is closed to visitors without reservations.

KUTSCHERSTUBEN IN HOTEL GNACKE 12/20
13 km northeast in Nordenau
57392, Astenstr. 6
(0 29 75) 8 30, Fax 83 70

Tables d'hôte: 30/59, à la carte: 39/73

At first sight, this spa hotel, with its black-and-white frame structure and profusion of red geraniums hanging from the window boxes, is just one of the many picture-book country inns that abound in this part of the Sauerland. But this traditional family-run hotel belongs to the top of its class, largely due to its high-quality cuisine that caters to the tastes of a conservative clientele. The rustic *"Kutscherstuben"* offers classic cuisine at moderate prices. Some dishes, like the *"Blankette"* of sole and sea trout with red beets and spinach beets, or veal fillet variations with ragout of asparagus and sweetbreads, are ambitious, but we've always liked the simpler, more classic dishes best. Service and wine list are satisfactory.

GNACKE 
13 km northeast in Nordenau
57392, Astenstr. 6
(0 29 75) 8 30, Fax 83 70

54, **S** 78/139, **D** 140/244,
APP 248/270, **½P** +22, **P** +35
Closed 20 November through 26 December, No Credit Cards

This beautiful old frame building looks more like a family inn than a modern spa hotel. Room numbers 60 to 85 face south and afford a marvelous view of the valley from their balconies. Two indoor pools, sauna and solarium, beauty treatments, café and guided hikes.

LANDHOTEL GASTHOF SCHÜTTE 12/20
8 km east in Oberkirchen
57392, Eddeweg 2
(0 29 72) 8 20, Fax 8 25 22 res.

P

Closed 26 November through 26 December. Tables d'hôte: 22/45L, 45/95D, à la carte: 34/83

Regional specialties and luxury cuisine are listed side by side on the menu of this country inn with its rustic exterior and elegant interior. The kitchen staff copes well with the demands of such an immense repertoire, although some flaws mar more extravagant dishes. Blood pudding with sauerkraut and Westphalian pea soup with smoked sausage are on the menu, as well as turbot fillet and anglerfish with caviar. Some highlights were crepes with asparagus and morel ragout, and veal fillet with asparagus. The service was excellent, and there is a new wine list.

LANDHOTEL GASTHOF SCHÜTTE

8 km east in Oberkirchen
57392, Eddeweg 2
(0 29 72) 8 20, Fax 8 25 22

59, **S** 100/155, **D** 180/350, **APP** 310/390, **½P** +26, **P** +36 *Closed 26 November through 26 December*

The lobby and lounges in the original building have low ceilings and the atmosphere of a 200-year-old country inn. The rooms in the new addition are modern and attractive. Opulent breakfast buffet.

STÖRMANN

57392, Weststr. 58
(0 29 72) 40 55/6, Fax 29 45

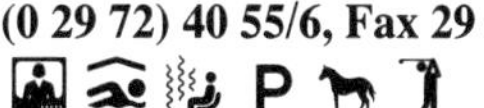

38, **S** 75/120, **D** 150/196, **APP** 196/240, **½P** +25, **P** +35
Closed 19—26 December, 19 March through 6 April

In one of the most beautiful little towns in the Sauerland, the Störmann has developed into a comfortable family hotel. An immense stone fireplace is the focal point around which dining rooms and salons with historic charm are grouped. The modernized rooms have shower baths, and some have balconies looking out over the Lennetal. Solarium, massage, recreation facilities. The restaurant offers good value.

WALDHAUS OHLENBACH 15/20

57392, Ortsteil Ohlenbach
(0 29 72) 8 40, Fax 84 48

Closed mid-November through 20 December. Tables d'hôte: 40/105, à la carte: 45/85

This hotel is tops in the Sauerland, and its cuisine the best. Sitting on the lovely terrace with a stupendous view over wooded mountains, we enjoyed excellent first courses and finished our meal with lovely sweet nothings in the old-fashioned and comfortable *"Schneiderstube"* inside. The kitchen prepares high-quality produce with creativity and expertise, and serves both light dishes and savory specialties. After three (!) appetizers, we had fish terrine, lobster with truffled vinaigrette, kohlrabi lasagna with salmon, anglerfish in warm vinaigrette with capers, venison with red currant sauce, and goat cheese.The service is friendly and competent, and the wine list shows the owner's interest in good vintages.

WALDHAUS OHLENBACH

57392, Ortsteil Ohlenbach
(0 29 72) 8 40 , Fax 84 48

50, **S** 100/130, **D** 200/260, **APP** 350, **½P** +30, **P** +50
Closed mid-November through 20 December

Once upon a time, a little house stood on the edge of a forest. Together with the pine trees that surrounded it, the house grew and grew to become a large and imposing hotel. The idyllic location and the stupendous view have remained the same. The lobby is a bit impersonal, but the rooms offer a lot of space and a lot of comfort. The suites in the annex can be recommended. Sports facilities, hiking paths, library. Ample breakfast buffet.

SCHÖNBERG Meckl.-Vorp.

Dassow 8 - Lübeck 12

HOTEL PAETAU

23923, Am Markt 14
(03 88 28) 2 13 10

20 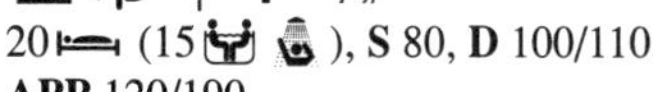 (15), **S** 80, **D** 100/110, **APP** 120/190
Closed Christmas Eve, No Credit Cards

The rooms of this hotel on the marketplace that opened in 1991 are pleasant and comfortably furnished. Breakfast: 10 DM. The ocean is only 10 minutes away.

SCHÖNECK Hessen

Hanau 6 - Frankfurt 10

STIER'S RESTAURANT 13/20

61137, Kilianstädten
Kirchplatz
(0 61 87) 9 15 34
A la carte: 31/58

Hiltrud and Gerald Stier's new restaurant is housed in a striking architectural ensemble in the middle of town. Urban flair and Old World atmosphere form the harmonious ambience of this old farm estate. The restaurant has the easy charm of a bistro or a café and reminds one of the Italian dolce vita. A great variety of simple, tasty, inexpensive dishes were on the menu, including homemade pasta with garlic and herb sauce, warm salmon tartare, salmon medallions with green sauce, and smoked sea trout with basil and cucumber sauce. Our beef fillet and rack of lamb were prepared just right, and the sauces were savory without being heavy. We don't understand, however, why such a good cook finds it necessary to supervise the charming and competent service staff, which does fine without him. We'd also like cuisine with a little more verve and ingenuity. The Stiers offer good wines at moderate prices, and some 20 to 30 wines by the glass. Very special and very good: the apple cider and sparkling wine made of apples.

SCHÖNWALDE Schl.-Holst.

Eutin 12 - Oldenburg 17

ALTES AMT 14/20

23744, Eutiner Str. 39
(0 45 28) 7 75 res.

P

Closed Tuesday, February. Tables d'hôte: 80, à la carte: 34/70, No Credit Cards

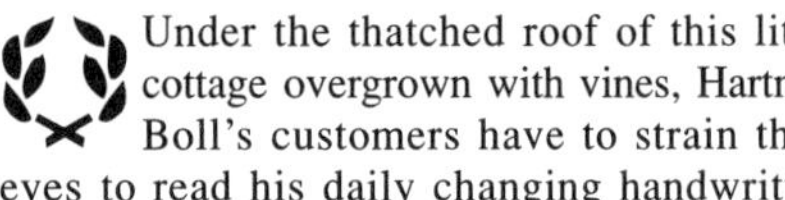

Under the thatched roof of this little cottage overgrown with vines, Hartmut Boll's customers have to strain their eyes to read his daily changing handwritten menu. But the consistently high-quality cuisine does more than make up for it. Our surprise prix-fixe included excellent saddle of lamb with seasonal salads, cucumber with fried shrimp, delicious saddle of wild boar with lovely bread dumplings, and tasty orange gratin with homemade vanilla ice cream and pink grapefruit. Boll has earned applause for his dishes, but also for his perseverance in cooking (almost solo) noon and night six days a week without lowering the high standard of his creative regional cuisine. The service in the two discreetly decorated dining rooms hung with precious engravings is circumspect. The informative wine list offers an impressive choice of German, French and Italian wines, as well as some English and Australian bottles.

SCHÖNWALDE Brandenburg

Bernau 12 - Berlin 21

DAMMSMÜHLE 12/20

16352, Schönwalde
(03 30 56) 8 25 02, Fax 8 15 05 res.

Tables d'hôte: 40/120, à la carte: 27/73

The ambience is lovely. Customers can either sit in the conservatory (if an art exhibition isn't taking place there) or in the equally pleasant dining room. We had an assortment of fine fish (salmon, pike-perch and scampi) and a succulent Canadian salmon gratin. Customers can also order Viennese schnitzel, fillet of beef, fried duck with homemade dumplings, venison medallions with cranberry sauce, or marinated legs of hare. The kitchen crew does its best to prepare all vegetables al dente.The meager wine list offered one highlight, a 1988 Gevrey-Chambertin, but the prompt service offered two highlights—namely, the two amiable waitresses.

DAMMSMÜHLE

16352, Schönwalde
(03 30 56) 8 25 02, Fax 8 15 05

P

15 (6), **S** 80, **D** 120,
APP 190/300

More and more visitors and tourists have spoiled the onetime peace and quiet of this hidden Baroque castle with a romantically landscaped park. Closed to the public for many years, the former residence of SS chief Heinrich Himmler, later a guesthouse for prominent East German officials, now offers six generously appointed suites and nine renovated rooms to the public. You can fish in the park's pond and play skittles in the former arcades.

SCHOPFHEIM Baden-Württ.

Lörrach 15 - Basel 25

ALTE STADTMÜHLE 17/20

79650, Entegaststr. 9
(0 76 22) 24 46, Fax 24 03 res.

Closed for lunch everyday except Sunday and holidays, closed Monday, Tuesday, Bad.-Württ. spring school holiday. Tables d'hôte: 60/120, No Credit Cards

Applause for Horst Kuhfuss, who adheres to vegetarian principles in his restaurant, and a standing ovation for his excellent cook, who practices what Kuhfuss preaches and manages to offer vegetarian haute cuisine. His sauces made only of vegetables were surprisingly good, and he created imaginative compositions that let us experience a variety of taste sensations, one after another. The repertoire included artichoke quiche, cream of squash soup with fresh ginger and poppyseed dumplings, basil tortellini with celery sauce, parsley root in nut crust with rosemary sauce, Savoy cabbage roulade with Chianti sauce, warm savarin with honey and vanilla ice cream, and plum compôte. A choice of prix-fixe meals is offered; there are no dishes à la carte. The four-course prix-fixe (for 60 DM) can be enlarged for an additional 15 DM per course. The multitalented Kuhfuss has opened a dressmaking studio in the rooms of the former bistro and tries to combat the recession with his own fashions for ladies and gentlemen.

MÜHLE ZU GERSBACH 12/20

79650, Gersbach
Zum Bühl 4
(0 76 20) 2 25, Fax 3 71

Closed Tuesday, closed for lunch Wednesday, closed 7 January through 17 February, 25 October through 3 November. Tables d'hôte: 28L, 94D, à la carte: 27/75

This genuine old mill house is located high on a hill 16 kilometers outside of Schopfheim. Visitors from the city like the country idyll and the smell of fresh hay. The small menu at noon, offering salad, delicate tomato soup, whitefish with potatoes, and vanilla ice cream with strawberries, makes way for the grandiose seasonal meals prepared by Martin Buchleither in the evening: fresh goat cheese fried in Parmesan and served with lamb's lettuce, pike-perch fillet with leek and cheese gratin and red wine butter, calf's liver with grapes, and wine sorbet with mascarpone cake. Customers who are nervous about the serpentine roads going down the mountain after such a good meal can stay overnight here.

SCHRANBERG BW

St. Georges 15 - Rottweil 25

HIRSCH 15/20

78713, Hauptstr. 11
(0 74 22) 2 05 30, Fax 2 54 46 res.

Closed Monday, closed for lunch Tuesday. Tables d'hôte: 35/79L, 79/95D, à la carte: 38/80.

Gebhard Kercher heads the kitchen of this particularly beautiful and elegant restaurant, and he achieves a synthesis of haute cuisine and Swabian cooking. Our first course was a dreamy terrine of guinea fowl, followed by stuffed artichoke, fish and vegetable salad; heavenly noodles with calf's-liver sauce; an excellent gratin of salmon, scampi and sole with spinach; and perfect Irish beef fillet with red-wine sauce. For dessert, we had a superb chocolate layer cake with apples and rum raisins stewed in white wine, served with vanilla cream.The wine list offers choice wines of the best quality from Germany, France and Italy, as well as many half bottles and an excellent choice of wines by the glass at moderate prices. Pleasant hotel rooms are available.

HIRSCH

78713, Hauptstr. 11
(0 74 22) 2 05 30, Fax 2 54 46

P

5 rooms, **S** 95/160, **D** 260

Centrally located in Schramberg, the Hirsch is a picturesque old building with all the atmosphere guests could wish for. The tastefully furnished rooms are spacious and have large bathrooms.

SCHRIESHEIM Bad.-Württ.

Heidelberg 8 - Mannheim 17

STRAHLENBERGER HOF 13/20

69198, Kirschstr. 2
(0 62 03) 6 30 76, Fax 6 85 90 res.

Closed for lunch, closed Sunday and holidays. Tables d'hôte: 98, à la carte: 58/92

High above the Schriesheim vineyards lies Strahlenburg castle. Down below, in the town, is the comfortable restaurant Strahlenberger Hof. Its ambience, wine list and service make this the best gourmet address in the Heidelberg region. The gigantic wine cellar can be visited, and the excellent wine list contains a good number of moderately priced wines. We didn't particularly fancy Schriesheim's Riesling, but the charming Christine Balais-Meyer very competently suggested alternatives. For our meal, she advised four different wines for a total of not more than 50 Deutsche marks! The restaurant's cuisine, however, has its problems. The bread crust of the foie-gras pâté was hardly edible, and the *tafelspitz* consommé was dark brown and salty. Venison and lamb were served with the same sauce and garnishes. But the foie gras and tender fillet of sea trout were of good quality, and the venison and lamb first-class. Nevertheless, this dull, tiresome meal called for two nightcaps rather than two toques.

SCHWABMÜNCHEN Bayern

Augsburg 26 - Memmingen 58

UNTERE MÜHLE 12/20

in Schwabmühlhausen
86853 Langerringen
(0 82 48) 12 10, Fax 72 79 res.

 P

Closed early to mid-August. Tables d'hôte: 38L, 80D, à la carte: 26/58

This idyllic mill house on the little river Singold is the object of many a family excursion on weekends. The staff speaks only the Swabian dialect, and the menu lists typically Swabian dishes. In case of (linguistic) doubt, order the *Sinklforelle* (brook trout), served either cooked or fried. Apart from that, we enjoyed the fried shrimps, an excellent pancake stuffed with vegetables, the crispy duck's breast with lemon sauce, pike-perch fillet, the saddles of venison and rabbit, and the opulent salad buffet. The wine list is typically Swabian as well: adequate quality at low prices.

Remember to reserve your table or your room in advance, and please let the restaurant or hotel know if you cannot honor your reservation.

SCHWÄBISCH HALL BW

Bad Mergentheim 54 - Stuttgart 68

EISENBAHN IN HOTEL WOLF 14/20

74523, Stadtteil Hessental
Karl-Kurz-Str. 2
(07 91) 21 12, Fax 4 22 36 res.

P

Closed Monday, 25 February through 5 March. Tables d'hôte: 50/88, à la carte: 43/58

In an elegant and inviting ambience, friendly waitresses serve light gourmet food and regional cuisine. We had excellent marinated salmon with lobster, salad and quail's egg with caviar, perfectly done foie gras in strudel with vegetable roots, succulent and tender pigeon, and delicious fruit ragout with white chocolate mousse. The wines by the glass recommended with the prix-fixe were excellent, and other interesting vintages were affordable.

SCHWAIGERN Bad.-Württ.

Heilbronn 10 - Eppingen 11

ZUM ALTEN RENTAMT 15/20

74193, Schloßstr. 6
(0 71 38) 52 58, Fax 15 23 res.

 P

Tables d'hôte: 50, à la carte: 33/77, No Credit Cards

This former accounting office of the Neipperg counts, with its beautiful old frame building and romantic garden, is a nostalgic dream come true. Hostess Heidi Stoltenberg-Schmeling makes her guests comfortable, and she serves and advises with charm and competence. Monsieur Bertrand presents his creations with solid craftsmanship and verve. We had baked mussels with croutons; pike-perch medallions with sliced potatoes and parsley sauce; a perfect entrecôte with red-wine butter, accompanied by delicate potatoes seasoned with caraway seeds; venison schnitzel with Riesling, truffles and spaetzle; and, finally, an ice-cream soufflé of oranges and Grand Marnier.High-quality and low-priced wines from the Neipperg estate are offered, and a good choice of wines by the glass is available. The exquisite hotel rooms are furnished with antiques.

BAD SCHWALBACH Hessen

Wiesbaden 16 - Idstein 22

RESTAURANT IM PARK IN HOTEL EDEN PARC 14/20

65307, Goetheplatz 1
(0 61 24) 51 60, Fax 51 63 31 res.

Tables d'hôte: 35, à la carte: 24/71

This extravagantly renovated villa in the spa park is a popular hotel for business meetings. Its restaurant is elegant and offers good cuisine at surprisingly low prices. Our fanned avocado with shrimps and cocktail sauce consisted of high-quality products and was tastefully prepared. The quality of steaks and fillets of beef, pork and lamb was good. Poularde and Barbary duck for two had to be ordered one day ahead. We liked the anglerfish medallions with black olive sauce in a nest of noodles and vegetable ragout. The service is perfect even when the house is full. The comprehensive wine list, although it's been somewhat reduced, is still impressive, and the prices are unusually low.

EDEN PARC

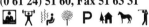

65307, Goetheplatz 1
(0 61 24) 51 60, Fax 51 63 31

82, **S** 158/198, **D** 198/398,
APP 350/638, **1/2P** +35, **P** +70

This hotel on the edge of the spa park has been lavishly renovated and now has marble bathrooms, a wine-tasting salon, nobly furnished suites and conference facilities with modern technology. Café, cocktail bar. Breakfast: 20 DM.

SCHWANGAU Bayern

Füssen 3 - Schongau 36

KÖNIG LUDWIG

87645, Kreuzweg 11
(0 83 62) 88 90, Fax 8 18 67

138, **S** 120/170, **D** 180/230,
APP 220/270, **1/2P** +10,
Closed 10—24 December, No Credit Cards

Located within easy reach of the famous royal Bavarian castles, this hotel offers a high degree of comfort in its rooms and generously proportioned suites. Excellent restaurant.

MEIER 13/20

3 km south in Hohenschwangau
87645, Schwangauer Str. 37
(0 83 62) 8 11 52 res.

Closed Tuesday, 7 January through 5 February. Tables d'hôte: 35L, 85D, à la carte: 20/53

Look up toward the mountains in Hohenschwangau, and you'll see the imposing castles. Look down into the valley, and you'll see the modest and inconspicuous Meier. Customers feel at home in the restaurant's two bright, pretty dining rooms or on the lovely garden terrace. Wolfgang Meier still serves low-priced standard dishes for tourists visiting the castles, but his menu also draws gourmets to Schwangau. They order carefully prepared salmon, anglerfish or pike-perch; high-quality entrecôte with ox marrow; tender lamb noisettes with red lentils; and an impeccably prepared breast of Barbary duck with orange and pepper sauce. Meier has an especially light touch with desserts, which include his delightful yogurt mousse with fresh fruit. The wine list limits itself to about two dozen regional wines. Whether served in bottles or by the glass, however, they are surprisingly low-priced.

BAD SCHWARTAU SH

Lübeck 9 - Eutin 25

OLIVE 12/20

23611, Am Kurpark 3
(04 51) 28 36 82, Fax 63 25

Closed for lunch Monday, closed 2 weeks in June. Tables d'hôte: 49/69D, à la carte: 31/60, No Credit Cards

It isn't necessarily a joke if somebody invites you to dine at the spa baths. In Bad Schwartau, it may mean good food. The explanation is simple: the spa complex, with its indoor swimming pool, also houses a restaurant that offers seasonal cooking. Most dishes are flawlessly prepared, like guinea fowl pâté with fried duck's liver, veal *tafelspitz* with chanterelles and *rösti*, and anglerfish medallions with Noilly Prat sauce. Portions are generous and prices are low. The service is quick and attentive, but the wine list must be improved to be adequate.

SCHWERIN Meckl.-Vorp.

Wismar 31 - Lübeck 60

BRASSERIE FRANCE IN EUROPA HOTEL

19061, Werkstr. 2
(03 85) 6 34 00, Fax 6 34 06 66
A la carte: 30/50

The attractive ambience of this restaurant, with comfortable cane chairs, large first-course buffet and well-spaced tables, suggests fine eating and drinking. But a French name alone doesn't guarantee good cuisine. The large menu and six *plats du jour* indicate prepared food and only seldom fresh products and dishes made on the spot. Our flavorful sugar-pea soup was acceptable but garnished with overdone salmon. Through a window that afforded a view of the kitchen, we saw our sole roulade with spinach being heated up in the microwave! The wine list, including only a few German and many French wines of unremarkable wineries and five (doubtful) wines by the glass, needs improvement. Inconspicuous service.

EUROPA HOTEL

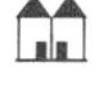

19061, Werkstr. 2
(03 85) 6 34 00, Fax 6 34 06 66
P
80, **S** 185/282, **D** 225/342, **APP** 282/342

The top two storys of a high-rise office building in an industrial area have been turned into a hotel. The spacious, extravagantly decorated lobby and rooms that are perfectly equipped for traveling businesspeople make customers soon forget the inhospitable surroundings. The Brasserie France restaurant has a wintergarten. Opulent breakfast buffet. Children up to 12 are free in their parents' room.

JAGDHAUS 13/20

19055, Güstrower Str. 109
(03 85) 86 32 51 res.
P
A la carte: 20/53

The name of the restaurant implies what the menu offers: Jagd means hunt, and customers have a large variety of game to choose from. Generous helpings of well-prepared, tasty food are served in rustic, comfortable surroundings. Commendable (and even creative) were warm chicken hearts with fresh salad and red wine vinaigrette, and wild boar medallions ingeniously garnished with smoked eel. Fresh fish from the region was also offered. The service is quick and attentive, but the wine list is barely adequate.

NIEDERLÄNDISCHER HOF 12/20

19061, Karl-Marx-Str. 12
(03 85) 55 52 11, Fax 5 50 74 82
P
A la carte: 17/43

The stylish dining room helps us forget the restaurant's dreary entrance. The cuisine no longer tries to meet gourmet standards. We recommend the daily menu, which offers hearty Mecklenburg specialities. These include such delicious dishes as cream of potato soup with marjoram and bacon, as well as a savory cream of red lentil soup with shrimp and chervil. The kitchen works as flawlessly as the well-trained service staff.The wine list disappoints in terms of both quantity and quality.

PRIMAVERA IN HOTEL PLAZA SCHWERIN 14/20

19063, Am Grünen Tal
(03 85) 3 48 20, Fax 34 10 53 res.
P
A la carte: 33/53

The extravagant decor creates an exuberant ambience, which the Italian cuisine here tried to match. Apart from a standard menu, the kitchen offered seasonal dishes. Customers should start with excellent antipasti from the buffet. We then enjoyed tender veal fillet with mozzarella and tomato noodles, and pike-perch with Chablis sauce and green asparagus. Most main courses are available as half-portions, a nice gesture that was appreciated by many customers. The wine list has greatly improved, and the service seemed motivated.

PLAZA SCHWERIN

19063, Am Grünen Tal
(03 85) 3 48 20, Fax 34 10 53

80 ⊨, **S** 240/270, **D** 280/310,
APP 450, **½P** +30, **P** +60

The nondescript exterior of this hotel, opened in 1992 and not far from the center of town, belies the luxurious ambience within. The spacious rooms will meet the expectations of the most fastidious guests. Fitness center, solarium, and conference rooms. Piano lounge. Children under 12 are free if staying in their parents' room. Breakfast: 18 DM.

SEEHOTEL FRANKENHORST

19055 Wickendorf
Frankenhorst 5
(03 85) 55 50 71, Fax 55 50 73

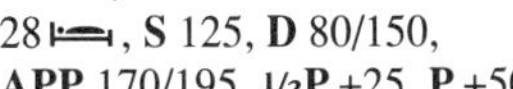

28 ⊨, **S** 125, **D** 80/150,
APP 170/195, **½P** +25, **P** +50

A favorite with former East German officials, this hotel stands on the shore of the idyllic Ziegelaussensee. Park, ferry to the Schwerin castle, well-equipped rooms, restaurant and café with terrace make this establishment attractive. Bike and boat rental.

WEINHAUS UHLE 12/20

19055, Schusterstr. 13-15
(03 85) 86 44 55, Fax 5 57 40 93 res.

Closed for dinner Sunday, à la carte: 30/59

Along with a large choice of wines, this *weinhaus* offers regional specialities. Dependable product quality and good cooking makes eating in these typical dining rooms with their domed wooden ceilings a pleasure. Highlights of our meal were pheasant breast with salads and excellently fried perch from Lake Schwerin. The service was impressive.

ZUM GOLDENEN REITER 13/20

19055, Puschkinstr. 44
(03 85) 81 25 54, Fax 81 25 54

Tables d'hôte: 26/32, à la carte: 21/50

With a lot of routine and sometimes a little creativity, the motivated kitchen crew cooks its way through a large international menu. Regular customers at the elegantly comfortable restaurant on the marketplace order the daily specials, like delicious cucumber soup with veal or duck terrine with red currants. We found our duck's breast stuffed with baked fruit especially commendable, and bread pudding and warm fruit for dessert concluded the meal in a typical Mecklenburg way. The service was obliging and professionally pleasant. Besides German and French wines, the cellar of the house also offered some interesting exotics.

SELTERS Hessen

Limburg 16 - Wiesbaden 48

STAHLMÜHLE 14/20

65618, Ortsteil Münster
Bezirksstr. 34
(0 64 83) 56 90, Fax 56 90 res.

Closed for lunch Wednesday and Thursday from October through April. Tables d'hôte: 56/135, à la carte: 47/82

More and more gourmets are learning to appreciate Roland Schauenburg's creative cuisine, served in a beautifully renovated old mill at the foot of the Taunus mountains. Strange and stunning combinations of different flavors are a welcome change from the usual gourmet-menu boredom. Some examples: a goose neck filled with Savoy cabbage and foie gras, oyster gratin with spinach, quail and prawns in lychee sauce with okra and ginger, and an enchanting mint mousse with candied kumquats, chocolate sauce and orange purée. Chef Schauenburg discusses each course with his customers, explains products and preparation and is quite willing to comply with other wishes. With an inviting daily prix fixe (four courses for 65 DM) and half portions, non-gourmets find the way to good cooking. The service is friendly, and the improved wine list deserves praise.

SENDEN Nordrhein - Westf.

Lüdinghausen 10 - Münster 18

AVERBECKS GIEBELHOF 16/20

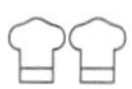

4 km southeast in Ottmarsbocholt
48308, Kirchstr. 12
(0 25 98) 3 93, Fax 7 79 res.

Closed for lunch except on weekends, closed Tuesday. Tables d'hôte: 95/185, à la carte: 80/125, No Credit Cards

To enjoy a gourmet meal here, customers have to come equipped with a good amount of money and lots of time. In Ottmarsbocholt they find first-class cooking and an impressive choice of wines, an elegant, countryfied ambience and charming service. Though only three tables were occupied on our last visit, we had to wait a long time for the menu and an even longer time (one hour!) for the first course. It was worth it: we had first-class turbot with lemongrass and a lovely salad, perfectly prepared sweetbreads in light puff pastry with savory morel sauce, and excellent sole fillet with slightly underdone spinach beets. The green string beans with a lovely lamb saddle were almost raw. Our desserts, wonderful warm chocolate ravioli and exquisite woodruff jelly with strawberries, were superb. The impressive wine list affords a lot of enjoyment, if customers can afford the prices.

SEUSSLITZ Sachsen

Riesa 10 - Meissen 11

LEHMANN'S WEINSTUBEN 11/20

01612, Elbstr. 26
(03 52 67) 2 36 res.

 P

Closed Thursday, January, à la carte: 12/32, No Credit Cards

This region north of Meissen is known as the Saxon Riviera thanks to its mild climate, and some of of the best wines grown in Eastern Germany come from here. In Lehmann's comfortable *weinstuben,* where wine has been served since the 16th century, the owner offers a grand variety of his own wines by the bottle and the glass. On warm days, customers sit on the terrace in front of the house under ancient chestnuts and enjoy the view of the Elbe river. The dining rooms are rustically furnished, but the kitchen has been modernized. Customers appreciate good, hearty dishes with lots of meat: pork or beef fillets were prepared just right, and both side dishes and sauces demonstrated quality and care in the kitchen. A small staircase leads upstairs to five comfortable rooms tastefully equipped with country-style furniture and modern comforts.

SIEBELDINGEN Rheinland-Pfalz

Landau 5 - Pirmasens 42

SONNENHOF 13/20

76833, Mühlweg 2
(0 63 45) 33 11, Fax 53 16

 P

Closed Thursday, 3 weeks in January. Tables d'hôte: 42/68, à la carte: 32/61

We enjoy the Sonnenhof best in summer, when we can sit under shady chestnut trees on the beautiful terrace and enjoy Volker Krug's light, fresh cuisine. The menu offers everything from little snacks and regional specialities to the delicate creations of sophisticated cuisine. We found no fault with the baked oysters, whipped sugar-pea soup, fish soup, lamb ribs, venison saddle, and fish platter with lobster, pike-perch and salmon. But we missed that decisive touch of originality that transforms good cooking into excellent cuisine. The service has always been very pleasant here, and the staff is learning more about wine. The wine cellar is stocked with the best wines from southern Pfalz. Quiet and tastefully furnished hotel rooms are available in the adjacent building.

SIEGBURG NRW

Bonn 9 - Köln 23

REMISE WEINBISTRO

53721, Haufeld 2a
(0 22 41) 6 29 96 res.

P

Tables d'hôte: 68, à la carte: 36/67

This refreshing wine bistro, decorated by the artist Johannes Helle, is characterized by its connection to Germany's best wine merchants, Fegers-Unterberg-Berts in Cologne and Siegburg. The wine list offers an excellent choice at relatively attractive prices, and the wines by the glass are of respectable quality. From time to time and without warning, Gerd Hansmann takes a few days off and closes his bistro. When it's open, he likes to serve pike-perch with a sauce of Riesling and herbs, brook trout with spinach and a stew of roasted duck's legs. When the weather permits, customers can sit outside as well.

SIEGEN Nordrhein-Westf.

Olpe 12 - Gießen 73

BERGHOTEL JOHANNESHÖHE

57072, Wallhausentr. 1
(02 71) 31 00 08, Fax 31 50 39

 P

Closed for lunch Saturday, closed for dinner Sunday. Tables d'hôte: 30/35, à la carte: 28/75

We had bad luck last time we climbed this mountain. Apparently the boss was out. We ordered the main courses advertised as daily specials and were bitterly disappointed by stringy anglerfish and oversalted broccoli (the menu announced spinach) and with dry saddle of rabbit and potatoes that tasted packaged, frozen and deep-fried. Even the wonderful view of Siegen from up here couldn't console us. Neither could the wine list and a formal (and somewhat immovable) service.

BERGHOTEL JOHANNESHÖHE

57072, Wallhausentr. 1
(02 71) 31 00 08, Fax 31 50 39

P

26 rooms, **S** 89/125, **D** 130/175, **APP** 125/210, **1/2P** +25, **P** +50

The modernized rooms facing south have balconies, and all offer the usual comforts, plus anti-allergenic furniture. Restaurant equipped with Empire furniture and rustic bar in front of a fireplace.

EFEU 12/20

57054, Marienborner Str. 7
(02 71) 5 64 33

P

Closed Monday, à la carte: 29/62

The service staff of this Italian restaurant with a German name decorated in the style of a French bistro is supervised by a charming Asian lady. The restaurant stands out conspicuously in the conservative gastronomic scene in Siegen. If you want to enjoy good pasta, nice scampi and respectable veal in a relaxed and relaxing atmosphere, you've come to the right place. We always order the special pasta dishes announced on the blackboard: the tortellini filled with ricotta and served with tomato sauce and pesto were excellent. Friendly service and a small wine list with a few very good Italian wines.

HAUS RÖDGEN 15/20

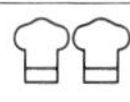

in 57234, Wilnsdorf-Obersdorf
Rödgener Str. 100 (B 54)
(02 71) 3 91 73 res.

P

Closed Monday and Tuesday, Tables d'hôte: 39/118, à la carte: 43/92

This restaurant with its bistro and hotel is the top address in the Siegerland. If this ambitious (and terrifically expensive) project is carried through, it will soon create a sensation and shake up the German competition. Chef Alexander Bulla has brought a first-class kitchen staff with him, and the phenomenal wine cellar has been stocked with choice yet moderately priced wines. Krug's Grande Cuvée, for example, costs just 185 Deutsche marks. The white wines are low-priced, but precious red vintages dominate. The entire operation is financed by a small group of industrialists.The menu isn't as extravagant as the outlay. Alexander Bulla keeps his feet firmly on the ground. He offers well-known products, but he prepares them much better than did his predecessors in Haus Rödgen. Prices are lower, too. We liked his light, delicate and finely balanced dishes. Bulla has high hopes, and so do we. He deserved two toques for a promising start. The service is impeccable.

PARK-HOTEL

57072, Koblenzer Str. 135
(02 71) 3 38 10, Fax 3 38 14 50

P

88 rooms, **S** 103/198, **D** 150/260, **APP** 184/368, **1/2P** +23, **P** +40

Just a 10-minute walk from the middle of town, this hotel has direct access to the convention center in Siegen. The rooms are functionally equipped and pleasant. Steam bath, massage. Nice bar, beautiful restaurant.

TEZETT 13/20

57078, Stadtteil Geisweid
Birlenbacher Str. 18
(02 71) 87 04 66

Closed Sunday, à la carte: 36/74

This restaurant is part of the new technology complex in Geisweid and is not easy to find: turn left at McDonald's in the direction of Freudenberg. The ambience is modern and tasteful, perhaps a bit cool and functional, but we liked it. It is refreshing to find in the strictly conservative gastronomic scene in Siegen a talented duo cooking light, modern food that fits the ambience of the restaurant: fish fried in olive oil, al dente tagliatelle and vegetables, and lighter sauces than the competition makes. The service is obliging, but the wine list is disappointing. Pretty terrace.

SIESEBY Schleswig-Holstein

Kappeln 14 - Eckernförde 24

SCHLIE-KROG 12/20

24351, Dorfstraße
(0 43 52) 25 31 , Fax 15 80 res.

Closed Monday, closed for lunch Tuesday, closed 1 February to early-March, 15—30 November, Monday though Thursday in January. Tables d'hôte: 35/45L, 75/95D, à la carte: 38/64, No Credit Cards

This old, comfortable *gasthof* has a thatched roof and is just a stone's throw away from the picturesque river Schlei. It is popular with gourmets and holidaymakers alike. The small menu lists what the region has to offer. Like many other customers, we preferred marvelous fish dishes, like pike terrine with crème fraîche and caviar, precisely prepared pike-perch with lemon butter, and fresh, perfectly fried turbot with truffled sauce. Ox fillet with herbs, and venison goulash with mushrooms and red cabbage were further proofs of Peter Möller's talents. The service is circumspect and takes pains to make even non-gourmets feel at home. The small wine list includes Californian wines by the glass served out of a magnum bottle.

SIMMERN Rheinl.-Pf.

Bingen 33 - Boppard 35

SCHWARZER ADLER 13/20

55469, Koblenzer Str. 3
(0 67 61) 1 36 11, Fax 96 01 08 res.

Closed Tuesday, 2 weeks each in January and July/August. Tables d'hôte: 38L, 65/95D, à la carte: 36/68

This black eagle (Schwarzer Adler) on the heights of the Hunsrück region is flying high. Fresh regional products dominate the menu. The talented cook Claudio Filippone has found his own style. After a rather inauspicious beginning, he's earned his first toque and can look forward to a higher rating next time. We enjoyed a light and tasty red lentil soup, followed by a still better fish stew with delicious shellfish, worth a rating of 15/20! Our mussels were good, and the quail and pigeon galantine tasty. Our rack of lamb was just a touch underdone, but the sauce served with it was delicious and flavorful. Hunsrück chicken was crispy and succulent, accompanied by perfectly cooked vegetables. Customers with a sweet tooth might not rave about it, but we found the tart and refreshing terrine of citrus fruit with its tangy sauce and fine orange sorbet superb. The service is unobtrusive but attentive. The wine list includes many wines from the Moselle, some of which are real finds.

SINGEN Baden-Württ.

Schaffhausen 20 - Donaueschingen 20

FLOHR'S RESTAURANT 16/20

in 78224, Überlingen am Ried
Brunnenstr. 11
(0 77 31) 2 84 88 res.

Closed for lunch Saturday, closed Monday. Tables d'hôte: 55/65L, 85/105D, à la carte: 47/91

This pretty country inn has grown still more beautiful and now offers hotel rooms for tired customers. Georg Flohr's vivacity in the kitchen is unabated. With such a good team, he can indulge his fancies in imaginative appetizers like pigeon with sugar peas served as pot-au-feu, for example. Flohr combines regional products and recipes with a distinctive Italian flair, with herbs, oil and vinegar creating stronger accents than butter, cream and salt. He's not afraid to be daring (how about artichoke cream with headcheese and oysters?) and dishes that sound simple are seldom plain. Red mullet, for instance, is fried simply in olive oil - and gets its kick out from two different kinds of vinegar. We loved delicate sweetbread ravioli with morels, and green asparagus with sweet arugula sauce, and our venison noisettes with a lovely sweet sauce highlighted with fig preserves and chestnut tortelloni. We stopped short of ordering a second helping of our exquisite champagne soup with fruit, strawberry dumplings and grape brandy parfait, because we still had to try the petits fours.There are enough bottles from three countries to drink a toast to the success of Flohr's Restaurant.

SALZBURGER STUB'N 14/20

4 km south
in 78239 Worblingen
Hardstr. 29
(0 77 31) 2 73 49, Fax 2 73 49 res.

P

Closed Thursday. Tables d'hôte: 38L, 45D, 130, à la carte: 30/56

A touch of Austria in Singen. A very light touch, since Austrian specialities are served sparingly or must be ordered ahead. Obviously and genuinely Austrian are the charming owners, who have decorated their elegant restaurant with colors and knickknacks from their native country. Chef Manfred Sobota isn't plagued by ingenuity, but his dishes are on the whole excellent and meet gourmet demands. His rabbit terrine with marinated green asparagus, anglerfish medallions coated with *rösti* and served with a delicate herb cream, and pancakes filled with Grand-Marnier parfait with puréed strawberries were delicious. Sobota also offers three prix-fixe meals that include the appropriate wines with each course. The service is charming and competent,and customers appreciate the good value for little money here. The wine list could use some more French wines but includes bottles from Baden to the United States and a large choice of wines by the glass.

SINN Hessen

Herborn 2 - Siegen 38 - Gießen 39

GASTSTÄTTE ARABIN 13/20

35764, Ortsteil Fleischbach
Edinger Str. 2
(0 27 72) 4 15 75 res.

P

Tables d'hôte: 60/80

This private restaurant in a 300-year-old historic building opens its door only if customers reserve far ahead, and offers neither menu nor wine list. In fact, it runs outside of competition, but because we enjoy our meals in these comfortable, cozy rooms so much, we don't want to keep it a secret. Ernst Arabin, a passionate 70-year-old amateur cook, prepares uncomplicated, honest, deceptively simple dishes with a lot of charm and loving care. His well-seasoned old-fashioned dishes are his best: fillet of beef, veal haunch and roast beef are all top-quality. Anneliese Arabin deserves the toque as much as he does for her charming and friendly service. The prices are very moderate here.

SINZIG Rheinl.-Pfalz

Bonn 26 - Koblenz 34

ALT-SINZIG (VIEUX SINZIG) 14/20

53489, Kölner Str. 5
(0 26 42) 4 27 57, Fax 4 30 51 res.

P

Closed for lunch Saturday and Tuesday, closed Monday, 1—8 January, 3—24 July. Tables d'hôte: 48/78, à la carte: 35/67

Ambition and creativity have made this restaurant popular, especially on weekends. The menu included the dishes Grandma used to make, prepared more delicately and with a lot more herbs: oxtail in aspic with green asparagus and vinaigrette, sorrel soup, goose consommé and nettles, and lamb with goat cheese steamed in turnip leaves. Not everything was perfect, however—a beef "Wellington" turned out to be dry roast of beef in a sticky crust. The service staff, in traditional French uniforms, was cheerful and pleasant. The wine list emphasized French wines, too, plus regional Ahr wines and cider.

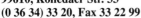

SÖMMERDA Thüringen

Weimar 33 - Sondershausen 40

ERFURTER TOR 14/20

99610, Kölledaer Str. 33
(0 36 34) 33 20, Fax 33 22 99

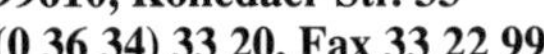

Closed for lunch every day except Sunday, closed 31 July through 20 August. Tables d'hôte: 20/25, à la carte: 19/47

Directly beside the old town wall, this pretty little restaurant with a beautiful terrace has established itself in the new hotel lobby. The owners take pains to make their customers feel at home and know enough about the international wines they offer. We had excellent catfish fillet with dill butter and lukewarm asparagus salad, fabulous little veal roulades with excellent basil cream sauce, tasty pork with gorgonzola, and an outstanding fruit salad gratin capped with meringue.

ERFURTER TOR

99610, Kölledaer Str. 33
(0 36 34) 33 20, Fax 33 22 99

41 rooms, **S** 60/110, **D** 90/135,
APP 135/165, **½P** +18, **P** +30

In the middle of the city next to the old town wall, this hotel offers individually furnished, comfortable, quiet rooms. Grand choice of breakfast foods.

MARKTSCHÄNKE 13/20

99610, Marktstr. 11
(0 36 34) 2 11 43,

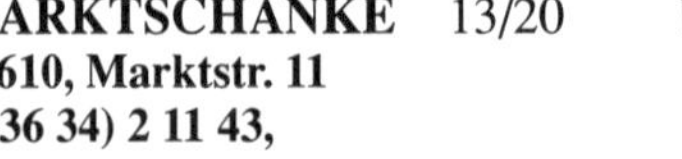

Closed for lunch Saturday, closed for dinner Sunday, à la carte: 19/44

Friendly, competent waitresses served carpaccio of cooked, smoked pork with delicately marinated raw vegetables; flavorful asparagus soup; plaice roulade filled with herbs and spinach, served with savory sage sauce; and fried veal slices with asparagus and fresh hollandaise sauce. The salad garnish on our plates was opulent — and superfluous. For dessert, we had delicious mascarpone with kiwis and strawberries.The wine list has become more international, and the prices are carefully calculated so that no bottle costs more than 40 Deutsche marks.

SOEST Nordrh.-Westf.

Paderborn 50 - Dortmund 52

BIERMANN'S RESTAURANT 15/20

59494, Thomästr. 47
(0 29 21) 1 33 10, Fax 1 32 34 res.

Closed Monday. Tables d'hôte: 55L, 79/115D, à la carte: 48/87

The shrill ambience of Biermann's restaurant seemed a little out of place in this sleepy little hamlet when it opened in the 1980s. Today, the cool, functional bistro is "in." The traditional salmon-pink decor of the gourmet restaurant with an abundance of mirrors pleases nostalgic bistro fans. Biermann's cuisine is up to date, however. He serves light cuisine with an Asian touch and vegetarian accents. We like to remember the tasty carpaccio with trout caviar, tuna sashimi, fabulous duck liver pâté with apple and Calvados jelly, white asparagus with salmon strips, a ragout of pike-perch and asparagus with morels served in a rice leaf, grilled scampi with garlic and noodles, beef fillet with truffled potatoes, and a deliciously simple rhubarb and strawberry soup with vanilla ice cream and candied puff pastry. Our nonchalant waiter had to be pressed into service. The international and moderately priced wine list was much more enjoyable.

SONNENBÜHL Bad.-Württ.

Reutlingen 23 - Hechingen 27

HIRSCH 13/20

72820, Ortsteil Erpfingen
Im Dorf 12
(0 71 28) 9 29 10, Fax 31 21

Closed Tuesday, closed for lunch Wednesday, 2 weeks in November, 1 week in July. Tables d'hôte: 52/110, à la carte: 27/80, No Credit Cards

The new wing of the Sonnenbühl houses a pretty banquet room with a fireplace, and

there's a new terrace and a shady summer garden outside. The old restaurant, however, has kept its Swabian flair, and Gerd Windhösel has maintained his high level of cooking. We had a lovely aspic of *tafelspitz* with crispy diced potatoes, a nicely marinated salad with scallops, asparagus soup with ravioli (and an irritating twig of marjoram), perfectly fried anglerfish with tomato and zucchini, a lovely-looking (but insipid) saddle of venison, and strawberries with rhubarb under a gratin of rice with honey. The wine list is good enough for big-city gourmet restaurants. The prices for half bottles and wines by the glass are astoundingly moderate. The service staff has its principles, but still remains prompt and pleasant.

SONTHOFEN Bayern

Oberstdorf 14 - Kempten 30

ALTE POST 13/20

87527, Promenadestr. 5
(0 83 21) 25 08,

Closed Friday, closed for lunch Saturday, closed 1 week in mid-January, 1 week in mid-June, à la carte: 17/55

A middle-class restaurant with better-than-middle-class fare, the Alte Post maintains its reputation. The salads were nice and fresh, and the tasty regional tidbits—like *Krautkrapfen* from the Allgäu and *Herrengröstel* from the Tyrolean Alps—are worth a try. We also liked the excellent salmon ravioli with spinach and the terrific trout, fresh from a mountain brook. The prices are reasonable, as is the choice of wines.

SPORT-UND KURHOTEL SONNENALP

3 km south in Tiefenberg
87527 Ofterschwang
(0 83 21) 27 20, Fax 27 22 42

220, **S** 364/390, **D** 522/685,
APP 704/1536 (includes 1/2P)
No Credit Cards

The hotel's superb amenities include a panoramic sun terrace and indoor and outdoor heated pools reserved only for resident guests. The spacious, comfortable rooms are just as exclusive. When other hotels in this region close down in November, this hotel starts a fine cultural program with concerts and art courses.

SPANGENBERG Hessen

Melsungen 13 - Bebra 25

BURGRESTAURANT IN SCHLOSS SPANGENBERG 13/20

34286, Im Schloß 1
(0 56 63) 8 66, Fax 75 67 res.

Closed for dinner Sunday, closed 1—10 January. Tables d'hôte: 49/56L, 86D, à la carte: 44/80

Now that the Wichmann family has invested time and money in rebuilding their restaurant, the food that comes out of the castle kitchen can be served in an appropriate setting. The decor is more elegant than it used to be, and the young and motivated service staff show how well-trained they are. The cook (mis)uses the menu to air his superior knowledge of gourmet cuisine, so some dishes sound more extravagant and eccentric than they really are. On the other hand, a few creations justify the bombastic descriptions on the menu. The ham of venison with sweetbreads on a salad of radishes with green-pepper vinaigrette, for instance, was a perfectly harmonious, if unusual, combination. We suspect, though, that the Burgrestaurant's customers prefer venison ragout and steak to pike with coriander or saddle of venison in strudel. We'll let the Burgrestaurant keep its rating and hope for improvement.

SCHLOSS SPANGENBERG

34286, Im Schloß 1
(0 56 63) 8 66, Fax 75 67

23, **S** 90/130, **D** 150/240,
APP 290, **1/2P** +42, **P** +68
Closed 1—10 January, 2 weeks during the Hessen summer school holiday.

From the outside, this 750-year-old castle looks romantically medieval. Inside, the hotel isn't the most modern, but it is agreeable and comfortable.

SPEYER Rheinl.-Pfalz

Mannheim 22 - Karlsruhe 57

BACKMULDE 12/20

67346, Karmeliterstr. 11-13
(0 62 32) 7 15 77, Fax 7 09 03 res.
Closed Sunday, Monday, mid-August to early-September. Tables d'hôte: 48/110L, 95/130D, à la carte: 40/80. Tables d'hôte with wine: 100/190

Ever since Gunther Schmidt opened his restaurant in a former bakery 10 years ago, our rating has been as varied as his performance in the kitchen. Sometimes we've eaten excellent meals here, and other times we've cursed the cook. Last time, we had light salmon slice with crème fraîche and cucumber, finely sliced beef (not fillet!) carpaccio in elderberry vinaigrette, perfectly fried duck's breast with excellent sage and honey sauce, lovely sweetbreads with green and white asparagus tips, heavy navarin lamb with insipid eggplant, and tripe with vinaigrette that just tasted sour. Schmidt's wine list deserved the award of excellence it got from the magazine *Wine Spectator* and is worth an extra trip. All wines "to go" at half price.

SPROCKHÖVEL NRW

Bochum 10 - Düsseldorf 45

RÔTISSERIE LANDHAUS LEICK 15/20

45549, Niedersprockhövel
Bochumer Str. 67
(0 23 24) 76 15, Fax 7 71 20 res.

Closed for lunch Saturday and Tuesday, closed Monday, 1—20 January. Tables d'hôte: 65L, 98/130D, à la carte: 58/100

With a talented new cook and more modern cuisine, this idyllic country restaurant is showing ambition and creativity. The menu offers only two prix-fixe menus, one regional and the other haute cuisine with an Asian touch. The courses, however, can be changed according to individual tastes. The regional prix-fixe is dedicated to the German writer of a well-known 19th-century cookbook and includes some of her recipes: warm salad of black salsify with sauerbraten and plum sauce, soup made of apples and red beets and garnished with baked eel, ox fillet topped with red onion marmalade and accompanied by green beans and risotto, and potato ravioli filled with goat cheese and served with marinated pear slices and quince mousse. The Eurasian alternative included asparagus and lemongrass savarin with fried salmon tartare, sole baked in almonds, and prawns with coconut milk mousse, mango chutney and jasmine rice. We liked both menus and promise the new chef a rating of 16/20 if he keeps up his high product quality, artistic presentation and expert cooking. The service has lost most of its stiff formality and takes pains to please customers in a more relaxed and natural manner. We liked the lowered prices and the 14 wines by the glass on the noble wine list.

LANDHAUS LEICK

45549, Niedersprockhövel
Bochumer Str. 67
(0 23 24) 76 15 , Fax 7 71 20

13, **S** 140/170, **D** 200/240, **APP** 320
Closed 1—20 January

Located in a quiet green park with spacious, individually furnished rooms, this country inn seems the perfect hotel-villa. The showers are small (except in number 1). Breakfast: 18 DM.

STARNBERG Bayern

München 25 - Garmisch-Partenk. 72

ILLGUTHS GASTHAUS STARNBERGER ALM 13/20

82319, Schloßbergstr. 24
(0 81 51) 1 55 77 res.

Closed for lunch, closed Sunday, Monday, 2 weeks after Christmas, first 3 weeks of the Bayern summer school holiday, à la carte: 13/42

This alpine pasture is a must. So is a reservation at this restaurant, because the comfortable dining rooms on two floors are usually filled not only with lovely antiques, but also with hungry Starnbergers and tourists. Thanks to the moderate prices, attentive and prompt service, and good cooking, Willi Illguth (proud of being born a

Stuttgarter) can count on satisfied customers. You can order Bavarian specialities, typically Swabian dishes and a large variety of meat. Most dishes can be ordered as half-portions as well. The wine list is large, and it also offers Swabian wines by the glass.

STEINHAGEN NRW

Bielefeld 9 - Gütersloh 14

ALTE SCHMIEDE 15/20

33803, Kirchplatz 22
(0 52 04) 70 01, Fax 8 91 29 res.

 P

Closed for lunch, closed Christmans Eve. Tables d'hôte: 69/82, à la carte: 45/73

The Alte Schmiede modestly presents itself as a wine store with restaurant, but most of the gourmets in this region associate its name with the high-quality, light, unpretentious cuisine that is served here. And perhaps also with the cramped but genuine historic ambience of the restaurant in this renovated half-timbered house. Our shrimp aspic tasted only faintly of shrimp, and the anglerfish with lobster sauce and nice salads was discouragingly insipid. Our eggplant canneloni with tomatoes was a little overdone. Much more impressive were veal *tafelspitz* with spinach beets and potato ragout, lamb with thyme sauce, Provençal vegetables, baked potatoes and pumpernickel mousse with rhubarb compôte, and a cheese dumpling with rum raisin ice cream and pear compôte. The expertly stocked wine cellar includes only German and Italian wines and, instead of just renowned names, offers some new discoveries.

STRALSUND Meckl.-Vorp.

Greifswald 31 - Rostock 74

VIER JAHRESZEITEN IN PARKHOTEL STRALSUND 12/20

18437, Lindenallee 61
(0 38 31) 47 40, Fax 47 48 60

 P

Tables d'hôte: 28L, à la carte: 28/45

Large windows, elegant and fragile-looking designer chairs, a blue-gray carpet and bright lights create a somewhat cool, sterile ambience. The kitchen offers regional and international dishes of varying quality. We had a flavorful, creamy soup of fresh tomatoes with basil, and ingenious curried sauerkraut with totally overdone scampi that couldn't even be rescued by an interesting cumin and ginger sauce. The service seemed sometimes well-trained and capable, sometimes obviously overtaxed. The small selection of French and German wines is of mediocre quality.

PARKHOTEL STRALSUND

18437, Lindenallee 61
(0 38 31) 47 40, Fax 47 48 60

 P

120 rooms, **S** 155/185, **D** 185/225, **APP** 200/800, **½P** +45, **P** +65

This new hotel is located in a residential area on the western outskirts of Stralsund. The elegantly furnished rooms are spacious and tastefully decorated. The complex offers rooms and halls for conferences, seminars, presentations and concerts. Fitness center, solarium, restaurant. Breakfast buffet: 17 DM.

STROMBERG Rheinl.-Pfalz

Bingen 11 - Bad Kreuznach 17

ALTE GERBEREI 12/20

55442, Kreuznacher Str. 1
(0 67 24) 89 76

 P

Closed for lunch Saturday, closed Monday. Tables d'hôte: 18/35, à la carte: 29/52, No Credit Cards

This beautiful framework house is one of the most pleasant country restaurants in this part of Germany. On warm days, we like to eat outside in the idyllic courtyard. The ambience is characterized by stone walls, oak beams and wooden paneling, as well as a few of host Alfred Wilbert's hunting trophies. He consciously avoids any celebration of haute cuisine, and instead keeps to savory and hearty regional cooking. His repertoire is simply delicious: well-seasoned lamb's-lettuce with bacon, tender maties herring fillets in cream, and generously portioned roast beef with crispy fried potatoes. The wine list emphasizes regional wines from the best producers of the Nahe at relatively moderate prices. There are wines by the glass as well.

LE VAL D'OR IN BURG-HOTEL STROMBURG 18/20

55442, Schloßberg
(0 67 24) 93 10 40, Fax 93 10 90 res.

Closed for lunch from Wednesday to Friday, closed Monday, Tuesday. Tables d'hôte: 135/165, à la carte: 60/113

Johann Lafer and his successful restaurant have moved from the valley in Guldental to a castle on a hill. He's kept the old name for his new restaurant, which opened at the end of 1994, and intends to serve the same excellent cuisine here. Try his classic dishes, like carpaccio of turbot and scallops, poularde with sweetbread, red mullet with artichokes and olive oil zabaglione, rack of lamb with pesto.

BURG-SCHÄNKE DEUTSCHER MICHEL

55442, Schloßberg
(0 67 24) 93 10 50

A la carte: 28/60

Maestro Lafer is going to celebrate bourgeois cuisine here and serve the (Austrian?) home-cooking he enjoyed as a boy: meatballs with *krautfleckerl* or paprika, fresh noodles with herbs, beef cheeks in red wine sauce, and schnitzel with warm potato salad. Draft beer, good wines and champagne by the glass will be offered. A little terrace and a larger biergarten are planned as well as occasional concerts in the castle courtyard with its splendid view of the Hunsrück landscape.

BURG-HOTEL STROMBURG

55442, Schloßberg
(0 67 24) 9 31 00, Fax 93 10 90

13 rooms, **D** 250/300, **APP** 450

The hotel lobby with fireplace and bar is the focal point of the castle complex. From there, customers enter the gourmet restaurant and the "Burg Schänke," the grandiose banquet hall, the wine store in the cellar, and find their way to the 13 rooms and suites. All rooms are named after famous cooks, like Escoffier, Brillat-Savarin and Walterspiel, and are equipped with all modern amenities. The three-room suite in the castle's tower is particularly appealing.

STUTTGART Baden-Württemberg

Karlesruhe 82 - Frankfurt 210 - München 215

ALTE POST 14/20

70174, Friedrichstr. 43 [B2]
(07 11) 29 30 79, Fax 2 26 07 57 res.

Closed for lunch Saturday and Monday, closed Sunday. Tables d'hôte: 59L, 98D, à la carte: 52/99

Wolfgang Pfeiffer and his kitchen staff are going strong. His vegetable polenta was fabulous, his venison pâté (filled with foie gras and served with an aromatic salad of brussels-sprouts leaves) perfectly seasoned, and his seafood consommé with lobster especially savory. His mélange of fine fish with saffron sauce was just delicious, as was the outstanding calf's liver with apples. After all these highlights, the millefeuille of prunes was slightly disappointing.The excellent choice of wines is international, headed by the best wines of the region. The wines aren't cheap, but they are adequately priced, in keeping with the high standard of cooking. The service is impeccable.

AM SCHLOSSGARTEN 14/20

70173, Schillerstr. 23 [C2]
(07 11) 2 02 60, Fax 2 02 68 88 res.

Tables d'hôte: 59L, 139D, à la carte: 50/96

The service in the elegant restaurant is back in shape; the wine list and the cuisine offer high quality. We had vegetable terrine with crème fraîche; trout galantine with chards and caviar; truffled consommé under a pastry crust; lovely carpaccio of scallops with lobster cream, green beans and rice; excellent quail cutlet with foie gras and delicate vegetables; savory blue-cheese terrine; and an artistic pastel composition with fruit and raspberry ice cream. We hope the kitchen keeps up this high-class cooking.

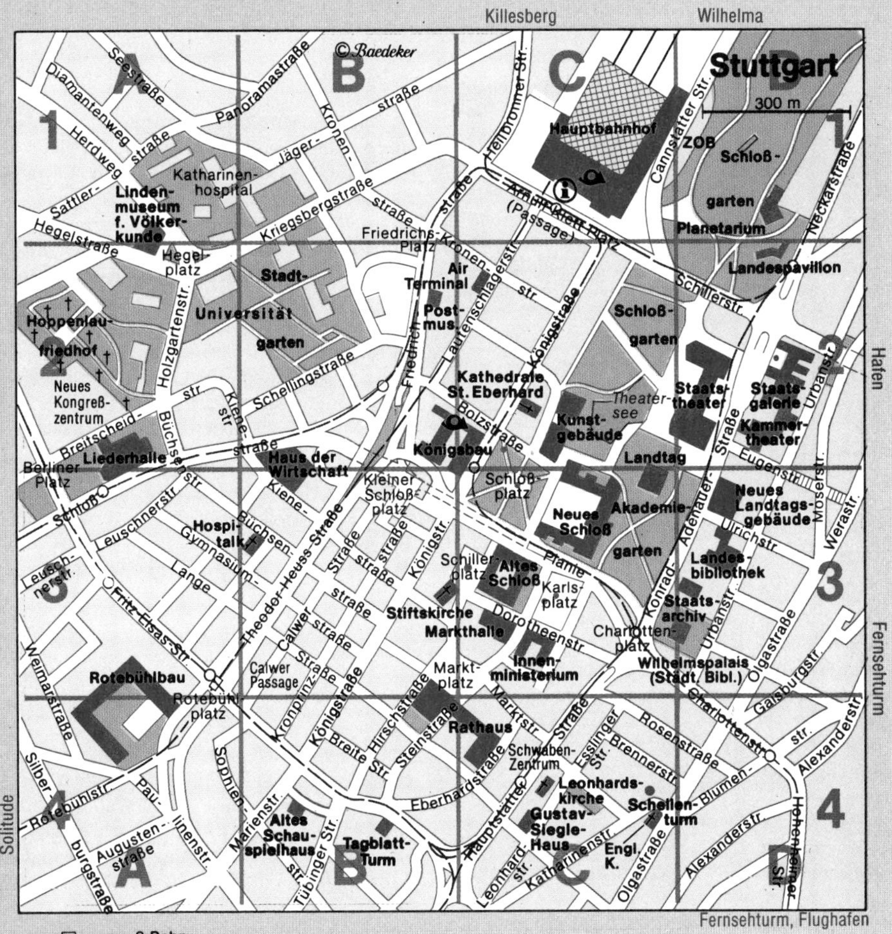

Killesberg
Wilhelma
© Baedeker
Stuttgart
300 m
A
B
C
D
1
2
3
4
Hauptbahnhof
ZOB
Schloß-garten
Planetarium
Landespavillon
Lindenmuseum f. Völkerkunde
Katharinenhospital
Hegelplatz
Stadtgarten
Universität
Hoppenlau-friedhof
Neues Kongreß-zentrum
Liederhalle
Berliner Platz
Air Terminal
Postmus.
Kathedrale St. Eberhard
Königsbau
Haus der Wirtschaft
Kleiner Schloßplatz
Schloßplatz
Kunstgebäude
Theatersee
Landtag
Staatstheater
Staatsgalerie
Kammertheater
Neues Landtagsgebäude
Neues Schloß
Akademiegarten
Landesbibliothek
Staatsarchiv
Hospitalk.
Schillerplatz
Altes Schloß
Karlsplatz
Stiftskirche
Markthalle
Innenministerium
Marktplatz
Charlottenplatz
Wilhelmspalais (Städt. Bibl.)
Rotebühlbau
Rotebühlplatz
Calwer Passage
Rathaus
Schwaben-Zentrum
Leonhardskirche
Gustav-Siegle-Haus
Schellenturm
Engl. K.
Altes Schauspielhaus
Tagblatt-Turm
Hafen
Fernsehturm
Solitude
Fernsehturm, Flughafen

S-Bahn

DELICE 17/20

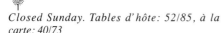

70178, Hauptstätterstr. 61 [C4]
(07 11) 6 40 32 22 res.

Closed Saturday, Sunday and holidays. Tables d'hôte: 125, à la carte: 72/106. Tables d'hôte with wine: 200, No Credit Cards

Chef Friedrich Gutscher buys only the best produce from ecological farms or firms. His gourmet meal started with exquisite snail strudel and chanterelles, followed by succulent baby chicken with delicate potato salad dressed with poppy-seed oil and muscat vinegar. We then had fried sturgeon with truffled sauce and *tafelspitz* with horseradish crust. We concluded our meal with a Stilton cheese and raisins in port wine. à la carte, we enjoyed a terrine of rabbit and foie gras with salads, lobster medallions with leek butter, and lamb saddle with beans and baked pigeon.The wine list offers a choice of more than 600 wines.

DAS FÄSSLE 15/20

70597, Stadtteil Degerloch
Löwenstr. 51
(07 11) 76 01 00, Fax 76 44 32 res.

Closed Sunday. Tables d'hôte: 52/85, à la carte: 40/73

The recession that makes other competitors fight for every guest has obviously bypassed Rudolf Schmölz's restaurant. Why do Swabian gourmets throng to this place? There is nothing special about the ambience; the plain, small tables are set close together and aren't even decorated with fresh flowers. The service is so-so; the hostess is, at best, friendly and distant, except with VIPs. The wine list, however, is astoundingly low-priced, and you get a lot of good food for relatively little money. This alone almost guarantees success among the reputedly thrifty Swabians. Regional specialities are best here. We had a wonderfully flavorful aspic of smoked fish with diced vegetables, chive sauce and tangy salads; saddle of veal (cut and served like a schnitzel) in a great cheese crust with spinach, sugar peas and homemade noodles; and iced cake with honey, pineapple and kiwi. If you don't like regional recipes, try something from the seasonal menu—Canadian lobster with broccoli, saddle of venison with red cabbage, or orange parfait with tropical fruit. We just loved our *trou de chef*, a fresh apple sherbet with a drop of Calvados, and the mini-*guglhupf* that was served with our coffee.

LA FENÊTRE IN RELEXA WALDHOTEL SCHATTEN 12/20

70569, Magstadter Str.
(07 11) 6 86 70, Fax 6 86 79 99 res.

P

Closed for lunch, closed Sunday, Monday, à la carte: 53/87

The cuisine has recently acquired a Eurasian touch, which can be problematic.We liked the salmon terrine with sprouts and lemon flavoring, for instance, but we could have done without the spicy sauces that almost killed the venison carpaccio and the otherwise excellent smoked swordfish. The glazed breast of guinea fowl might have called for Asian seasoning and chanterelle risotto, but it didn't harmonize at all with the bamboo shoots it was served with.The regional wines and vintages from neighboring countries are good and just affordable. The pleasant service staff distributes roses to the ladies.

LA FENICE 13/20

70195, Stadtteil Botnang
Beethovanstr. 9
(07 11) 6 99 07 03, Fax 6 99 07 03 res.

P

Closed Monday, closed for lunch Tuesday, closed first week in January

We like the cuisine of this pretty restaurant, the pleasant and flawless service, and the moderate prices on the menu. The wine list, however, has yet to follow this good example. Most wines are exorbitantly priced.We had a first-class veal carpaccio with a discreet vinaigrette and sliced mushrooms; fantastic pasta roulade with spinach and cheese, served with a fine tomato sauce and basil; excellent sturgeon with lime sauce; and an overdone turkey stuffed with chestnuts and served with a delicious sauce.

FONTANA 13/20

70563, Stadtteil Vaihingen
Vollmoellerstr. 5
(07 11) 73 00, Fax 7 30 25 25 res.

P

Tables d'hôte: 15/45, à la carte: 19/74

In addition to dining in the nicely furnished restaurant, guests can also eat in the new glassed-in veranda. The service is quick and friendly, but somewhat less than elegant. The low-priced menu offers good-quality cuisine and many Swabian dishes. The repertoire includes savory aspic of suckling pig with shallot vinaigrette, homemade noodles with scallops, salmon and anglerfish with vegetables, very good fish soup with crustaceans and garlic croutons, perfectly fried duck with broccoli, carrots and (overdone) potato gratin, *panna cotta* with caramelized pine kernels and exquisite Champagne parfait with puréed fruit.The international wine list hasn't a great deal to offer, but it is adequate. The choice of wines by the glass is good and moderately priced.

GAISBURGER PASTETCHEN 12/20

70188, Hornbergstr. 24
(07 11) 48 48 55, Fax 48 75 65 res.

P

Closed for lunch, closed Sunday and holidays, closed 1 week at Whitsunday, first 2 weeks of the Bad.-Württ. summer school holiday. Tables d'hôte: 60/100, à la carte: 47/87, No Credit Cards

The cuisine has improved somewhat since our last visit, but we still miss the creativity that would give a lighter touch to the opulent, rather heavy and hearty Swabian cooking here. Our appetizer, a little Savoy cabbage tart, was a massive welcome. It was followed by thickly breaded sweetbreads and heavily creamed sauerkraut soup, as well as saddle of rabbit wrapped in a coat of white bread. Highlights included the fabulous ravioli filled with blood pudding in the soup, perfect cheese and fresh apple tart with iced cream cheese.The service is pleasant, and Josef Kern competently takes on the duties of a sommelier. His internationally stocked wine cellar offers wines at fair prices.

HIRSCH-WEINSTUBEN 15/20

70567, Stadtteil Möhringen
Maierstr. 3
(07 11) 71 13 75, Fax 7 17 06 20

 P

Closed for lunch Saturday and Monday, closed Sunday. Tables d'hôte: 54/109, à la carte: 33/84

Congratulations for the second toque! This restaurant is characterized by impeccable service, a well-stocked wine cellar and expert advice, an impressive choice of liqueurs and excellent cuisine. We followed the meal suggestions of chef Martin Frietsch. He served lovely rabbit liver and kidneys with lentil salad as an appetizer, followed by an excellent terrine of sole with marinated sugar peas and shrimps with saffron butter, wonderful bass with basil sauce and mushroom julienne, superb-tasting deep-fried basil leaves with potatoes, flavorful fish consommé with oysters, prawns and anglerfish. After enjoying the tasty lamb medallions in an olive crust, we could choose from more than 20 different kinds of cheese. The final highlight was our dessert: citrus-fruit sherbet with peeled grapes, white ice-cream pralines with mango cocktail, all garnished with mango and raspberries. The wine cellar offers a choice of 65 half-bottles and excellent wines by the glass.

KREHL'S LINDE 13/20

70374, Stadtteil Bad Cannstatt
Obere Waiblinger Str. 113
(07 11) 52 75 67, Fax 5 28 63 70 res.

Closed Sunday, Monday. Tables d'hôte: 80/95, à la carte: 34/75. Tables d'hôte with wine: 120/150, No Credit Cards

This comfortable and nicely furnished restaurant offers pleasant service, good advice on choosing wines, and fine cuisine in the typically opulent Swabian style. Our appetizer, a tasty fish terrine with crème fraîche, was followed by an excellent beef carpaccio, flavorful mushroom consommé, nicely poached fillet of pike-perch with a delicious Riesling sauce and spinach, and veal medallions with lovely sherry sauce, accompanied by eight different kinds of vegetables. We loved our dessert of sherbets served in pineapple, so we didn't even try the soggy biscuit served with our coffee. Excellent wine list with moderate prices.

NECKARSTUBE IN HOTEL INTER-CONTINENTAL 13/20

70173, Willy-Brandt-Str. 30 [D1]
(07 11) 2 02 00, Fax 20 20 12

P

Tables d'hôte: 38/65L, 48/75D, à la carte: 24/61

We had bad luck on our last visit. During one of the most important fairs in Stuttgart, the restaurant of this first-class hotel managed to offer nothing but a reduced menu: two first courses, two soups, three main courses each of fish and meat, and three desserts. Shame! From this meager choice, we ordered fried fish and seafood with a seasonal salad; the latter turned out to be one shrimp, bits of salmon and anglerfish, and half a scallop on skimpily dressed salad leaves. Our cream of lamb's lettuce soup with sweetbreads, kohlrabi and carrots, however, was tasty, and the veal fillet was nicely done. The unsavory Turkish figs succumbed to the strong aroma of the rosemary ice cream they were served with.

SPEISEMEISTEREI 17/20

am Schloß Hohenheim
70599, Stadtteil Hohenheim
(07 11) 4 56 00 37, Fax 4 56 00 38 res.

P

Closed for dinner Sunday, closed Monday, 1—15 January. Tables d'hôte: 65/98L, 99/125D, à la carte: 52/94, No Credit Cards

Stuttgart has a new gourmet temple in its 200-year-old castle. We found an exquisite ambience here, impeccable service, and excellent and creative cuisine. A talented sommelier and a well-trained service staff in toreador uniforms set the stage for the taste sensations that followed. The large choice of wonderful breads impressed us, as did the asparagus mousse with salmon tartare that welcomed us. The variations of foie gras from the Périgord was fabulous: Foie gras was served with pearls of pears marinated in red wine, as a delicate terrine with grape salad, and as salad with truffles, decorated with nasturtium flowers. We had lobster with Beluga caviar, sugar peas and cauliflower purée, and fried sole with artichokes, tomatoes and herbs, followed by lamb fillet with shallot crust on pimento. The pastry was high-class as well, and offerings included date and chocolate strudel with vanilla sauce and Armagnac ice cream with plum preserves. For every course, the capable sommelier served exactly the right wine.The choice of wines is international and offers only the best names and vineyards. The prices aren't quite as grand as the ambience.

TOP AIR 15/20

70621, Flughafen
(07 11) 9 48 21 37, Fax 7 97 92 10

Closed for lunch Saturday, closed August. Tables d'hôte: 48L, 95/140D, à la carte: 50/98

The new chef of this elegant airport restaurant obviously feels at home in his kitchen. His little menu sounded interesting. On beautifully arranged platters, he served *gugelhupf* in Sauterne jelly (really first class!) with marinated artichokes, diced tomatoes and brioche. He enticed us with shish kebab of prawns with sherry sauce and lightly steamed cabbage and carrots, soothed us with poorly seasoned turbot fillet, and delighted us with his suprême of wild duck with gingerbread sauce, glazed pears, Brussels sprouts and dumplings. A large choice of cheese and a delicious dessert (almond soufflé with oranges and fresh raspberries) concluded this memorable meal. The coffee was only lukewarm, but the friandises and cake were lovely. We liked the moderately priced wines and the agreeable service.

WALLE & RAUL 14/20

70199, Stadtteil Heslach
Gebelsbergstr. 97
(07 11) 6 40 64 67, Fax 5 30 48 res.

P

Closed Monday, 1—12 January, 1—14 August. nmTables d'hôte: 88/110D, à la carte: 50/80. Tables d'hôte with wine: 90/150

In his cozy, comfortable restaurant with its distinct personal touch, charming Raul Va from Spain shows that he can do more than paint pictures. In addition to the paintings on the walls, he is responsible for the outstanding quality of service, while Walter (Walle) Hinzer's cuisine offers refined regional fare. We liked the opulent first-course platter with beef carpaccio, firm fish terrine, nicely fried foie gras, fresh smoked sheatfish garnished with a caviar of trout, ham and salad bouquet. After that, we had a light and tasty avocado soup with shrimps, perfect salmon with scampi and green asparagus, duck's breast with mushrooms, nice cheese and a dessert of different ice creams and chocolate mousse garnished with fruit.The wine cellar offers good and reasonably prices wines.

WEINSTUBE PFUND 12/20

70372, Stadtteil Bad Cannstatt
Waiblinger Str. 61
(07 11) 56 63 63 res.

P

Closed for lunch Saturday, closed Sunday and holidays. Tables d'hôte: 44L, 70/125D, à la carte: 39/82

International cuisine is served in this *weinhaus* built by a wine-cask maker at the turn of the century, and the cellar is traditionally well-stocked with moderately priced bottles and many good wines by the glass. The owner served parfait of smoked fish with soybean sprouts, a colorful mixed salad with small pieces of scallops and a strongly seasoned soy sauce vinaigrette, oxtail soup and a rather tasteless white-wine soup with prawns. Our curried rabbit with fried broccoli was delicious, but our tasty squab was full of bones.

WIELANDSHÖHE 17/20

70507, Stadtteil Degerloch
Alte Weinsteige 71
(07 11) 6 40 88 48, Fax 6 40 94 08

P

Closed Sunday and Monday. Tables d'hôte: 98/158, à la carte: 62/114

The sensitive, artistic Vincent Klink is no longer the sole shining star of Stuttgart's gourmet heaven, but the Wielandshöhe is still on top. Strong competition has motivated Klink to make a very special effort. After two appetizers, which might be a quiche lorraine or sushi with shrimp—Klink's kitchen served a combination of creative, classic luxury dishes. We ordered a typical meal: variations of headcheese, perfectly poached salmon in champagne sauce with spinach, red beets and a spoonful of Beluga caviar, Bresse pigeon with braised Belgian endives, and caramel apples glazed with cinnamon. Highlights we wouldn't want to miss were potato salad, foie gras and risotto. The service is perfect, and the wine cellar a treasure chest, with more than 400 choice wines.

DER ZAUBERLEHRLING 14/20

70182, Rosenstr. 38 [C/D4]
(07 11) 2 37 77 70, Fax 2 37 77 75 res.

Closed Sunday. Tables d'hôte: 48/98, à la carte: 27/72, No Credit Cards

The ambience of this new restaurant is enchanting, the service agreeable and pleasant, and the dishes artistically presented. We had wonderful salads with fresh lobster, great guinea fowl terrine, beautifully arranged leg of poularde with scrumptious sauce, and a fabulous saddle of venison. Waffles with cinnamon ice cream and cherries were ingeniously delicious. The wine cellar is well-stocked with international wines and is moderately priced. There are guest rooms for customers who don't want to drink and drive.

ZUR WEINSTEIGE IN HOTEL WÖRTZ 14/20

70184, Hohenheimer Str. 30 [D4]
(07 11) 2 36 70 01, Fax 2 36 70 07 res.

P

Closed Sunday and holidays. Tables d'hôte: 15/78L, 42/115D, à la carte: 23/72. Tables d'hôte with wine: 130/160

A questionnaire comes with the bill: How was quantity and quality of the food, did you like the drinks, and how good was the service? We can give the answers right here. Everything was good to very good, starting with Richard Scherle's appetizer (grilled shrimp with melon cream), continuing with the tasty lamb's-lettuce with bacon, croutons and slices of duck's breast, cream of lobster soup, beef medallion in horseradish crust, and ending with a variety of cheese and a bombastic dessert with Amaretto parfait, warm date strudel with vanilla cream, chocolate mousse, and ice cream with fresh fruit and puréed fruit.The gigantic wine list describes all wines accurately. The prices are incredibly low, and the choice of wines by the glass is fantastic.

HOTELS

AM SCHLOSSGARTEN

70173, Schillerstr. 23 [C2]
(07 11) 2 02 60, Fax 2 02 68 88

P

121, **S** 255/335, **D** 385/470,
1/2P +45, **P** +90

The central location—a stone's throw from the railway station and airport terminal, next to the opera and the city's art gallery—is the main asset of this hotel. An underground garage solves all parking problems. Rooms facing the park are sought-after.

INTER-CONTINENTAL

70173, Willy-Brandt-Str. 30 [D1]
(07 11) 2 02 00, Fax 20 20 12

 P

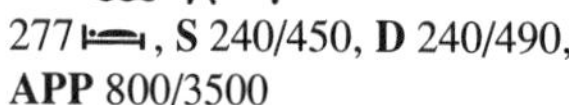

277, **S** 240/450, **D** 240/490,
APP 800/3500

This deluxe hotel in a first-rate city location offers all the many amenities of an efficient chain hotel. Unique pieces of furniture, however, and the finest materials create an individual style and a high standard of comfort. Convention center, ballroom for 800 guests, 24-hour service, fitness center, hairdresser, Lufthansa check-in and banking services. Breakfast buffet: 31 DM.

STEIGENBERGER GRAF ZEPPELIN

70173, Arnulf-Klett-Platz 7 [C1]
(07 11) 2 04 80, Fax 2 04 85 42

 P

240, **S** 245/345, **D** 345/385,
APP 650/1130, **1/2P** +45, **P** +90

This grand hotel with all the modern amenities is centrally located. The swimming pool on the fifth floor offers a marvelous view of the city and of a vineyard that extends almost into the middle of town. Large lobby, bar and nightclub. Restaurants. Room service brings an American breakfast: 30 DM.

SUHL — Thüringen

Coburg 55 - Eisenach 65

SUHL IN HOTEL THÜRINGEN 12/20

98527, Pl. d. Deutschen Enheit 2
(0 36 81) 30 38 90, Fax 2 43 79

P

Tables d'hôte: 27L, 35D, à la carte: 26/46

The ambience is modest but pleasant. The wine list is very small, the dining room colorfully decorated, the background music at least discreet, and the service pleasant. The menu doesn't offer any complete meals; you have to order á la carte. We remember a disappointing appetizer, good salmon tartare and tasty cream of asparagus soup, excellent fried salmon fillet with lemon butter, and flavorful lamb fillet with a not-more-than-cute assortment of side dishes.

THÜRINGEN

98527, Pl. d. Deutschen Enheit 2
(0 36 81) 30 38 90, Fax 2 43 79

P

124, **S** 170/195, **D** 200/240,
APP 350/380, **1/2P** +25, **P** +50

The renovated, modernized rooms are adequately comfortable, but the prices are now higher. Conference rooms, three restaurants, pub, bar, café with terrace. *Forbes* magazine elected the charming owner of this hotel its female manager of the year in 1992.

SULZBURG — Bad.-Württ.

Müllheim 10 - Freiburg 28 - Basel 50

HIRSCHEN 18/20

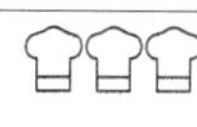

79295, Hauptstr. 69
(0 76 34) 82 08, Fax 67 17 res.

P

Closed Monday, Tuesday, 9—26 January, 25 July through 10 August. Tables d'hôte: 50L, 114D, 155, à la carte: 68/128, No Credit Cards

Hans Paul Steiner's gourmet temple is the most expensive restaurant in southern Baden—and is still as popular (and overrun) as ever. Ever since Steiner took flight toward the heights of culinary achievement, he has been strong competition even for the Alsatian experts across the nearby border. This French oasis in the Markgräfler region is neither flamboyant nor trendy. We blindly trusted Steiner and were never disappointed, neither with the expert service nor with the excellent cuisine full of personality and style. Steiner fans like the mushroom galantine with venison, sea bream and foie gras, sorrel soup with salmon soufflé, venison with Savoy cabbage, and the variety of lovely desserts. We agree wholeheartedly. We didn't even mind paying 58 DM for his wonderfully fried asparagus with veal fillet, spinach and pancake roulades filled with ham and cheese. Beer, mineral water and wines by the glass are amazingly cheap. The wine list is grand.

SILENCE WALDHOTEL BAD SULZBURG
79295, Badstr. 67
(0 76 34) 82 70, Fax 82 12

35, **S** 88/98, **D** 140/182,
APP 184, **1/2P** +34
Closed mid-January through mid-February

The old building dating from 1800 and the new addition built in 1979 offer all the modern amenities guests can ask for, including indoor pool with spa water, lovely garden terrace, idyllic paths for strolling, and absolute peace and quiet. Ambitious restaurant, famous for its pastries.

LA VIGNA 15/20

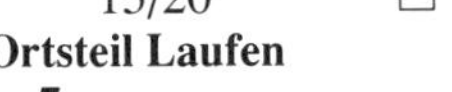

2 km west in Ortsteil Laufen
79295, Weinstr. 7
(0 76 34) 80 14, Fax 6 92 52 res.

Closed Sunday, Monday, Christmas Eve through 6 January, 3 weeks during the Bad.-Württ. summer school holiday. Tables d'hôte: 46L, 68D, 125, à la carte: 52/87, No Credit Cards

If you like Italian food, this restaurant is a must. In a typical old-fashioned house, customers enjoy an exclusive ambience at only six tables. Antonino Esposito can't manage more than that by himself, and customers need patience here. There is no spaghetti or pizza on the menu; instead, you will find rabbit fillet, shellfish soup, lamb saddle with olive sauce, and truffled pasta. We enjoyed salad with sea bream, salmon and anglerfish, tender duck, savory saltimbocca with delicious vegetables and yogurt cream, exquisite petits fours and good espresso. Italian wines at respectable prices dominate the wine list.

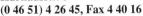

SYLT Schleswig-Holstein

For car ferry information in Niebüll call
(0 46 51) 2 40 57
Husum 81 - Kiel 125

AHNENHOF
in 25999, Kampen
Kurhausstr. 8
(0 46 51) 4 26 45, Fax 4 40 16

13, **S** 110/140, **D** 200/280
Closed 20 November through 20 December, mid-January through mid-February

A comfortable guesthouse near the beach adjacent to a natural preserve. Offers individually furnished, comfortable rooms facing the ocean. Typical island garden.

ALEXANDERS RESTAURANT 12/20
in 25980, Westerland
Johann-Möller-Str. 30
(0 46 51) 2 66 42, Fax 2 83 13

Closed for lunch, closed Tuesday. Tables d'hôte: 65/95, à la carte: 34/72

In his beautifully restored turn-of-the-century villa, Alexander Blume tries to recapture past grandeur, at least where the cuisine is concerned. He's engaged a new cook who can't deny his French education, but who lacks some of that expertise necessary for great cooking. Our bouillabaisse could have been more substantial, and the fish better done, but the scallops and scampi served with a fine salad were tasty. The prices were reasonable, and many main courses were offered as half portions as well. The pleasant service staff needed some wine education.

BENEN-DIKEN-HOF

in 25980, Keitum Süderstr.
(0 46 51) 3 10 35, Fax 3 58 35

P

39, **S** 140/280, **D** 235/380,
APP 360/650

Reserve rooms well in advance, since this hotel is almost always full. Its homey atmosphere and its extensive grounds make it a favorite with families. This romantic hotel has a game room for children and abundant leisure facilities for adults. Ample breakfast buffet and nice, light suppers.

BISTRO HAUS MEERESRUH 12/20
in 25999, Kampen
Braderuper Weg 4
(0 46 51) 4 13 83 res.

P

Closed Thursday. Tables d'hôte: 75L, à la carte: 42/104

This little restaurant is open only in the evenings and is an institution in the changing gastronomic scene here. Especially popular because of the many lobster dishes, the menu also includes courses with an Italian touch, like anglerfish fried in olive oil with noodles, and with a regional emphasis, like half a duck with red cabbage and dumplings. Competent service and a modest choice of wines.

FISCHE-FIETE 12/20

in 25980, Keitum
Weidemannweg 3
(0 46 51) 3 21 50, Fax 3 25 91 res.

 P

Closed November/February, à la carte: 30/87, No Credit Cards

We don't know which to admire more: the size of the menu or the obstinacy of those customers who, year after year, squeeze into these small dining rooms to enjoy traditional German fish dishes. We've often had bad luck with overdone and underdone food, soggy side dishes and careless presentation of dishes that could be at least good plain fare if the kitchen were more careful and motivated. The service ranges from pleasant to too busy to be pleasant. Our only comfort was the grandiose choice of wines.

FRANZ GANSER 13/20

in 25980, Westerland
Bötticherstr. 2/corner of Boysenstr.
(0 46 51) 2 29 70 res.

 P

Closed for lunch every day except Sunday, closed Monday, 26 November through 12 December, 21 February through 21 March. Tables d'hôte: 62L, 120D, à la carte: 53/98

The first courses are spectacular here. Our lobster salad with Champagne and tarragon dressing, duck consommé with liver quenelles, and scallop gratin with tomatoes and artichokes were all flawlessly prepared, finely seasoned and attractively arranged on our plates. Some main courses suffered from slip-ups in the kitchen, however: overdone fillet with an inappropriate Calvados cream sauce, and a burnt striped mullet. The service is attentive and quick. The choice of wines, especially the Italian ones, is interesting.

GOGÄRTCHEN 14/20

25999, Kampen
Strönwai
(0 46 51) 4 12 42, Fax 4 11 72

 P

Closed 1 November through 20 December, 9 January theough Easter, à la carte: 48/97

There's a new chef here every year, but it still doesn't help clever and enterprising Rolf Seiche to meet the demands of a first-class gourmet restaurant. On our last visit, we enjoyed classic cuisine with a touch of the new trend for hearty, savory cooking: fried sole, beef roulade with red cabbage, breast of ox, and sauerbraten. We also tried consommé of fine fish, scampi ravioli with pimento cream, and fish with the usual trendy sauces. Our rating is a compromise between dishes that are worth 12/20 and those that deserve 16/20. The service staff takes pains to please.

GOLF-UND LANDHAUS KAMPEN

in 25999 Kampen
Braderuper Weg 12
(0 46 51) 4 69 10, Fax 46 91 11

P

9, **S** 320/360, **D** 370/410,
APP 550/660

This fashionable new Frisian building offers comfortable rooms and suites with fireplaces and terraces. Bar, café and breakfast terrace. The owners also run the Village Kampen, with 12 rooms.

HARDY AUF SYLT 12/20

in 25980, Westerland
Norderstr. 65
(0 46 51) 2 27 75, Fax 2 95 20 res.

P

Closed Monday, 26 November through 22 December, 9 January through 1 April. Tables d'hôte: 45, à la carte: 32/60

New chef Oliver Saar was a catch for André Speisser. He even prepared time-tested Alsatian specialities in a light, tasty fashion. But Saar isn't satisfied with just improving standard dishes, he also creates attractive daily specials, like lamb kidneys with mustard cream sauce, mushrooms and *rösti*, black ravioli with delicate basil mousse, pheasant terrine with perfectly marinated salads, and delicious blueberry tarts with vanilla ice cream. Beside the fairly priced wine list, which features wines from France and Baden, there's also a list of rarities, with some bottles from the 1960s. Pleasant, competent service.

HINKFUSS AM DORFTEICH 13/20 
in 25996 Wennigstedt
Am Dorfteich 2
(0 46 51) 54 61 res.

Closed for lunch Tuesday, closed Monday, mid-Jaunary through mid-February, mid-Novemebr through mid-December. Tables d'hôte: 44/139, à la carte: 49/112

Other restaurants may complain of empty tables, but customers still wait in line to eat at this restaurant run by a genuine Berliner. Plain, hearty bourgeois German meals are served at noon, whereas the evenings are reserved for a "grand parade" that includes classics like pike quenelles, turbot fillet with champagne mustard sauce and morels, and lamb saddle with rosemary sauce, but also features seasonal dishes like crayfish cooked in court-bouillon and seasoned with cumin, and red mullet with ratatouille and noodles seasoned with rosemary. The service is quick and motivated and doesn't lose control of things even when the house is full. The wine cellar is well-stocked with reasonably priced German wines, whereas international bottles and wines by the glass have highly exaggerated prices.

100 JAHRE ALTER GASTHOF 12/20
in 25992 ListAlte Dorfstr. 5
(0 46 51) 72 44

Closed Monday, Tuesday afternoon during the winter, à la carte: 36/88

This 300-year-old Frisian cottage at the northern tip of the island attracts a crowd of regular customers who feel at home in the small dining rooms and in the lovely Frisian garden outside, and appreciate the unaffected hospitality offered here. The cuisine is straightforward and doesn't court fancy names, products or garnishes, but tries to carefully combine traditional cooking with modern accents. Our mussel soup was finely seasoned with curry, lobster was served on a bed of spinach and homemade noodles with mozzarella on top, and white chocolate ice cream came with delicious blueberry compôte. The small wine list includes some bottles from California and Chile and some wines by the glass at acceptable prices.

LANDHAUS STRICKER 14/20 
in 25980, Tinnum
Boy-Nielsen-Str. 10
(0 46 51) 3 16 72, Fax 3 54 55 res.

Closed Monday, closed for lunch Tuesday. Tables d'hôte: 34/44L, 65/149D, à la carte: 66/97

Time has stood still in this squat old Frisian house with its dark wooden beams and comfortable, cozy little dining rooms furnished with antiques. In keeping with this idyllic ambience, the kitchen offered technically perfect classic dishes, discreetly seasoned with creativity. After our rather subtle lobster soup we had seafood doughnuts with champagne and vinegar sauce and succulent anglerfish saltimbocca with truffled noodles and flavorful tomato mousse. Our parfait perfumed with wild roses and strawberries and ginger chocolate was a lively extravaganza we won't forget in a hurry! The service has its ups and downs, and the wine list features choice German wines. Beginning in spring 1995, the owners are also offering exclusive apartments on the upper floor of the country cottage.

MOBY DICK 13/20
in 25980 Munkmarsch
Munkhoog 14
(0 46 51) 3 21 20 res.

Closed Wednesday, closed for lunch Thursday, closed 22 November through 24 December. Tables d'hôte: 72/85, à la carte: 42/80

Refined, perfect regional cuisine with Swabian accents, an elegant ambience and genuine hospitality make a visit here a pleasure. We enjoyed a pot-au-feu of sole and turbot, delicious seafood ravioli with saffron sauce, and exquisite hazelnut parfait with a purée of peach and mangoes. Fans of Swabian cooking can also order a tasty traditional roast beef with onions and fresh spaetzle. Some customers just take a snack outside to the terrace and enjoy the marvelous view of the sea shallows. Moderately priced choice of wines with an emphasis on Baden.

NÖSSE 13/20

in 25980, Morsum
Nösistig (Am Kliff)
(0 46 54) 15 55, Fax 16 58 res.

 P

Closed Monday from September through March, 3 weeks in November/December. Tables d'hôte: 69L, 138D, à la carte: 71/101. Tables d'hôte with wine: 80

In spite of an auspicious beginning, the cuisine here has yet to find its own style. The new chefs from Düsseldorf obviously weren't yet feeling quite at home on a cliff in the middle of a nature preserve. Our thinly sliced, overdone pigeon breast with aniseed sauce and dry catfish fillet with delicately creamed lentils disappointed us, but excellent anglerfish piccata with artichokes and basil and tomato sauce, and tender, succulent fried saddle of suckling pig with ale sauce revived our dampened spirits. The tables were opulently decorated, but the size of the helpings was barely sufficient. The service was dependable and competent. The choice of wines was interesting, especially the young white wines and some nice Italians, but the wine list is much too cumbersome to handle.

NÖSSE-BISTRO 13/20

in 25980, Morsum
Nösistig (Am Kliff)
(0 46 54) 15 55, Fax 16 58

 P

Closed Monday from September through March, 3 weeks in November/December. Tables d'hôte: 45L, 65D, à la carte: 44/88. Tables d'hôte with wine: 80

If customers want good value for relatively little money, they avoid the restaurant and visit the bistro instead. Whether we ate in the small, somewhat cramped dining rooms or on the sheltered terrace, all the dishes we tried were tasty and flawlessly prepared. Although the Nösse chef offers his bistro clientele more regional dishes, the menu here was just as impressive. We tried delicious ratatouille salad with perfectly fried lamb fillet, a choice of homemade terrines (lamb, duck and quail), succulent striped mullet with a mild garlic sauce, and enticingly flavorful hazelnut dumpings with orange sauce. The service is competent and particularly nice to children. Avoid the mediocre wines by the glass and order a bottle from the choice wine list instead.

PICCOLO IN HOTEL WALTER'S HOF 14/20

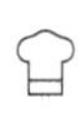

25999, Kampen Kurhausstr.
(0 46 51) 44 90, Fax 4 55 90

 P

Closed for lunch. Tables d'hôte: 75/130, à la carte: 53/97. Tables d'hôte with wine: 48/128

A new cook every season has been the recipe of this restaurant so far, but the management should hold on to this one. Jenns Dannenfeld´s light Mediterranean cooking is simply sublime. Our crispy fried pike-perch with marinated lentils, refreshing sorrel soup garnished with seafood, tender sweetbreads with chanterelles salad, and king prawns with tarragon all deserved at least a rating of 14/20. The panoramic view overlooking Kampen´s heath landscape to the ocean shallows near List was just as impressive as the cooking. The service was competent and the wine list comprehensive.

LA PROVENCE 12/20

in 25980 Westerland
Maybachstr. 24
(0 46 51) 2 31 01 res.

P

Closed Tuesday, 10 January through 10 February, 20 November through 15 December, à la carte: 40/75

With their Provençal cuisine, the owners have apparently found their niche. They have quite a few regular customers and fans on this island, which is literally flooded with restaurants. Small rooms in a brick house with wooden floors, old tiles and playful furniture are the perfect setting for the rich, opulently seasoned traditional dishes the dedicated French chef creates. We tried a savory fish soup with herb croutons and garlic, rabbit ragout seasoned with thyme and rosemary and served with fresh chanterelles and noodles, and an excellent lavender and honey parfait with strawberry salad and caramel and almond sauce that was a treat for the eye. The choice of wines included some rarities from Provence and regional wines. The service was cheerful and personal.

RESTAURANT JÖRG MÜLLER 19/20

in 25980 Westerland
Süderstr. 8
(0 46 51) 2 77 88/9, Fax 20 14 71 res.

Closed Tuesday, closed for lunch Wednesday, closed Wednesday from November through April, 20 November through 25 December. Tables d'hôte: 78/138L, 138/178D, à la carte: 65/127

After years at the very top of his profession in Germany, and defending this position not in Munich or Hamburg but on the northernmost island of the country, Jörg Müller has to be one of the great men in his profession. Only true superiority survives the inevitable seasonal ups and downs and the capricious demands of nouveau riche customers. We were captivated with Müller's attempts to create new compositions like a wonderful casserole of king prawns and sweetbreads, juicy anglerfish cutlet with delicious balsamic butter, and mildly smoked salmon with unparalleled potato salad seasoned with basil. We also loved our sliced sole with prawns and subtle saffron sauce, and squab with lobster and finely sliced sugar peas. Everything, however, was eclipsed by an unforgettable paillard of suckling lamb stuffed with chanterelles—a fine balance of the most delicate tastes! Four appetizers to start such a meal and excellent petits fours to end it are almost a matter of course. The wine list is one of the most comprehensive and interesting in Germany. The service is perfect and charming, without being forced or stiffly formal.

PESEL 15/20

in 25980, Westerland
Süderstr. 8
(0 46 51) 2 77 88/9, Fax 20 14 71 res.

Closed Tuesday, closed for lunch Wednesday, closed Wednesday from November through April, 20 November through 25 December. Tables d'hôte: 59L, 64D, 86, à la carte: 38/84

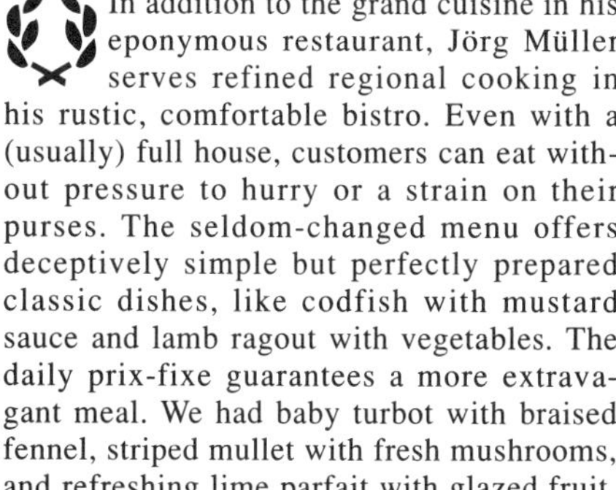

In addition to the grand cuisine in his eponymous restaurant, Jörg Müller serves refined regional cooking in his rustic, comfortable bistro. Even with a (usually) full house, customers can eat without pressure to hurry or a strain on their purses. The seldom-changed menu offers deceptively simple but perfectly prepared classic dishes, like codfish with mustard sauce and lamb ragout with vegetables. The daily prix-fixe guarantees a more extravagant meal. We had baby turbot with braised fennel, striped mullet with fresh mushrooms, and refreshing lime parfait with glazed fruit. There are wines by the glass, but customers can also ask for the grand wine list of the restaurant.

RESTAURANT KARSTEN WULFF 13/20

in 25980, Keitum
Museumsweg 4
(0 46 51) 3 03 00, Fax 3 57 38 res.

Closed Monday, mid-January through mid-February. Tables d'hôte: 59D, à la carte: 38/78, No Credit Cards

Karsten Wulff was born in Keitum, left it as a young boy, and returned as a widely traveled and experienced cook a few years ago to turn a former café into a restaurant. The focal point of the dining room is an open high-tech kitchen, where Wulff prepares and cooks his fish dishes in a manner similar to Fisch-Fiete next door. But, unlike the competition, Wulff changes his small menu every week, and all products are fresh. We had excellently seasoned and generously garnished cream of fish soup, excellent medallions of Atlantic bass with celery and potato mousse, and warm smoked saddle of lamb with basil yogurt and garden salads.

The service is discreet and circumspect. The choice of wines should include more than is usually offered on the island.

IL RISTORANTE 11/20
in 25999, Kampen
Kurhausstr. 1
(0 46 51) 49 51
P
A la carte:32/72

The enterprising Giorgio Morelli has found crowds of fans for his third establishment here, with its cheerfully colorful bistro-type dining room and a sheltered garden terrace. His clever yet straightforward Italian cooking is a success. Morelli offers a great variety of antipasti, many pasta dishes, and everything, from striped mullet to lamb, that is available on the island or can be ordered from the mainland. The prices are fair, but we would have liked to see more Italian wines on his list. The service is more nonchalant than professional.

SANSIBAR 12/20
in 25980, Rantum (5km south)
(0 46 51) 4 17, Fax 4 55 res.
P
Closed Christmas Eve, à la carte: 37/97

Herbert Seckler's log cabin in the middle of the lonesome dike landscape magically draws tourists from far and near. Good business during the day turns into a full house in the evenings, when there's no hope of getting a table without a reservation made far in advance. One glance at the sensational wine list and customers usually know why: the choice of Italian wines especially is unmatched anywhere else. The kitchen features fondue specialities and fish, all prepared and cooked in a down-to-earth, simple way. The service staff is very competent and keeps its good humor even when the place is packed.

STADT HAMBURG 14/20
in 25980, Westerland
Strandstr. 2
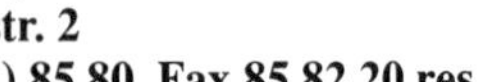
(0 46 51) 85 80, Fax 85 82 20 res.

P
Tables d'hôte: 85/105, à la carte: 48/96

This renovated restaurant with its precious English mahogany furniture, elegant curtains and choice antiques creates an elegant country-house ambience in which customers can still feel comfortably at home. The new cook gives impetus to the cuisine: classic and regional dishes are light and imaginative, even if some slip-ups could have been avoided, such as an oversalted potpourri of maties herring with endive salad, thick pasta with flavorful halibut and basil tomatoes and roughly cut cabbage. The professional service is traditionally formal but communicative and uncomplicated. The choice of wines is good.

BISTRO STADT HAMBURG 13/20
in 25980, Westerland
Strandstr. 2
(0 46 51) 85 80, Fax 85 82 29
P
Tables d'hôte: 35, à la carte: 35/63

The sun is shining in this beautiful new bistro: walls, curtains and china are a creamy yellow, upholstery brilliantly blue, and tablecloths and napkins cheerfully striped in orange and blue. A relaxed and cheerful service crew offers tasty dishes from the daily changing bistro menu, including salmon soup, salad with fried striped mullet, and cheese and berry strudel with walnut ice cream. There are 13 wines by the glass and draft beer to choose from.

HOTEL STADT HAMBURG
in 25980 Westerland
Strandstr. 2
(0 46 51) 85 80, Fax 85 82 20
P
72, **S** 205/281, **D** 366/476,
APP 521/566, **1/2P** +52

Like the restaurant, the hotel is run on traditional lines, with spacious and elegantly furnished rooms that complement the attentive service here. New and especially quiet suites are decorated in a countrified English style with antiques and fax hook-ups. 24-hour room service. Breakfast is served in the rooms all day. Prices are reduced from October to May.

STRANDHÖRN 14/20
in 25996, Wennigstedt
Dünenstr. 1
(0 46 51) 9 45 00, Fax 4 57 77 res.

Closed Wednesday, 15 January through 15 February, 20 November through 20 December. Tables d'hôte: 105/120, à la carte: 46/89

Visitors to the island obviously don't appreciate experimental cuisine as much as chef Robert Stolz thought they would, so the dishes with Asian touches that made such a good impression on us in the past have been drastically reduced. Warm home-smoked pigeon breast with refreshing bamboo salad (15/20!), lobster sushi, and tuna tempura with chili dip stand side by side on the menu with classic caper cream soup and sole roulade, char with artichokes, bean and olive doughnuts, and crispy squab with watercress risotto. The Holstein duck prepared Asian-style with vegetable crepe and soy and honey sauce was highly commendable. The wine list has a negligently stocked choice of German wines and ignores the new generation of winegrowers. The service is efficient and competent.

STRANDHÖRN
in 25996, Wennigstedt
Dünenstr. 1
(0 46 51) 9 45 00, Fax 4 57 77

22, **S** 140/215, **D** 250/330,
APP 290/580
Closed 15 January through 15 February, 20 November through 20 December, No Credit Cards

These two connected building complexes are just behind the dike of the western beach. The rooms are tastefully and elegantly furnished. Spacious suites are in the comfortable new addition, together with a fitness center, beauty farm and library.

TAPPES RESTAURANT 16/20

25999, Kampen
Strönwai
(0 46 51) 4 55 90, Fax 4 55 90 res.

Tables d'hôte: 112/136D, à la carte: 54/99

Continuity pays after all. Although Detlef Tappe accepts a new challenge every year (this time, it was a Driving Dinner Service with a kitchen in a specially built car), his main ambition has always been to make his restaurant, opened in 1989, one of the best in Germany. There is also continuity in the kitchen: Tappe has had the same cook for three years. Chef Holger Bodendorf creates new compositions with imagination, creativity and a sure instinct for quality and harmony. After five different appetizers, we enjoyed lovely seafood salad dressed with finely balanced olive oil, lasagna of chanterelles and John Dory with mushroom cream sauce, and (hats off!) succulent pigeon with green olives and artichokes. Even the most daring combinations were pure enjoyment. Extravagant china and artistic presentation underline the excellence of the cuisine. The service is pleasant and competent. The wine list features French wines at high prices.

VOGELKOJE 13/20
in 25999, Kampen
(0 46 51) 10 35, Fax 2 59 res.

Tables d'hôte: 60/125D, à la carte: 52/81

A young and unconventional team runs the idyllic Vogelkoje, sheltered by old trees and located between Kampen and List. Ten different breakfasts, light midday lunches in the lovely garden, irresistibly good cakes and an ingenious dinner menu attract many kinds of customers. Three- to five-course prix-fixes (and a small menu with alternatives) are served by romantic candlelight. We had beef carpaccio with pesto, Provençal tomato soup with red mullet, and white coffee parfait with cassis compôte. Each dish showed sensitivity and careful seasoning. The choice of wines is interesting. The friendly service staff takes pains to please.

WENNINGSTEDTER HOF
in 25996, Wennigstedt
Hauptstr. 1
(0 46 51) 9 46 50, Fax 4 39 88
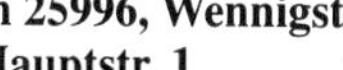
8 , **S** 120/240, **D** 160/280,
APP 180/360
No Credit Cards

The former Hotel Merk on the village pond was completely refurbished in 1993. It has retained the stylistic elements of the typical spa architecture, but the newly proportioned rooms have a modern Mediterranean flair. Bar, restaurant. Breakfast: 15 DM and up.

WOLFSHOF

in 25980, Keitum
Osterweg 2
(0 46 51) 34 45, Fax 3 11 39

13 (12), **S** 95/170, **D** 200/290

Closed 8 January through 10 March, 6 November through 22 December

This hotel is located on the outskirts of the most picturesque village on the island. The rooms are comfortably equipped, and the bar in front of the fireplace is cozy. Solarium, fitness center. Breakfast: 25 DM.

TECKLENBURG NRW

Ibbenbüren 8 - Osnabrück 24

PARKHOTEL BURGGRAF 13/20

49545, Meesenhof 7
(0 54 82) 4 25, Fax 61 25 res.

Tables d'hôte: 40/65L, 65/126D, à la carte: 38/69. Tables d'hôte with wine: 106/126

Maître Lattrich and his kitchen crew work at an efficient speed: before their hard-working colleague managed to bring the heavy blackboard-menu to our table, we were welcomed with bread, butter and vegetable aspic with cheese dip. Our seasonal (autumn) prix-fixe consisted of a well-dressed salad with red mullet and potatoes stuffed with leeks. Our lemon and pineapple consommé was a sweetish soup garnished with lobster-stuffed puff pastry. Wild duck's breast was more to our taste, even though some side dishes—red currant preserves and dry chestnut and almond dumplings —didn't seem appropriate. Crystallized rose ice cream with pear compôte, rubbery white and passable brown chocolate mousse concluded our meal. The wine list included many French and German wines, merely four Italians and a sufficient number of half bottles and wines by the glass, the cheapest costing 12 DM.

PARKHOTEL BURGGRAF

49545, Meesenhof 7
(0 54 82) 4 25, Fax 61 25

43, **S** 120/215, **D** 160/240, **APP** 198/360, **½P** +44, **P** +64

This modern hotel, located on a hill above the picturesque town, offers adequate comfort at reasonable prices.

TEGERNSEE Bayern

Miesbach 21 - Bad Tölz 22

DER LEEBERGHOF 15/20

83684, Ellinger Str. 10
(0 80 22) 39 66/7, Fax 17 20 res.

Closed Monday, closed for lunch Tuesday through Friday, mid-January through mid-February. Tables d'hôte: 65/78L, 88/99D, à la carte: 42/79

On a nice day, you can be happy just sitting on the terrace and looking at the beautiful Egern bay. But we were demanding about Markus Bischoff's cuisine as well, and we weren't disappointed. His sure sense of taste allows side dishes to complement rather than overwhelm the essential ingredients. And if your wishes run contrary to the courses he suggests, he'll even come out of his kitchen and talk to you about it. We were impressed: Even amid the hubbub of a full house, he managed to give priority to creating harmonious taste sensations. We had a finely balanced salad of sweetbreads and green asparagus; excellent anglerfish medallions with glazed Belgian endives and radicchio; lovely bouillabaisse with turbot, John Dory, salmon, shrimps and whitefish; passable rabbit leg with chanterelles, creamed Savoy cabbage and gnocchi; and finally, pineapple soufflé with coconut ice cream. The service is pleasant, and the wines are reasonably priced.

TEMPLIN Brandenburg

Prenzlau 30 - Oranienburg 63

FÄHRKRUG 12/20

17268, Fährkrug 1
(0 39 87) 4 80, Fax 4 81 11 res.

Tables d'hôte: 30, à la carte:18/74

We're glad to report that the cuisine finally measures up to the otherwise high standards of this modern, pleasant country hotel. Simple, hearty fare is on offer here. Delicious king prawns in white wine, fried pike-perch fillets and a well-seasoned salmon tartare stand out among the mainly meat courses on the menu. We had fried potatoes and fresh salad with our beer cutlet, and cèpes and rice with spicy beef cubes. The homemade hollandaise sauce did much to save a dry turkey breast. Customers who want a homemade dessert instead of brand-name ice cream should try the Armen Ritter.The wine cellar stocks only regional wines.

FÄHRKRUG

17268, Fährkrug 1
(0 39 87) 4 80, Fax 4 81 11

39, **S** 135/175, **D** 190,
APP 265/325, **½P** +20, **P** +40

The Uckermark, with its many lakes and beautiful forests, needed this hotel. The homey rooms are comfortable, and all face the lake. You can stroll through an idyllic landscape and participate in excursions. Rooms for seminars. Breakfast: 15 DM.

TETTNANG — Baden-Württ

Friedrichshafen 10 - Ravensburg 13

LANDGASTHOF RITTER

88069, Ortsteil Laimnau
Ritterstr. 5
(0 75 43) 55 30

Closed for lunch every day except Sunday, closed Monday, à la carte: 20/38

Our knight (Ritter) has thrown off his shining gourmet armor. Instead of sweetbreads and foie gras, the new owner offers amusing little regional specialties to go with Tettnanger beer and simple wines. The prices are low enough for whole families. Swabian ravioli with savory stuffing in all variations were served with hearty sauces. Fresh salads, scampi fried in dough, whitefish breaded with hazelnuts, and all sorts of beef and pork dishes made up the plain bourgeois repertoire. The service was amiable, and the ambience of this historic country inn makes it recommendable, even though it doesn't cater to gourmet tastes any more.

TEUPITZ — Brandenburg

Königs Wusterhausen 22 - Lübbenau 42

SCHLOSSHOTEL TEUPITZ 14/20

15755, Kirchstr. 8
(03 37 62) 4 76 00, Fax 4 76 55

P

Closed 1—14 January. Tables d'hôte: 35L, 40D, à la carte: 31/59

Half the kitchen crew of the Berlin Hilton works here and brings fresh impetus to the cuisine behind the medieval castle walls. Under the new management, a biergarten has been added to the hotel restaurant, the service has become more professional, and the menu (changed every two weeks) is one of the big gourmet attractions in Brandenburg. Roy Augustin's creative team has made creamy sauces lighter and expertly prepares fish and meat. On our last visit, the repertoire included smoked piglet leg with homemade dumplings, lovely fried duck's breast with lightly creamed Savoy cabbage, pike, pike-perch, eel or sea trout from Teupitz served with flavorful saffron sauce, and a succulent catfish from the Havel drowned in tomato and caper sauce. For dessert we recommend fresh figs with delicious mascarpone cream, nuts and honey. The wine list has definitely improved.

SCHLOSSHOTEL TEUPITZ

15755, Kirchstr. 8
(03 37 62) 4 76 00, Fax 4 76 55

38, **S** 65/160, **APP** 185/205,
Closed 1—14 January

This hotel offers an idyllic refuge just an hour's drive from the center of Berlin. Located on a peninsula on Lake Teupitz, this complex combines the ruins of a medieval castle with modern buildings. Some rooms do not have their own bathrooms. Sauna, table tennis, skittle alley. The house has its own pier for water sports and transfer service to the Berlin airports. Breakfast: 15 DM.

THOLEY Saarland

Saarbrücken 37 - Trier 56

HOTELLERIE HUBERTUS 16/20

66636, Metzer Str. 1
(0 68 53) 9 10 30, Fax 3 06 01 res.

Closed for dinner Sunday, closed Monday, closed for lunch Thursday, 1 week at the end of the Saarl. summer school holiday. Tables d'hôte: 75/98L, 78/140D, à la carte: 58/96

The low ceiling of the restaurant is meant to suggest a vaulted cellar, and ingenious lighting and exquisite floral decorations create a comfortable, elegant ambience. With creativity and expertise, Josef Hubertus prepares choice dishes and presents them decoratively on beautiful china. After a delicious appetizer—a light, lovely salmon terrine with a little salad bouquet—we started our prix-fixe (for 105 DM) with excellent foie gras. It was followed by fried liver with truffled sauce, mousse covered with pumpernickel crumbs, pâté, and a slice of brioche with pâté and jelly. We also liked the tasty turbot served with scampi and spinach, followed by delicious saddle of lamb in a (slightly oversalted) crust of herbs with red wine sauce. The combination of warm, light semolina soufflé with tangy orange ragout, praline ice cream, fresh black raspberries and flavorful passion fruit purée was fantastic.The service is attentive, and the choice of wines is comprehensive, intelligent and expensive: a 1987 Phélan-Ségur for 115 DM, a 1988 Baron de L for 145 DM, and a 1984 Grillet for 175 DM.

HOTELLERIE HUBERTUS

66636, Metzer Str. 1
(0 68 53) 9 10 30, Fax 3 06 01

9 rooms, **S** 60/90, **D** 110/160

This extravagantly renovated hotel is located on a main thoroughfare, but the landscape surrounding it is idyllic and the swimming pool magnificent. Good breakfast.

SCHAUENBURG 13/20

66636, Am Schaumberg 19
(0 68 53) 25 88, Fax 3 01 46 res.

Closed Tuesday, closed for lunch Wednesday, 23 January through 8 February. Tables d'hôte: 37/93, à la carte: 27/74

Customers can choose between the plain, rustic *gaststube* or the elegant new salon here. The comprehensive menu offers small, simple dishes for wandering holidaymakers and fine cuisine for gourmets. Our tasty food was served in generous portions. Salmon consommé with fresh salmon cubes had an obvious fish taste, but the pike-perch with spinach and delicately seasoned sauce with herbs was delicious. The orange sauce harmonized perfectly with the breast of guinea chicken, home-made noodles and glazed vegetables. Sweet nougat parfait with tart rhubarb mousse and fresh strawberries was a perfect combination. The wine list offers a choice of 208 wines, with emphasis on Moselle, Rhône, Burgundy, Beaujolais and Bordeaux.

TIEFENBRONN Bad.-Württ.

Pforzheim 15 - Stuttgart 40

BAUERNSTUBEN 14/20

75233, Louis-Pfeffinger-Platz
(0 72 34) 85 35 res.

Closed Tuesday, 14 days at Carnival. Tables d'hôte: 42, à la carte: 24/82

Customers quickly feel at home in this quaint, homey *gaststube* with its old pictures, antiques and tiled stove, and appreciate the perfect, personal service. We could see Jürgen Ludewig cooking in the kitchen—and he must have had fun watching us enjoy his dishes. We had salmon in the form of a tartare with herb sauce, mildly marinated with mustard sauce and smoked with fresh horseradish, accompanied by fresh salad and prawns with garlic dip. After a delicate beef consommé with well-seasoned spinach and cheese quenelles, we had pike-perch dumplings with beurre blanc, spinach and chopped tomato, slightly overdone fillet of veal with mushroom sauce, and Grandma's icecream *guglhupf* with tropical fruit.

LE GOURMET 14/20

4 km north in 71299
Wimsheim Austr. 48
(0 72 34) 4 13 23

Closed Monday, 1 week early January, 2 weeks during the Bad.-Württ. summer school holiday. Tables d'hôte: 35L, 50/115D, à la carte: 37/73

If the ambience weren't so stiffly formal here, we'd enjoy Frank Widmann's amazingly tasty creations even more. We liked delicious fried chicken livers with fresh salad and walnut dressing, fabulous saffron cream soup with diced salmon, a somewhat overdone slice of salmon with chervil butter, a perfect combination of brill, sole and lobster with saffron and Chablis sauce, hare fillet with cassis sauce, a great entrecôte with well-seasoned shallot sauce, homemade honey parfait with wonderful cherry zabaglione, and a fabulous dessert platter with everything from mousse to a plum terrine coated with marzipan. The wine list is small but international and includes good wines by the glass. The service is pleasant and sometimes a little shy.

HÄCKERMÜHLE 16/20

75233, Im Würmtal 5
(0 72 34) 42 46, 61 11/1, Fax 57 69

Closed for lunch Monday and Tuesday, closed 2—16 January. Tables d'hôte: 42/140L, 62/160D, à la carte: 41/95

It was love at first sight. After delicious fresh bread, we had wonderful quail's breast with beans and quail's egg, superb pigeon breast with balsamic vinegar, sliced truffles and lamb's lettuce, turbot, mussels in their shells, and lobster. Our lamb noisettes, garnished with lightly fried herbs and served with Savoy cabbage and black bread dumplings that tasted of smoked ham and nuts, were heavenly. The artistic Georg Häcker arranged a colorful sensation on our plate: brown mousse, raspberry sorbet, almond ice cream, plum ice cream in a puff pastry, punch terrine, rhubarb parfait with puréed fruit and mango slices, peeled grapes and an "fan" of strawberries.Inge Häcker's service staff is discreet but pleasant and recommends wines at moderate prices. Customers can spend the night in beautiful, quiet hotel rooms. Lovely terrace with a view of the valley.

OCHSEN-POST 14/20

75233, Franz-Josef-Gall-Str. 13
(0 72 34) 80 30, Fax 55 54

Closed Sunday and Monday. Tables d'hôte: 52/120, à la carte: 38/83

Helmut Weis likes to prepare hearty regional dishes that rely on what he buys at the market or what's in season. We enjoyed terrine of hare with cider jelly, fish terrine with watercress mousse, excellent sautéed scampi with a wonderful saffron sauce, saddle of venison, and a fabulous dessert platter including delicate parfaits, three kinds of sorbet, brown mousse, and tropical fruits with vanilla sauce.The service takes pains to please in the beautiful old dining rooms and in the elegant wintergarten. The comprehensive wine list has adjusted prices to the noble ambience of this luxurious country inn, but the wines by the glass are offered at reasonable prices.

OCHSEN-POST

75233, Franz-Josef-Gall-Str. 13
(0 72 34) 80 30, Fax 55 54

19 rooms, **S** 89/110, **D** 135/160

Charming, rustic rooms with geraniums on the balconies and plenty of fine old timbering.

TIMMENDORFER STRAND

Lübeck 20 - Eutin 22

KLEINES LANDHAUS 15/20

23669, Strandallee 73
(0 45 03) 6 08 59, Fax 6 08 60

Closed for lunch from Tuesday through Friday, closed Monday, 2—30 January. Tables d'hôte: 79/114L, 104/134D, à la carte: 59/96

This little slate-roofed outbuilding of the Landhaus Carstens houses an elegant restaurant that seats 30. With its open fireplace, exquisite furniture, elegantly laid tables and pleasant colors, it is the perfect setting for Manfred Führer's light, fresh cuisine. The menu does not promise flamboyant creations, just convincingly good cooking: scampi and lobster terrine with basil cream, caviar and salad, marinated asparagus with herb vinaigrette and delicately dressed veal haunch, succulent John Dory with an interesting tomato sauce and leeks, and ice cream with mangoes and black raspberry purée. The service is pleasant and unobtrusive. The large wine list concentrates on renowned wines and fat expense accounts (a 1988 Romanée Conti is priced at 1,660 DM!) and offers only a few reasonably priced red Bordeaux, ignoring the Italian alternatives.

MARITIM GOLF & SPORTHOTEL

23669, An der Waldkapelle 26
(0 45 03) 60 70, Fax 29 96

203 rooms, **S** 153/297, **D** 216/428, **APP** 570/780, **½P** +40, **P** +70

The hotel building is an appalling eyesore, but once inside, you will enjoy the friendly service and the high standards of comfort. Comprehensive range of recreational and sports facilities.

ORANGERIE IN MARTIM SEEHOTEL 16/20

23669, Strandallee 73b
(0 45 03) 60 55 55, Fax 29 32 res.

Closed for lunch everyday except Sunday, closed Monday, February. Tables d'hôte: 48/83L, 104/133D, à la carte: 53/106

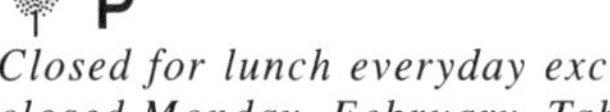

Chef Lutz Niemann's young, ambitious kitchen crew has carte blanche to realize its lofty goals. A promising appetizer of paprika mousse, veal aspic and courgettes started one Orangerie prix-fixe. Other offerings: Holstein quail (terrine, leg and breast), calf's tail ravioli with crayfish and fried basil, John Dory with onion confit and puréed parsley (exquisitely simple and sensational: 17/20!), tender lamb with heavenly mild garlic sauce and ratatouille, a gigantic choice of perfectly ripened cheeses, light cheese dumpling with rhubarb compôte and praline ice cream, and refreshing apple soup with Calvados sorbet. The desserts might not quite reach the standard of the first courses and main courses, but Niemann is well on the way to his third toque. The service is as perfect as the teamwork in the kitchen. The wine list is impressive, and the wines are served at the right temperature in lovely glasses.

MARITIM SEEHOTEL

23669, Strandallee 73b
(0 45 03) 60 50, Fax 29 32

241 rooms, **S** 173/297, **D** 246/438, **½P** +40, **P** +68

The best place to be in Timmendorfer Strand is inside this hotel—it is the only way you can avoid looking at this concrete blot on a beautiful landscape. Comfortable rooms and pleasant service.

TÖGING AM INN Bayern

Mühldorf 3 - Altötting 7

SCHOSSBÖCK'S RESTAURANT 13/20

84513, Dortmunderstr. 2
(0 86 31) 9 94 29, fax 9 52 68 res.

Closed Tuesday, 6—27 June. Tables d'hôte: 39/77, à la carte: 25/65

You'll find this new suburb just before you leave Töging for Landshut, and it isn't a particularly pretty sight. Schossböck's ambitious cuisine, however, makes eating here a pleasure. We enjoyed the asparagus salad with fried polenta, as well as the pike and pike-perch terrine with scampi and salad. For the main course, the same kinds of fish are available - prepared, for instance, as fillets poached in turnip broth or served in a crust of potatoes. You can even have shark fillet in zucchini crust, but we preferred trout and char from the nearby Aubach. After that, we had medallions and lamb sausages with blood pudding as well as a somewhat overdone veal *tafelspitz* with capers and vegetables. More than 350 wines are offered at very moderate prices. The choice of champagnes and liqueurs is extensive.

BAD TÖLZ — Bayern

Rosenheim 52 - München 54

JODQUELLENHOF 

83646, Ludwigstr. 13-15
(0 80 41) 50 90, Fax 50 94 41

81 , **S** 155/220, **D** 260/440,
½P +45, **P** +70

The hotel, which caters to holiday visitors and spa guests, is famous for its superb swimming-pool complex. Restaurant.

ZUM ALTEN FÄHRHAUS 14/20 

83646, An der Isarlust 1
(0 80 41) 60 30, Fax 7 22 70

 P

Closed Monday and Tuesday. Tables d'hôte: 85/130, à la carte: 45/78, No Credit Cards

First of all, you have to find the place. If you're coming from Munich, take the road that turns right off the state road at the end of Tölz. At the end of a winding road, you'll find this restaurant, located on the bank of the Isar river. The shaded terrace is wonderfully quiet, and the old-fashioned and rustic dining room is comfortable.The prices are high, but so is the quality of the food: marinated salmon with avocado and potato pancakes, a lovely pike-perch fillet with savory white-wine sauce, fish lasagna and fried anglerfish with zucchini sauce. We also enjoyed the fillet of venison, the breast of guinea fowl with sherry sauce and the leek tart. Our unusual dessert consisted of rhubarb, apricot and cream strudel.The wines by the glass are good but not cheap. The service is pleasant.

TRIBERG — Baden-Württemberg

Villingen 25 - Freiburg 49

PARKHOTEL WEHRLE 14/20

78094, Gartenstr. 24
(0 77 22) 8 60 20, Fax 86 02 90

 P

Tables d'hôte: 49/59L, 79/97D, à la carte: 38/90

A new chef has pulled things together here by combining tradition with progress. The abbreviated lunch menu is a Wehrle tradition: a single prix-fixe consisting of three or four courses and a few alternatives, none of it of great interest to gourmets. The evening repertoire ranges from delicate duck liver mousse to a country salad with bacon and croutons, rabbit saddle with a crust of pine needle tips, and a bombastic ice-cream cake. The service has improved. The wine list is large and highly priced.

PARKHOTEL WEHRLE 

78094, Gartenstr. 24
(0 77 22) 8 60 20, Fax 86 02 90

54 , **S** 85/150, **D** 145/260,
APP 360/490, **½P** +30/60

A few generations of buildings are combined here—from the early 17th century to the present day—to form a homogeneous hotel complex surrounded by trees in the center of Triberg. Indoor and outdoor pools. Breakfast: 19 DM.

TRIER — Rheinland-Pfalz

Saarbrücken 90 - Frankfurt 180

DORINT HOTEL TRIER 

54292, Ports-Nigra-Platz 1
(06 51) 2 70 10, Fax 2 70 11 70

P

106 , **S** 202/222, **D** 300/320,
½P +37, **P** +62

On the edge of the pedestrian district and facing the famous Porta Nigra, this hotel offers spacious, comfortable, functional rooms. Casino on the premises.

PFEFFERMÜHLE 

54292, Zurlaubener Ufer 76
(06 51) 2 61 33 res.

P

Tables d'hôte: 55L, 80D, 115, à la carte: 56/92

The Pfeffermühle is indisputably the best restaurant in Trier, but owner Siegbert Walde could use a little more serious competition. His cooking is almost perfect, but it has never been particularly creative. We also detected signs of carelessness: The lobster was too cold, the potato gratin totally tasteless, and the veal medallions were dry. Nevertheless, the mildly seasoned maties salad, perfectly done sweetbread, delicate asparagus with hollandaise sauce and artistically designed desserts (with a chocolate clef as the chef's signature on every dish) justify our rating.The service is as pleasant, competent and helpful as ever. Wines from Moselle, Saar, Ruwer and Bordeaux are available.

TROISDORF NRW

Bonn 18 - Köln 23

FORSTHAUS-TELEGRAPH 13/20

53842, Mauspfad 3
(0 22 41) 7 66 49, Fax 7 04 94 res.

Closed for lunch Saturday, closed for dinner Sunday, closed Monday, 1—23 January. Tables d'hôte: 69, à la carte: 46/82

This new restaurant is located in a former telegraph station in the middle of a forest, and for some years now this country inn has enjoyed a reputation as a place where fine cuisine is served. Thomas Pilger's menu is well-balanced, and his high-quality products are carefully and creatively prepared. In every dish, customers taste Pilger's love of southern France, as in a delicious Mediterranean fish soup or in a pair of scallops in their shells served with leeks. With the perfectly cooked duck's breast in a balsamic vinegar sauce, only one thing was missing: a spoon. The desserts, whether mousses, fruit purées or parfaits, were creative and tasty. The service was uncomplicated and pleasant, and the wines were fairly priced.

TÜBINGEN Baden-Württ.

Stuttgart 40 - Ulm 140

DOMIZIL

72072, Wöhrdstr. 5-9
(0 70 71) 13 90, Fax 13 92 50

P

80, **S** 110/145, **D** 160/205,
APP 230/290

You have a picture-postcard view of the Old Town and the Neckar from the exquisite rooms of this hotel. Fitness center, solarium. Restaurant.

KRONE

72072, Uhlandstr. 1
(0 70 71) 3 10 36 , Fax 3 87 18

P

48, **S** 135/185, **D** 180/300,
APP 320/380, **1/2P** +30, **P** +55
Closed 22—30 December

A hotel with a long and proud tradition, the Krone offers its customers every modern amenity behind its Renaissance facade. Ample breakfast.

WALDHORN 17/20

72074, Ortsteil Bebenhausen
Schönbuchstr. 49
(0 70 71) 6 12 70, Fax 61 05 81 res.

Closed Monday, Tuesday, 2 weeks during the Bad.-Württ., summer school holiday. Tables d'hôte: 75/160, à la carte: 56/104, No Credit Cards

The Schillings offer their customers genuine hospitality and the very best haute cuisine. We indulged in warm sole and lobster terrine with caviar cream, perfect foie gras (in many forms: coated with cornmeal, fried and served with Pomerol; raw and marinated; or as a parfait with truffles and tasty port wine jelly), vegetable risotto with shrimps, and turbot in a crust of herbs with an exquisite tomato butter. We enjoyed lamb saddle from the salt meadows with green and white beans and yellow peppers, as well as venison fillet with a savory sauce, celery soufflé, Brussels sprouts and homemade spaetzle. A fantastic gratin of curd with oranges and Grand-Marnier concluded our meal. Our favorite regional dishes were Swabian ravioli, boiled beef with horseradish sauce, and a delicious ice cream *guglhupf* with sour cream and berries. The choice of wines is impressive and includes some rarities from the region as well as from Bordeaux and Burgundy, sufficient half bottles and many wines by the glass at reasonable prices. Applause for expert cooking and pleasant service.

TUTZING Bayern

Starnberg 15 - Weilheim 15

FORSTHAUS ILKAHÖHE 15/20 

82324, Oberzeismering
(0 81 58) 82 42, Fax 28 66 res.

Closed Monday (from May through September open for dinner), Tuesday, 23 December through mid-January, à la carte: 27/75, No Credit Cards

From the Ilkahöhe, you have a fabulous view of lake Starnberg and the Alps. While the superb view attracts hordes of tourists, the outstanding cuisine of the Forsthaus draws almost as many connoisseurs to this restaurant. This is one reason you should always reserve a table—unless, of course, you prefer serving yourself in the biergarten. Customers sit almost cheek-to-cheek in the comfortable but small dining room and on the terrace, but nobody seems to mind—as long as the food is this good. The menu is small and the food always correctly prepared. The prices have even gone down, so we could enjoy our Swiss ham and light ricotta terrine without qualms. We liked the succulent rabbit, tender bass fillet and *rote Grütze*, a cold soup of delicious berries.The wine list offers pleasing wines by the glass and carefully selected wines by the bottle; prices range from average to high. The service is quick and attentive.

HÄRING'S WIRTSCHAFT IM MIDGARDHAUS 11/20

82327, Midgardstr. 3
(0 81 58) 12 16, Fax 79 35 res.

 P

Closed Monday during the winter, November, à la carte: 24/89

Chef Franz Häring charges high prices for carelessly prepared food. The service is mostly pleasant, often supercilious, and sometimes incredibly incompetent. Why do people like this place and pay good money for food of little value without complaining? Maybe it's because of the nice view, or because the house newsletter prints the juiciest gossip about Munich's "in" crowd. We've seen people positively enjoy sitting on the dark, damp terrace facing the lake, wrapped in shocking-pink blankets, while listening to the bigwigs and celebrities of Munich partying it up in the banquet room inside.

BAD ÜBERKINGEN BW

Göppingen 20 - Ulm 37

ALTES PFARRHAUS 15/20

73337, Badstr. 2
(0 73 31) 6 30 36, Fax 6 30 30

 P

Closed 9—22 January. Tables d'hôte: 49L, 80/98D, à la carte: 40/77. Tables d'hôte with wine: 60/160

We're glad to see that Rainer Jöckle's cuisine has reverted to old traditions. We've always enjoyed dining in this 400-year-old rectory, with its carefully renovated and historic rooms.Delicious breads accompanied the appetizers—mushroom tartare with asparagus salad and warm galantine of guinea fowl. After this opulent welcome, we had an excellent warm lobster with a ragout of trout caviar and cucumber. The consommé with lamb fillets and sliced thyme bouchées was redolent of fresh morels. The breast of Bresse pigeon, baked in strudel and served with sweet and sour kohlrabi, was impeccably prepared. The iced pralines with the millefeuille of nougat mousse as well as the fresh strawberries and raspberries in wafer-thin leaves of white and brown chocolate were superb. The service is perfectly competent, and the excellent wine list offers many half-bottles and a number of wines by the glass at impressively low prices.

ALTES PFARRHAUS 

73337, Badstr. 2
(0 73 31) 6 30 36, Fax 6 30 30

  P

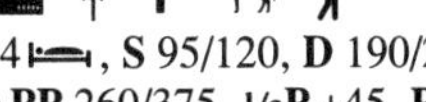

14, **S** 95/120, **D** 190/205, **APP** 260/375, **½P** +45, **P** +85

Closed 9-22 January

This golf hotel, a pretty, old half-timbered ensemble, offers lessons for beginners and advanced golfers.

BAD-HOTEL 

73337, Badstr. 12
(0 73 31) 30 20, Fax 3 02 20

P

20, **S** 130/140, **D** 190/220,
APP 260, **1/2P** +40, **P** +60
Closed 24—30 December

The 400-year-old half-timbered buildings here have been painstakingly renovated. The hotel, located on the main street of the town, offers spacious, extravagantly furnished rooms. Free use of the spa pool nearby. Restaurant. Breakfast: 18 DM.

ÜBERLINGEN Bad.-Württ.

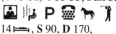

Friedrichshafen 32 - Basel 165

HECHT 13/20

88662, Münsterstr. 8
(0 75 51) 6 33 33, Fax 33 10 res.

P

Closed for dinner Sunday, closed Monday, 10—30 January. Tables d'hôte: 31/85, à la carte: 28/67

Chef Erich Surdmann has heeded his critics and now serves respectable portions of carefully prepared, high-quality food at acceptable prices. The menu includes traditional dishes like pike dumplings, chicken and beef roulade, which compete with Asian-inspired creations prepared in Surdmann's wok and with prosaic classics like fillet of suckling lamb in horseradish crust with smoked garlic and celery purée, and homemade foie gras consommé with a puff-pastry hood à la Paul Bocuse. Not everything is perfect, however: our carpaccio was too sour, the caviar too salty, and a sorbet was lumpy. But our ox cheek slices with a salad of asparagus and fresh sprouts were flawless, and fish dishes were precisely done, tasty and light. The service is adequate, and the wine list emphasizes wines from France and Baden.

HECHT

88662, Münsterstr. 8
(0 75 51) 6 33 33, Fax 33 10

14, **S** 90, **D** 170,
1/2P +35, **P** +70
Closed 10-30 January

This hotel's brochure rapturously extols its "romantic accommodations." There may be something to it, but the cramped bathrooms and the church clock that strikes the hour all night might soon put an end to romance. A choice of 10 special teas makes breakfast an adventure.

JOHANNITER KREUZ 13/20 

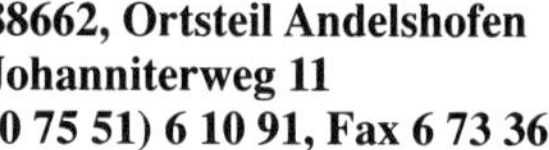

88662, Ortsteil Andelshofen
Johanniterweg 11
(0 75 51) 6 10 91, Fax 6 73 36

Closed Monday, closed for lunch Tuesday. Tables d'hôte: 88, à la carte: 42/69

Johanniter monks used to feed hungry wayfarers here in the 17th century. Today, Egon and Jutta Liebig pamper their gourmet customers in an elegant wintergarten, and their regular customers in the more rustic grill room with open fireplace. Homemade spaetzle and fish from the lake belong to the repertoire, but mostly the menu offers what would have been called nouvelle cuisine a while ago. Hungry customers would do better to order generous portions of steak à la carte, and leave gourmets to rave about perch roulade with salad and leg of suckling lamb with mint noodles. The highlights of our gourmet prix-fixe were excellent stuffed morels in lovely chive cream sauce, anglerfish medallions with mild garlic sauce, rabbit saddle with kidneys and green asparagus, and heavenly cheese soufflé with rhubarb mousse and puréed strawberries. In spite of a few snags, the ambitious modern Johanniter is trying for higher honors. The wine list emphasizes regional wines and offers a fantastic choice of wines by the glass.

JOHANNITER KREUZ 

88662, Ortsteil Andelshofen
Johanniterweg 11
(0 75 51) 6 10 91, Fax 6 73 36

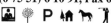

P

26, **S** 92/155, **D** 160/260,
1/2P +43

This recently restored, 300-year-old country inn with its new annex is located in a quiet, rural setting and has been tastefully and comfortably redecorated. Ambitious restaurant.

PARKHOTEL ST. LEONHARD

88662, Obere St. Leonhardstr. 71
(0 75 51) 80 81 00, Fax 80 85 31

145, **S** 127/185, **D** 226/270,
APP 300/380, **1/2P** +35, **P** +60

Located on a hillside high above the old town, the hotel is surrounded by open countryside and offers a magnificent view across the lake to Mainau Island and the Swiss Alps. Beauty farm, ample breakfast buffet. Restaurant.

SEEGARTEN

88662, Seepromenade 7
(0 75 51) 6 34 98, Fax 39 81

21, **S** 90/120, **D** 160/230,
1/2P +32, **P** +44
Closed 1 December through 15 February

As the name implies, staying here is like living in a garden bordering a lake, with the lapping of the waves against the shore to send you to sleep. Cordial hospitality and comfort.

ULM Baden-Württ.

Stuttgart 85 - München 130

ST. MARTIN'S SCHLÖSSLE 14/20

89079, Stadtteil Wiblingen
Schloßstr. 12
(07 31) 4 67 56, Fax 48 18 39 res.

Closed Monday, closed for lunch Tuesday. Tables d'hôte: 59L, 89/115D, à la carte: 47/85

The dishes we ordered during our last visit reminded us of the grand cuisine that was once served here. Karlheinz Schuhmair served beef carpaccio and nicely fried duck's liver with pine kernels and a tasty little salad, as well as ravioli filled with sweetbread ragout, served with a delicate morel sauce and surrounded by fresh white asparagus tips. Our fillet of sole was overdone, however, and the oyster mushrooms served with the leg of lamb had been fried much too long. The wine cellar is expertly stocked, and the French, German and Italian wines are reasonably priced. There's a good choice of half bottles and wines by the glass as well. The service rests on the shoulders of a single waitress, who does her work with such charm and enthusiasm that we gladly overlooked some shortcomings.

SCHLOSS-CAFÉ-RESTAURANT 14/20

12 km southwest in
89155, Erbach Am Schloßberg 1
(07 31) 69 54

Closed Monday, closed for lunch Tuesday, 2—24 January, 1—15 August. Tables d'hôte: 85D, à la carte: 41/70

The Lanza family offers genuine hospitality in the spacious salons of their beautifully situated Renaissance castle. The service is personal and attentive here, and everything is done to make guests feel at home. We love to sit in the garden under old chestnut trees.Tasty little salads were skillfully dressed and served with goat-cheese croutons. The cream of asparagus soup was delicious, as were the perfectly done anglerfish medallions with a wonderfully harmonious, interesting, light and tangy rhubarb sauce. Our veal kidneys—served with Dijon mustard sauce and excellent corn cakes, sugar peas and stuffed tomato—were superb, and the rhubarb sherbet with fresh strawberries, dates and kiwis was simply exquisite.The wine list emphasizes Alsacian wines, but it also offers German and European vintages at reasonable prices. There are many bottles that cost less than 30 Deutsche marks, and the choice of liqueurs is large.

ULMER SPATZ

89073, Münsterplatz 27
(07 31) 6 80 81/2, Fax 6 02 19 25

40 (35), **S** 90/110, **D** 140/160,
1/2P +25

After an undisturbed night's rest you wake up within sight of the famous cathedral to a good breakfast—all for relatively low prices. Restaurant with Swabian specialities.

ZUR FORELLE 12/20

89073, Fischergasse 25
(07 31) 6 39 24, Fax 6 98 69 res.

Closed Sunday. Tables d'hôte: 75, à la carte: 26/74

From these low-ceilinged old rooms on the bank of the Blau, customers look out at the weeping willows and towers of the nearby cathedral and it is clear that eating can be more than a culinary experience. We were sorry to see that the furniture and wood paneling were not better cared for. The international wine list is adequate. The choice of wines by the glass is large but expensive.Many regional dishes have been taken off the menu, but fans still find typical Swabian ravioli, *Gaisburger Marsch* and the famous onion roast.

USEDOM Meckl.-Vorp.

Rostock 118 / cars via Wolgast

FORSTHAUS LANGENBERG 13/20

in 17429, Seebad Bansin
(03 83 78) 3 21 11/1, Fax 2 91 02

Closed 2—31 January, à la carte: 23/47

This island in the Baltic has a lot to offer: beautiful, wild forests, romantic sea spas with lovely beaches and attractive restaurants. The elegant Forsthaus Langenberg is one of the best. The menu offers fried eel, pike-perch, trout fillet, and halibut with light béarnaise sauce, the traditional *labskaus* (a sailor's dish of salted pork and herring), a large choice of game in season and homemade desserts. Small but nice choice of wines.

FORSTHAUS LANGENBERG

in 17429, Seebad Bansin
(03 83 78) 3 21 11/1, Fax 2 91 02

36 rooms, **S** 80/100, **D** 145/165,
APP 195/270, **1/2P** +20, **P** +40

Closed 2—31 January, à la carte: 23/47, No Credit Cards

This hotel, located two kilometers from the beach in a beech woods, offers a lovely view of the surrounding natural beauties. The rooms are adequate. The hotel has its own private beach and yacht.

HOTEL DIANA

in 17424, Seebad Heringsdorf
Delbrückstr. 14
(03 83 78) 3 19 52, Fax 3 19 53

11 rooms, **S** 90/200, **D** 120/250,
APP 150/440

This fabulous villa, built in the last century, has become an exclusive refuge for holiday guests. Its picturesque location and extravagant architecture are the perfect setting for the luxurious ambience. The hotel has its own beach, fitness center and solarium. Opulent breakfast. Airport shuttle to Heringsdorf. Reduced rates for children (free under six years).

OSTEEHOTEL AHLBECK

in 17419, Seebad Ahlbeck
Dünenstr. 41
(03 83 78) 2 82 21, Fax 2 82 22

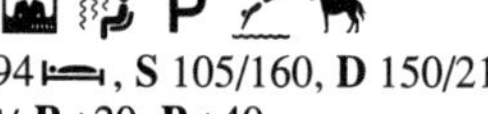

94 rooms, **S** 105/160, **D** 150/210,
1/2P +20, **P** +40

Closed January and February

Located on the ocean promenade, the completely renovated hotel offers comfortable, modern rooms, half of them with a view of the sea. Restaurant, bar, wintergarten with café. Breakfast: 15 DM.

RISTORANTE MANTOVANI 13/20

in 17429, Seebad Bansi
Seestr. 55-56
(03 83 78) 3 20 83

A la carte: 26/50

With its drab, block-like exterior and its rustic pizzeria ambience full of kitschy decorations inside, this restaurant isn't particularly inviting. But we were pleasantly surprised at the great variety of typical Italian dishes and a small but interesting choice of regional specialities, like leg of venison with chestnuts and young pork with croquettes. We liked our fruity tomato soup and found our seafood salad (unparalleled in quality even by many Italian colleagues in Western Germany) to be positively superb! The service is pleasant and charming, but the wine list desperately needs attention.

STRANDHOTEL 

in 17429, Seebad Bansin
Bergstr. 30
(03 83 78) 2 23 42, Fax 2 23 43

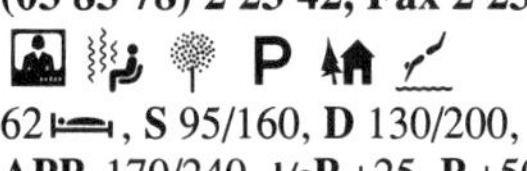

62, **S** 95/160, **D** 130/200,
APP 170/240, **1/2P** +25, **P** +50

This renovated hotel is located in direct proximity to the nudist colony and offers comfortable rooms, skittle alley, hairdresser, solarium, restaurant, café and pub.

WALD UND SEE 12/20

in 17424, Seebad Heringsdorf
Rudolf-Breitscheid-Str. 8
(03 83 78) 3 14 16/7, Fax 2 25 11

Closed 12—26 December. Tables d'hôte: 25L, à la carte: 28/55

Comfortable Nordic elegance in tasteful colors characterizes the ambience of this hotel restaurant. A cleverly compiled menu makes a can opener in the kitchen almost superfluous. Fresh regional products are prepared here, and, apart from a few snags, the cooking is dependably good. We liked fish soup and cod fillet, whereas our pike-perch was a bit overdone. Friendly and obliging service and a wine list that needs to be improved.

WALD UND SEE 

in 17429, Seebad Heringsdorf
Rudolf-Breitscheid-Str. 8
(03 83 78) 3 14 16/7, Fax 2 25 11

43, **S** 90/120, **D** 130/160,
APP 230/250, **1/2P** +25

With true Danish flair, this hotel about half a kilometer from the beach offers attractively furnished rooms, whirlpool, solarium, café and bar.

VERDEN Niedersachsen

Bremen 37 - Hannover 86

PADES RESTAURANT 15/20 

27283, Anita-Augspurg-Platz 7
(0 42 31) 30 60 res.

Closed for lunch, closed Sunday, 1—12 January, 3 weeks during the Nieders. summer school holiday. Tables d'hôte: 52/84D, à la carte: 47/83

Wolfgang Pade is known as one of the most ingenious cooks in northern Germany. Daring ideas are turned into delicious gourmet dishes. The new "fishburger" of marinated salmon with sweet arugula salad and cheese offered an unusual new taste sensation—not exactly to our taste, however. We liked our calf's cheeks with potato salad and artichokes and a Fontina cheese with a cap of potatoes much better. The combination of lemon sole fillets with herbs and semolina is another example of Pade's unconventional cuisine, which some conservative customers may term frivolous. The service is personal and amiable as well as competent. The prices are still surprisingly reasonable. Good espresso.

VERL Nordrhein-Westfalen

Gütersloh 8 - Bielefeld 17

BÜDEL'S RESTAURANT 16/20 

33415, Kirchplatz 5
(0 52 46) 79 70, Fax 8 14 03 res.

Closed Sunday, Monday, 2 weeks during the NRW Easter holiday, 3 weeks during the NRW summer school holiday. Tables d'hôte: 45L, 82/118D, à la carte: 40/85

This carefully restored half-timbered building at the foot of the village church has a promising future. Bernhard Büdel guarantees quality with amazingly dependable, first-class cooking. His rather conservative customers in Gütersloh appreciate consistency above all else. Büdel won't ever dare to remove from the menu his lobster soup with pike-perch quenelles, his marinated salmon with dill and mustard sauce, or his lamb saddle with a crust of herbs. This clever immigrant from Hessen cleverly caters to the parsimony of his conservative clientele and keeps them coming for low-priced (30 DM) lunch prix-fixes. Büdel also wins over the gourmets with his wonderfully light rabbit terrine, his pike-perch soufflé with chive sauce, Savoy cabbage and glazed potatoes, beef fillet tips with oyster mushrooms, and strawberry mousse in puff pastry. The service is competent and the choice of wines includes good, affordable wines from Germany, France and Italy.

VERSMOLD NRW

Bielefeld 32 - Münster 42

ALTE SCHENKE 16/20

in 33775, Bockhorst
Bockhorst 3 (by the church)
(0 54 23) 85 97, Fax 4 23 50 res.

 P

Closed for lunch every day except Sunday, closed Monday, Tuesday (from January through March and July through October), 2 weeks during the NRW summer school holiday. Tables d'hôte: 38/49L, 60/80D, à la carte: 33/63

In times when gourmet cooks groan about the recession that keeps customers away and profits low, Emil Sickendiek can just lean back and relax. His regional cuisine draws throngs of regular customers and ensures popularity. But Sickendiek does more than preserve old traditions. With his perfectionist chef, Erhard Wendt, he carefully but consistently incorporates new ideas. We'd bitterly miss his sweet and sour pig's ears with potatoes, his potato and sauerkraut soups and best of beef if they weren't on the menu! But we appreciated the new taste sensations: a pike-perch terrine with leeks or a turkey terrine with shallot marmalade. We loved our confused heap of spinach beets, potatoes and buckwheat noodles with fried pike-perch, and our ribeye steak in red wine sauce with glazed onions and vegetable ravioli. Sickendiek offers German wines exclusively, but only the best, along with some new discoveries. Some wines are served by the glass. For those who like beer, Grandma Sickendiek serves it from the tap. The service is nimble and friendly. There are three comfortable rooms for customers who want to stay the night, providing they book far ahead. One of the best hotel breakfasts in Germany is served here. Single rooms: 85 DM, Doubles 160 DM.

VIERNHEIM Hessen

Ludwigshafen 20 - Frankfurt 78

PFEFFER UND SALZ 13/20

68519, Neunlache 8-10
(0 62 04) 7 70 33

P

Closed for lunch Saturday, closed Sunday and holidays. Tables d'hôte: 125, à la carte: 43/106

It was love at first sight—the garden was beautiful, the ambience rustic and comfortable, the restaurant full, the service pleasant. A closer look dampened our spirits: The prices on the menu and wine list were exorbitantly high. What is on the menu today has been on it for years. This indicates continuity but can also mean lack of imagination. The crawfish were really fresh, but the warm salad served with them was just a pile of soggy leaves. The foie gras was disappointing. The extravagantly expensive sole stuffed with lobster was well prepared, as was the saddle of venison with chanterelles. The staff tired toward the end of our meal, neglecting to fill our water glasses and bringing us coffee and the bill only after repeated reminders.

VILLINGENDORF Bad.-Württ.

Rottweil 5 - Oberndorf 14

GASTHOF LINDE 13/20

78667, Rottweiler Str. 3
(07 41) 3 18 43, Fax 3 41 81 res.

 P

Closed for dinner Monday, closed Tuesday, 2—15 January, first 2 weeks of the Bad.-Württ. summer school holiday. Tables d'hôte: 35/90, à la carte: 32/69

This unpretentious *gasthof* is nice and comfortable, the service is pleasant, and the international choice of wines moderately priced. Our little gourmet prix-fixe included a wonderfully fresh terrine of regional fish with a lovely mustard and dill sauce as appetizer, salad of asparagus and Belgian endives with tomato vinaigrette and (slightly overdone) chicken livers, generously garnished clear oxtail soup, very tasty salmon wrapped in pancake strips and served on a bed of leeks, tenderly fried lamb saddle with a thick crust of herbs, and a delicious dessert platter with ice-cream cake covered with marzipan, strawberry ice cream, chocolate mousse, and marinated and fresh fruit.

VÖHRENBACH Baden-Württ.

Furtwangen 8 - Donaueschingen 21

GASTHOF ZUM ENGEL 13/20

78147, Schützenstr. 2
(0 77 27) 70 52 res.

Closed Monday, closed for lunch Tuesday, 7—17 January, 3 weeks during the Bad.-Württ. summer school holiday. Tables d'hôte: 75, à la carte: 30/85

The trout filled with delicate fish mousse was delicious and the French farmyard chicken with lovely spinach ravioli and mushrooms tasty—exactly what we had expected from such a highly praised establishment. Most of the hearty, savory regional specialities remain on the menu year after year, so we were especially grateful to find some new dishes. We liked our leek and potato soup with crispy bacon, salmon terrine, fresh salad with white fish fillet, and exquisite dessert creations. The service in this 200-year-old *gasthof* is pleasant, and the wine list is intelligently stocked with a little bit of the best of everything.

VÖLKLINGEN Saarland

Saarbrücken 10 - Saarlouis 12

ORANGERIE IN PARKHOTEL VÖLKLINGEN 17/20

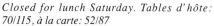

66333, Kühlweinstr. 70
(0 68 98) 2 70 54/6, Fax 2 36 55 res.

Closed for lunch Saturday. Tables d'hôte: 70/115, à la carte: 52/87

Perfect service, stylish decor, elegantly set tables and a nice view of the extensive park from the windows of this restaurant make this the perfect setting to enjoy the imaginative, artistic creations that come out of Reiner Starck's kitchen. Our appetizer, for example, consisted of shrimp: a tiny shrimp quiche, shrimp tartare seasoned with dill, and shrimp salad with a small salad bouquet. The "best of rabbit" was a perfect combination: rabbit liver with subtly delicate shallot sauce, terrine of rabbit liver, and an excellent rabbit roulade with liver pâté, garnished with avocado, along with a salad dressed with raspberry vinaigrette. His creamy Riesling sauce harmonized perfectly with the appetizing roulade of salmon and turbot with spinach and diced tomato. The succulent and tender veal fillet and sweetbreads with a creamy truffled sauce and a savory port wine sauce was superb. The dessert variations were fantastic, too. The service is so competent and quick that we hardly had time to take a deep breath between courses. Customers appreciate the well-stocked wine list, which includes a remarkable choice of half bottles and wines by the glass.

VOGTSBURG Baden-Württ.

Breisach 10 - Freiburg 25

GASTHAUS ZUM KAISERSTUHL 12/20

in 79235, Niederrotweil
Niederrotweil 5
(0 76 62) 2 37 res.

Closed for dinner Sunday, closed Monday, 10-20 March, 5—30 August. Tables d'hôte: 45L, à la carte: 27/67, No Credit Cards

Lothar Koch (means cook) is famous in the region for his love of fresh herbs. His plain *gaststube* has only six tables, which are usually reserved far in advance. Customers like his savory regional cooking with a strong emphasis on fresh and sometimes rare herbs, so strong that they sometimes overpower the main ingredient. But besides many ingeniously seasoned creations, we always enjoy typical regional dishes and the fresh bread that is served with them. Some dishes, however, seem more improvised than planned, like a tender kid roast coated in herbs that tasted like oregano. The service is nice, and the wines from the Kaiserstuhl wonderful.

SCHWARZER ADLER 15/20

79235, Oberbergen
Badbergsstr. 23
(0 76 62) 7 15, Fax 7 19 res.

Closed Wednesday, Thursday, closed mid-January through mid-February. Tables d'hôte: 85/150, à la carte: 41/96

Lothar Koch (means cook) is famous in the region for his love of fresh herbs. His plain *gaststube* has only six tables, which are usually reserved far in advance. Customers like his savory regional cooking with a strong emphasis on fresh and sometimes rare herbs, so strong that they sometimes overpower the main ingredient. But besides many ingeniously seasoned creations, we always enjoy typical regional dishes and the fresh bread that is served with them. Some dishes, however, seem more improvised than planned, like a tender kid roast coated in herbs that tasted like oregano. The service is nice, and the wines from the Kaiserstuhl wonderful.

STEINBUCK 14/20

79235, Bischoffingen
Steinbuckstr. 20
(0 76 62) 7 71, Fax 60 79 res.

 P

Closed Tuesday, closed for lunch Wednesday, closed 15 January through the end of February. Tables d'hôte: 48L, 78D, à la carte: 29/69, No Credit Cards

Our careful first rating doesn't express it, but we're confident this Steinbuck will soon meet or beat the competition of the Schwarzer Adler. Thomas Wernet has enough ambition to try, at any rate. And he has an ace up his sleeve: his rustically renovated hotel restaurant is located in the middle of a beautiful vineyard. Apropos: the restaurant stocks only local wines; they're good enough, but they have their limits. We liked the food served by the charming service crew. Highlights of our prix-fixe with wine for 98 DM included pike-perch from the Rhine cooked just right in light morel cream sauce, and a carpaccio of ox fillet marinated with walnut oil and homemade vinegar. Applause for the chef for the hearty and refined regional dishes, like ox tongue salad, warm headcheese, wine soup with saffron and foie gras, vine-smoked trout fillet, veal saddle with kidneys and sweetbreads, and venison ragout with cherries and red currants.

ZUR KRONE

79235, Achkarren 15
Schloßbergstr. 15
(0 76 62) 7 42, 69 19, Fax 87 15

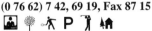

P

22, **S** 65/75, **D** 95/105,
½P +24, **P** +36
No Credit Cards

The rooms are plain but completely quiet. Restaurant, café and Schlossberg-Grotto.

WADERSLOH NRW

Lippstadt 12 - Beckum 14

BOMKE 16/20

59329, Kirchplatz 7
(0 25 23) 13 01, Fax 13 66 res.

 P

Closed for lunch Saturday, closed Thursday, 3 weeks during the NRW summer school holiday. Tables d'hôte: 29/45L, 49/96D, à la carte: 27/90

The nondescript gray house opposite the neo-Gothic church is easy to find, even if it doesn't look like one of the best addresses for true Westphalian hospitality. But the countrified elegance of the dining rooms creates the perfect setting for Jens Bomke's ambitious cuisine. He serves simple regional delicacies like homemade sausages, schnitzel or pork headcheese with fried potatoes and salads, and doesn't charge more than 15 DM for each dish. For more demanding gourmets, he sets off a fireworks of culinary sensations. After a daring but unsuccessful appetizer of fried scallops in buttermilk, we enjoyed excellent sweetbread salad with crayfish and watercress savarin, fillet of rabbit with chanterelles and chive cream, outstanding bass with ginger, shallots and parsley, kid with artichokes and sage sauce, and a fig tart with baby pineapple and champagne ice cream. Bomke's taste sensations are subtle rather than flamboyant; this is haute cuisine without pretensions. The plastic-covered wine list (including 370 different wines) and the repetitive background music were irritations in this setting. The quality of the food deserved better. The prices, however, were as welcoming as our hosts and the charming service crew. Ten of the champagnes cost less than 100 DM.

BOMKE 

59329, Kirchplatz 7
(0 25 23) 13 01, Fax 13 66

21, **S** 79/105, **D** 140/175,
APP 125/210, **½P** +40, **P** +62

The drab gray facade is misleading; it hides a tastefully decorated reception area and modern rooms, which are quieter toward the back of the house. There is no swimming pool, but there is a much-used skittle alley in the house and four golf courses nearby.

WAGING AM SEE Bayern

Traunstein 12 - Laufen 22

EICHENHOF

83329, Angerpoint 1
(0 86 81) 40 30, Fax 4 03 25

34, **S** 90/135, **D** 190/240,
APP 240/320, **1/2P** +30, **P** +60

This hotel offers spacious rooms furnished country-style, with large bathrooms and balconies. Water sports, beauty farm, driving range and tennis courts. Bike and boat rental. Restaurant.

KURHAUSSTÜBERL 19/20

83329, Am See
(0 86 81) 40 09 12, Fax 40 09 25 res.

Closed for lunch (except for Sunday from October through May), closed Monday, Tuesday, mid-January through the end of February. Tables d'hôte: 119L, 149D, à la carte: 70/97

While other gourmet cooks are trying to think of ways to make their cheap appetizers look more expensive, Alfons Schuhbeck throws two large handfuls of chestnuts into a pan and offers the fresh-roasted nuts to his customers. His menu doesn't offer creative fireworks, but we found some new dishes, like the rustic Bavarian sausages boiled with onions or marinated and fried with sauerkraut as refined gourmet courses. On our next visit, we'll have to order the pea soup flavored with mint again, as well as smoked fish with vegetables, and ox shoulder braised in red wine with apples and potato purée. The wine list has been cleverly revised. Hopefully, the service will revert from the stiff hotel formality it exhibited on our last visit to its original cheerful and sprightly attitude.

WALDMOHR Rheinl.-Pf.

Homburg 8 - Kaiserslautern 35

LE MARMITON 12/20

66914, Am Mühlweiher 1
(0 63 73) 91 56

Closed Monday, closed for lunch Tuesday. Tables d'hôte: 48/85, à la carte: 35/70

This restaurant has its merits. It is located near the autobahn between Saarbrücken and Mannheim, its terrace offers an enchanting view of a little lake, the service is pleasant and competent, the food is straightforward and good, and the prices are reasonable. The cooking isn't particularly imaginative, and the menu offers the same dishes year after year. Chef Louis Bour has brought a bit of his native Alsace to Waldmohr. He offers quiche lorraine, lamb's-lettuce with croutons, asparagus salad with (deep frozen?) shrimps, fresh John Dory with champagne sauce, excellent duck's breast and simple but good desserts. In his choice of wines, Bour shows a preference for his native France, and he offers half-bottles and wines by the glass.

WALLERFANGEN Saarland

Saarlouis 4

VILLA FAYENCE 17/20

66798, Hauptstr. 12
(0 68 31) 6 20 66, Fax 6 20 68 res.

Closed for lunch Saturday, closed Monday. Tables d'hôte: 52L, 79D, 130, à la carte: 41/89

This historic villa is hidden among ancient trees in a beautiful park, and the restaurant is housed in a lovely wintergarten. In summer, customers can dine in the park itself. The appetizing menu offers imaginative combinations that are artistically arranged and decorated. We enjoyed oyster parfait with green asparagus and diced tomatoes, piquant paprika soup with julienne and eggplant ravioli, salmon strudel with creamy Riesling sauce decorated with small shallots braised in red wine, a generous helping of saddle of rabbit stuffed with liver and served with a savory mustard sauce and fabulous side dishes, and, finally, sponge-cake soufflé with tangy orange compôte and exquisite vanilla ice cream. The choice of wines limits itself to good and very good wineries, and offers a large number of wines by the glass, half-bottles and liqueurs. The prices are fair; a few examples: a 1982 Yquem, 450 DM; 1976 Mouton-Rothschild, 450 DM, 1988 Vosne-Romanée (Jean Gros), 115 DM.

VILLA FAYENCE

66798, Hauptstr. 12
(0 68 31) 6 20 66, Fax 6 20 68

4, **S** 155, **D** 240,
APP 220/300

Three rooms and a suite in a villa surrounded by a park: restaurant customers who want to stay the night couldn't wish for more.

WALTROP NRW

Lünen 11 - Dortmund 12

RÔTISSERIE STROMBERG 14/20

45731, Dortmunder Str. 5
(0 23 09) 42 28 res.

Closed Monday. Tables d'hôte: 45/70, à la carte: 38/80

If you like sound, reliable cooking more than exciting experimental cuisine, you've come to the right place. The Strombergs preserve tradition and don't scare their staid, conservative clientele with culinary extravagance. At the most, they risk a little flirt with international fine cuisine. The faint touch of Italy in some dishes, for instance, caused a sensation in Waltrop: bass fillet was fried in sesame seeds and honey, breast of poularde was coated with potato crust, and delicious gratins were offered as first courses (lobster, scallops and asparagus) and as dessert (red fruit with coconut parfait). The Stromberg family refines traditional regional recipes and offers, for example, red lentils with glazed apple slices and savory blood pudding. We also recommend the fresh fish courses and opulent desserts. The choice of wines is small due to slight demand, and the service is amiable and obliging.

WANGEN/ALLGÄU BW

Lindau 20 - Ravensburg 24

ALTE POST

88239, Postplatz 2
(0 75 22) 9 75 60, Fax 2 26 04

19, **S** 100/125, **D** 180/200,
APP 220

With five centuries of proud history behind it, this traditional inn now offers comfort and a range of modern amenities. Restaurant.

VIERK'S PRIVAT-HOTEL 13/20

88239, Bahnhofsplatz 1
(0 75 22) 8 00 61, Fax 2 24 82

Closed Sunday, closed for lunch Monday. Tables d'hôte: 30L, 70D, à la carte: 34/70

It is very irritating when a kitchen doesn't even meet its own standards. Our cream of asparagus soup was tasty enough, but the consommé of *tafelspitz* with ravioli was insipid. Our entrecôte must have died of old age, and the thin and bitter asparagus with the pike-perch fillet was accompanied by congealed hollandaise sauce. The wine list offers a good choice of wines. The service takes pains to please, but what can they do when the kitchen takes pains to irritate and the owner so successfully hides her charms?

VIERK'S PRIVAT-HOTEL

88239, Bahnhofsplatz 1
(0 75 22) 8 00 61, Fax 2 24 82

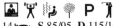

14, **S** 85/95, **D** 115/160

The atmosphere of this small, comfortable house is very private. Most rooms are renovated and are comfortably and pleasantly furnished. The breakfast isn't opulent, but good. Solarium.

The prices quoted in this guide are those whick we were given by the restaurants and hotels concerned. Increases in prices are beyond our control.

WARBURG Nordrhein-Westfalen

Kassel 35 - Paderborn 41

ALT-WARBURG 14/20

34414, Kalandstr. 11
(0 56 41) 42 11, Fax 6 09 10 res.

P

Closed Sunday, Monday, 1—16 January, 1—10 August. Tables d'hôte: 40/72, à la carte: 48/81

Hermann Fritz from Freiburg, who took over this picturesque framework house, cooks the best food between Kassel and Paderborn. Modestly and without much fuss, he serves light, tasty creations that reveal his love for Baden and Italy. We had a piquant, colorful choice of antipasti, then pike dumplings with lobster sauce, snail ragout with Champagne noodles, followed by saddle of lamb with artichokes. A delicious mint and ginger parfait concluded our meal. We recommend following the chef's meal suggestions, however, since ordering dishes à la carte can be very expensive. We liked the creamy potato and leek soup (served refreshingly cold in summer) and the wafer-thin sliced tongue with tangy tomato vinaigrette, but the anglerfish with onion was strangely tasteless. The wine list is comprehensive and the service agreeable.

ALT-WARBURG

34414, Kalandstr. 11
(0 56 41) 42 11, Fax 6 09 10 res.

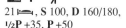

21, **S** 100, **D** 160/180,
½P +35, **P** +50

The individually furnished and comfortable rooms are on the second floor of this lovely house built in 1510.

WARENDORF NRW

Münster 26 - Osnabrück 41

HOTEL IM ENGEL 14/20

48231, Brünebrede 35-37
(0 25 81) 9 30 20, Fax 6 27 26 res.

Closed for lunch Saturday, closed Thursday, 3 weeks in July. Tables d'hôte: 39/98, à la carte: 26/73

The choice of wines here is heavenly: connoisseurs find the best of everything, especially German white wines and red Bordeaux. Customers can trust to the advice of their host Werner Leve, who recommends good, moderately priced bottles, but also offers an impressive number of wines by the glass, which alone make a detour to this hotel worthwhile. The cuisine was more down-to-earth: the kitchen made good plain fare without creative flights of fancy —just carefully prepared, straightforward regional specialities. The service is pleasant and competent.

HOTEL IM ENGEL

48231, Brünebrede 35-37
(0 25 81) 9 30 20, Fax 6 27 26

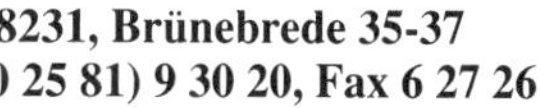

22, **S** 95, **D** 145,
APP 150/250, **½P** +25, **P** +50

This hotel was established 350 years ago and has been run by the same family for three centuries. The rooms (but not all bathrooms) are generously proportioned (numbers 124, 126 and 216 are very spacious). Whirlpool.

WARNEMÜNDE Meckl.-Vorp.

Rostock 14

HANSE HOTEL

18119, Parkstr. 51
(03 81) 54 50, Fax 5 45 30 06

74, **S** 125/170, **D** 180/220,
APP 265/380, **½P** +28

The buildings located on the sea promenade have been completely renovated. The rooms are tasteful and modern. Opulent breakfast buffet.

HOTEL NEPTUN

18119, Seestr. 19
(03 81) 77 70, Fax 5 40 23

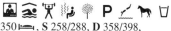

350, **S** 258/288, **D** 358/398,
APP from 690, **½P** +38, **P** +68

All the rooms in this luxuriously renovated hotel have balconies and overlook the ocean. The beach is a few meters away. Fitness center, bar and discotheque.

SEEMANNSKRUG IN HOTEL NEPTUN 11/20

18119, Seestr. 19
(03 81) 77 77 61, Fax 5 40 23

P

A la carte: 31/63

A hotel of this caliber should be able to afford a better restaurant. Uncomfortable wooden chairs covered with imitation leather in a rustic and definitely not elegant ambience were as uninviting as the familiar menu, which has survived the years without significant changes. The more elegant hotel restaurant, the Koralle, seems to be used only as a breakfast or brunch room. The comprehensive menu offers enough choice and features fish, but everything we ordered took a long time to get to the table. We had nicely done fish and salad without dressing, cream of lobster soup that lacked substance, and noncommittal side dishes that did nothing to enhance our poached turbot fillet. A large service crew didn't mean the service was efficient. The wine list is large and features German wines and even some exotics.

WARNEM INNER DEEL 12/20

18119, Am Strom 75
(03 81) 5 41 06

A la carte: 20/52

This restaurant is packed every evening, regardless of the season: a compliment to its cooking. The menu is varied and features all kinds of seafood, but offers some meat and game courses, too. All dishes were creatively and carefully prepared and excellently cooked. Salmon and sole roulade with delicious Champagne sauce were cooked just right, the leek cannelloni stuffed with fish and served with lobster sauce was ingenious, and the fresh scallops with saffron sauce were fabulous. Reasonable choice of wines and service that is charming even when the house is full.

WARSTEIN NRW

Meschede 13 - Soest 28

DOMSCHÄNKE 13/20

59581, Dieplohstr. 12
(0 29 02) 25 59, Fax 8 84 09 res.

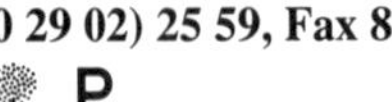

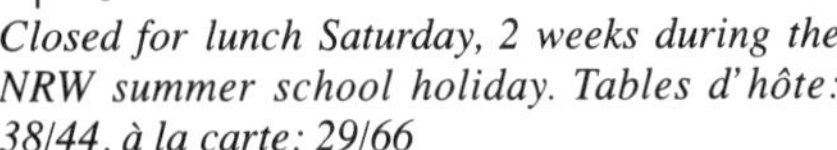

Closed for lunch Saturday, 2 weeks during the NRW summer school holiday. Tables d'hôte: 38/44, à la carte: 29/66

Among the many establishments run by the local brewery, this is the most representative. The restaurant is located in the original founder's manor house, built in 1753. The ambience is characterized by Hanseatic distinction, underlined by strictly correct and stylish service (the maître d'hôtel dressed in black, the waiters in red vests). We enjoyed the light cream of curry soup with ham, the delicious venison ragout with cherry sauce and the plum terrine with almond yogurt, although the opulent helpings brought us close to surrender. We also recommend the excellent fish gratins. At noon, a reduced choice of dishes is offered.

GASTHOF CRAMER

59581, Hirschberg
(0 29 02) 20 41, Fax 20 19

Closed Tuesday, closed for lunch Wednesday, 3 weeks during the NRW summer school holiday. Tables d'hôte: 22/34, à la carte: 26/49, No Credit Cards

In a natural preserve a few kilometers farther south, Warstein's brewery runs another restaurant located in a beautiful old half-timbered country inn. Tourists and natives meet in the traditionally furnished *gaststube* with its scrubbed wooden tables and rustic bar. More elegant tables for dining are set in the back near the big stove. At noon, the menu lists only low-priced prix-fixes with salmon, breast of ox, Königsberg dumplings or sauerbraten. The choice is larger in the evening, though your best bet is always the abundant game here. We also liked our broccoli soup and leg of lamb with tarragon sauce and leeks. In addition to some good wines by the glass, you can enjoy draft beer. The restaurant has a few hotel rooms.

WARTENBERG Bayern

Moosburg 10 - München 50

BRÜNDLHOF 17/20

85456, Badstr. 44
(0 87 62) 35 53 res.

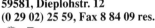

Closed Tuesday, Wednesday, 1—11 January, 21 August though 14 September. Tables d'hôte: 62/130, à la carte: 42/78

This country restaurant is only 20 kilometers away from the Munich airport, in the green belt of Wartenberg. The dining rooms are comfortable, and the warm wooden decor and terra-cotta floors create an agreeable atmosphere. The service is friendly and attentive. The quality of Jean-Luc Garnier's light and graciously simple French cuisine has improved enormously. The mushroom terrine with savory truffle sauce was captivating. It was followed by excellently fried scampi with salad, a delicious carpaccio of scallops with red pepper, and finely boned and delicately fried quail with potato gratin. The fricassee of kid with sugar peas, carrots and homemade noodles was a rare pleasure. Desserts and pastries are of the finest quality; these include black raspberry gratin, lemon soufflé, marinated oranges, crepes, tarts and sherbets. The choice of cheese was excellent.The wine list grows larger every year. In addition to young and light wines from France, there are also some aged Bordeaux and Burgundys at moderate prices. The Bründlhof offers simple guest rooms as well.

WASSENBERG NRW

Erkelenz 14 - Roermond 18

BURG WASSENBERG 12/20

41849, Kirchstr. 17
(0 24 32) 40 44/5, Fax 2 01 91 res.

Tables d'hôte: 50/60, 80/120D, à la carte: 47/94

The lords and ladies of this castle learn quickly. They have cleared away the racy (and anachronistic) paintings in the medieval dining hall and are hard at work trying to raise the quality of the cooking to match their high prices. A few tips: the mousse platter for 17.50 DM should consist of more than two teardrops of brown and white mousse with a few pieces of fruit, and the cream of asparagus soup shouldn't taste only of the red beets decoratively laid on top of it. The cook apparently has a laissez-faire attitude: our stuffed quail's leg wasn't stuffed, and the balsamic vinegar was sadly lacking in flavor. The stuffed salmon increased our misgivings: the puff pastry crust surrounding it was factory-made. The service is slightly disorganized. The wine chests are well stocked, however.

LA MAIRIE 17/20

41849, Am Roßtor 1
(0 24 32) 51 30, Fax 40 92 res.

Closed for lunch every day excepy Sunday, closed Thursday, 2 weeks in July/August. Tables d'hôte: 99/119, à la carte: 57/83

The justice of the peace married many a couple in this former town hall. Today, they get married elsewhere, but they still return to La Mairie for their wedding celebrations. Wolfgang Eickes arranges banquets and wine tastings. The wine list already consists of two volumes and is being further enlarged with more Austrian and South African wines. A large choice of half bottles and a small but exclusive list of wines by the glass are in keeping with the high-quality cuisine.The menu has been condensed into two large prix-fixe meals, whose courses can be switched and changed, giving customers a large choice after all. For about 100 DM, customers can order a wonderful dinner that shows the scope of Eickes' cuisine. Supposedly rustic dishes, however, only seemed simple. We discovered haute cuisine behind such deceptively plain-sounding dishes as pig's cheeks with lentils, headcheese with capers and fried potatoes, potato and cucumber salad with fried blood pudding and baked apples, pike-perch and salmon with bacon and sliced potatoes, and bean stew with turbot and lobster. Whether he cooks rustically or more elegantly, each dish has a gourmet surprise, like *tafelspitz* aspic served with iced consommé and tomato chutney, a subtly seasoned curried pasta sheet under a mildly seasoned anglerfish, a lovely sweetish sauce with a taste of rutabagas with young wild boar saddle in puff pastry. We admit we're addicted to Eickes' desserts. Why can't every restaurant be as competent as this one?

WEGBERG Nordrhein-Westf.

Erkelenz 9 - Mönchengladbach 16

MOLZMÜHLE 12/20

41844, Rickelrath
Im Bollenberg 41
(0 24 34) 2 43 33, Fax 2 57 23 res.

Tables d'hôte: 25L, 49D, 89, à la carte: 29/66

The Schwalm-Nette nature preserve north of Erkelenz abounds with mills. The

Molzmühle is one of the oldest and most remarkable, but customers enjoy not only the romantic surroundings of this renovated old building but also the honest, straightforward and satisfying cooking. The menu offers the usual cuts of beef and veal, quail, duck, rabbit and lamb, plus a touch of Alsatian cuisine and some recipes borrowed from Grandma. Diners who aren't looking for gourmet sensations can have heartily seasoned and generously portioned food: nicely dressed salads, well-done vegetables, a delicious potato soup with smoked salmon, and a large platter of breaded fish. The service is attentive. The wine list is more interesting than the cuisine and features wines from Alsace and South Africa, as well as renowned wines from France. Comfortable hotel rooms are offered.

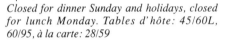

WEIDEN Bayern

Regensburg 85 - Nürnberg 98

L'ESCARGOT IN HOTEL EUROPA 13/20

92637, Frauenrichter Str. 173
(09 61) 2 50 51/3, Fax 6 15 62 res.

  P

Closed for dinner Sunday and holidays, closed for lunch Monday. Tables d'hôte: 45/60L, 60/95, à la carte: 28/59

Johannes Franz doesn't have an easy time of it: he has to cook for gourmets, bourgeois families who want their usual Sunday dinner and the nouveau riche, who want something hearty and lots of it. His menu offers a little something for every taste. Once the kitchen has understood what you want, everything actually tastes much better than our rating warrants at first sight. The ambience doesn't sweep customers off their feet, and neither does the wine list.

EUROPA

92637, Frauenrichter Str. 173
(09 61) 2 50 51/2/3, Fax 6 15 62

 P

26 🛏, **S** 65/95, **D** 120/180, **½P** +25, **P** +50

Individual furnishings in every room and loving attention to detail belie the functional impression the hotel exterior gives. Ample breakfast buffet.

WEIL AM RHEIN BW

Lörrach 4 - Basel 5

ZUM ADLER 16/20

79576, Hauptstr. 139
(0 76 21) 7 50 55, Fax 7 56 76 res.

Closed Sunday, Monday, early- to mid-January, early- to mid-August. Tables d'hôte: 48L, 98D, à la carte: 56/112

People in Baden usually raise a great outcry against modern experiments. Perhaps that is why they feel right at home in the comfortable, traditional Adler. They don't mind if the upholstery is worn thin, glasses are plain and cutlery looks secondhand. And instead of ordering expensive bottles from the wine list (prices only upon request), they order respectable, reasonably priced wines by the glass. The kitchen slips into a comfortable routine when the chef is "out." Our oxtail consommé was excellent, unlike the tasteless foie gras ravioli that garnished it. The turbot filled with smoked salmon probably swam an extra lap in the kitchen, whereas the grilled scallops with paprika and saffron were perfect. It didn't take long for the kitchen to realize that peeling peppers costs both time and effort, and our overdone saddle of lamb showed that the cooks still have a lot to learn about cooking times and temperatures. The cuisine here definitely doesn't deserve three toques, but, because we remember the good times we've had here, we'll lower the rating just one point for now. The service staff is either expert in the art of understatement or badly in need of training.

ZUM ADLER

79576, Hauptstr. 139
(0 76 21) 7 50 55, Fax 7 56 76

  P

23 🛏, **S** 110/150, **D** 130/250

One of the oldest inns in Germany, the Adler is famous for its nice little extras. The renovated, quiet rooms are tastefully furnished and equipped with largesse.

WEIMAR Thüringen

Erfurt 22 - Jena 21

CHRISTLICHES HOTEL AMALIENHOF

99423, Amalienstr. 2
(0 36 43) 54 90, Fax 54 91 10

  P

22, **S** 125/150, **D** 186/196, **APP** 160/250

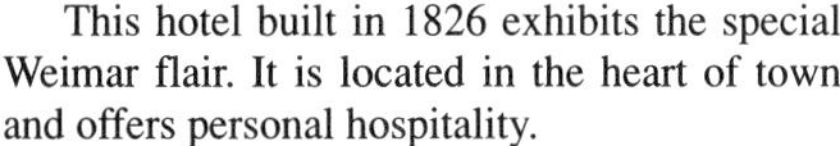

This hotel built in 1826 exhibits the special Weimar flair. It is located in the heart of town and offers personal hospitality.

ESPLANADE IN HOTEL WEIMAR HILTON 12/20

99425, Belvederer Allee 25
(0 36 43) 72 20, Fax 72 26 99

Tables d'hôte: 35/65L, 39/110D, à la carte: 27/58

The tables of the Esplanade and the adjacent Trattoria are set with festive elegance. We tried fried calf's liver strewn over a heap of summer salads, generously garnished beef consommé, grilled shrimp and scampi with a heavy butter sauce, tough veal schnitzel with tomatoes, ham and mushrooms, and a small choice of desserts. We couldn't figure out why we only got a canned pear and a maraschino cherry in a season when fresh fruit abounds and why nobody noticed the perpetually slamming doors to the kitchen. Another puzzle: why is a 4 DM parking fee charged with each meal? The choice of wines includes bottles from Germany, France and Italy, and none are cheap. The service is attentive, competently firm and friendly.

WEIMAR HILTON

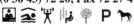

99425, Belvederer Allee 25
(0 36 43) 72 20, Fax 72 27 41

294, **S** 250/310, **D** 270/330, **APP** 580/1010

This hotel located on the Goethepark offers pleasantly furnished rooms, modern conference facilities, 24-hour room service, beauty treatments and hairdresser, solarium, massage and boutiques on the premises. Bar, restaurants.

RESTAURANT ANNA AMALIA IN HOTEL ELEPHANT 14/20

99423, Markt 19
(0 36 43) 80 20, Fax 6 53 10

Tables d'hôte: 40/50L, 50/90D, à la carte: 40/62

The new decor here includes marble floors, elegantly set tables, comfortable chairs, spaciously placed table, and 10 beautiful woodcuts by a renowned artist. We enjoyed a lovely salad, excellent potato gnocchi with fish ragout, delicious veal roulade filled with mozzarella and eggplant, good cheese with peeled and pitted grapes, and white chocolate mousse with raspberry compôte. The choice of wines is good, and the service has improved and is getting better.

ELEPHANTEN-KELLER 11/20

99423, Markt 19
(0 36 43) 80 20, Fax 6 53 10
A la carte: 16/41

This well-known cellar restaurant offers traditional fare. But not everything tasted as good as it sounded on the menu. Our "marinated slices of beef saddle with mustard cream and salads" turned out to be unmarinated, raw meat and dry salad leaves with cream and mustard seeds, and our rabbit leg in buttermilk sauce accompanied by creamed Savoy cabbage and potato gratin was overdone and stringy. This is a place where hungry people come for inexpensive meals.

HOTEL ELEPHANT

99423, Markt 19
(0 36 43) 80 20, Fax 6 53 10

102, **S** 190/210, **D** 260/380, **APP** 480, **½P** +30, **P** +60

This traditional 16th-century hotel is popular with businesspeople. For those in search of culture, there are guided tours of the city. Breakfast: 25 DM.

RUSSISCHER HOF 

99423, Goetheplatz 2
(0 36 43) 77 40, Fax 6 23 37
P

87 rooms, **S** 145/160, **D** 220/290,
APP 400, **½P** +20, **P** +40

Besides a spacious lobby, this lovely hotel offers restaurants, salon, bar and conference center. The rooms are quiet, and the service is very pleasant. Ample breakfast buffet.

ZUM WEISSEN SCHWAN 13/20 

99402, Am Frauenplan
(0 36 43) 6 17 15, Fax 20 25 75 res.

Tables d'hôte: 38/54L, 56/125D, à la carte: 23/69

When kings, queens, princes and politicians dine here (and there is enough TV coverage), Herbert Frauenberger exerts himself to please his customers. Our rating is an average of various impressions. The dishes Frauenberger cooks are worth 15/20 when he takes pains to please prominent customers or personal acquaintances. We've had lovely rabbit terrine with tongue and plums, marinated plaice with coriander and chili and delicious orange cream, cream of asparagus soup with poularde quenelles, fried king prawns with wild asparagus, quail with vegetables and dumplings, and rhubarb with vanilla ice cream. Everything was delicious! But if the chef thinks you're not important enough to bother about, everything is boring. The choice of wines includes Germany's finest and good bottles from Italy and France, all moderately priced, and a sufficient number of half bottles and wines by the glass.

WEINBÖHLA — Sachsen

Meißen 10 - Dresden 18

LAUBENHÖHE 14/20 

01689, Köhlerstr. 77
(03 52 43) 3 61 83
P

Closed Monday, 14—28 February. Tables d'hôte: 35/75, à la carte: 23/56

Even on a rainy day, this is a nice place to spend some time. Straightforward and down-to-earth dishes with a high standard of quality are offered. Our marinated asparagus with smoked fillet of poularde was delicious without being showy, and the clear consommé generously garnished with meat and poached quail's egg was savory and flavorful. A little less saffron would have underlined the flavor of the excellent anglerfish medallions more effectively, but our veal fillet with vegetables and potatoes seasoned with truffled oil was just perfect. The "Saxon pudding" we had was a fabulously light cream cheese soufflé with melted chocolate, rhubarb compôte and delicate vanilla sauce. In summer, customers can sit in a wonderful garden with a marvellous view of the Elbe river landscape. The service is pleasant. The wine list features German regional wines, a few Italian and French bottles at friendly prices, and a dozen or so wines by the glass.

WEINGARTEN — BW

Karlsruhe 16 - Heidelberg 46

WALK'SCHES HAUS 15/20

76356, Marktplatz 7
(0 72 44) 70 37 00, Fax 20 34 res.
 P

Closed for lunch Saturday and Monday, closed Sunday and holidays, 1—22 January. Tables d'hôte: 45L, 65/88D, à la carte: 39/88. Tables d'hôte with wine: 110

After some changes in management and with a talented young chef in the kitchen, things are looking up here. We enjoyed flavorful fried sweetbreads with ham, a not absolutely fresh turbot with kohlrabi crust, a first-class, fresh pike-perch with "scales" of potatoes, and venison saddle sausage with plums and red cabbage. The petits fours were lacking in refinement. The wine list made us blush: the prices for Burgundy and Bordeaux are exorbitant.

WEISSENSTADT — Bayern

Hof 28 - Bayreuth 36

EGERTAL 14/20

95159, Wunsiedler Str. 49
(0 92 53) 2 37, Fax 5 00

Closed for lunch from Monday to Friday, closed Tuesday, 3 weeks in January/February. Tables d'hôte: 45/98, à la carte: 39/75

Continuity often precludes creativity. Customers who prefer conservative cooking enjoy this restaurant, which offers well-known luxury products prepared in the classic way. The repertoire consists of sole, pike-perch, salmon, and noisettes and fillets of lamb, beef and veal. The kitchen's performance is technically perfect: fish and meat are impeccably prepared, the soups aren't too heavy, the sauces light enough, the desserts exemplary.The wine list is also reliable and includes well-known regions and famous names. The service is strangely aloof and familiar at the same time, the decor of the dining rooms nostalgic with a touch of kitsch.

WELCHENBERG Bayern

Deggendorf 13 - Straubing 20

LANDGASTHOF BUCHNER 14/20

94559, Freymannstr. 15
(0 99 62) 7 30, Fax 24 30 res.

 P

Closed Monday and Tuesday, Tables d'hôte: 65/85, à la carte: 34/71

In an old 16th-century brewery, Ingrid and Josef Achatz enthusiastically celebrate their new and light cuisine (at somewhat lowered prices). With competent charm, Josef Achatz advises his guests and suggests wonderful meals. We had cream soup with pike-perch ravioli and trout caviar as appetizers, followed by consommé with basil dumplings, mild maties tartare with quail's egg, and homemade noodles with flavorful morels. We appreciated Achatz's expertly prepared fish dishes, and we were surprised by how delicious sturgeon fillet with Savoy cabbage and horseradish sauce could be. The chef also served an excellent lamb saddle and succulent beef fillet in pastry crust. Waffles with cream cheese and fruit as well as coffee parfait with marinated figs were memorable desserts.The service was amiable, and we were glad to see that the wine list had grown. Achatz offers about 150 (mostly young) wines from Germany, France and Italy, as well as some remarkable Austrian vintages.

WERL Nordrh.-Westf.

Soest 13 - Dortmund 30

WIENER HOF IN PARKHOTEL 12/20

59457, Hammer Str. 1
(0 29 22) 26 33, Fax 64 48 res.

 P

Tables d'hôte: 46, à la carte: 35/76

The Austrian cook Wolfgang Farendla doesn't differentiate between first courses and main courses on his menu, but between meat and fish courses. He offers a little bit of everything for every taste: the menu ranges from Wachau ham tart to salmon ravioli and from Hamburgian fried fish to poularde breast with rosemary sauce. Farendla offers popular Austrian specialties as well, including *Palatschinken* (sweet dessert pancakes), veal schnitzel with flavorful potato salad, and *tafelspitz* in different versions (warm with horseradish, as aspic, salad and soup). Our generously portioned fish salad could have used a little more flavor from the balsamic vinegar it was supposed to be dressed with. The service is attentive. The informative wine list is as helpful as a sommelier would be.

WERNIGERODE Sachs.-Anh.

Braunlage 25 - Halberstadt 25

GOTHISCHES HAUS

38855, Am Markt 1
(0 39 43) 37 50, Fax 37 55 37

P

Tables d'hôte: 25/95, à la carte: 23/55

The historic ambience of this little restaurant near the beautiful town hall at the edge of the marketplace is unique: the oldest parts of the house were built 1400 years ago. The choice of wines is good and sufficient, and includes no great but many respectable wines by the glass from 6 DM to 8 DM. That was the positive aspect. The service isn't always competent and is often absent, and the kitchen seems to prepare many dishes far ahead.

GOTHISCHES HAUS

38855, Am Markt 1
(0 39 43) 37 50, Fax 37 55 37

P

118, **S** 140/155, **D** 190/245, **APP** 245/275, **1/2P** +25, **P** +50

The old, half-timbered original building offers a number of prettily renovated rooms; the new annex is more modern. Prices are high for rooms and apartments. Breakfast is adequate.

WERTHEIM Baden-Württ.

Würzburg 36 - Frankfurt 80

SCHWEIZER STUBEN 19.5/20

97877, Ortsteil Bettingen
Geiselbrunnweg 11
(0 93 42) 30 70, Fax 30 71 55 res.

 P

Closed for lunch, closed Tuesday, January. Tables d'hôte: 138/198, à la carte: 65/145

Even at the risk of boring our readers, we can't help but repeat our praises of Fritz Schilling's genius and expert craftsmanship. Together with owner Adalbert Schmitt, he celebrates Provençal cuisine with a Mediterranean touch. This not only sounds like sunny southern cuisine, but also looks and tastes like it. To get into the proper mood for this gourmet experience, customers can take a walk around the beautiful park before they enjoy their food on the lovely terrace with a view over sunflower fields and the Main river, or in the unobtrusively elegant restaurant inside. Everything on the menu is light yet substantial: cannelloni filled with salt codfish in spinach beet sauce, John Dory flavored with juniper berries and lemon sauce, Brittany lobster in Sauternes with fried asparagus, foie gras with Banyul cherries, artichoke soup with gruyère mousse and truffles, tomato mousseline with scampi and baked basil, guinea fowl suprême with white elderberry sauce, rack of lamb with Mediterranean vegetables, cherry soup with cheese soufflé, cream with candied citrus fruit, and coconut cream ice and a nougat pyramid with fig nectar. Schilling shows us all he's capable of and lets us taste all the imaginable flavors of his exquisite compositions, in which natural flavors always take precedence. The service supervised by Pedro Sandvoss, who also has the key to all of the treasures in the wine cellar, is perfect and charming.

SCHOBER 15/20

97877, Ortsteil Bettingen
Geiselbrunnweg 11
(0 93 42) 30 70, Fax 30 71 55

Closed Wednesday, Thursday, January. Tables d'hôte: 59/74, à la carte: 29/63

The kitchen staff in this comfortable country inn can't afford to take it easy, especially with the Schweizer Stuben and La Vigna next door. Another incentive for a high performance is the "culinary trilogy" offered to hotel guests who want to try all three restaurants. The Swiss bourgeois cooking here holds its own against Provençal gourmandise and Italian grandezza and achieves respectable success. The hit of the menu is the four course prix-fixe "A.S.," which consists of everything owner Adalbert Schmitt likes to eat himself, all purchased fresh at the marketplace fresh that very day. Trust his good taste, and he won't disappoint you. Neither will the wine list.

TAVERNA LA VIGNA 18/20

97877, Ortsteil Bettingen
Geiselbrunnweg 11
(0 93 42) 30 70, Fax 30 71 55

Closed Sunday, Monday, February. Tables d'hôte: 98, à la carte: 53/91

Hardly anyone has such instinctively good taste as Adalbert Schmitt. He's spent decades trying the best food the famous Italian regions have to offer and has brought his favorite dishes back with him to Wertheim. Along with his talented cook Christoph Johnen (who knows exactly how Schmitt's favorite Italian chef Cesare cooks), he serves his favorites to an enthusiastic clientele. In this the best Italian restaurant in Germany, we enjoyed tomato and bread salad with fried guinea chicken, salad of fried vegetables with octopus and stuffed squid, John Dory with Bottarga sauce and spinach beet gratin, braised farmyard duck with fried Savoy cabbage and polenta, goat cheese with Barolo onions and panettone cassata with orange salad. Unpretentious dishes on the menu turned into sensational cuisine on our plates. The wine cellar is in keeping with the cuisine's high quality.

SCHWEIZER STUBEN

97877, Ortsteil Bettingen
Geiselbrunnweg 11
(0 93 42) 30 70, Fax 30 71 55

33 rooms, **S** 225/345, **D** 275/395,
APP 465/990

Luxurious and distinguished, the Schweizer Stuben offers its guests the full range of comfort: comfortable rooms in the "hotel," luxurious one in the "villa," and pure noblesse in every detail in the "landhaus." Grandiose breakfast. The half board offer, which includes meals at one of the hotel's three restaurants, is very tempting. Tennis and driving range for golfers.

WERTHER Nordrhein-Westf.

Bielefeld 10

GASTHOF WÖHRMANN 14/20

33824, Alte Bielefelder Str. 24
(0 52 03) 9 70 90, Fax 50 40 res.

P

Closed for lunch, closed Sunday and holidays, 27 December through 10 January (except for New Years Eve), 9—25 April, 23 July through 8 August, 15—24 October. Tables d'hôte: 74/105, à la carte: 48/81

This ensemble consisting of hotel, restaurant, bistro and pub in an old Westphalian country inn is designed in a modern American style, inconspicuous perhaps in Santa Monica or West Palm Beach, but striking in Werther. The modern ambience is at least a more appropriate setting for the Asian cuisine we enjoyed here than for our umpteenth lamb in olive crust with sauce and vinaigrette. The hosts are charming and the wine cellar well-stocked. The enchantingly eccentric hotel offers individually furnished rooms with all modern amenities at reasonable prices.

WESEL Nordrhein-Westf.

Emmerich 39 - Düsseldorf 80

LIPPESCHLÖSSCHEN 12/20

46485, Hindenburgstr. 2
(02 81) 44 88 , Fax 47 33

Closed Tuesday, Tables d'hôte: 48/69, à la carte: 35/67.

Whether this building can be called a castle or not depends on the viewer's standards (and imagination). In any case, the river Lippe flows by the back of the house, and green meadows invite customers to take a stroll along the shore. After complete renovation, the restaurant has rejected a historic ambience in favor of a youthful, elegant atmosphere. A menu in French doesn't guarantee gourmet cooking, but our crayfish with spinach, soufflé of perch from Lake Victoria, and sliced duck's breast glazed with veal juices gave us an indication of just how well lords and ladies of the castle can eat here. The choice of wines is aristocratic, but the prices belong (thankfully) to a lower class: Where else would you get a bottle of Nicolas Feuillatte for 68 DM?

WALDHOTEL TANNENHÄUSCHEN

4 km north in Feldmark
46487, Am Tannenhäuschen 7
(02 81) 6 10 14, Fax 6 41 53

46 rooms, **S** 160/180, **D** 190/230,
APP 225/325, **1/2P** +68, **P** +90
Closed 24 and 25 December

This hotel is located far from the hue and cry of the city and is sometimes difficult to find: turn off the B 8/Emmericher Strasse into the Ackerstrasse. Impressive indoor pool and ambitious restaurant. The rooms are furnished in a traditional style that, at its worst, seems a bit kitschy.

WETZLAR Hessen

Gießen 15 - Limburg 42

BÖMISCH ECK

35578, Fischmarkt 4
(0 64 41) 4 66 46, Fax 7 33 52

Closed for lunch every day except Saturday, closed Sunday, during the Hessen summer school holiday, à la carte: 21/47, No Credit Cards

Manfred Tasch, a former star among the cooks of this region, is still successfully dedicated to genuine (and genuinely good) Hessian cooking in his comfortable and unpretentious *gasthaus*. Inhabitants of Wetzlar like it here and order generously garnished beef soup, sandwiches of smoked ham and fried eggs, liverwurst on homemade bread with radishes, or cutlets with sauerkraut. The menu also includes more substantial courses like savory loin of veal and more refined dishes like salmon strudel and seasonal specials. Customers drink Bohemian beer to go with their meal or a wine by the glass. Tasch has brought some of his best wines to this rustic restaurant and offers his customers a choice of good bottles if they ask for them.

HAUPTWACHE
35578, Fischmarkt 4
(0 64 41) 4 85 04 , Fax 7 33 52

P

A la carte: 18/38, No Credit Cards.

Fresh and crispy *rösti* are a hit in this (almost always) packed bistro on the Domplatz. While our host serves rösti in every conceivable way, we follow the daily suggestion on the blackboard, which is always appetizing and tasty, and sometimes imaginative and deserving of a toque. The service is relaxed and friendly, and you can always get something good and low-priced to eat and drink.

BÜRGERHOF
35578, Konrad-Adenauer-Promenade 20
(0 64 41) 90 30, Fax 90 31 00

P

62, **S** 98/125, **D** 160/80

Wetzlar's most picturesque hotel is also its most comfortable. One of the rooms on the first floor has the finest stucco ceiling found in this part of the country, and the Baroque staircase is a historic gem.

TAPFERES SCHNEIDERLEIN 14/20

35578, Garbenheimer Str. 20
(0 64 41) 4 25 51 res.

 P

Closed for lunch, closed Sunday, Monday, 2 weeks during the Hessen Christmas holiday, 3 weeks during the Hessen summer school holiday. Tables d'hôte: 54/98, à la carte: 31/69, No Credit Cards

This little tailor *(Schneiderlein)* is cutting back: the restaurant is now closed at noon, and offers a prix-fixe entitled "seven at one stroke" (from Grimm's fairytale) but consisting of only six courses that cater to less discriminating tastes. Even with a toned-down cuisine, however, the Schneiderlein is still the best restaurant in Wetzlar. We missed ingenious ideas and highly flavorful compositions and found Jürgen Schneider's creativity somewhat drowned in routine, but we liked our rabbit confit with mushrooms and sweet arugula salad, (lukewarm) bouillabaisse, excellent anglerfish with mediocre ravioli, and tender *tafelspitz* with chive sauce and overdone asparagus. Our last dessert—plums in red wine with sesame and caramel ice cream and a curd pudding—was superb!

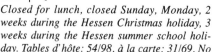

WIEFELSTEDE Nieders.
Bad Zwischenahn 9 - Oldenburg 13

HÖRNER KROOG 13/20
26215, Gristeder Str. 11
(0 44 02) 62 44, Fax 6 07 79 res.

 P

Closed for lunch, closed Tuesday, 1 week drunning the Nieders. Easter holiday, 2 weeks in August. Tables d'hôte: 55/80, à la carte: 35/69

This pleasant and tastefully decorated country restaurant offers good food and unusually attentive service. One of its big attractions is the low prices. Where else can you get, for less than 55 Deutsche marks, a four-course meal that can compete in quality with the offerings of bigger and more expensive restaurants? On our last visit, we had lovely maties tartare with well-dressed salads, foamy cream of sugar-pea soup, pigeon with a wonderful morel sauce and mint parfait for dessert. The beans, however, were a little salty, and the pigeon legs somewhat tough. The repertoire also includes fish soup with saffron and pike-perch ravioli, rabbit fillets filled with (raw!) onions and, alas, warmed-up spaghetti.Small but good and low-priced choice of wines.

WIESBADEN Hessen
Frankfurt 40 - Mannheim 90

BRASSERIE BRUNO 15/20
65183, Taunusstr. 49
(06 11) 5 12 51, Fax 52 09 29 res.

Closed for lunch every day except Saturday, closed Sunday and Monday, 2nd half of August, à la carte: 27/66, No Credit Cards

Bruno's brasserie is highly popular with the "in crowd" of Wiesbaden, who appreciate good, refined bourgeois cooking. The restaurant has a genuine bistro atmosphere and is always packed. Bruno's creations, if not new, are at least expertly prepared. Examples are the grandiose fresh salads with delicately marinated smoked salmon and great horseradish, outstanding maties herring with potatoes (too al dente!), and perfect, flavorful lamb cutlets with wonderful spinach and potatoes. The generous portions are comparatively cheap, considering the location.

CAPRICORNE IN HOTEL SCHWARZER BOCK 17/20

65183, Kranzplatz 12
(06 11) 15 50, Fax 15 56 52 res.

P

Closed for lunch Sunday. Tables d'hôte: 42L, 78/98D, à la carte: 55/87

We were glad to see chef Alois Köpf aiming high again after years of keeping a low profile. The menu differentiates between the creative new cuisine and classic French dishes, but both are made of high-quality products prepared with precision and fine attention to detail. Our tender rabbit with chanterelles and kohlrabi was accompanied by a wonderful sauce laced with white port wine, and the perfectly cooked turbot with seaweed and al dente asparagus deserved applause. We would have liked an encore of lobster lasagna with artichokes and tomatoes, and our roulade of Scottish beef with leeks and foie gras earned a standing ovation. A thickly breaded foie gras seemed a somewhat overwhelming partner for a delicate chicken, but our deceptively simple-sounding dessert was a spectacular fireworks of flavors.The menu is an ugly piece of cardboard, and the wine glasses aren't much prettier. At least they can be filled not only with renowned, expensive as well as respectable vintages in a lower price category. The service staff creates a relaxed atmosphere and takes pains to please the customers. The tables by the windows are particularly popular, but even they are empty when tables are set in the courtyard in summer.

DIE ENTE VOM LEHEL IN NASSAUER HOF 18/20

65183, Kaiser-Friederich-Pl. 3-4
(06 11) 13 36 66/7, Fax 13 36 32 res.

P

Closed for lunch, closed Sunday, Monday, first week in January, 4 weeks during the Hessen summer school holiday. Tables d'hôte: 130/170, à la carte: 72/118

Thanks to its stylish ambience, flawless service and always superb cooking, this duck *(Ente)* is still flying first-class in Germany's gourmet scene. The Ente has definitely grown a bit more staid, but it remains an impressive monument to its founder, Hans-Peter Wodarz. The appetizers weren't just a little welcome from the kitchen but a mini-collection of choice delicacies that took our breath away. We liked the sushi with rice, a first course that looked and tasted superb, and the absolutely perfect turbot with caviar and chive sauce and lobster mousse. Only the very best fish is allowed into the pots and pans of the Ente. And the best has its price: 62 DM for a slice of turbot with spinach and fried asparagus, for example! Other highlights were anglerfish medallions with paprika and pesto gnocchi, fresh salmon and smoked salmon, flawlessly fried pigeon with chanterelles and foie gras, and an ingenious fillet of beef with a crust of ginger and horseradish. Whatever you eat in the Ente, leave a little room for fantastic dessert creations like wild strawberry charlotte with orange parfait and puréed kiwi. The wine list still contains a choice of 1,250 wines, 70 champagnes and 45 sparkling wines, but the appearance (and weight) have changed: the smaller format is supposed to make the list easier to handle, but copper plates as a cover make the wine list literally heavy reading. Excellent sommelier service.

BISTRO ENTE VOM LEHEL IN NASSAUER HOF 16/20

65183, Kaiser-Friederich-Pl. 3-4
(06 11) 13 36 66/7, Fax 13 36 32 res.

P

Closed Sunday, Monday, first week in January, 4 weeks during the Hessen summer school holiday. Tables d'hôte: 170/170, à la carte: 48/89

We were lucky: Placido Domingo gave a live concert in front of the Kurhaus, and he supplied the background music for our meal on the bistro terrace of the famous Ente in Wiesbaden. For appetizers, we had a slice of veal saddle with tuna mayonnaise and headcheese croquettes. In true bistro style, we had opulent and colorful salads, composed of everything fresh and seasonal, served with piquant dressing and garnished with, for example, sautéed mushrooms, duck-liver parfait and fried (but not crispy) leg of guinea fowl. We also liked our duck galantine with raw marinated cabbage and a hearty bacon and onion dressing. This was followed by an unbelievably savory consommé with just-as-unbelievably large marrow quenelles. All the main courses offer proof of expert cooking and creativity. These included wild carp fried in almonds and served with Savoy cabbage and horseradish sauce, and a gratin of rabbit saddle with leeks and pine kernels. The menu in the bistro is smaller than that of the Ente restaurant, but it offers many of the same dishes.

ESTRAGON 14/20

65185, Wilhemstr. 12
(06 11) 30 39 06, Fax 37 32 02 res.

Closed for lunch Saturday and Sunday, closed Tuesday. Tables d'hôte: 59L, 72D, 98, à la carte: 60/97

You find restaurants like this only once in a blue moon. Chef Mohamed "Samy" Elzein is a passionate and intuitive cook, who seems to have as much fun preparing his dishes as his customers do eating them. And his customers would rather tolerate a mistake than indifference. This highly ambitious cook propagates unadulterated products, and consequently he serves meat almost rare (or at most, medium rare). His classic French cuisine incorporates influences from his own adventurous past (Dakar, Paris, Beirut, Frankfurt), leading to exciting ethnic tension in his food. We liked the pronounced Asian and Oriental taste sensations, and enjoyed mint in our ravioli and couscous with our fish. Every time you eat here, be prepared for some surprises. Samy's commitment also means that he doesn't serve more than six tables in one evening, although he could seat many more customers. The wine list attempts variety but reveals uncertainty in choice and pricing. The service is agreeable and discreet, creating a familiar atmosphere.

KÄFER'S IN KURHAUS WIESEBADEN 13/20

65189, Kurhausplatz 1
(06 11) 53 62 00, Fax 53 62 22 res.

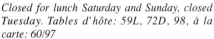

A la carte: 30/75

It's difficult to find a place to sit here in the evenings. At noon, it's somewhat easier, although the (almost) genuine French bistro ambience is extremely popular in Wiesbaden. Customers enthusiastically praise Käfer's dish of *rösti* with Sevruga caviar and sweet arugula, boiled eggs, onions and lime crème fraîche. Käfer's salad is mighty, not always easy to eat with decorum, and usually liberally covered with fried (when business is hectic, sometimes burnt) fillet of beef. On Käfer's grill platter, we found fillet of beef and lamb cutlet side by side with salmon fillet and shrimp. One course is usually enough to satisfy hungry customers. The same menu is offered in the casino's restaurant.

LANDHAUS DIEDERT 11/20

65195, Am Kloster Klarenthal 9
(06 11) 46 10 66, Fax 46 10 69 res.

Closed for lunch Saturday, closed Monday. Tables d'hôte: 55/75, à la carte: 41/86

This is a nice restaurant—both inside and in the garden—on the outskirts of the city. But you have to be hungry to enjoy the food here. We had well-dressed salad of immense proportions, maties herring tartare with a soggy potato pancake, dry salmon and pike terrine with a bitter green sauce, tough *tafelspitz,* and duck's breast with inedible skin. The vegetables were prettily prepared, and the choice of wines was good.

ORANGERIE IN NASSAUER HOF 15/20

65183, Kaiser-Friederich-Pl. 3-4
(06 11) 13 36 33, Fax 13 36 32

Tables d'hôte: 54L, 112D, à la carte: 42/94

Do yourself a favor and order a prix-fixe here. The kitchen readily complies with individual wishes, new combinations of dishes and switches. After a Japanese sushi as appetizer, we had Balik salmon with caviar and potato pancake, duck salad with liver mousse, turbot with puréed beans, generously garnished savory lobster soup, flawlessly prepared veal medallions with chanterelles in cream, and excellent lamb cutlets with a shoestring potato crust and tomato and basil sauce. Regional German cuisine was at its best: blood pudding terrine and foie gras with salad of Jerusalem artichokes, rich Swabian beef soup, homemade kid sausages with noodles, and suckling pig with sauerkraut and puréed green peas. The choice of wines is good and the service pleasant and obliging.

PANTUSO 13/20

65189, Kl. Frankfurter Str. 10
(06 11) 30 01 30, Fax 30 82 24 45 res.

P

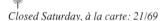

Closed for lunch Saturday, closed Sunday, à la carte: 43/83

The cordial welcome and friendly atmosphere of this restaurant, with its pretty new wintergarten and tastefully and elegantly laid tables, put us into a good mood right away. The menu is a farce; regular customers don't even bother to look at it, but instead follow the suggestions of the charming hosts. Whatever you order, don't miss the antipasti platter, on which eggplant, tomatoes, artichokes, peppers and mozzarella cheese play the main parts. The homemade pasta is wonderful but filling. This is the best Italian restaurant in town. It offers a middling choice of renowned Italian wines.

WEIHENSTEPHAN 13/20

65203, Stadtteil Biebrich
Armenruhstr. 6
(06 11) 6 11 34, Fax 60 38 25

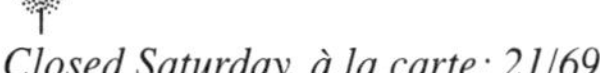

Closed Saturday, à la carte: 21/69

This is still one of the most popular restaurants in Wiesbaden, even though it's situated far from the heart of the city. Business executives eat here at noon, and the evenings draw customers who want good but plain fare and a break from fine cuisine. You get good food, and plenty of it, at moderate prices. Everything is well-prepared and nicely presented, without any indulgence in modernistic flights of fancy. You can have the original Weihenstephan beer here, but the wine list offers a choice of good Rheingau wines as well.

HOTELS

NASSAUER HOF

65183, Kaiser-Friederich-Pl. 3-4
(06 11) 13 36 30, Fax 13 36 32

202, **S** 325/295, **D** 415/480,
APP 680/2500

Wiesbaden's most prestigious hotel is located on a boulevard lined with exclusive shops and facing the park. The rooms offer the highest standard of comfort and an elegant ambience. There are thermal baths and a sun terrace on the top floor with a view over the city. Sauna, massage, beauty farm, restaurants, excellent bar. Breakfast buffet: 26 DM.

SCHWARZER BOCK

65183, Kranzplatz 12
(06 11) 15 50, Fax 15 56 52

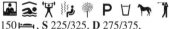

150, **S** 225/325, **D** 275/375,
APP 375/525, **½P** +36/46, **P** +70

If you like an elegantly styled, Old World-style hotel, this 500-year-old institution is the right address for you. Germany's oldest grand hotel offers old-fashioned luxury and style with comfortable rooms, spacious bathrooms and modern conference technology. Thermal spa waters and beauty farm.

WIESENTTAL Bayern

Bamberg 38 - Bayreuth 54

FEILER 15/20

91346, Ortsteil Muggendorf
Obere Markt 4
(0 91 96) 92 92 50, Fax 3 62 res.

Closed for lunch Monday, closed Monday through Thursday from November through March. Tables d'hôte: 59L, 89D, à la carte: 68/88

With its pretty framework facade and flowers on the windows, the Feiler restaurant radiates a down-to-earth charm. As they did 100 years ago, customers still crowd into the traditionally furnished dining room. There are antlers on the walls, various stuffed victims of the maître's hunting passion and dry little bouquets of herbs from the surrounding countryside. The trademarks of Feiler's cuisine are wild herbs, wild berries and mushrooms. Be it fresh morels, fern tips or a sort of wild spinach made from a mixture of herbs, almost all the dishes created by chef Klaus Mönius (Feiler's son-in-law) are characterized by the strong flavors of homegrown greens. Other products are grown or raised in the region as well; these include brook trout, salmon trout, lamb, veal and game. The soups and consommés are unsurpassed, the first courses and main dishes always harmonious. The strudels, soufflés and wild-berry gratins are enticing temptations that we seldom manage to resist. If you like cakes and tarts, try Käthe Feiler's cake buffet on Sunday afternoons. The service is unusually personal, attentive and almost familiar. You can trust Christina Mönius to choose the right wines for your meal.

WIESLOCH Baden-Württ.

Heidelberg 15 - Karlsruhe 47

LA CHANDELLE IN HOTEL MONDIAL 15/20

69168, Schwetzinger Str. 123
(0 62 22) 57 60, Fax 57 63 33 res.

Closed for lunch, closed Sunday and holidays, 1—16 January, 3 weeks in July/August. Tables d'hôte: 110, à la carte: 53/92

This restaurant seems slightly out of place here; the rustic mentality of the area looks askance at La Chandelle's modern design. Apart from a few business executives with cosmopolitan horizons, very few inhabitants frequent the best restaurant in Wiesloch. Maybe the modern decor frightens them off. We, however, like this decor much better than the usual rustic ambience. The impressive wine list is beyond criticism. It offers wines not only from the region, but also from across neighboring borders (France and Italy) at reasonable prices. At beautifully set tables, we enjoyed delicious Scottish salmon, freshly cooked lobster and scallops, excellent venison, and pigeon with rose-hip sauce, as well as exquisite pastries with impeccable sherbets and soufflés. The service is (almost) perfect.

FREIHOF 12/20

69168, Freihofstr. 2
(0 62 22) 25 17, Fax 5 16 34

Closed for lunch every day except Sunday and holidays, closed Monday. Tables d'hôte: 38L, 65/85D, à la carte: 39/73

How wonderful it would be to enjoy good food in this historic restaurant, with its lovely summer terrace—if only the kitchen would perform adequately! The service has seen better days as well. Cold cucumber soup and watercress cream soup were tasteless first courses, but the marinated salmon with mustard-and-dill sauce and potato pancake was tasty, and the duck-liver mousse, apart from its sticky consistency, was good. The Barbary duck's breast and medallions of young wild boar were well prepared, even if their sauces were somewhat indefinable. The service seems as indifferent as the cuisine.

PALATIN

69168, Ringstr. 17-19
(0 62 22) 5 82 01, Fax 58 25 55

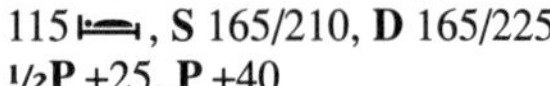

115, **S** 165/210, **D** 165/225, **½P** +25, **P** +40

A typical business and convention hotel. Fitness center, sauna, solarium, restaurant and bar on the roof.

BAD WIESSEE Bayern

Bad Tölz 20 - München 54

FREIHAUS BRENNER 12/20

83807, Freihaus 4
(0 80 22) 8 20 04, Fax 8 38 07 res.

A la carte: 25/75

Customers have to adjust their expectations according to the seasons and the weather. In summer, when tourists throng to this restaurant, the quality of the food drops markedly (but remains far above the average of similar restaurants). In any case, after the steep ascent to the Freihaus, the view of the Tegernsee is exquisite, and the atmosphere of the picturesque little *gasthof* is comfortable and cozy. Due to the high frequentation in summer, many dishes are prepared beforehand. We remember with pleasure the aspic of chanterelles with fried venison fillet and cassis-confit, as well as a marvelous caramelized blueberry pancake with vanilla ice cream. The wine list is well stocked and, for the most part, reasonably priced.

WILDBAD Baden-Württemberg

Calw 21 - Pforzheim 25

BELLA VISTA IN SOMMERBERGHOTEL 13/20

75313, 3 km west
Auf dem Sommerberg
(0 70 81) 17 40, Fax 17 46 12

 P

Closed Monday, à la carte: 36/66

From the summer terrace, you have a wonderful view over the pine trees of the Black Forest and into the lovely valleys. The menu has a definite Italian touch; it includes, for instance, linguine with mozzarella, tagliatelle, or *braciole à la pizzaiola.* Regional cuisine is also available. The Bella Vista offers Swabian ravioli, soup with pancake strips, and trout from the lakes of the Black Forest. On our last visit, we enjoyed lamb fillet with ratatouille as an appetizer, followed by a variety of first courses, excellent rolled char with sea-trout ragout, tender breast of quail with savory sauce, and a delicious mango charlotte and raspberry sherbet. The service is pleasant and attentive. The international choice of wines is fairly priced and offers many low-priced wines by the glass.

SOMMERBERGHOTEL

75313, 3 km west
Auf dem Sommerberg
(0 70 81) 17 40, Fax 17 46 12

100, **S** 127/175, **D** 254/328,
APP 368/404, **1/2P** +32, **P** +47

This new hotel offers spacious, lavishly equipped rooms with balconies and fine lounges. If you like a more rustic yet comfortable atmosphere, book a room in the "Jägerhof," with its handpainted country furniture. Children up to 12 years sharing their parents' room are free.

WILLSTÄTT Bad.-Württ.

Kehl 5 - Offenburg 10

GASTHOF ENGEL 12/20

77731, Hauptstr. 87
(0 78 52) 23 08 , 79 54, Fax 50 19

Closed for lunch Saturday, closed Friday, 24 February through 4 March, 18 August through 4 September. Tables d'hôte: 40/46, à la carte: 33/60

Not far from the French border, this restaurant isn't ashamed of being a plain *gasthof* rather than a gourmet temple. Paper napkins, picturesque kitsch on the walls, a lot of regular customers from the village and appropriately low prices create an ambience that may be somewhat disquieting to gourmets. But Friedrich Arbogast, whose family has run this restaurant for close to 150 years now, cooks like one of those dedicated few who make trips to Italy to buy just the right olive oil and truffles. Most customers order one of the conventional veal and beef dishes, with maybe a creamy snail soup as a first course, a platter of smoked fish or a mild and too subtle salmon tartare, with sorbet, parfait or fruit for dessert. Arbogast's fish dishes come close to deserving a toque. We enjoyed a creamy tuna mousse as appetizer, fried turbot fillet with Chardonnay sauce, and sturgeon fillet fried in butter with wonderful asparagus and a heavenly hollandaise sauce. The choice of wines features regional bottles and a great number of half-bottles and wines by the glass.

WISMAR Meckl.-Vorp.

Lübeck 48 - Rostock 58

ALTER SCHWEDE 12/20

23966, Am Markt 20
(0 38 41) 28 35 52 res.

P

A la carte: 29/51

On their last visit, Sweden's king and queen dined here in state, but that was probably because of the rich traditions of this imposing old house with a beautiful gabled facade. The kitchen offers noncommittal international cuisine that could use some new impetus. Sole with buttered potatoes, wild boar goulash, and seafood salad aren't particularly creative dishes, but at least they are prepared well. The service staff is well-trained, and the wine list includes mostly dry wines from Germany, France and Italy.

ALTES BRAUHAUS

23966, Lübsche Str. 37

(0 38 41) 21 14 16/7, Fax 28 32 23

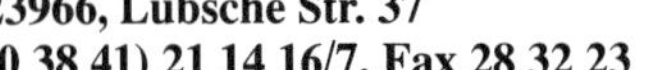

16 beds, **S** 85/95, **D** 120/160

This former brewery built in 1550 has been carefully renovated. The new rooms have a rustic flair.

AM MARKT IN HOTEL STADT HAMBURG 13/20

23966, Am Markt 24

(0 38 41) 23 90, Fax 23 92 39

Tables d'hôte: 39, à la carte: 24/57

This is Wismar's best (and only) address for gourmets. The restaurant lies behind a modern bistro-café and is furnished with comfortable cane furniture in the front room and formal, stiff-backed chairs in the back. Two different menus for the differently furnished parts of the restaurant seem a little fatuous. The more interesting offers international dishes, including excellent anglerfish medallions with Riesling sauce and savory ratatouille, but we also enjoyed an appealing prix-fixe. The service takes pains to please, but is still a little unsure of itself. The choice of wines is good.

TO'N OSSEN IN HOTEL ALTER SPEICHER 11/20

23966, Bohrstr. 12a

(0 38 41) 21 47 61, Fax 21 17 47

Tables d'hôte: 35/50, à la carte: 20/67. Tables d'hôte with wine: 50

Here today, gone tomorrow: shortly after it opened, this new restaurant cooked itself to the top in Wismar. Today, only the elegant ambience reminds customers of past ambitions. The kitchen offered nondescript steak dishes, salmon and two mediocre soups (insipid ham soup and oversalted cream of salmon). Our "fairytale prix-fixe" told an uninspiring story of curried beef liver mousse, tartare of smoked pork with kale, ostrich fillet with red beans, and ice cream. The restaurant is understaffed, and the choice of wines is meager.

ALTER SPEICHER

23966, Bohrstr. 12a

(0 38 41) 21 47 61, Fax 21 17 47

75 beds, **S** 110/140, **D** 160/250, **APP** 280/450, **½P** +35, **P** +60

The largest and most modern hotel in Wismar opened in 1993 in the center of the Old Town. The hotel has retained its beautiful original facade, but modern comfort reigns inside. Fitness center, solarium. Restaurant, pub and café on the premises. Breakfast buffet: 20 DM.

WITTLICH Rheinland-Pfalz

Trier 37 - Koblenz 90

WALDHOTEL SONNORA 18/20

8 km southwest in 54518, Dreis

Auf dem Eichelfeld

(0 65 78) 4 06, Fax 14 02 res.

Closed Monday, Tuesday, 10 January through 10 February. Tables d'hôte: 125/158, à la carte: 70/112

There's no doubt about it: Helmut Thieltges is one of the most talented cooks in Germany. His success is largely due to the support of his family: father Vinzenz Thieltges greets guests and does the honors, fiancée Ulrike Schmitz supervises her well-trained service staff and makes her guests feel at home, Helmut Thieltges cooks and controls every dish that leaves his kitchen, and his mother helps out where it's needed. The appetizer (oysters gratin) was worth a round of applause. After that, we enjoyed shrimp in tomato aspic, tartare of smoked eel and smoked salmon, quail's egg with béarnaise sauce, and baked headcheese with balsamic vinegar. All these dishes could be prepared in a different, but not in a better, way. The asparagus salad with foie gras and sweetbreads in aged balsamic vinegar was excellent, and our Brittany lobster with curry and coriander sauce was ingenious. Dessert was a surprise—delicious warm and cold variations of cream cheese with jellied rhubarb compote.The chef's highlights were baked king prawns on a bed of garden herbs, grilled anglerfish with ragout of artichokes and black olives, and finally, superb suckling kid of unparalleled quality. The wine list is dominated by the best Moselle wines, but high-quality producers from other regions are listed. You can choose among red Bordeaux and Burgundys, but you'll also find good wines at good value from Portugal and Spain.

WALDHOTEL SONNORA 

8 km southwest in 54518, Dreis
Auf dem Eichelfeld
(0 65 78) 4 06, Fax 14 02

18, **S** 70/80, **D** 130/150,
APP 300/350
Closed 10 January through 10 February

Formerly, the restaurant was just a part of this hotel. Today, one of the most outstanding restaurants offers its customers the opportunity to spend the night.

WÖRLITZ Sachsen-Anhalt

Dessau 13 - Wittenberg 20

ZUM STEIN 14/20

06786, Erdmannsdorffstr. 228
(03 49 05) 2 03 54, Fax 2 03 54

Closed Christmas Eve. Tables d'hôte: 25/50, à la carte: 24/50

After a lovely walk or a canoe excursion in the beautiful park of Wörlitz castle, we like to return to this unpretentious restaurant for tasty red wine aspic with mayonnaise and fried potatoes, delicious grilled salmon with fresh asparagus, lightly salted beef tongue with Burgundy sauce, and crepes with vanilla ice cream, strawberries and chocolate sauce, all of it priced very reasonably. The choice of about 50 wines is moderately priced as well.

ZUM STEIN 

06786, Erdmannsdorffstr. 228
(03 49 05) 2 03 54, Fax 2 03 54

55, **S** 118/145, **D** 160/180,
APP 180/220, **½P** +20, **P** +40

This small family-run hotel is located in a lovely landscaped park with ponds and waterfalls. All rooms are spacious and recently renovated with modern bathrooms.

WOLFRATSHAUSEN Bayern

Starnberg 16 - Bad Tölz 26

PATRIZIERHOF 13/20

82515, Untermarkt 17
(0 81 71) 2 25 33, Fax 2 22 46 res.

A la carte: 30/62

The ambience of the newly decorated Patrizierhof is tasteful and inviting. Radically reduced prices and an unpretentious cuisine make this restaurant seem particularly hospitable. We had savory sorrel soup, well-seasoned consommé with pancake strips, venison carpaccio with cèpe-flavored oil, arugula salad with truffled oil and king prawns, anglerfish with lemon balm, and sole fried in almond butter. Well-done lamb saddle and veal fillet with morels and spaetzle left little room for the delicious sherbets and strawberries with Grand-Marnier zabaglione. The service is attentive and pleasant, and the wines from Germany, Italy and France are moderately priced.

WOLFSBURG Niedersachsen

Braunschweig 28 - Berlin 88

ALTE MÜHLE 13/20

9 km northwest
in 38442, Weyhausen
Wolfsburger Str. 72
(0 53 62) 6 20 21 , Fax 77 10

Tables d'hôte: 45/65, à la carte: 32/58

Obviously, the recession hasn't left this restaurant unscathed. The size of the menu has been reduced, and the Alte Mühle now accepts conventions and business meetings. In spite of this, the kitchen crew hasn't cut down on the quality of the food served here, and the service is as pleasant and attentive as ever. We enjoyed the salad with chicken livers, as well as the tasty (if not tender) marinated salmon. The kitchen had some difficulty preparing fish just right, but the meat courses were well done. The desserts sometimes seemed touching in their simplicity. The prices are modest, too.

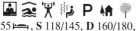

ALTE MÜHLE

9 km northwest
in 38442, Weyhausen
Wolfsburger Str. 72
(0 53 62) 6 20 21 , Fax 77 10

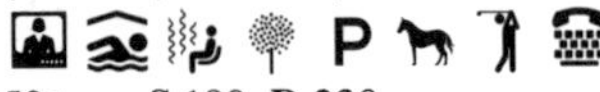

50, **S** 180, **D** 230,
APP 270, **½P** +35, **P** +70

Spacious, bright rooms with all modern amenities. The architecture of the octagonal entrance hall is interesting. Breakfast buffet.

LA FONTAINE IN HOTEL LUDWIG IM PARK 15/20

38442, Fallersleben
Gifhorner Str. 25
(0 53 62) 5 10 51, Fax 35 15 res.

Closed for lunch, closed Sunday, Monday, 3 weeks during the VW work holiday. Tables d'hôte: 98/138, à la carte: 58/96

The service and cuisine are as agreeable as ever, but the prices have gone up. The wine list has also grown, but it still doesn't have the quality warranted by the inappropriately high prices. The kitchen still cooks time-tested standards, to which we don't object, as long as the quality is good. The appetizer of salmon tartare with savory tomato mousse was nice and tangy, the salad with rabbit livers nicely decorated and the beef carpaccio with asparagus a little insipid. The salmon that followed wasn't particularly exciting either, but our lamb fillet with a flavorful crust of herbs was simply perfect. For dessert, we had a wonderful cheese soufflé with ice cream and rhubarb. Pralines with coffee were reserved for only a few (selected?) guests. The service is nice, but the staff shouldn't put a rejected wine on the bill.

LUDWIG IM PARK

38442, Fallersleben
Gifhorner Str. 25
(0 53 62) 5 10 51, Fax 35 15

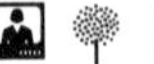

40, **S** 165, **D** 210,
APP 290

The pleasant rooms of this hotel are furnished with antiques. The rooms on the park side are quieter. Breakfast buffet.

HOLIDAY INN

38440, Rathausstr. 1
(0 53 61) 20 70, Fax 20 79 81

207, **S** 278/338, **D** 358/418,
APP 624/650

The rooms of this centrally located hotel are furnished according to American chain-hotel standard. Restaurants.

NEUE STUBEN 13/20

38442, Fallersleben
Bahnhofstr. 13
(0 53 62) 9 69 00, Fax 96 90 30

Closed for lunch Saturday. Tables d'hôte: 35/50D, à la carte: 21/48, No Credit Cards

Daddy made his dream come true: talented young Stefan Baer now owns his own restaurant and hotel. With good taste and no expense spared, his father, an architect and a gourmet, rebuilt a lovely half-timbered ensemble in the old part of town. A few months after a successful opening, Stefan Baer has had to gear down his ambitions, and not only because the Volkswagen managers from the nearby factory are scrimping and saving. He's still the best cook far and wide and keeps up high standards in his elegant Italian restaurant. After a somewhat disappointing first course, a tomato and bread salad with scampi, we were consoled by a delicious fish soup, excellent black pasta with seafood, and a superb red mullet fillet with warm spinach spaghetti. Our poached fillet of beef with wonderful roasted vegetables was fantastic, and not quite topped by a creamy vanilla ice cream with fruit. The service was remarkably unsure of itself, the choice of wines small but good.

WORMS Rheinland-Pfalz

Mannheim 20 - Mainz 44

RÔTISSERIE DUBS 16/20

67550, Stadtteil Rheinduurkheim
Kirschstr. 6
(0 62 42) 20 23, Fax 20 24 res.

Closed for lunch Saturday, closed Tuesday, 1—15 January, 3 weeks during the Rh.-Pf. summer school holiday. Tables d'hôte: 65/100L, 95/135D, à la carte: 66/99. Tables d'hôte with wine: 100, No Credit Cards

People like to call this restaurant an institution in this part of the country, since chef Dubs has done pioneer work with his fine cuisine. But some institutions can crumble, and if the Dubs don't shape up their restaurant, this is exactly what might happen in Worms. Standard dishes—like lamb ribs with a crust of herbs, salmon with caviar on potato pancake, sugar-pea soup with shrimp, and cream of asparagus soup—were either refined or prepared with a strong regional accent. We greatly enjoyed Dubs's unusual creations, such as fried John Dory with puréed white beans, blood pudding with walnuts and cakes of potatoes and apples, or saddle of venison with foie gras carpaccio and Madeira. But we were greatly irritated by raw sliced asparagus in vinaigrette, bitter parfait of foie gras and salty duck confit. The service has its weak points as well. The wine list is comprehensive and offers a fine choice of renowned wines.

WORPSWEDE Niedersachsen

Bremen 25 - Hannover 140

EICHENHOF

27726, Ostendorfer Str. 13
(0 47 92) 26 76/7, Fax 44 27

18, **S** 115/125, **D** 168/198,
APP 220

Closed 19 December through 23 February

For once, the claims of the enthusiastic hotel brochure are true: here are extensive grounds, ancient trees, picturesque ponds, total peace and quiet, cozy furniture and comfortable rooms with rustic charm.

WÜRZBURG Bayern

Nürnberg 105 - Frankfurt 120

BERNARDO 14/20

97070, Dompassage
(09 31) 1 80 90, Fax 1 80 92

Closed Sunday and Monday, 1—9 January, 31 July through 28 August. Tables d'hôte: 29L, 52/99D, à la carte: 25/72

Customers like the light and airy ambience of the restaurant with a glass-domed roof located on the first floor of a shopping mall. Modern still-life paintings create a stylish ambience. Roland Popp's cuisine sounds more Italian than it is. We enjoyed delicately marinated beef carpaccio with pesto and Parmesan, velvety and flavorful cream of cèpes soup, gratin of fresh fine fish (sea bream, anglerfish and pike-perch), saddle of veal with lemon and white wine sauce and vegetables and polenta, and plums with ricotta ice cream and lovely vanilla sauce. Choice, moderately priced Italian wines accompanied our meal. The service is excellent: competent yet relaxed.

BÜRGERSPITAL

97070, Theaterstr. 19
(09 31) 1 38 61, Fax 57 15 12

Closed Tuesday, August. Tables d'hôte: 28, à la carte: 20/50, No Credit Cards

Wander through the 10 adjoining dining rooms here until you find the perfect nook to sit in. The kitchen offers fried sausages with sauerkraut, boiled sausage in vinegar, boiled beef with horseradish sauce, and a hearty sandwich platter with lots of wurst and ham. The service staff in dirndls and local costumes offers a choice of 30 great wines at moderate prices. Wine tastings can be arranged.

JULIUSSPITAL

97070, Juliuspromenade 19
(09 31) 5 40 80, Fax 57 17 23

Closed Wednesday. Tables d'hôte: 12/19, à la carte: 19/52, No Credit Cards

An archbishop founded this former hospital and wine estate in the 16th century. Today, it's the third largest winery in Germany, and the names of its best vineyards are famous the world over. You can taste some of the prestigious wines in this restaurant and have typically Franconian regional cooking to go with them, including boiled sausage in vinegar (called *"blaue Zipfel"*), ham and cheese on toast, and marinated cheese.

REBSTOCK

97070, Neubaustr. 7
(09 31) 3 09 30, Fax 3 09 31 00

81 rooms, **S** 176/248, **D** 280/350, **APP** 450/525

The Rebstock ranks as Würzburg's best hotel. The magnificent rococo facade has recently been restored, and the interior is elegant and polished. The rooms vary according to their size, but all are comfortable, and some bathrooms are extravagant. Restaurant.

SCHLOSS STEINBURG

6.5 km northwest
97080, Auf dem Steinberg
(09 31) 9 30 61, Fax 9 71 21

52 rooms, **S** 120/140, **D** 180/240, **APP** 320/340, **½P** +40, **P** +65

This isn't a castle, just a former villa with a stupendous view of the city and the Maintal. Some rooms are furnished with Oriental rugs and antiques. Restaurant, café, solarium, wine tastings, skittle alleys.

WITTELSBACHER HÖH

97082, Hexenbruchweg 10
(09 31) 4 20 85, Fax 41 54 58

P

75 rooms, **S** 115/175, **D** 160/300, **APP** 210/300, **½P** +28/32, **P** +50

Another vantage point with a breathtaking view over Würzburg. Small, cozy rooms. Restaurant with terrace.

WUNSIEDEL Bayern

Selb 24 - Hof 36

JÄGERSTÜBERL 16/20

95632, Luisenburg 5
(0 92 32) 44 34, Fax 15 56 res.

P

Closed for lunch every day except Sunday, closed for dinner Sunday, closed Monday, 3 weeks in September. Tables d'hôte: 49L, 59/89D, à la carte: 40/71. Tables d'hôte with wine: 60/150

The Jägerstüberl is one of the most original restaurants in Bavaria. Beate and Heinrich Schöpf want to get away from the image of the traditional gourmet restaurant and are realizing another (and more attractive) concept. In the two opulently decorated dining rooms, the customers are the focal point of the evening. In a comfortable aperitif-bar, you discuss what you want to eat and drink with chef Schöpf and wife Beate. Individual suggestions and wishes are readily complied with, and the choice of wines is as important as the courses of the meal. Beate Schöpf, an expert on wines, offers some surprising (and always harmonious) discoveries from, for instance, California and Italy. Heinrich Schöpf's cuisine is aromatic and fresh, exhibits a distinct Mediterranean preference and does without any kind of culinary acrobatics. We loved the beef fillet with truffled vinaigrette and roasted pine kernels, and the fish with vegetables in pastry. His fine Bohemian dumplings with apricot or plum filling are superb! Schöpf works with the flavors and colors of his products, but he presents them without artificial artiness. In winter, Schöpf offers Sunday brunch with wine tastings; in summer, guests can dine on the terrace.

WUPPERTAL NRW

Düsseldorf 38 - Essen 40

ALTER WASSERTURM 13/20

42119, Südstr. 49
(02 02) 43 50 53 res.

Closed for lunch Saturday, closed Sunday. Tables d'hôte: 60, à la carte: 47/74

It would be unfair to concentrate on the architecture as the most remarkable feature of this restaurant, but there is a lot to be admired in the building. The service staff freely distributes charm and smiles, but chef Hans-Joachim Arschel, who prepared his dishes with care and precision, isn't particularly free with new ideas. The menu offers French country cooking with lots of mustard and even more herbs, lamb prepared in manifold ways, rumpsteak and fillet, excellent carpaccio, different salads and soups, health foods and a large variety of desserts. We followed the special suggestions and were not disappointed with sardines stuffed with herbs, anglerfish in Savoy cabbage, and grouper, a little-known fish from the South Seas. The sauces were light and delicate and the fish prepared just right. The choice of bottles is small, but there are a large number of wines by the glass at low prices.

GOLFHOTEL JULIANA

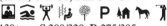

42279, Stadtteil Barmen
Mollenkotton 195
(02 02) 6 47 50, Fax 6 47 57 77

139, **S** 200/320, **D** 275/395,
APP 350/450, **1/2P** +35, **P** +70

This is one of Germany's very few golf hotels, with its own 18-hole golf course. The rooms are small but comfortable enough. Solarium, conference rooms, pub and *bierstube*.

SCARPATI 13/20

42327, Stadtteil Vohwinkel
Scheffelstr. 41
(02 02) 78 40 74/5, Fax 78 98 28 res.

Tables d'hôte: 59L, 88D, à la carte: 60/92

Aniello Scarpati, the Italian owner, has a new German cook. His sweetbread mousse and fried pigeon with morel cream sauce were worth a rating of 14/20. Our technically flawless sauté of fresh John Dory and not-so-fresh scallops in sage butter showed promise, and so did the wonderful tomato tagliolini with oily marinated salmon and scampi. We enjoyed aspic of duck with marinated lentils, foie gras mousse covered with apples, sole with pine nuts, and fillet of beef in an olive crust. The pastries are charming. The choice of wines in bottles, half bottles and by the glass is one of the highlights of this restaurant.

WUSTROW Meckl.-Vorp.

Ahrenshoop 3 - Graal-Müritz 20

OSTSEEHOTEL

18347, Fischländer Weg 35
(03 82 20) 62 50, 2 93, Fax 2 94

109, **S** 55/162, **D** 74/210,
APP 150/240, **1/2P** +25
No Credit Cards

This hotel and apartment complex is located right on the beach and offers tasteful, modern rooms. Surfing, sailing, waterskiing, fishing. Restaurant, dancing, café and bistro-pizzeria. Breakfast: 15 DM.

XANTEN NRW

Kleve 28 - Moers 28

HOTEL VAN BEBBER 12/20

46509, Klever Str. 12
(0 28 01) 66 23/5, Fax 59 14

Closed 30 January through 16 February. Tables d'hôte: 32/73, à la carte: 47/73

In one of the rustic dining rooms here, Winston Churchill pored over his operational plans. Frederick the Great studied accounts in the royal suite with stuccoed ceilings. A wine jug displayed in the 400-year-old vaulted cellar is a piece of Roman history. This house is steeped in history, but since the present owners took over in 1987, they have been trying to create a modern ambience. Comfortable hotel facilities are a part of the overall concept, along with modern cuisine that pleases a variety of tastes but hasn't yet succumbed to the feeding of busloads of tourists. The products are of high quality: game from the hotel's hunting grounds, fowl from the farmyard, fish and crayfish from nearby ponds and brooks. The attractive menu still offers some eccentric, flamboyant dishes like fillet of lamb wrapped in a rice leaf and served with port wine sauce, or pike-perch fried in grated coconut and accompanied by pineapple juice. Aside from these superfluous flights of fancy, customers can enjoy sauerbraten and saddle of suckling pig with ale sauce. An excellent pigeon with pistachio quenelles was just fantastic, and our venison with rose-hip sauce, sugar peas and noodles was delicious. Friendly, helpful service and an intelligently stocked wine list make this restaurant a haven of true hospitality.

LANDHAUS KÖPP 17/20 

46509, Ortsteil Obermörmter
Husenweg 147
(0 28 04) 16 26 res.

P

Closed for dinner Sunday, closed Monday, 2—21 January. Tables d'hôte: 69/112, à la carte: 62/86

We has some qualms about awarding Jürgen Köpp a third toque this time. It takes ages to eat here: we spent more than two and a half hours at a four-course dinner—with only three other customers in the dining room! Why? Chef Köpp is dealing with the recession by cutting back not on quality products, elegant ambience, a good selection of wines or his own efforts, but on kitchen and service staff. With such long waits between courses, however, the fine balance of logically arranged meals topples, leaving only an unconnected string of highlights. The pauses, which demand a lot of patience even from gourmets used to drawn-out dinners, have another unwelcome effect: customers get hungry. They are likely to remain so because Jürgen Köpp still prepares his dishes in the mini-portions once favored by advocates of nouvelle cuisine. He doesn't even offer trendy new regional dishes to assuage wild hunger pangs, though we'd like to see what he makes out of blood pudding, sauerkraut and pig's knuckle. He still deserved a rating of 17/20 because, in spite of small portions and long waits, we enjoyed a grandiose meal, and because Köpp is a brilliant cook. His laconically titled "anglerfish with stuffed celery" turned out to be sheer poetry: fabulous fried anglerfish in a nest of *rösti*, accompanied by a piece of lobster and slices of celery root stuffed with spinach (the white celery was colored with red beet juice) and served with two superb sauces. The rest of our meal was (almost) as incomparable: vegetable mousses, smoked salmon and shellfish of perfect consistency, roasted sweetbreads, foie gras, Bresse pigeon sausage, and chocolate-coated pineapple parfait. The service is competent and pleasant, but we didn't like being asked twice during every course if we liked our food.

ZERBST Sachsen-Anhalt

Dessau 20 - Magdeburg 41

PARK-RESTAURANT VOGELHERD 14/20 

39261, Lindauer Str. 78
(0 39 23) 78 04 44, Fax 22 03

 **P**

Closed Monday and Tuesday. Tables d'hôte: 50L, 70D, à la carte: 21/60

First impressions are important, and the Vogelherd had the best chances to begin with. The hotel, which has a lovely terrace, is located on the edge of a pond in beautiful natural surroundings, and a glance at the wine list showed a good selection from Germany, France and Italy, as well as half bottles and wines by the glass at astoundingly moderate prices. The kitchen didn't disappoint us either. After a tasty, light omelet with fresh chanterelles, we enjoyed delicious cream soup garnished with vegetables and potatoes and salmon quenelles, lightly fried pike-perch fillet in a lemon and herb crust with wine sauce and noodles, and a superb leg of rabbit with mushroom cream sauce, dumplings, pears and fabulous red cabbage. Walnut parfait with chocolate rum sauce and pear salad with raisins concluded a fine meal.

ZINGST Meckl.-Vorp.

Ahrenshoop 27 - Stralsund 43

SKIPPER 12/20

18374, Alte Reihe 5a
(03 82 32) 6 80

P

A la carte: 20/42

They like contrasts here: the entrance is glaringly white and brightly illuminated, while the dining room, with its brass lamps and model boats, is as dusky as the lower deck of a ship. The menu is large and varied, forcing the kitchen to open a few cans and frozen packages instead of using only fresh ingredients. We liked our Atlantic bass garnished with shrimps much better than the rubbery scampi with leeks, rice and garlic. The service is flawless, and the interesting German wines are well-cooled in wine chests.

BAD ZWISCHENAHN NS

Westerstede 10 - Oldenburg 17

APICIUS IN JAGDHAUS EIDEN AM SEE 16/20

4 km northeast
towards Wiefelstede
26160, Ortsteil Aschhauserfeld
(0 44 03) 69 84 16, Fax 69 83 98 res.

Closed for lunch, closed Sunday and Monday, closed January. Tables d'hôte: 100, à la carte: 52/93

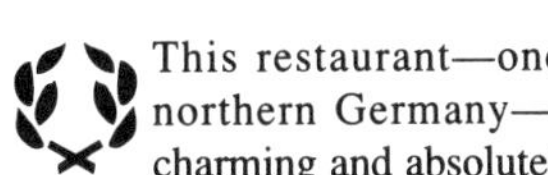

This restaurant—one of the best in northern Germany—has a naturally charming and absolutely perfect service staff, which can also give competent advice on wine. After a delicious appetizer of maties herring with caviar and cream on a tiny potato pancake, we had delightful roulade of eel, a daring veal *tafelspitz* with lobster, and an excellent rabbit pot-au-feu. The fish dishes are better than ever—the wonderful turbot fillet with crayfish, for example. The variety of cheese is adequate, and the desserts are fabulous. The choice of wines is enormous, but the prices are reasonably low.

JAGDHAUS EIDEN AM SEE

4 km northeast
towards Wiefelstede
26160, Ortsteil Aschhauserfeld
(0 44 03) 69 80 00, Fax 69 83 98

63 rooms, **S** 103/142, **D** 157/227,
APP 280/290, **½P** +36, **P** +51

Housed under the same roof as the casino and the Apicius restaurant, this hotel offers comfort and absolute quiet. The location is one of the most beautiful in northern Germany.

HOTEL AM KURGARTEN

26160, Unter den Eichen 30
(0 44 03) 5 90 11, Fax 5 96 20

17 rooms, **S** 135/155, **D** 210/290

A comfortable hotel that still looks like a private residence. Beauty farm, solarium, bar, breakfast room for non-smokers.

SEEHOTEL FÄHRHAUS

26160, Auf dem Hohen Ufer 8
(0 44 03) 60 00, Fax 60 05 00

56 rooms, **S** 108/113, **D** 180/225,
APP 240/350, **½P** +35, **P** +55

The spectacular view of the lake from the extravagantly renovated rooms of this popular hotel is alone worth a visit. Restaurant.

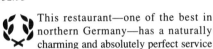

GLOSSARIES & INDEXES

MENU SAVVY

VORSPEISEN—APPETIZERS

Pastete	minced meat pie
Schinken	ham
Geräucherte Forelle	smoked fillet of trout
Sülze	aspic
Kartoffelpuffer	potato pancakes
Carpaccio	raw slices of meat, fish or vegetables, dressed with oil and vinegar
Feldsalat	lamb's-lettuce
Frisée, Endiviensalat	Belgian endive
Schnecken	snails
Gänseleber	goose liver, foie gras
Matjeshering	young herring, slightly salted and served in fillets or pieces

FLEISCH, WILD UND GEFLÜGEL —MEATS, GAME AND POULTRY

Lamm	lamb
Rindfleisch	beef
Schweinefleisch	pork
Wachtel	quail
Rebhuhn	guinea fowl
Fasan	pheasant
Ente	duck
Hase	hare
Kaninchen	rabbit
Reh	doe
Hirsch	male deer
Ziege	kid
Wildschwein	wild boar
Frischling	suckling wild boar
Leber	liver
Kalbsbries	sweetbread
Nierchen	kidneys
Stubenküken	squab
Huhn, Hähnchen	chicken

FISCH UND SCHALENTIERE —FISH AND SHELLFISH

Austern	oysters
Muscheln	mussels
Jakobsmuscheln	scallops
Krebs	crayfish
Hummer	lobster
Languste	spiny lobster
Krevetten	shrimps
Langustinen	king prawns
Seezunge	sole
Scholle	plaice
Kabeljau	codfish
Rotbarbe	red mullet
Hecht	pike
Zander	pike, perch
Forelle	trout
Aal	eel
Lachs	salmon
Seewolf	bass
Seeteufel	monkfish, angler
Sankt Peters Fish	John Dory
Steinbutt	turbot
Heilbutt	halibut

TYPICAL GERMAN DISHES

Spanferkel	roast suckling pig
Tafelspitz	boiled tenderloin of beef
Sauerkraut	fermented white cabbage with a sour taste
Sauerbraten	marinated and roasted beef
Maultaschen	large ravioli filled with different types of stuffing
Gugelhupf	a rich yeast cake baked in a special round mold with a hole in the middle
Eisbein	mildly pickled pork haunch
Saumagen	lining of a pig's stomach filled with pork stuffing, ham, potatoes, bread and spices, cooked and served in slices
Rösti	raw slivered potatoes, crisply fried
Eintopf	stew
Blutwurst	blood sausage, blood pudding
Geschnetzeltes	meat, usually veal, sliced thin and fried, served in a creamy sauce
Ochsenschwanzsuppe	oxtail soup
Hochzeitssuppe	a rich beef soup with noodles and vegetables
Rollmops	marinated rolled herring
Semmelknödel	bread dumplings
Kartoffelklöße	potato dumplings

GEMÜSE—VEGETABLES

Blumenkohl	cauliflower
Spargel	asparagus
Mangold	Swiss chard or spinach beets
Erbsen	sweet peas
Grüne Bohnen	green beans
Pfifferlinge	chanterelles
Steinpilze	yellow boletus
Pilze	mushrooms
Rüben	turnips
Lauch	leeks
Möhren	carrots
Weißkraut	white cabbage
Rotkohl	red cabbage
Rote Beete	red beets
Wirsing	savoy cabbage

FRUCHTEN—FRUITS

Ananas	pineapple
Kirschen	cherries
Erdbeeren	strawberries
Himbeeren	raspberries
Brombeeren	black raspberries
Holunderbeeren	elderberries
Pfirsich	peach
Pflaumen	plums
Trauben	grapes
Mirabellen	yellow plums

NACHSPEISEN—DESSERT

Mousse	foamy whipped cream desserts made of anything from chocolate to fruit
Saucenspiegel	different fruit purées arranged on a plate
Sorbet	sherbet
Eis	ice cream
Flammeri	soufflé
Torte	layer cake
Kuchen	cake
Plätzchen	cookies
Gebäck	pastry
Apfelstrudel	pastry roll filled with stewed apples and served warm with vanilla sauce
Quark	sweet curds

GETRANKE—BEVERAGES

Saft	juice
Apfelwein	fermented apple cider
Spätlese, Auslese	white wine made from

	very mellow grapes, usually some degrees sweeter than normal
Tafelwein	a plain red 'or white table wine
Bier vom Fass	draft beer (from a barrel)
Flaschenbier	bottled beer

USEFUL TERMS

Breakfast	Frühstück
Lunch	Mittagessen (usually means a noon dinner)
Dinner	Abendessen
The menu, please	Die Speisekarte, bitte
The wine list	Die Weinkarte
Waiter	Ober
Waitress	Bedienung, Fräulein
Tip	Trinkgeld (is generally included)
The check, please	Die Rechnung, bitte
To reserve a table	Einen Tisch reservieren
Dish	Gericht
Three course dinner	Drei- Gänge- Menü
Prix fixe	Menü
Appetizers	Vorspeise
Main course	Hauptspeise
Desserts	Nachspeise
Cheese	Käse
Fork	Gabel
Spoon	Löffel
Knife	Messer
Plate	Teller
Glass	Glas
Napkin	Serviette
Pre-dinner drink	Aperitif
White wine	Weißwein
Red wine	Rotwein
Mineral water	Mineralwasser (carbonated), Stilles Wasser (not carbonated)
Draft beer	gezapftes Bier, Bier vom Fass
After- dinner drink	Dijestif
Salt	Salz
Pepper	Pfeffer
Mustard	Senf (mustard is sweet in Bavaria)
Oil	Ol
Vinegar	Essig
Bread	Brot
Rare	Blutig
Medium	Medium
Well-done	Durch
Cold	Kalt
Hot	Heiß
Coffee	Kaffee
Tea	Tee
Sugar	Zucker
Milk	Milch
Honey	Honig

WINE SAVVY

INTRODUCTION

Grapevines have a long history in Germany, going back to ancient times, when they grew wild along the banks of the Rhine river. In the first or second century, after the Romans conquered the region, they introduced *vitis vinifera*, the species of vine that includes all of Europe's great winemaking grapes. Later, in the era of Charlemagne, wine growing received further impetus through its support of the spread of Christianity. Many monastic orders devoted vast quantities of land and labor to cultivating vineyards. The wine trade reached its zenith by the end of the Middle Ages, when an increasing population, needing more living space, began to claim vineyard land.

The era of modern German winemaking began after World War II. The area under vine dramatically expanded, as did the yield per acre permitted under German wine law. So more vines have been planted and those vines are producing more grapes than ever before. With over a quarter of a million acres under vine, Germany produces less wine than either France or Italy. It exports about 30 million cases a year, with the United Kingdom its leading customer, followed by the Netherlands, Japan and the U.S.

THE GRAPES

Being so far north (on the same latitude as Labrador), Germany has a relatively cool climate that marks it as one of the most marginal regions on earth for successfully growing wine grapes. Consequently, the ancient viniculturists paid particular attention to planting the most favorable sites with the most appropriate grape varieties. Red Bordeaux or Rhone varietals were out; they would never fully ripen in the cool climate. So unlike the majority of the wine growing regions in the world, white wine grapes account for nearly 90 percent of Germany's wine production.

Germany makes the finest Rieslings in the world; in fact, they are the standard by which all New World Rieslings are judged. If Cabernet is the king of grapes, then Riesling is the queen, Chardonnay's recent rise in popularity not withstanding. Riesling produces a wine of incomparable fragrance, rich character and delightfully crisp acidity. The sweetness level can range from imperceptible to incredibly unctuous, depending on the ripeness of the grapes. Most California Rieslings, which are vinified in an unbalanced, cloyingly sweet manner, bear little relationship to the real thing.

Silvaner was once an important white grape in Germany but its acreage has been declining; when planted in the right sites, it can produce a concentrated, flavorful and long-lived wine. Ruländer is the name given to Pinot Gris here and is noted for its rich, full-bodied, sweet style. Grauburgunder denotes Pinot Gris vinified in a drier, more food-friendly style. Weissburgunder is the name given to Pinot Blanc which has a fine fruitiness, good acidity and a dry finish. Scheurebe is another variety that is being increasingly cultivated by quality-minded producers; it has exuberant flavors of black currants along with ripe grapefruit-type acidity. Müller-Thurgau, a cross of Riesling and Silvaner, is the mostly widely planted white wine grape. Like most hybrids, it was bred to

The German Wine-Growing Regions

be a more prolific producer that requires less sun and ripens early. It makes generally light, undistinguished wines of the lowest quality.

Red wine grape plantings, such as they are, are dominated by Spätburgunder, which is analogous to Pinot Noir. Its style has become more French-oriented, with higher alcohol, more flavor extraction and barrel aging. Lemberger and Trollinger are also planted, though the up-and-coming Dornfelder produces a better quaffing, Beaujolais-style wine.

Sparkling wine, called Sekt, is produced from a variety of exclusively German grapes; they are usually less austere, lower in alcohol and more lively than their French counterparts.

UNDERSTANDING GERMAN WINE LABELS

German wines, even to the most wine savvy American, still remain a puzzling riddle. We are probably spoiled by the deceptively simple California wine label, where the grape variety (Chardonnay, for example) is the most prominently displayed, followed by the winery, with lesser importance attached to the district or region. German wine labels, many of them gothic and ornate, feature very specific and precise information about their origin, quality, level of dryness/sweetness, as well as the variety of grape. On first glance, this surfeit of information can be overwhelming or at least intimidating, particularly stated in an unfamiliar and, to most of us, unwieldy language.

Branded wines, like "Blue Nun" and "Black Tower," the first taste of German wines for most Americans, were one answer to the label confusion. Quite simply, you didn't need to know anything about German wines or regions, you just bought a brand that was consistently blended and bottled to a price point meant to compete with California jug wines. Most such Liebfraumilch is a mass produced, low alcohol, moderately sweet wine designed to appeal to novice wine drinkers.

Unfortunately this marketing ploy was a double-edged sword for the German wine industry. Those who liked Liebfraumilch continued to buy the brands, seeing no need to explore the great diversity of flavors in German wines. Those who found Liebfraumilch too flabby and cloying improperly assumed all German wines were cut from the same cloth and perhaps wrote off German wines altogether.

The German Wine Law of 1971 was meant to facilitate an understanding of the labels and exactly what was in the bottle. However the way the law was framed seemed to give a governmental blessing and authentication to even the lowest quality wine. Paradoxically it has further increased the confusion it was designed to eliminate. There are however some basic label terms that generally define the type, style and quality of German wine. Ripeness is largely the key to assessing the quality levels of German wine, broken down into two main groupings: Tafelwein and Qualitätswein.

Deutscher Tafelwein (table wine): a simple table wine made from ripe grapes. It's the lowest level of blended wine meant for everyday enjoyment and primarily consumed in the region where it was grown. Sugar may be added before fermentation to raise its alcohol content.

Deutscher Landwein (country wine): a slightly more upscale version of Tafelwein that has a bit more character and body than a simple Tafelwein; comparable to a French vin de pays. Sugar may also be added at fermentation.

Qualitätswein has two main categories, with several sub categories. Qualitätswein bestimmter Anbaugebiete (QbA), or quality wines from one of the thirteen specified wine growing regions, includes the largest quantity of German wines. The grapes must be the approved varieties and reach a minimum level or ripeness to assure that the wine will be indicative of the traditional style and taste of that region. They are fresh, fruity and meant to be consumed young. Again, the law allows sugar to be added at fermentation.

Qualitätswein mit Prädikat (QmP), or "quality wines with distinction," are the highest level of quality wines. The main distinction between QbA and QmP is that the latter are made from grapes ripe enough that sugar is not added at fermentation and is, in fact, prohibited by law in this category. Every wine's "Prädikat" (distinction) is designated on the label by one of the following terms, listed in ascending order of ripeness at harvest:

- ***Kabinett:*** A fine wine made from ripe grapes and generally light and delicate; it may be dry or off-dry.
- ***Spätlese:*** Literally "late harvest," these wines are made from superior quality grapes that are picked after the main harvest, thus they are even riper than normal. This results in more intense and concentrated flavors in the wine. Often these wines may be sweet, though increasingly they are being made in a drier style.
- ***Auslese:*** One step riper than Spätlese, these wines are made from hand-selected bunches of grapes that are particularly ripe. Very intense but not always sweet.
- ***Beerenauslese (BA):*** A wine made from individually selected over-ripe grapes. Sweet but balanced, this is a dessert wine.
- ***Trockenbeerenauslese (TBA):*** A wine made from individually selected over ripe grapes, dried almost to raisins. A rare dessert wine, made in years when nature cooperates.
- ***Eiswein:*** Literally "ice wine," it is made from grapes left on the vine and naturally frozen. Pressed before they thaw, the nectar extracted is intense and honey-like. A rare dessert wine.

Additionally, with the trend toward drier wines, the terms Trocken and Halbtrocken are more frequently appearing on labels. Troken indicates a dry wine, while Halbtrocken will have a slight sweetness. Erzeugerabfullung means that the wine was bottled by the producer, be it a grower, winery or cooperative. Gutsabfullung is more specific, meaning "estate bottled," permitted only when the grapes are harvested, made and bottled on the winery site.

The "A.P. number" shown on the label of "Quality" (QbA and QmP) wines is the German government's seal of authenticity. It verifies the level of ripeness at harvest and (in blind tastings) that the color, aroma and flavor of the wine is consistent with the vintage, region, grape variety and ripeness stated on the label. Every "Quality" wine will name its region of origin on the label. Just as California has many different wine growing regions, so too does Germany. Its thirteen regions are distinct and have their own styles and specialties. The label may also indicate the sub region, collective site, village and vineyard. The name of the village is followed by the name of the vineyard; for example, the popular Zeller Schwarze Katz wines are from the Schwarze Katz (literally "black cat") vineyards in the town of Zell. The famous Bernkasteler Doctor comes from the Doctor vineyards in the village of Bernkastel.

With so many names and designations on the label, there are a few good rules of thumb for finding quality German producers. If you find a wine you like from a particular winery, try their other offerings, which are likely to be made in the same style by the same winemaking talent. Second, there are two major importers bringing German wines into the U.S.: Rudi Wiest imports through Cellars International, ILNA Selections in Carlsbad, Ca. and Terry Theise imports through Milton Kronheim & Co. in Washington D.C. Both have great palates and many years of experience with German wines; every year they literally taste hundreds of wines before deciding which ones they will import. In a sense, their wines have been preselected to represent the best. They are among the best distributed winesof excellent quality.

Finally many of the best wineries are members of Verband Deutscher Pradikatsweinguter (VDP), an association of QmP producing estates founded in 1910.

While not every quality producer belongs to the organization, many of the 165 winery members are among the best. The association's symbol, a spread eagle, and the VDP abbreviation, are easily recognizable on the wine bottle capsules and are a good indicator of quality.

GERMAN WINE REGIONS AND WINERIES

German vineyards are planted in thirteen specified regions, between Lake Constance, all along the Rhine river tributaries, almost up to Bonn in the north and from the French border in the west to the Elbe river in the east. Wine growing regions are particularly concentrated in the southwest corner of Germany, many of the most famous vineyards located favorably near rivers. Wines in the north tend to be light, fruity, fragrant with fresh acidity, while wines from the south seem richer with fuller body and intensity. There are over 1,400 wine villages and 2,600 vineyards in Germany, so it's a veritable wonderland for wine lovers. Many quality wineries are within an hour or two's drive from Frankfurt.

Here are brief descriptions of the thirteen wine regions, starting in the north near Bonn, along with selected wineries in each region.

Following are selected wineries in the thirteen wine growing region. They have been selected because they offer visitors centers and their products are exported and therefore available outside of Germany. Don't forget to check restaurant and hotel recommendations in each major city and surrounding areas corresponding to each wine region.

AHR

Southwest of Bonn, steep hillside vineyards line the Ahr river as it flows into the Rhine in one of Germany's smallest wine growing regions. While Riesling and Müller-Thurgau are produced here, red wine is king. Velvety Spätburgunder and light weight Portugieser are the quaffers of choice, nearly all consumed locally.

Selected Wineries

Weingut Deutzerhof-Cossman-Hehle
53508 Mayschoss, 02643-7264
Mon.-Sat. 0800-1800.

Weingut Kreuzberg
Benedikt-Schmittmann-Strasse 30,
53507 Dernau, 02643-1691
Mon.-Fri. 0800-1900; Sat. 1100-1600.

Weingut Toni Nelles
Goppinger Strasse 13,
53474 Heimersheim, 02641-24349
Mon.-Fri. 0800-1830; Sat. 1000-1200.

Weingut Sonnenberg-Gorres & Linden
Heerstrasse 98,
53474 Bad Neuenahr, 02641-6713
Mon.-Fri. 0900-1800; Sat. 1000-1500;
Sun. 1000-1200.

Staaliche Weingut-Domane Marienthal
Klosterstrasse,
53507 Marienthal, 02641-978633
Mon.-Fri. 0900-1200 and 1300-1600.

MITTELRHEIN

Directly south of Bonn as the Rhine river flows and extending for about 60 miles downstream, this is a picturesque region of steep, terraced vineyards and ancient castles. Mittelrhein accounts for less than one percent of Germany's annual production and the vast majority of vineyards are planted to Riesling. Very little wine is exported; most is drunk locally by visitors who come to view the castles and ruins in the small villages of Bacharach, Oberwesel and Boppard. The wines are fresh though more austere than fruity with high acidity. Much of the harvest is used to produce Sekt or sparkling wine, which is quite popular in the area.

Selected Wineries

Weingut Toni Jost-Hahnehof
Oberstrasse 14,
55420 Bacharach, 06743-1216
Mon.-Sun. Call for hours.

Weingut Goswin Lambrich
Auf der Kripp 3,
55430 Oberwesel-Dellhofen, 06744-8066
Mon.-Sun. 0800-1900.

Weingut August Perll
Oberstrasse 11,
56164 Boppard, 06742-3906
Mon.-Fri. 0800-1900;
Sat. and Sun. 0900-1800.

Weingut Walter Perll
Ablassgasse 11,
56154 Boppard, 06742-3671
Mon.-Fri. 0900-1700;
Sat. 0900-1900; Sun. 1000-1200.

Weingut Ratzenberger
Blucherstrasse 167,
55422 Steeg, 06743-1337
Mon.-Fri. 0800-1800;
Sat. and Sun. 1000-1700.

Weingut Sonnenhang
56348 Dorscheid bei Kaub, 06774-1548
Mon.-Fri. 0730-1800.

MOSEL-SAAR-RUWER

The Mosel river is the focus of this region, from the city of Trier in the south, where the Romans originally planted vineyards, to Koblenz in the north. The wines of the Mosel and its tributaries, the Saar and Ruwer are fragrant and fruity, although it's hard to generalize, since the area is so large. The wines of the Saar, which is southernmost, tend to be more steely and austere; the wines of the Ruwer, which is the smallest of the three, can be flowery, delicate and elegant. The majority of vineyards in this fourth largest wine region are planted to Riesling and Müller-Thurgau. Some of Germany's greatest wines are produced here, particularly those of Auslese quality and above. Wonderful Eiswein is made here nearly every year.

Selected Wineries

Weingut Fritz Haag
Dusebmonder Strasse 44,
54472 Brauneberg, 06534-410
Mon.-Sat. Call for hours.

Weingut Willi Haag
Hauptstrasse 111,
55470 Brauneberg, 06534-450
Mon.-Sat. Call for hours.

Weingut Joh. Jos. Prum
Uferallee 19,
54470 Bernkastel-Wehlen, 06531-3091
Mon.-Fri. 0800-1600.

Weingut Schloss Saarstein
54455 Serrig, 06581-2324
Mon.-Fri. 0800-1700.

Gutsverwaltung Von Schubert
54318 Grunhaus-Mertesdorf, 0651-5111
Mon.-Fri. 0830-1200 and 1300-1645;
Sat. 0900-1200.

Weingut Selbach-Oster
Uferallee 23,
54492 Zeltingen, 06532-2081
Mon-Sat. Call for hours.

Weingut Wwe.
Dr. Thanisch-Erben Thanisch
Saarallee 31,
54470 Berkastel-Kues, 06531-2282
Mon.-Fri. Call for hours.

Weingut Forstmeister Geltz-Zilliken
Heckingstrasse 20,
54439 Saarburg, 06581-2456
Call for appointment.

Bischofliche Weinguter
Gervasiusstrasse 1,
54290 Trier, 0651-43441
Mon.-Fri. 0800-1700.

Weingut Friedrich-Wilhelm-Gymnasium
Weberbach 75, 54290 Trier, 0651 978300
Mon.-Fri. 0900-1800; Sat. 0900-1400.

Weingut Von Hovel
Agritiusstrasse 56,
54329 Konz-Oberemmel, 06501-15384
Mon.-Fri. 0800-1800.

Weingut Dr. Pauly-Bergweiler
Gestade 15,
54470 Bernkastel-Kues, 06531-3002
Mon.-Fri. 0900-1630; Sat. 0900-1900.

RHEINGAU

Cradled by the Mainz and Rhine rivers, the Rheingau is the most central wine region (nearest Frankfurt) and home to some of the oldest vineyards. Many monastic orders chose this area for winemaking in the Middle Ages. Riesling is overwhelmingly the grape of choice, being planted near the Rhine as well as back in the interior valley. The wines are refined yet lively with great character and elegance. The most famous wine villages are Hochheim (from which the British derived the generic term Hock to refer to German wines), Eltville, Erbach, Hattenheim, Hallgarten, Oestrich and Winkel. The famous German enology school and center for wine research is located at Geisenheim.

Selected Wineries

Weingut Robert Weil
Muhlberg 5, 65399 Kiedrich, 06123-2308
Mon.-Fri. 0800-1700.

Weingut Scholoss Vollrads
Schloss, 65375 Oestrich-Winkel,
06723-660
Mon.-Thurs. 0830-1200 and 1300-1600;
Fri. 0830-1200.

Weingut Schloss Reinhartshaysen
Schloss Reinhartshausen,
65337 Erbach, 06123-676333
Mon.-Sat. 0900-1800; Sun. 1100-1700.

Weingut Freiherr Langwerth Von Simmern
Kirchgasse, 65343 Eltville, 06123-3007
Mon.-Fri. 0800-1700.

Weingut Franz Kunstler
Freiherr-von-Stein-Ring 3,
65239 Hochheim, 06146-82570
Mon.-Fri. 1400-1900; Sat. 0900-1700.

Weingut Schloss Johannisberg
Schloss, 65366 Johannisberg,
06722-70090
Mon.-Fri. 1000-1300 and 1400-1800;
Sat. 1000-1300.

Weingut August Eser
Friedensplatz 19,
65375 Oestrich-Winkel, 06723-5032
Mon.-Fri. 0900-1200 and 1300-1700;
Sat. 0900-1200.

Weingut Georg Breuer
Grabenstrasse 8,
65385 Rudesheim, 06722-1027
Mon.-Sat. 0900-1800.

NAHE

The Nahe, planted on both sides of the river of the same name, is bordered by the Rheinhessen on the east, with the Mosel further west. A peaceful agricultural area of vineyards, orchard and meadows, the Nahe produces quite a diverse number of wines because of its geography and range of soil types. Müller-Thurgau, Riesling and Silvaner are the predominant grape varieties; the wines combine the flowery aromas of the Mosel coupled with the full flavor and elegance of the Rheinhessen. Bad Kreuznach is the main town while other popular wine villages are Schlossböckelheim, Niederhausen and Rüdesheim.

Selected Wineries

Schlossgut Diel
55452 Burg Layen, 06721-45045
Mon.-Thurs. 0800-1700; Fri. 0800-1400.

Weingut Crusius
Hauptstrasse 2, 55595 Traisen,
0671-33953
Mon.-Sat. 0800-1800.

Weingut Paul Anheuser
Stromberger Strasse 15-19,
55545 Bad Kreuznach, 0671-28748
Mon.-Fri. 0800-1700; Sat. 0900-1200.

Weingut Michael Schafer
Hauptstrasse,
55452 Burg Layen, 06721-43097
Mon.-Fri. 1500-1900;
Sat. and Sun. 1000-1800.

Weingut Jacob Schneider
Winzerstrasse 15,
55585 Neiderhausen, 06758-6701
Mon.- Sun. 0900-2000.

Weingut Reichsgraf Von Plettenberg
Winzenheimer Strasse,
55545 Bad Kreuznach, 0671-2251
Mon.-Fri. 0900-1600.

Weingut Emrich-Schonleber
55569 Monzingen, 06751-2733
Mon.-Fri. 0800-1800; Sat. 0900-1700.

Don't forget to check restaurant and hotel recommendations in each major city and surrounding areas corresponding to each wine region.

RHEINHESSEN

Bordered on the west by the Nahe river and on the north and east by the Rhine, this valley of rolling hills is Germany's largest wine producing area, representing 20 percent of the total crop. Charlemagne, who had a fortress at Ingelheim, was one of the early promoters of this region. Due to its varying soil types and climates, all the major grape varieties are planted here. The wines are often soft, pleasant, easy to drink and generally undistinguished. It is the home of Liebfraumilch, originally made from the vineyards surrounding The Church of Our Lady in Worms. The Liebfraumilch designation today has become synonymous with mild, innocuous white wine. There are, however, a number of dedicated vintners in the region whose quality wines are exported. The main wine-growing communities are Worms, Alzey, Mainz and Bingen.

Selected Wineries

Weingut Gunderloch
Carl-Gunderloch-Platz 1,
55299 Nackenheim, 06135-2341
Mon.-Fri. 0800-1700.

Weingut Keller
67592 Florsheim-Dalsheim, 06243-456
Mon.-Sat. 0800-1800.

Weingut Kiuhling-Gillot
Olmuhstrasse 25,
55294 Boddenheim, 06135-2333
Mon.-Fri. 1000-1200 and 1400-1800.

Weingut J. Neus
Bahnhofstrasse 96,
55207 Ingelheim, 06132-73003
Mon.-Fri. 0800-1200 and 1300-1800;
Sat. 0900-1200.

Niersteiner Winzergenossenschaft EG
Karolingerstrasse 6,
55283 Nierstein, 06133-97070
Mon.-Fri. 0800-1800; Sat. 0900-1300.

Weingut Rappenhof-Dr. Muth
Bachstrasse 47,
67577 Alsheim, 06249-4015
Mon.-Fri. 0800-1700.

Weingut Sankt Anthony
Worrstadter Strasse 22,
55283 Nierstein, 06133-5482
Mon.-Fri. 0800-1200 and 1400-1700.

Weingut Schales
Alzeyer Strasse 160,
Florsheim-Dalsheim, 06243-7003
Mon.-Fri. 0800-1200 and 1300-1700;
Sat. 0800-1300.

Weingut Heinrich Seebrich
Schmiedgasse 3,
55283 Nierstein, 06153-58211
Mon.-Fri. 0900-1800; Sat. 0900-1400.

Weingut Wittmann
Mainzer Strasse 19,
67593 Westhofen, 06244-7042
Mon.-Fri 0800-1800.

PFALZ

The Pfalz starts at the southern end of Rheinhessen and extends south through Landau and to the border of Alsace. This pretty region is almost one uninterrupted vineyard for nearly 50 miles. While it's the second largest region in terms of size, it is the largest wine producer, accounting for about 25 percent of the country's output. Müller-Thurgau and Riesling are the most widely planted grapes, though Silvaner, Scheurebe and Portugieser are taken seriously too. Most of the wines tend to be mild and well rounded but can be aromatic and full bodied when from the top producers. Home to one of the first Weinstrasse (wine roads) in the 30s', the 73km road passes through nearly every important wine village from Schweigen, near the French border, to Bockenheim at the northern end.

Selected Wineries

Weingut Josef Biffar
Niederkircher Strasse 13-15,
67146 Deidensheim, 06326-5028
Mon.-Fri. 1000-1200 and 1300-1800;
Sat. 1000-1600.

Weingut Dr. Burkin-Wolf
Weinstrasse 65,
67157 Wachenheim, 06322-8955
Mon.-Fri. 0800-1200 and 1300-1700;
Sat. 0930-1200 and 1400-1800;
Sun. 1400-1800.

Weingut Kurt Darting
Am Falltor 2,
67098 Bad Durkheim, 06322-2983
Mon.-Fri. 0800-1900; Sat. 0800-1800.

Weingut Dr. Deinhard
Weinstrasse 10,
67146 Deidesheim, 06326-221
Mon.-Fri. 0800-1730; Sat. 0930-1700.

Weingut Lingenfelder
Hauptstrasse 27,
67229 GroBkarlbach, 06238-754
Mon.-Sat. 0800-1900.

Weingut Herbert Messmer
Gaisbergstrasse 132,
76835 Burrweiler, 06345-2770
Mon.-Fri. 0900-1130 and 1330-1700;
Sat. 0900-1700.

Weingut Muller-Catoir
Mandelring 25, 67433 Haardt,
06321-2815
Mon.-Fri. 0800-1200 and 1300-1700.

Weingut Pfeffingen-Fuhrmann-Eymael
Weinstrasse,
67098 Bad Durkheim-Pfeffingen,
06322-8607
Mon.-Sun. 0800-1800.

Weingut Karl Schaefer
Weinstrasse Sud 30,
67098 Bad Durkheim, 06322-2138
Mon.-Fri. 0800-1200 and 1300-1800;
Sat. 0900-1200.

Weingut Heinrich Vollmer
Gonnheimer Strasse 52,
67158 Ellerstadt, 06237-6611
Mon.-Fri. 0800-1200 and 1300-1700.

Weingut Dr. Wehrheim
Sudliche Weinstrasse 8,
76831 Birkweiler, 06345-3542
Mon.-Fri. 0900-1100 and 1400-1900;
Sat. 1000-1600.

Weingut Werle Erben
Weinstrasse 84, 67147 Forst, 06326-8930
Mon.-Fri. 0800-1200 and 1400-1800.

Weingut Wilhelmshof
Queichstrasse 1,
76833 Siebeldingen, 06345-1817
Mon.-Fri. 0800-1800; Sat. 0900-1700.

FRANKEN

Before German reunification, Franken was the country's easternmost wine region. Located 40 miles east of the Rhine, in Bavaria, most of the vineyards are planted on the slopes of the Main river and its tributaries. Due to the colder climate and earlier winter frosts, very little Riesling is planted here; instead the earlier ripening Müller-Thurgau and Silvaner are predominant. The colder weather is also responsible for the unique wines: less aromatic, steely, earthier and more full-bodied. Most Franken wines are easily recognizable by their traditional bottle, a Bocksbeutel, a squat green or brown flagon with a round body. Würzburg is the most important hub, while Castell, Iphofen, Eschendorf, Thungersheim and Randersacker are also interesting wine villages.

Selected Wineries

Weingut Burgerspital Zum Heiligen Geist
Theaterstrasse 19,
97070 Wurzburg, 0931-35030
Mon.-Thurs. 0800-1200 and 1300-1800;
Fri. 0900-1200; Sat. 0900-1300.

Furstlich Castellsches Domanenamt
Schlossplatz 5, 97335 Castell,
09325-60160
Mon-Fri. 0730-1700; Sat. 1000-1600.

Weingut Michael Frohlich
Bocksbeutelstrasse 41,
97332 Escherndorf, 09381-2847
Mon.-Sun. 0800-1800.

Weingut Rudolf Furst
Hohenlindenweg 46,
63927 Burgstadt, 09371-8642
Mon.-Fri. 0800-1800; Sat. 0800-1600.

Weingut Juliusspital
Klinikstrasse 5,
97070 Wurzburg, 0931-3084147
Mon.-Fri. 0900-1800; Sat. 0900-1300.

Weingut Johann Ruck
Marktplatz 19, 97346 Iphofen,
09323-3316
Mon.-Sat. 0800-1200 and 1300-1800;
Sun. 1000-1200.

Weinbau Egon Schaffer
Astheimer Strasse 17,
97332 Escherndorf, 09381-9350
Mon.-Sat. 0800-1900.

Weingut Schmitt's Kinder
Am Sonnenstuhl,
97236 Randersacker, 0931-708303
Mon.-Sat. 0800-1800.

Weingut Robert Schmitt
Maingasse 13,
97236 Randersacker, 0931-708351
Mon.-Fri. 0800-1800, Sat. 0900-1700.

Staatlicher Hofkeller
Residenzplatz,
97070 Wurzburg, 0931-3050923
Mon.-Fri. 0830-1730, Sat. 0830-1200.

Weingut Josef Storrlein
Schulstrasse 14,
97236 Ranmdersacker, 0931-708281
Mon.-Fri. 0800-2000; Sat. 0800-1800.

Weingut Hans Wirsching
Ludwigstrasse 16,
97346 Iphofen, 09323-3033
Mon.-Fri. 0800-1800; Sat. 0900-1800;
Sun. 1000-1300.

Weingut Zehnthof
Kettengasse 35,
97320 Sulzfeld, 09321-23778
Mon.-Sat. 0800-1800.

HESSISCHE BERGSTRASSE

One of the smallest wine regions is centered around the small towns of Heppenheim and Bensheim, with the Rhine river on one side and the forest next to Baden on the other. Close to the outskirts of Frankfurt, the wine road starts at Darmstadt with the vineyards coming into view at Seeheim. The wines, pleasant and easy to drink, are made primarily from Müller-Thurgau and Riesling. Due to their small production, these wines are almost always consumed by locals and their visitors.

Selected Wineries

Weingut-Weinhandel H. Freiberger OHG
Hermannstrasse 16,
64646 Heppenheim, 06252-2457
Mon.-Fri. 0880-1230 and 1330-1830;
Sat. 0800-1300.

Weingut Simon-Burkle
Wiesenpromenade 13,
64673 Zwingenberg, 06251-76446
Mon.-Fri. 0900-1200 and 1500-1800;
Sat. 0900-1300.

Staatsweingut Bergstrasse
Grieselstrasse,
64625 Bensheim, 06251-3107
Mon.-Thurs. 0730-1700; Fri. 0700-1500.

Weingut Der Stadt Bensheim
Darmstadter Strasse 6,
64625 Bensheim, 06251-14269
Mon.-Fri. 0800-1630; Sat. 1000-1200.

WÜRTTEMBERG

Württemberg, east of the Rhine and situated between the Tauber river valley and Baden, has vineyard plantings mainly along the slopes of the Neckar river. Red wine varieties comprise over half the region and include the little seen Trollinger and Müllerrebe, along with the more widely planted Spätburgunder, Portugieser and Dornfelder. The whites include the ubiquitous Müller-Thurgau and Riesling. The wines here tend be sound, everyday drinking wines, prized for the quaffing qualities; consequently, very little is found outside the region. Stuttgart is the main commercial hub.

Selected Wineries

Weingut Graf Adelmann
Burg Schaubeck,
71711 Kleinbottwar, 07148-6665
Mon.-Fri. 0900-1200 and 1400-1700;
Sat.-Sun. 0900-1200.

Weingut Amalienhof
Lukas-Cranach-Weg 5,
74074 Heilbronn, 07131-51735
Mon.-Fri. 0800-1800; Sat. 0800-1700.

Weingut Und Schlosskellerei
Burg Hornberg,
74865 Neckarzimmern, 06261-5001
Mon.-Fri. 0800-2000;
Sat.-Sun. 0900-2000.

Weingut Drautz-Able
Faisstrasse 23,
74076 Heilbronn, 07131-177908
Mon.-Fri. 0880-1200 and 1330-1800;
Sat. 0900-1600.

Weingartnergenossenschaft Flein-Talheim
Romerstrasse 14, 74223 Flein,
07131-59520
Mon.-Fri. 0880-1700; Sat. 0800-1200.

Weingartnergenossenschaft Grantschen
Wimmentaler Strasse 9,
74189 Weinsberg-Grantschen,
07134-98020
Mon.-Fri. 0880-1200 and 1300-1700;
Sat. 0800-1200.

Weingut Karl Haidle
Hindenburgstrasse 21,
71394 Kernen im Remstal, 07151-42503
Mon.-Fri. 0800-1200 and 1300-1800;
Sat. 0800-1300.

Schlossgut Hohenbeilstein
Im Schloss, 71717 Beilstein, 07062-4303
Mon.-Fri. 0900-1130 and 1400-1700;
Sat. 0900-1200.

Schlossgut Graf Von Neipperg
Im Schloss, 74190 Schwaigern,
07138-5081
Mon.-Fri. 0800-1130 and 1300-1600;
Sat. 0900-1130.

Staatliche Lehr-Und
Versuchsanstalt Weinsberg
Traubenplatz 5,
74189 Weinsberg, 07134-5040
Mon.-Fri. 0800-1600.

Weingut Wohrwag
Grunbacherstrasse 5,
70327 Unterturkheim, 0711-331662
Mon.-Fri. 0800-1800; Sat. 0900-1300.

Wurttembergische Hofkammer-Kellerei
Schloss Monrepos,
71634 Ludwigsburg, 07141-22550
Mon.-Fri. 0800-1130 and 1300-1600.

BADEN

Baden is a long thin strip of a wine region that borders Franken on the north, Württemberg on the east and all the way down to Lake Constance on the Swiss border. This area, encompassing the Black Forest is the third largest wine region and arguably the most diverse. While Riesling is the queen of grapes in many other areas, here the Pinot and its many offshoots are popular: the red Spätburgunder (pinot noir) and the white Ruländer (pinot gris) and Weissburgunder (pinot blanc). The reds range from velvety to intense, while the whites are fragrant, aromatic and spicy. In the northern part of Baden, Heidelberg is perhaps the most well-known city. The heart of the region though, stretches from Baden-Baden south to the border. Wine cooperatives, where many small growers sell their harvest to be blended with other growers, are primarily responsible for the reputation of the wines.

Selected Wineries

Weingut Abril
Talstrasse 9,
79235 Bischoffingen, 07662-255
Mon.-Fri. 0730-1200 and 1400-1800.

Affentaler Winzergenossenschaft
An der B3,
77815 Buhl-Eisental, 07223-98980
Mon.-Fri. 0730-1200 and 1330-1700; Sat. 0800-1200; Sun. 1100-1500 (May-September).

Weingut Bercher
Mittelstadt 13, 79235 Burkheim, 07662-212
Mon.-Sat. 0800-1200 and 1300-1800.

Winzergenossenschaft Bickensohl
Neunlindenstrasse 25,
79235 Bickensohl, 07662-93110
Mon.-Fri. 0730-1700; Sat. 0900-1300.

Winzergenossenschaft Bischoffingen
Bacchusstrasse 14,
79235 Bischoffingen, 07662-93010
Mon.-Fri. 0830-1200 and 1330-1730; Sat. 0830-1200.

Winzergenossenschaft Britzingen
Markgrafler Strasse 25,
79379 Britzingen, 07631-4011
Mon.-Fri. 0800-1200 and 1400-1730.

Winzergenossenschaft Durbach
Nachweide 2, 77770 Durbach, 0781-93660
Mon.-Fri. 0800-1200 and 1330-1800; Sat. 0900-1200, Sun. 1000-1200.

Weingut Dr. Heger
Bachenstrasse 19,
79241 Ihringen, 07668-205
Mon.-Sat. 1000-1200.

Winzergenossenschaft Konigschaffhausen
Kiechlinsberger Strasse 2,
79346 Konigschaffhausen,07642-1003
Mon.-Fri. 0800-1200 and 1330-1700; Sat. 0900-1200.

Weingut Schloss Neuweier
Mauerbergstrasse 21,
76534 Baden-Baden, 07223-06770
Mon.-Fri. 0900-1200 and 1300-1700;
Sat. 0900-1300.

Weingut Salwey
Hauptstrasse 2,
79235 Oberrotweil, 07662-384
Mon.-Sat. 0800-1230 and 1400-1800.

Weingut Stigler
Bachenstrasse 29,
79241 Ihringen, 07668-297
Mon.-Fri. 0900-1200 and 1400-1800;
Sat. 0900-1300.

Graflich Wolff Metternich'sches Weingut
Grohl 2-6, 77770 Durbach, 0781-42779
Mon.-Fri. 0800-1700; Sat. 0900-1200.

SAALE-UNSTRUT

The northernmost wine growing area in Germany has a long tradition of winemaking. Ironically the first American rootstock vines were planted here in the late 19th century, after the root louse *phylloxera* affected their vineyards. Located equidistant between Weimar and Leipzig, the vineyards are clustered around the banks of the Unstrut river and the nearby intersecting Saale river. Being so far north, the cooler climate and longer growing season has a strong influence on the type of varieties cultivated and the ripeness they achieve. It's rare to find Spätlese and Auslese quality wines here, for example. The workhorse is the Müller-Thurgau, but Silvaner is important and perhaps a better grape for showing what this region can do in a marginal grape-growing climate.

Selected Wineries

Landesweingut Kloster Pforta
Saalhauser, 06628 Bad Kosen,
034463-273
Mon.-Sun. 1000-2000.
Weingut Lutzkendorf
Saalberge 31,
06628 Bad Kosen, 034463-772
Mon.-Sun. 1000-1800.

Don't forget to check restaurant and hotel recommendations in each major city and surrounding areas corresponding to each wine region.

SACHSEN

This is the smallest wine growing region as well as the most easterly. The vineyards are planted on the banks of the Elbe river, down to the southern German border. The climate is marginal for grape cultivation, with the great possibility of late spring frost decimating the vineyards. Early ripening varieties like Müller-Thurgau and Weissburgunder are preferred and the resulting wines are fruity and dry. The small production is consumed locally, much of it by tourists who come to visit Dresden, see the local porcelain factories and, to their surprise, discover a number of charming wineries and historic inns.

Selected Wineries

Weingut Schloss Proschwitz
01665 Proschwitz uber Horder,
03521-452096
Mon.-Fri. 0800-1530.

Sachsisches Staatsweingut
Schloss Wackerbarth
Im Schloss, 01439 Radebeul,
0351-722728
Mon.-Sun. 1000-1800.

INDEX

A

C

D

E

F

G

H

I

J

K

L

M

N

O

P

Q

R

S

T

Y

Z

RECEIVE A FREE SUBSCRIPTION TO "TASTES"

BY FILLING OUT THIS QUESTIONNAIRE YOU'LL RECEIVE A COMPLIMENTARY ONE YEAR SUBSCRIPTION TO **"TASTES,"** OUR INTERNATIONAL NEWSLETTER.

NAME ______________________________

ADDRESS ______________________________

CITY ____________________ STATE ______________

ZIP ______________ COUNTRY ____________________

PHONE (   )   -

The AGP/Gault Millau series of guidebooks reflects your demand for insightful, incisive reporting on the best that the world's most exciting destinations have to offer. To help us make our books even better, please take a moment to fill out this anonymous (if you wish) questionnaire, and return it to:

Gault Millau, Inc., P.O. Box 361144, Los Angeles, CA 90036;
Fax: (213) 936-2883.

1. How did you hear about the AGP guides? Please specify: bookstore, newspaper, magazine, radio, friends or other.

2. Please list in order of preference the cities or countries which you would like to see AGP cover.

3. Do you refer to the AGP guides for your own city, or only when traveling?

A. (Travels) ....   B. (Own city) ....   C. (Both) ....

(Please turn over)

4. Please list, starting with the most preferred, the three features you like best about the Gault Millau guides.

A. ....

B. .... C. ....

5. What are the features, if any, you dislike about the Gault Millau guides?

6. Please list any features you would like to see added to the Gault Millau guides.

7. If you use other guides besides Gault Millau, please list below.

8. Please list the features you like best about your favorite guidebook series, if it is not Gault Millau.

A. ....

B. .... C. ....

9. How many trips do you make per year, for either business or pleasure?

Business: International .... Domestic ....

Pleasure: International .... Domestic.........................

10. Please check the category that reflects your annual household income.

$20,000–$39,000 .... $40,000–$59,000 ....
$60,000–$79,000 .... $80,000–$99,000 ....
$100,000–$120,000 .... Other (please specify) ....

11. If you have any comments on the Gault Millau guides in general, please list them in the space below.

12. If you would like to recommend specific establishments, please don't hesitate to list them:

Name	*City*	*Phone*

We thank you for your interest in the Gault Millau guides, and we welcome your remarks and recommendations about restaurants, hotels, nightlife, shops, services and so on.

317/95

NOTES